P9-CEU-490

Mrs. Appleyard's
FAMILY KITCHEN

BOOKS BY LOUISE ANDREWS KENT

The Terrace
Paul Revere Square
Mrs. Appleyard's Year
Mrs. Appleyard's Kitchen
Country Mouse
" . . . with Kitchen Privileges"
The Summer Kitchen *(with Elizabeth Kent Gay)*
The Winter Kitchen *(with Elizabeth Kent Gay)*
The Vermont Year Round Cookbook
Mrs. Appleyard and I
Mrs. Appleyard's Family Kitchen *(with Polly Kent Campion)*

STORIES FOR YOUNG PEOPLE

Douglas of Porcupine
The Red Rajah
Two Children of Tyre
He Went with Marco Polo
He Went with Vasco da Gama
He Went with Magellan
He Went with Christopher Columbus
Jo Ann, Tomboy *(with Ellis Parker Butler)*
In Good Old Colony Times *(with Elizabeth Kent Tarshis)*
The Brookline Trunk
He Went with John Paul Jones
He Went with Champlain
He Went with Drake
He Went with Hannibal

Mrs. Appleyard's FAMILY KITCHEN

A Treasury of Vermont Country Recipes

by

LOUISE ANDREWS KENT

and

POLLY KENT CAMPION

Illustrations by Polly Alexander

VERMONT LIFE MAGAZINE / MONTPELIER, VERMONT

Published in association with

HOUGHTON MIFFLIN COMPANY / BOSTON

Copyright©1977 by Polly Kent Campion. All rights reserved. No part of this book may be reproduced without written permission from the publisher, except by a reviewer who may quote brief passages or reproduce illustrations in a review; nor may any part of this book be reproduced, stored in a retrieval system, or transmitted in any form or by any means electronic, mechanical, photocopying, recording, or other, without written permission from the publisher.

This book is published by Vermont Life Magazine, 61 Elm St., Montpelier, Vermont 05602 in association with (for distribution outside of Vermont) Houghton Mifflin Company, 2 Park St., Boston, Massachusetts 02107 and has been produced in the United States of America: composed by The Burlington Free Press and printed and bound by the Arcata Book Group.

Designed by Linda Dean Paradee

FIRST EDITION: November 1977

Library of Congress Cataloging in Publication Data

Kent, Louise Andrews, 1886-1969.
Mrs. Appleyard's family kitchen.
Includes index.
1. Cookery, American—Vermont.
I. Campion, Polly Kent, joint author. II. Title.
TX715.K358 641.5 77-13436

ISBN 0-395-25771-9

Contents

Introduction

ON this bright, changeable afternoon, as I sit down to introduce this book, I feel just as a writer of cookbooks should feel: brisk and hungry, authoritative and amiable, generous yet confidential. It has been threatening to rain all day. Luminescent clouds billowing into ominous looking towers of gloom move in towing patches of azure to raise the spirits, only to overspread the horizon with murky forms once again. I walked with my son during a brief respite from the thunderheads and, as he lies sleeping beside me, I am content with the world.

The history of this book has much the same profile as this changeable day has had. The *Family Kitchen* began looking very bright and encouraging. After numerous postponements and changes of author clouding its progress, it has been completed in an aura of glistening hopefulness.

It all started, actually, with a Massachusetts pioneer named Remember Kent who, in 1797, crossed a blazed trail into central Vermont and laid claim to a spot that was to "burgeon" into the settlement known as Kents Corner. Primarily, however, Mrs. Appleyard, as she came to be called, began with the birth of Louise Andrews on a warm spring day in Boston in 1886. Now all of Grandmother's life was, of course, remarkable, but the existence of Mrs. Appleyard became assured when Louise met, courted and married Remember Kent's great grandson, Ira Rich Kent, and moved to Kents Corner as Rich's wife.

It wasn't long before Grandmother, more commonly known as Mrs. Kent or Lulie, made a place for herself and became an influential source of energy for Kents Corner. She was frequently the inspiration and organizer for the town's most festive events — such as holding memorable square dances by candlelight on Valentine's Day with vast and succulent feasts prepared for the ravenous dancers. Many of the social occasions motivated by my Grandmother had as their central feature, rich and savory forms of fare. Her expertise in the kitchen became known and respected as quickly and as firmly as did her reputation for being the warm and irreplaceable core of Kents Corner.

From the sound of it, Louise Kent's life involved only friends and food; it was not so. She painted; she read (nearly a book a day!); she restored antiques, made miniature rooms, gave guest lectures, gardened, took photographs; she avidly watched birds; she stencilled walls in her house and in the historic tavern next door; she raised her and Rich's three children: Elizabeth (Kenty), Hollister (Sam), and Rosamond (Posy); and she wrote. Grandmother thought of herself primarily as a writer. She wrote numerous children's books, including a series of eight "He Went With . . ." books. She wrote books for adults and she wrote cookbooks. She collaborated with her daughter Elizabeth Kent Gay on a series of articles about cooking for the *Ladies' Home Journal.* She also wrote cooking articles for the *Boston Herald.* And it was because of the *Herald* articles that Mrs. Appleyard came to be.

In the late 1930's it was Rich who suggested to his wife that she compile some of her *Herald* articles into a cookbook. She decided to do so but thought it best to limit the book to seasonal articles, and to group the book around one central character. "How does Mrs. Applegate sound?" she asked her husband. "Not bad," he replied, "but that sounds as if you shut people out. She ought to welcome them in. Call her Mrs. Appleyard." And with her usual wifely obedience (hah!), Grandmother launched the existence of Mrs. Appleyard, her alter ego.

During the next twenty years, Grandmother produced *Mrs. Appleyard's Kitchen, Mrs. Appleyard's Year* (a novel), *Mrs. Appleyard's Summer Kitchen* and *Mrs. Appleyard's Winter Kitchen,* the last two in collaboration with Elizabeth. In 1968, Louise Kent published her autobiography, *Mrs. Appleyard and I,* written in the same whimsical and lyrical style as her former works. From 1962 to 1969, she also wrote the tantalizingly good Mrs. Appleyard food page for each quarterly issue of *Vermont Life* magazine. Grandmother's *The Vermont Year Round Cookbook* was published in 1965, in part a compilation of the *Vermont Life* articles.

It was after her four previous cookbooks had gone out of print that Grandmother began work on this book. With much prompting from her family and a plethora of requests from her readers, she set out to produce a final book. It was to be a collection of the best of her previous cookbooks and numerous new rules. She initiated work on this massive undertaking shortly after completing the manuscript of *Mrs. Appleyard and I.*

After working diligently on the manuscript in her Massachusetts winter home, Grandmother made her usual summer move to Vermont. As fate would have it, she had somehow misplaced the manuscript and spent the entire summer looking for it, finding it in September only with the help of her favorite clairvoyant, Luvia. She continued work on it through the next winter and early summer while living with my family. With her usual industry, Grandmother surged ahead until her death in August of 1969.

At this point you may be wondering who I am and how I became involved in a book of this nature. Sam Kent was my father, Louise Kent my grandmother. After my Grandmother's death in 1969, *Vermont Life* retained her manuscript in the anticipation that one of her offspring would want to complete it. Grandmother had produced very active children, however, who were all too involved in other ventures to devote the necessary time to the completion of the *Family Kitchen.* Elizabeth was working as a psychiatric social worker and making plans to go back to school; Sam (my father) was planning a reconstruction project for the country of Jordan and died in July, 1974 during a mountain search for a lost friend; and Posy was teaching philosophy in South Carolina and England. The next logical step was to look to the succeeding generation.

I was enthusiastic about the prospect of working on a cookbook. Having always been interested in cooking and nutrition, I was contemplating compiling a book of my own. I was living in Kents Corner at the time and was, therefore, surrounded with Appleyardian lore and the proper atmosphere for writing. So, when Brian Vachon, *Vermont Life's* editor, approached me in the spring of 1975, I was only too happy to delve into the rewriting and completion of my Grandmother's work.

The writing of and experimenting with the *Family Kitchen* have brought me many hours of joy and my husband many unique meals. I have tried to clarify directions as much as possible in order to facilitate the cooking. I have annexed numerous rules of my own making and a number that have come to me through a variety of paths.

It has taken three generations to bring this book to its final form. During my work on it, I completed my Bachelor of Arts degree and gave birth to Kieran, a member of the fourth generation. Please enjoy the cross-generational results and feel free to adopt or adapt any rule you wish.

With love of course —
Polly Kent Campion

To Jay and Sam

To the former, without whose continued support,
I would not have been able to work.
To the latter, without whose lifelong love and teachings,
I would not be.

Mrs. Appleyard's
FAMILY KITCHEN

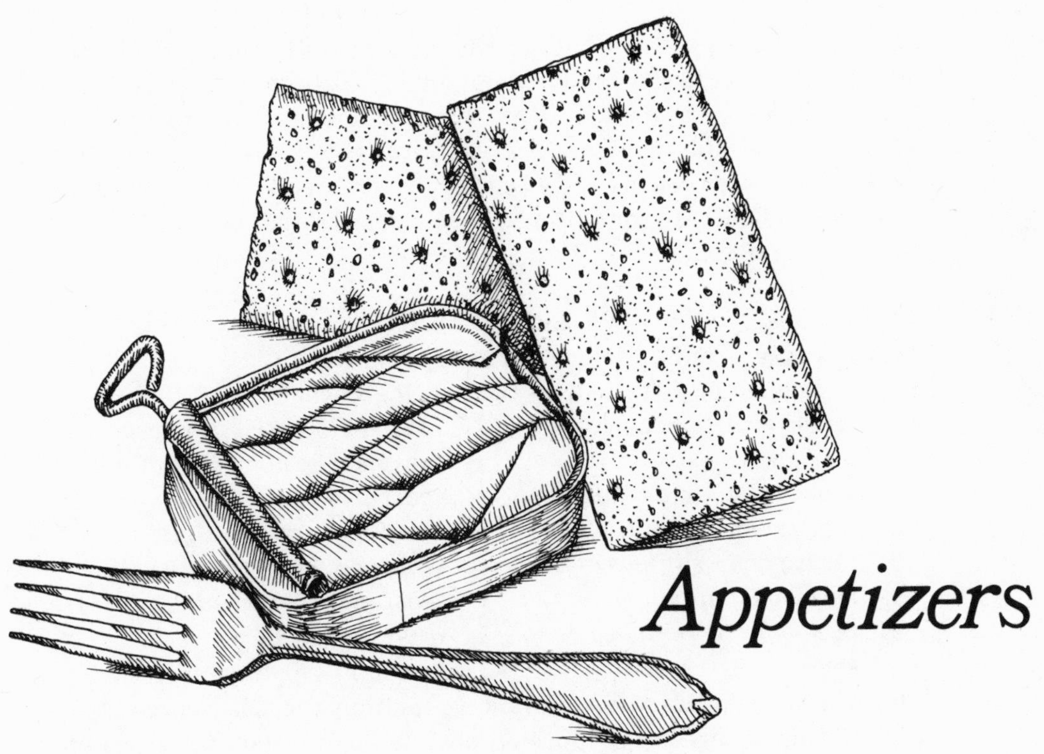

Appetizers

MRS. Appleyard used to say that appetizers were a seductive and inaccurately named form of fare. "If one is not hungry, an appetizer will simply make him less so," she'd say, and I have trouble finding fault with her logic. If you're hungry, it seems foolish not to consume something substantially more, well, substantial. But not practicing her own recommendations, Grandmother would produce an elaborate array of hors d'oeuvres accompanying or preceding an equally elaborate meal, one dinner party after another. It seems little has changed in that department. I'd much prefer making a repast of hors d'oeuvres alone and leave the main course for the more famished members of the household or dinner guests.

Though appetizers are a delusionary delight and though Grandmother's assessment of their appellation seems fairly indisputable, they were definitely not strangers in her kitchen. Nor are they in mine. Herewith are some of the favorite temptations to which Appleyards willingly yield:

ARTICHOKES, BEANS AND MUSHROOMS-VINAIGRETTE

1 10-ounce package frozen green beans cut in pieces
1 10-ounce package frozen artichoke bottoms (hearts)
1 tablespoon onion, minced
1 tablespoon butter
½ pound mushroom caps, washed and sliced
1 tablespoon flour
½ teaspoon paprika
Pinch of nutmeg
½ cup light cream

Start the beans cooking, using as little water as possible. The water should all cook away. Cook the artichokes according to the directions on the package, until tender but not mushy. Sauté the onion in the butter until it is straw colored — about five minutes. Add the mushrooms. Sauté for five minutes over medium heat. Rub the flour and seasonings into the mushroom mixture, stir in the cream. Add the beans and artichokes as soon as they are cooked. Add any cooking water and cook the mixture down until the sauce is quite thick. While the vegetables are still hot, pour over them some:

VINAIGRETTE SAUCE

This is really a rather acid French dressing.

Shake together in a jar with a tight fitting cover:

- 1 *tablespoon tarragon vinegar*
- 1 *tablespoon lemon juice*
- 2 *tablespoons cider vinegar*
- 6 *tablespoons safflower oil*
- ½ *teaspoon paprika*
- ½ *teaspoon Worcestershire sauce*
- 1 *teaspoon parsley, minced*
- ½ *teaspoon lemon rind, grated*
- ½ *teaspoon sugar*
- ½ *teaspoon dry mustard*
- ¼ *teaspoon black pepper*
- 1 *teaspoon salad herbs, minced*
- ½ *teaspoon garlic powder*
- 1 *teaspoon chives, minced*

This makes just over ½ cup of dressing, multiply the rule as necessary.

Chill the appetizers in the sauce at least 24 hours. Drain the sauce off and save. Serve them cold with slices of homemade bread.

Use the same sauce for:

MUSHROOM VINAIGRETTE

- 1 *pound button mushrooms, washed and sliced vertically*
- 2 *tablespoons onion, minced*
- 2 *tablespoons butter*
- 1 *cup Vinaigrette Sauce*

Sauté the mushrooms and onions in the butter for about five minutes. Pour the sauce over them. Put the entire mixture into a jar and chill for at least 24 hours. Serve cold with minced parsley and basil sprinkled over them.

ASPARAGUS VINAIGRETTE

Cook a 2½ pound bunch of asparagus, standing up in two inches of boiling water for ten minutes. Then cook, covered by boiling water for another seven or eight minutes. Do not overcook or the tips will break off. Drain the asparagus, and while it is still hot, cut the stalks into half inch pieces. Cover with Vinaigrette Sauce. Chill at least 24 hours. Serve them cold, garnished with grated egg yolk and strips of pimento.

SHELL BEAN VINAIGRETTE

Use the beans with the caramel blotches on the pods. They ripen in late August in New England. Lima beans may be used if you prefer them; they are more readily available.

- 2 *cups beans, measured after shelling*
- 1 *tablespoon onion, minced*
- 1 *tablespoon butter*
- 1 *cup Vinaigrette Sauce*

Cook the beans in rapidly boiling water until almost soft — about 25 minutes. Sauté the onion in the butter until straw colored. Pour four tablespoons water from the beans over the onion and cook until the water is all gone. Don't be absent-minded about this or the onions will be truly caramelized. Pour the Vinaigrette Sauce over the beans and onions. Chill at least 24 hours before serving.

The Vinaigrette Sauce may be used in the same way on other vegetables or combinations of vegetables. Drain them before serving and pour the sauce back into the jar. It may then be used in various ways. Add some to French Dressing,* or pour it over fish before broiling. Or add a little to cocktail sauce. Keep it cool and shake it well before using. It's sure to come in handy.

CHEESE AND CHUTNEY APPETIZERS

¼ pound butter

Rounds of bread toasted on one side
½ pound cheddar cheese, grated
*½ cup Mrs. Appleyard's Chutney**
1 tablespoon onion, finely minced

½ teaspoon Worcestershire sauce

Butter the bread thinly on the toasted side. Mix the rest of the ingredients and spread the rounds of bread with the mixture. Put the rounds on a baking sheet and bake them at 375° until the cheese melts — about five minutes. This rule makes about two dozen appetizers.

CHEESE CUBES

(approximately 2 dozen)

2 slices of homemade bread, ¾ inch thick
1 egg, beaten
2 tablespoons melted butter
1 cup dry cheddar cheese, grated

Cut the crusts off the bread. Cut the bread into ¾ inch cubes. Mix the egg and melted butter. Roll the cubes in the mixture until coated on all sides. Then roll them in the grated cheese. Put them on a buttered baking sheet. Bake at 375° until they start to brown — about 5-7 minutes. It might be wise to double the rule, as they disappear rapidly.

CHEESE BALLS — BAKED

½ cup cheddar cheese, grated
½ cup blue cheese, grated
1 egg, beaten
½ cup soft crumbs of white bread
1 teaspoon Worcestershire sauce
1 teaspoon dry mustard
1 cup dry bread crumbs, rolled very fine
½ teaspoon paprika
¼ teaspoon black pepper
1 egg, beaten lightly with 1 teaspoon water

Mix both kinds of cheese with the beaten egg, soft bread crumbs, Worcestershire sauce and mustard. Roll the mixture into balls about one inch in diameter. Then roll the balls first in the fine dry crumbs, mixed with the pepper and paprika, then in the egg beaten with the water. Finally roll the balls in the crumbs again.

Chill the balls in the refrigerator for at least ten minutes.

*See Index for pages where recipes can be found.

Light oven: 450°. While the oven is warming, arrange the balls in a lightly buttered iron frying pan. They must not touch each other. Bake them for five minutes. Turn them carefully using two spatulas.

Bake until brown. The total baking, including turning, takes about 12 minutes. If you prefer that they be browner, run them briefly under the broiler. Do not overcook them or they will be tough and stringy.

CHEESE AND CRACKERS

For reasons both social and economic, the trend of buying in bulk is growing rapidly nationwide. The food co-op I am active in has a rotating selection of fine cheeses available at reasonable prices.

From this and other sources I frequently arrange a tray of cheese and crackers that includes a selection of Swedish Jarlsberg, Greek Feta cheese, Swiss Colony Blue Cheese, Bordon's Liedercranz, Crème Damia from Denmark, Gouda from Holland and, of course, an ample supply of well-aged Vermont cheddar.

All of these cheeses are improved by being allowed to stand at room temperature for at least one hour before serving.

To accompany these cheeses, split Cross crackers, butter the halves well and bake them at 350° until they just start to brown — about 12 minutes. Since the crackers are served cold the baking can be done ahead of time. Other crackers might be used to enhance the cheese tray. I suggest using Triscuits, Wheat Thins, rice, rye or sesame wafers.

CELERY — STUFFED WITH CHEESE

Use only the best and crispest inner stalks of the celery bunch. Save the outer ones for soup.

Make a filling of equal amounts of cream cheese and Roquefort cheese blended together with enough sour cream (or yogurt) to make the mixture stick together. Fill the celery stalks ahead of time, wrap them in aluminum foil and keep them chilled until it is time to serve them. Arrange, unwrapped, on a platter and sprinkle with minced chives.

CANAPÉS

According to Webster, a canapé is ". . . a slice or piece of bread fried in butter or oil, on which anchovies, mushrooms, etc., are served. They originated about 1880 in France."

The English and Mrs. Appleyard both borrowed the idea, but did away with the excessive habit of frying the bread, and decided to toast it instead. From there, Grandmother expanded to include a number of toppings that Webster probably never encountered. Or at least he didn't include them in his unabridged book.

One such topping is:

CAVIAR CANAPÉS

Reportedly, these were the first to vanish in Boston or Appleyard Center, even when the caviar was really cod roe dyed black, or salmon roe in its own natural coral color.

For 12 canapés use:

12 rounds of firm, thin bread cut with a cooky cutter
¼ pound butter (unsalted), softened
1 4-ounce jar of caviar
1 teaspoon onion, minced
Juice of ½ lemon
1 hard-boiled egg, white and yolk chopped separately
4 large stuffed olives

Toast the rounds of bread lightly on one side. Spread them thinly with the softened butter, then generously with the caviar mixed with the onion and lemon juice. Caviar spread too thinly is frustrating. Decorate the canapé around the edge with the finely chopped egg white. Sprinkle the yolk over the middle and put a slice of stuffed olive in the center.

CAVIAR TOMATO CANAPÉS

Make these like the Caviar Canapés above, but first cover the buttered round of bread with a thin slice of tomato, thinly spread with mayonnaise.

MUSHROOM AND BACON CANAPÉS

1 pound mushroom caps, chopped
1 tablespoon onion, minced
4 tablespoons butter
2 tablespoons flour
1 tablespoon sherry
2 tablespoons thick sour cream
6 slices of bacon

Chop the mushrooms and onions and fry them slowly in the butter. When tender, sprinkle the flour over them and cook for three minutes over very low heat, rubbing the flour well into the liquid. Add the sherry, turn off the heat, stir in the cream. Toast the rounds of thinly sliced bread on one side. Cut the bacon into small squares and cook until they are not quite crisp. Drain them on paper towels.

Spread the untoasted side of the bread with the mushroom mixture. Put a square of bacon on each canapé. Cook them briefly under the broiler until the bacon is crisp and serve hot.

PEANUT BUTTER AND BACON APPETIZERS

These were originally intended for children, but you'd be wise to make plenty of them because grown-ups, too, take a childlike interest in them.

A number of Appleyards, frustrated with the commercially hydrogenerated and homogenized peanut butters, would make their own. I'm thankful, however, to have numerous real peanut butters available to me through food co-ops and natural food outlets. Strangely enough, these are made out of just peanuts!

Toast the rounds of bread on one side. Cut the bacon into small squares, and fry them until they are translucent. Spread the untoasted side of the rounds of bread with peanut butter. Top each one with a bacon square. Put them on a cookie sheet. Just before serving time, put the sheet under the broiler and cook until the bacon is crisp, 2-3 minutes. Watch them though: as Grandmother used to say, "carbon comes quickly." Serve hot.

POPCORN

Children consider this an appetizer. My brothers and I would put away popcorn by the handful and then fall upon a dish of Bouillabaisse as if we had never seen food before. When this happened at Grandmother's house, she used Bear-Paw popcorn, the kind that comes off an ear shaped like a bear's paw. You are supposed to rub two ears together until the kernels run into a tin pan like hail on the porch roof.

Fortunately for me, inept at the sport, popcorn may also be purchased in a package.

To the Appleyards, popcorn is more than an appetizer. We enjoy it sprinkled lightly with salt and melted butter, or with cinnamon sugar. We have been known to eat it for dessert with chocolate sauce or maple syrup. Grandmother would eat it with soup instead of crackers, and she was rumored to have sprinkled a little garlic powder on it once in a while. Confidentially — if I can be confidential about garlic — one of her favorite people once wrote to her kindly, but firmly, about her habit of sprinkling garlic powder around. Mrs. Appleyard apologized and added that she would start to work at once on a new cookbook in which she would make it abundantly clear that *garlic is optional.* Now, if only her family would catch on.

Unless you have an automatic popcorn popper, with directions that come with it, use a gallon kettle, stainless steel, with a tight fitting lid.

Melt two tablespoons of butter in the kettle. Pour enough popcorn to cover the bottom of the kettle well. Clamp down the lid firmly, and shake the kettle over a hot flame. Popcorn has to be coaxed into suddenly exploding. Soon the first pop comes and a grain hits the top of the kettle. Keep shaking it until no noise of popping is heard.

Remove the kettle from the flame before it scorches and let it stand for two minutes before taking off the cover. It's more crisp and tender if it is not allowed to cool slowly.

TINY CREAM PUFFS

Tiny Cream Puffs make some of the best appetizers. The rule for Cream Puffs* in the chapter on Desserts will make about 20 small puffs, depending on how deft you are in shaping them. They will not take quite as long to bake as the larger ones but — like the larger ones — they must be baked until there are no longer any iridescent bubbles showing on them.

Split the puffs on one side as soon as they are baked. Fill them when they are cool with either lobster, shrimp or crabmeat salad, or a combination of all three; or the Mushroom and Bacon Canapé* mixture; or chicken salad with the chicken and celery very finely cut; or various kinds of Pâté.* Any number of fillings are delicious, but Grandmother liked this one best:

RED CAVIAR FILLING

1 4-ounce jar red caviar
4 tablespoons sour cream
2 teaspoons onion, grated
Juice and grated rind of ½ lemon
1 teaspoon paprika
Watercress

Mix the caviar, sour cream, onion and lemon. Split the cream puffs halfway through and fill them. Put a small dab of the filling on top of each puff and sprinkle a dash of paprika on it. Wreathe them with watercress. Keep them cool till serving time.

SALAD A LA MAX

Many years before I was around, Max had a small restaurant in Boston. As soon as someone sat down, a plate of this salad was set before him.

To make this delicacy, arrange four or five crisp leaves of Boston lettuce on each plate. Over the lettuce place four fillets of anchovy. In and around the anchovies lay thin slices of radishes and stuffed olives, some green and some ripe. Place a single large shrimp (cooked) in the center of each plate and sprinkle grated egg yolk over the entire arrangement.

Unfortunately, Max did not give away the rule for his red wine and sugar dressing. However, Grandfather's French dressing went well with this combination. You might want to use the plain French Dressing* rule or its anchovy version.

Either brown bread, cucumber or watercress sandwiches are excellent served with this salad.

DIPS

My mother considers dips one of the best modern laborsaving inventions ever devised. I agree with her wholeheartedly. Dips may be prepared in advance and taste all the better for standing a while in the refrigerator. They are easily mixed and easily served and even allow you time to converse with the guests.

Mother supplies a variety of things for dipping including an arrangement of crackers, and fresh vegetable spears (carrots, celery, broccoli, cucumber or even apple slices). I've noticed, however, that finger size pieces of homemade bread, dried slowly in an oven till a gold color, are the first to disappear.

BACON DIP

6 *slices of bacon, cooked slowly till crisp, drained, cooled and crumbled*
Juice and grated rind of 1 lemon
1½ *cups sour cream*
1 *tablespoon parsley, minced*
2 *teaspoons onion, crushed through a garlic press*
1 *tablespoon chives, finely cut*

Mix all the ingredients together in a pottery bowl. In the summer the flavor may be varied by adding a little minced fresh tarragon or dill. Serve well chilled in a bowl of contrasting color.

CAVIAR DIP

(For 12)

1 *8-ounce package cream cheese*
1 *cup sour cream*
1 *tablespoon onion, minced*
2 *4-ounce jars red caviar*
2 *tablespoons chives, cut fine*

Mix all the ingredients. Chill. Serve with Melba Toast.*

CHEESE DIP

(For 8)

Into the blender put:

½ cup sour cream
2 tablespoons milk
1 3-ounce package cream cheese
4 sprigs parsley
3 drops Tabasco sauce
2 ounces blue cheese
1 clove garlic, peeled

Blend until smooth. Serve very cold.

GREEN DIP

(For 8)

½ cup mashed ripe avocado
½ cup watercress, cut fine
1 teaspoon onion, minced
1 teaspoon chives, minced
Juice and grated rind of 1 lemon
1 tablespoon cream
1 cup mayonnaise
½ cup sour cream

Put into the blender: avocado, watercress, onion, chives, lemon juice and rind. Blend for 15 seconds. Add the cream. Blend five seconds more. Add this mixture to the mayonnaise. Add the sour cream, stirring it in well. Chill and serve cold with a sprinkle of paprika on top.

SARDINE DIP

(For 12)

12 ounces sardines
2 tablespoons olive butter
1 cup mayonnaise
1 teaspoon lemon juice and a little grated rind
1 cup sour cream
*1 tablespoon Oyster Sauce**

Mash the sardines. Mix all the ingredients. If it seems too thick for dipping add extra mayonnaise. Chill.

This same mixture may also be used for hot canapés. Spread it on rounds of bread toasted on one side and buttered. Run them under the broiler until they just start to brown. Obviously, it's much more restful to serve it as a dip.

SMOKED OYSTERS AND OLIVE DIP

1 8-ounce package cream cheese
¾ cup mayonnaise, more as needed
1 tablespoon lemon juice
¼ teaspoon onion powder
1 3½ to 4 ounce tin smoked oysters
½ cup ripe olives

Soften cream cheese (at room temperature) with mayonnaise. Mix in lemon juice and onion powder. Chop oysters and olives and mix in. If mixture seems too thick for dipping, add more mayonnaise. Pile into serving dish and chill until serving time. Good with celery and carrot sticks and with plain crackers.

When she served 12 or more people, Grandmother would often tease their appetites with Flounder Balls and a choice of two dips.

FLOUNDER BALLS

It is wise to make these the day before they are to be served. First make a Court Bouillon:

Bones and trimmings from 2 pounds of fresh, filleted flounders
2 sliced carrots
1 teaspoon mixed herbs
2 onions, chopped
1 bay leaf

Simmer this mixture in water to cover for ¾ of an hour. Then add ¼ cup of white wine and simmer five minutes more.

For the Flounder Balls use:

2 pounds flounder, filleted
1 small onion, ground
½ teaspoon salt
2 eggs, beaten
2 Cross crackers (crumbs rolled fine and sifted)
¼ teaspoon pepper

Put the fish through the grinder, or if you have a blender that will puree, use that. Grind or blend the onion with the fish. Add the seasonings and the eggs, working them in thoroughly with your hands. Add the cracker crumbs and shape the mixture into balls. Use only about a teaspoon of the mixture for each ball. They will double in size.

Strain the court bouillon through cheesecloth. Put the bouillon into a large sauce pan. Put an Italian open leaf strainer — the kind with the adjustable legs — into the pan. Bring the bouillon to the boiling point, lower the strainer filled with the flounder balls into the steaming liquid. Cover tightly. Cook for ten minutes.

Cook the balls in several batches, adding a little water to the bouillon accordingly so it won't dry out. Lay the balls on a big platter and chill them overnight.

RELISH TRAYS

For groups of people who are apt to nibble, and how many groups aren't, use a large tray with separate dishes surrounded by sprays of parsley and watercress and serve any of the following combinations.

1. With Beef Pie*
   Shell Bean Vinaigrette,* Mint Sauce,* Mrs. Appleyard's Chutney,* preserved kumquats.
2. With Real Chicken A La King*
   Cubes of cold Gaspé salmon with Caviar Dip,* Cheese and Chutney Appetizers,* raw broccoli flowerets, mayonnaise, Melba Toast.* Halves of hard-boiled eggs stuffed with a paste of the yolk, Mrs. Appleyard's Deviled Ham* and a little mayonnaise. Small tomatoes stuffed with a mixture of cream cheese, olive butter and chopped chives moistened with a little cream.
3. With Convent Pie *(Vermont Year Round Cookbook,* p. 143)
   Tiny sausages baked in the oven for half an hour, finished under the broiler; large stuffed olives wrapped in bacon and broiled; oysters done the same way; mushroom caps dotted with butter and broiled.
4. With cold sliced ham and turkey or chicken
   Tiny Cream Puffs* stuffed with Chicken Liver Pâté;* Tomato

Conserve;* a small hot dish of baked potatoes, cubed, seasoned with onion, pepper, paprika and baked in thick cream then spread with black caviar.

5. With Scalloped Haddock*
   Toasted mushroom sandwiches; grilled shad roe cut in chunks, wrapped in bacon, skewered with skewer sticks and broiled; Mrs. Appleyard's Chutney;* and ripe stuffed olives.

Before a light supper of cold meat and salad, to warm the guests, you might serve:

HOT MEAT BALLS

(For 8)

1 cup soft bread crumbs
½ cup milk
2 tablespoons onion, minced
2 tablespoons butter
½ teaspoon paprika
Pinch of nutmeg
½ teaspoon black pepper
Pinch of dill
1 clove garlic, peeled and crushed
1 egg, beaten
1 pound beef, bottom of the round, put twice through the grinder
2 ounces deviled ham
Extra butter

Soak the bread crumbs in the milk for five minutes and squeeze dry. Sauté the onion in the butter until soft but not brown. Mix the bread crumbs, seasonings, garlic, onion and egg thoroughly with the beef and ham. Make into balls no bigger than a horse chestnut. Sauté them in the extra butter until they are well browned all over. Drain on a paper towel. Insert toothpicks. Serve hot.

CHICKEN LIVERS AND CHESTNUTS

½ pound chicken livers
1 cup chicken broth
2 tablespoons soy sauce
2 tablespoons sherry
9 slices bacon (½ pound) cut crosswise in thirds
1 14-ounce can water chestnuts, drained and sliced

In saucepan, over moderate to low heat, simmer chicken livers in broth about 15 to 20 minutes until firm. Drain well. In small bowl combine soy sauce and sherry and add chicken liver. Marinate one hour. Wrap a piece of bacon around each piece of liver (cut in bite size pieces) with one slice of water chestnut and secure with toothpick. Place on rack in broiler pan and broil in preheated broiler 4 inches from source of heat for 15 minutes or until bacon is crisp, turning once. Serve hot. May be reheated in a 350° oven about 5 minutes.

Baking

MRS. Appleyard spoke often of her first triumph in baking — a pan of biscuits. She was very surprised when they turned out crisp and golden brown outside and soft inside. She was not from a family that was brought up learning to bake, and so her first attempt at baking came somewhat late in her life. However, by the time I knew my Grandmother as a person, not just as "Grandmother," she had more than made up for her lack of early training. I was inundated early in my life with the fragrances of cookies, bread, cakes, biscuits and a variety of other goodies. I now think that that anticipatory exposure to the irresistibility of baking has made me an addict. I frequently bake a loaf of sweet bread or a pan of muffins even if I don't plan on eating any of the final product myself, I just can't seem to go too long without at least the smell of warm bread coming from the oven.

There must be others like myself. Assuming there are, I include here a few notes on baking.

If you've never baked before, it is probably best to begin where high school home economics teachers begin.

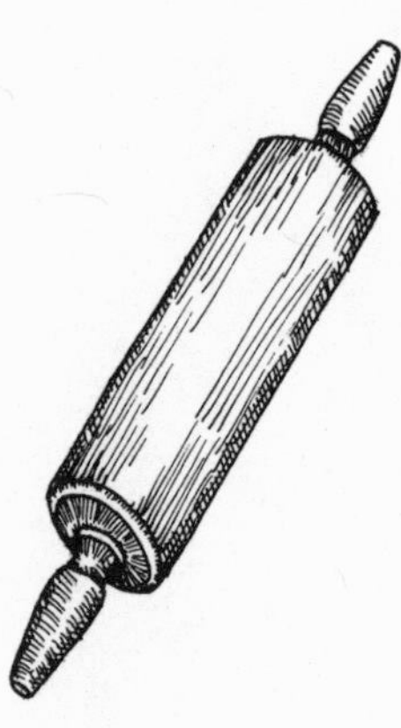

BAKING POWDER BISCUITS

2 cups unbleached flour
½ teaspoon salt
2 teaspoons baking powder
2 tablespoons butter
¾ cup rich milk

Sift the flour once, measure it, flour your new bread board with what's left over. Sift it three times more with the salt and baking powder. With a pastry blending fork work in the butter until it is in rather small grains. Still using the pastry fork, work in the milk. Toss the dough on a slightly floured board, or cloth. Knead it briefly and gently. Roll out the dough — also gently — about three quarters of an inch thick. Light oven: 450°. Handling it as little as possible and using a fluted or straight-sided cookie cutter, shape it into biscuits. Lay them on a buttered or teflon baking sheet. Bake them until golden brown — about 12 minutes.

For shortcake increase the butter to one-third of a cup. Cut and bake them as above.

If your oven is not hot enough, the gas formed by the baking powder will escape without letting the biscuits rise. If you are planning to use them for chicken pie or pan dowdy, do not roll them out. Add a little extra milk and push fair sized lumps off a spoon onto the bubbling liquid in the pan of chicken.

For herbed biscuits, stir in:

¼ teaspoon rosemary *¼ teaspoon basil* *⅛ teaspoon marjoram*

with the dry ingredients after sifting. These are excellent with poultry or for topping a chicken pie.

SOUR CREAM BISCUITS

Learning to make these is a trial and error process. Grandmother learned from her husband's mother to use only just enough soda to neutralize the acidity of the buttermilk and sour cream and to add baking powder to help with the rising process. The amount of soda needed varies with the acidity of the milk and cream. If you get it right, the biscuits will be deliciously light, golden and tender. If you put in too little soda, they won't rise and if there's too much, they will be greenish and taste terrible. You must taste the milk and cream after you've mixed the soda with them. This takes courage. There should be no sour taste and no taste of soda either. If there is too much soda, add more milk. Of course in that case, you'll need more flour and so on. It's a knack. It takes learning, but in these days of commercial sour cream and consistent soda, we have a distinct advantage. If you get the knack, I think the trials will have been worth it.

Start with:

2 cups flour (or more), use any left over for rolling out
½ teaspoon salt
2 teaspoons baking powder
¾ cup buttermilk
½ cup sour cream
½ teaspoon soda

Sift the flour, measure it. Sift it three times with the salt and baking powder. Light oven: 475°. Mix buttermilk, cream and soda. Taste it. Add more sour cream, a teaspoon at a time, if it tastes at all of soda. When it is right work it into the flour mixture lightly with a pastry fork. Add more flour if necessary. The mixture should be stiffer than for baking powder biscuits because there is no butter to melt. Push lumps of dough off the end of a large spoon onto a buttered baking sheet. Bake at 475°. Check at the end of eight minutes. Reduce heat to 450° if the biscuits are browning too fast. They should be done in about ten minutes.

DEVILED BISCUITS

Mix dough for baking powder biscuits. Light oven: 450°. Roll the dough rather thin. Brush half of it with melted butter. Lay the other half on top of it. Cut dough into small squares. Bake at 450° until lightly browned — about 12 minutes.

Make this filling:

1 4-ounce tin deviled ham
1 cup grated mild cheese
1 tablespoon mayonnaise
1 egg, beaten
1 teaspoon onion, put through garlic press
Softened butter

Mix ham, cheese, mayonnaise, beaten egg and onion together well. While biscuits are warm, split them. Spread insides of the top halves with softened butter, and the lower halves with the filling. Put the halves together again. At serving time put them into a 400° oven just long enough to heat them through. Serve hot.

CHEESE AND CHUTNEY BISCUITS

Make these like the Deviled Biscuits above but use this filling:

½ cup chutney, Mrs. Appleyard's, or Major Grey's*
1 egg, beaten
1 teaspoon onion, put through garlic press
1 cup grated cheddar cheese
½ teaspoon curry powder

Use extra curry powder if you like them very hot.

Mrs. Appleyard learned to make these muffins from her favorite philosopher, who also happened to be her daughter, Sally. It's a healthy thing to have recipes pass in both directions on the family tree.

BRAN MUFFINS

1½ cups bran
1 cup milk
1 cup flour
4 teaspoons baking powder
4 tablespoons butter
½ cup sugar
½ cup molasses
2 eggs, beaten

Soak the bran in the milk for five minutes. Sift flour and baking powder and stir them into the bran and milk. Cream butter and sugar, stir in the molasses and the beaten eggs. Beat this mixture into the flour mixture. Light oven: 400°. Heat iron gem pans or teflon muffin pans with small bits of butter in them. Pour mixture into the heated pans. Fill two-thirds full. Bake for about 20 minutes. This amount makes a dozen or more muffins according to the size of your pans. Any left over are good split, buttered and heated through to melt the butter.

**See Index for pages where recipes can be found.*

BLUEBERRY MUFFINS

These used to be seasonal, but with frozen blueberries, you can have them at any time of the year. I still like the blueberries best picked off a convenient mountain top.

Heated iron gem pans with plenty of butter melted in them make these muffins beautifully browned all over.

Start with:

¼	*cup butter*	2⅔	*cups flour*
⅓	*cup sugar*	4	*teaspoons baking powder*
2	*eggs, beaten*	1	*heaping cup blueberries*

1 *cup milk*

Cream butter, working in sugar. Add the beaten eggs, beat well. Sift the flour, measure it, sift it three times more with the baking powder. Flour the berries with about a quarter of a cup of the flour. Alternating with the milk, beat the rest of it into the egg mixture. Gently stir and fold in the blueberries. Use a spoon with holes in it or a rubber spatula. Light oven: 450°. Put the gem pans with pieces of butter in them into the oven until the butter is melted. Fill gem pans two-thirds full. Bake until the muffins have risen above the tops of the pan and are a handsome tan, punctured here and there by spots of imperial purple — about 25 minutes. Serve them with the main course or for dessert with Foamy Sauce.*

MRS. APPLEYARD'S DATE NUT BREAD

2 *cups graham or whole wheat flour*	1 *cup sour cream*
1 *cup white flour*	2 *large eggs*
1 *teaspoon baking powder*	1 *cup dates, cut in pieces and floured*
1 *teaspoon baking soda*	1 *cup walnuts, chopped and floured*
1 *cup dark molasses*	

Butter a bread tin, lightly flour it. Sift the flour, measure it. Sift it three times with the baking powder and soda. (Don't discard the bran, as I once made the mistake of doing in my Grandmother's kitchen, stir it back in.) Light oven: 375°. Stir the molasses and cream together. Add the eggs, well beaten. Now add the dry ingredients. Keep beating, with an electric mixer. Stir in the floured dates and nuts. Put the entire mixture into the bread tin. Bake one hour, reducing the heat to 350° after the first 15 minutes.

Serve slightly warm with cottage or cream cheese and fruit. This is considered an adequate dessert by the simple dwellers of Appleyard Center, who also like it buttered and eaten with a salad.

SOUR CREAM GRAHAM BREAD

I have always had a secret ambition to make graham (whole wheat) bread as good as my Grandmother's Grandmother. That secret was never written down, but my Grandmother, through trial and error, claimed to have reached a pale shadow of that happy memory. Now, never having tasted the elder Appleyard's version, I think that the following rendition is not bad — as I have learned to say from my Vermont neighbors. Please overlook this conceited expression and try it sometime.

Begin by buttering and flouring two pans and lining them with waxed paper.

2	*cups graham or whole wheat flour*	2	*teaspoons soda*
2	*cups unbleached white flour*	2	*eggs, well beaten*
2	*teaspoons baking powder*	½	*cup sour cream*
		1½	*cups buttermilk*

1⅓ cups light molasses

Sift dry ingredients together. Light oven: 375°. Beat eggs well. Stir cream, milk and molasses into them. Add the sifted flour. The batter should be quite stiff. Add a little more graham flour if necessary. Fill pans two-thirds full with the mixture. Bake one hour, reducing heat to 350° after the first fifteen minutes. Test with a straw of dried tall timothy grass. When it comes out clean the bread is done.

This bread is good buttered and even better served as a warm dessert with powdered maple sugar and thick cream.

An excellent special bread for holidays or gift-giving is Cranberry Bread. My sister-in-law, Chris, baked a loaf for my husband, Jay, at Christmas time. Unfortunately, as was the custom, the gift was left under the Christmas tree while the entire family was eating a delectable Christmas dinner. A new Labrador puppy made his dinner that afternoon of cranberry bread, and Jay never got a chance to sample Chris' gift. The puppy wasn't too happy about the incident in the end, either, for he spent the remainder of the day locked out of the festivities.

CRANBERRY BREAD

2	*cups sifted flour*	1	*egg, beaten*
1	*cup sugar*	¾	*cup orange juice*
1½	*teaspoons baking powder*	1	*teaspoon grated orange peel*
1	*teaspoon salt*	1½	*cups light raisins*
½	*teaspoon baking soda*	1½	*cups whole fresh cranberries*
¼	*cup butter or margarine*		

Sift the first five ingredients together three times. Cut in the shortening with a pastry knife until crumbly. Mix the egg, orange juice and orange peel in a separate bowl and pour into flour mixture. Stir just until the mixture is moist. Fold in the raisins and cranberries.

Spoon into a buttered 9x5x3-inch loaf pan. Bake at 350° for one hour and ten minutes. Test for doneness with a straw. When it comes out clean, the bread is done. Remove from the pan and cool on a rack. You may use all cranberries in place of half the raisins if you like; it makes for a more colorful bread.

BREAD WITH YEAST

A great moment it was when I cut into the first real loaf of bread that I had baked myself! It was hard to believe the loaf of fragrant, golden, crusty bread was something that I had produced. Luckily the pleasure comes again with almost the same excitment and more confidence every time I bake more. Recently, I have taken to using a bread mixer. It is a labor-saving device, if there are two people to take turns, one cranking and one holding the mixer down to the table. Happily, my husband seems to enjoy this exercise so that every now and then we bake four loaves of bread.

We begin by wetting the rubber feet on which the mixer stands. This is supposed to make it stick firmly to the table, and so it does until we are about exhausted from cranking, when it starts to skid. This is when another pair of hands, especially one stronger than mine, is appreciated. If you haven't a bread mixer, it is still possible to knead bread by hand, which I do quite often.

BASIC WHITE BREAD

2½	*cups milk*	*3*	*envelopes active dry yeast (or 3 tablespoons)*
⅓	*cup butter*	*¼*	*cup lukewarm water*
¼	*cup sugar*	*13*	*cups flour, measured after sifting*
1	*tablespoon salt*		
2	*cups cold water*		

Put milk and butter in a deep sauce pan. Scald milk. Remove from heat. When butter is entirely melted, pour milk into mixer (or large mixing bowl). Stir in the sugar and salt. When they have dissolved, add the cold water. Dissolve the yeast in lukewarm water (85-105°). A drop of it on your wrist should feel just barely warm. If you are unsure about the quality of your yeast, add a teaspoon of sugar to the yeast-water mixture. Let it sit for 5-8 minutes — it should begin to show some activity (bubbling). If it does not, don't use it, you'll only waste your flour.

When the milk is lukewarm too, stir in the dissolved yeast mixture. Add the sifted flour, a cup at a time. Clamp top tightly on the mixer and crank it for 15 minutes (or knead for 8-10 minutes by hand, turning the dough towards you and into itself). Check the contents of the mixer after ten minutes of cranking. If a ball has not formed on the crank, add a little more flour, about half a cup. If kneading by hand, use additional flour and continue until no flour is needed to prevent dough from sticking to board and hands. Dough should be smooth and elastic.

Finish cranking or kneading; set the mixer, or bowl, in a warm place. The top of a radiator with a layer of newspaper on it is ideal. Cover the mixer or bowl with a clean towel, wrung out in warm water. Your gas oven, if it has a pilot light and is large enough, is good too. Or set the bowl in a cold oven with a pan of warm water on the shelf beneath it. What you want is a temperature of about 80°. The dough should double in about two hours.

When the dough has doubled in bulk, punch it down with a few turns of the crank, or your fist, then rub a little butter on your hands, get the dough off the crank and the sides of the mixer. Put the dough on a floured slab or cloth. Knead the dough for two or three minutes. Let it rest briefly: there's a mixer to wash and four pans to butter. Divide the dough into four parts, knead, punch with the knuckles, turn and fold each one until it is the right size and shape for the pan. Put each one, seam side up, in a pan, then turn the dough so that the smooth side is oiled and on top, pushing it well towards the corners of the pan.

Set the pans on a tray, back on the radiator, or other warm spot, so the bread will rise again at 80° for about an hour. When it is well risen, light oven: 400°. Melt some butter and with a pastry brush, gently paint the tops of the loaves. Bake for 15 minutes at 400°, then reduce to 350° and bake until the bread is golden brown and sounds hollow when tapped on the bottom — about 30-40 minutes longer. Turn off the oven. Turn the bread upside down in the pans or set on a rack, and let it cool slowly. Cut the crust off one of the loaves, butter it and share it with your helper.

Veteran bread bakers know of a vast number of variations frequently made on yeast bread. Most often, my bread is a result of a combination of the most readily available ingredients. Any number of ingredients might be substituted in order to come up with an entirely original delicious bread. For example:

Substitute as much as half of the white flour with:
- whole wheat flour
- cooked hot cereal; oatmeal, Wheatena, cream of wheat, etc.
- wheat germ
- uncooked rolled oats
- rye, millet or barley flour
- or any combination of the above.

Substitute the sugar with:
- honey — decrease the liquid by ¼ cup
- molasses
- brown sugar

Substitute the milk with:
- potato water
- soup stock — for herbed bread

Be inventive and experiment. Once you have a good feel for a successful loaf of white bread, you'd be surprised at the success you might experience with new ingredients.

Another variation of yeast bread that comes out a deep rich auburn color with a full-bodied flavor is:

WHITE BREAD WITH SOY FLOUR

Start with:

2 *tablespoons dry yeast*
½ *cup warm water*
6 *tablespoons honey*
4 *tablespoons melted butter*
4 *cups scalded milk*
2 *cups soy flour*
10 *cups unbleached flour (about)*
3 *teaspoons salt*

Dissolve the yeast in lukewarm water (85°-105°) and set in a warm place. Put the honey, melted butter and salt in a large bowl and add scalded milk, stirring until all has melted. When this mixture has cooled to lukewarm, add the yeast mixture, soy flour and two cups of the white flour. Stir well until the batter is smooth. Slowly add more flour, stirring until the dough leaves the side of the bowl.

Turn the dough out onto a well-floured breadboard and knead until it picks up no extra flour. Set the dough to rise until double in size. Cover with a clean, damp towel. Knead down and set to rise again. Shape into loaves as for the Yeast Bread above, let rise again for one hour and bake at 425° for about 35 minutes, until a straw comes out clean and a tap on the bottom of the loaf brings a hollow sound. The soy flour causes the loaves to brown more quickly than usual, so you should check them after 20 minutes, and if they are browning too fast cover with aluminum foil for the remainder of the baking time. If you want a soft crust, spread melted butter over the crusts with a pastry brush.

FOUR GRAIN BREAD

This is a very substantial bread, somewhat coarse and 100% more nutritious than a typical loaf of white sponge bread commonly purchased at the grocery store. The Appleyards have spent many free moments dreaming of uses for that foul substance, but most would be unacceptable to the common consumer. Ah well, at least one positive step towards better bread is to begin with:

3	*tablespoons dry yeast*	2	*cups scalded milk*
½	*cup warm water*	1½	*cups hot water*
½	*cup vegetable oil, or butter*	12	*cups flour: 6 white, 2 rye,*
½	*cup honey*		*2 cornmeal and 2 whole*
4	*teaspoons salt*		*wheat (about)*

Dissolve yeast in warm water and set in a warm place to begin working. Put shortening, honey and salt in a large bowl. Pour the scalded milk and hot water over these ingredients and stir until all is dissolved. Let cool to lukewarm and add the yeast mixture. Add enough flour to the mixture to make a batter, stir briskly. Keep mixing in more flour until you can't work it with a spoon. Then, turn the dough out onto a floured board or cloth and knead until the dough picks up no extra flour. Place the dough in a greased bowl, cover with a clean towel and let rise until double in size (about 45 minutes). Knead the dough down and set to rise again (about 30 more minutes). Divide the dough into four equal pieces and shape into loaves as for Yeast Bread. Place in well-greased bread pans and set to rise again (about 20 minutes). Bake for 35 minutes at 425° and test as for Yeast Bread.

Having once made a batch of bread, anything seems possible. You'll want to try rules that your neighbors give you. One of Mrs. Appleyard's neighbors once gave her this particular rule for:

CINNAMON BUNS

½	*cup sugar*	¼	*cup lukewarm water*
1	*teaspoon salt*	8	*cups sifted all-purpose flour*
¼	*cup butter*	2	*eggs, well beaten*
2	*cups boiling water*	1	*teaspoon cinnamon*
2	*tablespoons dry yeast*	¾	*cup brown sugar*
1	*tablespoon sugar*	½	*cup currants*

Dissolve ½ cup sugar, salt and butter in the boiling water. Cool to lukewarm. Dissolve the yeast and one tablespoon sugar in the ¼ cup of lukewarm water. Add to the first mixture. Add four cups of the flour.

Add the beaten eggs and the rest of the flour. Stir thoroughly. Let rise in a greased bowl till twice the bulk. Use at once or store for refrigerator rolls. For cinnamon buns, roll out the dough, spread with butter, cinnamon, brown sugar and currants, if desired. Roll up and into a log shape and cut into ¾ inch slices. Lay cut side down in greased pans. Let rise in a warm place until it has doubled in bulk. Bake at 400° for 10-15 minutes, depending on size. Also good baked in individual muffin pans. Good for breakfast with scrambled eggs.

KOLACKY — NUT BREAD

8 cups flour (about)
⅔ cup sugar
3 tablespoons dry yeast dissolved in ½ cup lukewarm water
¾ pound butter, melted
2 cups milk scalded, lukewarm
3 level dessert spoons salt
4 eggs
1 cup pecans
1 cup sugar

Mix all but the pecans and one cup of sugar, together. Knead well on a floured board or cloth. Let rise in a warm place till doubled or more in bulk. Cut into 10 or 11 pieces and put on a floured breadboard. Roll each piece out to eight or nine inches square. Mix the chopped nuts with one cup sugar and enough water to spread easily. Spread each square with the mixture. Roll up like a jelly roll and place all the rolls in an oblong pan. When all the rolls are in place, brush each one with melted butter. Bake at 400° for ten minutes until light golden brown. Reduce the heat to 350° and bake until done — about 20 minutes longer.

CRESCENT ROLLS

Use the Kolacky dough above cut into smaller pieces. Roll out to 3x3 inches square. Dip in melted butter, shape into crescents, sprinkle with poppy seed, bake at 400° for ten minutes. Reduce heat to 350° Bake until done — about 20 minutes longer.

FRENCH BREAD

(With an American Accent)

Use Kolacky dough above. Shape into two long loaves like French loaves. Bake on a cookie sheet. The loaves will not, of course, be of the consistency or texture of real French bread, but they are, according to Mrs. Appleyard, quite palatable. They bake in a somewhat shorter time than loaves of bread in tins — ten minutes at 400° and about 30 minutes longer at 350°.

I sometimes cut one loaf part way through, in diagonal strips, put garlic butter in the cracks and reheat it. This is delicious served with cold meat and a tossed salad on a warm evening. On a cooler evening, it goes well with a hearty soup. I sometimes use a loaf for:

CURRIED BREAD

Cut a loaf of your French bread in ½ inch slices almost all the way through. To ¼ pound of softened butter, add ¼ teaspoon of garlic powder and ½ teaspoon of curry powder. Spread the seasoned butter between the slices. This may be done ahead of time. Just before you serve it, put the bread in a pan in a 400° oven and bake till it smells irresistibly pungent — about eight minutes. Don't overbake it: the centers of the slices should be rather soft.

MELBA TOAST

Your own bread, when it is a few days old, makes the best Melba toast. Grandmother used to tell me stories of Madame Melba, a singer, singing in Symphony Hall more than half a century ago. It was her opinion that it was better that Madame Melba be remembered by the toast and Pêche Melba than by any scratchy old recordings that may still exist.

At any rate, for Madame's toast, trim off the crusts of the bread you plan to use. Keep every crumb, of course, for future use in casseroles. Cut each slice into four triangles, put them into a large pan in a 200° oven to dry. This takes about two hours. At the end of the first hour change their position in the pan so that they will all dry evenly.

POPOVERS

Popovers are cheering on a cold evening, and much easier to prepare than the popular mystique allows you to believe. They may be made triumphantly by starting them in cold pans in a cold oven, I'm told, but I haven't had much luck in using this method. I recommend the hot technique. It's somewhat like being a water witch: you have to find your own method of success and stick to it.

The most important part of the process is to make sure that the muffin tins are filled exactly half-full. One way of ensuring that's happening is to start with a clean wooden tab, the kind you might use for marking young plants. Find out by filling a cup with water and pouring off half of it, where the halfway level comes on your cups. Then mark this on your wooden tab. It works well to help produce popovers evenly baked and uniform in size.

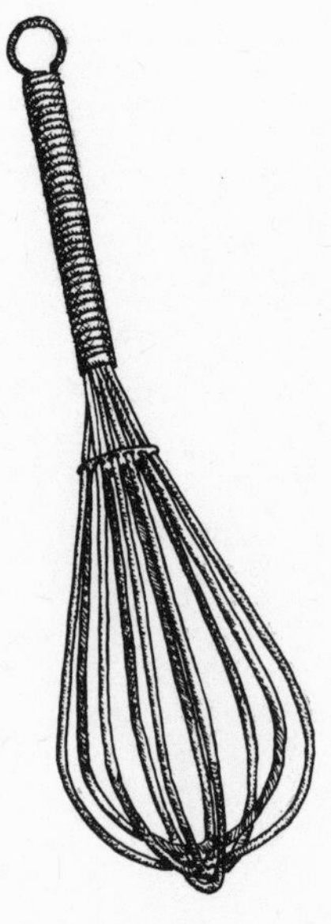

Start with iron muffin pans or ovenproof custard cups set on a cookie sheet. Put half a teaspoon of melted butter in each cup. Set the pan or cookie sheet in a preheated 450° oven. Then set to making the batter.

6 teaspoons melted butter — for pans
1½ cups milk
3 eggs
1½ cups flour, sifted, measured, sifted three times with
½ teaspoon salt
1 tablespoon butter

Put the milk, eggs, a tablespoon of butter and the sifted flour and salt all into your blender. Blend for three minutes, or beat with a wooden spoon. If any flour sticks to the side, push it into the batter with a rubber scraper and blend again for a few seconds. Using your wooden measure, fill each preheated muffin or custard cup half full. Return the cups or iron pans to the oven. Bake 30 minutes at 450°. Reduce the heat to 350° and bake until well-browned — 15-20 minutes longer. Remove from the pans. Make small slits in the side with a sharp knife. This lets the steam escape. Turn off the oven. The popovers not used at once may be kept in a warm oven without getting soggy.

Eating them with butter is only one way of using popovers. You may fill them with Real Chicken a la King,* or with Mushrooms in Cream* or with Shrimp Newburg* and serve them for lunch with a salad. They may also be used for dessert as if they were cream puffs. I like them filled with vanilla ice cream and laced with Chocolate Sauce.*

YORKSHIRE PUDDING

This is actually a close relative to the popover. The resemblance is not always noticed, though, because the pudding is so often soggy and limp. This is unnecessary if you use this method for baking.

Start with:

1 cup flour	*3 eggs*
Salt to taste — about ½ teaspoon	*1 cup milk*

Sift the flour and salt together four times. Put them in blender with the eggs and milk, and blend just under three minutes. Check at the end of the first minute and push any flour that has stuck to the side of the blender into the batter with a rubber scraper.

If you are serving this with roast beef, test the beef with a meat thermometer and note when the beef reaches the temperature at which you like it. Just under 145° for the Appleyard family. Pour fat from the beef, half-inch deep, into a nine-inch cast iron frying pan. Keep the fat hot on top of the stove. Pour in the batter (carefully, it may spurt at you).

Assuming that the meat thermometer shows the beef to be almost done, it does the roast no harm to remove it from the oven ahead of time. It will continue to cook slowly and is easier to carve than if it is hot. Set the pan with the batter in the oven and bake the pudding for 20 minutes at 400°. Baste the pudding with the pan juices after 20 minutes and occasionally after that. It should be crisp and a dark golden brown in about 15 more minutes.

After coping with Yorkshire Pudding, you might like to experiment with some:

PARSLEY PIN WHEELS

2 cups flour

1 teaspoon baking powder	*4 tablespoons ice water*
1 8-ounce package cream cheese (at room temp.)	*¼ cup minced parsley (no stems)*
4 tablespoons butter with extra butter — about 2 tablespoons	*2 tablespoons minced chives*
	1 teaspoon onion powder
	3 tablespoons cream

Sift the flour three times with the baking powder. Cut in the cream cheese and butter with a pastry fork. Work in the ice water with a fork. Add the parsley, chives and onion powder mixed with the cream. Mix thoroughly and toss mixture on a floured pastry cloth or board. Roll the dough out ¼ inch thick in a 12x8-inch rectangle. Cut in thirds the short way. Dot with butter. Pile the outer two pieces on the center one. Turn the cloth 90 degrees. Roll out the dough again. Cut in thirds again and repeat this turning, rolling and cutting process three times. Roll up like a jelly roll. Slice pieces from the roll ½ inch thick. Put the slices on a baking sheet. Bake at 400° for ten minutes. Reduce the heat to 350°. Bake until puffed and delicately browned — about 25 minutes longer.

ENGLISH MUFFINS

If you have a heavy griddle, the type you also use for pancakes, you might like to try baking some English Muffins. I was once told that English Muffins are just a myth; that they don't exist in England and never did. Perhaps they are like some American habits of speech: 17th century English was still spoken in parts of New England a generation ago. Television has made that all but vanish, along with old ballads and old contra dances. Although, there seems to be a resurgence of contra dancing in the area surrounding Appleyard Center, and perhaps in other areas, too. Might we also start a resurgence of English Muffins?

A friend insists that these are really more like crumpets. Of course by that time he had eaten three, two plain buttered and one with strawberry jam. And even if they are, since there is no such thing as an English Muffin, how did he know? At any rate, here is how Grandmother made these possibly Anglican delicacies.

1	*tablespoon, or 1 package dry yeast*	*1½*	*cups milk, scalded*
		2	*tablespoons sugar*
½	*cup lukewarm water*	*1*	*egg, beaten*
¼	*cup butter*	*6*	*cups sifted flour*

Dissolve the yeast in the lukewarm water. Melt the butter in the scalded milk. Add the sugar and stir until it is dissolved. Cool this mixture until it is lukewarm and add the yeast mixture and the beaten egg. Beat in, gradually, three cups of flour. When the batter is smooth, stir in the other three cups of flour. Butter a large bowl well. Put the dough in it. Turn the dough over so that all sides are greased. Cover the bowl with a clean towel and let the dough rise until double in bulk — about one and a half hours.

Roll the dough three-quarter inch thick on a floured board. Cut into rounds with a three inch cutter and put the rounds in a big iron dripping pan, not too close together. . . . Cover and let rise in a warm place again until they are very light — about 20 minutes.

When the muffins are well risen, bake them on a moderately hot griddle. You may grease it with shortening, or polish it with the cut side of a raw potato. Cut off and discard a thin slice from time to time, so that you will have a fresh potato surface.

Getting the muffins from the dripping pan to the griddle without dropping them is a rather special skill. They seem determined to lead their own lives. The air bubbles formed escape easily. Be firm but gentle, I would say, and use two spatulas.

Turn the muffins often on the griddle so they will bake evenly all the way through. This rule makes about two dozen. Eat them hot or cold. Split, toast and butter them like any English Muffin — or crumpet for that matter. Or, split them with a stainless fork, butter them generously and run them under the broiler. Watch them carefully, they turn to carbon speedily.

MUFFINS WITH CHEESE AND CHUTNEY

For a change of pace light lunch, try these English Muffins* along with a tossed salad.

For four muffins split, use:

- 2 *tablespoons of butter*
- 1 *cup cheddar cheese, grated*
- ½ *teaspoon paprika*
- 4 *tablespoons Mrs. Appleyard's Chutney**
- 1 *teaspoon dry mustard*

Melt the butter. Remove the pan from the fire. Stir in the grated cheese. When the cheese is soft, stir in the chutney and seasonings. Heap some of the chutney and cheese mixture on the toasted muffins. The mixture will tend to spread, so keep it in the center. Put the muffins on a baking sheet. Run them under the broiler till the cheese begins to bubble — about two minutes.

COFFEE CAKE

- 2 *tablespoons dry yeast*
- 1½ *cups milk*
- ¼ *cup butter*
- 1 *cup sugar*
- 6 *cups flour*
- 3 *egg yolks*

Dissolve the yeast in ¼ cup of lukewarm water. Scald milk and melt the butter in it. Cool to lukewarm. Mix with yeast and four tablespoons of sugar. Stir in three cups of the flour, sifted, and beat well. Put in a large well-buttered bowl, and reverse the dough so that it will be greased all over. Cover with a clean towel. Set in a warm place and let rise until it doubles in bulk — about two hours. Then add the egg yolks, the rest of the cup of sugar and the other three cups of flour. Toss on a floured board and knead well for seven minutes, letting it rest once for a minute. Put back into the buttered bowl and let rise again until doubled — about an hour and a half.

In the meantime make this mixture:

- 2 *cups sugar*
- ¼ *pound candied fruit*
- ½ *teaspoon nutmeg*
- ¼ *cup each of currants, seedless raisins and chopped walnuts*
- 1½ *teaspoons cinnamon*

Butter an angel cake tin well, punch down dough and tear off tablespoon size pieces of it. Dip them into the fruit, sugar and spice mixture and pack them lightly into the angel cake tin. Cover, set in a warm place and let rise till double in bulk — about 40 minutes. Scatter the remaining mixture over the top of the dough. Dot with butter, about two tablespoons, in small bits. This amount will fill two medium size angel cake tins. Bake at 375° for 25 minutes. Reduce heat to 325° and bake delicately brown — about 15 minutes.

ALMOND COFFEE CAKE

(For 6)

This is a filling and somewhat richer version of the above coffee cake. Use the same dough as above. Set about three-quarters of it to rise for its second rising in a deep round pan about seven to eight inches across. When it is well risen, tear it into four pieces. Roll each one out into a half inch thick circle that will fit easily into the pan. Put one layer into the greased pan and spread a layer of almond paste, then some raspberry and some currant jelly, then a layer of blanched and toasted almonds. Next, put another circular piece of dough on top of the last and repeat until all four pieces are in the pan. Finish the top layer with plenty of almonds, sprinkle on a little sugar, and dot with small bits of butter.

Let the dough rise again in a warm place until doubled in bulk. Bake at 400° for ten minutes. Reduce the heat to 350° and bake until the top is brown — about 35-40 minutes longer. If it seems to be browning too quickly, make a tent of aluminum foil and remove it in the last 15 minutes of baking.

With the remaining quarter of the dough, I made half a dozen individual cakes in muffin tins. Reheated, they are a welcome addition to breakfast. If you have some Crème Damia cheese to eat along with the cake, you will need little else to sustain you, except perhaps a long brisk walk afterward — half uphill if possible.

After about a week's time you might feel in the mood to try a:

CROUSTADE

This is really Bread with Yeast,* except that it is baked in a Dutch round, enameled, iron casserole instead of in a regular loaf pan. Bake it the day before you plan to use it.

When the time comes to serve it, slice the top off the lightly browned loaf. This will be the lid of the croustade. Remove all the soft part from the center of the bread. (You may save it and stuff a chicken with it another day.) Butter the inside of the lid and the croustade. Just before filling it, set it into a 350° oven for five minutes so that it will be warm when the filling goes in. Different kinds of filling may be used: Real Chicken a la King,* curried chicken, or Lobster Newburg,* for instance. This makes a complete lunch or light supper accompanied by a green salad.

BREAD CUPS

These are junior size croustades. You can make them from your own bread, thinly sliced, or from Arnold or Pepperidge Farms bread. Cut the crusts from bread. Spread both sides with butter or, if you like, garlic butter. Press the slices into lightly greased muffin pans. Trim the edges neatly, saving the crumbs and the crusts, that is if you're frugal. If not, you may proceed on your path of dissolute extravagance. Bake at 400° until golden brown — about ten minutes. Use to hold creamed chicken, creamed mushrooms, or seafood.

BREAD STICKS

2¼ cups flour
2½ teaspoons baking powder
1 tablespoon sugar
¾ cup milk
Extra butter

Sift flour with baking powder and sugar four times. Cut in the butter with a pastry fork. Work in the milk. Toss the dough on a floured board or cloth, knead it ten times. Roll it out in a rectangle 12x8 inches. Cut it into three sections. Put the side sections on the middle one. Turn dough

90 degrees. Roll out, cut and turn twice more. Chill briefly while you heat oven to 450° and melt four tablespoons of butter in the ends of two 9x13-inch pans. Now, roll out the dough once more. Cut it into sticks, turn each over in the melted butter. Lay the sticks in rows in the pans. They may be sprinkled with sesame seeds if you like. Bake them at 450° for ten minutes, then until well browned — 15 or 20 minutes longer. Serve with soup or salad. Makes about three dozen. The number depends on how they are cut. If you cut them too narrowly, they will break.

CROUTONS WITH CURRY

Remove crusts from four slices of bread. Cut them into quarter inch cubes. Melt butter in an iron frying pan. Toss in the cubes until they are delicately browned. Sprinkle them with a mixture of one teaspoon of garlic powder and half a teaspoon of curry powder. These are especially good with cream of chicken soup.

CORNMEAL IN BAKING

What is corn? Strangely, as I was growing up, I never had any doubts about the substance intended when the term "corn" was employed. Now all of a sudden, I've become aware that "corn" holds a number of different meanings to persons of different nationalities. The English, correctly Grandmother believed, call the seeds of wheat "corn." In Scotland and Ireland oats are also called corn. Where did all the confusion come from over such a seemingly simple substance? Well, as I eventually found out, corn is simply the name for our most important grain, whatever it may be. So, I can again assume that I am correct in calling corn, in my distinctly Americanized English, corn. After all, it was the American Indians' most important grain, so important that the "Pilgrim Fathers" (and mothers) called it corn as soon as they began to grind it up and make Hasty Pudding out of it. Those who had servants in the early days had to give them a certain amount of Hasty Pudding each day, and it had to be "lawful pudding." This meant that there had to be suitable amounts of cornmeal in proportion to the water in which it was cooked so that the pudding stick, with which it was stirred, would stand straight up in the kettle. A real "stick to your ribs" kind of sustenance.

The closest thing to Hasty Pudding now eaten is what we call:

CORNMEAL MUSH

4¼ cups boiling water

Salt to taste, about one teaspoon
1 cup cornmeal, yellow or white

When the water is boiling hard in the top of a double boiler, add the salt. Then sprinkle in the cornmeal so slowly that the water never stops boiling. Keep stirring it constantly until the mixture is smooth. Set the pan over the bottom half of the double boiler containing rapidly boiling water, and let it cook until it has absorbed all the water and is quite thick, about 30 minutes. This makes a strengthening breakfast, and is tasty with butter and maple syrup. My brother also likes it with milk and brown sugar. It is especially helpful when you have to face a strong wind and a temperature of 30° below zero.

The best part, however, comes the next day. If you had any mush left over, and packed it into buttered orange juice cans, or larger cans if you prefer, you have the makings for another meal. When you use the mush, cut into half inch slices. Butter an iron frying pan. Dip the slices, just enough to dust them, in flour seasoned as you like. (I prefer a pinch of nutmeg.) Put the floured slices in the buttered pan and bake them at 400°, turning them after the first ten minutes. If you like, you may cook them on top of the stove on a greased griddle. Whichever way they are cooked, they should be a rich golden brown.

Serve the cakes with butter and maple syrup and either sausages or bacon. Your backbone should feel as strong as a pudding stick standing upright in a "lawful pudding."

In the *Vermont Year Round Cookbook*, Mrs. Appleyard included a rule for Vermont Johnny Cake on page 63. The Appleyards are fond of it, but even more so of:

THIN SCALDED JOHNNY CAKE

1 cup cornmeal, yellow or white
2 tablespoons butter
Salt to taste, about ½ teaspoon
1 cup boiling water, more if needed
Extra butter, about two tablespoons

Light oven: 475°. Put the cornmeal, butter and salt into a warm bowl. Bring it close to the rapidly boiling water, which should be as hot as possible when it strikes the meal. Pour the water over the meal a little at a time, returning the saucepan to the fire after each addition. When the butter is melted and the meal has absorbed enough water so that it is smooth and thick but not too wet, put it on a greased baking sheet in small lumps and spread them out. Use a round-ended spatula for this job. Dip it in hot water from time to time. Put a good dot of butter in the middle of each cake.

Bake the cakes until they are well browned — about ten minutes. When you check them, if you think they might absorb more butter, add it if you like. Some cakes may brown more quickly than others Remove these when they are done at once. They are best when served hot, but may be reheated briefly. They go well with soup or salad or afternoon tea.

RHODE ISLAND JOHNNY CAKE

Hazard's *Johnny Cake Papers* give some idea of how delicious this form of cornmeal can be. Grandmother reportedly has cooked these in the old-fashioned way on a board tilted in front of a fire of glowing coals. She had no doubt that they and the scent of perfect coffee had a strange effect on the Dauphin of France. I have yet to read this classic and form my own opinion, but I have made these cakes in the less hectic way on the gas stove.

This rule was given to Mrs. Appleyard's Grandmother by a kind Rhode Island friend more than one hundred years ago. Her mother frequently produced these johnny cakes and set her off on a cold hike to school with her pockets warmed with an extra cake and her spirits warmed by the memory of their odor while baking.

2	*cups real white Rhode Island cornmeal*	2	*cups boiling water (or a little more)*
1	*teaspoon salt*	½	*cup milk, heated, not boiled*
2	*tablespoons butter*		*Extra butter for frying*

Light oven: 325°. Put a warm bowl on the stove and put the meal, salt and butter into it. Have the water boiling hard in a sauce pan. Be sure it is really boiling as you pour it on the meal, stirring all the time. The meal must absorb all the moisture it will take, so let it stand a minute or two and add the milk. Let it stand a minute longer. Add more boiling water if necessary. The batter should be soft but not wet. Drop it by heaping tablespoons on a pre-heated, well-buttered griddle. When the cakes look brown around the edges turn them, add more butter, and brown them on the other side. Have a buttered dripping pan ready in the oven. When the cakes are brown on both sides put them into the dripping pan. A little baking improves them, but be careful not to dry them out. They should be a glazed dark amber on the outside, soft, hot and white inside.

Some people serve molasses or maple syrup with them. I like them just split and buttered. They may also be served with sausages, bacon, creamed dried beef or creamed chicken, and taste extra good.

SPIDER CORN CAKE

This takes care of all things made with sour milk, but when it is done right, it has the taste of ambrosia, and once the technique is learned, it is never lost.

1⅛	*cups yellow cornmeal*	1¼	*cups sweet milk*
½	*cup white flour*	1	*egg, beaten*
3	*teaspoons baking powder*	2	*tablespoons melted butter*
1½	*teaspoons baking soda*	1	*cup buttermilk*
½	*cup sour cream*	½	*cup sweet cream*

Light oven: 400°. Sift the dry ingredients together three times. Pour in half the sour cream and half the sweet milk. Beat well. Stir in the beaten egg. Stir in the rest of the milk, sour cream and buttermilk. Melt butter in a 10-inch black iron frying pan. Pour the batter into the preheated pan. Taste the mixture. If you detect any flavor of soda, add a little more sour cream. Pour the sweet cream over the top, not stirring it in. Bake for ten minutes at 400°. Reduce the heat to 350° and bake until the corn cake is well browned — about 30 minutes longer. It should be firm outside but creamy and moist in the center.

Set it right on the table in the spider (pan) on an iron trivet. It goes well with broiled or fried chicken. A tart jelly such as raspberry or currant is good with it, but maple syrup or some butter certainly do it no harm.

The spider corn cake is not unlike spoon bread. The rule for spoon bread was given to Mrs. Appleyard under the name of "Southern Spoon Bread." But as she had no proof that it was actually from the South, she merely asserted that this is the way they make it in the southern part of Appleyard Center. That is, south of the old brick tavern on the old stage road to Canada, though slightly north of the goldfish pond and the barn with the painting of the Morgan horse on the door. With these directions I hope that you'll be able to drop in and have some pretty soon.

SPOON BREAD

1 cup cornmeal, preferably white, but yellow will do	*2 teaspoons baking powder*
2 cups boiling water	*6 tablespoons melted butter*
1 teaspoon salt	*1 cup milk*
	3 eggs, beaten

Light oven: 375°. Scald meal mixed with water, salt and baking powder. Add four tablespoons of the melted butter, then the milk and the eggs, beaten together. Put the rest of the butter into a hot baking dish. Pour in the batter. Bake until well browned — about 35 minutes.

Spoon bread is good instead of potatoes with broiled swordfish, fried chicken or cold turkey. The brown scrapings at the bottom are especially popular. Serve the spoon bread in the dish in which it is cooked.

CORN DODGERS

1 cup cornmeal	*3 cups boiling water*
1 scant teaspoon salt	*1 tablespoon butter*

Add meal and salt slowly to boiling water and cook till the mixture is thick. Add butter and beat well. Drop by spoonfuls on a buttered sheet. Bake about 25 minutes in a 450° oven.

They should be crisp outside. But look out for the inside; it will burn your tongue.

CORN DROP BISCUITS

These are similar to Corn Dodgers but a little lighter and easier to handle.

¾ cup flour	*2½ tablespoons butter*
⅓ cup cornmeal	*⅓ cup sugar*
1 teaspoon salt	*1 egg, beaten*
2 teaspoons baking powder	*½ cup milk*

Sift flour, cornmeal, salt and baking powder together. Light oven: 425°. Cream butter, beat in sugar, egg and milk. Add dry mixture and beat well. Drop batter from a tablespoon on a buttered cookie sheet. Bake until they spread out and are brown around the edges — about 25 minutes.

CORNMEAL MUFFINS

This rule is for the lucky owners of iron gem pans or iron ear-of-corn pans, the kind deeply engraved with the pattern of an ear of corn. Both pans must be heated with butter before the batter is poured. The butter should also be evenly distributed with a pastry brush.

1 cup cornmeal	*¼ cup sugar*
1 cup white flour	*1 cup milk*
½ teaspoon salt	*2 eggs, beaten*
4 teaspoons baking powder	*2 tablespoons softened butter*

Extra butter for pans

Mix and sift the dry ingredients. Light oven: 425°. Add milk, eggs and butter to the dry mixture. Beat well with an electric beater. Fill your buttered iron pans half full with the mixture. Bake for ten minutes at 425°. Reduce the heat to 375° and bake until lightly browned — about 15 minutes longer. This amount makes a dozen good-sized muffins. They should be golden brown and crusty outside, soft inside. What do you have to put on them? Honey? Strawberry jam? Orange marmalade? Any of them will be good with plenty of butter.

CORNMEAL MUFFINS WITH HONEY

These are a richer and heartier version of the above rule. They make a light supper with a robust soup and a green salad. I invented these in the midst of my self-proclaimed war against processed sugar. They may not be too much better for you, but they have a delicately sweet and nutty flavor of their very own.

¾	*cup cornmeal*	1	*cup milk*
½	*cup whole wheat flour*	1	*egg, well beaten*
½	*cup white flour*	2	*tablespoons butter, melted*
3	*teaspoons baking powder*	⅓	*cup honey*
¾	*teaspoon salt*		*Extra butter for pans*

Mix and sift the dry ingredients, putting the wheat bran back into the mixture after it is sifted out. Light oven: 425°. Mix the milk, egg, melted butter and honey together with a wire whisk. Add the wet ingredients to the dry mixture and beat well with an electric beater. Fill the pans half full with the batter. Bake ten minutes at 425°. Reduce heat to 375° and bake until lightly browned — about 15 minutes longer. This rule also makes about a dozen good-sized muffins. Watch them carefully; the honey makes them brown more quickly than usual. Serve hot.

For an even richer corn muffin, replace the baking powder with one teaspoon soda and two teaspoons cream of tartar. In place of the milk, use one cup yogurt or heavy sour cream and ¼ cup milk.

CORN PUDDING

(For 6)

Grandmother concocted this one day when she didn't have enough corn to go around for a group of unexpected visitors. I can't determine whether it is a kind of bread or a vegetable, so I'll leave it up to the chef's discretion and menu.

1¼	*cups corn, cut from the cob*	½	*teaspoon salt*
6	*tablespoons butter*	2	*cups boiling water*
1	*cup yellow cornmeal*	1	*cup milk, part cream*
2	*teaspoons baking powder*	3	*eggs, beaten*

Cut the corn from the cob, or use canned or frozen if no fresh corn is available. Melt two tablespoons of the butter in an iron enamelled baking dish. Sift the baking powder and salt with the cornmeal. Light oven: 400°. Add the rest of the butter to the meal. Scald it with the boiling water. Add the milk and the beaten eggs. Beat well. Add the cut corn; stir it in well. Put the mixture into the hot buttered baking dish.

Bake until well browned — about 25 minutes. It's especially good with ham or sausage. When my garden is depleted of corn — how soon the raccoons and summer's end come — I make corn pudding from frozen or canned whole kernel corn. I also add a teaspoon of sugar to replace some of the sweetness of freshly picked corn.

Grandmother, in her days of corn adoration, thought that it would be good to get back on the Golden Corn standard, as were the early settlers of Massachusetts. I think if you try any of the aforementioned corn dishes, you might actually agree with her.

SOUR CREAM DOUGHNUTS

Grandmother was notorious for her contempt of fried foods of any kind, including doughnuts. However, her mother-in-law was known to make doughnuts using either sour milk and butter or sour cream that even her daughter-in-law was seen to test on an occasional morning. As a result, I feel obliged to include this rule for sour cream doughnuts for those who enjoy them: they are delicious, though high in cholesterol.

	Crisco for frying	*¼*	*teaspoon cinnamon*
4	*cups flour*	*½*	*teaspoon nutmeg*
3	*teaspoons baking powder*		*Pinch of ginger*
½	*teaspoon soda*	*3*	*eggs, medium size*
½	*teaspoon salt*	*1¼*	*cups sugar*
¼	*teaspoon cloves*	*1*	*cup sour cream*

The fat should be hot enough to brown a one-inch cube of bread in one minute (365-370°). Sift the flour once and measure it. Sift it again twice, together with the dry ingredients. The spices may be varied according to taste. Beat the eggs well, beat in the sugar, stir in the cream, and sift and stir in the flour mixture. Chill the dough while the fat is heating.

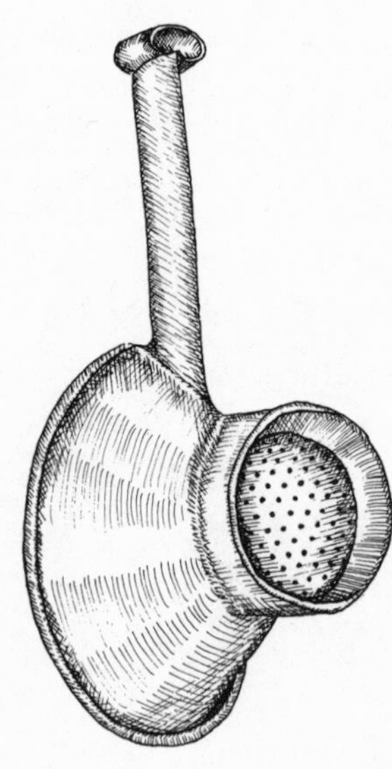

The dough may be refrigerated overnight for early morning doughnuts. Roll out the dough, half-inch thick, and cut with a lightly floured doughnut cutter or glasses of two different diameters. Cut out four and cook only four at a time. Slip the doughnuts gently into the hot fat. When they rise to the surface and are beginning to brown underneath, turn them carefully. Be careful never to pierce the surface of the doughnut for it will allow an avenue for grease to enter. They should be turned several times. When they are a rich golden brown, but not overdone, remove from the pan, letting the surface grease drip back into the kettle.

Have two pans full of crumpled paper towels. Drain the doughnuts first in one pan on one side, then move them to the second pan to drain the other side.

Check the heat of the fat. When it reaches 370°, put in four more doughnuts. When the doughnuts are all cooked, cook the doughnut balls, as rolling the dough out more than once makes them tough.

If you like your doughnuts sugared, shake them in a bag with sugar when they are well drained and just barely warm. Either powdered or granulated sugar may be used. Add half teaspoon mixed spices (cinnamon, nutmeg, allspice) to a cup of sugar, for spiced doughnuts. I have even dipped them in melted honey, and if this is done deftly, they come out with a fine coating of honey, just sweet enough.

Doughnuts are not the only baked foods that are both traditional and delicious as breakfast or brunch foods. So, before I leave baking, I'll include these last few rules for pancakes and other breakfast foods. A good basic recipe to begin with is:

SOUR MILK GRIDDLE CAKES

(Four 4-inch cakes each for 4 people)

⅞ cup flour	*1 tablespoon sugar*
¾ teaspoon baking powder	*1 large egg*
½ teaspoon salt	*1 cup sour milk*
½ teaspoon baking soda	*2 tablespoons butter, melted*

Taste the milk. If it is not very sour, reduce soda to ¼ teaspoon and increase baking powder to one teaspoon, or use one cup sour cream and omit butter.

Sift flour once. Measure it. Sift twice more with dry ingredients. Beat egg light with wire whisk. Quickly beat in milk and melted butter, then flour mixture. Do not overbeat. Heat iron griddle or well-seasoned iron frying pan. Don't grease the griddle but wipe a raw potato over the surface while griddle is warm. Heat griddle until drops of cold water dashed on it sputter and steam. Pour on batter in 4-inch circles. After two or three minutes the cakes will begin to bubble and bubbles will burst; the edges should be getting dry. Lift cakes with pancake turner. Check to see if they are well-browned, turn them and bake until they are well-browned on the other side. Remove them to a warm platter set in an open warm oven. Cut a thin slice from the potato, discard it and wipe griddle with the freshly cut surface. Do this between baking each batch of cakes. Stack in heaps of four. Serve with maple syrup or thick cream and granulated maple sugar.

BLUEBERRY PANCAKES

If you'd like to make blueberry pancakes as a special treat, use the same batter as above and one cup of frozen or fresh blueberries. Do not mix them with the batter or you will end up with batter a strange color green. Pour batter on hot griddle, spoon on blueberries, cover with more batter. Or flour the berries with ¼ cup of the flour before mixing them in. Brown cakes on both sides. Serve with Vermont sausage and butter, add maple syrup if you like the combination of tastes.

BANANA PANCAKES

For those who like bananas in any form, these will delight and surprise you.

⅞ cup flour	*½ teaspoon salt*
¼ teaspoon baking soda	*1 egg*
1 teaspoon baking powder	*1 ripe banana*
¼ teaspoon each nutmeg and cinnamon	*1 cup milk*
	2 tablespoons melted butter

Sift flour once. Measure it. Sift twice more with dry ingredients. Beat egg light with wire whisk. Blend banana with milk in blender and mix into egg, then add melted butter. Quickly beat in flour mixture. Do not overbeat. Brown cakes on both sides on a hot griddle and serve with butter and either Orange Sauce* or maple syrup.

BREAD CRUMB GRIDDLE CAKES

1½ cups scalded milk
1½ cups dry bread crumbs, browned in oven and rolled fine
2 tablespoons butter
2 eggs
½ cup flour
3 teaspoons baking powder

Scald milk over medium heat, add butter and stir until it melts. Pour over bread crumbs. Add eggs, well-beaten. Sift flour, measure and sift twice more with baking powder. Beat into milk mixture. Drop by spoonfuls on a hot griddle, turn once. Serve with butter and maple syrup.

SOUFFLÉD PANCAKES

3 eggs, separated
½ cup sour cream
¼ cup flour
1 tablespoon sugar

Beat egg yolks until light, add sour cream. Sift flour, measure, sift once more with sugar and beat into egg and cream mixture. Beat egg whites until stiff and fold into batter. Bake on a not too hot griddle in a small amount of butter. Brown on both sides. Serve with strawberry jam, melted butter mixed with confectioner's sugar and cream cheese.

ORANGE PANCAKES

A refreshing change for a Sunday brunch or even as a glamorous dessert.

2 eggs
¼ cup oil
1 cup whole wheat flour
1 cup white flour
½ teaspoon baking soda
½ teaspoon salt
2 cups orange juice, reconstituted frozen or fresh

Mix eggs and oil with a wire whisk. Sift flours once, separately, and measure. Sift twice together with other dry ingredients. To the eggs, add dry ingredients alternately with orange juice. Mix until well-blended. Bake on a hot griddle until golden brown on both sides. Serve with Orange Sauce, below. Serves four generously.

ORANGE SAUCE

1 tablespoon cornstarch
¼ teaspoon salt
2 tablespoons freshly grated orange rind or 1 tablespoon dried
1 cup orange juice
¼ cup honey
1 tablespoon butter
1 orange sectioned and cut into 1-inch pieces

In a small saucepan, mix cornstarch, salt, orange rind, orange juice and honey. Bring to boil over medium heat, stirring constantly until thickened.

Remove from heat. Stir in butter until it melts. Add orange pieces. Keep the sauce warm until pancakes are ready. Great with Orange Pancakes, above. Good also with waffles or Banana Pancakes.*

STUFFED PANCAKES

(For 4)

A sustaining luncheon dish, it is made up of three parts. First make the stuffing:

1 pound sausage meat	*¼ cup cream*
½ cup celery, cut fine	*1 cup white meat of turkey*

6 chestnuts, broken

Cook sausage meat in a frying pan until done. Drain off fat and crumble meat finely. Sauté celery in a small amount of sausage fat. Mix celery and meat with cream, turkey and chestnuts. Mix well and set aside. If the stuffing is too moist add enough bread crumbs to absorb the excess liquid.

Next make the cheese sauce:

3 tablespoons butter	*1½ cups rich milk*
3 tablespoons flour	*½ cup tangy cheese, grated*

Paprika and pepper to taste

Melt butter in the top of double boiler over hot, not boiling, water. Add flour and seasonings and cook 3 minutes. Gradually stir in milk and cook until thick and creamy. Keep warm until ready to use and add grated cheese at last minute, stirring until melted.

Now make the pancakes:

2 tablespoons butter	*½ cup flour*
1 cup milk	*1 teaspoon baking powder*
2 eggs, lightly beaten	*¼ teaspoon salt*

Melt butter and mix with milk. Stir in eggs. Add flour sifted with baking powder and salt. Beat well. Bake on a hot griddle until cakes bubble. Turn and brown lightly. Let them cool slightly and assemble.

Spread each cake with stuffing. Roll up and place seam side down in shallow casserole. Cover with cheese sauce. Put the dish under broiler until sauce bubbles, about 5 minutes, and serve with green salad.

Variation: For a sweeter filled pancake for breakfast or dessert, make batter as above and fill with a filling made of:

8 ounces cottage cheese	*2 tablespoons sugar*
6 ounces cream cheese	*1 tablespoon soft butter*

2 eggs

Mix all ingredients together. Fill pancakes with stuffing, roll up and serve with sour cream and wild strawberry jam.

WAFFLES

2 cups flour	*3 eggs, separated*
2 teaspoons baking powder	*1¼ cup milk*
½ teaspoon salt	*1 tablespoon melted butter*

Sift flour, measure and sift twice more with dry ingredients. Beat egg yolks and add milk and butter. Add to dry ingredients and beat well. Beat egg whites until stiff and dry and fold into batter. Put into a glass measuring pitcher and use one cup batter for each waffle. Bake in well-heated iron for 4 to 5 minutes or until steaming stops. Do not raise the cover of the iron while waffle is baking. Serve for breakfast with butter and maple syrup or for lunch or light supper with Welsh Rabbit,* Dried Beef in Cream,* Real Chicken a la King,* or Shrimp Newburg.*

A change of pace from toast to be served with scrambled eggs, or just coffee, is Grandmother's:

MAPLE TOAST

Allow one slice of toast for each person to be served. Toast on one side. Butter the other side and sprinkle generously with maple sugar, but don't put it too near the edge as it tends to spread. Put under broiler, 3 inches from flame, and broil until sugar melts. Sprinkle slices with coarsely chopped pecans. Serve with thick sweet yellow cream or sour cream. Use either white or whole wheat bread, whichever you prefer. You need firm bread for Maple Toast and homemade is the best.

Beverages

IT would have been quite unlikely to find Grandmother at a wine tasting ceremony giving her opinion of the Luze Montrachet of '64 or the Latour Pouilly-Fuissé of that same year, rolling a drop or two around on her tongue. As a matter of fact, her favorite drinks were water, orange juice and Bristol Cream sherry, in that order. I suppose I take after my Grandmother in that respect, delighting in liquids of a simpler nature.

But I have come to be unreasonably fussy about the water I drink. In Appleyard Center, for instance, the water tastes like water, not like chlorine or any other disinfectant, nor like a stagnant pool too long filled with thirsty fish.

In the Vermont Year Round Cookbook, Mrs. Appleyard told all she knew about making tea, coffee, chocolate and several other drinks. However, if you still feel thirsty, I hope you'll find something with which to indulge your taste buds here. If not, drop in at Appleyard Center and just help yourself to a glass of delicious water.

CIDER — COLD OR HOT

Grandmother maintained the idea that the real reason Adam and Eve had to leave Eden was because the serpent suggested to Eve that she ought to filter cider and pasteurize it. If this is so, and I have severe doubts, she undoubtedly deserved her reward. That clear, unchangingly handsome, tasteless liquid is not cider, in my opinion.

Cider should be slightly cloudly. It should taste of apples, tart ones growing on gnarled, gray trees, loaded with drifts of pale pink blossoms in spring and hung with bright pink and gold globes in the autumn. A bear got most of ours last year. I was fascinated to discover that the bear and I are just about the same height.

"This," I thought one starry night as I looked up past the apples on an old Dutchess tree to Cassiopia's chair, "is how cider looks to a bear before it is cider."

Then I promptly went in and drank a glass of cider. The cap of the jug sighed as I twisted it open. The cider hissed a little as it filled the tall glass. It was, in fact, just right and I couldn't help feeling a little sympathy for the bear, for he would never get to taste cider that way. Nor would he, I suppose, ever get it this way either:

HOT SPICED CIDER

(For 12-16)

- 1 *gallon cider*
- 2 *4-inch sticks cinnamon, broken*
- 12 *whole cloves*
- ½ *teaspoon allspice*
- 1 *teaspoon grated nutmeg*

Let the fizzy cider stand with the spices in it for at least half an hour. Bring it to a boil in a large kettle but do not boil it. Ladle it into pottery mugs and watch your tongue.

Another way of using hot cider in a delectable punch is in the following formula:

HOT SPICED PUNCH

(For 20)

- 1 *quart water*
- 2 *tablespoons loose tea*
- 1¼-2 *cups sugar*
- 1 *2-inch stick cinnamon*
- 12 *whole cloves*
- 1 *6-ounce can frozen lemonade*
- 2 *6-ounce cans frozen orange juice*
- 3 *quarts cider*

Bring quart of water to the boil. When it boils hard, throw in the tea. Boil exactly one minute. Strain over sugar, spices and fruit juice. Let it stand at least 10 minutes. Longer will do no harm. Add cider. Heat. Serve hot in pottery mugs. I prefer the lesser amount of sugar in my punch, but you may want a sweeter punch. Sweeten it to your taste.

I served this punch to 80 at my graduation from college, some of it spiked with rum, and had no complaints.

CIDER AND RUM PUNCH — HOT OR COLD

(For 50)

- 24 *lemons*
- 4 *pounds lump sugar*
- 1 *gallon water*
- 3 *tablespoons orange pekoe tea*
- 1 *quart rum*
- 4 *ounces apricot brandy*
- 4 *ounces yellow chartreuse*
- 2 *ounces curaçoa*
- 2 *gallons fizzy cider*

Take the peel off the lemons and make it as thin as possible. Put it into a large kettle with the sugar. Put the water on to boil. While it is heating, squeeze the lemons and strain the juice over the peel and sugar. Just as the water reaches a full bubbling boil, throw the tea into it and boil it exactly one minute, no more, no less. Too long boiling makes it bitter and too short boiling fails to bring out its full flavor. Use a timer and watch it. Remove from the heat and strain it over the lemons and sugar. Stir hard until sugar melts. Add rum, apricot brandy, chartreuse and curaçoa and keep stirring.

Now set the punch in a cool place (not the refrigerator) to mellow and ripen for at least a day. Strain it into scalded jugs, and keep until you are ready to use it. If it is to be used within two days, add a little more rum or brandy to the top of each jug.

When serving the punch cold, put ice cubes into a large bowl. Add diced fresh pineapple, strawberries or raspberries, a few stoned black cherries or — when in season — slices of fresh peach. Freshly sliced orange and lemon may be used, but not too much fruit, please. This is a drink, not a fruit compote.

Add the cider. Decorate the bowls with sprays of fresh mint.

For hot punch: at serving time reheat the basis of the above punch with the cider in a large kettle. Do not add any fruit except for a few lemon slices. Ladle right out of the kettle into mugs.

Serve with either Huckleberry Gingerbread,* or Appleyard Center Gingerbread.*

THE MAGIC COCKTAIL

There has recently been a movement to make cranberry juice the official drink of the Commonwealth of Massachusetts. Perhaps it would have had more of a chance for success if it had been diluted as in the magic cocktail. The formula for this tribute to the cranberry came from a famous magician to a distinguished surgeon, who revealed the secret to his friend, Mr. Appleyard, giving permission to tell Mrs. Appleyard, who passed it on to me.

The first step is to locate the cranberry cider. For this you must either go to Cape Cod, or make your own, starting with a quart of cranberry juice from your local grocery store. Begin by pouring out a quarter of the juice. Substitute for the juice an equal amount of grain alcohol, shake it up, let it stand in a cool place to blend for a few days.

For each cocktail use:

3 ounces fortified cranberry juice
1 ounce Jamaican rum
Dash lime juice

Shake well with ice and serve it up. It comes out a handsome pale pink. Be sure to warn any unsuspecting guests of its lack of innocence and drink a toast to the Commonwealth of Massachusetts.

DANDELION WINE

Cranberries are scarce in Appleyard Center, but fortunately dandelions are not. When lawns first turn green, dandelions are putting forth the

*See Index for pages where recipes can be found.

beginnings of their leaves. Pick four quarts of the flowers, loosely packed, on a sunny day early in the season. Then take:

Thin rind and juice of 6 lemons
1 *gallon boiling water*
3 *pounds sugar*
2 *10-ounce packages frozen raspberries*
2 *packets (2 tablespoons) dry yeast*

Wash and scald a two gallon pottery crock and a cover. Put in the flowers (and only the flowers, any greens will make a very bitter liquid) and the thin lemon rind (no white) and pour the boiling water over them. Let the crock stand in a cool place overnight. In the morning strain out juice, pressing it out through the strainer. Put the dandelion juice and the juice of the lemons and the raspberries on to boil with the sugar. Boil 20 minutes and pour it back in the crock. Dissolve the yeast in lukewarm (85-105°) water. When the dandelion juice is also lukewarm, add the yeast mixture to it. Cover the crock. Let the juice ferment till it stops hissing — about ten days. Using a funnel with a filter paper in it, strain the juice into scalded cider jugs. Let it stand three days to settle. Tops should be in place but not tightened. Strain once more through filter paper into sterilized quart bottles. Filter again if necessary. When it is perfectly clear, faintly pink in color, cork the bottles tightly and leave it in the cellarway or other cool place until Christmas.

RHUBARB WINE

Cut up enough stalks of young pink rhubarb into inch pieces to make one gallon. Pound it into pulp with a wooden paddle, or other available wooden utensil. Add a gallon of boiling water. Let stand several hours. Strain it through a fine sieve and measure it. For each quart of liquid, add three cups of sugar. Put it into a large well-scalded crock. It will soon start fermenting and will keep doing so for about three weeks. When it stops bubbling and hissing, strain it into sterilized cider jugs, using a funnel and filter paper. Let it stand about three days to settle, with the tops in place but not tightened. Strain and filter again into sterilized quart bottles. If it is not perfectly clear, filter it once again. Then cork the bottles tightly and store them in a cool place. It should be ready to use by Halloween.

ELDERBERRY WINE

This is made very much like the dandelion wine but it comes out a deep rich tyrian purple. The berries should be very ripe. A gallon of berries is a good quantity to begin with. Making sure you've removed all stems and leaves, mash them well with a wooden paddle and put the juice to drip through a jelly bag. To each quart of juice add a pint of water and the rind of one large lemon. Bring the liquid to a boil and boil for five minutes. To each gallon of liquid add two pounds of sugar. Stir well till sugar is dissolved. Cool. When lukewarm, add to each gallon two tablespoons of dry yeast dissolved in lukewarm water. Put the liquid in a crock and follow the directions as given above for fermenting, straining and filtering the dandelion wine. Be sure it has stopped working before you tighten the corks.

With the approach of summer, punch is served at Appleyard Center a good many times. I recall many an August spent with my Grandmother during her punch-making times. I would often stand just out of the way of a party in order to get a glimpse of the "secret" ingredients that went into all of her punches, and wonder why there was always a bowl for the "grownups" and another for the children. I found out why one evening as my older brother Bruce bravely commandeered several glasses from the wrong bowl. This was the night of a concert at Appleyard Center, and luckily for Bruce, the children usually sat outside the museum on the lawn in order not to disturb the concert. He barely made it up to the lawn and promptly fell asleep to the delightful strains of a Bach Concerto. Following the concert, all the guests and musicians made their way to Mrs. Appleyard's house for a party replete with punches in her Grandfather's Chinese bowls, and assorted other delicacies including Oatmeal Lace Cookies.* One of the children's punches from which many adults sipped on a very hot evening was:

GRANDMOTHER APPLEYARD'S LEMONADE

12 lemons
4 oranges
16 cups water (spring, if possible)
4 cups granulated sugar

Slice the lemons and oranges as thinly as possible, and sprinkle sugar over them from time to time to prevent their coloring. When all the fruit and sugar are in a large bowl, take a wooden paddle, or spoon, and "scrunch" them. (That's right. Scrunching consists of crushing the fruit with a circular motion so that the sharp crystals of the sugar grind the juice out of the fruit and the flavor out of the rind.)

Don't work the fruit too long or the white pith under the rind will make the juice bitter. What you want is a thick syrup that has all the tang of the fruit but none of the bitter taste. Three or four minutes of scrunching is enough if the fruit is sliced really thin. To this base, add water in two forms, liquid and frozen.

For an afternoon gathering, put the lemonade in a Sandwich glass pitcher or a cut glass pitcher through which the sun strikes rainbows. The rule may be multiplied to serve more; one gallon serves about twenty. Sponge Cake* goes well with it.

As I grew old enough to contribute, my contribution to the making of the punch was the combining of the crushed fruit and sugar with the infusion. This makes:

APPLEYARD CENTER PUNCH BASIS

(For 60)

12 lemons
4 oranges
4 cups granulated sugar
1 gallon spring water
3 tablespoons of loose tea

Slice the lemons and oranges very thin. Add the sugar gradually and crush the fruit with it for three or four minutes. Bring a gallon of spring water to a fast bubbling boil. Throw in the loose tea (Earl Gray's mixture is good) and let it boil exactly one minute.

Have the bowl of fruit ready nearby, and strain the tea infusion over the fruit. Put the mixture into a five gallon kettle. Set it in a cool place until you want to use it. The day before you use it stir in two gallons of cold water at once.

Using this basis, the punch may be varied in many ways. For instance:

FOURTH OF JULY PUNCH

(For 40)

*2 gallons Punch Basis**
2 cups pineapple juice
2 6-ounce cans frozen lemonade, diluted
2 6-ounce cans frozen orange juice, diluted
2 quarts ginger ale
2 cups brandy
2 cups Almaden white wine
¼ teaspoon peppermint extract
1 quart fresh strawberries, slightly crushed with ½ cup sugar
2 quarts of Punch Basis or pineapple juice frozen in quart juice cans
Sprays of mint

The advantage of using the frozen basis or pineapple juice is that the punch does not weaken as the frozen blocks melt. Mix all liquid ingredients, add the frozen blocks at serving time and decorate with sprays of mint.

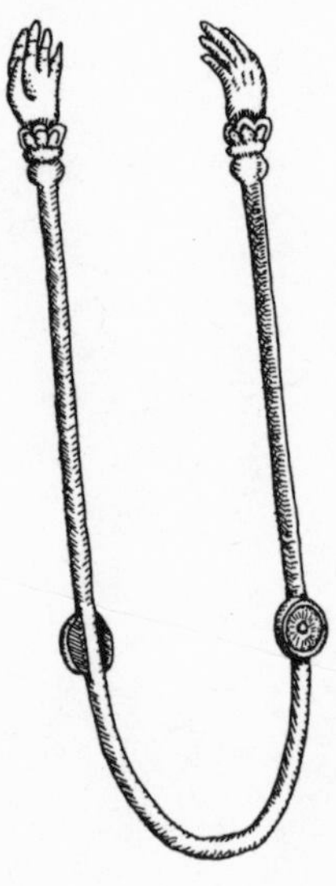

LABOR DAY PUNCH

(For 40)

*2 gallons Punch Basis**
2 quarts pale dry ginger ale

Using frozen concentrate make:

2 quarts orange juice
1 quart pineapple juice
2 quarts lemonade

By this time in the punch season, I usually have some quart pineapple juice cans in my freezer filled with punch left over from an earlier day. They make excellent ice blocks. Put the blocks into a large punch bowl, mix the Punch Basis, the fruit juice and the ginger ale and pour the mixture over the frozen punch. Of course, if you have any punch left over, refill the juice cans for a future punch. This could go on indefinitely and, like sherry, there might always be a tang of the ancestor of all Appleyard Punch in each bowl.

Unfortunately for the system, sometimes a very hot night coincides with a concert at the museum, after which the guests walk to Grandmother's to meet the musicians. On a recent summer evening, a Prokofiev concert proved to be especially thirst-provoking. There wasn't a drop left.

CROQUET COOLER

(For 20)

For a hot afternoon after a match has taken place on the back lawn, use:

¼ cup mint leaves, slightly crushed
2 tablespoons sugar
*1 gallon of the Punch Basis**
1 quart white wine
1 quart pale dry ginger ale
Tray of ice cubes
Sprays of mint

Crush the mint with the sugar. Add it to the Punch Basis. Add the wine and ginger ale, both well chilled, and ice cubes. Decorate with sprays of mint. Float a few strawberries in it if you like.

WHITE GRAPE JUICE PUNCH

(For 20)

12 ounces frozen orange juice
1 quart water
1 quart pale dry ginger ale
2 quarts white grape juice
*1 gallon of Punch Basis**
Cubed fresh pineapple
Tray of ice cubes
Mint sprays

Mix orange juice and water. Add ginger ale and white grape juice, both well chilled. Mix into Punch Basis. Add pineapple and ice cubes. Decorate with mint.

LIME AND LEMON PUNCH

(For 40)

When you make your Punch Basis, substitute 12 limes for the oranges.

2 quarts pineapple juice, frozen in cans
1 tray ice cubes
*1 gallon Punch Basis**
1 quart soda water
2 quarts pale dry ginger ale
1 quart white wine
1 quart orange juice
1 pint dark red cherries, stemmed and stoned
6 drops peppermint extract

To mix two large bowls of punch, put one of the frozen quarts of pineapple juice and some ice cubes in each bowl. Pour over each, half a gallon of the basis, half the chilled soda water, ginger ale, white wine and orange juice. To each bowl add three drops of peppermint extract and half a pint of dark red cherries. Substitute two packages of frozen raspberries if cherries are not available.

If a smaller group comes along, a tempting punch to serve is:

CHAMPAGNE PUNCH

(For 8)

For each quart of champagne:

1 quart club soda
2 ounces curaçoa
4 ounces Bristol Cream sherry
2 ounces brandy
Large block of ice
1 6-ounce can frozen orange juice
1 tablespoon lemon juice
1 tablespoon sugar
1 tablespoon orange bitters

Chill champagne and soda for several hours. Mix all the other ingredients and chill them too. At serving time put the block of ice in the punch bowl. Pour the mixture over it. Add the soda. Last of all add the champagne.

Even if you, like me, are a chronic non-dishwasher, do not serve this punch in paper cups.

If you are in the habit of keeping a pitcher of something on hand in the refrigerator in case someone drops in on a hot afternoon, Mint Cup will draw them from miles away.

MINT CUP

1 cup sugar
½ cup water
1 cup of fresh mint leaves, slightly crushed
Juice of 3 lemons
Juice of 3 limes
Strips of thin peel of lemons and limes
2 quarts ginger ale, chilled

Make a syrup by boiling the sugar and the water five minutes. Pour it over the crushed mint and the lemon and lime peel. Let stand two hours. Strain into a tall glass pitcher. Add the fruit juice. Keep chilled till needed. At serving time add a few ice cubes and the ginger ale. Have a bunch of fresh mint at the top of the pitcher.

During the ripe tomato season, in place of Mint Cup in the refrigerator, you might have a pitcher of what Grandmother called:

MINT TULIP — FOR A HOT AFTERNOON

1 lemon, sliced thin
2 tablespoons sugar
1 quart of strained tomato juice, fresh or canned
¼ teaspoon ginger, ground
½ teaspoon garlic powder
Ice cubes
1 cup pale dry ginger ale
Sprigs of mint

Crush lemon slices slightly with the sugar and pour the tomato juice over them. Stir in the ginger and the garlic powder (optional, all). Keep chilled. At serving time add a few ice cubes, the ginger ale and the sprigs of mint.

TOMACHICKO — FOR A COLD EVENING

(6 cups)

3 cups jellied chicken stock
3 cups tomato juice
1 onion, sliced
1 leaf each of rosemary, basil and tarragon
Pinch of curry powder
Sour cream

Make the chicken stock anytime you have a chicken carcass on hand. After simmering the stock down to three cups, strain it and later remove all the fat from the top. Now pour the tomato juice, canned or fresh, over the sliced onion. Add the herbs. Let stand in the refrigerator at least two hours. At serving time heat the chicken stock with the herbed juice a few minutes, then strain the onions out and stir in the curry powder. Serve it in pottery mugs. Pass sour cream with it to dab on the top.

Good for both hot or cold days is:

MRS. APPLEYARD'S TOMATO COCKTAIL

(For 6)

1 cucumber peeled and diced
4 tablespoons chopped green onion and tops
Thin peel of 2 lemons
1 tablespoon prepared horse-radish
6 cups tomato juice
Lemon slices
Juice of 2 lemons
2 teaspoons sugar
Ice cubes
3 drops Tabasco sauce
1 tablespoon Worcestershire sauce

Put the cucumber, onions and tops, lemon peel and horseradish into the blender. Add one cup of the tomato juice, blend while you count to ten slowly. Put the rest of the tomato juice, the lemon slices and juice, sugar and ice cubes into a tall glass pitcher. Stir in the juice from the blender. Put in the Tabasco and Worcestershire sauce. Stir well. Chill till serving, or leave out ice cubes, heat for a few minutes and serve in mugs.

VEGETABLE JUICES

Grandmother used to keep her juice extractor extremely active. Her favorite drink was carrot juice with a variety of herbs and lemon juice added to it. One day the herbs might consist of basil, marjoram, thyme and parsley. On another day they might be snips of tarragon, chives, rosemary and comfrey. She would sometimes add a small beet to the carrot juice and also put in a combination of dill leaves, parsley, chives and tarragon. These juices may be poured over ice cubes and used cold. Or they may be heated and served with sandwiches for lunch on cold days, or added to a thin soup base. The only way to determine your own tastes in vegetable juices is to experiment with what you have.

MRS. APPLEYARD'S PEP-UP

This is not a beverage to be served to a large number of guests at an evening party. Rather, it is a thoroughly wholesome and tasty manner by which to nourish oneself. Many of the ingredients can be purchased at a nearby health food store. My Grandmother was mixing up this concoction for many years before I was aware of it. She insisted on offering it around. At age ten, I was much more interested in lemonade than Pep-Up, but I now drink Pep-Up regularly in order not to miss any vital nutrients in my diet. There are many variations to this rule, and you might want to be innovative and come up with your own way of making it tasty.

Into the blender put:

Peel and juice of 1 large lemon (no seeds)
2 *tablespoons safflower oil*
2 *eggs*
2 *tablespoons soya lecithin (optional)*
1 *tablespoon wheat germ oil*
½ *cup brewer's yeast powder*
1 *tablespoon honey*
½ *cup yogurt*
1 *teaspoon vanilla*
¼ *teaspoon nutmeg*
1 *6-ounce can frozen orange juice, undiluted*
¼ *cup calcium lactate*
½ *teaspoon magnesium oxide*
1 *quart whole milk*

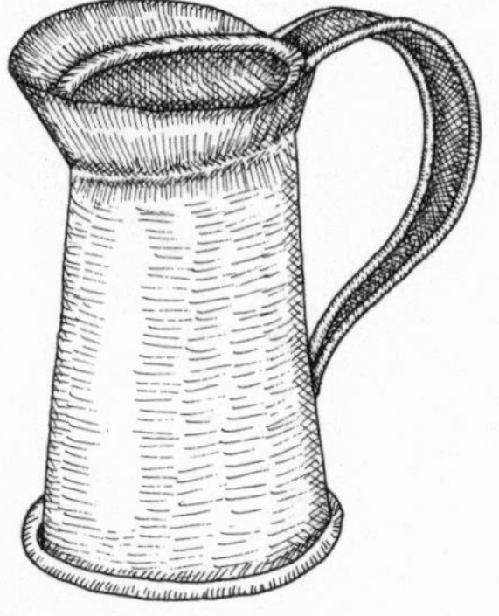

Blend everything but the milk for ten counts. Pour half the mixture into a mixing pitcher. Blend the remaining half for five counts, pouring in one pint of whole milk while it runs. Pour half of this mixture out into the mixing pitcher. Blend the remaining portion five counts, pouring another pint of whole milk into the blender while it is running. Pour all into the pitcher and stir well. This almost fills a two quart jar.

The taste of calcium lactate, magnesium oxide and brewer's yeast are sometimes hard to get used to. I suggest starting with smaller amounts and gradually building up to the written amounts. This mixture is especially good for pregnant women and lactating mothers, but it certainly won't *hurt* anyone.

VERMOUTH CASSIS

Cassis is really just black currant juice. I've tried making it by crushing some of the native currants with sugar, but think it is more practical to buy black currant syrup. Into each highball glass put:

1 ounce dry vermouth
½ ounce black currant syrup
2 ice cubes

Fill up the glass with club soda and stir.

BLOODY MARY

This rule is included in response to a special request from my father-in-law. He drinks Bloody Marys rarely, but they are an essential beverage on several traditional occasions throughout the year; the Christmas tree cutting party and the Fourth of July Sunday trout brunch in particular.

It is difficult to give a definitive rule for a Bloody Mary, as the mixture is a matter of individual taste more than anything else. The rule below is for a single drink; for more than one at a time, simply multiply the quantities and season to taste.

Ice cubes
1 jigger vodka
5-6 ounces tomato or V-8 juice
Worcestershire sauce
Tabasco sauce
Salt and pepper
¼ lemon or lime
Parsley sprig

Put ice and vodka into a highball glass. Fill with tomato or V-8 juice. Season to taste with Worcestershire, Tabasco, salt and pepper. Squeeze in lemon or lime juice and garnish with a sprig of parsley.

EGGNOG

(For 12)

Christmas time in Appleyard Center brings with it a vast variety of eggnog rules. There is usually at least one for the adults and one for the younger folks, or those not wishing to indulge (Mrs. Appleyard counted herself among the latter). This rule has been on hand for a number of Christmas celebrations and I must warn that it is quite vibrant.

12 egg yolks
2 cups granulated sugar
1 fifth whiskey (bourbon)
1 cup Jamaican rum
2 quarts heavy cream
2 cups milk

Make this in the morning of the day it is to be consumed. Beat egg yolks light with a wire whisk. Beat in sugar. (You may use less sugar if you prefer; I think one cup is plenty.) Stir in whiskey and rum and let the mixture stand in a cool place for at least three hours. Then stir in cream and chill mixture again. Just before serving the eggnog, stir in the milk. Doing this requires a little judgment. The eggnog must be of a drinkable consistency, not too thick, not too thin. The temperature and the strength of your beating arm make a difference to the mixture. Add the milk slowly, stirring rather than beating. Add a little extra if necessary. Serve in clear punch glasses with a little nutmeg sprinkled on top of each one.

Cakes

GRANDMOTHER professed to have run a constantly changing kitchen filled with cooking students. What may have been closer to the truth was that she loved to experiment, and loved to even more when there were others around to observe and make suggestions. She did give many people their first lessons in baking, as there was a constant stream of cooks, novices and even experts, traveling through her home.

She would begin with baking powder biscuits and slowly work her students up to the baking of a cake. Frequently, the students had already baked one of their own — clandestinely, from a packaged mix. But those cakes so often tasted like the package from which they came, that the novices were anxious to try their skill at producing a cake of true original quality.

My own impulse to bake came in the spring, and according to my Grandmother, that was as natural as the flowers of Poor Man's Daphne accenting gray stone walls.

Along with a concern about gaining excess weight, the overconsumption of cholesterol and the soaring cost of food, there has been a decline in the frequency of cake baking — especially cakes containing ingredients without which a cake wouldn't really be a cake. Rather poor cakes, in fact, are made without the inclusion of real butter and real eggs. I've made it my own personal rule never to bake a cake if I am feeling at all economical. Rather, I will serve fresh fruit with cheese, or topped with yogurt and honey, or go without. There is really nothing noble about baking a cake with one egg in a large shallow pan. Cakes should rise, and your spirits along with them if you use plenty of eggs.

Enough! I will stop all the qualifiers and simply begin. For whatever reason you have to bake a cake, do it in the spirit of joy that will indeed make it rise well.

I will begin with a cake that threatened me for years. Once I mustered the courage to attempt the baking of a sponge cake, I was embarrassed by its simplicity.

So, get your biggest angel cake pan and begin. Grandmother called this her:

SPRING SPONGE CAKE

	Grated rind and juice of one lemon	1½	*cups flour, sifted three times and measured*
1	*6-ounce can frozen orange juice, melted but not diluted*	1½	*cups sugar, sifted once*
		10	*large eggs, separated*
			Extra sugar, about ⅓ cup

Grate and squeeze lemon. Mix grated peel and juice with thawed orange juice. Sift flour three times and measure it. Sift sugar once and also measure. Preare a large angel cake pan, lightly floured but not greased.

Beat egg whites with an electric beater to soft peaks that just hold their shape. Beat four tablespoons of sugar into egg whites. Light oven: 325°. Without washing the beater, beat egg yolks until thick and lemon colored. Beat in rest of sugar alternately with fruit juices and rind. Fold first some of the whites then a little flour gently into the yolks using a wire whisk. Continue alternating whites and flour till both are used. It is important to fold gently so that the bubbles you have beaten in will not break. Their expansion is what causes the cake to rise.

Put the batter into the pan. Heap it in lightly, turning pan constantly. Sift the extra sugar over the top.

Put the cake into the pre-heated 325° oven. It will take at least an hour to bake the cake. Open oven door as little as possible but check the cake at the end of half an hour. If it is browning too much, reduce oven heat to 300°. The cake should shrink from the edges of the pan and the top should feel firm. If you have any doubt about its being done at the end of an hour, turn off the oven and leave the cake in for 15 more minutes.

I'd like to suggest two ways in which to cool the cake. The first is to let it cool, inverted, over a cake rack. Tease it away from the pan gently with a narrow spatula. Invert it again hoping it will fall out. On lucky days it does, but often I have to tailor a fragment back into place because it stuck to the pan. Turn it over again, sugar side up, on a round dish.

The second method takes somewhat more courage, but is an effective way of removing the cake from the pan. Invert the tube pan over the neck of a sturdy bottle. This method lets plenty of air circulate around the cake to cool it. When the pan feels lukewarm, remove from bottle, loosen the cake from it using a thin knife around the tube and a spatula around the outside. The cake is now supposed to fall gently from the pan to a cookie sheet below.

My experience has shown that it often needs more encouragement from knife and spatula. Again, tailoring may be in order. When serving, don't try to cut sponge cake. Tear it into succulent wedges with two forks.

ANGEL CAKE

1½ *cups egg whites*	1½ *teaspoons cream of tartar*
1½ *cups cake flour*	1 *teaspoon real vanilla*
1⅞ *cups sugar*	1 *teaspoon almond extract*

Let the egg whites stand at room temperature for one hour. Light oven: 350°. Sift the flour once before measuring, then four times with half a cup of the sugar. Beat the egg whites till foamy. Sprinkle cream of tartar into egg whites and beat till stiff enough to make soft peaks, but still moist and glossy. Add the rest of the sugar, about two tablespoons at a time, counting to 25 slowly, while you beat in each addition. Add the flavorings. Use two teaspoons of whichever flavorings you prefer. Beat in while you count to ten slowly. Add the flour and sugar in five additions. Fold them in with a wire whisk, turning the bowl slowly. Use 15 complete, gentle foldover strokes each time. Do 20 additional strokes after the flour is all in.

Heap the batter into an angel cake pan and bake at 350° for one hour. Reduce the heat after the first 15 minutes if the cake is browning too fast. Test with, preferably, a straw of tall timothy grass. The cake is done when the straw comes out clean. Invert it on a cake rack or sturdy bottle neck as for sponge cake. Let stand until cool, about one hour. Loosen around the outside edge with a spatula, and around the tube with a flexible silver knife.

Tastes tend to differ about which side up you should serve it. I rather like to see the macaroon-like top crust, but that means turning it over a second time on a plate. Suit yourself.

The one unfortunate thing about baking an angel cake from the start is that one then must think up ways to use 13 or so egg yolks. For this reason, I've used a packaged mix from time to time. If you follow the instructions exactly, the results can be quite good. My cousins all learned to do this quite competently as soon as they were old enough to read the directions. This was almost in preparation for Grandmother's further instructions in baking. One of the uses I make of an angel cake made from a package is:

ANGEL CAKE WITH RASPBERRY CREAM

1 *envelope (tablespoon) gelatin*	2 *10-ounce packages frozen raspberries, defrosted*
¼ *cup cold water*	1 *Angel Cake* sliced horizontally into thirds*
½ *pint heavy cream*	

Dissolve the gelatin in the cold water. Strain off the juice from the defrosted raspberries and add it to the dissolved gelatin. Add the berries to the mixture. Chill till quite stiff. Whip the cream and fold it into the gelatin mixture. Spread the resulting mixture between the layers of cake and on the top and sides. Chill briefly and serve.

If you had really made your own angel cake you might dispose of some of those egg yolks by creating:

**See Index for pages where recipes can be found.*

COFFEE ANGEL CAKE

1	*tablespoon plain gelatin*	1	*teaspoon real vanilla*
¼	*cup cold water*	2	*cups heavy cream*
1	*cup powdered sugar*	1	*Angel Cake**
2	*tablespoons instant coffee*	¾	*cup blanched and toasted almonds*
8	*egg yolks*		

Soak gelatin in the cold water. Put it in the top of a double boiler. When the gelatin is dissolved, add the sugar. Mrs. Appleyard used to make her own powdered sugar in a small but active grinder. Add the coffee — any of the more concentrated instant coffees will work for this purpose. Beat egg yolks till light and lemon colored. Add vanilla. Fold in the gelatin and coffee mixture. Cool. Whip the cream and fold it into the gelatin mixture. Cut the angel cake in thirds, horizontally. Spread the slices with the coffee cream. Spread some on top. Sprinkle the toasted almonds over the cake. Chill briefly and serve.

FLAMING ANGEL CAKE

*1 large Angel Cake**

1	*quart vanilla ice cream*	7	*lumps sugar*
2	*packages frozen strawberries, slightly thawed*	2	*tablespoons pure grain alcohol*

Split the angel cake into three layers, horizontally. Spread the ice cream between the layers. Set the cake on a round tray, covered with aluminum foil, and put it into the freezer for at least half an hour. Thaw the strawberries and, at serving time, spread them over the top and around the sides of the cake with a spatula. A few fresh whole berries enhance the cake, if available.

Turn off all the lights in the dining room. Soak the sugar lumps briefly in the alcohol. Fish them out with sugar tongs and place them in a circle on the top of the cake. Light them. Carry the cake in, blazing blue. Then sit back and enjoy the congratulations.

Following the baking of an angel cake, the next step is to bake cakes with butter in them.

ON CAKE BAKING

Eggs should be fresh and so carefully separated that no spot of yolk clouds the white. If you break them one at a time over a small bowl and then slide the white into the bowl in which you are going to beat them all, you will save yourself some disasters. Have the butter at room temperature but not too soft. The sugar should be sifted and free of lumps, the flour dry, measured after one sifting, then sifted three more times.

I find an electric beater a great help in cake-making. I have also started to use teflon pans with good results. Be careful not to use those pans which have a scratched teflon surface. If you use other kinds of pans, be sure they are *well* buttered, lightly floured, and for rich pound cake and fruit cake, lined with plenty of wax paper.

Never bake or mix a cake in a hurry. The baking is as important as the mixing. Even well-mixed cakes of the best materials can be spoiled by being shoved into the oven and neglected.

Remember that oven temperatures recommended in recipes are based on the author's own stove, and yours may be different. Check your oven with an oven thermometer. See how closely the temperature coincides with the temperature at which you have set the dial. Always take the difference into consideration when you are baking.

Divide the baking of a cake into four periods. In the first it is rising. Treat it gently: don't open the oven door and let cool air in on it. In the second quarter, it continues to rise and starts to brown. Now open the oven door gently. Reduce the heat if the cake is browning too quickly. During the third period the cake goes on browning. If it is browning unevenly the pan may, with great care, be turned around. In the fourth period the cake is getting baked inside. It is drying out a little. It shrinks from the pan. It is baked if a testing straw comes out clean. Alleluia!

If the oven is too cold at first, the cake may rise too fast. It may even run over the sides of the pan. If the oven is too hot, it may split on top. This may happen if one uses too heavy a hand with the flour. Use less all-purpose or bread flour in baking than you would use cake flour for the same rule, about seven eighths. As soon as you take the cake from the oven, turn it upside down on a wire cake cooler. If it seems as if it were going to stick to the pan — and this happens sooner or later to everyone including Mrs. Appleyard — keep calm. Loosen it around the sides with a spatula. Put a tray of ice cubes, aluminum side down, on top of the pan. Hope for the best. If the cake leaves a piece behind, regard it as part of a picture puzzle. Put the broken piece into place with the spatula. Give the cake a good adhesive coat of frosting.

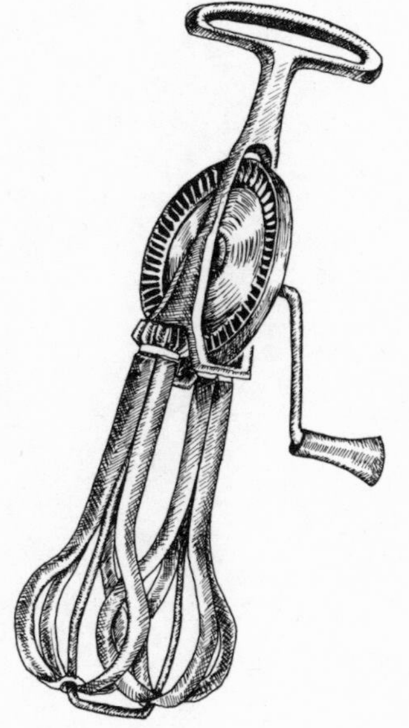

If the frosting you use is the cooked kind, put it on while the cake is still slightly warm. If you use uncooked frosting, the cake may just as well be cool.

Cupcakes are easier to bake than loaf cakes. They take a slightly hotter oven and a shorter time to bake than do larger cakes.

Perhaps good cupcakes to begin with are:

MADELEINES

(2 dozen)

1 cup cake flour
1 teaspoon baking powder
4 eggs
1 cup sugar, sifted
½ cup butter, softened until just melted, over hot water
Powdered sugar, or your choice of frosting
1 teaspoon vanilla

Sift the flour, measure it. Sift it with the baking powder three times more. Beat the eggs well. Add the sugar and keep beating. Add the melted butter and the vanilla. (Avoid using artificial vanilla if you wish the best flavor for your madeleines.) Beat some more. Butter and lightly flour small cake tins. Fill them half full. Bake in a fairly hot oven (375-400°), till they spring back when lightly touched with a finger — about 15 minutes.

Frost with Seven Minute Frosting,* Boiled Frosting,* or Almond-Butter Frosting.* Decorate with candied cherries, almonds, pecans, chocolate chips or whatever you like.

Sometimes Grandmother would bake these in real madeleine pans, heavy pans which seem to have sea shells pressed into them. They would not be frosted but just dusted with powdered sugar. One of her friends doubled the rule, made four dozen, baked them in small pans and frosted and decorated each dozen differently. She reported that they were popular at church suppers and food sales, and why not? After all, these are not unlike the madeleine that Proust dipped into a cup of tea. The haunting flavor started his remembrances. Be prepared as you try them: anything might happen.

Use no baking powder when making:

LEMON QUEENS

1¼ cups flour
¼ teaspoon nutmeg
½ cup butter at room temperature
1 cup sugar, sifted
Grated rind of one lemon
2 teaspoons lemon juice
1 teaspoon brandy
4 large or 5 medium eggs, separated

These are really small pound cakes. Sift the flour and measure it. Add the nutmeg. Sift three times more. Cream butter, which should be at room temperature, and beat in the sugar, a little at a time. Light oven: 375°. Add lemon rind and juice and the brandy. Keep beating. Add the egg yolks, beating them in one at a time, and beat in the sifted flour. Wash the beater. Beat egg whites stiff but not dry. Fold them into the mixture gently with a wire whisk. Fill small cake tins, preferably teflon, half full with the mixture. Ordinary tins should be buttered and lightly floured. Bake 20-25 minutes at 375°.

Sprinkle the cakes with powdered sugar or frost with two tablespoons of thick cream in which powdered sugar has been mixed until it is thick enough to spread. Flavor the frosting with vanilla or with three drops of lemon extract or use Almond Butter Frosting.* More trouble but best, I think, is Boiled Frosting.* The cakes may have a small piece removed from the center and be filled with Lemon Filling.* Cover the filling with the crusty top of the piece that was cut out and dust the whole top with powdered sugar. The crumbly pieces left over are the property of the cook only, but I've noticed that interested gourmets suddenly appear just in time to share them.

Properly baked Lemon Queens are almost level on top. Their consistency is that of a very delicate pound cake. A careless hand with the flour is fatal to them.

CHOCOLATE PEPPERMINT CUPCAKES

These delightfully surprising small cakes are the invention of Mrs. Appleyard. The surprise comes when you bite into the cake to find a peppermint lurking below the surface of the frosting. The first time that I attempted to bake chocolate peppermint cupcakes, the baking urge came upon me in a whim and I found myself with no peppermints in the house. I ran (drove, actually) to the nearby store which is usually amply supplied with nearly all emergency ingredients. Unfortunately, the emergency peppermints had been on hand for an untold number of months and were quite stale and hard. But naively, I assumed that they would soften up when exposed to the warmth of the cakes. They didn't. That evening, there were six people politely gnawing on vari-colored pieces of hardtack in search of a soft chocolate cake. Jay almost chipped a tooth. Since that time, I have become a connoisseur in the art of peppermint picking and my friends and family have been much happier as a result.

Start with:

1¼	*cups flour*	¾	*cup sugar*
¼	*teaspoon soda*	2	*eggs, beaten*
2	*teaspoons baking powder*	1	*cup milk*
2	*squares unsweetened chocolate*	1	*box peppermints, the size of a half-dollar, white or a variety of colors*
¼	*cup butter*		

2 *teaspoons vanilla*

Sift the flour, measure it. Sift it three times with soda and baking powder. Cream the butter with sugar. Grate the chocolate and melt it over boiling water (in the top of a double boiler). Add butter, sugar and the well-beaten eggs to the chocolate. Keep beating. Light oven: 375°. Add sifted flour and milk alternately in small amounts, beating each addition in thoroughly. If batter seems too stiff add a little extra milk, about a tablespoon. Last of all, add the vanilla. Fill small cupcake tins, greased and lightly floured, half full. Bake for 20 minutes at 375°. If these cakes are mixed and baked carefully, they should be quite level. If they rise too high in the middle, cut off small pieces before putting peppermints on, one on each cake. Cover them with Chocolate Cream Cheese Frosting.*

Luckily the tide of family culinary recipes can flow up as well as down. This fudge cake is something that Cicily taught *her* mother to make.

FUDGE CAKE

2	*eggs, separated*	1	*cup sugar*
2	*cups sifted flour*	3	*squares unsweetened chocolate (melted)*
½	*teaspoon soda*		
3	*teaspoons baking powder*	1¼	*cups milk*
½	*cup butter (room temperature)*	1	*teaspoon vanilla*
		24	*real Marshmallows**

Butter three medium layer cake tins. Flour them lightly. Beat the egg whites to soft peaks. Sift the flour with soda and baking powder. Cream the butter, add the sugar, beat till light. Light oven: 350°. Add egg yolks, well beaten, and the melted chocolate. Add flour and milk. Beat smooth after each addition. Add the vanilla. Fold in the egg whites. Fill pans half full. Bake at 350° for 20-25 minutes. The cake should spring back when lightly touched with a finger. Remove the layers from the pans and set them to cool on cake racks. While the layers are still warm, pave each one neatly with pieces of marshmallows whisked briefly through cold water.

When cool, fill and frost the cake with Mrs. Appleyard's Fudge Frosting.*

As this cake will be eaten before you know it, perhaps you had better make a little:

APPLEYARD CENTER GINGERBREAD

2½	*cups sifted flour*	1	*cup sugar*
1	*teaspoon soda*	1	*cup dark molasses*
½	*teaspoon ginger*	⅔	*cup melted butter*
½	*teaspoon nutmeg*	1	*cup sour milk*
1	*teaspoon cinnamon*	2	*eggs, well beaten*

12 *real Marshmallows**

Sift the flour and measure it. Sift three times more with soda and spices. Light oven: 400°. Mix together the sugar, molasses, butter and milk. Beat the dry ingredients with the wet ones. Add the well-beaten eggs. Fill two buttered, lightly floured, large layer cake tins half full. Bake for 20-25 minutes at 400° until a straw inserted into the center comes out clean.

I usually reverse the position of the pans about halfway through the baking, but one layer usually feels springy to the touch before the other, nonetheless. Place this on the dish on which it is to be served. A large earthenware platter with crinkled blue edges is the Appleyard's favorite, but it would still be delicious on a paper plate.

Spread the first layer of gingerbread lightly with butter while it is still hot. Then tear about a dozen marshmallows into pieces and scatter them over it. (Not caring for the contemporary marshmallow, constructed of glue, cornstarch and plastic, Grandmother made her own. If she had a little crystallized ginger, or some of her own Candied Grapefruit and Orange Peel,* she shredded it into the spaces between the marshmallows.) Place the second layer over the first and set the dish into the still-warm oven with the door open. The gingerbread keeps hot and the marshmallows soften while the family is eating, perhaps, Scalloped Haddock.*

This is a filling dessert and goes well with a meal that is not too heavy. Sometimes whipped cream and crystallized ginger or other candied fruit are served with the gingerbread. Some gourmets prefer sour cream to the whipped cream. Either way, there never seems to be a crumb left over at the end of the meal.

Fruit cake is a little more durable than gingerbread, perhaps because there is more of it. I bake it in the evening when the oven is not needed for other purposes. A favorite fruit cake in the Appleyard family is affectionately known as:

HUCKLEBERRY GINGERBREAD

(Appleyard Fruitcake)

4	*cups sifted flour*	1	*teaspoon nutmeg*
1	*pound seeded raisins*	½	*teaspoon soda*
1	*pound currants*	3	*cups sugar, sifted*
¼	*cup citron, thinly sliced*	1½	*cups butter, creamed*
½	*cup nuts (optional)*	6	*eggs, separated*
1	*teaspoon cloves*	1	*cup milk (or ½ cup strong coffee and ½ cup brandy)*
1	*teaspoon cinnamon*		

½ *cup dark molasses*

Sift flour. Measure it. Flour fruit with half a cup and sift the rest three times with the dry ingredients. Add the sifted sugar to the creamed butter.

Beat till light. Light oven: 275°. Add egg yolks, beaten thick. Add milk and other liquids. The molasses should be mixed in with whatever liquid is used. Add the floured fruit and fold in the egg whites, beaten to stiff peaks.

Bake the cake in a large enamelware pan lined first with buttered brown paper, then with waxed paper. Bake it for three hours at 275° for the first hour, 250° the other two. Have a pan of hot water on the bottom shelf of the oven. Put the cake on the middle shelf. When the baking is through, cover a breadboard with waxed paper. Put the board over the top of the pan and reverse both.

Let the cake sit overnight. The next morning, peel off the brown and waxed paper. Frost the cake with Boiled Frosting.* This cake is said to be better if it is kept for a week before being eaten. The Appleyards have rarely been as patient as that and have discovered that it is very palatable if eaten the very next day.

WHITE FRUIT CAKE

(A Bride's Cake)

½	*pound each; candied citron, orange peel, lemon peel, cherries*	1½	*pounds blanched almonds, slivered (keep 24 whole for decorating)*
½	*pound pitted dates, cut fine*		*Juice and grated rind of two lemons*
2	*pounds seedless Sultana raisins*	½	*cup brandy*
		1	*pound butter*
½	*pound dried figs cut fine with scissors*	4	*cups sifted flour*
		12	*eggs, separated*
2	*teaspoons almond extract*	1	*pound granulated sugar*

½ *teaspoon nutmeg*

Put fruit and almonds in a bowl. Pour the lemon juice and rind, almond extract and brandy over the mixture. Let it stand while you cream the butter very smooth and beat in half of the sifted flour. Separate the eggs. Beat the yolks till lemon-colored and beat in the sugar. An electric beater is extremely useful for this step. Light oven: 300°. Sprinkle the rest of the flour, sifted with the nutmeg, over the fruit mixture. Wash the beater. Beat the egg whites till they form stiff peaks. In a large bowl combine flour/butter and egg/sugar mixtures. Fold in alternately the floured fruit and the egg whites. Put the batter into two lightly greased and floured angel cake pans. Bake until a testing straw comes out clean — about four hours. It may bake in one very large pan without a tube but it will take longer — probably five hours. Reduce the heat to 275° if it starts to brown too quickly. When done, invert and let cool on cake racks.

Frost the cakes with Boiled Frosting.* Decorate it with whole almonds.

WEDDING CAKE

(Mrs. Appleyard's)

Mrs. Appleyard's daughter, Sally, was married in August. By the end of June, Mrs. Appleyard and Patience Barlow had the wedding cake all baked. It consisted of three layers, each baked in a different sized pan.

The largest was an enameled milk pan 14 inches across. The second was a smaller milk pan ten inches across and the top layer was in an enameled pan seven inches across. The pans were all greased, then lined first with heavy brown paper, then greased and next lined with four layers of waxed paper.

For this elaborate cake, begin with:

2 pounds seedless raisins
2 pounds seeded raisins
1 pound Sultana raisins, seedless
1 pound currants
½ pound each of candied orange, lemon peel and candied cherries
1 pound citron
¼ pound candied ginger
1 cup blanched almonds, slivered
Grated rind of 2 lemons, 2 oranges
1 cup orange marmalade
4 tablespoons lemon juice
4 tablespoons orange juice
2 cups white wine
1 cup brandy
1 pound butter
2 pounds sugar
12 eggs
4 cups flour
2 teaspoons cinnamon
½ teaspoon each: cloves, mace, and allspice
1 teaspoon nutmeg
2 squares unsweetened chocolate, melted with ½ cup strong coffee
2 teaspoons vanilla
2 teaspoons almond extract

1 cup molasses

Prepare the fruit the day before baking the cake. Grandmother used to cut and slice the citron and the candied orange peel, but I now buy them in neat, transparent, half-pound containers. Dump them all in a very large mixing bowl, add the almonds (or chopped pecans if you prefer), the different kinds of raisins and the currants. Add the grated orange and lemon rind, the marmalade, fruit juices, wine and brandy. Cover the bowl and leave it in a warm place overnight. By morning the fruit should have absorbed most of the liquid.

The next morning begin with the rest of the preparations. Have the butter at room temperature. Using an electric beater, cream it till fluffy and beat in the sugar. Then beat in the eggs one at a time. While you are doing this, your helper (if you are fortunate enough to have one) is attending to the flour. He/she sifts it, puts it into a shallow pan and sets it into the oven at 250° to warm and dry it for ten minutes. Leave the oven door open. Stir the flour several times. Then sift three cups of the flour with the spices and beat it slowly into the egg mixture. Dredge the other cup, which should be quite hot, over the fruit. Melt the chocolate with the coffee and add them to the batter. Add the vanilla, the almond extract and the molasses.

I found a helpful hint for coping with molasses in an old cookbook the other day:

"Pour in molasses while you sing one verse of 'Nearer My God to Thee,'" it said. "In cold weather you sing two verses."

Not being a natural songbird, I set the molasses bottle in a warm place, poured it into a warm cup and then poured it in rich golden silence into the cake batter.

Then stir the fruit mixture into the batter. When everything is mixed, if the batter can be stirred only by a circus weight lifter, add a little more brandy to moisten it.

Set a pan of boiling water into the bottom of the preheated oven. Spoon the batter into the three paper-lined pans. It should very nearly fill them. This cake is not going to rise a great deal. It is going to amalgamate, consolidate and blend flavors.

Cover the pans during the first part of the baking with sheets of buttered brown paper. Any rising the cake does will be done during the first half hour. It will take at least five hours to bake. Keep a little hot water in the pan at the bottom of the oven for the first four hours. At the end of four hours, remove the pan of water and the buttered brown papers, too. Test each cake with a straw, and when it comes out clean, the cake is done.

Have three cake coolers, large enough to cover the entire pans, or cover three pastry boards with waxed paper. Place each cooler or board over a pan. Reverse each in turn. This takes only about as much coordinated energy as Rudolf Nureyev uses to dance for half an hour. Cover the pans with cloths wrung out in cold water and some ice. Perhaps you might like to rest while the cakes decide when to fall from the pan. No matter what you do, the cakes should be left alone until they leave the pans on their own. When the cakes have fallen, peel the paper from the cakes, tasting an occasional stray crumb. Better do this alone, I think, or the cakes will soon look as if a crocodile had been around.

If the wedding day is more than a few days away, it is better to store the cakes wrapped in brandy soaked cheese cloth and aluminum foil. They will "cure" nicely kept in a cool place.

The day before the wedding, (or the day of, if you are in calm control), unwrap the cakes and pile the three layers into a tower on the big Sheffield tray on which they will appear at the wedding. Put triangles of wax paper under the bottom layer to be pulled out when the frosting is over. The plate will be spotless.

Transform the bronze tower of spice into a sugary white tower with Boiled Frosting.* Make four times the usual amount called for. One of Mrs. Appleyard's neighbors, who had a pastry bag, a generous heart and a steady hand, dropped in to help change the tower for Sally's wedding. She made it into a work of art with swirls and flowers and initials. From that point on, whenever Grandmother felt another wedding coming on, she made sure that this genius was present at the frosting bee.

The last time she came, two cakes were baked, one for the bride and groom to cut, and one to be divided up for the guests. One was baked at Mrs. Appleyard's and the other across the road in Cicely's Pioneer Cottage. Cars drove through a sort of fog of sugar and spice. Some drivers paused to inhale it. That winter Mrs. Appleyard's house was ingeniously entered by an extremely small opening suitable for a small, undernourished burglar. The only thing taken was fruit cake. After that, in the breezeway, she posted notices giving fruit cake statistics. These told how much fruit cake she had made this year and how it had been distributed.

Such a notice read: "1967 — I made 15 pounds of fruit cake this year. All used at Minerva's wedding. Hope you had some."

This thoughtfulness saved a good deal of trouble. No one squirmed in through her wood box as long as she continued to make fruit cake. Mrs. Appleyard's last batch was not frosted but was soaked in brandy instead and put in a large covered box. A large chunk of it was used as plum pudding at Christmas time. She made Hard Sauce* to go with it. I remember it well and wish that she had made more cake.

ALMOND RING

Make this in a plain, smooth, circular mold or tube pan that holds a quart. Don't try it in a fluted mold or you will rue the day. A glass mold is best, but they are hard to find.

Shortening for greasing mold
2 *zwieback, rolled very fine, sifted, rolled again*
6 *ounces almonds, blanched and chopped fine or ground through a medium cutter or food grinder*
Whites of five large eggs
1 *teaspoon almond extract*
1 *cup sugar*
8 *candied cherries*
Extra whole almonds, for decorating, lightly browned in butter

Begin by greasing the mold with shortening. There must be no bare spots. *None. Not any.* Pour in the powdered zwieback and tip the mold around till every bit of it is coated. Light oven: 325°. Beat the egg whites to a good froth. They should be slippery and slightly sticky rather than fluffy. Add the almond extract, with a rubber spatula, fold in alternately the sugar and the chopped almonds. Pile lightly and evenly into the mold. Bake for half an hour or until the top looks like a macaroon. Remove from the oven. Press cherries and toasted almonds lightly into the top. Let stand exactly one minute. Loosen with a spatula around the outside edge, pushing spatula underneath as far as it will go. With a flexible silver knife, loosen ring carefully around the inner edge. Invert ring at once on a cookie sheet. Even with the most careful handling, you will sometimes find that a small piece has stuck to the mold. Do not grieve. I have had it happen to me, too. Simply stick the stray piece carefully back into place.

Invert the ring again on the serving plate so it will be macaroon and cherry side up. You might serve either coffee ice cream or a bowl of vanilla ice cream with frozen peaches and raspberries with the ring.

Giving kitchen privileges, as Mrs. Appleyard did to young medical students and their families for ten years, had many interesting features. One was that something was always going on in the kitchen. It might be that the washing machine had exploded again in clouds of white fluff, or that the twins had new dresses, both different (their mother was a woman of imagination), or that someone had been making:

CHOCOLATE ICE BOX CAKE

There it was in a pyrex loaf pan in the refrigerator. The pan was lined with waxed paper with the paper neatly folded over the top. The contents were a mystery and remained so until Phyllis unveiled the cake for an admiring and hungry audience. While the last crumb disappeared she told

Grandmother just how her mother had taught her to make it. It calls for lady fingers, which are not always easy to find. Mrs. Appleyard sometimes baked her own, or used finger-shaped strips of her own Sponge Cake* with pretty good results.

4½ tablespoons hot water

¾	*pound Nestle's chocolate chips*	6	*large (or seven small) eggs*
		1	*teaspoon vanilla*
3	*tablespoons powdered sugar*	1½	*dozen lady fingers*
		½	*pint thick cream, whipped*

Put the hot water and the chocolate chips into the top of a double boiler. Cook over simmering water till the chocolate melts. Stir in the sugar, when it melts, add the egg yolks, lightly beaten, and keep cooking until the mixture thickens and coats the back of the spoon — about seven minutes. Remove from the fire, and add the vanilla. Set the pan into cold water with ice cubes in it while you beat the whites stiff but not dry. Fold them gently into the chocolate mixture.

Line the pyrex loaf pan with wax paper. Leave enough at the sides and ends to fold over the top. Line the bottom, sides and ends of the pan with lady fingers. Spoon in half the chocolate and egg white mixture. Add the rest of the mixture. Finish with lady fingers. Fold the paper over. Put the pan in the refrigerator for at least four hours. When it is time to serve it, undo the paper, turn the loaf out of the pan on a platter. Frost it with whipped cream. This is deadly to the silhouette, but tasty!

If you are in the mood for chocolate and feeling adventurous try:

CHOCOLATE ROLL

A little butter

1	*tablespoon hot water*	1	*teaspoon real vanilla*
3	*squares unsweetened chocolate*		*Shortening for greasing*
6	*eggs, separated*	1	*tablespoon flour*
1½	*cups sugar*		*Powdered sugar for dusting*

For filling:

Whipped cream   *2 peppermint sticks, crushed*

Lightly butter a small saucepan. Put in a tablespoon of hot water and the chocolate. Melt it over hot water. Cool chocolate to lukewarm. Light oven: 350°. Beat egg yolks well in a bowl large enough to contain the whole mixture. Beat in the flour, sugar, chocolate and vanilla.

Grease a 9x13-inch pan. Line the pan with heavy brown paper. Grease the paper. Beat the egg whites to stiff peaks and fold them lightly into the chocolate mixture. Put the batter into the pan, tipping it to distribute the batter slowly. Bake the roll at 350° for 17 minutes. Watch it. If it starts to brown around the edges, reduce heat to 325°.

Dust a clean cloth, slightly larger than the pan, well with powdered sugar. Take cake, paper and all from the pan. Trim the edges well with kitchen shears. This makes it easier to peel off the paper. You must do it while the cake is still warm. As soon as the paper is peeled off, lay the cake on the sugared cloth till you are ready to use it. Roll up cake, cloth and all. Then unroll it. Fill it with whipped cream mixed with two peppermint sticks crushed fine, then roll cake and serve it sliced, with Chocolate Sauce.*

Less of a nervous strain to bake is:

GREEN MOUNTAIN CAKE

This cake used to be made with butternuts, but cracking them is regarded by a good many people, including myself, as work. They must be picked off the ground in the fall of one year and shelled the next year. Two flatirons, either of which might fall on your toe with painful results, enter into the cracking process. Not wishing to have a permanent limp as I cross from my Grandmother's winter kitchen into her summer one, with delight I welcome nicely shelled pecans to the Green Mountains.

2	*cups flour*	¼	*teaspoon nutmeg*
2	*teaspoons baking powder*	2	*eggs*
¼	*teaspoon soda*	1	*cup soft maple sugar*
1	*teaspoon cinnamon*	1	*cup sour cream*

Grease two eight-inch layer cake tins. Light oven: 375°. Sift the flour, baking powder, soda and spices four times. Beat the eggs with a wire whisk until light. Beat in the maple sugar. Stir in sour cream and then the flour. Pour batter into cake tins and bake until the cake shrinks slightly from the pan and springs back when pressed with the finger — about 20 minutes.

Frost with Maple Frosting* and decorate with pecans, between layers and on top.

LADY BALTIMORE CAKE

When Mrs. Appleyard ate her first piece of this cake in Baltimore in 1906, her cooking experience consisted of one pan of somewhat scorched fudge. The cake, brought from Charleston, South Carolina, was so good that a deep-seated prophetic impulse prodded her to ask her fellow guest for the rule and she copied it down in clear, purposeful handwriting. Evidently she intended to make it and she claimed that she did so about fifty years later.

"You need," she would say, "three ten-inch layer cake tins, complete leisure — no book to write — no birds to paint on the wall — and a gold and blue summer day with occasional puffs of sailing clouds casting their shadows on the forget-me-nots." I would become a congenial apprentice, and would try to be of some help.

There are three stages in making a Lady Baltimore Cake. The first is the mixing of the cake batter, then a syrup, and last of all the frosting and filling.

To begin, make batter:

	Shortening for greasing pans	2½	*cups sifted sugar*
		5	*large eggs*
4⅓	*cups sifted flour*	1¼	*cups milk*
5	*teaspoons baking powder*	2¼	*teaspoons almond extract*
1¼	*cups butter*	2½	*teaspoons vanilla*

Grease the three large cake tins. Sift the flour four times with the baking powder. Light oven: 350°. Using an electric beater, cream the butter, beating the sugar into it. Break the eggs into the butter and sugar, one at a time, and beat well. Beat in the flour alternately with the milk, using a rubber spatula to keep the batter away from the sides of the bowl. Add the almond and vanilla flavorings. Distribute the batter evenly in the three pans. Each one should be filled about half full. Bake for 30 minutes, reducing the heat to 325° after the first ten minutes. The layers should be only lightly browned and are done when they shrink from the pan a little and are flexible when gently pressed. Allow cakes to cool in the pans for twenty minutes. Remove layers from pans.

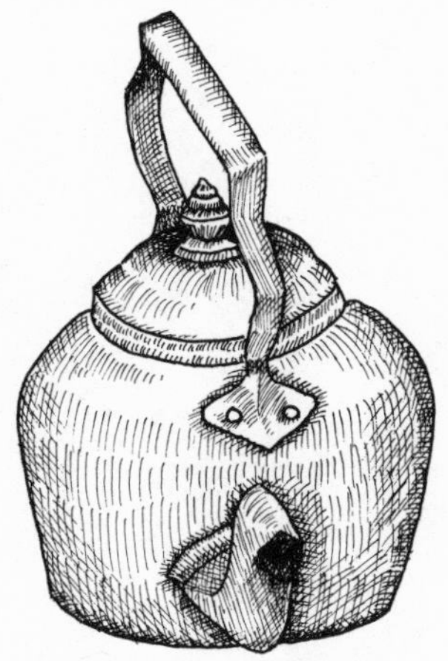

Next, make the syrup from:

1¼ cups sugar
¾ cup water
½ teaspoon almond extract
½ teaspoon vanilla

Combine all ingredients and cook to 234°, soft ball stage, on a candy thermometer. Don't let it discolor. Cool the mixture slightly and spread it while still warm on the layers which should also be slightly warm. The purpose of the syrup is to keep the frosting from making the layers soggy.

The final stage is the making of Lady Baltimore Frosting.*

I suggest that now is a good time to relax and read Owen Wister's *Lady Baltimore*. It does not throw much light on how to make the cake but it gives an accurate idea of how people feel when they eat it, as if you were eating a few pages of lyric poetry flavored with moonlight and magnolias. Of course, the cake is substantially more moist than pages of poetry could ever be. It's not just a cake — it's an experience.

After having tried Lady Baltimore, I find it rather relaxing to make a:

POUND CAKE

1 pound of flour (4½ cups)
1 teaspoon grated nutmeg
1 pound of butter (2 cups)
1 pound of sugar (2¼ cups)
1 pound of eggs (10 large)
2 tablespoons brandy
Juice of 1 lemon (2 tablespoons)
Grated rind of 1 lemon

Have two well-greased loaf tins, 9x5x2¾-inches, lined with wax paper. Then begin with the pounds. First sift the flour, measure it, sift with nutmeg three more times. Cream the butter, add sugar. Beat till fluffy. Beat in the egg yolks, add the brandy, lemon juice and rind. Wash the beater. Light oven: 325°. Set the flour to warm in the oven with the door slightly open while you beat the egg whites to stiff peaks. Remove flour from the oven. Stir it well. Fold the flour into the batter alternately with the egg whites. Fill two pans with the batter. Bake at 325° for half an hour. Reduce the heat to 300°. Bake until a testing straw comes out clean, 35-40 minutes longer. The cake should be light golden brown. It should not be used for at least 24 hours after it is baked, if you can stand the suspense. Keep it tightly covered in a tin box. If it is properly wrapped to prevent drying, it can be kept in the freezer until needed. If it is to be used soon, sprinkle the cake while still slightly warm with powdered sugar.

WHITE CAKE

- ¾ *cup butter*
- 2 *cups sugar*
- 1½ *teaspoons almond extract*
- 1¼ *cups milk*
- 4½ *teaspoons baking powder*
- 3 *cups cake flour, sifted four times*
- 6 *egg whites*
- *Shortening for greasing pans*

Begin by greasing three eight-inch layer cake tins. Cream the butter till light and fluffy. Add 1½ cups of the sugar. Mix the almond extract with the milk. Beat the milk in alternately with the flour that has been sifted with the baking powder. Light oven: 375°. Beat the egg whites to stiff peaks. Fold the remaining half cup of sugar into the egg whites, and fold the mixture into the batter. Distribute the batter evenly in the layer cake tins. Bake the cake until it shrinks slightly from the edges of the pans and is flexible when lightly pressed — about 25 minutes. After the cake has baked 15 minutes, change the position of the pans in the oven so that all layers will be evenly cooked. Reduce the heat to 350° if they are getting too brown. The idea is to cook them thoroughly but keep them as light in color as possible.

Frost with Strawberry Icing* or with Almond Butter Frosting.*

My husband, Jay, created this cake and proudly makes it for my birthday each year. It has almost become a tradition, and a delicious one at that.

CARROT-APPLESAUCE CAKE

Begin with:

- ¾ *cup unbleached white flour*
- ½ *cup whole wheat pastry flour*
- 1 *tablespoon cocoa powder*
- ½ *teaspoon salt*
- ½ *teaspoon baking powder*
- 1 *teaspoon baking soda*
- ¼ *teaspoon nutmeg*
- ⅛ *teaspoon cloves*
- ½ *teaspoon cinnamon*
- ½ *cup honey*
- ¼ *cup vegetable oil*
- 2 *eggs*
- 3 *tablespoons water*
- ¾ *teaspoon vanilla*
- 1 *cup grated carrots*
- ¾ *cup raisins*
- ¾ *cup applesauce*

Sift the flour twice, and twice again with the cocoa, salt, baking powder, soda and spices. Set aside. Mix the liquids: honey, oil, eggs, water and vanilla (a wire whisk is sometimes helpful in breaking up the honey). Add the carrots to the liquid mixture. Beat with an electric beater on medium speed for one minute, or 150 hand strokes. Stir the raisins and applesauce into the liquids and then stir the dry ingredients into the wet until well blended. Turn the batter into a greased eight-inch square baking tin. Bake in a moderate oven, 350°, for about 30 minutes or until a testing straw comes out clean. Cool on a cake rack and frost with Browned Butter Frosting,* cream cheese frosting, or Boiled Frosting.*

CAKE FROSTINGS AND FILLINGS

Frostings are a magical substance that are capable of blanketing the most dog-eared cakes or enhancing the beauty of an already perfect cake. They can be plain in appearance, reaping any benefit from good taste alone, or in the hands of a creative froster, transform a simple cake into a tower of sugar and spice fit for any occasion. I tend to be the type that goes in for the simpler type of frosting preparations, relying on their good taste and the good will of the recipients. One of Jay's sisters, Christine, is now in the throes of a cake-decorating course and is producing a steady stream of the most artistic masterpieces in cakes ever seen. Whatever your bent, I hope you'll find a rule or two here to fit your fancy.

I'm not always in the mood to test my courage and patience by making cooked frosting, after having baked a cake and assured myself that I have triumphed over the forces of nature that conspire to keep bakers humble. Uncooked frosting can be very good and it is certainly more enjoyable to make than it is to watch a candy thermometer. This statement in no way indicates that I am opposed to thermometers. I consider them an absolute necessity in the kitchen — but there are hot afternoons, even in Vermont, when breathing steam is unappealing to me.

It was on such an afternoon that Grandmother invented:

STRAWBERRY ICING

- ¾ *stick sweet butter (6 tablespoons)*
- 3 *cups confectioner's sugar*
- 4½ *tablespoons thick cream*
- 1½ *tablespoons orange juice*
- ½ *cup mashed strawberries, pulp and juice*
- 12 *whole strawberries*

Cream the butter. An electric beater helps in this endeavor. Beat in the sugar, cream, orange juice, and strawberry pulps, until creamy. Put the frosting between layers, on the sides and on top of a three layer White Cake.* Decorate with whole berries.

ALMOND BUTTER FROSTING

- ½ *cup butter*
- 2 *cups confectioner's sugar*
- 2 *egg yolks*
- 1 *teaspoon almond extract*
- ½ *cup blanched, toasted, finely chopped almonds*
- 12 *whole almonds*

Cream the butter, beat in the sugar and the egg yolks. Add the flavoring and the chopped almonds. Put between layers and on top of the cake. Decorate with whole almonds.

SOUR CREAM ALMOND FROSTING

This is a country cousin of Almond Butter Frosting and even easier to make because there is no butter to cream. Simply substitute half a cup of sour cream for the butter and proceed as above.

The simplest of all frostings to make is:

UNCOOKED WHITE FROSTING

- 1 *egg white*
- ½ *cup confectioner's sugar*
- ½ *teaspoon vanilla*

Beat the egg white until stiff. Add the sugar gradually, beating all the time. Add the flavoring. Beat till the mixture is smooth and ready to spread. This quantity is for a dozen cupcakes. Double the rule for a layer cake.

CHOCOLATE CREAM CHEESE FROSTING

Any chocolate frosting requires melted chocolate, but that is the extent of the cooking this frosting needs.

4 ounces cream cheese
2 tablespoons heavy cream
2 cups confectioner's sugar
3 squares unsweetened chocolate, melted
1 teaspoon vanilla

Mash the cream cheese. Beat into it the cream, sugar, and melted chocolate.

This is delicious on Chocolate Peppermint Cupcakes.* A good variation if used for such is to substitute three drops of peppermint extract for the vanilla.

MRS. APPLEYARD'S FUDGE FROSTING

This is more trouble than uncooked frosting but both the flavor and the texture are good enough to warrant the effort. Delicious on either white or chocolate cake.

2 squares unsweetened chocolate
⅔ cup thin cream
2 tablespoons maple syrup
2 cups sugar
2 tablespoons butter
1 teaspoon vanilla
6 marshmallows (optional)
¼ cup chopped nuts (optional)

Grate the chocolate. Put it into a saucepan with the cream, maple syrup and sugar. Stir away from the sides till the sugar is dissolved, then cook without stirring till a candy thermometer registers soft ball stage — 234°. Remove the pan from the fire. Add the butter. Cool the mixture by setting the pan into a pan of cold water. Add ice cubes to the water if you are in a hurry. When the frosting is cool, add the vanilla. Beat until it is ready to spread. Put bits of marshmallows on the cake before frosting. Swirl the frosting on. Sprinkle the chopped nuts over the top if you wish.

ORANGE FROSTING

¾ stick sweet butter (6 tablespoons)
3 cups confectioner's sugar
1½ tablespoons lemon juice
6 ounces frozen orange juice, melted but not diluted
Grated rind of one lemon
Crystallized orange peel

Cream the butter. Beat in the sugar, orange and lemon juices and rind. Add more sugar if necessary to make it thick enough to spread. Spread the frosting between layers and on the sides and top of a three layer White Cake.* Decorate with crystallized orange peel. I sometimes add a little crystallized ginger also.

CARAMEL FROSTING

¾ cup brown sugar
2 tablespoons butter
⅓ cup heavy cream
½ teaspoon vanilla
2 tablespoons caramel syrup
3 cups confectoner's sugar (about)
Whole pecans (optional)

For caramel syrup: heat two tablespoons of the brown sugar in a small black iron frying pan until dark brown. Add one tablespoon of water and stir to a dark golden brown syrup.

Over a low fire, melt the butter, stir in the cream and brown sugar and cook until the sugar is dissolved. Remove the pan from the fire. Stir in the vanilla and caramel syrup. Cool. Gradually work in enough confectioner's sugar to make a stiff frosting, about three cups. Put between the layers and on the top of a white cake. Decorate with pecans or toasted almonds if you prefer.

BROWNED BUTTER FROSTING

1½ tablespoons butter
1 cup confectioner's sugar
2-3 teaspoons milk
½ teaspoon vanilla
2 tablespoons chopped raisins

Heat the butter in a saucepan slowly until lightly browned. Remove it from the heat and stir in the sifted sugar alternately with the milk. Stir in the vanilla and the chopped raisins. Add more milk if necessary to obtain a good spreading consistency.

Spread the frosting while still warm over the top of a Carrot-Applesauce Cake.* It may dribble down the sides of the cake, which is all the better.

SEVEN MINUTE FROSTING

This is the simplest of all the cooked frostings, and always more popular with the young, who seem to like to bury their faces in it, than with Grandmother, who rarely indulged in any frostings.

¾ cup granulated sugar
1 egg white, unbeaten
3 teaspoons cold water
1 teaspoon vanilla or other flavoring

Put all the ingredients except the vanilla into the top of a double boiler. Beat them with an egg beater over boiling water for exactly seven minutes — no more, no less. Remove from the fire, and add the flavoring. Beat the mixture until cool and thick enough to spread.

This may be used on small cakes. Decorate them with candied cherries, bits of citron, chocolate chips, candied ginger, candied orange peel or nuts.

BOILED FROSTING

This is perhaps the most difficult frosting to make and also the most delicious, with the possible exception of Lady Baltimore Frosting.* It is necessary to have either a good friend or an electric mixer at hand: I much prefer the former.

1 cup sugar
½ cup cold water
½ teaspoon vanilla or lemon extract
1, 2 or 3 egg whites

Put both the sugar and the water into a sauce pan. Heat them while keeping crystals from forming on the sides of the pan by wiping them away with a clean pastry brush wrapped in cheese cloth. Do this until the sugar is dissolved. Then boil the mixture without stirring it. You *must* use a candy thermometer. If using one egg white, cook the syrup to 238°. If two egg whites, the syrup must be hotter — 244°. If three egg whites are used — hotter still — 254°.

Remove the syrup from the fire and let it cool slightly and stir in the flavoring. Meanwhile, beat the egg whites till stiff. Now pour the syrup into the egg whites in a thin steady stream, beating steadily. This is the moment when an extra pair of hands is a help. Continue beating until all the syrup is mixed in with the egg whites, and the frosting is thick enough to spread.

Boiled icing is especially good on wedding cake, or as an icing for cream puffs.

CHOCOLATE ICING FOR CREAM PUFFS

1 cup sugar
5 tablespoons cold water
1 square unsweetened chocolate
½ teaspoon vanilla

Put sugar and water in a sauce pan to make a syrup. Stir the crystals away from the sides of the pan till the sugar is dissolved. Cook till it just reaches soft ball stage — 234°. Stir in the vanilla. Melt the chocolate over hot water. Cool. Stir the chocolate into the sugar mixture with a wooden spoon till it is well mixed. Put the mixture in a pan over hot water and beat until it will spread with ease. Paint it on Cream Puffs* with a pastry brush.

MAPLE FROSTING

⅔ cup maple syrup
⅓ cup sugar
2 egg whites

Stir together the maple syrup and the sugar. Cook slowly to the soft ball stage — 234°. Use a candy thermometer. (Don't answer the telephone or there will be a fragrant caramelized sweetness all over the stove. Clean it at once when this happens, I'd advise, and start all over.)

Beat the egg whites to soft peaks. Pour the cooked syrup into them in a thin steady stream, beating all the time with an electric beater. Keep beating until the frosting starts to cool. Then put pecan halves on one layer of a Green Mountain Cake,* and cover it with frosting. Place the second layer on top of the first one and swirl with frosting. Decorate with pecan halves.

LADY BALTIMORE FROSTING

The night before making either the cake (Lady Baltimore*) or the frosting, mix:

3 cups seeded raisins, chopped fine
½ cup candied cherries
1 cup sliced blanched almonds
2 cups chopped pecans
15 figs, cut in small bits

Cover the fruit with:

½ cup brandy
1 teaspoon vanilla
1 teaspoon almond extract
1 tablespoon lemon juice

Stir the mixture occasionally so that the fruit will absorb the liquid.

The next morning, beat three egg whites until they make soft peaks. Mix one cup water, half teaspoon cream of tartar, and three cups sugar.

Using a candy thermometer, cook the sugar syrup until it forms a soft ball when dropped into cold water — the syrup should be about 234°.

Pour the syrup slowly on the beaten egg whites while your helper keeps the beater going all the time. Add the fruit and nuts. Cover your most beautiful round plate with four triangles of wax paper, with the points toward the center. They should be pulled out when the frosting, which you put between the layers and on the top, has had time to set.

ALMOND CUSTARD FILLING

1	*cup milk*	1	*tablespoon butter*
½	*cup sugar*	½	*teaspoon almond extract*
1	*tablespoon instant flour*	1	*cup chopped, blanched almonds*
2	*egg yolks*		

Bring the milk to a boil. Sift sugar and instant flour together. Beat the egg yolks till light and beat in the sifted sugar and flour. Pour the hot milk over them, beat well. Add the butter. Put the mixture into the top of a double boiler and cook until it thickens. Stir in the almond extract and blanched almonds.

("Coats the back of a spoon," is the classic expression. Mrs. Appleyard was frequently criticized by her friends and relatives for using that expression. They claimed that the spoon is either always coated, or it never is. All I can say when thus challenged by a superlative cook, is that if the filling is not cooked until it is thick, it will make the cake soggy, and if it is cooked too long it will curdle.)

To return to the matter at hand, once the filling is thickened, it may be spread between the layers of a layer cake, with Almond Butter Frosting* on the top, and all recipients will rejoice.

ORANGE FILLING

2½	*tablespoons instant flour*	¼	*cup orange juice*
½	*cup sugar*		*Grated rind of 1 orange*
2	*egg yolks*		*A little grated lemon rind*
½	*tablespoon lemon juice*	1	*tablespoon butter*

Sift the flour and the sugar together. Add the egg yolks, well beaten, the fruit juices, the rind and the butter. Cook on the top of a double boiler, stirring carefully until the mixture thickens. I advise that you look at the back of the spoon.

A large Sponge Cake,* sliced, with this filling between the layers and Orange Frosting* on the top, is rather palatable.

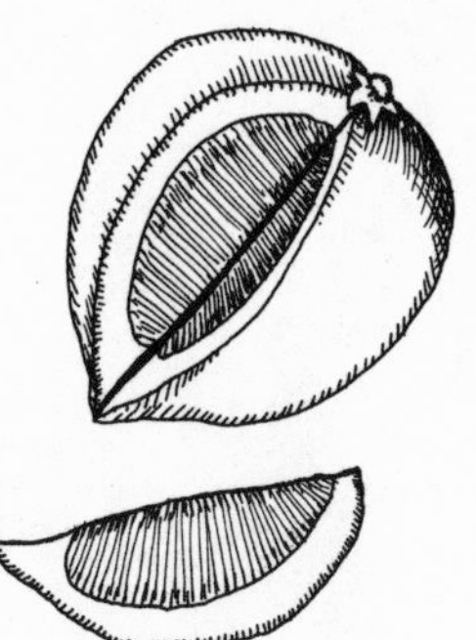

LEMON FILLING

This may be made like the orange filling above, substituting lemon juice for the orange juice. I think that it is even better when made with no flour, and thickened only by the mixture of the eggs and the lemon. It is, however, more likely to separate if it is cooked even a few seconds too long, so watch it carefully.

2	*ounces sweet butter*	¼	*cup lemon juice*
⅔	*cups sugar*	3	*egg yolks, well beaten*

Grated rind of 1 lemon

Put the butter in the top of a double boiler. As it melts, stir in the sugar, then the lemon juice and, last, the beaten egg yolks. Keep stirring steadily until the mixture — yes, you guessed it — coats the back of the spoon. Remove it at once from the fire and cool slightly before using it.

CHOCOLATE FILLING

- 2 *tablespoons butter*
- ¼ *cup heavy cream*
- 6 *ounces semi-sweet chocolate chips*
- 2 *cups powdered sugar*
- 2 *egg yolks*
- 1 *teaspoon real vanilla*
- *Pecans (optional)*

Put the butter and cream into the top of a double boiler. As the butter softens, mix in the sugar and beat well. Add the chocolate chips. Continue beating. Add the beaten egg yolks and cook till mixture thickens. Remove from the fire. Stir in the vanilla. Either a two layer white or chocolate layer cake is good with this between layers and on top. Decorate with pecans if you like.

Candy

I have long thought that anyone eating a piece of candy from a professional box was taking an unnecessary risk. In order to fortify my resolution not to eat any, I read the list of contents. This in itself is no easy task. Such a box has six sides and the list has been placed where it is as hard as possible to find.

Fortunately, or unfortunately, as the case may be, I am near-sighted and so can read the contents. When I do, it is usually aloud and in a frightening tone. I've decided that if I'm going to eat candy, I'd better make my own. It may contain sugar, or better yet, honey, but at least it won't be composed of mono or diglycerides and corn syrup. Besides, the making of candy provides a certain amount of exercise.

Having worked myself into a state of mind in which making candy has become a domestic virtue, I'll begin with:

APRICOT ROLLUPS

1 12-ounce package dried quick-cooking apricots
Extra sugar for rolling — about one cup
1 cup sugar

Begin by covering the apricots with water and cooking them until they are quite soft — about 15 minutes. When they are soft, make the apricots into a pulp using an electric blender. Do not put in too many at a time, but rather grind them in small batches, using part of the cooking liquid each time and running the blender about two minutes. The result should be a bowl full of apricot pulp, not too wet, not too dry, to use for the rolls or in Apricot Sauce,* or Apricot Soufflé.*

In making the rolls, first light oven: 450°. Stir a cup of sugar into the apricot pulp. Put the mixture into a saucepan and continue stirring it over a low flame until the sugar is dissolved. Next, spread it as thin as possible, using two nylon spatulas, in teflon cookie pans with edges. Half the amount given above will cover two 10x14-inch pans. It should be spread so thinly that you might think there was a sheet of colored cellophane over the pan. When it is as thin as you can possibly get it, put the pans in the oven. After five minutes reverse the position of the pans in the oven — the upper one on the lower shelf, the lower one on the upper shelf. Turn the heat off, shut the oven door and leave the pulp to dry overnight.

The next morning the pulp should be dry enough to roll. If it is not dry enough to be lifted from the pan and retain its shape, light the oven again for three minutes, turn it off, leaving the pans in the oven for another half-hour. The pulp should feel just slightly sticky, rather like scotch tape and not much thicker.

Score the pulp with a spatula into 2x3-inch pieces. Sprinkle the entire pulp with sugar. Put some more sugar on a shallow plate.

Remove the apricot oblongs with a spatula and lay them, one at a time, unsugared side down in the plate of sugar. Then roll them up tightly over the sugar. Have a candy box ready, lined with wax paper and pack the rolls neatly, sprinkling sugar between the layers and separating them with wax paper.

PRUNE TORTOISE SHELL

1 pound quick-cooking prunes
½ cup sugar
Juice and peel of half a lemon
Sugar for rolling out, about one cup

Simmer the prunes till it is easy to remove the pits — about half an hour. Then use exactly the same method as with the Apricot Rollups in the recipe above. Use the blender, spread the pulp on the pans, dry in the oven till it looks like bronze tortoiseshell on the pans. The prune strips may be rolled around blanched or toasted almonds if desired. The results are not only tasty but nutritious, and filled with iron.

STRAWBERRY ROLLUPS

1 16-ounce box frozen strawberries
Sugar for rolling, about ¾ cup

Thaw the strawberries. Pour them into the blender and run it until they are thoroughly pureed. The resulting pulp is moister than either the apricot or the prune pulp, so must be simmered in a saucepan before being spread evenly in teflon cookie pans. Light oven: 450°. Place the pans in the oven and after five minutes, turn the heat off and leave them overnight to dry. If the pulp is still too sticky to handle in the morning,

**See Index for pages where recipes can be found.*

light the oven again at 250° and turn it off after five minutes. In about half an hour the pulp should be just tacky enough to make it into 2x3-inch oblongs. Remove them from the pans, and roll them in the sugar as directed for the apricot and the prune pulp (above).

Strawberry rollups may be served for dessert with a combination of cream cheese broken up with a fork and some thick Vermont cream stirred into it. On such an occasion you should make sure that the rollups have every advantage in the making. For instance, have either Brahms' Clarinet Quintet or Bach's Harpsichord Concerto in D Minor, on the record player, and pine grosbeaks visiting highbush cranberries prickly with hoarfrost outside the window.

The thought of highbush cranberries reminds me of:

CANDIED CRANBERRIES

1 cup cranberries
1 cup sugar
1 cup water
Extra Sugar

Pick over a quart of cranberries and choose the biggest and best berries. The others may be used in Cranberry Orange Relish.* Prick those chosen in several places with a needle. This helps them to absorb the syrup and retain their shape. Cook the sugar and water together for three minutes in a saucepan with the pan almost covered. Insert a candy thermometer. Don't stir the syrup or it will get grainy. Cook it to the firm soft ball stage — 238°. Put the cranberries into the syrup and cook until they are almost clear rubies — about ten minutes. Spread them to cool and dry overnight on a teflon cookie pan. The next morning roll them in the sugar. Save any left over syrup to add to punch.

CANDIED GRAPEFRUIT OR ORANGE PEEL

Peel of 2 grapefruit or 4 large oranges
1 tablespoon salt
1 cup sugar
½ cup water
Extra sugar

Cut the peel of two grapefruits or four large oranges in quarter-inch sections. Soak them overnight in four cups of cold water with one tablespoon salt added. The next morning, drain the peel and rinse in cold water. Cover with cold water, bring to the boiling point and cook for 20 minutes. Drain again and repeat the process until the peel has no bitter taste — at least four times. Then cook the peel until tender, an hour or more. Drain and cook slowly in a syrup made by mixing one cup sugar and half a cup water. Use a candy thermometer and cook the syrup until it registers 238°. Put the peel into the syrup and cook till transparent. Remove the peel using a spoon with holes in it. Spread the peel to cool on aluminum foil. Roll in granulated sugar. Store in a tightly covered tin box or a glass jar with a tight lid.

Separate batches of orange peel and grapefruit peel may be made, or they may be combined into one batch — one grapefruit and two large navel oranges. They make welcome Christmas gifts packaged in attractive glass jars and tied with red silk ribbon.

Every now and then, when cold winds were screaming around the house, Grandmother would live dangerously and make:

CHOCOLATE CARAMELS

- 3 *tablespoons butter*
- ¾ *cup light cream*
- 1 *cup sugar*
- 1 *cup molasses*
- 4 *squares unsweetened chocolate*
- ½ *teaspoon vanilla*
- ¼ *cup chopped pecans (optional)*

In a heavy stainless steel saucepan, melt the butter, add the cream, sugar and molasses. Bring to a boiling point. While doing so, melt the chocolate, two squares at a time, in a wooden spoon held over the steam. Stir the chocolate into the other mixture. Using a candy thermometer, cook the entire mixture to 244°. It should make a firm ball when some is dropped into cold water. It must be watched constantly. Even a little too much cooking will make it too hard for caramels.

Remove the pan from the heat. Add the vanilla. If you like it with nuts, stir in the pecans as soon as the pan is taken from the fire. Pour the mixture ¾ of an inch deep into a well-buttered shallow pan. Cool. When it is cool enough to handle, cut it into cubes. Use a sharp knife and finish with scissors. Wrap each caramel in wax paper. Put them in a covered tin box and set them to harden in a cold place.

Vanilla caramels may be made in the same way, omitting the chocolate and adding an extra quarter-cup of cream.

HOREHOUND CANDY

The making of this candy will be a virtuous act if any of your family or friends has a cold. A kind neighbor of Grandmother's used to make it more than forty years ago and would make winter pleasant by giving it to her friends.

- ¼ *ounce horehound*
- 2 *cups boiling water*
- 3 *cups granulated sugar*
- ½ *teaspoon cream of tartar*

Pressed horehound herb may be bought in a package at a drug store. Cut off about a quarter of an inch of the herb, pour the two cups of boiling water over it and let it steep for three minutes. Strain it through fine cheesecloth over the sugar mixed with the cream of tartar. Use a saucepan with a large evaporating surface. Let the mixture come to a boil, scraping the crystals away from the sides of the pan till the sugar is dissolved. Then using a candy thermometer, boil without stirring till it reaches 290°. It will be brittle when you drop a little on a cold plate. Spread about ⅜-inch deep in a well buttered, shallow pan. Crease the candy in half-inch squares before it is cool. Make deep creases. When it is cold, crack it sharply in pieces and store it in a tin box with a tight cover between layers of wax paper.

Make this candy on a bright crisp day with blue shadows on the snow. It looks like the amber drops of resin found on pine trees on a cold crisp day. It is excellent if you have a cough, or even if you haven't.

The only time she was ever in Texas, Mrs. Appleyard was greeted near the Rio Grande by a reader of her works who brought her a box of pralines she had made herself. She gave her the rule and also told her that pralines were named after the French Marshal, César du Plessis-Praslin, who liked almonds cooked in sugar. In New Orleans pecans were substituted, and Grandmother's friend made them like this:

PRALINES

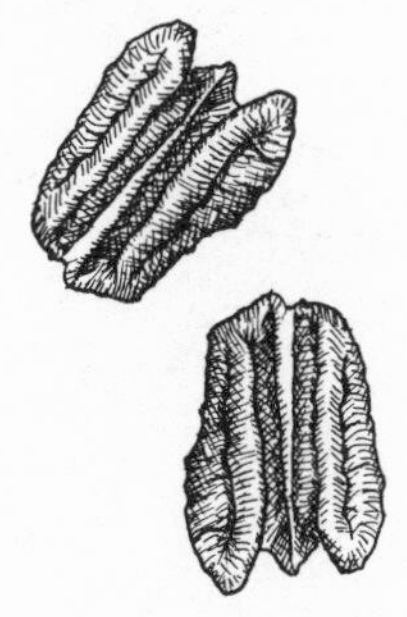

2	*cups light brown sugar, well packed*	1¼	*cups light cream*
1	*cup white sugar*	1	*teaspoon real Mexican vanilla*
½	*teaspoon cream of tartar*	1½	*cups whole pecans*

Combine the sugars, cream of tartar and cream and cook to the soft ball stage, 238° on a candy thermometer. Remove the syrup from the heat and let stand till lukewarm. Add the vanilla and pecans and beat it until it starts to lose its glossy look. Drop from a tablespoon onto wax paper, making 3-inch circles. Let it stand until firm. Store in a tightly covered tin box with wax paper between the layers of pralines.

MARZIPAN FRUIT

Grandmother started making marzipan after she bought a charming basket of it without reading the label. She had eaten a tasteless piece of it before reading what was in it — corn syrup, cracker crumbs and artificial flavoring — among other things. Remembering fondly the marzipan of her childhood, she decided to make her own. She used:

12	*ounces of shelled almonds*	1	*tablespoon soft butter*
3	*cups finely powdered sugar*	3	*teaspoons pure almond extract*
¼	*teaspoon cream of tartar*		*Extra powdered sugar*
3	*unbeaten egg whites*		

Begin by making your own powdered sugar in a small grinder. It tastes better than ordinary powdered sugar because there is no cornstarch in it. Note: If you don't make your own powdered sugar, use confectioner's sugar, as it is more finely ground.

Blanch and peel the almonds. Light oven: 250°. Cover cookie sheets with paper towels, spread the almonds on the towels and dry them for 15 minutes in the preheated oven. Then spread the nuts on fresh paper towels and let them cool. They must be thoroughly dry. When dry, grind them. This can be done by putting them through the finest attachment of a meat grinder. A small coffee grinder will work also. Do small amounts at a time. Before long you should have about three cups of loosely packed almond powder.

Next, make the uncooked fondant. Sift the three cups of powdered sugar and the cream of tartar together. Work in the egg whites one at a time, then the butter and the almond extract. Mix in the powdered almonds. A pastry fork makes this job easier. Dust your hands lightly with sugar and knead the marzipan thoroughly. It should be quite stiff. Wrap it in aluminum foil when stiff and store in a cool place overnight.

The next day fix your palette of vegetable colorings. Mrs. Appleyard used to use a large platter for this and small paint brushes kept for this purpose only. Have at least three glasses of water for rinsing the brushes, and change the water often so that the colors will stay clear. First put the red, yellow, green and blue food colorings on your palette. Next mix orange (red and yellow); carrot color (yellow, a dash of red); pear color (green with a touch of red); brown (red and green); and strawberry color (red with a touch of yellow).

Shape the marzipan into small apples, pears, bananas, carrots, peaches, pea pods — half open and showing the peas — and potatoes. Strawberries are shaped about like medium-sized berries and seem huge compared with the other fruit.

Have at hand: whole cloves, bits of candied angelica for leaves and strawberry hulls. Mix powdered sugar, cocoa and a little cinnamon to roll the potatoes in. If angelica is not available, make the strawberry hulls out of heavy green paper. Whichever you use, fasten the hulls on with the small ends of toothpicks dipped in green or brown coloring. Toothpicks are also useful in modeling. Suggestions for the forming of a number of fruits are given below, let your imagination go and invent your own fruits or vegetables.

Apples: Dilute yellow coloring and paint the apples all over. Blend in a touch of green around the stem end. Dilute red a little and paint one cheek of the apple. Add a few darker red stripes. Use a clove for the blossom end. Fasten on leaves with a brown (toothpick) stem.

Carrots: Engrave a few lines around them with a toothpick. Paint with carrot color. Touch the tops with green. No leaves or stems are needed.

Tangerine, Orange: Make little pits all over the surface with the fine point of a toothpick. Paint them a deep orange color all over. No leaves. No stem.

Peaches: Paint yellow, not diluted. Paint one cheek red with a touch of blue blended in. Fasten leaves with a brown stem.

Pears: Dilute yellow coloring and paint all over. Paint one cheek with pear green and touch the other with red. Use a clove for the blossom end. Fasten on leaves with a brown stem.

Bananas: Paint with a slightly diluted yellow. Stripe and dot with brown. Touch the end with green.

Peas: For both the partly opened pod and the peas inside, paint with a diluted green.

Strawberries: Paint all over with strawberry color. Dot with green for seeds. Fasten on hulls with green toothpick stems.

Potatoes: Make several depressions with the blunt end of a toothpick. Touch these with brown. Do not paint the rest of the potato but roll it in the sugar, cocoa and cinnamon mixture.

An enjoyable and sometimes efficient way in which to make a large number of marzipan fruit is to invite friends and relatives of all ages to participate. It can be turned into a family project, with the head cook first making a model of each fruit desired and then turning the production over to grandchildren and other innocent passers-by. I've spent many a snowy day at my Grandmother's painting marzipan fruit — perhaps that is where my interest in painting stemmed from.

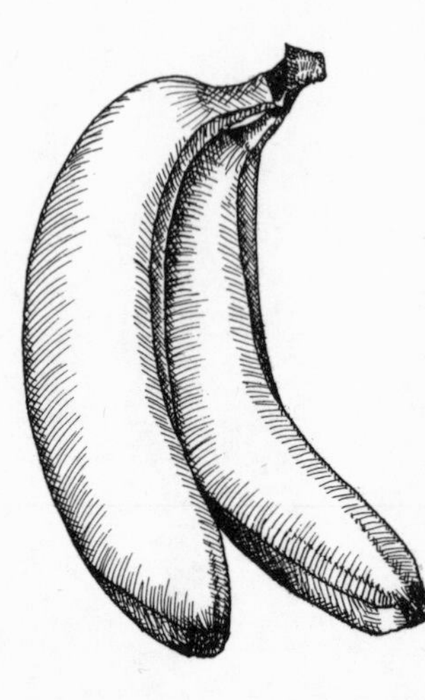

Strawberry baskets lined first with aluminum foil and then with crumpled green tissue paper and filled with an assortment of marzipan fruit, make delightful Christmas gifts. And, unlike the collection that inspired Grandmother to undertake the initiation of yet another tradition, the gay looking fruit also tastes quite good. What a coincidence!

SALLY APPLEYARD'S FUDGE

When her youngest child began to supply the Appleyard family with this nourishment, Mrs. Appleyard felt that Sally had a great career in cooking before her.

"You will be known internationally," she was heard to have said.

She was right of course, though, to be accurate, it was not fudge but a book of Sally's on *Plato's Use of Fallacy* that had recently been reviewed in Japan and Germany. The fudge is still excellent.

3	*squares unsweetened chocolate*	*1⅓*	*cups white sugar*
¼	*pound butter*	*1½*	*cups light brown sugar*
1	*teaspoon vanilla*	*⅔*	*cup milk, part cream*
		½	*cup pecans (optional)*

Grate the chocolate. Save a tablespoon of it and a tablespoon of butter and the vanilla. Boil everything else in a large sauce pan. Scrape the mixture away from the edges of the pan so that it will not form crystals. Do this until all the sugars have dissolved. Then boil without stirring till it forms a soft ball when dropped in cold water — 238° on your candy thermometer. Take the pan from the fire. Drop in extra butter and chocolate. Let fudge cool a few minutes. Add the vanilla and beat fudge until some will hold its shape when dropped from the spoon. If you like nuts in it, add them now. Pour the fudge out quickly on a buttered pan. Crease in squares, set to cool in a hidden spot, and give any small boys the pan to scrape.

MARSHMALLOWS

Having indulged in the distasteful habit of reading the ingredients on a package once again, Grandmother decided to make her own marshmallows.

2	*tablespoons (envelopes) gelatin*	*1*	*cup sugar*
¼	*cup cold water*	*¾*	*cup hot water*
		½	*teaspoon real vanilla*

Soak the gelatin in the cold water. Dissolve the sugar in the hot water. Cook the sugar mixture without stirring to 238° (soft ball) on a candy thermometer. Cool slightly. Add the vanilla. Pour the mixture on the softened gelatin, beating with a wire whisk. Beat till fluffy. Put the mixture in a teflon pan, eight inches square, and smooth it down. Chill at least three hours in refrigerator. Cut in cubes. Use them plain or dip them in chocolate syrup made by dissolving six ounces of Nestle's chocolate chips in a quarter-cup of hot water. Place them on wax paper. Cool. Place them between layers of wax paper in a tightly covered tin box.

FRENCH FONDANT

This is the foundation of all cream candy.

2	*cups sugar*	*½*	*cup water*
		⅛	*teaspoon cream of tartar*

Mix the sugar and water, and dissolve over low heat. Add the cream of tartar. Wash away crystals from the sides of the pan with a clean pastry brush wrapped in cheesecloth. Cover. Boil four minutes without stirring. Test temperature with a candy thermometer. It should just touch 240°.

Stir until creamy. Set the pan in another of cold water and cool until you can just touch it without burning your finger. Turn it out on a metal, enameled or — better — a marble slab. Don't scrape the pan or let the last — possibly grainy — drops of syrup run out. Knead the mixture with your hand till it is soft and very creamy. Put it in a bowl lined with wax paper. Cover the bowl with a slightly moistened pastry cloth. Don't let the cloth touch the fondant.

Set away to ripen. The next day, or several days later, heat the desired quantity in a double boiler, stirring constantly. Cool till it can be shaped into balls. This recipe makes one pound.

CHOCOLATE CREAMS

Flavor the fondant with vanilla. Form balls and dip them in melted Nestle's semi-sweet chocolate. Use two forks to dip unless you have a real candy dipper. Put on wax paper to cool and harden.

WALNUT OR PECAN CREAMS

Form fondant into balls. Press each ball between two nut halves. Or make balls with sugared almonds, and form the fondant around blanched toasted almonds or pecans.

UNCOOKED FRUIT BARS

1 cup figs
1 cup dates
1 cup raisins
1 cup dried coconut
1 cup nuts (walnuts)

Grind all the ingredients together in a meat grinder. Press the mixture into an eight-inch square teflon pan. Refrigerate for at least two hours. Slice into bars or squares and serve.

I found this rule while visiting a New England Natural Foods Association convention. It had been prepared for a recipe contest and won second prize in its category. Not only are the bars tasty and satisfying for a sweet tooth, but they are nutritious. But don't tell the recipients, or they might not try them.

Cheese

GRANDMOTHER thought she had covered the topic of cheese rather thoroughly in her *Vermont Year Round Cookbook*. However, her filing system, a box confusingly labeled "Paradise Kittens" and containing cards arranged in a pretty nearly alphabetical order, still showed treasures that made my mouth water and my stomach grumble. So, I include here a selection of cheese recipes from the *Year Round Cookbook*, as well as a number of other suggestions for your use.

Cheese should be given the respect and honor it deserves. I frequently find myself making use of a variety of cheeses, most often Vermont cheddar, almost without thinking about its value and versatility. I have changed this ungrateful pattern with the acquisition of a capricious milking Toggenburg goat.

Jay and I obtained Jenny from a nearby goat farm nearly two years ago. Jenny was approaching six weeks of age at that time and quickly won the hearts of anyone whom she approached. We bought Jenny with the intention of breeding her in order to have access to a constant supply of milk. However, she did not follow our plan for a full year and a half. She became a family joke of sorts, and the most lovable and expensive pet that we might possibly want. Jenny quickly outgrew her original quarters, and would "entertain" me by leaping over her pen wall, running as quickly as possible to the front porch and waiting quietly until she was noticed. At which time she would be brought back to her pen to begin the process all over again. It was not long before Jay had constructed a "goat-proof" pen and Jenny was contentedly browsing in the field under skies of azure.

Finally, after what had seemed an eternity, Jenny became pregnant and is now the proud mother of an equally capricious buck goat and is supplying us with enough milk to use for all purposes including cheese-making. We soon found ourselves at the mercy of the somewhat distinctive flavor of goat's milk cheese after the long, drawn-out process of having produced it. I now rarely use any cheese without thinking of the love, devotion and hard work that must have gone into the making. But, I still love Jenny and use her milk in many other ways.

Cheese must always be cooked at low temperatures and watched carefully. If not, it will all too soon become tough and stringy.

An easy way to begin the practice of watching a cheese sauce with precision is with the making of:

CHEESE CROUSTADE

(For 4)

2 tablespoons soft butter
4 rounds homemade bread
4 extra rounds each cut with a doughnut cutter to make a hole in the center
1 extra tablespoon butter
3 tablespoons thick cream
4 tablespoons grated cheddar cheese
½ teaspoon mustard
½ teaspoon paprika
¼ teaspoon Worcestershire sauce

Butter each round of bread on one side. Put those with the holes on top of the others, both butter side up. Bake these at 350° until they are lightly browned — about ten minutes. In the meantime make the filling. Over very low heat soften the extra butter. Add the cream, the cheese and the seasonings. Stir well until melted. Fill the croustades. Put them back in the oven until the cheese starts to bubble — about five minutes. Serve with a tossed salad containing the five kinds of lettuce in your garden and small bits of fresh herbs.

Another rule requiring the close watching of cooking cheese was one of Mr. Appleyard's favorites:

WELSH RABBIT

(For 6)

2 tablespoons butter
1 cup beer
2 teaspoons Worcestershire sauce
2 teaspoons dry mustard
½ teaspoon salt
¼ teaspoon cayenne
2 pounds mild soft cheddar cheese cut into small pieces
6 English muffins, split
2 egg yolks, lightly beaten

Grandfather used a silver chafing dish, but an electric skillet or a cast iron skillet over a low flame both make good substitutes. The primary thing to remember is that cheese reacts badly to high heat or long cooking.

Melt the butter. Pour in the beer and bring it quickly to a boil. Add the seasonings. Reduce the heat. Add the cheese. Stir well so that the small cubes into which you have cut it will melt quickly. Meanwhile, your assistant is toasting English muffins. She/he also beats the egg yolks in a small bowl and presents them at the right moment. Add a good dollop of melted cheese to the egg yolks and beat them together with a fork. Add the mixture to the contents of the skillet. Stir well until it thickens. The muffins should be ready, hot and buttery.

Dunk one into the rabbit. It will emerge veiled in ambrosia and gold, dripping, pungent, and succulent, ready to go on a hot plate and receive a final spoonful of rabbit. Serve hot to all those waiting, with tall glasses of beer and Mrs. Appleyard's Chutney* or Major Grey's Chutney.

VERMONT CHEESE FONDUE

No doubt, if I were in Switzerland, I would find a Swiss cheese that would make me think of Alpine flowers and wind and sunshine and towery white peaks. Unfortunately, in the Swiss cheese I encounter here, the holes seem to have the most taste. I prefer fondue made out of cheese that has the flavor of green, blue and purple Vermont hills, grass with wild strawberries and four-leaf clovers growing in it.

Grandmother made her fondue in an electric skillet with no complaints from customers. I still prefer my red enamel fondue pot, or a special cheese fondue pot, heated first on the stove and kept warm over an alcohol burner. Either way, the results are luscious.

1 clove garlic, peeled
1½ cups white wine
1 tablespoon kirsch
2 pounds cheddar cheese cut in small cubes
½ teaspoon fresh pepper
Nutmeg to taste
Your own genuine imitation French Bread, sliced half inch thick and toasted*

Split the clove of garlic and rub the pan with it. Pour in the wine and the kirsch and heat till the liquid starts to bubble. Add the cheddar cheese. Lower the heat to 200°. Stir till cheese is melted and the mixture is smooth. Add the seasonings. Have a helper who makes the toast and then makes some more. Give everyone a plate, a fork (a fondue fork if possible) and let them dip pieces of toast into the fondue. Lower the heat below 200° so the fondue will keep warm but not curdle. Ultimately all that will be left will be some crisp golden crust on the bottom of the pan. Luckily this is almost the best part: the customers will scrape practically all of it off so the pan won't be hard to wash. A fresh green salad tops off the meal, with glasses of cool dry white wine.

CHEESE PUFFS

1 cup water
½ cup butter
½ teaspoon paprika
Salt to taste — about ½ teaspoon
¼ teaspoon garlic powder (optional)
1 cup flour, sifted three times
4 eggs, unbeaten
¾ cup cheddar cheese, finely grated

Put water, butter and seasonings into a fairly deep saucepan. When the water boils, dump in the flour, all at once. Stir hard until the mixture leaves the sides of the pan. Remove pan from the heat. Cool slightly. Add the unbeaten eggs one at a time, beating hard after adding each one. Beat in the grated cheese a third at a time. Beat some more. Light oven: 400°.

*See Index for pages where recipes can be found.

Drop the batter by teaspoonfuls on a teflon cookie sheet, in a circular shape. Heap them up in the center. Keep them an inch and a half apart. This amount of batter will make 18 small puffs or 12 good-sized ones.

Bake at 400° for ten minutes. Then reduce the heat to 350° and bake till they are done. They will collapse if taken out too soon. Be sure there are no bubbles of moisture on them and that they have stopped hissing before taking them out of the oven.

The small puffs are good to serve with a salad just as they are. If your digestion is like that of an ostrich, you may like the larger ones filled with:

CHEESE CUSTARD FILLING

3 tablespoons butter
3 tablespoons instant flour
½ cup of thick cream
¼ teaspoon pepper
½ teaspoon paprika
¾ cup grated cheese
2 egg yolks

Cut a slit in the sides of the puffs as soon as you take them from the oven. Melt the butter, rub in the flour, cook over low heat for one minute. Remove from heat. Blend in the cream and the seasonings. Return to low heat. Cook until the mixture starts to thicken. Add the cheese and stir until the cheese melts. Remove from fire. Beat the eggs. Add a tablespoon of the sauce to the eggs. Stir it in well, then add the eggs to the cheese mixture. Cook for one minute over low heat, stirring all the time. Cool.

When filling the puffs, open the slits in the sides and fill them with some of the sauce. Put a little of the sauce on top and return the puffs to the oven for five minutes. Serve hot with new grilled tomatoes and Mrs. Appleyard's Chutney.*

Easier to make on a busy day are:

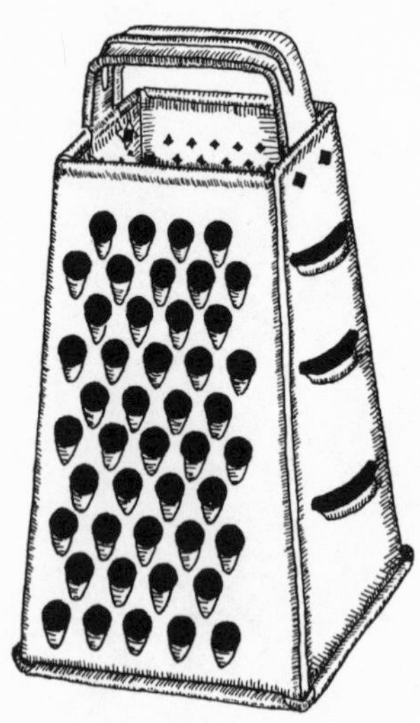

CHEESE CUBES

¼ cup butter
6 drops Worcestershire sauce
½ teaspoon paprika
1 egg, beaten
12 cubes real bread, ¾ inch square
½ cup grated cheese

Cream the butter, add the seasonings and the egg lightly beaten. Mix well. Light oven: 375°. Dip the bread cubes in the mixture and then roll them in the grated cheese. Put the cubes on that teflon sheet you remembered to buy and bake them until the cheese melts and the cubes begin to brown — about eight minutes. These are good either hot or cold with soup or salad.

Good too with either soup or salad are:

CHEESE RUSKS

For a dozen rusks, allow:

1 teaspoon butter
1 teaspoon salad oil
2 teaspoons red wine — tarragon vinegar
1 teaspoon onion powder
1 teaspoon paprika
1 teaspoon dry mustard
1½ cups grated cheese

Melt the butter over low heat, add the salad oil, vinegar and seasonings. Stir in the grated cheese and stir until the mixture is smooth. Spread it on rusks — or if you prefer, on English muffins lightly toasted, or on Cross crackers split, buttered and lightly toasted. Put the rusks on the pan of an electric broiler and broil until the cheese mixture bubbles. Serve very hot.

CHEESE CLUB SANDWICHES

(Open-Faced Style)

For each person to be served:

- 1 *slice of homemade bread*
- *Mayonnaise*
- 1 *slice of Vermont cheddar cheese*
- 1 *thin slice of a large mild onion*
- 1 *thin slice from a large tomato*
- *A little finely chopped green pepper*
- 2 *slices of bacon, partly cooked, drained on paper towels*

Spread the slices of bread with mayonnaise. Light oven: 375°. Put the tomato on the bread, followed by the cheese, then the onion. Sprinkle with the green pepper. Lay slices of bacon over everything. Bake for 15 minutes, or until the bacon is as crisp as you like it.

CHEESE RING

A cheese ring is a refreshing cool lunch on a hot day. Served with a salad and Parker House rolls, it is complete and welcomed.

- 2 *tablespoons gelatin*
- ½ *cup cold water*
- 9 *ounces cream cheese*
- ½ *pound Danish blue cheese*
- ½ *teaspoon onion powder*
- 1 *cup heavy cream*

Soak the gelatin in the cold water in a small saucepan. Place it over hot water, stir occasionally till gelatin dissolves. Lightly oil a ring mold. Mash together the cream cheese and the Danish blue, add onion powder. Whip the cream. Mix it with the cheeses. Add the gelatin. Pour the mixture into the mold. Chill at least two hours. Serve surrounded by oak leaf lettuce. Decorate platter with Radish Roses* and stuffed olives and matchstick carrots.

Some of my favorite dishes are made from homemade cottage cheese. I know this is a controversial subject. People are sharply divided into two groups, both vocal — those who like cottage cheese and those who don't. Few are indifferent. If you do not care for it, you will sympathize with a small boy, who once took a mouthful of some Grandmother had made, under the impression that it was popcorn. Being a child of character, he swallowed it, and having done so, he remarked quietly: "This popcorn has a dampish sour taste."

Great-Grandmother called it Dutch Cheese and this is the way she made it:

COTTAGE CHEESE

Begin by scalding a five-quart milk pan and pouring into it three quarts of whole milk (unpasteurized). Let it stand in a cool room until a thick clabber is just starting to whey off — about two days. There is no way to hurry the process. If you do, you will produce a rubbery substance excellent for the compost heap or perhaps for making glue-all, but something certainly not edible. Cream will have risen on it. It will make ivory shadows in the finished cheese.

Set the pan of curds in the sink. Fill the pan with boiling water. Let it stand until cool. The whey will separate and the curd will sink to the bottom of the pan. Take a pinch of the curd occasionally between your thumb and forefinger. When it feels just slightly rough, it is ready. If, when it is cool, it still feels slippery, add a little more hot water. Add two tablespoons of salt. Put the curd in a colander. Pour cold water through it and let it drain. Put it in a bowl. If it seems too dry, add a little thick cream, sour or sweet, whichever you prefer.

You now have the basic material for:

GLAZED STRAWBERRY CHEESE CAKE

I'll admit, you can save everyone a lot of trouble by buying some cottage cheese. Even I seldom chase a Guernsey cow out of the forget-me-nots these days. Although, I do from time to time chase a goat out of the dandelions for the same purpose.

1 tablespoon butter

½ cup wheat germ mixed with ½ cup sugar
¼ teaspoon nutmeg
4 eggs, separated
1 pint cottage cheese
½ cup light cream
½ cup heavy cream
2 teaspoons vanilla
1 8-ounce package cream cheese
1 tablespoon flour
1 cup sugar

For the glaze:

1 10-ounce package frozen strawberries, defrosted
1 8-ounce glass currant jelly
1 tablespoon instant tapioca

Use a 9x13-inch pyrex dish. Butter it well, leaving no bare spots. Mix the wheat germ, ½ cup sugar and nutmeg. Use two-thirds of the mixture to coat the buttered dish. Save the other third for topping.

Beat the egg whites to stiff peaks. Light oven: 300°. Mix the cottage cheese and light cream. Beat till smooth. Add the heavy cream, vanilla, cream cheese, flour and sugar and mix well. Add the egg yolks beaten thick, and stir them in. With a wire whisk gently fold in the beaten whites.

Put the mixture in the coated dish. Top it with the remaining wheat germ mixture. Bake one hour at 300°. Cool thoroughly. For the glaze: use a cup of juice from the defrosted strawberries. Add the currant jelly and cook in the top of a double boiler till jelly is melted, add the instant tapioca. Cool till it starts to thicken. Top the cheese cake with the drained whole berries. Add the glaze, spooning it over each berry, and over the whole cake. Chill in the refrigerator at least one hour.

You can make as many variations on this rule as you can think up some long winter evening with the symphony playing Berlioz' "Romeo and Juliet," apple tree wood burning on the hearth and frost pictures of white forests forming on the windows. For the crust you may use graham crackers or finely rolled Cross crackers or very finely sifted bread crumbs all mixed with sugar. You may put fresh or frozen peaches on top of the cake and glaze them with peach juice and currant jelly and instant tapioca. You may add very ripe bananas, well-mashed, to the cheese cake mixture. You may sweeten it with honey and use raspberries instead of strawberries for the glaze.

A cookbook plainly called *The Art of Cooking Made Plain and Easy*, written in 1760, suggests the use of "two perfumed plums in rose or orange flower water" among other obscure ingredients, for the making of a "fine cheese cake." I've not been able to obtain any perfumed plums and so I've persisted with further variations employing more readily available components.

CHEESE SOUFFLÉ

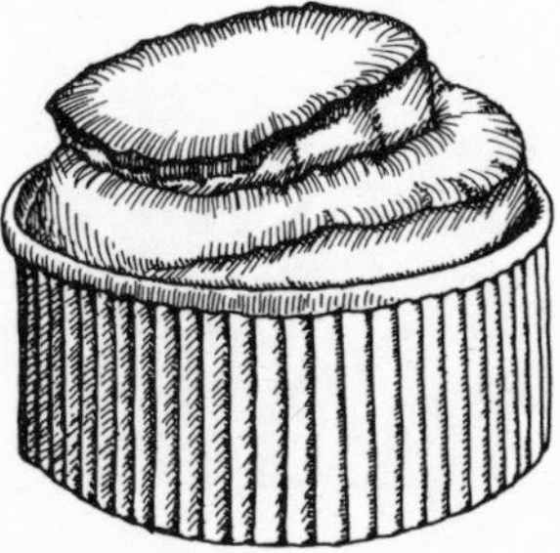

½	*cup butter*	*1½*	*cups milk*
6	*tablespoons flour*	*½*	*cup cream*
1	*teaspoon paprika*	*2*	*cups (scant) grated cheddar cheese*
½	*teaspoon mustard (optional)*	*1*	*extra tablespoon butter*
	Pepper and salt to taste	*6*	*eggs, separated*

Make a roux of the butter and the flour sifted with the dry seasonings. Cook over low heat for three minutes, remove from the heat, blend in the milk smoothly. Cook over low heat until it is thick and smooth. Add the cream and the cheese. Cook until the cheese melts. Cool slightly. Light oven: 350°. Put the extra tablespoon of butter in a two quart straight-sided casserole or soufflé dish. Set the casserole in the oven. Add the beaten egg yolks to the cheese mixture. Beat the egg whites so stiff that they stick to the bowl. Fold them gently into the cheese mixture and fill the casserole. The butter in the casserole should be hot but not brown.

Start the soufflé on the lower shelf of the oven. After 20 minutes move it gently to the upper shelf. If it browns too fast, reduce the heat to 325°. Bake until it ceases to make any sound of hissing and bubbling. Listen carefully! You must hear nothing. It takes nearly 50 minutes to reach this happy silence. Recipients must wait.

Variations: Instead of cheese you may use a cup and a quarter of finely minced ham or chicken or pureed spinach or finely flaked flounder in the soufflé. Most people seem to prefer cheese. Tiny baking powder biscuits spread with a mixture of mayonnaise and Underwood's deviled ham and run briefly under the broiler, go well with it. So do freshly picked green peas from the garden or a salad of several kinds of lettuce, tossed with French Dressing,* and Garlic Croutons.* Chutney harmonizes well with it, so does tomato conserve. Soufflés are versatile, luscious, and too appetizing for me to continue writing.

CHEESE CROQUETTES

(for 8)

Mrs. Appleyard never had the courage to fry anything in deep fat. However, her daughter Cicely is somewhat tougher on that score and so coerced her mother into including this rule in *The Winter Kitchen.*

I fluctuate from abhorrence to mild tolerance of deep frying, and happen to enjoy the results of the following rule.

6	*tablespoons butter*	1	*teaspoon Worcestershire sauce*
½	*cup flour*	6	*egg yolks*
1⅓	*cups milk*	1	*cup dry cheese, grated (cheddar or parmesan)*
	Salt and pepper to taste	1	*cup mild cheese, cubed*
½	*teaspoon paprika*	2	*extra egg yolks*
1	*teaspoon dry mustard*		
	Few grains of cayenne		

1 *cup fine dry bread crumbs*

Make a white sauce of the butter, flour, milk and seasonings. When it is smooth, add the egg yolks, unbeaten. Add the dry cheese and stir well. Add the mild cheese. Do all this over rather low heat and take the pan off the fire as the cubes begin to melt. Don't overcook or the cheese will be tough and stringy.

Pour the mixture into a 9x13-inch pan. Spread it out evenly. Cool. Mark the mixture in oblongs. Beat the extra two egg yolks and two tablespoons of water together with a fork. Roll each oblong of the cheese into a cylinder. Dip them first into the dried bread crumbs, then into the egg mixture, then into the crumbs again. Chill briefly. Fry the croquettes in deep fat (Crisco) at 380-390° until they are golden brown — about one minute. Do a few at a time taking care not to let them get too dark. They should be crisp outside and a little like Welsh Rabbit inside.

GNOCCHI

(For 3)

2	*cups milk*	2	*eggs, beaten*
½	*cup farina*	2	*tablespoons butter*
1	*teaspoon salt*	½	*cup grated cheddar cheese*
2	*teaspoons sugar*	½	*cup parmesan cheese, grated*

Heat the milk in the top of a double boiler and stir in the farina. Add the salt and sugar. Cover and cook for 20 minutes. Remove the pan from the heat and stir in the beaten eggs, butter, and the grated cheddar cheese. Beat together well and pour into well-buttered pyrex pie plate or an unbuttered teflon one. Cool. Refrigerate overnight. The next day sprinkle with parmesan cheese, dot with butter and bake in a 350° oven until delicately brown on top — about 30 minutes. Serve with a green salad for a light lunch.

Another cheese dish for a light lunch or a full brunch, is a variation on French toast.

CHEESE FRENCH TOAST

(For 2)

½	*cup heavy cream*	¼	*teaspoon nutmeg*
½	*cup cheddar cheese, grated*	2	*eggs, well beaten*
⅛	*teaspoon pepper*	6	*triangles of bread*

Mix the cream, the cheese grated rather coarsely, and the seasonings and cook in double boiler over hot water a few minutes, stirring, until the cheese melts. Cool by setting pan into cold water. Beat the eggs with a wire whisk and beat them into the mixture. Grease a baking sheet well with butter. Dip slices of bread into the cheese mixture one at a time, coating both sides. Place them on the baking sheet and bake at 375° until they are light brown and bubbly — about 15 minutes. Serve very hot with a tossed salad. For a slightly tangier result, replace the cream with yogurt.

CHEESE QUICHE

(For 6)

A quiche, like a soufflé, is a dish that seems to throw cooks into fits of anxiety, by the simple mention of the name. That is effective until you have tried the preparation yourself and find how truly simple it is. A quiche is basically an open-faced custard pie that may have various ingredients in it in addition to the rudimentary mixture of eggs and cream. A real French quiche is served in a pastry that stands alone. Americans are less adventurous and usually serve the quiche in the dish in which it was baked.

Begin by lining a 9-inch pie plate with pastry, either the packaged variety or Mrs. Appleyard's variety found in the chapter on Pies. Cover the pastry with aluminum foil, weight it down with dry beans and bake at 400° for eight minutes.

Next make the filling:

- *6 slices bacon*
- *¼ cup chopped chives*
- *4 eggs*
- *2 cups light cream*
- *1 cup sharp cheddar cheese, coarsely grated*
- *Nutmeg, cayenne, pepper, salt to taste*

Cook the bacon in a 350° oven until crisp but not overcooked. Discard the beans used in baking the pastry. Scatter the bacon in small pieces over the bottom of the cooked pastry shell. Sprinkle chives over the bacon. Beat the eggs and cream together. Stir in the cheese and the seasonings and add to shell. Bake at 400° for ten minutes. Reduce the heat to 325° and bake until a knife will come clean from the middle — about 25 minutes longer. The bacon and chives will come to the top which should be puffed and golden brown. Quiche may be served as a main course for a light meal, or cut into thin slivers and used as an appetizer.

Variations: Instead of cheese, use a large mild onion sliced very thin and sautéed in butter until yellow and transparent. Spread the thin slices of onion over the bacon. Add a pinch of marjoram to the seasonings.

Substitute for the cheese a cup of mushroom caps, sliced thin and tossed in butter for three minutes with a little minced onion.

Substitute four tablespoons Roquefort cheese and six ounces cream cheese for the cheddar cheese. Mash them together with a pastry fork and blend cream and beaten eggs into the cheese. Omit the bacon. Sprinkle pastry with minced chives and parsley.

Substitute a good Swiss cheese for the cheddar cheese, or use a mixture of cheeses, such as Gruyère and Emanthaler.

Substitute chopped, cooked ham, turkey or chicken for the cheese, changing the seasonings to suit your tastes.

Make up your own combination of ingredients — the blends are infinite.

BAKED CHEESE PIE

This is similar to a cheese quiche, but begins with no pastry shell. It provides a filling and creamy rich main course and is good served hot or cold.

- *½ cup kidney beans, cooked*
- *¾ cup raw brown rice, cooked*
- *1½ cups onions, thinly sliced*
- *1 tablespoon butter*
- *1 cup milk*
- *2 eggs, beaten*
- *1 cup cheddar cheese, coarsely grated*
- *¾ teaspoon Worcestershire sauce*
- *1 teaspoon salt*
- *1 teaspoon dried tarragon*
- *2 tablespoons sherry*
- *Yogurt*

Cook the beans and rice. Meanwhile, sauté the sliced onion in butter until yellow and transparent. Set aside. Beat together the milk, eggs, cheese and seasonings, including sherry. Fold the onions, rice and beans into the egg and milk mixture. Turn the whole mixture into a buttered 10-inch pie plate. Bake at 325° for 25-30 minutes, or until the custard has set and the edges are a golden brown. Let cool for eight to ten minutes before serving. Excellent with a dab of plain yogurt on top and great served cold the next day for lunch, if you have any left over.

This rule is subject to many of the same variations as described above for the quiche. Sliced, cooked vegetables, such as carrots or broccoli also enhance this dish.

CHEESE BISCUITS

A favorite with the Appleyard family whenever five or more are gathered together for any excuse of a party whatsoever.

- *½ pound grated mild cheddar, about two cups*
- *½ pound butter*
- *2 cups flour*
- *1 teaspoon dry mustard*
- *1 teaspoon paprika*
- *¼ teaspoon baking powder*
- *1 teaspoon Worcestershire sauce*

Have cheese and butter at room temperature. Sift the flour with mustard, paprika and baking powder three times. Cream the butter with an electric mixer, add the Worcestershire sauce, cream in the cheese. Add the flour and keep beating until mixture is well blended. On a pastry cloth or very lightly floured board, make a long roll of dough, about 1¾-inches in diameter. Wrap the dough in wax paper and chill at least two hours. It may be chilled overnight if that is more convenient.

At baking time, preheat the oven to 325°. Slice off circles from the roll of dough, ⅓ of an inch thick. Make into small balls. Flatten them slightly. They should be about one inch across. They will spread, so allow space between them. Keep two pans going. Bake for eight minutes. Do not overbake. The biscuits should not brown except slightly on the bottom. They will have a somewhat orange-yellow color due to the paprika in the dough. This rule makes about four dozen and a few extra that always seem to disappear before they can be stored.

Cookies

COOKIES have delighted the tastes and hearts of children of all ages for generations. Grandmother munificently taught her children and grandchildren the joy and ease of producing a savory batch of cookies. As the baking was a righteous act, I was restricted to the role of observer for a number of years before I was invited to become a participating member. The corner behind the pantry door leading to the winter kitchen was a particularly opportune location for out-of-the-way observation. From that vantage point I was also treated to bowl licking and the heavenly aroma of the baking delicacies. However, once I was allowed to dip my hands in Oatmeal Lace Cookie* dough, I felt that I had become a full-fledged member of the family. Since my initiation years ago, I have produced innumerable batches of cookies, of as many types and qualities.

Although potentially as deadly — in terms of calories and sweets — as other forms of desserts, cookies somehow escape the condemnation freely given heartier desserts. It *is* possible to eat just one cookie and commit only a small crime of eating. It is also possible to create cookies that do indeed have nutritional validity, by adding ingredients in varying amounts to just about any cookie recipe.

ALMOND BALLS

2	*cups sifted flour*	*1*	*teaspoon vanilla*
¼	*cup sugar*	*2½*	*cups finely chopped blanched almonds*
½	*cup butter*		

1 teaspoon almond extract

Sift the flour and sugar together. With a pastry fork, work in the butter, almond and vanilla flavorings and two cups of the chopped nuts. Shape the dough into balls about ¾ of an inch in diameter. If the dough seems too dry to shape, work in up to two tablespoons of cream. Dip the tops and sides of the balls in the rest of the chopped almonds. Place them on a teflon cookie sheet. Bake at 325° until delicately browned — about 25 minutes. Leave some plain if desired, and when cool, dip them in Nestle's chocolate chips, melted over very low heat.

ALMOND SHORTBREAD

¼ pound butter
½ cup powdered sugar
1 teaspoon almond extract
2 cups flour, sifted
½ cup ground almonds

Cream the butter, beat in the sugar and the almond extract. Combine the flour and the almonds and work them in with a pastry fork. Roll the dough out about ⅜ of an inch thick. Cut with a fluted cookie cutter and prick all over the top with a fork. Bake at 350° until delicately brown — about 25 minutes. Check at the end of ten minutes and reduce the heat to 325° if they seem to be browning too fast.

BENNE (SESAME) SEED COOKIES

¾ cup butter
1½ cups light brown sugar
1 teaspoon vanilla
¾ cup flour, sifted
1 cup toasted Benne (sesame) seeds
1 egg

Soften the butter. Beat into it the sugar, the vanilla and the egg. Stir in the sifted flour. Chill briefly. Light oven: 375°. Roll out the cookie dough, using a lightly floured pastry cloth and covered rolling pin. Cut out cookies. Sprinkle with toasted Benne seeds. Bake until lightly brown — about 12 minutes. These cookies have a delicate crunchy flavor, delicious with a glass of fresh milk.

BRANDY SNAPS

These must be made on a crisp day with a slight breeze from the northwest. Grandmother used to make these while the rest of her family had taken sandwiches and gone to Camel's Hump. She would fantasize that they were being pursued by musk oxen or glancing catamounts' tails swishing through the ferns, or meeting bears in caves. She was just as content to be safe at home preparing Brandy Snaps for their hungry return. I much preferred to be the subject of my Grandmother's fantasy and continue running up a mountain stream in search of musk oxen.

Whatever your fantasy, begin with:

½ cup butter
⅔ cup sugar
1 cup dark molasses
2 tablespoons brandy
¾ cup flour, sifted three times
½ teaspoon nutmeg
½ teaspoon cinnamon
⅔ cup coconut

In a deep saucepan, boil the butter and sugar, molasses and brandy together for 20 minutes. Watch it carefully, stirring occasionally. Mix in the flour, spices and the coconut. Boil an additional ten minutes, stirring all the time. Cool slightly. The mixture should be quite thick. Light oven: 350°.

*See Index for pages where recipes can be found.

Drop the mixture by half teaspoonfuls on teflon cookie sheets. The cookies will spread to about 2½-inches in diameter, so be sure to give them room. Bake them until they bubble hard. Remove the sheets from the oven. Let them stand at least one minute. Test the edges with a nylon spatula. Remove them from the sheets and lay them flat on a cold platter. Or, choosing the right stage of pliability — which can only be learned by experiment — roll them into cornucopias or curl them around the handle of a wooden spoon. Store them in a tightly covered box between layers of wax paper.

If you are really deft, you might serve cornucopia-shaped snaps filled at the last minute with freshly whipped cream. This taste might quickly become habit-forming, but I have never reached the proper stage of agility, and so avoid the temptation.

Sometimes even the deftest (most deft) cook feels it would be more restful to make:

CLASSIC BROWNIES
(Cake-Type)

There are several kinds of brownies: some are rather like a rich chocolate cake; some like baked fudge; some have nuts; some do not; some have chocolate chips instead of nuts; and some don't have any chocolate at all. I've come across a remarkable collection of brownie recipes and include here some of the best.

Use an electric mixer for these.

2 squares unsweetened chocolate
½ cup butter
1 cup sugar
2 eggs
½ teaspoon vanilla
½ cup chopped walnuts (optional)
½ cup sifted flour

Melt the chocolate over hot but not boiling water. Cream the butter. Light oven: 375°. Cool the chocolate slightly by setting the pan in another containing cold water. Beat the chocolate into the creamed butter. Let the mixture cool while you butter and lightly flour an 8x8-inch aluminum pan. Beat in the sugar, the eggs and the vanilla. Flour the nuts with two tablespoons of the flour. Beat the rest of the flour into the mixture. Add the floured nuts. Put the mixture into the buttered pan. Bake for 15 minutes at 375°, then at 350° until the brownies shrink from the edges of the pan and spring back when touched — about 30 minutes longer. Cut into 16 squares.

BROWNIES
(Easier Version)

If you don't like to wash dishes and like a moister brownie, use the quantities listed above but make the mixture all in one pan.

Melt the butter over hot water, using a pastry fork, add chocolate and stir until it melts. Remove the pan from the heat. Add the sugar and keep stirring. Add the vanilla. Light oven: 375°. Grease and lightly flour an 8x8-inch aluminum pan. Break the eggs one at a time into the mixture and beat with a pastry fork. Beat in the flour. Again, the nuts are optional, if you use them add them now.

Put the mixture in the pan. Bake at 375° for 15 minutes. Reduce the heat to 350°. Bake until mixture shrinks from the sides of the pan — about 25 minutes longer. Do not overbake. Make creases for 16 squares but do not cut all the way through or remove them from the pan for several hours. They will be quite sticky.

BAKED FUDGE BROWNIES

(Triple Rule)

For a 9x13 inch pan:

¼	*cup warm water*	1	*cup walnut meats, broken (optional)*
1½	*cups butter (three sticks)*	6	*eggs, slightly beaten*
6	*squares unsweetened chocolate*	3	*teaspoons vanilla, or ½ teaspoon peppermint extract*
3	*cups sugar*		
1½	*cups flour, sifted*		

Extra sugar, about ¼ cup

Heat the water to the simmering point, add butter and chocolate, and stir over low heat until they are all melted and blended. Add the sugar, beat well. Cool. Light oven: 350°. Butter and flour a 9x13-inch baking pan. Flour the nuts with half a cup of the flour. Beat the eggs with a wire whisk until they are well mixed. Add them and the vanilla to the chocolate mixture. Continue beating. Add the flour and the nuts. Spread the mixture evenly in the baking pan. Scatter the extra quarter cup of sugar over the top. Bake until the mixture shrinks from the edges of the pan, is crusty on top and firm to the touch in the center — about 40 minutes. Do not overbake. When you think they are quite done, take the pan out. Chill, mark in 48 squares. Do not try to cut the brownies through or remove them from the pan for several hours or — better — the next day.

These are my favorite brownies. They taste very much like deep chocolate fudge with that extra something.

CHOCOLATE CHIP BROWNIES

Mrs. Appleyard invented these. The idea is to bake them at a temperature hot enough at the beginning to give the batter a chance to rise but low enough all the way through so that the chocolate chips will retain their own texture and flavor when the baking is over. The mixing is easy: baking has to be done with great care.

½	*cup water*	½	*cup walnuts (optional)*
½	*cup butter*	½	*cup Nestle's chocolate chips*
2	*squares unsweetened chocolate*	¼	*cup flour, extra*
		1	*teaspoon vanilla*
1	*cup sugar*	2	*eggs*
½	*cup flour, sifted*	1	*tablespoons sugar, extra*

Heat the water. When it is simmering add the butter and chocolate. Turn off the heat but leave the pan on the burner. Stir until the butter and chocolate are melted. Add the sugar. Stir until it is well mixed. Place pan into another pan containing cold water and leave until mixture is just lukewarm. Light oven: 350°. Butter an 8x8-inch aluminum pan and dust it lightly with a tablespoon of flour.

To the lukewarm mixture add half a cup flour. The walnuts should not be broken up too finely. Add them to the mixture. Add the vanilla. Break two eggs into the mixture and beat well. Pour the mixture, which will look rather like very thick molasses, into the floured pan. Tilt the pan to even it. Is your stove level? If it slopes, your cakes will not bake evenly.

Bake at 350° for ten minutes. Sprinkle the top with the extra sugar. Turn the pan one quarter of the way around. Reduce the heat to 325° and bake 20 minutes. Turn the pan again. Reduce the heat to 300°. Bake 10-15 minutes longer. The center should be firm to the touch but soft. Do not overbake. Remove from the oven. Let stand five minutes. Mark in 16 pieces. Let stand five minutes more and cut through to the pan but do not remove the brownies. Chill thoroughly, preferably overnight, at least for several hours before removing the brownies from the pan. The chilling makes them fudgier.

If done carefully, the chocolate chips will retain their personality and you will find yourself eating a piece of chocolate fudge cake in which you encounter pieces of semi-sweet chocolate. I hope you will like the experience.

Recently, I asked a friend of mine who had lived in Africa, what Christmas was like there and was told: "It's about the same as here — only with fewer pagan rites."

Perhaps a good thing, I reflected for a moment — no Christmas Eve office party for instance. Still, I would miss the mistletoe and the holly, the smell of a fir balsam tree when the candles are lighted, the sound of my relatives ringing the sleigh bells that hang near the front door, the taste of a flaming plum pudding. I would even, I thought, miss the Christmas baking.

In fact, on that crisp December morning, I felt so sentimental that I got out the cookie cutters that had belonged to my Grandmother: the star, the tree, the gingerbread man. Then I creamed butter, sifted flour, blanched almonds, produced sugar cookies, a white fruit cake and some extremely sinister gingerbread men. All this to the sound of my own voice humming "Hark the Herald . . ." I began with:

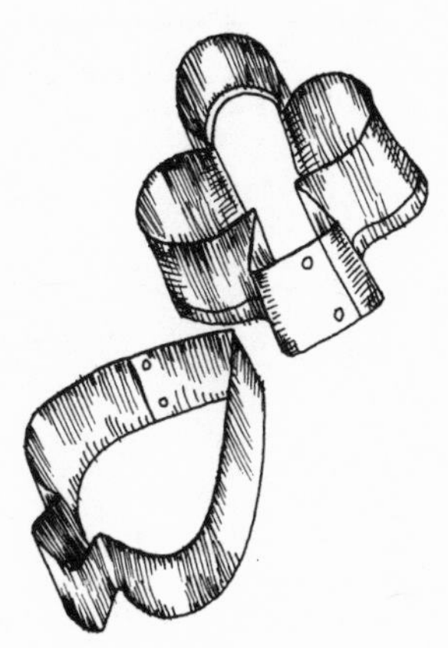

SUGAR COOKIES

1/4	*pound butter*	1 3/4	*cups flour*
1	*cup sifted sugar*	2	*teaspoons baking powder*
1	*tablespoon lemon extract*	1/8	*teaspoon salt*
2	*tablespoons cream*		*Extra sugar, with cinnamon to taste*
1	*egg*		

Set out materials ahead of time to reach room temperature. (I use a bowl big enough to hold the entire mixture and my small electric beater.) At very low speed, cream the butter, beat in the sugar. Stir in the lemon extract, cream and the lightly beaten egg. Sift the flour, baking powder and salt three times. Measure — there should now be two scant cups, no more. A heavy hand with flour spoils these cookies. Sift the dry ingredients into the butter/sugar mixture, beating well till all is used. Wrap the dough in wax paper. Chill in the refrigerator for several hours; overnight if you prefer.

Use a third of the dough at a time, leaving the rest to chill as needed. Roll it out very thin, using a pastry cloth and covered rolling pin, both very lightly floured. Light oven: 350°. Cut the cookies in tree and star shapes (or others as desired). Bake them on teflon cookie sheets. Sprinkle them with cinnamon sugar. Bake until just delicately browned around the edges — about seven minutes. Keep at it until all the dough is used.

If you still have any energy, make:

GINGERBREAD MEN

½ cup butter
¾ cup molasses
¼ cup sugar
1 egg, lightly beaten
3 cups sifted flour
1 tablespoon ginger
¼ teaspoon nutmeg
½ teaspoon cinnamon
¼ teaspoon salt
3 teaspoons baking powder
Seedless raisins — for eyes and buttons

Melt the butter. Stir in molasses, sugar and beaten egg. Stir in the flour, sifted with spices, salt and baking powder. Chill the mixture in refrigerator at least two hours. Roll out dough, not too thin, using a pastry cloth and covered rolling pin. Use as little flour as possible. Cut dough with gingerbread man cutter. Lift with two nylon spatulas and place on a teflon cookie sheet. Roll up small bits of raisins for eyes and buttons and push them into the dough. Use the edge of a spoon to make marks for the nose, mouth, chin and collar. Bake at 375° for about ten minutes. Be sure they do not scorch. Cool.

With loops of gold cord, hang the finished men on your Christmas tree, or make a fence of them in front of it. This amount of dough will make about 16 men. The same mixture, rolled rather thicker, may be used for a gingerbread house if you are in the architectural mood. My father was an architect, among other things, but I don't recall seeing his designing any gingerbread houses. I hope that the real houses he designed were sturdier than was my gingerbread house. But then, just about anything would be, my house was eaten by a dog.

CHOCOLATE CRISPS

6 ounces Nestle's semi-sweet chocolate chips
2 cups Kellogg's Special K cereal (one of the more nutritious)

Melt the chocolate in the top of a double boiler. Remove from the heat: add the Special K cereal. Stir in carefully. Shape neatly in teaspoonfuls on wax paper. Chill at least half an hour. If you like a slight mocha flavor add half a teaspoonful of instant coffee to the melting chocolate.

CHOCOLATE CHIP COOKIES

Mrs. Appleyard used to say that adding soda to this type of cookie, and indeed to most kinds, and to some kinds of cake, is just a nervous habit. It's a hangover from the old days, when butter came in tubs and often did not have all the buttermilk washed out of it. Its rancid flavor was somewhat obscured by the soda. Today's pasteurized butter needs no such treatment, of course. If you like the taste of soda and enjoy a soft stuffy cookie, go right ahead and throw some soda into the batter. These cookies spread out into crisp lacy circles. Please use teflon cookie sheets and you will have no trouble getting the cookies off the pan.

- ½ *cup butter*
- 6 *tablespoons granulated sugar*
- 6 *tablespoons light brown sugar*
- 1 *egg, beaten*
- ½ *teaspoon vanilla in ½ teaspoon warm water*
- 8 *ounces Nestle's chocolate chips*
- ½ *cup chopped pecans or walnuts (optional)*
- 1 *cup sifted flour*

Light oven: 375°. With a blending fork, mix the butter, sugar, and beaten egg. Blend in the flour and vanilla. Stir in the chocolate chips and nuts. Drop by half teaspoonfuls, well separated, on the pans. It takes only eight to ten minutes for a batch to bake. Watch them carefully. Let them stand for one minute before taking them off the pan. Use two nylon spatulas. Keep cookies in a tightly covered tin box between layers of wax paper.

COCONUT CAKES

For years these were made by a shop in Boston so that they were, in flavor and texture, as they had always been as long as Grandmother could remember. I never had the opportunity to taste the originals from Boston, but very much enjoy the version invented by my Grandmother. She had ordered some from the shop not long ago, and decided that they were not as she had expected. With some difficulty, she found the label and read it. No wonder they tried to conceal it! In the cakes lurked various chemicals and corn syrup. Mrs. Appleyard called the manager more out of nostalgia than anger. He assured her that "all additives were non-toxic" and that the customers loved the new cakes. She did not agree with the other customers and so came up with her own rule:

- 1¼ *cups sugar*
- *Meat of two coconuts (best), ground not too fine, or 3 cans or packages Baker's moist coconut*
- *Whites of four large or five small eggs, unbeaten*
- ¼ *cup water*

Cook the sugar and coconut in a double boiler, stirring well to blend them, until the sugar melts — about eight minutes. If you use fresh coconut, press out any excess liquid before you use it. The kind in the can is about the right moisture, but naturally the fresh has a better flavor. I think the difference is worth the trouble, especially if one of your friends or husband does the work.

Add the unbeaten egg whites to the coconut and sugar. If you use canned coconut, add a quarter cup of water. Cook until the mixture is very sticky — about ten minutes. Moisten a 9x13-inch aluminum pan. Spread the mixture evenly in the pan. Cover it with wax paper. Chill in the refrigerator for one hour or longer.

Light oven: 350°. Mark the coconut mixture in 24 squares.

Set a pan of cold water beside you. Moisten your hands slightly and form each square into a ball, dipping your hands into the water from time to time. This helps to smooth the cakes and keep them in shape. They may be baked on a cookie sheet greased with shortening, not butter, but a teflon pan is better. (By this time you may think that the Appleyard family gets a commission. Such — alas — is not the case!)

Bake at 350° until the cakes are lightly browned — about 25 minutes. Let them stand three minutes. Remove them from the pan with a nylon spatula. Cool. Keep in a tightly covered box between layers of wax paper.

COCONUT CUBES

These are less trouble than Coconut Cakes:

Cut homemade bread into 1½-inch cubes. Dip each cube first into extra thick Vermont cream, then into sugar, then on all sides in coconut. Put them on a teflon cookie sheet in a 350° oven and bake until lightly browned — about 20 minutes. Let them cool at room temperature.

DATE NUT SQUARES

¼ pound butter
1 cup sugar
2 tablespoons molasses
3 eggs, beaten
1 teaspoon vanilla
½ cup pecans, broken
½ cup dates, stoned and finely cut up
1 cup flour, sifted, with pinches of nutmeg and cinnamon, 2 teaspoons of instant coffee

Soften the butter over warm water, stir in the sugar and molasses and mix until smooth. Cool slightly. Add the beaten eggs and the vanilla. Light oven: 350°. Flour the dates and nuts with a quarter cup of the flour. Work the other three-fourths cup of flour into the mixture. Stir in the nuts and the dates. Spread the mixture evenly in a 9x9-inch pan, lightly greased and floured. Bake until delicately brown and firm to the touch in the center — about 45 minutes. Cool slightly. Cut into 24 squares. Non-chocolate eaters like these.

PECAN BRANDY BALLS

½ cup butter
¼ cup granulated sugar
¾ cup flour
1 cup pecans, finely chopped
1 tablespoon brandy
½ cup confectioner's sugar
Extra confectioner's sugar

Cream the butter, beat in the sugar, flour, nut meats. Add the brandy. Light oven: 300°.

Press the mixture into an 8x8-inch pan. Cut it into 32 pieces. Make each piece into a ball. Sugar your hands lightly with confectioner's sugar while doing this. Put the balls on a teflon cookie sheet. Bake for 30-35 minutes. They should not be brown except where they have touched the pan. Remove from the oven. While still warm, roll the balls in confectioner's sugar. Cool. Roll in confectioner's sugar again. Use extra sugar if necessary. Keep them in a tightly covered tin box between layers of wax paper.

SAND TARTS

¼	*pound butter*	1	*teaspoon almond extract*
¾	*cup sugar*	1¾	*cups sifted flour*
3	*egg yolks*		*Extra sugar, about ¼ cup*
1	*egg white*	½	*teaspoon nutmeg*

Cream the butter. Beat in the sugar and the egg yolks and white, beaten together with a wire whisk. Add the almond extract and the flour. Cut the flour in with a pastry fork. Roll the dough in a cylinder in wax paper. Chill in the refrigerator at least two hours. Slice into slices ⅜-inch thick. Lay the slices on a teflon pan. Mix the sugar and nutmeg and sprinkle the sand tarts with it. Bake at 375° until the tarts brown lightly around the edges — about 12 minutes. Do not overbake.

These are somewhat like the sand tarts in texture:

SCOTCH SHORTBREAD

½	*pound butter at room temperature*	½	*cup sugar*
		3	*cups flour*

Cream the butter until it stand in soft peaks. Using a pastry blending fork, work in the sugar slowly. Work in one cup of the flour by tablespoonfuls. Flour a pastry board, put the dough on it and knead in the rest of the flour. The more you knead it, the "shorter" it will be, so add it in small amounts, turning the dough around and over from time to time. Light oven: 350°. Scrape every bit of the dough together and press it into a 9x13-inch teflon pan. The dough should be about ⅜-inch thick. Mark it off into triangles. Prick them all over with a fork. Bake for 20 minutes. Remove any triangles around the edges of the pan and any that have begun to brown at all. Separate the others and bake for ten minutes longer. Again remove those that are delicately brown. The last half dozen will probably need an extra five minutes baking. Cool thoroughly before storing them in a tight lidded box.

OAT CAKE

This is a type of American Cousin to Scotch Oat Cake which I sometimes make when real Scotch oats are not available (an event that occurs quite frequently). Put regular oats through your coffee grinder or flour mill and use:

1	*cup flour*	2	*cups ground oats*
1	*teaspoon baking powder*	½	*cup butter*
	Salt to taste	3½	*tablespoons cold water*
¼	*cup sugar*	2	*tablespoons butter (extra)*

Sift the flour with baking powder, salt and sugar and add the oats, stirring all well together. Work in the butter, which should be at room temperature, with a pastry blending fork. Add the water, cut it into the mixture. Light oven: 325°. Spread the dough in a round black frying pan. Crease the cake into wedge-shape pieces. Dot with extra butter. Bake until delicately browned. Check at the end of ten minutes. Turn the pan around. The baking may take five minutes longer to complete.

SWEDISH COOKIES

These cookies are like a rather light shortbread. To make them, get a Swedish cookie press and follow the directions that come with it exactly. Grandmother thought that this was a piece of equipment well worth having. The cookies are delicious and a large number can be made in a comparatively short time, much more quickly than if they are rolled and cut.

OATMEAL LACE COOKIES

Mrs. Appleyard has given the rule for these a number of times, always — I think — improving it slightly. Through this evolutionary process she had — after more than 20 years — reached a recipe from which she did not deviate. After having tested a good many of my Grandmother's rules, I do not intend to attempt to improve upon this recipe.

There are certain requisites if you wish to produce these golden brown crisp circles of sweetness and light. You must make them on a blue and white and golden day. If there is a breeze it should come from the northwest. If you have not already yielded to the Appleyard persuasion about teflon pans, you must buy them now and get the nylon spatulas to go with them. You must use butter — not any of the lower-priced spreads — and regular Quaker Oats or Mother's Oats, not the instant kinds. Having accomplished all of this you may feel like taking a nap, but now is the time to begin:

½	*pound butter*	*1*	*tablespoon flour*
2	*cups white sugar*	*1*	*egg*
4	*tablespoons molasses*	*2*	*tablespoons water*
2½	*cups regular oats*	*½*	*teaspoon real vanilla*

In a saucepan big enough to hold all the ingredients, melt the butter over low heat. Stir in the sugar and molasses and mix thoroughly. Remove the pan from the heat. Add the oats and flour. Cool. Form a well in the batter. Break an egg into the well and beat the egg slightly with the water and vanilla and work into entire mixture. Light oven: 360°. Set the pan in the refrigerator for five minutes. Using a half-teaspoon, put 12 small lumps of the mixture on a teflon cookie sheet. Put the sheet in the oven. Put 12 lumps on a second sheet and put that sheet in the oven. In about ten minutes the cookies on the first sheet should have spread out to about 2½ inches in diameter, be bubbling and starting to turn deep golden brown. Take the sheet out. Let it cool a minute or two. Test the edges of the cookies with a spatula. They will soon slip off the pan easily. Put them first on a large cool platter. When they have thoroughly cooled, transfer them to a large tin box, with wax paper between the layers. Keep both pans going. Don't answer the telephone. Don't stop to go to the door and accept a food cooperative order blank. And don't go outside to shovel snow or weed your garden. After all, you don't make 12 or 14 dozen oatmeal cookies every day.

It is possible to bake part of the cookies in the morning, put the saucepan in the refrigerator and finish the rest in the afternoon or evening.

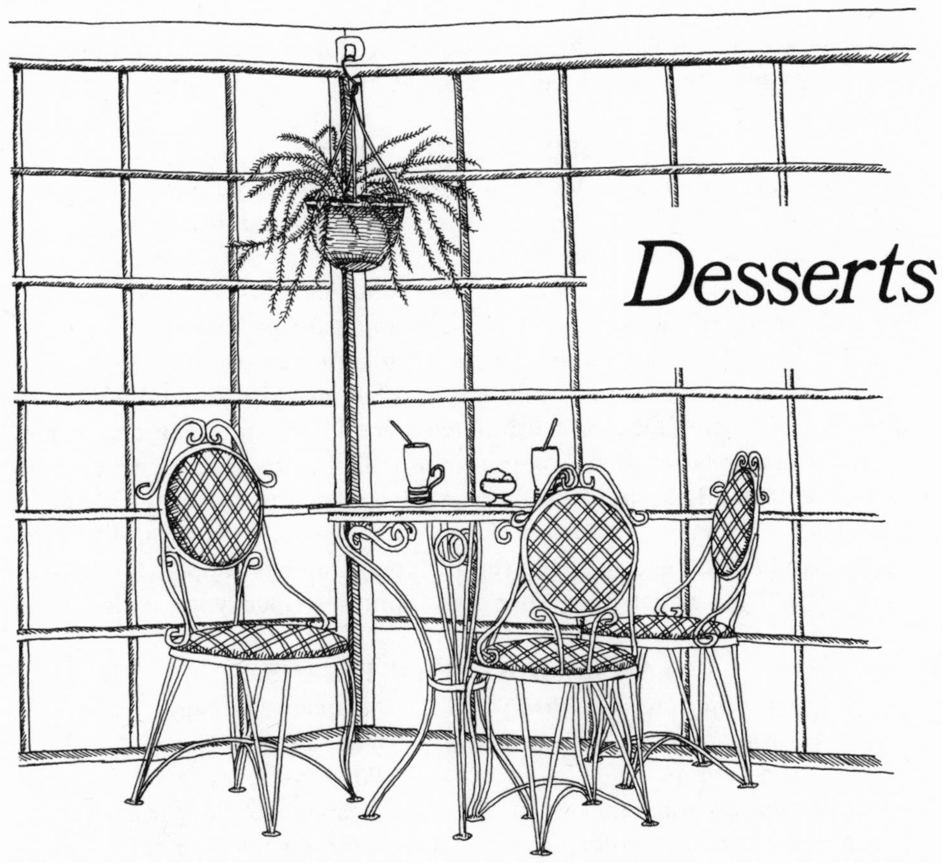

Desserts

DESSERTS are the subject of mixed feelings, and are in themselves a muddled blessing. They can be the perfect ending to the perfect meal, or the gilding of the lily, or a necessary part of one's nutrition, or unneeded calories. There was a time, among ordinary families, when the dessert was a way to dress up the meal while using up stores of provisions, such as apples in many forms, simply to clean out the larder. For others, they have always been the elegant, or at least complicated finalé expected of the cook.

As there are very few people who actually need desserts to fill out their profiles, I feel that desserts should be looked on as a part of the meal, containing things necessary to the making of a good diet — eggs, milk, fruit and cheese. I am usually content with fruit and cheese, but there are occasions when a specially designed dessert helps an otherwise uninteresting meal. I don't think that all the things about which people are less enthusiastic should go into one meal, just as not all the good things should go into another. For instance, when you serve a meat loaf, you should cheer it up with asparagus, or freshly picked corn and with a dessert especially popular with the indulgers — a short cake, or an apple pan dowdy perhaps. The day you serve the Roast Ducklings* (and that doesn't happen frequently) is the time for fruit, Melba Toast* and some Crème Damia cheese.

I include a wide selection here not because I expect anyone to make them every day, but so that you may have a broad choice for happy occasions. And what do I mean by happy occasions? Why simply every meal when people who like each other sit down and eat together, and at those times the deserving should get their just desserts.

APPLESAUCE MARIE

2 quarts applesauce from early tart apples
½ cup Sultana seedless raisins
½ cup Kellogg's Special K cereal, crumbled
½ cup light brown sugar
¼ teaspoon cinnamon
¼ teaspoon nutmeg
Pinches of clove and allspice
2 tablespoons butter
12 marshmallows

Put the applesauce into a well-buttered baking dish. Light oven: 350°. Stir in the raisins. Mix the crumbled cereal, brown sugar and spices together and scatter them over the top. Dot with butter, cover with marshmallows. Bake until the marshmallows start to brown — about 12 minutes. This may be made with canned applesauce if you aren't lucky enough to have an ever-bearing (up till now) Dutchess apple tree in your front yard from which to gather rosy apples striped with pink flesh.

APPLE TART WITH PECANS

Butter for greasing dish
4 large apples, pared, cored, sliced thin
1 cup white sugar
2 tablespoons molasses
¼ teaspoon nutmeg
½ teaspoon cinnamon
Pinch of cloves
1½ teaspoons instant tapioca
1 tablespoon lemon juice
Grated rind of half a lemon

Light oven: 400°. Grease a pyrex pie dish, nine inches across. Mix the spices, sugar and tapioca. Mix the molasses with the apples and add the sugar mixture. Mix well and pour into the prepared pan. Sprinkle the lemon juice and grated rind over all. Put the dish in the oven and bake until the apples are soft — about 30 minutes. While it is baking make the pecan topping:

½ cup flour
½ cup wheat germ
¼ cup butter, melted
Pinches of cinnamon and nutmeg
½ cup chopped pecans
12 whole pecans

Mix all the ingredients except the whole pecans and cover the tart with the mixture leaving a two-inch space in the center for the steam to escape. Bake till the mixture bubbles — about 15 minutes. If you like it browner, run it briefly under the broiler. Decorate with whole pecans, especially in the center. Serve warm, not hot, with vanilla ice cream or cheese or both!

BAKED APPLES

Core tart apples. Bake with brown sugar, pinches of spice and dots of butter in the centers, at 350°. While they are baking, simmer the cores in water with sugar and a little spice. Use half a cup of granulated sugar to six cores. When the syrup begins to thicken, strain it over the baking apples. Baste them with it several times until they are soft. When the apples are cool they will have a sort of spicy jelly around them.

Serve ice cream, sweet cream, sour cream, or yogurt with them. And how about a slice of Huckleberry Gingerbread,* which contains — according to Mrs. Appleyard's father, who used to enjoy an occasional slice when he was over 80 years old — everything necessary to the nourishment of the human system.

APPLE LILIES

(For 6)

I inherited from my Grandmother, among other sundry goodies, an almost new apple cutter. It is strong, sharp and when pushed down hard over a large red apple, cores it and transforms it into eight red and white petal sections all at once. If you are not so lucky as to own such a device, the apples may be cut into "lilies" by hand.

6 red apples
2 tablespoons butter
1 cup Sultana seedless raisins
½ cup blanched almonds
½ cup sugar
1 tablespoon molasses
Extra sugar — about half cup for light syrup
Pinches of spice

Push the cutter down almost all the way over the apples so that the "lilies" will still hold together after you cut away the core.

Butter six small baking dishes or custard cups that will keep the "petals" from falling apart too far. Fill centers with raisins and almonds. Mix the sugar and molasses and spoon some over the centers of the apples.

Bake at 350° until apple pieces are soft but not mushy — about 40 minutes.

Make the syrup by simmering the cores with water, the extra sugar and the pinches of spice. When it begins to thicken, strain some over the center of each apple.

Serve cold with thick cream and perhaps a square of Appleyard Center Gingerbread.*

CRANBERRY APPLES

(For 8)

8 fine tart apples
2 tablespoons lemon juice
2 cups water
2 whole cloves
Pinches of nutmeg and cinnamon
2 cups sugar
2 cups cranberries
Butter for greasing dish

Wash, peel and core the apples. They should be perfect but not outsized. Brush them with lemon juice and set them in a cool place while you are cooking the peel and cores in water seasoned with the spices. Also mix the two cups of sugar and water and bring mixture to the boiling point. Add the cranberries and cook until they all pop. Put the apples in a shallow pyrex baking dish, lightly buttered.

Fill the centers of the apples with the popped cranberries and pour one tablespoon of cranberry syrup over each apple. Set the dish in a 350° oven and bake until the apples begin to soften — about 25 minutes. Now mix the juice from the apple peelings — it should have cooked down to half a cup — with the same amount of cranberry syrup. Use this mixture

*See Index for pages where recipes can be found.

to coat the apples as they finish cooking. It will slide off the backs of the apples but keep spooning it over them every five minutes, until apples are tender — about 25 minutes longer. Put them in a serving dish. Add some of the cooked cranberries to any of the apples that do not look well filled. Pour all the juice in the pan over them. Chill.

Use the cranberry apples as a dessert or as a garnish with roast turkey, duck or chicken.

BAKED APPLE DUMPLINGS

(For 6)

Pare and core six small apples. Brush them with lemon juice and fill them with sugar sifted with pinches of cloves, cinnamon and nutmeg. Set them in a cool place while you make the dough.

2 tablespoons butter
2 cups flour
2 teaspoons baking powder
Pinch of salt
¼ teaspoon nutmeg
1 cup milk (about), part cream

Using a pastry fork, cut the butter into the flour sifted three times with the baking powder, salt and nutmeg. Work in the milk. Do not make the dough too wet: it should be rather stiff. Toss it on a floured board, knead it a minute and roll it out into an oblong. Light oven: 350°. Cut the dough into six squares. On each one put an apple, draw dough up around it and press the points together with a wet fork. Put the dumplings in well-buttered muffin tins or glass dishes, with the rough sides down. Bake until lightly browned — 30-40 minutes.

BROWN BETTY

(For 6)

Once, overcome with enthusiasm and immodesty, Grandmother labeled this in her notebook "Perfect Brown Betty." Realizing that she was just beginning to be considered a Vermonter (after only 40 years) and not wishing to jeopardize her position, she promptly apologized for her mistake. There are as many rules for brown betty in Vermont as there are catamounts (imagined or real) in the Green Mountains. I happen to believe that this one is pretty good and blush for having again bragged about a family recipe.

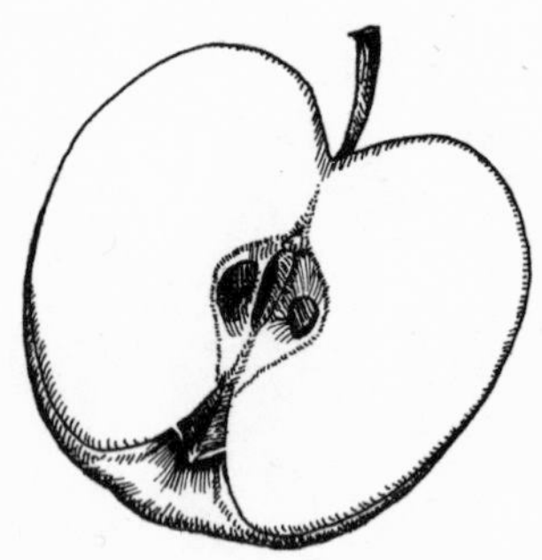

2 cups cubed homemade bread (no crusts)
2 tablespoons melted butter
3 cups pared and thinly sliced apples — four large Macs or six medium
1 cup white sugar
½ teaspoon nutmeg
⅛ teaspoon cloves
¼ teaspoon cinnamon
2 tablespoons butter, in small dots
Grated rind and juice of one lemon

Put a layer of cubed bread into a straight-sided, buttered baking dish, either a French soufflé dish or a Swedish enameled iron dish, that will hold one and a half quarts. Mix the apples, sugar and spice. Cover the bread with a layer of the mixture. Dot with butter, add a little lemon juice and rind. Put in more layers, alternating bread cubes and the apple mixture until the dish is well heaped. Finish with cubed bread. Cover.

Bake at 375° for half an hour. Uncover. Bake until the apples are tender and the crumbs golden brown — about half an hour longer. Serve at once with thick cream or vanilla ice cream. Like a soufflé, it will collapse if allowed to stand.

APPLE ROLY-POLY

(For 6)

6 apples
2 tablespoons lemon juice
Grated rind of one lemon
1 cup sugar
2 teaspoons molasses
Pinches of cinnamon, cloves, nutmeg
Extra sugar and spice
1 tablespoon butter

Core and slice the apples into eighths. Peel them. Cut each slice in half lengthwise. Sprinkle with lemon juice and rind. Mix the sugar with molasses and spices.

Make the same dough as used in the dumplings (see above). Light oven: 375°. You will need some extra sugar and spice and about two tablespoons extra butter for greasing the pan. Roll the dough out into an oblong, sprinkle it with a little extra sugar and spice. Cover it with the apple mixture. Roll it up like a jelly roll. Cut it in two-inch slices. Put the slices in a teflon baking dish. Sprinkle with a little more sugar and spice and dot with butter. Bake at 375° for ten minutes, then reduce the heat and bake until the slices are well browned — about 25 minutes longer.

Serve with vanilla ice cream or sour cream.

APRICOT ALMOND TRIFLE

12 ladyfingers, split
1 cup apricot pulp, sweetened (see below)
4 ounces almonds, blanched, peeled
1 cup cream
3 eggs
1 teaspoon almond extract
2 tablespoons soft butter
2 tablespoons sherry
4 tablespoons candied fruits, diced
1 cup sugar

Split the ladyfingers and spread them with the sweetened apricot pulp. Put them in a glass bowl in which you will serve the trifle. Put the blanched, peeled almonds in the electric blender. Add the cream and run until the almonds are finely cut. Add the sugar, eggs and almond extract and run the blender until the mixture begins to thicken. Add the butter in small pieces and run the blender until the mixture is rather like thick custard. Stir in the sherry. Pour the mixture over the ladyfingers and chill the trifle in the refrigerator until serving time. Chill at least three hours. Decorate with candied fruit and toasted almonds.

APRICOT PULP

1 12-ounce package of dried apricots
Juice and grated rind of half lemon
½ cup sugar

Cover the apricots with water and soak overnight. They will have absorbed most of the water. Add more water, enough so that they will not scorch, and simmer until the apricots are tender. Do not drain them but put apricots, sugar, lemon juice and rind into the blender and blend until it is smooth and thick. It may be used in a variety of ways: in a trifle, as a sauce for vanilla ice cream or orange sherbet or in an:

APRICOT SOUFFLÉ

A well-buttered straight-sided French soufflé dish is necessary for this soufflé.

3 tablespoons butter	*⅓ cup sugar*
¼ cup instant flour	*A little almond or vanilla extract — or both — or neither*
1 tablespoon butter, extra	
1 cup milk, scalded	
½ cup Apricot Pulp (above)	*5 eggs, separated*

Melt the butter, turn off the heat. Rub in the flour. Light oven: 350°. Put the extra butter in a soufflé dish and set the dish into a pan of warm water in the oven. Scald the milk and stir it into the butter and flour mixture. Do this slowly, stirring all the time so there will be no lumps. (If there are any they must be strained out.) Cook the mixture over low heat for two minutes. Cool slightly. Add the apricot pulp mixed with the sugar and flavoring. Beat the egg whites to stiff peaks. Without washing the beater, beat the yolks thick and lemon colored and mix them thoroughly into the apricot mixture. Fold the egg whites into the mixture, using a rubber scraper. Use it also to heap the mixture in the slightly warmed dish.

Set the dish on a wire rack in a pan of warm water on the lowest shelf in the oven and bake 20 minutes. Reduce the heat to 325° and move the dish gently to the upper shelf. You may breathe while doing this but not too hard. In another 20 minutes the soufflé should be done. Listen to it! It should not even be whispering. The family will just have to wait for it, as with other soufflés; they seem to do so willingly.

SOUFFLÉ IN A DOUBLE BOILER

This is somewhat more relaxing to make than an oven-baked soufflé. It can be kept warm for a short time over hot, not boiling water, if necessary.

4 egg whites	*Grated rind of one lemon*
*3 tablespoons sweetened Apricot Pulp**	*Grated rind of one orange*
	½ tablespoon butter
4 tablespoons sugar	*Slivered almonds (optional)*

Beat the egg whites until they make stiff peaks but are not dry. Mix the apricot pulp, sugar, lemon and orange rinds together well. Butter the top of a double boiler. Put in the mixture. Cook for one hour over water that is just boiling.

Three tablespoons of orange marmalade may be used instead of the apricot pulp. In either case save the egg yolks with which to make Foamy Sauce,* and serve with the soufflé. Garnish with slivered almonds, if desired.

APRICOT PARFAIT

1	*29-ounce can apricots*	2	*egg whites, beaten stiff*
½	*tablespoon gelatin*	2	*tablespoons lemon juice*
½	*cup sugar*	½	*pint heavy cream, whipped*

Drain the apricots, reserving syrup. Soak the gelatin in two tablespoons of the syrup. Cook the rest of the syrup with the sugar to the thread stage (less than 225° on your candy thermometer — or until syrup threads when dripped from a spoon). Pour the syrup on the beaten egg whites. Stir them all the time with a wire whisk. Chill thoroughly. Whip the cream. Fold it into the apricot mixture. Put the whole thing into a melon shaped mold. Cover and put it into the freezer. Freeze for three hours. Stir the mixture three times during the first hour to prevent crystals from forming.

Unmold the parfait on a round dish. Surround it with scoops of Orange Ice* and with heaps of fresh raspberries sprinkled with powdered sugar, or in winter with frozen raspberries slightly thawed.

PIN WHEEL PUDDING

First, make a jelly roll. Of course you might buy it ready made and thus keep up with other activities. Jay likes to know what his food contains and so makes his own using:

1	*cup currant jelly or raspberry jam*	1	*cup sugar*
	Shortening for greasing dish	2	*tablespoons lemon juice*
5	*large eggs, separated*		*Rind of one lemon, grated*
		⅔	*cup cake flour*

½ *cup extra sugar, powdered*

Set the glass of jelly or jam into warm water. Grease a 9x13-inch pan and line with two thicknesses of heavy brown paper. Grease the paper. Light oven: 350°. Put egg yolks into a bowl large enough to hold the whole mixture. Put the whites into another bowl and beat them to stiff peaks. Without washing the beater, beat the yolks thick and lemon colored. Beat in the sugar, lemon juice and rind. Fold in some egg white, scatter in the flour and fold it in, and fold in the rest of the whites.

Pour the batter into the pan. Tip the pan to distribute the batter evenly. Bake for 15 minutes or until it springs back when pressed with a finger. Reduce the heat to 325°. It should not brown. When done, remove from the pan, trim the edges, and peel off the paper. Sugar a pastry cloth with powdered sugar. Put the cake on it. While it is still warm, spread it with the warmed jelly and roll it up. Let it cool while you make the Orange Custard Cream.*

Slice the jelly roll and line a large glass bowl with the slices. Pour in the orange custard. Chill overnight. When you serve it, unmold it on a large round platter. Surround it with Temple orange slices, strawberries, raspberries, frozen pineapple chunks and Conserved Apricots* in small heaps. Top the heaps with blanched almonds. It is supposed to have whipped cream swirled over it but I think you've already created a masterpiece without it.

One thing to be said for the desserts inaccurately and confusingly called trifles, is that they are made ahead of time so there is no last minute fluster about serving them.

LEMON TRIFLE

1 tablespoon gelatin
4 tablespoons lemon juice
5 eggs
½ cup sugar
2 teaspoons grated lemon peel
1 cup heavy cream
2 packages ladyfingers

Soak the gelatin in the lemon juice. Dissolve it over hot water. Place the eggs, beaten with the sugar, in a double boiler over simmering water. Beat till the mixture thickens — four or five minutes. Remove from the heat. Add the gelatin and lemon peel. Beat for ten seconds. Cool in the refrigerator. When cool, whip the cream and fold it in gently. Chill.

In the meantime put into the blender:

6 tablespoons Conserved Apricots cut up*
3 tablespoons orange marmalade
2 tablespoons butter
2 tablespoons frozen orange juice, melted, no water added
1 tablespoon lemon juice

Blend until well mixed. Spread the mixture on the ladyfingers, or if you prefer, on strips of pound cake. Line a large glass bowl with them. Add half the custard cream. Cover it with ladyfingers or strips of pound cake and spread with the rest of the fruit mixture. Put in the second half of the custard cream. Cover with ladyfingers. Scatter blanched slivered almonds over the top. Chill at least four hours.

There are, of course, many variations on the "trifle" theme. This one Mrs. Appleyard made after reading Thomas Mann's *Buddenbrooks*, and finding out what that family had for dessert at Christmas time. That was also where she got the idea of trimming her Christmas tree with madonna lilies, tinsel and small electric bulbs that look like fireflies.

It was by this light that she would serve her family:

MACAROON TRIFLE

1 9-inch sponge cake
½ cup currant jelly
1 cup sherry
24 small macaroons
1 cup candied fruit (orange peel, lemon peel, cherries)
½ cup blanched almonds

For the custard:

6 egg yolks
½ cup sugar
4 cups scalded milk
½ teaspoon almond extract
1 teaspoon vanilla

Make the custard and let it cool while you are arranging the trifle. Beat the egg yolks slightly with a wire whisk. Add the sugar, a little at a time, and beat it in. Pour on the scalded milk, stirring all the time. Cook in a double boiler till the mixture thickens and coats the back of a spoon. It must be stirred constantly or it will curdle. Add flavoring. Chill.

Now pick your handsomest bowl. Grandmother used to favor a large one of thousand-eye Sandwich glass which rings, when struck, like a bell buoy in the fog on Frenchman's Bay.

Cut the sponge cake in rather thin slices, spreading each one with currant jelly, irrigating them with sherry and sticking blanched almonds into them as you go along. Line the bowl with them. Put in a layer of macaroons and sprinkle them with candied fruit. Repeat this arrangement

— first the cake then macaroons — until the bowl is full. Macaroons should be on top. They will lurk above the custard, which you now pour on, like rocks at low tide. You don't have to do another thing except chill it for three or four hours and eat it.

FLOATING ISLAND

In Grandmother's day this innocent dessert was a favorite with children. At present it is grownups, suffering from nostalgia perhaps — who croon happily when they see it. It should be served in a large rather shallow bowl so that there will be room for plenty of islands.

First make the meringue:

8 egg whites
⅓ cup granulated sugar, sifted
1 quart milk, scalded
½ teaspoon vanilla or almond extract
½ cup sugar, also sifted

Put the egg whites into a well-chilled bowl. Beat them to a stiff froth and beat the ⅓ cup of sifted sugar into them. Put the milk into a large shallow pan, add the flavoring and the half cup of sugar and bring it just to a boil. Drop heaping tablespoons of meringue into the boiling mixture. Use half of the meringue and poach the "islands" over low heat, three minutes on each side. Remove them with a skimmer or a large spoon with holes in it. Drain them on paper towels. Repeat the poaching with the other half of the meringue. Watch it every minute. The milk is just waiting — if you turn your head — to whirl all over the stove.

Save the milk and make the custard next of:

2 cups scalded milk (approx.)
½ teaspoon vanilla or almond extract
8 egg yolks
½ cup sugar

Taste the milk in which you poached the meringues. Add the half teaspoon of flavoring or more if you like. Beat the egg yolks well with sugar. Strain the milk over them through a very fine sieve. Put the mixture into the top of a double boiler. Cook it, stirring carefully, until it coats the back of a spoon — or reaches 175° on a candy thermometer. This should happen in about five minutes.

Pour the custard into a cool shallow bowl. Put the islands on top of the custard and sift a little sugar over them. Chill till serving time.

If you are in a situation where you have acquired egg whites without yolks, I think you had better make:

MERINGUES

1 teaspoon vanilla
1 cup granulated sugar
5 egg whites

The day must be chosen carefully. Meringues, like myself and my relatives, feel best when the barometer is rising. A bright blue day with the shadows made by a northwest breeze rippling over long timothy grass is a suitable one. Mrs. Appleyard, who had in her time turned out her share of flabby and sticky meringues, gave the following instructions.

Beat the egg whites in a cold bowl till they are thick but not stiff. Light oven: 275°. Add the sugar to the egg whites, a tablespoon at a time, beating it in well until you have used ¾ of a cup. Fold in the remaining quarter-cup of sugar and the vanilla. If you do not have a teflon cookie sheet, cover an aluminum sheet with a double thickness of white typewriter paper. (This was Mrs. Appleyard's favorite use for this substance. She always used the best grade.) In these times of recycling everything, I use a brown paper bag cut to fit.

Spoon the mixture onto the cookie sheet (covered with whatever) in circular heaps. Bake them until there are no shiny bubbles on them. Not *any*. It will take at least one hour. If your oven does not bake evenly, turn the pans around after half an hour. Do this gently and as fast as possible so that cold air does not strike them at any time. When they are done, remove them immediately from the pan, peel off the paper. You may have to lay the paper briefly on a damp towel in order to loosen the meringues. Store the meringues in a tightly covered tin box until serving time.

ABSENTMINDED MERINGUE

5 egg whites
1 teaspoon cream of tartar
1½ cups sugar
1 teaspoon vanilla

Beat the egg whites until they thicken and begin to make stiff peaks. Sprinkle in the cream of tartar. Beat until the whites are thick. Beat in half the sugar, a little at a time. Fold in the rest. Add the vanilla. Light oven: 350°. Put the mixture into an 8x8-inch pan lined with two thicknesses of white typewriter paper, and bake the mixture for half an hour. Turn off the oven. Forget the meringue and leave it in the oven all night.

You will have to arrange your own system for overlooking this delicacy. I did it one day while testing my Grandmother's rule and suddenly realized that it was past milking time. I turned off the oven (recalling some faded grandmotherly instructions) and dashed out to the barn to milk the goat. As I had finished and was walking across the road to the house with milk pail in hand, Roger Willard drove into the driveway for a brief, but friendly visit. After I had been updated on all the goings-on about town, relative to the work being done on neighbors' houses, we parted ways. Luckily, I then became involved with dinner preparations, another visitor and a complex book on child development. In the morning, as my Grandmother would say, the meringue was a "delicately tinted square of crispness." I split it, filled it with coffee ice cream and served it with chocolate sauce.

Variations, such as filling the meringue with vanilla ice cream and serving with fresh or frozen raspberries, are also good. Suit yourself.

If you are in the mood for chocolate, try Mrs. Appleyard's

CHOCOLATE MOUSSE

¼ cup hot water
6 ounces Nestle's chocolate chips
6 egg yolks
6 egg whites

Put the hot water in the top of a double boiler. Add the chocolate chips, put over hot but not boiling water, and stir them until they melt. Using a wire whisk, beat in the egg yolks. The hot water in the bottom of the double boiler should not touch the top part of the double boiler. Remove the chocolate and egg mixture from over the water as soon as the chocolate is entirely melted and the eggs have all been beaten in.

Beat the whites to stiff peaks and fold them gently into the mixture until no white shows. Pile in small serving glasses and set them into the refrigerator till serving time. If you like a mocha taste, you may stir in a teaspoon of instant coffee while the mixture is still over hot water. No doubt you will add whipped cream if you feel like it. I prefer it plain. I sometimes serve it as the filling for the center of an Almond Ring.*

Perhaps you might like:

CHOCOLATE MOUSSE — FROZEN

If you have only egg yolks on hand — instead of folding in whites, cool the egg and chocolate mixture and add a cup of cream, whipped. Put the mousse into a rather deep round pan. Set it into the freezer. Freeze it for two hours, stirring it four times during the first hour, to break up the crystals.

You might also combine the frozen chocolate mousse with a plain mousse, also frozen. When they are frozen, pack a melon mold with the chocolate mousse and then in the center put the:

PLAIN MOUSSE

½ pint cream
¾ teaspoon vanilla
¼ cup powdered sugar
¼ cup marrons, cut up
Or ¼ cup dried macaroon crumbs
Or ¼ cup crushed peanut brittle

Whip the cream with vanilla. Sprinkle over it the powdered sugar and stir it in. Fold in with a wire whisk, the marrons or macaroons or peanut brittle. Put the mixture in a fairly deep round pan. Put the pan into the freezer and freeze for two hours, stirring thoroughly to break up crystals — four times during the first hour.

Cicily Bradshaw was in the habit of preparing this delicacy for family get-togethers at Thanksgiving. She claims that it is actually restful to make:

APPLEYARD CHOCOLATE TORTE

1 6-ounce package of cream cheese
2 tablespoons milk
2 tablespoons cream
12 ounces Nestle's chocolate chips
3 egg yolks, beaten
1 teaspoon vanilla
1 medium sized sponge cake, cut in four thin layers
Blanched almonds, browned in butter
1 tablespoon hot water

Soften the cream cheese with the milk and cream. Melt the chocolate with the hot water. Beat the egg yolks till thick. Combine the chocolate and the egg yolks. Cook over hot water to 170° on a candy thermometer. Stir in the cheese mixture, and add the vanilla.

On the plate on which you will serve it, lay four triangles of wax paper so that the wide ends cover the edges of the plate. Pile on the layers of cake, coating each in turn with the chocolate custard. Decorate the top layer with the toasted almonds. Chill for at least half an hour. Pull out the paper triangles and serve.

MOCHA MERINGUE TORTE

This requires a little more energy than the above rule. The filling is the same as above with the addition of one heaping tablespoon of granulated coffee and two tablespoons of softened butter beaten into it when the filling is almost cool. Chill it thoroughly before spreading it on layers of meringues. For the meringues use:

3 egg whites
1 cup sugar
1 teaspoon almond extract
1 cup cream, whipped
¼ cup unsweetened chocolate shavings

Beat the egg whites stiff. Beat in the sugar a little at a time. Beat in the almond extract. Butter three 8-inch layer cake pans and line them with white typewriter paper. Spread meringue evenly in each pan. Bake at 250° until the layers are a delicate pale tan and have no iridescent bubbles on them — about one hour.

Cool. Remove the paper. Set the meringues briefly on a towel wrung out of very cold water, if necessary. When putting the torte together, cover the plate with triangles of wax paper. Put on a layer of meringues — spread it first with the mocha filling, then with the whipped cream. Repeat this with the other two layers. Sprinkle the top layer with shavings of bitter chocolate. Pull out the paper triangles. Serve.

CHOCOLATE SOUFFLÉ

(For 4)

4 ounces Nestle's chocolate chips
1 square unsweetened chocolate, grated
3 tablespoons water
2 tablespoons butter
3 tablespoons instant flour
5 tablespoons sugar
1 tablespoon extra butter
5 egg yolks
1 teaspoon vanilla
5 egg whites
Grated unsweetened chocolate, extra
¾ cup rich milk

Melt the chocolate chips and grated bitter chocolate with the hot water in the top of a double boiler. Melt the butter in a separate pan, stir in flour. Cook over low heat for one minute. Remove from heat. Stir in the milk. Stir in chocolate mixture and three tablespoons of sugar. Stir until the sugar is dissolved. Cook while you butter a straight-sided soufflé dish with the extra butter. Dust it with the other two tablespoons of sugar.

Make a collar of strips of white paper lined with wax paper, big enough to go around the soufflé dish.

Beat the egg yolks in a bowl big enough to hold the whole mixture. Add the chocolate mixture. Keep beating. Add the vanilla. Wash the beater. In a separate bowl, beat the egg whites to very stiff peaks. Light oven: 350°. (Check it with oven thermometer). Fold the whites into the chocolate mixture. Don't stir them in but don't leave white patches either. Put the mixture into the soufflé dish. Fasten the collar on with paper clips. It should come about two inches above the rim of the dish.

Set the soufflé on a rack in a pan with a little hot water in it. This will all cook away by the time the soufflé is done. Bake for 45 minutes. Reduce the heat to 325° after the first 15 minutes. Do not open the oven door for 45 minutes. Then open door briefly and listen to it: it should not be making any noise. Give it an extra five minutes if necessary. The smells usually keep the customers happy while waiting for it. Remove the collar, dust the top of the soufflé with powdered sugar, garnish with extra bitter chocolate, if desired, and serve.

LEMON SOUFFLÉ

(For 8)

8 eggs, separated in two bowls, the yolks in the larger one
2 cups powdered sugar, sifted
4 tablespoons lemon juice
Grated rind of two lemons

Beat the egg whites to stiff peaks. Beat in a cup of the sugar, a tablespoon at a time. Without washing the beater, beat the yolks till thick and lemon colored. Add the lemon juice and rind, still beating. Beat in the rest of the sugar, about a quarter-cup at a time. Fold in the whites. Be gentle but thorough.

Put the mixture into one large or two small straight-sided soufflé dishes. Bake it as above. With the wax paper collar clipped on, a pan of hot water on a rack, and the oven first at 350° and turned down to 325° after 15 minutes.

Mrs. Appleyard was once asked by an impertinent relative (what other kind did she have?) whether she had ever found any paper clips in a soufflé. She said no, but recommended scotch tape for those nervous cooks.

During the last few minutes of baking, while my cooperative and well-trained guests are clearing the table, I make Foamy Sauce* to go with the soufflé.

BAKED ALASKA

This may be started in either of two ways, the day before you are going to serve it. You may either bake a Pound Cake,* or drive into town and buy one made by Sara Lee, with real butter and eggs. I've discovered that both methods take about the same amount of time.

For two baked Alaskas use:

1 pound cake
Meringue (see below)
2 1-quart bricks of ice cream (any flavor you prefer)

If you have bought your pound cake, its tin makes an excellent form for the Alaska. If not, use small loaf pans. Line two pans with wax paper and slices of pound cake. Fit a one-pound brick of ice cream into each pan, and cover with additional slices of cake. Put the pans, covered with aluminum foil, into the freezer to harden for the next day.

When the time comes make the meringue:

6 large egg whites
¼ teaspoon cream of tartar
¾ cup sugar
1 teaspoon vanilla

Beat the egg whites till frothy with the cream of tartar. Add the sugar, a tablespoon at a time, beating after each addition. Beat till the whites stick to the bowl and form peaks. Add the vanilla. Light oven: 450°.

To assemble, remove the loaves from the pans, peel off the wax paper. Set the loaves on a cookie sheet. Cover the sides and tops with meringue. Smooth it a little along the sides, but heap and swirl it lightly and casually on top. Bake each for three to five minutes at 450°, until the top just starts to brown. Serve at once. It should be warm outside, cold inside. Two loaves serve 12 generously. And how else would you want to serve them?

If you have any doubts about appetites being satisfied, you may serve Chocolate Sauce* or crushed strawberries with it — depending on the flavor of the ice cream inside.

CREAM PUFFS

Grandmother had not tried to improve on this classic rule for cream puff batter. She did however adapt it to modern equipment and so made it easier for me and other "modern" cooks to follow. The rule for the batter is:

1 cup boiling water | *1 cup flour*
½ cup butter | *4 eggs*

Bring the water to the boiling point in a quart saucepan. Add the butter at once. As soon as the mixture boils again, dump in the flour, all at once. Remove the pan from the heat. Stir hard and constantly till the mixture leaves the sides of the pan. It seems occasionally that this moment will never occur — but stand fast — it will. Light oven: 375°. Now transfer the batter to the large bowl of your electric mixer (if you have one — if not use another large bowl and your hand electric beater). Set the dial at the speed for creaming butter (low). Break in the eggs, one at a time, beating half a minute after each addition and scraping the batter in towards the beaters carefully with a rubber scraper.

Beat the batter at least one minute after the last egg is in. Put the batter by spoonfuls on a teflon cookie sheet. If you have a steady hand and eye you may be able to get a neatly spaced design of 12 similar puffs. I frequently end up with about nine — of a variety of sizes.

Bake them for half an hour at 375°. Turn the pan so they will bake evenly, and bake until there are no iridescent bubbles left on them — about half an hour longer. If you have any doubts about their being done, remove the smallest and least symmetrical puff and see what happens. If it is not done, it will soon collapse. If it holds its shape give the others another five minutes: then they may come out also.

Slit each puff along the side and when you serve them fill them with whatever you like best. For dessert, people seem to prefer them filled with vanilla ice cream and semi-sweet chocolate melted outside. Of course the correct filling is:

CUSTARD FILLING FOR CREAM PUFFS

2 eggs, well beaten | *¼ cup flour*
½ cup sugar | *2 cups hot milk*
½ teaspoon vanilla

Mix the beaten eggs with the sugar and flour. Pour the hot milk over the mixture and stir. Cook over hot water until the mixture coats the back of a spoon (170°). Add the vanilla. Fill the cream puffs. The outside may be either chocolate or Boiled Frosting.*

Variation: For chocolate filling add two squares unsweetened chocolate, melted, to the custard mixture. Increase the sugar to ¾ cup. Proceed as above.

If the puffs are to be used as appetizers, make them smaller and fill them with any of the suggestions put forth in the chapter on Appetizers.

There was a summer at Appleyard Center known as the Cheese Cake Summer. Everyone had his or her specialty and brought it to Pot Luck suppers, croquet tournaments and to picnics on mountain tops or near waterfalls. It was Mrs. Appleyard who invented:

BANANA CHEESE CAKE

Cheese cake comes in three parts — the crust, the custard and the topping. The dish used in each case is a 8x11-inch pyrex dish.

Begin by making the crust:

- 2 *tablespoons butter, softened*
- ¼ *cup sugar*
- 1¾ *cup wheat germ*
- ¼ *teaspoon nutmeg*

Grease the dish thoroughly with the butter. Mix the sugar, wheat germ and nutmeg. Put this mixture in the dish and tip it around until the dish is well coated all over. Light oven: 350°.

Next make the custard:

- 1 *banana, well-ripened*
- 8 *ounces cream cheese*
- 1 *cup light cream*
- 3 *eggs*
- 2 *tablespoons lemon juice*
- ¼ *cup sugar*

Begin by slicing one well-ripened banana very thin and putting the slices all over the bottom of the dish. Then put the cream cheese, cream, eggs, lemon juice and sugar in the blender and blend for two minutes. Pour in the custard. Bake for 30 minutes at 350°. Remove from the oven and let cool for ten minutes.

Turn the heat to 450°. Make the topping:

- ½ *cup sour cream*
- 2 *tablespoons sugar*
- 2 *tablespoons heavy sweet cream*
- 1 *teaspoon vanilla*

Blend until smooth — about one minute. Pour it over the top of the cheese cake. Bake for five minutes. It will be of an ivory smoothness. Chill the cake for five minutes in the freezer and at least two hours in the refrigerator.

My friends and I once indulged in gluttonly by serving this already delicious cake with fresh strawberries — tasty, but unnecessary.

Simpler to make than cheese cake if you have the proper French baskets is:

COEUR À LA CRÈME

(For 6)

- 6 *ounces cream cheese*
- 1 *pound cottage cheese*
- 1 *cup heavy cream*

Mix and beat with an electric mixer. Fill six small heart-shaped baskets, first lining them with three thicknesses of cheese cloth. Set them on a rack in a pan. Cover the pan with cheese cloth. Set the pan in the refrigerator and let the cheese drain into the pan all night.

The next day, unmold the individual cheese molds, peel off the cheese cloth and serve with home-powdered sugar and fresh raspberries, strawberries or peaches.

PINEAPPLE UPSIDE DOWN CAKE

My favorite weapon for this dessert is an iron frying pan big enough to hold seven slices of canned pineapple. Other kinds of pans may be used but most of them are not big enough.

Begin with what is going to be the topping when the pan is reversed.

½ cup butter

1¾ cups sugar
4 tablespoons molasses
1 large can (7 slices) of pineapple

Small jar of maraschino cherries

Light oven: 375°. Melt the butter in the frying pan. Stir in the sugar and melt it. Stir in the molasses. Arrange pineapple slices in the pan. Put the cherries in the centers of the slices and in the spaces between the slices. Add a tablespoon of the maraschino liquid. Set the pan in the oven.

Now make the batter and when the butter and sugar mixture begins to bubble, pour this over the pineapple. Batter:

1 cup milk
1½ cups sugar
6 tablespoons melted butter
3 eggs
2½ cups flour, sifted three times and measured
2½ teaspoons baking powder sifted with the flour

1 teaspoon vanilla

Mix the milk, sugar, butter, eggs and vanilla and beat with a hand beater — or an electric beater — until they are all well blended. Beat the sifted flour and baking powder in gradually. Keep on beating till the batter is smooth. Pour it over the bubbling fruit and bake at 375° until a testing straw comes out clean — about 35 minutes.

Turn the cake upside down on a platter big enough to hold it. This takes courage, speed and a strong wrist. Have a helper if you can. Good fortune be yours this day.

Serve the upside down cake hot with thick cream, vanilla ice cream or Foamy Sauce.* An estimate of the calories contained in this dish would be depressing. "Seldom but superb" is my motto.

PEACH UPSIDE DOWN CAKE

Make this just as you would the Pineapple Upside Down Cake, but flavor the batter with half a teaspoon of almond extract instead of the vanilla. Halve fresh peaches; fourteen halves is the number prescribed by Grandmother for the large frying pan. Canned peach halves may be used, but fresh peaches are far superior. Put a cherry — I sometimes use fresh black cherries, stoned — in the hollow of each half. Place the peach halves cut side down in the hot butter and sugar mixture. This may be accomplished with the use of two pancake turners. Place the pan in the oven, and when the butter and sugar are bubbling, pour the batter over the cake, and bake at 375° until a testing straw comes out clean — about 35 minutes. Serve the cake with thick cream or vanilla ice cream, or with a sauce made by crushing raspberries with sugar, or with Foamy Sauce.*

You may think that the upside down cakes are made with an excess of butter and sugar. Be warned, I once tried to reduce the amount of both in the making of a peach cake. The taste was good, but when I flipped the cake onto my best round platter, I found I was gazing upon what looked like a picture of moon craters. All the peaches had stuck to the too thick mixture in the bottom of the pan. One by one, I picked out the peaches and tried to puzzle which crater each one had come out of. The original amount of butter *is* necessary.

PEACH AND RASPBERRY SHORTCAKE

Grandmother had help in inventing this. She asked a young gentleman whether he would like peaches or raspberries on his shortcake. He replied promptly, "Both."

The shortcake is, of course, real Vermont shortcake made of biscuit dough, not any of the cake-like subterfuges that masquerade under that honorable name.

Jay and I have just been to a "Strawberry Festival" in a nearby town. This event has become a method of sharing some of the joy of strawberry season with contributions to a church most in need of fiscal relief. The festival consists of one serving of either strawberry shortcake *or* strawberry sundae and as much hot coffee as you can drink on a hot July day, in exchange for a not-so-nominal fee. The shortcake was good, but not of the quality that I remember from other festivals in and near Appleyard Center. Perhaps, it was not so much the taste of the food, but the nostalgic memories of bingo games, horseshoe tosses, frisbee throws, and the smells of midsummer clover and hay being cut and bailed in the field next to the church — "Quickly before the thunderhead breaks!"

Somehow, and I have never been quite sure how, the taste and texture of all these events managed to become a part of the unlimited strawberry shortcake that was available along with all of the activities. Or was it just one serving even then? No matter, it was enough, and I think that the following rule will be quite enough whether haying and horseshoe tosses are part and parcel or not. Ah yes, strawberries may be used in place of the peaches and raspberries.

Begin with the shortcake:

2 cups flour, sifted three times
4 teaspoons baking powder
¼ teaspoon nutmeg
½ teaspoon salt
⅓ cup butter
¾ cup milk
Extra butter

Sift the flour, baking powder, nutmeg and salt together. Work in the butter with your fingertips until the mixture feels like coarse meal. Cut the milk in with a pastry fork. Since different kinds of flour absorb milk differently, you may need another tablespoon of milk, or perhaps one less. (I use whole wheat pastry flour and so need two tablespoons more of milk to reach an adequate consistency.) The dough should be soft and pliable, not sticky. Toss it on a lightly floured board. Knead it briefly, roll it out gently. Handle the dough as little as possible. Cut it with a good-sized biscuit cutter. Grandmother's was an antique square model, but I have turned out excellent shortcakes in circular form. (Oh — where has my modesty gone?)

If you prefer one large shortcake, roll out two 8-inch circles of dough and place the first in a buttered 8-inch cake pan, butter it and place the second on top. Bake the biscuits — for that's what the smaller ones are — at 450° until lightly browned; 12 to 15 minutes. The larger form may take up to 20; it should spring back in the center when touched. Split them, butter them with the extra butter which should be soft but not melted. Have the fruit ready in a warm — not hot — place.

The peaches must drip when cut into. Perhaps those handsome deceivers that are fuzzy inside and out might be used, well dried, for insulating radiators during Vermont winters. At any rate, slice the peaches very thin. Put the slices on the cut lower half of a shortcake, squeeze a little lemon juice over them and sprinkle them lightly with powdered sugar. Put the other biscuit layer on top, cut side up, put raspberries mashed with sugar on the top layer. Next, whisk over them a light cloud of whipped cream and top with a raspberry similar to an uncut ruby. The creation is complete but for the eating.

Once this invention was introduced in Appleyard Center, there was rarely another type of shortcake served without protest. So, beware and be prepared for the demands that you will open yourself up to, once your family has tasted of this ambrosia.

Grandmother did not always frown upon the use of cake. "It can be used to advantage," she would say solemnly, "as a cousin of shortcake, as a pan dowdy." It is easier to make than shortcake because there is no last minute work to be done.

APPLE PAN DOWDY

(For 12)

½ pound butter	*¼ teaspoon nutmeg*
3 cups sugar	*¼ teaspoon cinnamon*
3 tablespoons molasses	*3 pounds tart apples cut in eighths, peeled (2 cups)*
2 cloves	

Thin peel of ½ lemon

Light the oven: 475°. Melt half the butter in a large dish. Mrs. Appleyard used an ancestral milk pan, white with scarlet edges. Add 2 cups of the sugar and molasses and mix well. Add spices. Put in apples and dot with ¼ of the butter cut in small pieces. Chop lemon peel and sprinkle over apples. Put the pan in the oven. Meanwhile, make biscuit dough. Use either the rule for Baking Powder Biscuits* or Sour Cream Biscuits.* When mixture bubbles hard, cover apples with biscuit dough, mixed soft and dropped from the spoon in small lumps. When biscuits have risen, sprinkle them with remaining sugar and dot with the rest of the butter. Bake until biscuits are well-browned — about half an hour longer.

Serve warm with thick cream or vanilla ice cream.

The rule for Rhubarb Pan Dowdy is in the *Vermont Year Round Cookbook,* p. 86.

PEACH PAN DOWDY

(For 10)

This may be made satisfactorily with canned Alberta peaches, but what I really like are fresh peaches from North Carolina. A friend there had the generous habit of sending my family a bushel basket every summer. I now order bushels through the nearby food cooperative, and even help unload the truck when it arrives in Plainfield directly from North Carolina. It is a treat just to put your head into the cellar way while they are ripening. The thought makes me hungry, so I begin with:

½ pound butter
2 cups sugar
4 tablespoons molasses
¼ teaspoon nutmeg
16 peaches, sliced
Baking Powder Biscuit dough or Sour Cream Biscuit dough**
½ teaspoon almond extract

Light the oven: 450°. Melt half the butter in a large enameled pan. The pan should not be too deep as you want lots of biscuit in proportion to the fruit. Add 1½ cups of the sugar and molasses and mix well. Do this over medium heat so mixture will start bubbling. Add nutmeg and almond extract. When mixture is bubbling hard, drop in sliced peaches. Put some butter in between slices. Now set the pan into the oven. Make biscuit dough. It should be mixed with enough milk so that it can be pushed from a spoon in small soft lumps. Be sure mixture in pan is bubbling hard before you spoon on batter. Return dish to oven. When the biscuits are well-risen — about 7 minutes — sprinkle them with remaining sugar and dot with the rest of the butter. Bake until biscuits are well-browned — about 20 minutes longer.

BLUEBERRY PAN DOWDY

(For 8)

¾ cup butter
1 tablespoon molasses
1 tablespoon instant flour
1 cup sugar
¼ teaspoon nutmeg
3 cups blueberries
1 teaspoon powdered orange rind
1 teaspoon powdered lemon rind
*Baking Powder Biscuit dough**

Melt ½ cup of the butter in an enameled baking dish, add the molasses. Mix instant flour with ½ cup of the sugar and stir it into butter and molasses. Sift the nutmeg into the mixture with the flour. Make biscuit dough. Light the oven: 400°.

Stir blueberries into the pan, sprinkle powdered orange and lemon rind over them. Set the pan in the oven. When fruit is bubbling hard, push small lumps of dough from a spoon on top of the fruit. Dot dough with remaining butter and sprinkle the rest of the sugar over it. Bake at 400° until well risen — about 10 minutes. Reduce the heat to 325° and bake until well browned — about 25 minutes longer. Serve with Brandy Hard Sauce* if you like, but the pudding really makes its own sauce.

MAPLE GLACÉ BISQUE

(For 6)

1	*cup maple syrup*		*Strips of sponge cake*
5	*egg yolks*	1	*cup heavy cream*
1	*cup light cream*	⅓	*cup chopped pecans*

¼ *cup maple sugar, crushed*

Cook syrup to 230° on the candy thermometer. Beat egg yolks with the light cream. Pour syrup on them in a thin steady stream, beating all the time with a hand electric beater. Cool mixture by setting the pan into a larger one containing water and ice cubes. Beat until it thickens. Chill in refrigerator while you line dessert glasses with strips of sponge cake. Whip the heavy cream and fold it into the mixture. Fill glasses. Scatter maple sugar and chopped pecans over them.

If you have no maple sugar on hand — a lack that occurs even in well-regulated homes occasionally — it is possible to buy maple candy and pound it up, not too fine.

FROZEN DESSERTS

The mention of ice cream must conjure up dream-like visions in almost everyone, Mrs. Appleyard believed that you are missing the greater part of the enjoyment if your visions don't include the making of the ice cream itself with all its attached duties and privileges. These begin with picking the strawberries, bright plump crimson packages of pure sweet ambrosia; milking the cow and separating the cream afterwards, seeing the creamy liquid spinning round and round and coming out in two separate streams, one of pure snowy white and the other unmistakably a creamy yellow. Next comes the pleasure of packing the freezer with rock salt and ice (of course the ice is never in convenient shapes and must be broken with a mallet) and finally pouring the cream, fruit and sugar into the freezer, taking turns cranking and checking to determine how much longer it is going to be. When the cranking is done and rhythmic songs have been sung, a feeling of breathless anticipation hangs in the summer's air as Dad unscrews the top of the freezer and ever-so-slowly doles out small portions of the delectable coldness. The luckiest person is the recipient of the freezer paddle, tasting the ice cream in every one of its stages.

The thought of all that lip-licking has made me ravenous. I feel fortunate to have inherited my Grandmother's small electric freezer that fits neatly into the freezer compartment of my refrigerator. Of course, any of the following rules may be made in a hand-cranked ice cream freezer. I admit I miss all the accompanying activities of the more traditional ice cream production, but I needn't wait for a crowd or a clear, sunny, lightly breezy day to make — among other things:

REAL STRAWBERRY ICE CREAM

This rule contains nothing but strawberries, cream and sugar. You will find no isinglass, for instance, to stick it together. This is a substance which is used somewhat like gelatin. It comes out of a sturgeon. I suppose that if you grow your own caviar you could probably have isinglass also.

This form of isinglass would not be too useful to put into the windows of an old-fashioned cast iron stove. These windows look like and are even called isinglass, but they are really mica. Grandmother did not think that either of these substances should be in ice cream. Neither should it contain cornstarch, powdered eggs, artificial vanilla nor glue.

Ah — yes, the rule:

2	*cups crushed strawberries*	1	*pint heavy cream, not beaten*
½	*cup sugar*		

Put the strawberries and sugar through the blender. Mix with cream. Pour mixture into electric freezing unit, or hand-crank unit, and follow the directions that come with it. Freeze until the paddle will no longer turn.

I make ice cream ahead of time and store it in the deep freeze. A quart of ice cream is supposed to serve six people. It is my duty to tell you this is not so with real ice cream. It is better to make plenty.

If you have not obtained an electric freezer you can still make:

STRAWBERRY MOUSSE

2	*cups crushed strawberries*	1	*pint heavy cream, whipped*
½	*cup sugar*		

Put the strawberries and sugar into blender and blend till smooth. Chill. Whip the cream till it stands in soft peaks. Fold whipped cream into the strawberry mixture until you have a beautiful even color like snow at sunset. Put mixture into a pan at least three inches deep and place it in the freezer. Stir it thoroughly to break up the ice crystals, at least five times during the first hour of freezing. An extra stir does no harm. Freezer temperatures vary. The mousse should be ready in two hours, but better allow three.

Any of the ice cream or sherbet (I use the words sherbet and ice interchangeably) recipes given below may be made in the same way as the mousse, following the above method.

MACAROON ICE CREAM

2	*cups macaroon crumbs*	2	*teaspoons vanilla, or 1 teaspoon vanilla and 1 teaspoon brandy*
¾	*cup sugar*	2	*cups thick cream*
2	*cups thin cream*		

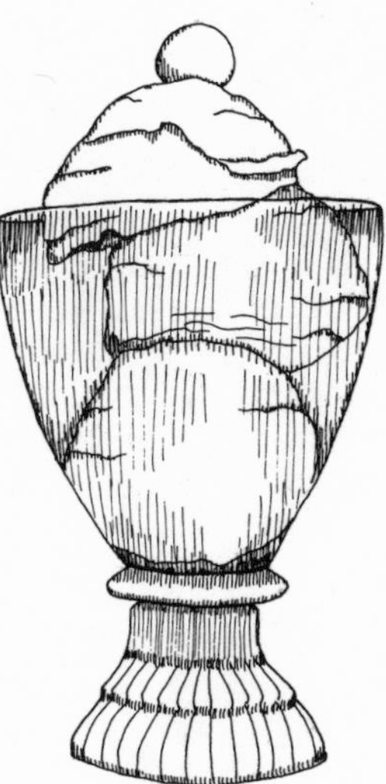

Dry two dozen macaroons for two hours in a very slow oven — 250°. Pound them. Measure crumbs. Mix with sugar. Stir them into the cream. Add the flavoring. Don't put in too much brandy. It is only there to bring out the flavor of the macaroons. Freeze in the electric cylinder or as a mousse in a pan three inches deep.

If you have some orange or raspberry ice on hand, line a one and a half quart melon mold with it. Then fill the mold with the macaroon ice cream. This is a nice project for a spring morning. Mrs. Appleyard made some one morning while four men were putting up a portable garage in her backyard. They finished before she did. The garage is still there, but the mold of ice cream and sherbet vanished that evening. She maintained that it was worthwhile.

RASPBERRY SHERBET

2 cups raspberry juice	*2 cups water*
2 tablespoons lemon juice	*1 cup sugar*

It takes about four cups of raspberries, crushed and strained, to make two cups of juice. Mash them and strain through a very fine sieve. Add lemon juice. Make a syrup of the sugar and water and boil until it is quite thick, about 12 minutes. Don't scorch it. Cool the syrup. Add raspberry juice. Freeze in the electric cylinder.

ORANGE ICE

1 cup sugar	*1 teaspoon grated lemon rind*
1 cup water	*2 cups orange juice*
Grated rind of 2 oranges	*¼ cup lemon juice*

Cook the sugar and water together until syrup is thick — about 12 minutes. Watch it carefully. Add grated orange and lemon rind. (Never grate the rind of any oranges that are marked "color added." Mrs. Appleyard used to make her sherbet from Temple oranges sent to her by the man who grew them. She said that grated orange peel out of a bottle is better than what comes off artificially colored oranges.)

Let the lemon and orange peel stand in the syrup while it is cooling. When it cools, strain it, add the fruit juices and freeze in the electric cylinder, or in a refrigerator tray.

PEACH ICE CREAM

Some ice creams are all right made with a custard, but not peach or strawberry. The fresh flavor of the fruit is so delicate that it takes very little to change it. Never use any fruit for ice cream that you would not like to eat plain. This does not necessarily mean using the largest and handsomest fruit, but ice cream is no better than the ingredients from which it was made.

Really good sliced peaches with some Vermont cream poured over them are, in my opinion, much better than any peach ice cream you can buy; or anything you can make yourself, out of peaches seemingly made of wool and rubber. Alas, both of these substances can lurk under a skin of beauty. So begin by taking:

2 peach kernels	*1 cup sugar*
2 cups peach pulp and juice from perfect peaches	*2 cups heavy cream*
	2 cups light cream

Crack two peach stones, blanch the kernels, let them stand a few minutes in the cream. I doubt that this ritual has any real effect. Perhaps two drops of almond extract would do just as well. Anyway, remember to take the kernels out again.

Put peach pulp and juice in the blender. Add sugar. Combine with the cream. Freeze in the electric cylinder or as a mousse. Macaroons are good with it. So are Mrs. Appleyard's Oatmeal Lace Cookies.*

In the wintertime, Grandmother used to use some of her frozen peaches and raspberries to make:

PEACHES CARDINAL WITH ORANGE ICE

(For 8)

Begin the day before by making a quart and a half of Orange Ice* and packing it into a melon mold. Rinse out the melon mold with water before packing in the sherbet and set it into the deep freeze.

The next day take:

- *2 12-ounce packages frozen peaches*
- *2 10-ounce packages frozen raspberries*
- *¾ cup sugar*
- *½ teaspoon almond extract*
- *1 tablespoon Bristol Cream sherry (optional)*
- *½ cup blanched, slivered almonds*

Defrost peaches for several hours in the refrigerator. Boil the raspberries with the sugar. Strain them through a very fine sieve to remove seeds and boil syrup till it is quite thick. Chill.

At serving time add the almond flavoring and sherry, if used, to the raspberries. Unmold the sherbet in a large shallow bowl. Arrange thawed peaches around the sherbet. Sprinkle almonds over the peaches. Pour raspberry sauce over the sherbet and peaches and serve.

A good variation to this theme consists of using Conserved Apricots* instead of the peaches, and using the raspberry sauce and orange sherbet in the same way.

COFFEE ICE CREAM

- *2 cups thin cream*
- *2 tablespoons instant coffee crystals*
- *1¼ cup sugar*
- *4 egg yolks*
- *2 cups thick cream*
- *½ cup pecans, broken (optional)*
- *1 tablespoon instant flour*

Put the thin cream and the coffee crystals in the top of a double boiler. When coffee is dissolved, sift sugar and flour together and stir them into the coffee mixture. Cover the pan and cook mixture over simmering water for ten minutes, stirring occasionally.

Beat egg yolks slightly with a wire whisk. Pour a little of the coffee mixture into them, beat, add a bit more of the mixture, then stir egg yolks into the coffee mixture. Cook for two minutes, stirring well. Scald but do not boil the thick cream and stir it in. Cook the mixture until it coats the back of the spoon (170°). Add pecans, if you are using them. Freeze in the electric cylinder. Some customers like this with Chocolate Sauce* on it.

CHOCOLATE ICE CREAM

- *2 cups rich milk*
- *3 squares unsweetened chocolate, grated*
- *1 cup sugar*
- *3 tablespoons instant flour*
- *4 egg yolks*
- *2 cups thick cream*
- *2 teaspoons vanilla*

Put the cold milk and grated chocolate in the top of a double boiler and stir well over hot but not boiling water, until the chocolate is melted. Sift sugar and flour together and stir them into the chocolate mixture. Cover the pan and let mixture cook slowly for ten minutes, stirring occasionally.

Now beat the egg yolks slightly with a wire whisk. Pour a little of the chocolate mixture into them and beat a little more. Then add a little bit more of the chocolate, then stir the egg yolks into the chocolate mixture. Cook for two minutes, stirring well. Scald but do not boil the thick cream and stir it in. Cook it until it coats the back of a spoon. After all, you are making a custard. The temperature should be 170° on a candy thermometer. Add the vanilla. Put the mixture into the electric cylinder and freeze it.

The cylinder's being warm does the ice cream good rather than harm — the extra heat will help make the good contact that is essential to this kind of freezer. Did any kind friend ever tell you to touch the tip of your tongue to metal on a zero degree day? If so, you will understand why your cylinder has to have a hot surface to make it stick tight to the frosty one.

NUT GLACÉ

If you are serving a group of guests with mixed tastes, those who don't like nuts in ice cream and those who crave them, you can please them both by serving Nut Glacé with plain ice cream. Make the glacé with:

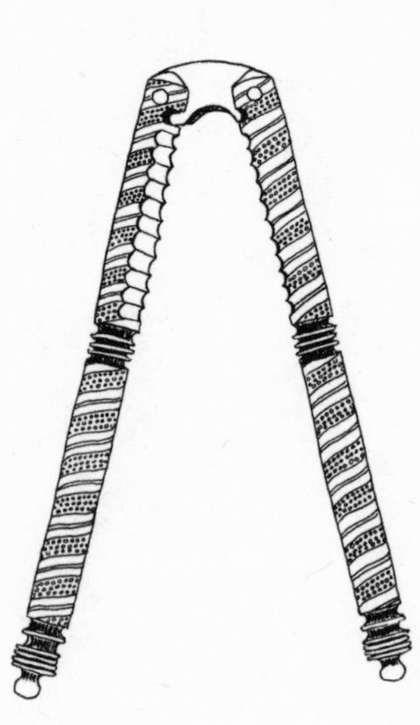

½	*tablespoon butter*	1	*cup nuts, broken in pieces*
		1	*cup sugar*

The nuts may be pecans, blanched and toasted almonds, walnuts, cashews or mixed nuts. Do not include peanuts in the mixture or it will taste only of peanuts. Use them separately if you like.

Make the glacé on a crisp bright day and begin by buttering a medium-sized black frying pan. Pour in the nuts. In a separate pan, melt the sugar. When it is golden brown pour it over the nuts. Let the combination cool. Remove it from the pan and pound it up into a rather fine powder. Grandmother had noticed this was a task a member of the younger generation was always willing to help with. It does not, however, always make as much as you had thought it would when nibblers do the cooking. Perhaps you had better make it yourself.

Mrs. Appleyard had been known to buy vanilla ice cream and pack it in her ice cube tray, put it in the freezer compartment with the temperature indicator at its coldest setting for one hour. She would then cut the ice cream into rather thick slices and roll them either in pounded nut glacé or in powdered macaroon crumbs. She would then put the slices on a cold platter, sprinkle more glacé over them and bring them to the table with all the speed she could muster — which, she claimed at that stage of her development — was about that of a polar bear on a hot day.

BANANA ICE CREAM

3	*ripe bananas, enough to make up one cup, mashed*	1	*tablespoon lemon juice*
		1	*tablespoon Cointreau*
1	*cup thin cream*	½	*cup sugar*
½	*teaspoon grated lemon rind*	2	*cups thick cream*

Peel bananas, cut them up. Put thin cream, lemon rind and juice, Cointreau and sugar into blender. Blend till smooth. Mix with thick cream and freeze in the electric cylinder. Or make it as a mousse as above, beating the cream first and mixing it in well, stirring the mixture during freezing. Orange sherbet is good served with it.

As a variation, you might serve a melon mold of orange sherbet with bananas, sliced horizontally, around it in small heaps. Alternate these with scoops of vanilla ice cream. Orange slices preserved in a whiskey sauce are placed on the ice cream and the sauce is poured over it. This is a very nourishing dish, Grandmother had been heard to remark, adding that she was planning to have milk toast for supper. She was a strong advocate of the adage: "Do as I say, not as I do."

CRANBERRY-STRAWBERRY ICE CREAM

(For 6)

Grandmother invented this one hot October day. There was almost always one such day a season, even when snow has already frosted Mt. Mansfield's sharp blue profile.

- *1 cup whole cranberries*
- *1 cup water*
- *2 cups sugar*
- *1 10-ounce package frozen strawberries or raspberries*
- *2 cups heavy cream*

Cook cranberries in the water until they pop. Add sugar. Put the mixture into blender. Blend till smooth. Leave some of the mixture in the blender. Add the partly thawed strawberries and blend till smooth. (If you use raspberries, soften them over low heat and strain them through a fine sieve to remove seeds). Add the heavy cream to the mixture and freeze it in the electric cylinder.

It may also be frozen as a mousse in a pan three inches deep. Beat the cream before you stir it into the fruit mixture. Stir it three times during the first hour, once during the second hour. It should be ready to eat in two hours.

ORANGE AND LEMON SHERBET

- *2 cups sugar*
- *2 cups water*
- *1 teaspoon grated lemon rind*
- *2 6-ounce cans frozen orange juice not diluted*
- *½ cup lemon juice*
- *2 egg whites*

Make a syrup of sugar and water. Boil five minutes. Add the lemon rind. Cool. Add the frozen orange juice and lemon juice. Put the mixture into your electric cylinder and freeze for half an hour. Beat egg whites to stiff peaks. Remove mixture from the cylinder and fold the egg whites into it. Freeze again until paddle stops turning — about one and a half hours longer. Heat the face of the cylinder well both times to establish a good freezing contact. This may be done by running hot water over it.

LIME AND LEMON SHERBET

- *2 cups sugar*
- *2 cups water*
- *1 teaspoon grated lemon rind*
- *2 6-ounce cans frozen lemon juice, not diluted*
- *½ cup lime juice*
- *2 egg whites*

Make this like the orange-lemon sherbet above. Pack it into a melon mold. Serve it surrounded by sprays of fresh mint leaves and large whole strawberries or heaps of fresh raspberries — sprinkled with powdered sugar.

GRAPEFRUIT WITH SHERBET

(For 6)

1	*pint fresh strawberries*	4	*Temple oranges*
½	*cup powdered sugar*	1	*quart sherbet — orange,*
3	*grapefruit*		*lemon and lime, or lemon*

Sprigs of mint

Save out six large strawberries for decorating. Cut the others in halves. Put them in a bowl and scatter powdered sugar on them. Remove seeds from grapefruit and oranges. Take out the fruit sections and mix them in a bowl with the strawberries. Cut and scrape out all the skin that divides the sections of the grapefruit, leaving only the shell. Save juice for drinking.

You should have the sherbet on hand, homemade if possible, but I frequently buy it following moments of lethargy. Divide the mixture of grapefruit, orange and strawberries among the grapefruit shells. Cover the fruit with the sherbet. Decorate them with sprays of mint and the large whole strawberries dipped in powdered sugar.

This is a pleasantly cooling dessert, especially after having eaten one of Mrs. Appleyard's curries.

RASPBERRY SHERBET BOMBE

1	*quart raspberries*	1	*cup sugar*
¾	*cup water*	3	*egg whites*

1 *tablespoon lemon juice*

Mash raspberries. Strain them through a very fine sieve to remove the seeds. Make a syrup of the water and sugar. Boil to 238° on candy thermometer. Beat egg whites stiff. Pour syrup on them, beating all the time. Fold in strained raspberry pulp and lemon juice. Freeze in a three-inch deep pan in the freezer, stirring four times the first hour.

Line a melon mold with the sherbet. Fill the center with Plain Mousse.* Keep in the freezer till needed. Defrost in the refrigerator an hour before serving. Surround with spun sugar.

Mrs. Appleyard was tantalized for years by the idea of making spun sugar herself. All you need, she was told, is two clean broom sticks laid across the backs of two chairs, three feet apart, plenty of clean white wrapping paper on the floor, a wire whisk, two cups of sugar and a cup of water with a pinch of cream of tartar and a sugar spinner. Whew!

You spin the syrup back and forth across the broom sticks and it is supposed to fall on the white papers. If no small children, puppies or kittens come in, everything should go smoothly — or crisply anyway.

I am now in the position to tell you that I buy spun sugar from my favorite caterer. It is an economy, in the long run, not to cut the heads off two new brooms. And if you buy spun sugar in a box, it is very unlikely to land on your Grandmother's Bristol Delft pottery or on that shimmering collection of Waterford crystal. Nor does it crackle stickily under your shoes. I should have known all this before I tried it.

Every summer Jay's family has a reunion on the Fourth of July. It has been dubbed Wimblewood, as one of the prime activities for any interested person is tennis. With forty to fifty people in the house and tents outside, and predictable rainy days, activities other than outdoor ones need to be thought of. There is usually singing, bridge, basketball in the barn and this year, the ice cream afternoon. This involved three ice cream freezers, hand-cranked of course, going at the same time with one of the older cousins commandeering the beginnings in the kitchen. There was an ice cream that came out of that afternoon that was strictly for adults, the taste of which was exquisite. I offer this rule:

MOCHA CHIP ICE CREAM

2 cups thin cream
1 cup sugar
2 tablespoons instant flour
4 egg yolks
¾ cup Kahlua coffee brandy, or to taste
¾ cup semi-sweet chocolate, grated
2 cups thick cream

Put thin cream into top of double boiler. When scalded, sift sugar and flour together and stir them into the cream. Cover pan and cook mixture over simmering water for ten minutes, stirring occasionally.

Beat egg yolks slightly with a wire whisk. Pour a little of the cream mixture into them, beat, add a little more of the mixture, then stir egg yolks together with the cream mixture. Cook for two minutes, stirring well. Scald but do not boil the thick cream and stir it in. Cook until it coats the back of the spoon (170°). Mix in the coffee brandy. Freeze in electric cylinder until cool, then add grated chocolate and continue freezing. If you add chocolate before the custard is cool, it will melt into the custard — a much nicer consistency is reached with flakes and chips of chocolate lurking in the custardy coldness.

We reserved this delicacy for adults with the phrase "Oh, but there's alcohol in it," to the smaller fry. If you have enough to go around, I'm sure children would also enjoy it.

FRUIT DESSERTS

Fruits are an excellent form of nutrient for any meal or occasion. Orange juice or sections bring sunshine to breakfast, a fruit salad for lunch sparkles up an omelette, and a potpourri of fruit in wine adds a touch of glamour and lightness to dinner, whether simple or elaborate. Grandmother's favorite dessert was often simply a Temple orange or a Royal Riviera pear from Oregon. However, when the season for those treasures was over — how brief it seems — she was to be found tampering with fruit; fresh, canned or frozen, according to her own ideas.

The hills and valleys of Vermont are filled with different varieties of fruit; raspberries, strawberries, blueberries, pears, rhubarb, grapes and of course, an unending supply of apples. All of these are available for a short period of time while fresh, after which the fresh taste must be recalled through other means. For an assortment of fruit desserts, consult the following rules. For instance:

MINTED PEARS

8 canned pear halves
½ cup juice from the can
½ cup sugar
5 drops peppermint extract
¼ teaspoon green food coloring
1 tablespoon lemon juice
Grated rind of one lemon
Sprays of mint

Boil pear juice and sugar till thick and syrupy — 230° on the candy thermometer. Add the green coloring, lemon juice and rind and peppermint extract. Add eight pear halves, two at a time. Turn them gently in the syrup until they are evenly colored. Remove them with a slotted spoon and a slotted pancake turner. Hold the pear over the pan and let all the syrup drain back into the pan. Then place all the pears on a cold plate. Chill thoroughly.

They may be served in dessert glasses with lime or lemon sherbet and decorated with fresh sprays of mint. They seem pretty good on a hot evening when the swallows are diving over the pond catching their favorite dessert on the wing. On a cooler night they might be used, resting on half circles of cranberry sauce wreathed in watercress as a garnish for cold roast ham.

PEARS IN MAPLE SYRUP

(For 6)

6 fresh pears, peeled, halved and cored
¼ teaspoon nutmeg
Juice and grated rind of half lemon
½ cup maple syrup

Simmer the peels and cores of pears in two cups water for half an hour. Put pears, cut side down, in a lightly buttered shallow baking dish — a round pyrex pie plate for instance. Squeeze lemon juice over them. Sprinkle over the grated rind and nutmeg. Pour liquid from the peelings and cores over the pears. Light oven: 225°. Spoon maple syrup over the pears. Bake for two and a half hours, basting twice during the first hour. Chill. Serve with sour cream.

BAKED RHUBARB WITH ORANGE SLICES

4 large, or 6 small, Temple oranges peeled and sliced
4 cups rhubarb, washed, cut in inch long pieces
2 cups sugar
1 tablespoon lemon juice
Thin rind of one lemon cut in a long twist
Butter

Light oven: 375°. Remove seeds from orange slices and place slices on an earthenware baking dish. Fill it with alternate layers of rhubarb and oranges, sprinkling sugar and lemon juice in between. Bury lemon peel in the center. Dot butter over top. Bake at 375° for ten minutes. Reduce the heat to 350° and bake until it bubbles stickily around the edges — about 35 minutes longer. Serve hot with Brandy Hard Sauce* or cold with sour cream.

BAKED RHUBARB AND STRAWBERRIES

Substitute a quart of strawberries, cleaned and hulled, for the orange slices and proceed as above. This may be served hot with Brandy Hard Sauce* or cold with scoops of vanilla ice cream or sour cream.

FRESH PEACHES IN BRANDY

(For 6)

Peel peaches dipping them briefly in boiling water. As soon as you have skinned them, halve them and put them into a bowl containing a can of frozen lemonade concentrate diluted with one can of water. (This supplies sugar and enough lemon juice to keep the peaches from turning brown). For six people allow nine peaches. Add to the bowl half a cup of brandy and one teaspoon almond extract. Chill until serving time. Garnish with slivered blanched almonds.

HONEYDEW MELON

Slice a chilled perfect honeydew melon crosswise in half-inch slices. Remove seeds. Lay each slice on a cold plate. Fill the centers with heaps of mixed fruit. A good combination is bananas, sliced and peeled, slices of peaches, fresh raspberries and ripe fresh pineapple. Top the heaps with thin strips of candied ginger. For an added treat put a dollop of sour cream on the fruit.

POTPOURRI OF FRUIT IN WHITE WINE

4 *fresh peaches, sliced*

1 *ripe cantaloupe*
1 *10-ounce package frozen raspberries*
1 *10-ounce package frozen strawberries*
1 *12-ounce can frozen orange juice, not diluted*
1 *cup seedless grapes*
⅓ *cup clover honey*
3 *tablespoons chopped mint leaves*
6 *drops mint extract*
2 *cups white wine (red wine may be used if you prefer)*

Mix all ingredients together in a large bowl. Chill for at least two hours. Serves six to eight.

This same mixture is delicious topped with plain yogurt, or as a light lunch mixed with yogurt. It may be used as a sauce for lemon or pineapple ice, when made with half a cup of white wine and one can of water. Or it may be used as a topping for vanilla ice cream. Again, numerous substitutions may be made without detracting from the flavor.

For another hot evening serve:

FRUIT COMPÔTE

(For 8 or more)

2 *ripe bananas*
2 *peaches*
Juice of half a lemon
½ *pound ripe dark cherries*
2 *tablespoons brandy*
5 *drops peppermint extract*
2 *containers frozen cut up fruit*
½ *pound seedless green grapes*
8 *ounces frozen raspberries*

Sprigs of mint

This may, of course, be varied according to what fruit is available. This is a good combination and easy to prepare because the troublesome work of cutting grapefruit and orange sections has already been done.

Slice bananas, peel and slice peaches. Squeeze the lemon juice over them. Stone the cherries and cut them into a tall glass compôte, add brandy and the peppermint extract. Add bananas, peaches and other fruit. Garnish with sprays of mint.

TUTTI FRUTTI

Hot evenings in Vermont are so rare that they are long remembered. Tutti Frutti, a sustaining mixture, would usually be more appropriate for not-so-warm evenings.

- *½ pound pitted dates*
- *½ pound figs*
- *½ pound Conserved Apricots**
- *¼ pound pitted prunes*
- *¼ pound Sultana raisins*
- *½ cup Vermont honey*
- *½ cup frozen lemonade, not diluted*
- *1 cup heavy cream*
- *½ teaspoon almond extract*
- *¼ pound blanched almonds, slivered*
- *3 tablespoons curaçoa*

Soak fruit for several hours in honey, lemonade and curaçoa. Just before serving, whip the cream, flavor it with almond extract. Add cream to the fruit mixture. Add slivered almonds. Chill briefly and serve.

ORANGE-BANANA WHIP

(For 4)

In the blender put:

- *1 6-ounce can frozen orange juice, not diluted*
- *¾ cup cold water*
- *1 very ripe banana, sliced*
- *¼ cup dried non-fat milk*
- *1 tablespoon lemon juice*

Run the blender for about one minute. Put the whip in dessert glasses. Chill. Garnish with slivered almonds.

Variation: Omit the almonds and put a scoop of Orange Ice* over the whip if you prefer.

Eggs

MRS. Appleyard spoke of an acquaintance, a gentleman and a scholar, who had paid her an unusual compliment.

"In ancient Egypt," he said, "choosing a wife was compared to putting your hand into a bag of vipers and hoping you would pull out an eel. I always," he added kindly, "think of you as an eel."

Mrs. Appleyard was so impressed by this tribute that she passed a restless night. Toward dawn she found herself riding a camel near the Sphinx and carrying a large sack full of something smooth, slippery and oval. She pulled out one of these objects and held it up to the rising sun: it was the only brown Vermont egg among a hundred white ones.

She woke happily, realizing that she was in Appleyard Center and the owner of two dozen eggs, ranging in color from deep pinkish brown to a freckled creamy tan. My hens had been busy the previous week and I had shared some of my bounty with my Grandmother. After she had told me of her odd dream, we decided together that there was no course but to have omelettes for lunch.

But before we get into the more glamorous methods of preparing eggs, the simplest ways are often the most difficult. If you can soft boil or poach or hard boil or fry, or scramble or make a plain omelette, more elaborate dishes need hold no terrors for you. The cook must have, in dealing with eggs, the qualities that are essential in any friendship — sympathy, understanding, patience and courage. With these on hand, equipment is a secondary consideration. Yes, Grandmother liked her teflon omelette pan, but I find that a seasoned black iron frying pan works just as well. I hear that there are stainless steel egg poachers with easy to handle individual cup-like pans, but I have poached plenty of eggs without them. A wire whisk is a handy tool but so is an old-fashioned egg beater or a spoon with holes in it.

An accurate timer is extremely helpful in the preparation of eggs but, if necessary, you can manage with the same tools your grandmother used.

You have one advantage over her; the eggs most people buy today are much more uniformly fresh than those she used. Be thankful for one blessing of modern times and begin with:

SOFT BOILED EGGS

The eggs should be removed from the refrigerator and stay at room temperature — 70° — for an hour before they are boiled. In these days of fuel shortages, room temperature may vary considerably from one room or home to another. In the winter our home is usually about 64° and eggs boil quite well. It also will do no harm to leave them out overnight, if you plan to use them the next day.

The water in which you start the eggs cooking should also be at room temperature, 65-70°. Do not begin until your customer — whether it's yourself or someone else — is ready to eat. The bitter orange marmalade should be on the table, the bread in the toaster and the sweet butter, slightly softened, ready to spread on the toast.

Slide eggs from a spoon into a saucepan of 70° water. Cover pan. Bring water to boiling. The minute it boils, remove pan from the fire. Let it stand exactly four minutes unless the eggs are liked so that the white is barely set, in which case two minutes is enough.

Serve eggs in warmed egg cups. Bring the hot toast. Pour the juice. This day has begun right.

HARD BOILED EGGS

Eggs should be at room temperature, and the water at 70°. Slide eggs into the water with a spoon. Cover the saucepan and bring eggs quickly to the boiling point. Remove pan from the heat as soon as they boil and let stand for 20 minutes. Plunge eggs into very cold water and keep cold water running over them for one minute. Roll eggs in the hands to loosen the shells. Do not peel shells off till eggs are cool or they will look rather moth-eaten. Begin peeling at the large end.

POACHED EGGS
(Without a Poacher)

Eggs done in small poaching pans are more neatly shaped than these and are good for dishes like Eggs Benedict.* Still, there is something homelike and genuine about eggs poached in the following fashion, and they taste just as good.

Butter a heavy pan. Fill it two inches deep with hot water. Bring it almost to a boil and let it simmer. Break four eggs, one at a time, on a saucer. Slide them into the water from the saucer, putting edge of the saucer under water. If you like your eggs firmly set, add a tablespoon of vinegar to the water before adding the eggs; it doesn't change the taste, but simply helps them retain their shape.

I'm sometimes heard announcing the names of friends for whom I intend each egg, as I do this. I am not really uttering an incantation; I'm just trying to remember their personalities so I'll take them out in the same order in which I put them in.

Don't crowd the eggs. Use two pans if necessary. Cover the pans. Cook

*See Index for pages where recipes can be found.

for three to five minutes according to how firm you like them. Have buttered toast ready on very hot plates. Remove the eggs from the water to the toast with a slotted spoon. Serve.

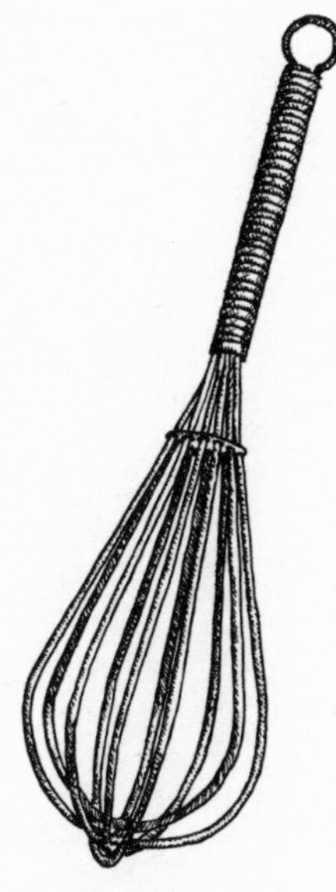

SCRAMBLED EGGS

(For 4)

1 *tablespoon butter*	*Salt and pepper to taste*
3 *tablespoons heavy cream*	9 *medium eggs*

In top of a double boiler, melt butter over hot water. Add cream and seasonings. Break eggs on a saucer one at a time and slide them in. With a wire whisk, stir the eggs from the bottom. They may be mixed until the white barely shows, the way Jay likes them, or a little more vigorously and thoroughly so they are yellow all through. Use a double boiler large enough to give you room to work. If eggs are not well stirred from the bottom they will be dry and the top slippery.

Eggs may, of course, be scrambled in a frying pan directly over the fire but they easily get dry and tough. If you do them in the double boiler five minutes cooking is about enough.

I find that variations in seasoning of scrambled eggs makes them a favorite breakfast dish for house guests. Try:

- 2 tablespoons chopped parsley and one tablespoon Worcestershire sauce or
- 1 teaspoon taragon or
- 2 tablespoons chopped chives and half a teaspoon celery salt or
- 1 teaspoon curry powder or
- 1 cup cottage cheese and four tablespoons grated parmesan cheese garnished with parsley sprigs or
- Mushrooms sautéed in butter or
- ¼ cup chopped green pepper and ¼ cup chopped onions, sautéed in butter

or — be innovative and come up with some original seasonings.

EGGS — SCRAMBLED AND BAKED WITH MUSHROOM SAUCE

½ *pound mushrooms*	2 *cups Bechamel Sauce**
¼ *cup chopped shallots*	¼ *cup cream*
4 *tablespoons butter and oil*	⅔ *cup cheese, grated*

8-9 eggs, scrambled as above

Chop mushrooms with a chef's knife, holding it by both ends, into sixteenth-inch cubes. Chop shallots. In a teflon or iron frying pan, put butter and oil. When butter stops fizzing it is the right temperature for browning. Brown mushrooms with shallots for one minute. If they are cooked too long they will be bitter.

Heat up bechamel sauce. Add cream slowly while stirring. Stir in one-third cup of grated cheese. Set aside.

Scramble eggs. Butter a 8x8-inch dish or shallow casserole. First put in a layer of eggs, followed by the mushroom mixture, another layer of eggs, and the cheese sauce. Sprinkle with grated cheese and dot with butter. Place under broiler for one to two minutes, till bubbling and just brown.

OMELETTES

Omelettes are a versatile and highly acceptable dish for any meal of the day. A plain omelette makes a filling breakfast or a nice brunch, fixed with cheese and served with a tossed salad it makes a fine lunch, and filled with cheese or mushrooms and served with a vegetable salad, Baking Powder Biscuits* or Bran Muffins* and covered with either Mushroom Sauce* or Onion Sauce,* it makes a light supper for a hot summer's day.

If the omelettes are to be served with a sauce, I would suggest that it be made first. Once the sauce is made, keeping warm and mellowing in the top of a double boiler, you may begin with the preparation of the omelettes. I use a seven and a half inch iron frying pan with curved sides, and it accommodates a three egg omelette perfectly. You may prefer a special omelette pan, useful but not necessary.

For each omelette use:

1	*tablespoon butter*	*2*	*tablespoons water*
3	*eggs*	*½*	*tablespoon minced chives*
	Pinches of salt and pepper		*and parsley*

Make one omelette at a time and reheat the first ones quickly in a warm electric broiler while making the last ones.

In the pan, heat butter over high heat, until it just starts to brown. This takes about half a minute and gives you time to beat the eggs with the salt, pepper, and water, using a table fork, until the yolks and whites are well mixed. Count to 30 slowly while you are doing this.

Swish the hot, frothing butter around in the pan so it covers the bottom and sloped sides. Tip in beaten eggs. Reduce heat slightly. Stir well with a fork. Shake the pan as you do this. Add the parsley and chives. Lift the edges of the omelette with fork or thin spatula allowing any uncooked egg to run under the cooked egg. As it begins to brown, roll the half of the omelette closest to the handle over the opposite half. Let it keep browning a few seconds at the lip of the pan. Then tip the pan over a warm platter or plate; with your right fist, give the handle of the pan three sharp blows and the omelette will slide out on the platter. If you prefer, you may guide it out with a spatula. I like the pounding method, not because it works any more efficiently, but it works out my hostilities.

Turn on the electric broiler. Make the other omelettes. When all of them are lying side by side on the warm platter, pour the hot sauce over them. Summon the guests. Put the platter briefly under the broiler till the sauce just starts to bubble. Garnish the platter with sprigs of parsley and serve.

There are, of course, endless variations on the omelette theme. Below are a few suggestions.

1. Before the omelette is flipped add a filling such as:
   - 4 tablespoons cheese, grated; cheddar, Gruyère, or other.
   - ¼ cup croutons sautéed in butter; or garlic cheese croutons.*
   - 3 tablespoons left-overs, i.e. chicken, fish, lobster, shrimp, mushrooms sautéed in butter and sherry, tomato, etc.
   - 4 tablespoons sautéed vegetables, i.e. sliced onion, green pepper, spinach, etc.

2. Omelette aux Fines Herbes:
   Add to the parsley and chives, half a teaspoon each: tarragon, basil and watercress. Or use any herb combination you think tasty.
3. Sweet omelette for dessert:
   Omit the seasonings and add to the egg mixture: One tablespoon powdered sugar and a scant half a teaspoon vanilla. Spread before folding with currant and raspberry jelly or marmalade — sprinkle with sugar.

Grandmother especially liked:

OMELETTES AND CAVIAR

Make the omelettes as above, but just before you roll each one of them, spread the middle with cod roe disguised as black caviar, or salmon roe picturesquely known as caviar. A slice of onion put through the garlic press may be mixed with the caviar. Garnish the platter with watercress and parsley.

If you have any real caviar, Grandmother would assume that you would be clever enough to spread it on a finger of buttered toast, and serve it with your eyes shut — pretending that it is 1913 and it might happen any day.

HAM AND ASPARAGUS OMELETTE

This is a particularly good luncheon dish.

For each omelette cooked as above, insert before it is folded:

1 thin slice cooked ham *3 asparagus spears*

Pour over the omelettes Cheese Sauce* made with Gruyère or Swiss cheese and parmesan. Garnish with watercress.

FRIED EGGS

Grandmother did not often cook fried eggs. She preferred the other kinds. However, one of her students taught her to cook one fried egg at a time — a method of which she approved. However, more often than not, you will be wanting to cook more than one egg at a time, and here is my method.

For four eggs (you may adjust for fewer eggs) in one large cast iron frying pan: melt two tablespoons of butter in pan over medium heat. Again, eggs should be at room temperature. Break the eggs, one at a time, into a saucer. When butter starts to brown and bubble, slide in the eggs. Cover and cook until the eggs are slightly brown around the edges and, on top, look rather like the sun seen through haze on a day when it's going to rain and the barometer is falling. It is the cook's privilege to serve it hazy-sunny side up, or turned and cooked very lightly on the other side. Remove the eggs, one at a time, to warm plates and serve. I usually succeed in breaking at least one yolk and so have learned to be satisfied with the egg any way it comes.

I recommend English Muffins* toasted and buttered, to go with the eggs. Gooseberry jam, or your own apple butter are tasty on them.

Now that you can hard boil and scramble and poach eggs, you will probably want to combine them with other things in various ways. Eggs are somewhat like people who — not witty themselves — are the cause of wit in others: they enjoy company.

EGGS BENEDICT

(For 6)

I would recommend making these with a minimum of three people on hand. They are not extremely complicated but rather involve a number of steps that should be completed simultaneously. All the more reason to serve them to and with your family and a few friends — not when you are at home alone studiously writing a book.

3	*English muffins, split, toasted and buttered*	6	*slices of baked ham, cut thin and to fit the muffins*
6	*large eggs*	6	*mushroom caps, grilled*

*Hollandaise Sauce**

The first member of the team toasts and butters the muffins and puts the ham on them. Another poaches the eggs, in poaching pans almost the size of the muffins. The third member grills the mushrooms, then makes the Hollandaise.

To assemble the eggs, first put the ham on the muffins, the eggs on the ham, the Hollandaise over it all and the grilled mushrooms on top. Then all that remains is to be seated and begin eating.

If you haven't any ham on hand, deviled ham may be spread on the muffins.

The process reminds me of a story by Dr. Suess, *Green Eggs and Ham.* Fortunately, Vermonters don't come across many green eggs, but might be entertained by Suess' description of the versatility of eggs, whether green, brown or white. As a matter of fact, I have recently come across some green eggs, produced by a farm family not far from Appleyard Center. They are supposed to be cholesterol free and higher in protein than are other colored eggs, and they are, in fact, green! Surprises will never cease.

EGGS APPLEYARD

These are similar to Eggs Benedict, above, but easier to assemble. For each two persons use:

	Garnish: asparagus tips, and/or mushroom caps	1	*tablespoon butter*
		¼	*cup cream*
2	*pieces of toast, crusts removed*	2	*eggs, at room temperature*
			Pinch of paprika
	Extra butter for toast		*Pinch of garlic powder*
2	*heaping tablespoons Chicken Liver Pâté**	2	*teaspoons tarragon vinegar*
		1	*egg yolk*

Parsley sprigs

Prepare mushroom caps or asparagus tips and keep them warm in a warm oven until needed. While they are cooking, toast bread lightly. Butter one side and spread about one tablespoon liver pâté on each slice. Keep them in the warm oven also.

When serving time comes, butter a skillet. Pour in cream. Place poaching rings in the skillet and break whole eggs into them. Baste eggs with cream while they are poaching. Remove eggs to pieces of toast, which should now be on a warm platter.

Now make the sauce. Fish out poaching rings. Add seasonings and vinegar to cream. Have pan over low heat. Beat egg yolk. When cream begins to bubble, delayer yolk with it until you have equal amounts of cream and eggs. Add this mixture to cream in the pan. Continue stirring and cooking over low heat until sauce thickens.

Put the garnish (asparagus tips, mushroom caps or other) around platter with the toast on it. Pour hot sauce over the eggs. Decorate with parsley sprigs and serve. With a tossed salad and a light dessert, this makes a nice lunch. White wine and/or coffee go well with it.

STUFFED EGGS

Choose large eggs at least two days old. The freshest ones are all but impossible to shell. Hard boil them and remove the shells. Cut eggs in half lengthwise. Remove yolks and mash them with a fork.

For four eggs allow:

2 tablespoons mayonnaise | *2 tablespoons deviled ham*

Blend yolks, mayonnaise and ham. Fill whites with the mixture. Cut each half in two widthwise. Chill. Happy picnic.

In the event that you still have some deviled ham on hand, you might like to make:

STUFFED EGGS IN ASPIC

(For 6)

6	*hard boiled eggs*	2	*tablespoons thick cream*
2	*cups jellied Beef Stock**	2	*canned pimentos*
2	*ounces deviled ham*	12	*stuffed olives*
	Finely cut chives		*Parsley sprigs*

While eggs are being cooked, heat the jellied stock — chicken will do if you have no beef — and pour a dessert spoonful of it into each of six custard cups. Set cups into refrigerator. Shell eggs when they are cool. Take out yolks and mash them with ham and chives. Moisten mixture with cream or mayonnaise if you prefer. Fill egg whites with this mixture. Save any left over mixture for a sandwich. Put halves of the eggs together and wrap a thin strip of pimento around them to conceal the cut place.

By the time you have performed this piece of first aid, the stock in the cups should have stiffened a little. Put a slice of stuffed olive at the bottom of each cup, the egg on top and the rest of the sliced olives around it. Fill the rest of the space with stock, set cups in the refrigerator for at least three hours. Unmold them on individual plates and add a sprig of parsley.

This may also be made in a ring mold. When you unmold it — a task demanding great courage and presence of mind — set the mold in a pan of just barely warm water for about a minute. Reverse it on one of your handsomest big round plates. If it does not fall out at once, caress the top quickly with a towel wrung out invery hot water. Fill the middle with a green salad of watercress and oak leaf lettuce and decorate the platter with Radish Roses.* Russian Dressing* goes well with this combination. It is a good deal easier to unmold six small aspics than to get a large one out of a ring. I just happen to know from a very unhappy experience.

EGGS STUFFED WITH CRABMEAT

4 hard boiled eggs

3	*tablespoons mayonnaise*	*¼*	*pound crabmeat*
1	*tablespoon finely minced green pepper*	*4*	*stuffed olives*
			Parsley

Hard boil four eggs by the method described in the beginning of this chapter. Shell them. Cut eggs lengthwise. Mash yolks with mayonnaise and mix in green peppers. Add more mayonnaise if necessary — mixture should be rather moist. Flake crabmeat and fill the whites with it. Top with mashed yolk mixture, swirling a little with a fork. Decorate with stuffed olives. Put them on a plate with sprays of fresh parsley around them.

Hard boiled eggs are a good basis for other sauces. They are good on toast with a rich Cream Sauce,* with a newburg sauce, or with a curry sauce and some of Mrs. Appleyard's Chutney.*

EGGS AND SPINACH

(For 6)

1	*10-ounce box frozen spinach, cooked*	*1*	*tablespoon lemon juice*
		3	*tablespoons butter, soft*
1	*teaspoon minced onion*	*6*	*eggs (room temperature)*
	Salt to taste	*½*	*cup dry grated cheese*
¼	*teaspoon nutmeg*	*2*	*tablespoons butter*
1	*tablespoon cream*	*¼*	*teaspoon paprika*

Cook spinach in as little water as possible. The water should cook down to about two tablespoons when the cooking is done.

Put spinach, cooking water, onion, salt, nutmeg, cream and lemon juice into blender and run it for a minute. Divide mixture into six portions. Put one portion in each of six well-buttered shirred egg dishes. Make a hollow in the spinach. Put a small lump of butter into each hollow. Break an egg on a saucer and slide it in on top of the butter. Cover the egg thickly with grated cheese. Dot it with butter and sprinkle on some paprika. Set dishes on a rack in a pan of hot water and bake eggs in a slow oven — 300° — until whites of the eggs are set — about 20 minutes.

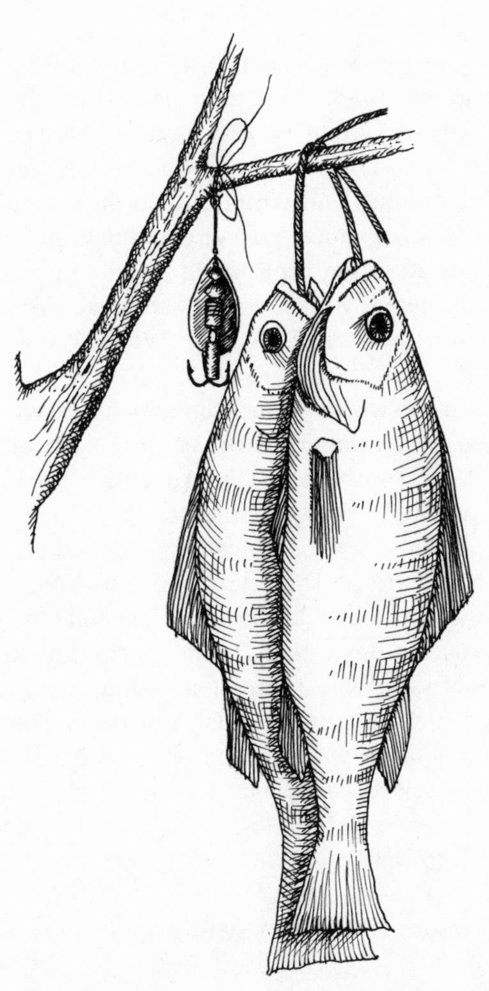

Fish

I hold a special sympathy for those people who are so unfortunately allergic to fish. For fish of any kind is one of my favorite forms of food. We of the "modern" age have advantages our foremothers and fathers didn't have. When the Appleyards first moved their belongings from Rehoboth, Massachusetts, in the late 1700's, salted fish was about the only form of seafood they could obtain when the local lakes and streams were empty. That is why you'll find such an abundance of rules for salt codfish dinners in New England cookbooks of an older vintage. Salt codfish is still available for those who have an attachment to it or to the past; luckily for the rest of us, fresh and frozen fish now reach many places where fish were seldom seen in edible condition twenty years ago.

The flesh of fish differs substantially from that of most land animals. It is much less fatty and has much thinner connective tissues, thereby cooking more quickly than either beef or chicken. You should be careful when cooking fish, as it does overcook easily and becomes tasteless. But broiled, baked, fried or steamed, if cooked with care most fish will delight you with the delicacy of its flavor.

I'll admit, it isn't easy to get really fresh fish in the middle of Vermont, but there is a saviour who appears once a week. He is a truck driver from Maine, who, every Friday, parks his truck on the strip of road unfondly referred to as the "miracle mile," in front of a rather run-down motel painted a ghastly flamingo pink. In spite of his selling location, the truck driver carries with him lobster and other delicacies from the sea, fresh enough to be eaten in rather simple ways as the natives of the Maine coast do every day. The lobster needs only to be boiled and served with plenty of butter to dip the pink and white chunks in as you pry them out of the shell. You need no wine sauce, no sautéed mushrooms and no greasy crumbs to distract your attention. You might possibly want to serve some freshly baked Garlic French Bread,* a tossed salad with two kinds of lettuce and spinach, a Potpourri of Fruit in White Wine* — nothing elaborate.

There are, of course, other places in the world fortunate enough to have a ready supply of fresh seafood available; Japan, Norway, the coast of mainland China, Taiwan and much of Southeast Asia. An entire book might be written that would be a simple compilation of the favorite seafood dishes from each of these places. Oh well, I must save something to do another day. For now I'll concentrate on the more traditional New England rules for the preparation of different kinds of fish, shell and otherwise. I'll try not to be as fanatically Bostonian about the treatment of fish as were a number of my relatives, who, without mentioning any names, refused to eat lobster much further west than Durgin Park. The rest of the country needs to enjoy seafood as well, and not everyone need be a fish zealot in order to delight in Mrs. Appleyard's rule for:

OYSTER STEW

(For 4)

Allow at least eight oysters to a person. The more recently opened they are the better the stew is.

1 quart oysters
½ cup butter
½ tablespoon salt
¼ teaspoon pepper
4 cups milk
2 cups cream

Clean oysters by putting them into a colander standing in a saucepan and pour three-quarters cup of cold water slowly through them. Strain liquid through a double thickness of cheese cloth into a pan large enough to hold the stew. Add butter and seasonings and bring mixture to the boiling point. In the meantime, in another saucepan, scald milk and cream.

As soon as oyster liquor is boiling, add oysters and cook until they begin to curl around the edges — about three minutes. Watch them every second — the change comes suddenly. Get the milk mixture as hot as you can without scorching it. I use a double boiler for this task — it is easier on my nerves.

When the oysters are ready, pour the hot milk over them. Have your tureen and its cover hot. Pour the stew into it.

Serve the stew with oyster crackers, or Cross crackers that have been buttered and put into the oven until the butter froths and the crackers just start to brown.

This rule serves four very generously. It might be made to serve more if all the recipients aren't from Boston or vicinity. I think perhaps even outsiders (myself included) will soon fall prey to its charms once allowed a taste of it. So, better make something else, or multiply the recipe.

**See Index for pages where recipes can be found.*

OYSTER SCALLOP STEW

Make this like oyster stew. Use half a pound of scallops to half a pint of oysters. Cook them in a quarter pound of butter until the edges of the oysters curl. Add pepper, paprika and a pinch of nutmeg. Add a quart of milk and two cups of cream, both scalded. Serve very hot with a Soufflé of Cross Crackers.*

LOBSTER STEW

(For 4)

1 pound fresh lobster meat
½ cup butter
1 teaspoon paprika
4 cups rich milk
2 cups cream

In a pan large enough for the whole mixture, sauté the lobster meat in the butter for two minutes. Sprinkle the paprika over it. Scald the milk and cream and pour them over the lobster meat and simmer for five minutes. Cool. Keep in the refrigerator for at least four hours. Reheat in a double boiler, bringing the stew just to the boiling point before serving it in a big hot, blue and white tureen.

Hot toasted crumpets go well with it.

MRS. APPLEYARD'S FRIED OYSTERS

Frying in deep fat was something that Mrs. Appleyard left to characters more daring than herself. However, she did invent a rule for a rather good imitation of fried oysters — and so much better for your health.

1 pint oysters
2 eggs, beaten
2 tablespoons cream
1 tablespoon butter, melted
¼ teaspoon mixed herbs
½ teaspoon paprika
1 cup fine dry crumbs of homemade bread
Extra butter for frying — about three tablespoons

Rinse oysters quickly in water. Remove any pieces of shell. Dry them between paper towels. Beat eggs till light. Beat in cream and melted butter. Add seasonings to the crumbs. Dip each oyster first into the egg mixture, then into the crumbs. Let them stand a minute and again dip them into eggs and then into the crumbs.

Melt the butter in an iron frying pan large enough to hold all the oysters in no more than one layer. When the butter starts to froth put the oysters in. Cook for one minute. Then set the pan under the broiler, not too near the heat, and cook until the crumbs are a golden brown. Turn the oysters carefully using two spatulas. Add more butter if necessary. Cook under the broiler till the oysters are golden brown. Serve.

BAKED OYSTERS

Allow six oysters apiece for these. Frozen ones will not do. They must be bought in their shells. Don't grumble about their costing a King's ransom — what king were you planning to ransom anyway? Just get your fish person to open them for you and fasten them together with rubber bands (not part of the finished product). Ask him to put them in a box for you, deep shell down.

Use shallow pyrex dishes large enough to hold six shells. They take more room than you think. You must have a dish for each person to be served. Fill the dishes with coarse rock salt and set them in the oven to heat. For four people take:

4 slices bacon, cooked till soft but not crisp
½ cup fine dry crumbs of homemade bread
¼ pound butter
2 tablespoons onion, finely minced
2 tablespoons white wine
1 teaspoon garlic powder
¼ teaspoon black pepper
⅛ teaspoon red pepper
½ teaspoon paprika
6 drops Worcestershire sauce
Juice of 1 lemon
24 oysters on the deep shell
1 tablespoon minced parsley

Cook bacon till soft. Drain. Cut in 24 small squares. Dry six thin slices of homemade bread in a slow oven, crust and all. Crumble and pound bread into fine crumbs. In a saucepan, melt half the butter and cook the onion until it is a pale straw color. Add the wine and seasonings, stir well. Cook for one minute. Add lemon juice and stir in the bread crumbs. If mixture seems too dry — add a little more wine but do not get it wet and mushy.

Open the oysters, keeping them deep shell down. Don't spill the juice. Sink shells into the heated salt, keeping edges above the salt. Cover each oyster with buttered bread crumbs. Sprinkle with parsley, or with minced chives if you prefer, and put a small square of the partly cooked bacon on top. Allow the top shells to rest where they will. Bake them for ten minutes at 500°.

Layer cake tins will do if you have no pyrex dishes. When serving them, set them on heat proof dishes. Those dishes of salt are *hot.*

These are something like oysters Rockefeller, only without the spinach and absinthe. Mrs. Appleyard never learned how to make them, and so did not pass the rule on to me. No matter — baked oysters are divine in themselves.

MRS. APPLEYARD'S SEAFOOD STEW

1 small onion, finely minced
½ cup butter
1 pound mushroom caps, sliced
1 green pepper, cut in thin strips and cut fine
¼ cup instant flour
½ teaspoon nutmeg
⅛ teaspoon cayenne
¼ teaspoon pepper
1 teaspoon paprika
1 tablespoon salt
2 cups rich milk
1 quart cream
Bit of bay leaf
½ pound lobster meat
1 pound crabmeat
1 quart oysters
1 quart bay scallops
2 cups oyster liquor
2 cups scallop liquor
2 egg yolks, beaten
½ cup white wine

Gently fry minced onion in butter until pale yellow. Slice mushroom caps vertically into parasol shapes. Add them and green pepper and cook until they are tender but not mushy, about five minutes. Push them to one side. Remove pan from the fire. Rub in flour, nutmeg, cayenne, pepper, paprika and salt. Work in milk and cream. Add bay leaf. Cook over low heat for five minutes. Add lobster and crabmeat. Set the pan in a warm, not hot, place until serving time.

Clean the oysters and scallops by pouring two cups of cold water through both the scallops and the oysters. Strain the liquor through a double thickness of cheese cloth. Bring it to a boil and cook scallops and oysters in it till edges of the oysters begin to curl. Do this in a kettle large enough to hold all the stew. Scallops, like oysters, should not be overcooked. Fortunately, both take about three minutes to cook. As soon as they are ready, stir in the lobster and cream mixture. Beat egg yolks well with a wire whisk. Spoon a little sauce over them, beat it in. Repeat. Stir yolk mixture back into the sauce in the kettle. Stir in wine. Simmer, but don't boil, till egg yolks thicken the sauce — about three minutes.

Be sure that no real cooking goes on after the addition of the wine and eggs or your sauce will separate. Chafing dishes over hot water are ideal for serving this stew, but it may also be served from a big tureen or from covered casseroles. It does not matter so long as the dish will keep hot for a reasonable length of time.

While you are heating the stew before serving it, have some extra cream on hand to add to the sauce if it seems too thick. There should be plenty of sauce. Be sure to taste the sauce as you go along, after all, a cook has kitchen privileges. Remove the bay leaf before serving the stew. Perhaps you forgot to put it in, as Mrs. Appleyard has been known to do on more than one occasion.

French Bread* cut about three-quarters of an inch thick — toasted and buttered — goes well with seafood stew, as do neat triangles of Melba Toast.* They look more lady-like and therefore are usually rejected on this ground by Jay and myself. We are so famished after preparation of a kettle of this stew, that nothing so delicate would be quite fitting.

This same combination of fish may be used to make a seafood Croustade.* It may also be served in a ring of rice — wild or tame. Or baked in a rather deep dish with a lattice crust of Mrs. Appleyard's 2000 Layer Pastry* criss-crossing it in flaky elegance. It is in fact a versatile dish, well worth the trouble it takes. When a shortcut is necessary I sometimes make:

SEAFOOD BISQUE

(For 6)

3 tablespoons butter
2 tablespoons instant flour
2 cups milk
1 cup cream
½ teaspoon paprika
⅛ teaspoon cayenne
1 minced onion
1 stalk celery, cut fine
2 tablespoons butter
1 6½-ounce can minced clams
1 pound lobster meat, frozen
1 pound shrimp, cleaned and deveined
½ cup blanched almonds
Minced chives and parsley
Slices of lemon

Make a white sauce of butter, flour, milk, cream and seasonings. Set aside. Sauté the onion and cut celery in two tablespoons of butter until the onion is translucent and pale yellow. Do not let it brown.

Add the clams, including liquid, and lobster and shrimp to the vegetables. Stir. When the fish is well heated, add white sauce and put the whole thing into the top of a double boiler over hot but not boiling water. Let it stand at least half an hour. Reheat it when serving time comes but do not let it boil. Put it in a big, hot tureen; garnish it with blanched almonds, chives, parsley and lemon slices.

Mrs. Appleyard dealt with the subject of fish and other chowders in the *Vermont Year Round Cookbook.* She seems to have forgotten about Bouillabaisse, which is defined by Webster as a "kind of stew of fish, vegetables, saffron, spices, oil, etc." Somehow it seems unrefined to call a dish so breathtakingly delicious, a stew. Grandmother was fond of bringing up Thackeray's lines about the dish whenever the name was mentioned. They are:

Green herbs, red peppers, mussles, saffron;
Soles, onions, garlic, roach and dace —
All these you'll eat at Terre's Tavern
In that one dish of Bouillabaisse

Not everyone may be able to follow Thackeray's rule to the "T," but there must be saffron in it. It takes only a little to flavor and color a whole kettle of fish, and it keeps its flavor and color well.

NEW ENGLAND BOUILLABAISSE — APPLEYARD

2 pounds of frozen haddock fillets
1 pound frozen halibut fillets
1 pound frozen flounder fillets
½ pound frozen lobster
1 cup salad oil, part olive
2 large mild onions, chopped fine
1 bunch leeks, cut in half-inch pieces
1 teaspoon garlic, minced
1 tablespoon minced celery
1 tablespoon lemon juice
3 tomatoes, skinned and cut fine
1 teaspoon thyme
2 bay leaves
½ teaspoon pepper
½ teaspoon paprika
1 cup white wine
1 4-ounce can of pimentos
1 pint oysters, frozen
1 pint cape scallops, frozen
1 pound crabmeat, canned
½ teaspoon saffron
1 tablespoon minced parsley
Half a long loaf French bread

Grandmother planned this mixture partly from the ballad, partly from an old French cookbook, partly from observation (having once eaten Bouillabaisse in a French restaurant). She knew that it was supposed to have mussels in their shells in it but neither she nor I liked either mussels or shells. If you really like shells in your chowder, I suppose you could put some small clams in the shell to steam in it and open them during the last part of the cooking. Jay was once served a Bouillabaisse with a whole lobster in it, in addition to a number of shells. He says it was delicious, but I still prefer mine "Sans shells."

To begin:

Thaw the fish for half an hour at room temperature — excepting the oysters and scallops. Cut up the partly-thawed fish into neat pieces — not too small. Cover them with boiling water and cook in a large kettle until the fish is tender — about 12 minutes. Set aside, water and all.

Put oil in a large frying pan. Fry onions, leeks, garlic, and celery in it until onions are a light straw color. Use green tops of the leeks as well as the white part. Add tomatoes, lemon juice and all the seasonings except saffron and parsley. Add fish stock, wine and pimentos cut in strips. Cover the pan and simmer for ten minutes. Add oysters and scallops. Cook them until the edges of the oysters curl — about three minutes. Add the cooked fish and crabmeat. Last of all, stir in saffron and sprinkle with parsley.

Put French bread, cut in one and a half-inch slices and toasted, into a large hot tureen or covered casserole. Pour hot Bouillabaisse over it. Serve the rest of the loaf of bread, some unsalted butter, radishes, olives, and raw celery with the Bouillabaisse. Have some white wine to drink with it. This is enough Bouillabaisse for eight to ten people. A simple dessert such as fruit and cheese, will be more than sufficient to top off the meal. I wonder if this dish was the originator of the expression "A fine kettle of fish."

GALLEY SLAVES FISH STEW

(For 6)

It was suggested to Grandmother by the inventors of this dish, that she write a cookbook about cooking on board a boat. As usual, she was charmed by the idea, and in dreams saw herself sometimes in a chef's cap and apron, sometimes neatly tailored in dark blue with brass buttons and a visored cap at just the right angle, serving delectable meals cooked on the bias to the background musical gurgle of water sounding against the hull. As time passed, there was splashing and dashing and also, eggs crashing to the floor as the boat pitched and rolled. Mrs. Appleyard would swab up what she had intended for an omelette — with fines herbes, of course. She would never order them in restaurants on shore because they cost 75 cents extra.

She was surprised and delighted to find, when she woke, that she had not been to sea at all. The nearest body of water was her goldfish pond in Appleyard Center. She breathed a silent sigh of relief and blessed that steady floor and the unsalted air.

Luckily, I discovered that this fish stew can be made at 1,199 feet above sea level (benchmark at Appleyard Center). It is an easy and delicious form of stew. Begin with:

2 *pounds frozen haddock fillets*
4 *large potatoes, peeled and thinly sliced*
Celery tops, a bay leaf, 2 whole cloves
3 *large onions, sliced*
⅛ *teaspoon dill*
¼ *teaspoon garlic powder, (optional)*
Salt to taste
½ *teaspoon pepper, from the grinder*
¼ *pound butter*
2 *cups boiling water*
½ *cup white wine*
1 *cup heavy cream*
1 *cup light cream*
Bread crumbs browned in butter
Extra butter
Minced parsley and chives

Put everything but the cream, parsley, chives and bread crumbs into a three-quart enameled iron baking dish with a cover. Bake covered for one hour at 375°. Scald the cream and add it. Bring the stew to the boiling point but do not boil. Sprinkle crumbs over top. Dot with extra butter. Put the dish, uncovered, under the broiler until the crumbs start to turn deep golden brown — about two minutes. Scatter the chives and parsley over the top. Serve with lemon slices and crumbled bacon.

COULIBIAC TART

This rule also came from the sea. It was not found by Grandmother, who continued to live happily in her hillside swamp, always wondering whether her house would crash into the basement some moist evening. Instead it was brought back by her daughter, Sally, from an ocean voyage on a large steady ship.

	*Half a rule, Mrs. Appleyard's 2,000 Layer Pastry**	¼	*pound fresh Gaspé salmon*
2	*hard-boiled eggs, sliced*	¼	*pound shrimp, cleaned, deveined*
1	*cup sour cream*	1	*teaspoon fresh dill weed, minced*

½ *teaspoon paprika*

Keep pastry in the refrigerator until it is needed. Remove half of it and roll it out between two very lightly floured sheets of wax paper. Roll a piece big enough to cover a ten-inch pyrex pie plate. Put it quickly into the dish, trim the edges neatly.

Spread the pastry with sliced eggs, dotting them with cream. Scatter in small pieces of salmon, adding cream as you do so. Then slice shrimp and put them over the salmon. Spread the rest of the cream over them and sprinkle with dill and paprika.

Light oven: 400°. Set the pie plate in the refrigerator while rolling out the rest of the pastry in a circle to make the top of the tart. Fold it. Cut two slits in the fold. Cover the tart, seal edges, tucking them inside the rim of the plate and crimping them neatly. Bake at 400° for ten minutes, then at 375° until lightly browned — about 40 minutes longer. Serve with a heated sauce made of a cup of sour cream, beaten with two egg yolks and seasoned with half a teaspoon dill.

FISH MOUSSE

(For 6)

Use a blender to mix this:

2	*cups rich milk*	¼	*teaspoon nutmeg*
1	*cup cream*	¼	*teaspoon pepper*
1	*slice onion*	1	*tablespoon lemon juice*
	Bit of bay leaf	1½	*pounds of flounder fillets, frozen, partly thawed*
¾	*cup jellied Chicken Stock**		
6	*eggs, beaten*		*Parsley or watercress*

Scald, but do not boil, milk and cream with onion and bay leaf. Add chicken stock. Beat eggs with nutmeg, pepper and lemon juice. Add flounder, cut into one-inch cubes, to egg mixture. Remove bay leaf and onion from the milk. Now, into the blender, put a cup of milk mixture and one cup of the egg and fish mixture. Blend for one minute. Pour it into a pitcher big enough to hold the whole mixture. Repeat twice or three times if necessary in order to blend the whole mixture.

Light oven: 350°. Set into it a large pan with a rack and an inch of hot water in the pan. Grease a large ring mold thoroughly with shortening. Pour the mousse into the mold from the pitcher. Cover the mold with aluminum foil.

Bake the mousse until a silver knife slipped into it comes out clean — about 35 minutes. Don't overcook or it will whey off (separate). Set the mold in cool water for ten seconds. Run a spatula carefully around the edges. Invert mold on a large circular plate.

Fill the center with Lobster Sauce,* Seafood Stew,* Hollandaise Sauce,* or Mushroom Sauce.* Garnish with sprays of parsley or watercress.

It may also be well-chilled and served cold with Ravigote Sauce.*

SALMON MOUSSE

This is made exactly like the Fish Mousse, substituting salmon for the flounder. Serve it with Hollandaise* or Egg Sauce* or cold with Raviagote Sauce.* It may be baked in a mold or in glass custard cups, rinsed out with cold water. Set them on a rack in a pan of hot water and bake till a silver knife slipped in comes out clean. Do not overbake. If baked in the cups, they should be cooked only about 20 minutes.

SALMON STEAKS WITH BURGUNDY

(For 4)

If you are fortunate enough to have access to several salmon steaks, a good way to serve them is baked in a burgundy sauce.

4 salmon steaks

4	*medium mushrooms, sliced*	*¼*	*teaspoon poultry seasoning*
4	*shallots, chopped, or two tablespoons onion and half teaspoon garlic, minced*	*1*	*tablespoon beef paste or one beef bouillon cube*
			Pinch of cayenne pepper
2	*cups burgundy wine*	*1½*	*tablespoons flour*
1	*tablespoon chopped parsley*	*4*	*tablespoons butter*
			Parsley to garnish

Heat oven: 350°. Set salmon steaks in a large cast iron frying pan, or other pan capable of being used in the oven and on top of the stove. Combine the mushrooms, shallots, wine, parsley, poultry seasoning, beef paste and cayenne in the same pan and bake all uncovered for ten minutes, or until steaks flake with a fork but are not dry.

Transfer the steaks to a serving platter and keep in a warm oven with the door open. Cook liquid down in the same pan on the top of the stove.

Thicken the liquid with a roux of one and a half tablespoons of flour and two tablespoons of butter. Take the pan off the heat and add two tablespoons of butter. Pour the sauce over the steaks and garnish with parsley sprigs. Serve at once with parsleyed new potatoes and a tossed salad.

SALMON AND FLOUNDER

Gaspé salmon is hard to come by these days. Last year I found only two slices weighing ¾ pound in all. I made it go further by buying a pound of flounder.

Cut flounder in strips about an inch wide. Cut salmon into cubes and wrap flounder around each one and fasten the fish together with toothpicks. Wrap them in a piece of cheese cloth, put them in a steamer, cover it and steam for about 12 minutes. While they are still warm pour over them a marinade of:

4	*tablespoons olive oil*	2	*tablespoons minced parsley*
2	*tablespoons vinegar*		*Salt and pepper to taste*
1	*tablespoon minced chives*	1	*teaspoon mixed herbs*

Chill the fish. Two hours before serving time add a sauce of:

1	*cup sour cream*	¼	*cup cucumber, finely sliced and diced*
1	*hard-boiled egg, cubed*		
1	*tablespoon chopped olives*		

Pack the marinated fish, mixed with the sauce, into a fish shaped mold rinsed out with cold water (if you happen to have inherited a fish shaped mold — if not, use a ring mold). Use an olive for the fish's eye. Chill well for at least two hours. At serving time set the mold in lukewarm water for ten seconds. Unmold it on a platter covered with oakleaf lettuce. Surround it with slices of peeled tomatoes, cucumbers, hard-boiled eggs — all of which have been sprinkled with French Dressing.*

Popovers are a harmonious addition.

THE NEWBURG FAMILY

Newburgs are slightly more elegant than chowders and stews, but they are easily made in an electric skillet. You must keep your wits about you in order to make them in a big iron frying pan over very low heat and then keep them warm in a double boiler. Either way, begin with:

LOBSTER NEWBURG

¼	*cup butter*	½	*teaspoon paprika*
1½	*pounds frozen lobster, cut up, not too small*	⅓	*teaspoon nutmeg*
			Few grains cayenne pepper
3	*tablespoons good sherry (NOT "cooking" sherry)*	1½	*cups light cream*
		½	*cup heavy cream*
1	*tablespoon cognac*	3	*egg yolks, lightly beaten*

Melt butter over low heat. Toss the lobster in it for two mintues. Add sherry and cognac, mixed with seasonings. Cook for two minutes. Mix the cream and beaten egg yolks in a bowl. Add a tablespoon of juice from the lobster mixture. Stir again, then pour the egg and cream mixture over the lobster. Cook gently without letting it boil, until the sauce is thick and smooth. Serve at once on a very hot dish surrounded by diamonds of Mrs. Appleyard's 2,000 Layer Pastry,* or in a ring of rice. If the mixture is allowed to boil, the egg will separate, and the sauce become thin.

I had often wondered from whence my Grandmother's passion for breaking eggs one at a time into a cup before separating them came.

It happened that Mrs. Appleyard and a friend were making Lobster Newburg for their husbands and two other men who had been invited to the friend's house for Sunday night supper. The friend had never dared make Newburg by herself, she said, so Grandmother was in the kitchen helping her. All went well until the friend (she remained nameless even after more than 40 years), separated the egg yolks from the whites all in one bowl, and poured the yolks all at once into the Newburg. The flavor that rose from the mixture was — in the words of James Russell Lowell, who must surely have had a similar experience — "a sulphurous mist of passion and woe."

One of the eggs, Grandmother thought, must have come from some old Chinese palace where it had been mellowing 40 or 50 years until needed for an appetizer, or perhaps the origin was an Egyptian pyramid.

"What shall we do?" moaned the friend, "What shall we do? I don't have another thing but a can of beans, and I promised Bob lobster for this time. He'll be furious, they're important clients of his."

"They shall have lobster," said Mrs. Appleyard grimly. "Where's the mustard?"

No record exists of how much mustard she put in nor how much Tabasco sauce, nor Worcestershire sauce, garlic, and brandy. Valiantly she tasted the mixture from time to time, alleging to her friend that King Tut would have loved it. (For a poultice perhaps.) When she was satisfied that no one would ever know, they heated up the beans — they had already made brown bread sandwiches to go with the Deviled Lobster — nee Newburg — and summoned the men to this pungent repast. Mrs. Appleyard and her friend ate generously of the beans and brown bread, leaving the lobster for the men. They loved it. One of them asked Grandmother for the rule.

This is the first time that it has ever been given.

Newburgs, except in the instance above, follow the same pattern — a rich cream sauce with sherry and brandy thickened only by the slightly cooked egg yolks.

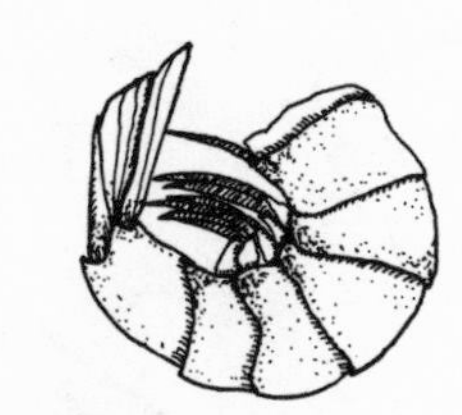

SHRIMP NEWBURG

(For 4)

Vary the quantity according to the number of people to be served. This may be made with either canned or frozen shrimp.

- 3 *tablespoons butter*
- 1 *pound shrimp*
- 2 *tablespoons sherry*
- 1 *tablespoon cognac or lemon juice*
- *A few grains of cayenne*
- 1 *cup light cream*
- ½ *cup heavy cream*
- 2 *egg yolks (broken separately and beaten)*
- ½ *teaspoon paprika*

Make as you would Lobster Newburg.* Serve it on homemade crumpets, split, toasted and buttered, or with a ring of rice. Serve with Mrs. Appleyard's Chutney.*

A newburg from crabmeat, scallops or a combination of shellfish may all be made following the pattern for Lobster Newburg. If they are followed by a fruit salad with crackers and a choice of cheeses, I think that you will be sustained for a while.

SHRIMP MOLD

(For 8)

- 2 *tablespoons plain gelatin soaked in half a cup ginger ale*
- 2½ *cups hot ginger ale*
- 4 *tablespoons lemon juice*
- 1 *tablespoon lime juice*
- 1 *cup celery, cut fine*
- 2 *teaspoons onion put through the garlic press*
- 1 *green pepper, minced*
- 2 *pounds frozen shrimp (cook according to directions)*
- *A little olive oil*
- *Watercress*
- 2 *10-ounce packages tiny green peas, frozen*
- 4 *Stuffed Eggs**

Soak gelatin in cold ginger ale. Dissolve it in the hot ginger ale. Cool. Stir in lemon and lime juice, celery, pepper, onion and shrimp. Brush a mold with olive oil. Add the mixture. Chill several hours. Unmold on a platter. Surround with watercress, tiny green peas, cooked and chilled, and the stuffed eggs. Serve mayonnaise with it.

In the summer I surround the mold with sliced tomatoes and cucumbers from my garden, along with sliced stuffed olives. Garnish the dish with sprays of fresh mint.

SHRIMP COCKTAIL WITH CRABMEAT AND AVOCADO

For each person to be served, have half a ripe avocado, brushed with lemon juice. Allow three shrimp halved, a tablespoonful of fresh crabmeat, half a teaspoonful of minced green pepper, and a little finely-minced onion for each person.

Mix all these together and add tomato cocktail sauce, and mayonnaise to the mixture. Allow two tablespoons of cocktail sauce to half a cup of mayonnaise. Heap the fish mixture lightly into the avocado halves. Garnish with watercress and serve.

DEVILED CRAB IN SCALLOP SHELLS

(For 6)

- 2 *tablespoons olive oil*
- 2 *teaspoons Worcestershire sauce*
- 1 *teaspoon dry mustard*
- ⅛ *teaspoon cayenne*
- 3 *drops Tabasco sauce*
- ½ *teaspoon pepper from the grinder*
- ½ *teaspoon sugar*
- 1 *pound fresh crabmeat free from shells*
- ¼ *pound butter*
- 2 *slices homemade bread, crumbled*
- 2 *Cross crackers rolled fine*
- 6 *scallop shells*

Mix the olive oil, Worcestershire sauce, mustard, cayenne, Tabasco, sugar and pepper. Pour them over the crabmeat and let it stand while you cream the butter and mix it into the bread and cracker crumbs. Mix this with marinated crabmeat and divide mixture among six well-buttered scallop shells. If the mixture seems too moist, add a few more bread or cracker crumbs and a few dots of butter. Bake at 400° until the crumbs are well browned — about 20 minutes. Watch it and reduce the heat if crumbs are browning too fast.

BROILED CRABMEAT

1	*pound crabmeat*	½	*teaspoon mustard*
½	*cup mayonnaise*	¼	*teaspoon curry powder*
¼	*teaspoon garlic powder*	1	*tablespoon lemon juice*

Arrange fresh crabmeat in a buttered, shallow, fireproof dish. Mix the mayonnaise with all the seasonings but lemon juice. Sprinkle the crabmeat with lemon juice and set it in the oven for five minutes at 350°. Then mark crabmeat with the seasoned mayonnaise. Run the dish under the broiler — six inches below the flame — until the mayonnaise is slightly brown and bubbly.

Serve with sandwiches of brown bread and cream cheese and a tossed salad of lettuce and spinach.

On the whole, Grandmother liked fish best when it was broiled. When daffodils, shadbush and forsythia were in bloom, you were likely to see her hurrying home after having caught a shad — for a certain price. By some mysterious accident it had just lost its bones and she would use it planked.

PLANKED SHAD — APPLEYARD

(For 6)

Actually she never used a plank but a large stainless steel platter with a wooden shell on which it rested when the fish was cooked and served.

6	*large potatoes, mashed with hot milk and butter*	6	*boned serving pieces of shad*
2 or 3	*large tomatoes*	¼	*cup butter*
8	*slices of bacon*		*Juice of 2 lemons*
	Match stick carrots	½	*teaspoon pepper, from the grinder*
3	*tablespoons sugar*	1	*teaspoon paprika*
1	*teaspoon molasses*		*Extra butter*
1	*10-ounce package tiny frozen peas*	½	*cup bread crumbs browned in butter*
1	*shad roe*		

Watercress

Begin by making plenty of good creamy mashed potatoes. Keep them hot in a double boiler. I use real potatoes, but if you like the packaged kind this is a good time to use them.

Slice enough tomatoes to give you six good slices. Cook bacon till soft but not crisp. Cook carrots, glazing them with the sugar mixed with molasses. Cook peas till they are not quite done, about five minutes, in very little water. Do not overcook the vegetables — they will get more cooking under the broiler.

Next lay the shad, skin side down, and the roe cut in six pieces on a large piece of heavy aluminum foil. Turn the edges of the foil up carefully to make a box that will keep the juice where it belongs — in the fish — not burned on the broiler. Put the box on a cookie sheet. Melt butter with lemon juice, add pepper and paprika and pour the mixture over the shad and roe. Broil for eight to ten minutes. If you use gas and can turn the flames down to pin points, have the fish one inch from the flame.

With an electric broiler it must be further away — about four inches.

Do not turn the shad, but at the end of five minutes turn roe and baste with lemon and butter. Test the fish for flakiness. Do not overcook it. Now put the aluminum foil box on your broiling platter. Spread out edges of the foil. Make a wall of mashed potato around the outside of the platter. Score potato lightly with a fork and dot with butter. Inside the potato ring, make another ring of heaps of peas and carrots brushed with melted butter and a third ring of the tomato slices, covered with browned crumbs and topped with partly cooked bacon. Put the whole platter under the broiler and cook until potato is golden brown — about three minutes. Watch it!

Decorate the dish with watercress and get a strong person to carry it to the table. This person must be trained to do so without slipping, tripping or spilling this work of art — for that is what it will be. Don't feel badly about eating it though, for the taste matches if not exceeds the beauty of the platter.

SHAD ROE, BROILED

(For 6)

When you are far from the sea and a little homesick for it, canned shad roe is handy to have in the pantry. I think that canned roe is better than fresh roe from fish too far from the sea. You need not wait till the shadbush is in bloom. Serve it any time. For six people you will need:

2 cans of shad roe
4 tablespoons melted butter
12 slices of bacon cooked almost crisp
2 tablespoons lemon juice
Sprigs of parsley and watercress
Lemon cut in eighths

Brush the roes with melted butter and lemon juice. Broil them for two minutes on the first side, three minutes on the second. I cook them on the stainless steel platter on which they will be served.

Add the partly cooked bacon during the last three minutes of cooking. At serving time, garnish the platter with watercress, parsley and eighths of lemon. With it serve, in season: Asparagus Country Style* or boiled zucchini. Inside-out Potatoes* go well with it, too. How about Lattice Cranberry Pie* for dessert? Or whatever *you* like.

BROILED HADDOCK, FROZEN

Use the kind of frozen haddock that comes in a one pound block. One block serves three people. Do not defrost the fish. Put the blocks in a heavy, well-buttered pan. Squeeze over them the juice of a lemon. Dot with butter and sprinkle with pepper and paprika.

Have the broiler very hot. Cook the fish without turning, three inches from the flame, until it starts to brown — about ten minutes. Turn and cook the other side until browned — five to seven minutes. Sprinkle the fish with minced parsley and pour juice from the pan over it. Surround with sprays of parsley and lemon cut in eighths. You may vary the seasonings sprinkled on the fish. Tarragon and basil are good additions to broiled haddock.

PLANKED FILLETS OF HADDOCK

Broil the fish on a stainless steel platter for about ten minutes. Turn it. Build a wall of mashed potato around it. Mark the wall with a fork and dot it with butter. Fill the space between the fish and potato with slices of tomato covered with buttered crumbs; mushroom caps, stem side up dotted with butter; and with slices of partly cooked bacon. Broil for five minutes. Decorate with parsley. Serve asparagus with Hollandaise Sauce* separately.

Flounder, halibut or mackerel may all be planked as described above. The first broiling time will vary slightly with the thickness of the fish and whether it is fresh or frozen.

MACKEREL IN MARINADE

Cook 12 fresh mackerel, cleaned and split, on a rack over boiling water in a covered roasting pan. Cook until a meat thermometer inserted into the fish reads 150°. This will take five to seven minutes, according to the size of the fish. Longer cooking only dries and toughens the fish. Remove the fish to a serving platter, and while still hot pour over it the following marinade:

- 6 *tablespoons olive or other salad oil*
- 2 *tablespoons tarragon vinegar made with white wine*
- 2 *tablespoons lemon juice and rind*
- 1 *small onion put through the garlic press*
- 1 *tablespoon piccalilli*
- ½ *teaspoon mixed herbs including basil, marjoram and dill seed*
- 2 *tablespoons cut chives*
- 2 *tablespoons minced parsley*
- 1 *teaspoon garlic powder*
- ½ *teaspoon each of dry mustard, sugar, paprika*

Pepper from the grinder

Chill the marinating fish for several hours. Serve surrounded by garden lettuce, and sliced tomatoes with Sour Cream Dressing.*

Haddock, halibut, and flounder are all good marinated and served the same way.

ROCK FISH

This is a delicious fish that makes its home in the waters around Portsmouth, Virginia. It is sometimes served to fortunate visitors. It may, as any other fish, be cooked in many ways but is at its best cooked in the following fashion.

Cook a thick slab on a rack over boiling water till a meat thermometer, inserted so it does not touch the backbone, registers 145° — about 12 minutes. Egg and Butter Sauce* seems its ideal companion.

In New England, rock fish is sometimes called bass. The change of name — or something else — makes it less succulent than its Virginian cousin. Still, when Jay or a friend brings a freshly caught bass into Appleyard Center, there is no harm in treating it like its aristocratic relative.

Mrs. Appleyard would frequently attend Pot Luck Suppers at the Community Club, as other descendents do now. She would sometimes take with her a dish, that gave her, until it was empty, a pleasant feeling of popularity. It contained:

SCALLOPED HADDOCK

(For 6)

- *2 one-pound blocks of frozen haddock*
- *¾ cup butter*
- *1 onion, finely minced*
- *¼ pound mushrooms, sliced vertically*
- *½ cup instant flour*
- *½ teaspoon white pepper*
- *¼ teaspoon nutmeg*
- *½ teaspoon paprika*
- *3 cups rich milk*
- *1 cup cream*
- *½ teaspoon minced parsley*
- *1 teaspoon thyme*
- *2 egg yolks*
- *½ cup homemade bread crumbs*
- *½ cup Cross cracker crumbs*
- *¼ cup Vermont cheese, grated*

Steam haddock for ten minutes. Flake it up not too fine. Melt half a cup of butter in a large saucepan. Sauté the onion and mushrooms in butter till onion is a pale straw color. Remove vegetables. Turn off the heat. Rub the flour sifted with pepper, nutmeg, and paprika into the butter in the pan. When mixture is smooth, work in milk, turn on the heat. Then add cream, parsley, thyme and cooked vegetables. About half a teaspoon of fresh thyme is best, but dried will do.

Cook the sauce over low heat until it just starts to bubble. Beat the egg yolks and slowly pour two tablespoons of the sauce into the egg yolks, beating constantly. Then stir this mixture into the sauce. Cook for one minute. Turn off heat while buttering a large enameled iron casserole.

Put in a layer of the sauce, then a layer of the cooked fish, and continue alternating layers finishing with a layer of sauce. Add the bread and cracker crumbs into which you have stirred the rest of the melted butter. Add a few more dots of butter if the crumbs seem too dry. Sprinkle grated cheese over all and bake at 375° for about 15 minutes or until the crumbs are well browned.

BAKED HADDOCK

You need a whole haddock for this, cut to bake — that is, cleaned and with head and tail removed.

- *1 five-pound haddock*
- *2 tablespoons melted butter*
- *½ teaspoon pepper*
- *1 teaspoon paprika*
- *¼ pound fat salt pork or beef suet*
- *6 slices bacon*
- *1 teaspoon minced parsley*
- *Watercress*

Stuffing:

- *¾ cup Cross cracker crumbs*
- *¾ cup homemade bread crumbs*
- *¼ teaspoon pepper*
- *1 teaspoon poultry seasoning*
- *½ teaspoon salt*
- *⅓ cup melted butter*
- *1 medium onion, finely minced*
- *1 egg, beaten*

Make the stuffing first. Roll crackers fine. Dry slices of bread and roll, crust and all, into the fine crumbs. Stir dry seasonings into the crumbs, then the melted butter, minced onion and beaten egg. The stuffing may seem rather dry, but it will absorb moisture from the fish.

Brush the fish inside and out with melted butter and sprinkle it with pepper and paprika. Put in the stuffing. There is no reason for sewing the fish closed, although cookbooks, possibly out of sadism, often advise sewing up fish prior to baking it. Of course, if you like to sew fish, go right ahead.

After having packed the stuffing in neatly, bake the fish on a stainless steel platter. It will not be moved again, so the stuffing, once in, will not fall out. Butter the platter lightly, lay the stuffed fish on it. Put salt pork or suet, cut in narrow strips, over the fish. Bake until the thermometer inserted into the thickest part, not touching any bones, registers 145°. The oven should be at 425°. The cooking should take about 40 minutes. Baste the fish occasionally with fat from the pan.

Cook bacon separately until almost done and garnish the fish with it during the last five minutes of cooking. Sprinkle it with minced parsley, and surround it with sprays of watercress.

I sometimes prefer the haddock with:

OYSTER STUFFING

½ cup Cross cracker crumbs
1 cup homemade bread crumbs
1 teaspoon mixed herbs
½ teaspoon paprika
½ teaspoon nutmeg
¼ cup butter, melted
1½ tablespoons chopped onion
½ cup celery chopped fine
1 cup frozen oysters, thawed
1 beaten egg
1½ tablespoon minced parsley

Roll out crackers into fine crumbs. Dry thin slices of bread at 200° and roll them out fine. Add dry seasonings. Melt the butter, toss onion and celery in it till onion is straw color. Add them to the crumb mixture. Cook oysters in their own juice until they start to boil. Skim out the oysters and add them to the stuffing. Cook juice down until there is only one tablespoon left. Add this to the stuffing. Add beaten egg and minced parsley. Stuff fish with the mixture and cook as directed above.

BAKED FISH WITH CHEESE SAUCE

(For 3)

This dish is simple to prepare and may be used with a variety of fish. Flounder or haddock take especially well to this rule.

1 pound fresh or frozen fish fillets
¼ cup cornmeal seasoned with paprika, salt and pepper
4 tablespoons butter
1 medium onion, sliced thin
*2 cups Cheese Sauce**
¼ cup dry white wine

Coat the fish with seasoned cornmeal. Sauté in butter, briefly, on both sides. Place fillets in a buttered casserole. Lay onion slices, sautéed in butter till straw color, over fish. Pour cheese sauce, mixed with wine, over all. Bake at 350° till fish just flakes but is not dry — about 20 minutes.

The results will be tender and quite tasty. A green salad goes well with it. Serve hot.

HALIBUT AND MUSHROOMS

(For 6)

2	*pounds halibut cut in fairly thick steaks*	¼	*teaspoon nutmeg*
¼	*cup butter*	½	*teaspoon onion powder*
½	*pound mushroom caps*	2	*tablespoons sherry*
2	*tablespoons instant flour*	1	*cup cream*
½	*teaspoon paprika*	12	*slices of bacon cooked as you like*

Sprays of parsley

Put the fish on a rack in a roaster over boiling water. Cover and steam it until thermometer shows an internal temperature of 140°.

Have ready a mushroom sauce made as follows: melt butter. Cook mushroom caps, sliced vertically, in the butter until tender but not mushy — about five minutes. Push them to one side of the pan. Work flour mixed with dry seasonings into the butter. Stir in sherry and cook for two minutes. Stir in cream. Do not let the sauce boil.

Now transfer the fish to a fireproof platter. Cover it with the sauce and set it into a 400° oven until the sauce just starts to bubble — about five minutes. Garnish the platter with cooked bacon and with sprays of parsley. Serve it very hot with toasted crumpets, or surrounded by scoops of rice.

FROGS' LEGS

Are frogs' legs fish — or are they meat? This has been a long standing controversy among those with nothing more substantial to controvert over. I do not intend to become involved. People who describe them often say they are "like chicken." Well, I admit, they are more like chicken than like roast beef, but actually they are like frogs' legs.

Another mistaken idea is that Mrs. Appleyard used to get them from her own goldfish pond. The thought is, of course, nonsense. Those frogs were her friends. In fact, I occasionally think I hear a note of melancholy in their croaks. Perhaps this comes from their missing the woman who would bend over the edge of the pond in order to rescue a goldfish caught in the forget-me-nots and gasping for breath, or to tickle a frog's head with a buttercup. She said that they loved it. At any rate, the frogs' legs she cooked or I cook are quite impersonal. I am not sure where they come from, but this is how I cook them:

2	*pounds frogs' legs*	½	*teaspoon pepper from the grinder*
½	*cup butter, melted*	1	*tablespoon minced parsley*
1	*tablespoon minced onion*	2	*egg yolks*
½	*cup white wine*	½	*cup cream*
1	*tablespoon lemon juice*	½	*cup blanched, slivered almonds*
	Grated rind of half a lemon		*Parsley sprigs*
1	*cup Chicken Stock**		
¼	*teaspoon nutmeg*		

Sauté the frogs' legs in melted butter for two minutes. Remove them and sauté onion in butter until onion is a pale straw color. Add white wine, lemon juice and rind, chicken stock and seasonings.

Return frogs' legs to the pan and simmer until the meat is tender. Put the frogs' legs on a hot fireproof platter.

Beat the egg yolks with a wire whisk until they are thick and lemon colored. Beat in the cream. Stir one tablespoon of the sauce into the egg and cream mixture. Stir in another. Stir egg mixture into the sauce and cook until it begins to bubble around the edges. Do not let it boil, but cook it over very low heat until it is thick — about two minutes. Pour it over the frogs' legs. Scatter slivered almonds over them. Wreathe the platter with parsley sprigs.

Serve Popovers* and a tossed salad of several kinds of garden lettuce. Perhaps you might like creamed potato with caviar with them instead, or asparagus with Lemon Butter.*

Mrs. Appleyard had an aversion to codfish. She would postpone the mention of it until necessary, as she didn't feel very fond of cod in any form except carved out of wood as a symbol of Boston. She was a vigorous Bostonian, but anxious not to have any form of codfish served with the mention of her name. Luckily for everyone, I suppose, she had already taken up the subject of fish hash, shad and of a salt codfish dinner, in the *Vermont Year Round Cookbook*. What else is there?

By chance there is an amazingly palatable manner of serving codfish if you have plenty of thick Vermont cream on hand.

CREAMED CODFISH

Freshen a pound of salt codfish by soaking it in cold water. Change the water several times. Do this at least two hours before you plan to serve it. When you cook it, start it in cold water, bring it to the boiling point and set it where it will keep hot but won't boil again. Meanwhile make a cream sauce of thick Vermont cream. You will need three cups of Cream Sauce* to a pound of fish. Season the sauce as you prefer, perhaps with one teaspoon of tarragon, salt, pepper and paprika.

Hard boil three eggs. Flake up the fish, discarding any tough pieces having the consistency of dried corn husks. Cut up the eggs and add them and the fish to the sauce. Serve baked potatoes or new potatoes with parsley butter with it.

FILLETS OF SOLE WITH BROCCOLI

(For 6)

2 bunches fresh broccoli
2 pounds sole fillets
*2 cups Bechamel Sauce**
¼ cup white wine
¾ cup grated cheddar cheese
Paprika

Cut the broccoli into long spears and steam until almost done. They should still be bright green in color and crisp. Fresh sole is best, but frozen may also be used. If you are using frozen fillets, thaw them before beginning this dish. Butter a shallow casserole. Wrap each fillet around one or two broccoli spears. Place them, with the seam down, in the casserole. Heat the already-made bechamel sauce in the top of a double boiler, stir in wine, and stir in grated cheese until it is melted. Pour the cheese sauce over the fillets. Sprinkle with paprika.

Bake in a 400° oven until the fish flakes with a fork and the sauce is bubbling and just beginning to brown — about 25 minutes. Serve hot.

This delicate flavor needs only a spinach and lettuce salad and Bran Muffins,* or new potatoes with parsley butter. Complete the meal with a Potpourri of Fruit in White Wine.*

CAGED LOBSTER

(For 6)

Winged lobsters (those flying over the mountains from Maine to Vermont) need cages.

Begin by making the cages out of unsliced homemade bread. They should be cubes three inches long, three inches wide and two inches high. A by-product will be a good many bread crumbs to be saved for bread pudding or a casserole.

Hollow out the cubes of bread, leaving a thickness of half an inch at the sides and bottom. Butter the cages inside and out with softened butter. Set them in a 350° oven for ten minutes or until they dry out and start to brown. Don't brown them too much — they are going back in the oven later.

Now make the filling. You may use Lobster Newburg,* creamed lobster, or lobster salad, whichever you prefer. Or use Lobster Sauce for Caged Lobster:

2 tablespoons butter
1 tablespoon instant flour
1 cup milk
1 cup cream
1 tablespoon white wine
1 teaspoon paprika
¼ teaspoon nutmeg
2 cups pre-cooked lobster meat cut up not too fine
3 egg yolks, beaten
6 lobster cages

Heat the butter, rub in the flour. Turn off heat and blend in milk and cream. Add wine. Bring sauce to the boil but do not boil. Simmer for three minutes. Add paprika, nutmeg and lobster meat. Beat egg yolks till thick, add one tablespoon of sauce to them, then another, and stir them into the mixture. Simmer until it thickens — about two minutes.

Fill the lobster cages. Spoon mayonnaise over the tops, set them on a fireproof pan and broil them fairly close to the heat. Watch them. One minute should be enough. The mayonnaise should bubble and just start to brown and puff.

You may extend your lobster filling by adding flaked, cooked haddock — a quarter cup of haddock to three-quarters cup of lobster. Sprinkle haddock well with paprika. Add strips of pimentos and a little juice from the pan and let the haddock stand for 20 minutes before adding it to the lobster mixture.

Variations: Make the cages the same way as for lobster but fill them with creamed crabmeat and mushrooms, with chicken salad, or with creamed chicken and mushrooms — in fact with whatever you like.

If you feel too languid to make the cages, you can hollow out hard dinner rolls, brush them with melted butter, and fill them. Mask the filling with mayonnaise and set the rolls briefly under the broiler. You will not need anything else to eat for quite a while.

The Lobster Sauce suggested above is a good one to serve with a ring of Fish Mousse.* It is also good served on toasted English Muffins* or simply on buttered toast.

RED SNAPPER ALMANDINE

(For 6)

This rule was first tried out when our neighborhood food cooperative very kindly offered cases of a variety of frozen fish from a Boston market. Jay and I greedily ordered a ten-pound box of Red Snapper fillets to share with a neighbor. Once we had tried it prepared this way, we found it irresistible and had it several times in succession. After we had taken a breather from it, I again remember it fondly. Snapper is a very delicate, tasty fish.

Begin with:

¼ cup flour
¼ cup cornmeal
1 teaspoon parpika
Salt and pepper to taste
2 pounds red snapper fillets
½ pound butter
3 tablespoons lemon juice
4 tablespoons slivered almonds sautéed in butter
Parsley sprigs

Mix the flour and cornmeal with paprika, salt and pepper. Dip the fillets lightly in the seasoned flour. Melt the butter in a heavy iron frying pan. Put fillets in pan and sauté over medium heat until a delicate brown. Squeeze lemon juice into the juices in the pan. Place the fillets in a lightly buttered fireproof casserole and pour the pan juices over them. Sprinkle with sautéed almonds and dust with paprika. Run the pan under the broiler for two minutes, or just until the almonds start to brown and the butter bubbles. Garnish with parsley sprigs and serve with baked potatoes and broccoli (the fish sauce makes a good sauce for the broccoli) or a symphony in green vegetables. And — beware — it is habit forming!

With this advice, I lay down my fishing tackle for the moment and go out to my Grandmother's pond to see how her goldfish are getting on. I saw Finfeather senior, Bianca d'oro, Rose Alba and Scarlet O'Hara. All seemed to be enjoying the fine hot morning. The swallows darting across the lupines to the pond, the Pekin lilac covered with ivory plumes and the great towers of white drifting clouds complete my contentment with the world in general and Appleyard Center in particular.

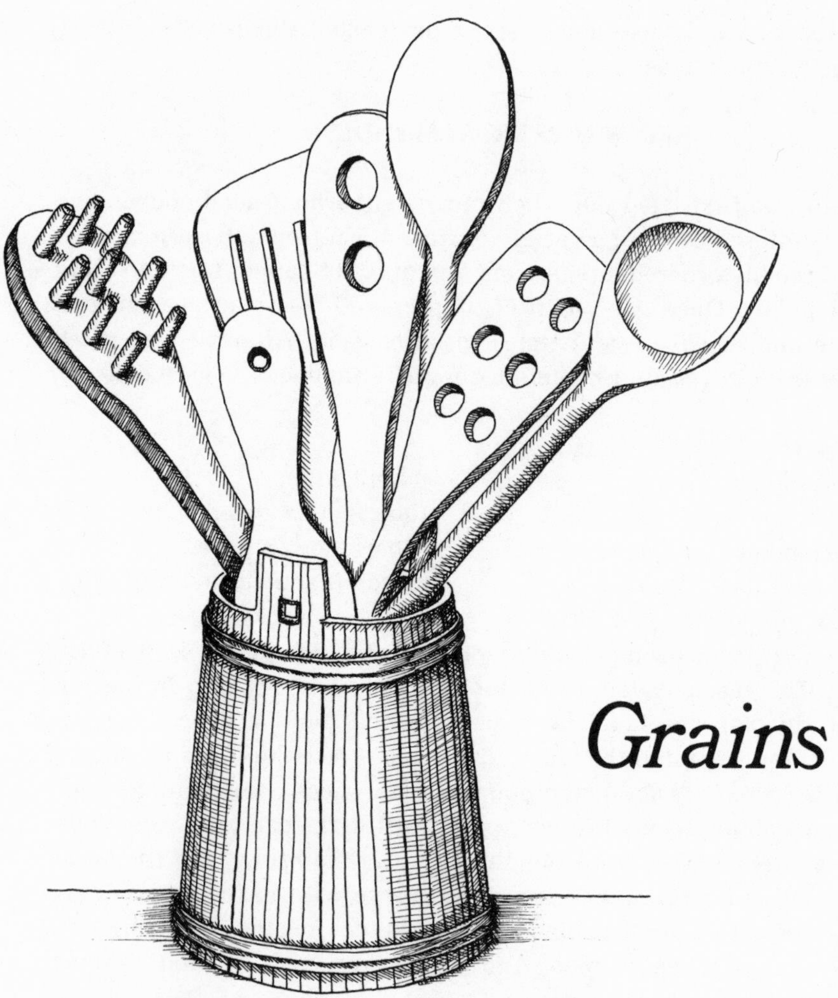

Grains

THE two major grains consumed throughout the world are wheat and rice. Generally speaking, those in the northern climes rely on wheat whereas those in the southern reaches depend largely on rice. This is a natural division due to the difference in climates and growing conditions.

For the most part, wheat is processed to one degree or another before being consumed in the form of wheat flour, processed cereals or as an additive to many other foods. Rice is generally eaten before it goes through processing. The two major kinds of rice consumed, white and brown, are actually the same seed. To make white rice, the hull of the brown rice is simply removed and the grain "polished." Unfortunately, in removing the outside covering, you are losing the main source of the food's nutrition, the B-complex vitamins contained in the hull. Those who eat white rice to the exclusion of brown rice must find other foods or vitamin supplements to fulfill their need for B vitamins.

Americans are fortunate in having a rapidly moving import system, therefore having access to rice and other grains not able to be grown in our part of the world.

In choosing grains to eat with your meals, please don't forget others equal or greater in food value than rice, such as millet, wheat berries, bulghur wheat, barley, oats or rye. Grains may frequently be used interchangeably for additional variety in your diet.

Since more than two-thirds of the world's population uses rice as a major part of their diet, let us start with the preparation of rice. There are two basic ways of cooking rice, or any grain for that matter. The first, the Chinese way, is to slowly stir rice into boiling salted water, taking care not to stop the water from boiling, and cooking it until tender. The second way, the Near Eastern manner, is to melt butter or oil in a pan with a tight cover, stir in the rice, getting every grain heated, then adding boiling water, covering the pan and simmering until the rice is tender. The purpose is to get the rice as hot as possible, without browning it, so that the water will continue to boil when introduced.

Use your own method and begin.

STEAMED WHITE RICE

(For 5 or 6)

Do not wash packaged rice as you lose some of the food value down the sink. If you buy rice in bulk, look it over for faulty grains and wash quickly in a collander, not letting rice stand in water.

2 cups boiling water
1 teaspoon salt
1 cup rice
1 teaspoon butter

Bring salted water to boil in a heavy saucepan. Slowly stir in rice so that the water never stops boiling. Reduce heat, cover and simmer until kernels are soft but not mushy when felt between thumb and forefinger — about 20 minutes. Do not lift the cover for 15 minutes since rice forms volcanoes in its cooking, and stirring or disturbing the grains will destroy the structural formation that keeps the grains separate.

Put rice into a colander, pour hot water quickly over it to remove excess starch created during cooking. Stir in butter and set the colander into a warm oven to fluff rice and to keep it warm until serving time.

STEAMED BROWN RICE

(For 5 or 6)

2 cups boiling water
1 teaspoon salt
1 cup brown rice

Follow the directions for cooking white rice above, except that brown rice needs to cook longer — 40 to 45 minutes or until tender. Do not remove cover for at least half an hour.

RISOTTO

(For 8)

1½ cups rice
*1½ cups Chicken Stock**
2 tablespoons butter
1 small diced onion
½ pound sliced mushroom caps
1 cup diced celery
2 tablespoons minced parsley
⅛ teaspoon ginger
¼ teaspoon nutmeg
½ teaspoon paprika

Lightly butter an iron frying pan in which risotto will be served. Put in rice and chicken stock and cook over medium heat, stirring occasion-

**See Index for pages where recipes can be found.*

ally, until rice has absorbed almost all the stock — half an hour for white rice, longer for brown. Test the rice. If it is not tender, add another ½ cup of stock and cook until it is absorbed. While rice is cooking, melt butter in another frying pan and sauté onion and celery for 3 minutes. Add mushroom caps. Cook 5 minutes, stirring occasionally. Vegetables should be slightly crisp, not mushy. Add minced parsley and seasonings. Stir mixture into rice. Rinse out pan with ¼ cup stock and add to rice. Keep rice warm until serving time. It will improve with standing. Reheat at serving time. Serve with ham, hot with Raisin Sauce,* or cold sliced.

STEAMED WILD RICE

Wild rice is not technically a rice at all, but a cereal grain. It is harvested by North American Indians only, thus raising the price far above that of other forms of rice. It is considered a luxury for that reason. It is especially good with poultry or game as it has quite a strong flavor.

2 cups boiling water | *1 teaspoon salt*
1 cup washed wild rice

Bring salted water to boil in top of a double boiler. Introduce rice slowly so as not to stop water from boiling. Cover and cook over hot water until tender yet firm — 1 to 1½ hours. Serve plain or with mushrooms, as in the recipe that follows:

WILD RICE WITH MUSHROOMS

(For 6)

1 cup wild rice
2 tablespoons butter
1 small chopped onion
½ pound sliced mushroom caps
2 pieces cooked crisp bacon

Cook wild rice. Slice mushroom caps and chop onion. Melt the butter in an iron frying pan, sauté onion 3 minutes, add mushrooms and sauté 5 minutes longer. Stir vegetables into warm, cooked rice. Spoon into serving dish and crumble bacon over top. Serve with Roast Duckling.*

BARLEY AND MUSHROOM CASSEROLE

(For 6)

1 finely minced onion
¼ cup butter
1 cup medium pearl barley
½ pound sliced mushrooms
*2 cups Chicken Stock**

Preheat oven to 350°. Sauté onion in butter over medium heat until straw colored. Add barley and cook, stirring, until it begins to turn golden. Add mushrooms and continue cooking and stirring until mushrooms wilt. Spoon the mixture into a buttered one-quart casserole and pour over it one cup stock. Cover and bake ½ hour at 350°. Uncover casserole and add remaining cup of stock. Cover and continue until barley is tender — about 30 minutes longer. Serve hot with steak in place of potatoes. For an added treat, lay thin slices of cheddar cheese over casserole in last few minutes of cooking.

Other grains are cooked in a manner similar to those described in the preceding pages. They may be made more interesting by the addition of herbs and spices during cooking, or vegetables previously sautéed and added in the last 5 minutes of cooking or cooked in with the grain with the addition of more liquid. Cooking grains in vegetable and other stocks also increases their flavor. Experiment.

BULGHUR WHEAT
(or Kasha)

2 tablespoons butter
1 cup bulghur wheat
1 teaspoon salt
2 cups boiling water

Melt the butter in a heavy pan with tight-fitting lid. Stir in bulghur and salt and stir until all grains have been heated. Pour boiling water over and stir to prevent from boiling over. Reduce heat and simmer until tender — about 20 minutes. Serve in place of rice, potatoes or other starchy food. Or add half a pound of mushrooms, a tablespoon minced onion, both sautéed in butter, and serve with roast venison.

Grandmother used to call this grain (actually parboiled cracked wheat) kasha, which is technically barley groats. She was very fond of serving kasha with a number of different menus, as well you might be once you've tasted it.

Contrary to the beliefs of many Americans, spaghetti was not invented in Italy but in China. And to prick another balloon, most pasta is not served with exceedingly rich tomato-based sauces, at least not in the north of Italy. Spaghetti is a regularly featured item on the menu, but it is most often served, before the main dinner is brought out, with sauces of subtle flavoring, combining primarily cream, eggs and cheese. There are many authentic Italian cooks in Vermont, descendents of the first granite workers who migrated to the "Granite Capital of the World," Barre, from Northern Italy. For that reason, Vermont seems to be filled with more than its share of good Italian restaurants. We're just lucky, I guess.

BASIC SPAGHETTI

Spaghetti is very simple to cook. Just boil salted water in a large kettle with 2 tablespoons of oil. Introduce spaghetti gradually into boiling water, making sure it is completely covered with water. Boil for about 10 minutes until tender but not mushy, al dente. One foolproof method of testing the doneness of spaghetti is to throw a single strand against the wall. If it sticks, it is done. You may not want to violate your walls in this way, but it works. Rinse spaghetti in warm water to remove any excess starch and serve with any sauce of your choice; clam, Taxi Driver's Tomato,* Mushroom* or Cheese Sauce.*

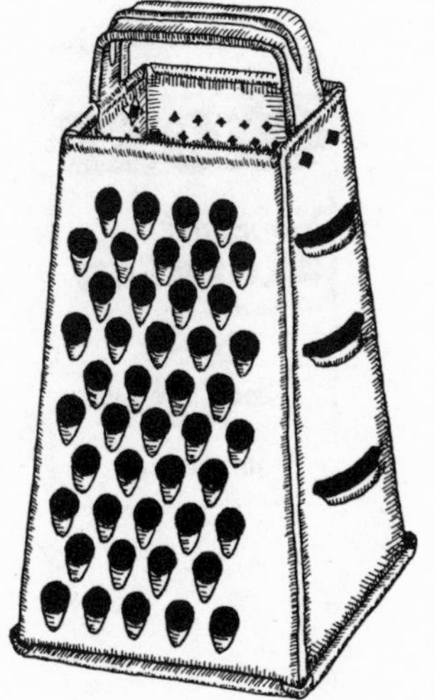

SPAGHETTI, EGGS AND CHEESE

Boil one pound of spaghetti for 10 minutes. Hard boil eggs and slice them. Place slices of large ripe tomatoes, dotted with butter, under broiler for a few minutes. Chop a large onion very fine, add it to two cups Cheese Sauce.*

Drain and rinse spaghetti. Put it on a fireproof platter. Lay tomatoes on spaghetti. Spread egg slices with deviled ham (2 jars) and put them between tomatoes. Cover the whole thing with cheese sauce. Sprinkle with paprika. Put under the broiler for one minute. Serve right away with a green salad and fresh fruit for dessert.

SPAGHETTI LOAF

¼ cup butter
1 cup soft bread crumbs
1 medium minced onion
1 cup light cream
2 tablespoons chopped green pepper
1 thinly sliced pimento
1 tablespoon finely chopped parsley
½ teaspoon finely chopped parsley
½ teaspoon finely chopped thyme
½ cup grated sharp cheddar cheese
3 eggs
½ cup cooked spaghetti
Salt to taste
*Mushroom Sauce**

Put butter, crumbs and seasonings in bowl. Scald cream and pour it over them. Mix well and stir in the cheese. Add well-beaten eggs and spaghetti. Put mixture in well-buttered loaf pan. Dot more butter over the top. Set in a pan of hot water and bake at 350° until firm, about 45 minutes. Turn out of pan, slice and serve with mushroom sauce.

SOUFFLÉD CROSS CRACKERS

The amounts for this side dish are nonspecific, it is simply the method that is worth noting.

Top (the puffier) halves of Cross crackers
Butter at room temperature
Water with ice cubes in it

You may use the bottom halves of the crackers, but Grandmother noted after making this for 20 plus years that the top halves puff more noticeably than do the bottom halves. Save the bottoms for making crumbs for casseroles, or toasting and eating. The amount of butter depends on how many crackers you use. Be generous with it. A quarter pound should be enough for 12 or more crackers.

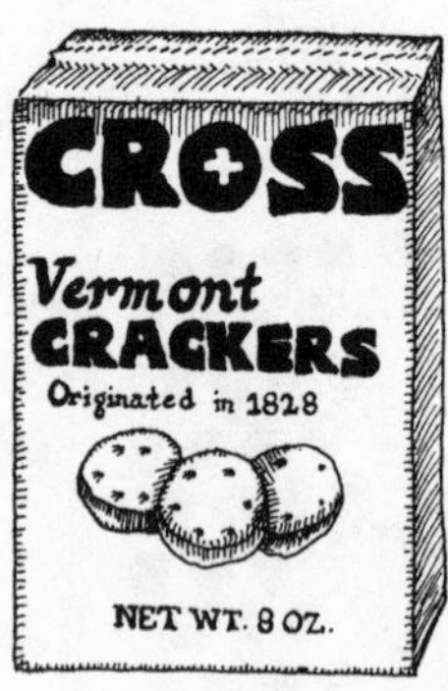

Put cold water and ice cubes into a large pottery bowl. As the ice melts, split crackers and drop top halves into the water, split side up. Light the oven to 450°. Watch crackers carefully. Have ready a cookie sheet with paper towels on it. At the end of 3 minutes, sooner if they seem to be softening too fast, remove crackers from water to the cookie sheet. Use a spatula or spoon with holes in it for this task. Set cookie sheet in refrigerator for 5 minutes.

Butter iron dripping pans or shallow casseroles and transfer crackers to the pans, working as quickly as possible. Dot them thickly with butter. Bake in preheated oven until they are puffed, crisp and golden brown. This will take at least 35 minutes, longer if you have more than one panful. Check at the end of half an hour, adding more butter if they look thirsty. Allow at least an hour for the whole process. If you try to hurry them you will end up with a panful of moist blotter paper. They should be as light and dry as a dandelion fluff ball. The sudden exposure of the soaked, chilled and buttered crackers to intense heat is the cause for the delightful results. Serve hot with just about anything, especially good with soups.

Herbs

GRANDMOTHER showed a lively interest in herbs. At one point she had almost learned to be fashionable and call them herbs with a roughly breathed "h." Her use of them was somewhat naive, however. As hard as she tried to be sophisticated about their use, she found herself constantly in need of well-informed advice. Luckily, her friend Alice Dobson had an herb garden. (She was the same friend whose marriage was saved by learning to make rhubarb pie from Mrs. Appleyard.) Alice generously shared both herbs and opinions with Grandmother.

I have no Alice Dobson with whom to experiment, but I do have limited access to the herb garden flourishing under the hands of the Appleyard Museum curate across the road. I'm allowed to snip unobtrusive samples all summer, but am given free reign on the small garden after the museum has closed for the season.

I realize that most people don't have ready entrée to their own private herb gardens, but everyone can obtain herbs from good stores and even grow a few plants inside on a window ledge. The smells and visions of the growing plants cheer up many a winter day. The combination of the above experiences has contributed to the following suggestions.

BASIL

Put some basil in French Dressing* for a salad that contains tomatoes. Add a leaf to tomato soup while it is heating but remove it before serving. Always bruise the leaf slightly before adding it. Add one or two bruised leaves to tomato juice cocktail while it is chilling. Remove leaves when serving. Add a few snips of basil to crumbs used on baked tomatoes and also in any tomato sauce.

Basil is a good ingredient for a tossed salad containing cucumbers. Sprinkle chopped basil over cucumber slices, or make sure to include it in a French Dressing* marinade to be used on cucumbers.

Sprinkle some dried basil in scrambled eggs while cooking. Use a bruised leaf or two in creamed eggs or sauces containing eggs. Soak some bruised leaves in lemon juice to be used on mackerel. Use a little in gravy for tongue and lamb. Also good in meat pies and stews. If making mayonnaise or cream sauce for shrimp, add a leaf of basil to either. Sprinkle dried, minced basil over Mushroom Vinaigrette* before serving.

BAY LEAVES

Boil one bay leaf in soups, stews or sauces, especially tomato sauce. Simmer a leaf in fish chowders. Add to meat pies. Always remove the leaf before serving.

CINNAMON

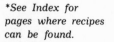

Use ground cinnamon to taste when making applesauce or other apple dishes, such as Brown Betty* or Apple Pan Dowdy.* Cinnamon sticks add a distinctive, sweet flavor to Hot Spiced Cider.* Use a cinnamon stick as a swizzler for hot chocolate. When making a chocolate parfait, heap homemade chocolate ice cream in a tall glass, top with whipped cream and over that scatter a teaspoonful of grated semi-sweet chocolate mixed with ⅛ teaspoon of cinnamon. When making Rice or Bread and Apple Pudding,* flavor the custard mixture with cinnamon.

CLOVES

The most familiar use of whole cloves is to mark off diamonds on a ham before baking it. Nothing tastes better than a real New England ham with this Oriental flavor.

Whole cloves are often recommended for meat gravies, but there is the problem of fishing them out again. Where "a few cloves" are suggested for gravy, I use a pinch, ⅛ of a teaspoon, of ground cloves. Tomato sauce, soup or juice also benefits by a pinch of cloves to a quart of liquid.

Ground cloves are also good in sweet, spicy pickles, spice cakes, cookies and other desserts, and in a mayonnaise dressing for cole slaw. Whole cloves add a touch of spiciness to hot wine or cider.

Another pleasant place to encounter cloves is in a pomander — an orange or an apple stuck thickly with whole cloves. I made one for my Grandmother years ago. She hung it in her closet and said she thought gratefully of the maker every time she opened the closet door. She made pomanders herself for Pomander Punch (*Vermont Year Round Cookbook*, page 15). They can be used for more than one batch of punch when kept in the refrigerator between times. Add a few fresh cloves and they are as good as new.

COFFEE

Perhaps you don't think of coffee as an herb, but I use it as one to intensify flavor, especially in the roasting of meat. A pinch of instant coffee in the flour you rub onto lamb, beef or turkey helps the skin to brown.

**See Index for pages where recipes can be found.*

I also use it mixed with the flour with which I thicken gravy. Brown gravy should be brown, not an anemic, grayish tan. Coffee helps both the color and the flavor as does caramelized sugar, a tablespoon to a quart of gravy.

Mrs. Appleyard found a can of baked beans rather uninteresting, and once made a sauce for them of:

½	*cup fizzy cider*	2	*teaspoons instant coffee*
¼	*cup sugar*		*Pinches of basil, thyme,*
1	*tablespoon molasses*		*marjoram and tarragon*

She pronounced it quite palatable.

COMFREY

Comfrey is a wonderful herb. It grows with leaves almost as long as your arm and bell-shaped flowers of lilac, pink or white. Comfrey, roughly speaking, is good for what ails you. Nicholas Culpepper, a skilled 17th century herbalist, spoke well of it, so Grandmother used it for several occasions. There was that time, for instance, when she decided that she had gout. Her daughter Cicely did not want to be left out, so she contracted the disease for several weeks. She even sent 25 cents for a pamphlet about this aristocratic disease. When Grandmother read it, she decided not to have gout after all. It seemed too much trouble. On Alice Dobson's advice, she made herself comfrey tea every afternoon.

Comfrey leaves do make good tea, and a few scrapes of comfrey leaf are a good addition to a tossed salad or a soup. The bellflower stalks look well in a bouquet of flowers. What more could be asked of an herb?

CUMIN

Cumin is a spice commonly found in Indian curries and savouries. It may also be used in Oriental or Mexican dishes, especially beans. I once was surprised to taste cumin in a batch of homemade granola cereal. The mother of the maker apologized profusely, but I actually enjoyed the different flavor it imparted. Cumin is an historical spice mentioned as far back as Isaiah's time and frequently in the work of Hippocrates. Experiment.

CURRY POWDER

Curry powder contains more spices than I know the names of — about 50 I think. Naturally, I use it when making Twelve Boy Curry,* but I also like it in other places. A pinch of curry powder in cream of pea soup for instance, plenty of it in Mrs. Appleyard's Chutney* and a little in dressing for Tossed Green Salad,* or combined with garlic powder to make Curried Bread.* It is also good in egg dishes and vegetable soups.

DILL

If you like dill, it is good used in many ways. If you don't like it, you're not likely to appreciate it in any form. The seeds are good in bread, especially rye bread. Make dill vinegar by soaking a tablespoon of dill seed in a cup of apple cider vinegar. Use the vinegar in salad dressing. Soak thin slices of green tomato in it and add them to a big bowl of tossed salad. Pour the vinegar over freshly cooked small beets thinly sliced. Use either dill seed or fresh dill weed in making dill pickles, especially dilled green beans.

Toss dill leaves in butter and lemon juice when you are making a sauce for lamb chops, breaded veal cutlets or for broiled fish. Ground dill weed is also good in many egg dishes.

FENNEL AND FENUGREEK

These are herbs cultivated for their aromatic seeds. Fennel is European and Fenugreek is Asiatic. The seeds are ground to powder and a little goes a long way in soup or salad dressing. They are also good in a marinade for broiled fish. They are most commonly seen in chutneys and curries, and fenugreek is one of the many ingredients in curry powder.

GARLIC

Is garlic an herb? Perhaps not in its raw state, but when it is dried and powdered, I regard it as one. Garlic is good with roast lamb. Combine ½ teaspoon of garlic powder with two tablespoons of flour and rub it all over a leg of lamb before putting the roast in the oven. Garlic powder is good also in salad dressings, sprinkled over vegetables while they are cooking and in sauces and soups.

When desired, whole garlic cloves may be used. They are excellent with cheese dishes. Split one clove and rub it on the inside of the pot to be used for preparing cheese fondue. To make garlic bread, slice a loaf of French Bread* almost all the way through in ½ inch slices. Melt ½ pound of butter in which one clove of minced garlic is sautéed. Brush each slice with the garlic butter, wrap loaf in aluminum foil and heat through in a moderate oven.

GINGER

Ginger is one of the oldest known Oriental spices. Fresh ginger root is sometimes hard to come by, but when available is well worth having.

Slice a few thin slices from a ginger root, sauté them in 3 tablespoons of peanut or vegetable oil and add partially cooked vegetables. Broccoli is particularly good. Continue cooking and stirring as you cook, making sure that the broccoli is exposed to the flavored oil on all its surfaces. Remove the ginger slices before serving. Fresh ginger is used in many Oriental poultry and fish dishes also.

Ground, ginger is a sweet spice used in spice cakes, gingerbread and ice cream. Gingerbread is sometimes served with slices of crystallized ginger and sour cream.

MARJORAM

Wild marjoram is really tame oregano, and is used in much the same manner. Good with lamb and mutton dishes, casseroles, soups and cooked green and yellow vegetables.

MINT

The classic use for mint is either in mint sauce for Roast Lamb* or in mint jelly to go with it. But mint goes well with different kinds of fruit also. Almost any fruit compote benefits by a touch of mint. It is especially delicious with fresh or canned pineapple.

In addition to its special excellence in Mint Tulip,* it is also good with other drinks, alcoholic or nonalcoholic. A bouquet of mint, not mashed but just gently crushed, blends well with white wine punch. A mint leaf or two is always welcome in a glass or pitcher of lemonade or iced tea.

A little mint is good in cream of pea soup, with Glazed Carrots* and in Chocolate Sauce* or Chocolate Mousse.* Dried mint leaves make an excellent tea for an uneasy stomach.

NUTMEG

Nutmeg is another of the sweet ground spices commonly used in sweet breads and cakes. It is also at home in cheese dishes such as fondue and Welsh Rabbit,* chicken dishes such as creamed chicken, or with mushrooms and chicken as in Coq au Vin.* Enjoy it in custards, Rice Pudding* and stewed fruit also. Sprinkled on Eggnog,* it adds the perfect touch.

OREGANO

Oregano is typically included in Italian and Spanish dishes, especially spaghetti and lasagna. A must for tomato sauces. See Marjoram for other uses.

PAPRIKA

Powdered Hungarian paprika is best but expensive. Use paprika in creamed meat and poultry dishes such as Real Chicken a la King.* Also good in egg dishes and salad dressings and as decoration and sparkle dusted over Stuffed Eggs,* creamed dishes and cream soups such as Pumpkin Soup.*

PARSLEY

Parsley is usually used as a garnish. Few people take advantage of its intrinsic flavor characteristics. It adds an ideal touch to cream or green soups, chowders, eggs and salad. Chop it finely and add it to creamed cottage cheese, or add it to melted butter for parsleyed potatoes.

Yes, as a garnish, it is perfect for meats, salads, fish and eggs.

ROSEMARY

Rosemary goes well in mixtures of herbs for stuffing fish or poultry. A pinch of it is good in a green soup, the kind Grandmother would make from whatever green things were in the garden at the moment. Cream of Spinach Soup* or pureed spinach both respond pleasantly to a little rosemary. A scissored leaf does no harm in a tossed salad.

SAGE

This word of many meanings is a favorite of mine, but the herb named sage is one to use with restraint. It is needed in stuffing for poultry, especially goose and duck. When making your own Sausage* it is, as the name implies, an absolute necessity, as it is in scrapple. It is also good in small amounts in scrambled eggs with cheese. However, it is easy to use too much. I enjoy the balance of sage and herbs in Bell's Poultry Seasoning and use it in most rules in which sage is called for.

SUMMER SAVORY

Savory is also an ingredient used in stuffings of various kinds. It is good in egg dishes when added "to taste." When I make an Omelette with Fines Herbes,* I include a little of it in the mixture of chives, parsley, thyme and rosemary that I gather as I go around the yard before lunch. In making a Spanish omelette with tomato sauce, I also include a variety of herbs — basil, summer savory, chives and parsley. I sometimes use a little when making buttered crumbs for the topping of a Scalloped Haddock* casserole and season other fish dishes lightly with it.

SESAME SEED

(Benne Seed)

Sesame seed is not exactly an herb, but it is used to enhance the flavor of a variety of foods. Generally, before using the seed, toast until golden brown in a 350° oven for 20 minutes or in a pan over low heat. Then use the seed as a garnish for casseroles, or fruit, vegetable, fish or chicken salads. Or brush bread and rolls with beaten egg and sprinkle generously with sesame seed before baking. Replace chopped nuts in rules for cakes and cookies with toasted seeds. Add some toasted seed to any breakfast cereal, especially granola. The toasted seed adds crunch, flavor and additional protein.

TARRAGON

Soak half a dozen leaves in white or red wine vinegar and use the vinegar in French Dressing.* A sauce to serve with broiled lamb chops made with tarragon was something enjoyed by Grandmother. She also thought it was good in the stock used in Aspic* jelly. It is good, too, with cheese and egg dishes such as Baked Cheese Pie.*

THYME

Thyme is one of those amiable flavors that fits in anywhere — stuffing, stew, soup and scalloped fish. Like sage it is also well-balanced in Bell's Poultry Seasoning.

VEGETABLES WITH HERBS

Green Beans with Garlic Croutons* are good with pinches of thyme, summer savory, parsley and rosemary

Broccoli is good served with a Mustard Sauce* to which thyme, basil, paprika and parsley have been added.

Glazed Carrots* — sprinkle them just before serving with basil, parsley, chives and comfrey.

Cauliflower is also good with the sauce described for broccoli.

Celery, Braised,* takes kindly to a mixture of parsley, marjoram, thyme and just a hint of sage.

Spinach, which is something like a green herb itself, is good with the addition of a little spice. To two cups of pureed spinach, add ¼ teaspoon of nutmeg, ⅛ teaspoon cinnamon and ½ teaspoon garlic powder.

I urge you to experiment with your own combinations of herbs and spices, to use a light hand with them and enjoy them in your own way, which may not be mine. A good many otherwise virtuous people know no seasonings but salt and pepper. Grandmother, who had not eaten any salt since 1948, said that "eating salt is largely an emotional habit and the careful use of herbs and spices is the best cure for the disease." People need some sodium in their diet, but unless you are doing hard physical labor in the hot sun you probably get all you need from natural sodium in meat, poultry, fish and cheese. There is even a good deal of sodium in certain vegetables, celery and beets for instance.

If you don't use salt for a week you might find at the end of seven days that for the first time in years you are tasting the actual flavor of vegetables and meat and fish — not just the salt, which was actually obscuring the flavor.

TO DRY HERBS

Herbs should be cut early in the season before the plants blossom and while the leaves are still young and tender. About 11 o'clock in the morning when the dew has gone from the grass, on a sunny day when a fresh breeze is blowing, cut the stalks and hang them for at least half an hour in a sunny, windy place. If you have an arched porch it will be just right for this. Afterwards, hang them in your dark shed-chamber or other dry out-of-the-way place, not too close together, and forget about them. When you remember them, they are usually dry. Take them down, crumble the leaves into glass jars and label them to be used in cold weather as a happy souvenir of summer.

POTPOURRI

Grandmother once planted what she thought was going to be a Silver Moon rose near Abdiel Appleyard's brick house. She thoughtfully supplied a trellis so that the rose's white and gold blossoms would show off nicely against the varied colors of the brick tapestry behind it. The rose bush, however, had a mind of its own. It decided to be a very fragrant prickly rugosa with large flowers of a slightly magenta coloring, which clashes with every shade of brick in the old wall.

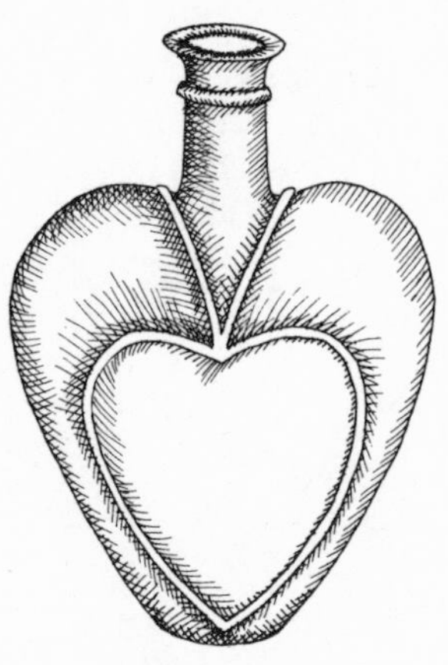

Grandmother, who liked people and plants with minds of their own, would grind her teeth only slightly over this color scheme and make potpourri out of the petals which keep their bright color even after they have dried.

To make potpourri, gather the roses in the middle of a clear, bright morning when the dew is off. If you have rose geraniums or lemon verbena, you may add their leaves, and the flowers of your spice pinks and a few syringea blossoms, carefully snipped off the stems. A few plumes of Pekin lilac may also be added. Be sure that you have at least four times as many rose petals as you do of the other flowers and leaves. Put the petals and leaves to dry in a warm place spread out on newspapers.

There should be about two quarts of dried petals. The other ingredients to stir in are:

½	*cup powdered rock salt*	1	*teaspoon oil of cloves*
½	*ounce powdered cloves*		*A few drops of oil of lemon*
½	*ounce whole cloves*	8	*drops oil of rose*
1	*ounce powdered orris root*	1	*teaspoon oil of cinnamon*
½	*ounce powdered cinnamon*	1	*teaspoon oil of lavender*
½	*ounce stick cinnamon, crushed*		*Thin peel of one orange, cut fine*
2	*ounces dried lavender*	¼	*pint brandy*

Many of the listed ingredients can be obtained from any good grocery store's spice shelf while others must be purchased from a pharmacy.

When the petals are thoroughly dry, sprinkle them lightly with salt. Let them stand for five days. Then stir in the dry spices and let stand covered for a day. Then add oil of cloves, cinnamon, lemon, lavender, rose, stirring well. The next day add orange peel and brandy. Transfer the whole mixture to a covered jar or jars and let stand in cool place for at least four weeks. Open the jars, take a long breath! Ah!

Potpourri was scattered among the sheets stored in the highboy the Appleyards dragged up from Massachusetts in 1797. You can treat your sheets likewise or keep a jar on your bureau and take the top off it occasionally. In fact, enjoy it any way you choose, as it will stay fragrant for years.

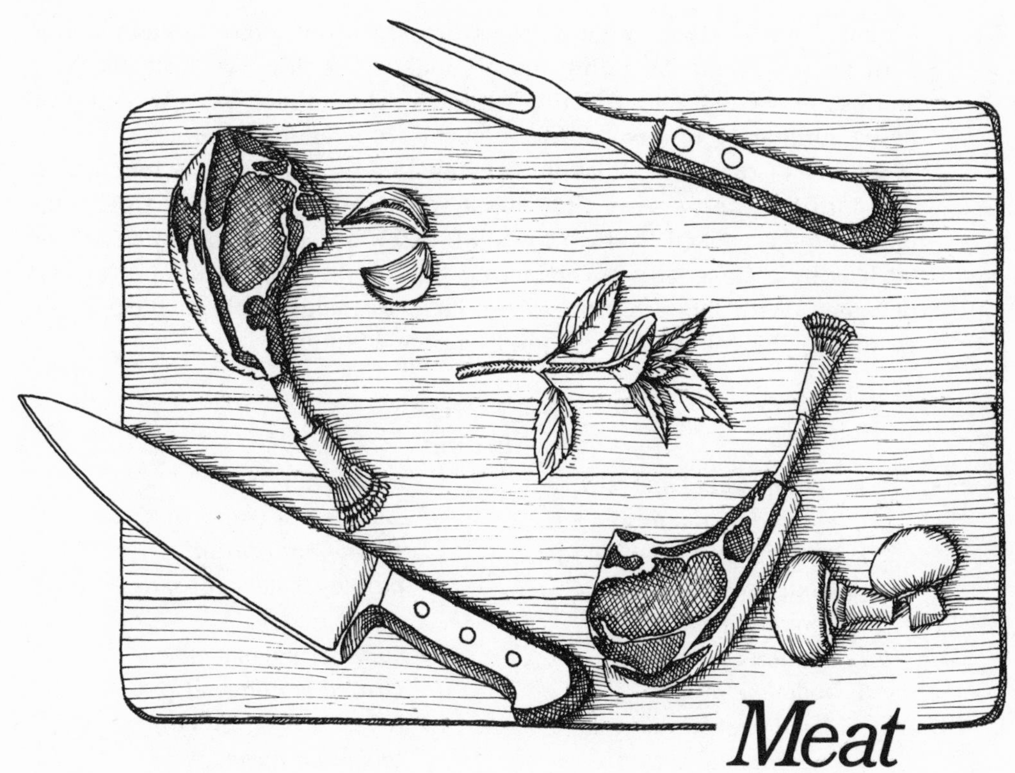

Meat

THE frequency of the use of meat has gone through many changes over the past several generations. Before days of refrigeration fresh meat was seldom served in winter. The pork was smoked or pickled in a salt brine and is still used this way in baked beans, in chowders and to lard lean meats. Some ingenious families, of course, discovered the deep freeze, namely the back buttery, as a place for hanging sides of beef for the long winter months, chiseling off portions as needed before the spring thaw. During the summer and autumn, small animals were freshly killed as needed, the farmer walking to his turkey coop on Thanksgiving day to "do in" a Thanksgiving gobbler.

With the dawn of refrigeration in homes, stores and methods of transport, a larger variety of meats has become available to a greater number of people at reasonable prices. This was the time during which Grandmother came upon most of her rules, and took for granted that others had the same access to meats that she did, and that the trend of availability would continue. However, during my lifetime, the prices have risen drastically and the availability of the choicer cuts has decreased. Therefore, the amount of meat regularly consumed by the normal family has declined. In addition, the scarcity of grain for the world population has made many people think twice about feeding beef animals the grain that could feed ten times as many humans as could the resulting meat. For many of the above reasons meat has become a special treat instead of a twice a day occurance. Therefore, I include a large number of different rules for those occasions, and a great choice for those who are able and interested in preparing meat frequently.

Since I am likely to mention the word *stock* quite often in connection with meat, I begin by telling how I make it. I think wistfully back to stories of my Great-Grandmother's kitchen where there was always a soup kettle simmering in a warm place on the iron range. Bones from a roast of beef or of turkey or chicken, vegetables, herbs and spices found their way into that kettle. Any time stock was needed she strained off some of the liquid, cooked it down for a while, chilled it and skimmed off the fat leaving a clear jelly never tasting like the last she made, but always delicious. With modern stoves, you have to make stock on purpose. In so doing, the following rule might prove helpful:

BEEF STOCK
(Brown)

3 pounds beef bones
1 pound veal bones
1 pound chicken wing tips and necks
½ pound ground beef
1 gallon cold water
5 whole cloves
½ inch stick cinnamon
1 carrot, sliced thinly
1 young turnip
3-4 radishes
1 large onion
Bouquet of stalks of: fresh thyme, marjoram, parsley, celery tops, tarragon and summer savory
Grated lemon rind
1 teaspoon instant coffee
¼ teaspoon nutmeg
1 tablespoon sugar, caramelized
2 bay leaves

Have beef bones sawed in short lengths. Put all the bones, skin, chicken wing tips and necks and ground beef in a large kettle. Add any other beef bones you may have, some from a roast, perhaps. Cover bones with cold water and set kettle over a simmering burner for three hours. Don't let the water boil.

Add to bones the cloves, cinnamon, carrot, turnip, radishes, onion and sliced odds and ends of vegetables you may have on hand, and water in which they were cooked. (You were supposed to have saved it, and have a jar of it in the refrigerator, remember?)

Add the bouquet of fresh herbs, tied together. If you have none of these herbs fresh, use dried herbs to taste. Add remaining ingredients and continue simmering.

When stock is cooked down to about two quarts of liquid, strain it off into quart jars. Chill. Remove the cake of fat from top. Eat the stock cold on hot days or hot on cold ones or use it for aspic jelly.

ASPIC

Aspic sounds mysterious but it is simply soup Stock* that is concentrated enough so it will jell.

Make the stock ahead of time and chill it. When it has jelled, remove every particle of fat from it. Keep it in a covered dish in the freezer until it is needed.

The best jellied stock for dishes containing veal is made from chicken and veal bones with gelatin added later. Don't make it with so-called

**See Index for pages where recipes can be found.*

bouillon cubes or with canned soup. Up until about 1940 canned consommé was made with beef. At present it contains so much MSG that it —and bouillon cubes — are simply an expensive way to buy salt. Add salt to your aspics according to taste and you will have much better seasoned jelly.

Jellied tomato juice or — for dishes containing beef — jellied beef stock also make satisfactory aspics. The jelly itself is not officially aspic — that is the term reserved for the finished product, the whole mold of meat or fish or vegetables shining on your best platter with decorations shining through the jelly.

Begin by melting jellied veal and chicken stock. Pour a little of it into a jelly mold, rinsed out with cold water. Tip it all around to coat the mold and chill it in the freezer till the coating thickens. In the meantime, make some much stiffer aspic with which you will coat your decorations.

JELLY FOR DECORATING ASPICS

2 ounces gelatin
1 tablespoon lemon juice
*5 cups strong, clear, well seasoned Stock**

Dissolve the gelatin in less water than the directions on the package call for. Let it stand and absorb the water. Heat the stock to the boiling point. Pour it over the gelatin, stirring well, till the gelatin dissolves. Add lemon juice. Set the mixture away in a cool place.

You can be as dramatic about arranging aspics as your artistic skill of hand and eye, time and strength permit. Being basically a lethargic type, I have seldom done anything more impressive than embedding a few hard boiled eggs and some salmon in a copper mold, shaped like a fish, in tomato aspic. Just getting it out again was such a dangerous and dizzying process that it takes my breath away as I mention it. However, great things can be done if you inherited a hat pin from your grandmother, have the genius of a sculptor, a steady hand and a melon-shaped mold.

When you plan your decorations, remember that if what you put into the mold is in very small pieces, you will need more jellied stock than you would if you were putting in large chunks of material. For instance, chicken and celery cut fine, as for salad, need more jellied stock around them than whole breasts of chicken or turkey. If pieces are small, a mold that holds six cups of water may need as much as five cups of stock. Have plenty of stock on hand. You'll always be able to find uses for it.

DECORATIONS FOR ASPIC

All right, you have your stock, your stiff jelly, your instructions and a hat pin. Grandmother's was topped with imitation jade. It rather resembled lime jello. Perhaps you have a fancy vegetable cutter, or just a sharp knife. Shape hard-boiled eggs into water lilies. Later you will dip them into the stiff jelly and put them facing outward into the chilled, coated mold. With the hat pin, pick up green peas, one at a time, dip them into the stiff jelly and arrange in a bunch like green grapes. Keep all these afterwards on a cold platter till you are ready to arrange your aspic. Radishes can become roses and tiny beets can be rosebuds. Parsley can look like ferns, watercress makes handsome foliage, carrots can be carved into flower shapes.

"What flowers did you have in mind?" I once skeptically asked of my Grandmother.

She attached a few bits of a beet and capers here and there to the slices of carrots and announced firmly: "Zinnias!"

Well, I'll concede at least they looked more like zinnias than they did gardenias. Everyone admitted that. So go right ahead, keep spearing asparagus tips and thin slices of cucumber and bits of pimentos or tiny oak leaves of lettuce.

The time has come to begin the assembly. Chill everything before you start to put your decoration in the mold. You must work quickly. Place flowers and ferns in their stiffened gelatin into the coated mold, facing outward. Fix another layer of almost thickened jelly over them to keep them in place. Deposit something handsome along the sides, water lilies perhaps, with ferns around them and bunches of grapes made out of peas. Then put in the main food — such as cubes of veal and tongue, arranged in layers with the jellied stock in between. When the meat is all in, pour in the jellied stock enough to fill the mold almost to the top. Set it in the refrigerator and chill at least two hours. If you have extra stiff jelly left over, score it into little cubes. You can now relax — briefly. The only problem now is to get the aspic out of the mold intact.

When the tense moment for unmolding arrives, you may be glad you have those little cubes on hand. Aspic sometimes melts too fast or sticks to the mold and those wounds can be concealed with spoonfuls of sparkling cubes.

Have your best silver platter ready, plenty of fresh sprays of parsley and watercress, oak leaf lettuce and slices of lemon. You also need Mayonnaise* or Green Mayonnaise.*

Set the mold into a pan of warm water. It should feel just warm to your fingertips — *not hot.* If you have any doubts, test the water with a thermometer before setting the mold into it. The mercury should not be above 97°. The water should come right up to the top of the mold. Hold your hands around the mold. Watch the jelly. In about a minute you will see it start to soften around the edges. Remove the mold from the water at once. Wipe the mold dry.

Put a platter over the mold and turn the whole thing upside down. (This dangerous exercise is enjoyed by those with a passion for excitement.) If the aspic does not leave the mold at once, you may wet a cloth with very hot water, wring it dry and lay it briefly on top of the mold. Have patience. Just when you think it's never coming out, it will — with a satisfying plop.

Lift off the mold and use the cubed jelly to repair any defects. Arrange the parsley, cress, lemon slices, oak leaf lettuce and spoonfuls of mayonnaise around it. Serve more mayonnaise separately. Set the platter in a cold place.

Let company come! When they look at the aspic they won't believe you made it. You probably won't either.

Before I leave you eating aspic, I will mention a few combinations that are pleasant to find in it.

1. Cubes of veal and fresh calf's tongue with truffles
2. Pieces of breast of chicken, boned and skinned, with cubes of Vermont ham and sliced stuffed olives
3. Thighs of chicken, boned, cooked with liquid smoke flavoring and cubes of calf's tongue
4. Fresh salmon with hard-boiled eggs
5. Shrimp and hard-boiled eggs with stuffed olives

Decorate all these molds with the jellied things described above — asparagus, peas like bunches of grapes, radish roses, "Zinnias," or whatever occurs to you, and enjoy the appearance as well as the taste.

Grandmother had some jellied brown stock on hand when she read a copy of *Godey's Lady's Book*, which she happened to find while straightening up a drawer full of this and that — for virtue is sometimes rewarded. This copy of *Godey's* showed fashionable ladies in crinoline, and it was printed before Mrs. Appleyard was born. I mention this because a polite young friend of Grandmother's, whose historical perspective was only slightly longer than her 17 years, had recently asked Grandmother what it was like when she wore hoop skirts and bustles. She seemed to think one wore both at once. She was disappointed when she heard that Mrs. Appleyard had never worn either except in a play.

At any rate, she had jellied stock on hand and she bought some bottom of the round for a pot roast, when she found the rule in *Godey's* for:

BEEF IN ASPIC

3 pounds bottom of the round | *1 tablespoon gelatin*
Butter | *2 cups jellied Stock**
1 tablespoon sherry

The bottom of the round should be tied up neatly for roasting. Brown roast all over in butter, then put it on a rack in a small roasting pan, covered tightly, set it in a preheated 250° oven and leave it alone for five hours.

During that time Grandmother worked on a miniature chest of drawers she was making, read some of *Persuasion*, picked a bouquet of calendulas and watched some crows through her new bird glasses — for cooking is exhausting work. She said that one of the crows was white. I don't quite believe this, but do trust that the beef was tender and delicious.

Grandmother's beef stock was jellied enough for cold soup and not quite enough for aspic. If yours is also, soak gelatin in a quarter-cup of stock, for five minutes, then heat stock with the sherry and dissolve the gelatin in it. Next, rinse out a melon-shaped mold with cold water and put in half a cup of stock. Set the mold in the refrigerator till the aspic is fully jelled. In the meantime, slice the beef diagonally across grain in slices about a quarter-inch thick. Lay these into the mold, pouring in stock from time to time, until it is full. Set mold in the freezer for five minutes, then refrigerate overnight.

Serve beef in aspic the next day on a large blue Canton platter. Surround it with oak leaf lettuce and bibb lettuce, sliced tomatoes, heaps of peas from the garden (cooked and chilled), garden cress and a few raw broccoli flowers. Serve it cut in thick slices, each composed of jelly and tender beef. The response will undoubtedly be gratifying.

BRAISED BEEF

	Beef suet, about ¼ pound	¼	*teaspoon cinnamon*
1	*large onion, chopped*	3	*pounds beef chuck cut in good-sized cubes*
1	*carrot, sliced*		
2	*stalks celery, cut fine*	2	*tablespoons parsley*
1	*cup sliced mushroom caps*	½	*teaspoon thyme*
½	*cup flour*	½	*teaspoon garlic powder*
½	*teaspoon nutmeg*	1	*bay leaf*
½	*teaspoon pepper*	2	*cups stock*
⅛	*teaspoon cloves*	1	*cup Zinfandel or other red wine*

Begin by cutting suet into small cubes. "Try them out" in a large frying pan over low heat till cracklings are golden brown. Remove them with a slotted spoon and set aside. Cook onion, carrot slices, celery and mushrooms in fat till onions are straw colored. Skim them out and set aside. Mix flour with nutmeg, pepper, cloves and cinnamon. Roll cubes of beef in flour and brown them in beef fat, putting them into a Dutch oven as they brown. Add mushrooms, celery, carrot, onion, parsley, thyme, garlic powder, and bay leaf. Pour beef stock and red wine over all. Simmer over low heat for two and a half hours, turning beef pieces over after one hour.

Half an hour before serving it, remove bay leaf and transfer beef and vegetables to a handsome casserole. Pour the gravy over them. Cover with:

2	*tablespoons butter*	¼	*cup Cross cracker crumbs*
¾	*cup homemade bread crumbs*	½	*cup dry cheese, grated*
			Beef cracklings

Melt the butter, toss bread and cracker crumbs in it. Scatter crumbs, grated cheese and beef cracklings over meat and gravy. Set casserole in the oven at 350° and bake until crumbs are well browned — about half an hour.

With the braised beef serve butternut squash, broiled tomatoes and a tossed salad of garden lettuce.

DRIED BEEF IN CREAM

½	*pound dried beef*		*Salt and pepper to taste*
2	*tablespoons butter*	2	*tablespoons sour cream*
3	*tablespoons instant flour*	1	*cup sweet cream*
½	*teaspoon paprika*	1	*cup rich milk*
		4	*hard-boiled eggs, sliced*

Freshen beef by pouring hot water over it, letting it stand for ten minutes and draining it. Make the sauce by putting butter in the pan over moderate heat and heating it until it melts and starts to froth. Remove pan from heat, rub in seasoned flour, return pan to heat and cook the roux for three minutes, stirring carefully. With the pan off the heat, add sour cream, sweet cream and milk. Now heat sauce until it starts to simmer, add the dried beef and sliced hard-boiled eggs. Cook until thick and creamy. There should be plenty of sauce. If it gets too thick, add a little more milk and cream.

Serve beef with new potatoes, boiled in their skins and then peeled and tossed in melted butter and minced parsley, or with baked potatoes in their skins or mashed potatoes. Grandmother once had it poured over well-browned French toast, at a friend's house. She reported that it was quite an experience; she herself served it with pancakes. Whatever vegetables are in season will go well with it.

BROILING BEEF

Never season beef — or any other meat — before broiling it. Salt and MSG both tend to toughen meat. Many people prefer their meat unseasoned, but those who do not may add seasoning to their own portions.

Use a meat thermometer if possible, carefully inserting it so as not to touch bone or fat. Never start to broil anything until you have figured as closely as possible when it is to be served.

Grandmother used to use the slow method of broiling, with the meat four inches from a very low flame and the oven door open. She believed that this was less nerve-wracking since it allowed some margin in case people arrived late. She was even known, on one occasion, to broil the meat on one side, remove the pan and keep it warm, not hot, in the oven, till she knew the guests would be ready at the right moment. The process may also be slowed down by putting the meat farther away from the flame.

If you like your beef rare, cook it to 145° on the thermometer. If you let it go above 155°, it might as well be baked.

FILET MIGNON

Remove filets from the refrigerator two hours prior to cooking time so they will be at room temperature. A good place to leave them is on the rack of a radiant electric broiler. Then all you need to do is turn the broiler on at the correct moment.

If you have more than one filet to cook, insert the thermometer into one of them and judge the rest by that one. The entire cooking time from the moment the broiler is turned on, till the thermometer registers 145° is approximately 12 minutes.

This includes searing the filets for two minutes on the first side, turning them, cooking them for two minutes on the other side, then broiling them for four minutes on the first side and three minutes on the second side again. The filets should be medium rare and the thermometer should register 145°.

If you like them quite rare, reduce the last part of the cooking time slightly and remove them from the heat when the thermometer is at 140°. Remember that both broiled and roasted meat continues to cook a little after it leaves the fire so serve it promptly. The guests must be at the table and the plates very hot.

I suggest the following vegetables to be served with the filets: large mushroom caps, also broiled, asparagus with Hollandaise Sauce* and

Inside-out Potatoes.* Celestial Pie* is an easy dessert because it is made the day before. Chocolate Sauce* goes well with the pie. Eat heartily!

PORTERHOUSE STEAK — PLANKED

Grandmother was fortunate enough to have owned an oak plank with a well and tree cut into it. It was big enough to hold a steak of noble proportions, a wall of mashed potatoes and a ring of vegetables. It rested on a platter of stainless steel. I think the plank isn't necessary. The various items may be cooked separately and arranged comfortably on any heat-proof platter still leaving room for the steak.

However it is served, it is still steak, and should be treated with the respect that its origins deserve. Mrs. Appleyard did not respect any steak less than two inches thick, and it had to be a Porterhouse with a really good slab of tenderloin on one side of the T-bone. There are different tastes in steak. If you like yours well browned outside, tender juicy with reddish pink inside, directions for achieving that happy state follow. Grandmother cooked not only by smell and sight, but also by ear. A steak sounds done. There is a certain vibrant, purposeful hiss and fizz from a steak that is ready to eat. Listen for it and train your ear to it.

To keep the juice inside the steak, instead of letting it run out and dry up, begin by searing the steak on both sides. The searing time depends on the size of the steak — that is the whole surface area, thickness and the steak's beginning temperature. For a large steak, weighing close to three pounds, starting out cool but not cold, allow two minutes on each side close to the flame of the electric broiler. If your broiler is gas, it must be turned low while the searing is going on. By the time it is seared on both sides, you should know by sight, smell, sound and how hot your cheek feels, how long the rest of the cooking will take.

In figuring when the steak will be ready to serve, include the time spent turning it. A clock with a moving second hand is a great help. Luckily Mrs. Appleyard had one left over from her career as an itinerant photographer.

The schedule for a 2¾-pound steak will run about like this:

Close to the flame: searing

- Side A: 2 minutes
- Turning: 1 minute
- Side B: 2 minutes
- Turning: 1 minute

Slightly further from the flame: for further cooking

- Side A: 5 minutes
- Turning: 1 minute
- Side B: 4 minutes
- Transfer to platter and garnishing: 2 minutes
- Total time: 18 minutes

Please note that side B will always receive a little less cooking time than side A. That is because it actually received some cooking from the heated broiler while side A faced the flame. If you expose side B as long as side A, your steak will be overcooked. If you listen to it while it cooks you will hear that this is so, as well as taste it later.

The schedule above is for any steak. For one to be served on a plank or a stainless steel well and tree platter, the principle is the same up to the second cooking of side B.

At this point, transfer the steak to the plank with side B uppermost. The plank should be rubbed well with salad oil. Quickly heap fluffy mashed potatoes around the edge. Between the potatoes and the steak, arrange mushroom caps dotted with butter, sliced tomatoes already partly cooked and covered with bread crumbs, little heaps of partly fried onion. This arranging will probably take five minutes, and as the steak will lose a little cooking momentum, you will have to give it five minutes under the broiler, instead of four minutes for a plain steak. This will make a five minute difference in the total time, making it 23 minutes instead of 18.

However, since no two steaks are exactly alike, this is merely a slightly more definitive guide than any Mrs. Appleyard has given before. A meat thermometer helps, but the best thing is to be able to train your ear to know when — by the hissing and spitting — the steak is done as *you* like it. Be sure that each side gets two turns at the flame. Perhaps you might even like it as I do with curly parsley around it.

ROAST BEEF

Mrs. Appleyard used to cook roast beef by the slow method. She would allow 25 minutes a pound and leave it cooking peacefully in a 250° oven while she did a certain number of other things — perhaps a dash of crewel embroidery or some reading, writing or arithmetic. These activities would take about three hours, at which time she would put the roast on a well and tree platter, turn the oven to 450° and make Yorkshire Pudding* in the pan in which the roast was cooked. After ten minutes, she would turn the oven down to 350°. During the last 15 minutes, before serving the beef and pudding, she would put the beef back into the oven to brown a little more.

You will probably not get into much trouble if you follow this method, but I feel it's my duty to tell you that the best roast of beef I ever cooked was done quite differently. It was a magnificent sirloin of beef weighing a little over 15 pounds. It had been kept at room temperature for several hours before the cooking started.

Begin by inserting a meat thermometer so that it touches neither fat nor bone. Then put beef into a 450° oven for half an hour. During the next two and a half hours baste it every 15 minutes and reduce the heat of the oven gradually every half hour: 400° — 350° — 325° — 200°. The meat thermometer should register 140° after approximately the first three hours of cooking. Times will vary with the cut, weight, etc.

Be sure you know exactly what the roast weighs.

For roasts with the bone in allow:

For rare: 13-15 minutes to the pound
For well done: 18-20 minutes to the pound

For roasts without bones, allow:

For rare: 15-18 minutes to the pound
For well done: 20-22 minutes to the pound.

I like, for basting, some hot broth made by simmering trimmings from the roast (the butcher will give them to you) with a carrot, onion, branch of celery, a few herbs, pinches of nutmeg and cinnamon. Stock* is also excellent for basting. If you make pan gravy to go with the meat, it will be especially good if the roast has been basted with stock. Make sure that the roast is basted with some kind of hot liquid for the first few bastings, hot water will also suffice. When fat begins to run into the pan from the roast, it will no longer be necessary to add more liquid until you make the gravy. When you do, use more hot stock.

Remember that the meat, especially if there are bones in it acting as heat conductors, will go on cooking inside after it leaves the oven. If your guests are late, cover it, let it stand till you are ready to serve it, then return it briefly to the oven.

Remove the beef to a stainless steel or other heat-proof platter and begin making Yorkshire pudding in the roasting pan. Half an hour before serving time, put the beef back in the oven to finish browning. It should come out just right. I found that I had noted in my notebook that mine had miraculously come out "perfectly" (an immodest term).

Part of this miracle was a good carver, a surgeon with a strong wrist, who was present. I supplied him with a well-sharpened carving knife. Even a well-cooked roast loses its personality if it is mauled by a well-intentioned person with a dull knife. With the roast I served Green Beans with Mushrooms* and broiled butternut squash. The dessert was simple, a Deep-Dish Apple Pie* with cheddar cheese. The guests appeared reasonably well-nourished. Another excellent accompaniment to roast beef is:

ROAST POTATOES AROUND THE MEAT

In a steamer cook potatoes in their skins for 20 minutes. Run cold water over them. Peel them. Cut them in halves. Melt some beef fat — from the jar you should have in the refrigerator — or some butter in a frying pan. Turn the potatoes over in this until they are buttery all over. Put them into the pan with the beef. Baste them when you baste the beef. Turn them occasionally so they will brown evenly. This takes 30-40 minutes, depending on the size. They should be crisp and brown outside and fluffy inside.

The next day I went on a trip to visit friends and took the rest of the roast beef with me, thus guaranteeing an enthusiastic welcome. It was excellent cold and before I left, I made:

ROAST BEEF HASH

Hash must always begin with the eating of a hot roast beef done to a delectable state of rareness. If you are fortunate enough to have meat left over, you have the makings of one of the most satisfying, delicious traditional meals. It is hard to prescribe exact measurements to the making of a truly good hash, as the amounts always vary with the available ingredients and individual tastes.

Begin by cutting the meat off the bone, in rather large chunks. Then put the meat and bones into the biggest kettle you have, add a large onion, quartered, and cover it all with cold water. Simmer this combination gently until most of the water has cooked away — about three hours.

If you are one to add salt to your meat, do so only during the last few minutes of cooking. If added earlier, it will toughen the meat.

When most of the water is cooked away, remove bones. Cook remaining broth until there is only about half a cup left. Pick over meat carefully. Remove gristle and large pieces of fat. At this point the meat should be tender enough to fall apart.

Next, cut fat into cubes and try them out in an iron frying pan. If you were prudent enough to have saved the juice that ran down from the roast, you may now put it to good use. It will consist of some garnet colored jelly with cream colored fat on top. Add jelly to the broth and the fat to the frying pan.

When cracklings are golden brown, skim them out and set aside. Leave the iron frying pan in a warm place while you cook some new potatoes in their skins. Cook enough potatoes to make about three cupfuls. While they are cooking, chop meat and large onion in a large wooden bowl. Don't chop too finely.

As soon as potatoes are done, remove skins and chop them in with the meat. They should be chopped rather coarsely. A good proportion for a large pan is two cups of meat to three of chopped potatoes. Add the combination of broth and gravy to this mixture. They should have been cooked down to about half a cup.

Now comes the cooking of the hash in its final form. Heat the fat in a frying pan. There must be plenty of it — enough to cover the pan about a quarter-inch deep. If there isn't enough fat add some butter. (This is not for calorie counters.) Put hash into the pan and mix well for a minute over a hot flame. Reduce the heat and put a flame tamer or flat metal toaster over low flame to keep hash from burning. Let hash cook for twenty minutes in this manner. Watch it ever so carefully. It is done all underneath when brown begins to show around the edges. It is then ready to serve.

Serving is in itself a feat requiring great dexterity. In theory, one should be able to loosen the hash all around with a spatula and take it out in one piece. The theory is a good one, but practice doesn't prove it out. Grandmother recommended the following method. Make a cut through hash — but not through the crust — across the middle of the pan at right angles to the handle. Rest pan on a hot platter. With a pancake turner, fold the half of the hash closest to the handle over the other half, as you would an omelette, then tease the whole thing out onto the platter. It should be a glazed beautiful brown, like an old cherry table. Scatter cracklings over it, wreathe it with parsley and serve. What better way to warm the souls and stomachs of those you love. But be careful not to warm them too quickly after removing hash from the pan, as burned tongues tend to deaden the compliments.

Another method of utilizing cold roast beef in an appetizing way is to serve slices of it with roast beef gravy with mushrooms.

Or, if you did not have Yorkshire Pudding* with the hot roast, you can make it to go with the cold beef. It takes about 50 minutes.

POT ROAST

Pot roast, I believe, is invariably better the second day. So I always begin its cooking on the first day — if you understand what I mean. The preparation takes two days.

On the first day use:

- *6 pounds beef chuck, bones and fat removed*
- *2 onions, sliced*
- *½ cup instant flour*
- *½ teaspoon pepper from the grinder*
- *½ teaspoon ginger*
- *1 teaspoon paprika*
- *Pinches of cloves and cinnamon*
- *1 teaspoon Bell's Poultry Seasoning*
- *1 teaspoon garlic powder*
- *3-4 tablespoons fat — butter or oil or tried-out beef fat*
- *2 cups burgundy or other red wine*
- *4 ounces tomato sauce*
- *1 bay leaf*
- *1 teaspoon instant coffee*
- *1 tablespoon sugar, caramelized*
- *1 carrot, sliced*
- *1 stalk celery, cut fine*
- *Celery tops*

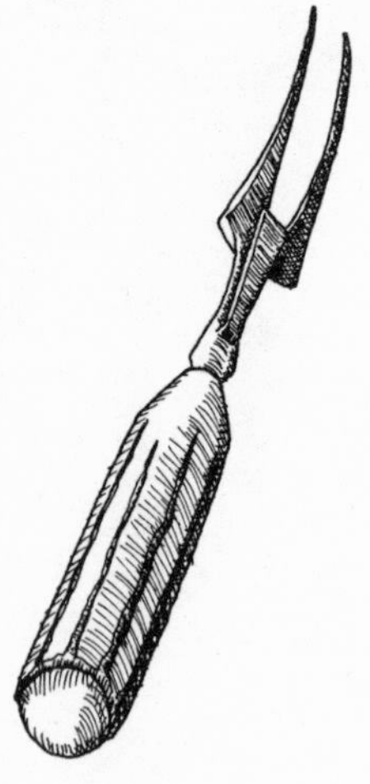

Keep bones and fat trimmed from the roast. Cut fat into small cubes and try them out in a frying pan large enough to brown the meat in. When they are golden brown, skim them out and set aside. Cook onion slices in pan till straw colored. Remove them and set aside. In a large, strong paper bag, put flour and dry seasonings, sifted together. Put roast into bag and move it around, patting all the flour into it. Put at least a quarter of an inch of fat in the pan. Add butter or oil if needed. Put roast in the frying pan and brown on all sides, turning it carefully with a pancake turner. When well browned, put it into a large Dutch oven or other fireproof cooking dish. Set it over a low flame on a flame tamer. Pour fat from pan into the cooking dish. Add bones and trimmings and pour hot, not boiling, water over it. Add wine, tomato sauce, bay leaf, cooked onions, coffee, caramelized sugar, carrot, celery and celery tops. Cover cooking dish and simmer till tender, four to five hours, turning roast after two hours. Remove meat to another dish. Pour a little gravy over it to keep it from drying out. Chill the rest of the gravy in the refrigerator.

Second day:

- *6 young carrots, sliced*
- *4 large onions, sliced*
- *1 cup celery, cut fine*
- *¼ cup young white turnips, diced*
- *6 small radishes*
- *2 cups young peas*

Start by removing fat that has hardened on the chilled gravy. Bring two quarts of water to a boil. Add all the vegetables except peas, and cook for 40 minutes. The radishes will not be recognized as such. They taste rather like delicate spicy turnips.

Put beef back into Dutch oven. Pour skimmed gravy over it, add cooked vegetables and cooking water. Cover, and simmer slowly — use a flame tamer — until meat is very tender — about one hour.

Cook peas in very little rapidly boiling water until they are done and water is all cooked away — about five minutes. After this dish has been given two days of a cook's loving care, it is surely worthy of your best platter, and the family's finest humor at serving time.

If the gravy needs last minute thickening, use an old friend, instant flour, and cook it in gravy for about three minutes. When all is ready, put beef on a warmed platter, the vegetables around the edges of roast, with peas on the outside. Remember to remove bay leaf. Scatter yesterday's cracklings over all, pour most of the gravy over meat and put the remainder in a gravy boat for second helpings.

Serve mashed potatoes with the roast, and whichever green vegetable is in season — Asparagus Country Style,* Green Beans with Garlic Croutons* or Beet Greens and Young Beets* cooked together.

BEEF CHOWDER — APPLEYARD

¼	*pound beef suet, diced*	4	*cups Beef Stock**
2	*large onions, sliced thin*	1	*tablespoon lemon juice*
3	*carrots, sliced*	1	*teaspoon instant coffee*
½	*teaspoon cinnamon*	2	*tablespoons sugar, caramelized*
¼	*teaspoon nutmeg*		

½ *teaspoon mixed herbs*

Dice beef suet and try it out in a frying pan over medium heat. Skim out cracklings and set aside. Spoon out three tablespoons of fat and set it aside. Add sliced onion and sauté until straw colored. Add carrots and sauté for two minutes. Add cinnamon, nutmeg, herbs, beef stock, lemon juice, instant coffee and caramelized sugar. Rinse out the pan in which you caramelized the sugar with a little stock. Cook the mixture over low heat until carrots are soft but not mushy — about half an hour.

While mixture is cooking, make meat balls:

1	*cup homemade bread crumbs*	1	*egg, lightly beaten*
½	*cup milk*	¼	*teaspoon garlic powder*
½	*pound Vermont sausage*	3	*tablespoons flour*
1½	*pounds ground chuck*	3	*tablespoons beef fat, from frying pan*
1	*small onion, minced*	2	*tablespoons minced parsley*
2	*tablespoons butter*		

Mrs. Appleyard used sausage that was made locally of excellent materials. It was finely ground and lightly seasoned.

Soak bread crumbs in milk for five minutes and squeeze them dry. Mix sausage and ground beef together well. Sauté onion in butter till transparent and yellow. Add egg, soaked crumbs, garlic powder and onion to the meat mixture. Mix well. Form mixture into small balls, pressing them firmly together. Put meatballs into a paper bag with flour. Shake the bag gently until balls are all well coated with flour. In the pan in which onion was sautéed, put tried-out beef fat. Put some of the meatballs into the pan and brown them on all sides over low heat. Remove them and repeat cooking until all balls are browned. Add butter if more fat is needed.

The vegetables should be done by now. Add meatballs to the vegetable mixture and simmer for five minutes. The chowder should now stand at least an hour, barely simmering. A flame tamer proves helpful. At serving time, if gravy does not seem thick enough, add two tablespoons of instant flour. Stir it in well, let mixture simmer for three minutes. Bring it to a boil and serve chowder in a hot soup tureen, very hot. Scatter diced cracklings and parsley over the chowder.

This is the basic rule for making chowder. It may be varied a great deal according to the materials at hand and individual preference. Part of the stock may be replaced with tomato juice. To the liquid in the kettle you may add mushroom caps sautéed in butter and a broth made from the stems and caps. Or add celery, cut fine, or a few small radishes, to the carrots while they are being sautéed. Occasionally, add dumplings for a change of taste and texture.

I sometimes make the meatballs to serve as hors d'oeuvres. Make them very small, brown them in salad oil or butter, and serve them, impaled on toothpicks, either plain or wrapped in partly cooked bacon and broiled on both sides, just enough to crisp the bacon.

GOULASH

Mrs. Appleyard called her beef chowder goulash, when she added tomato juice, sautéed tomatoes and sherry to it. She would vary the seasoning by adding pinches of allspice, cayenne and a teaspoon of paprika to the sauce. This version is a welcome change from the typical seasonings, and no more difficult to prepare.

BEEF STEW

(For 6)

- *5 pounds beef chuck, cut in one inch cubes*
- *½ pound beef suet (optional)*
- *2 cups jellied Beef Stock**
- *½ cup flour*
- *½ teaspoon oregano*
- *¼ teaspoon cinnamon*
- *½ teaspoon garlic powder*
- *½ teaspoon thyme*
- *½ teaspoon nutmeg*
- *¼ teaspoon cloves*
- *1 large onion, chopped*
- *6 new potatoes, cubed*
- *6 young carrots*
- *12 small white onions*
- *12 radishes*
- *1 cup peas*
- *2 tablespoons minced parsley*

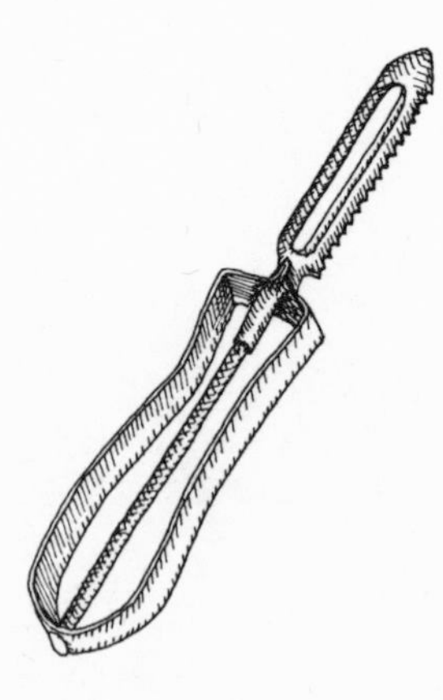

Grandmother was in the habit of making what she would immodestly call "Perfect Beef Stew." In recent years she admired it more than usual because she would make it from native Vermont beef which tastes of Vermont grass, clover and corn. "It is important," she would say, "that native beef — or any beef for that matter — should be hung long enough to ripen well before it is cut up." Your butcher might still give you good advice: follow it.

If your beef has little fat, buy half a pound of beef suet, cut it into small cubes and try it out. Drain cracklings, delicately browned, through a paper towel. Save them and the fat separately. This should be done, along with the making of the stock if needed, the day before you plan to make the stew.

The next morning, sift flour and seasonings into a paper bag. Add beef cubes and shake until they are well coated with seasoned flour. Melt beef fat in a large skillet and lightly brown chopped onion in it. Add floured meat and brown it on all sides, removing it to an electric skillet or other pan in which the stew will be served. Heat stock to the simmering point, and pour it over browned meat. Simmer on low, or at 200°, for two hours.

After one and a half hours, put one cup boiling water into a saucepan large enough to hold potatoes, carrots, small onions, radishes, and peas. Add all but peas and cook until vegetables are tender but not mushy — about 25 minutes. Let most of the water cook away. Watch it, and add more water if needed. Add peas. Cover the pan and cook until peas are tender — about 6-8 minutes.

Stir all vegetables and the water in which they were cooked into the stew. Simmer for five minutes, until all flavors have had a chance to blend. Taste it, and correct seasonings to taste. If the gravy seems too thin, add a little instant flour. If you intend to add salt, add it now, never when the meat is cooking. Your judgment about quantity will be better than mine, as I use no salt.

Scatter the stew with the cracklings and minced parsley. You may like to serve piping hot Popovers* with it.

BEEF PIE

- 5 *tablespoons instant flour*
- ¼ *teaspoon nutmeg*
- 1 *teaspoon Bell's Poultry Seasoning*
- ½ *teaspoon black pepper*
- ¼ *teaspoon cinnamon*
- 2 *pounds round steak cut in 1½ inch cubes*
- 5 *tablespoons butter*
- 6 *tablespoons chopped onions*
- 4 *cups tomato juice*
- 1¾ *cups Beef Stock**
- 2 *cups chopped carrots*
- 1 *cup green beans*
- 12 *small radishes*
- 1 *teaspoon sugar*
- 1 *teaspoon instant coffee*
- 1 *10-ounce package tiny frozen peas*
- *Baking Powder Biscuits* for topping*

Put flour and dry seasonings in a strong paper bag and shake cubes of steak in the bag until they are well coated. Melt butter in a frying pan. Cook chopped onion in butter till the onion is straw colored. Skim out onion. Set it aside, brown meat cubes in butter, turning them so they will brown on all sides. Cover meat with two cups tomato juice and three-quarters of a cup beef stock, return onion to pan and set it into a 250° oven. Cook covered until the meat is tender — about three hours.

During the last hour prepare carrots, beans and radishes and cook them in one cup of beef stock and two cups of tomato juice. Add sugar and coffee to the liquid and add the whole mixture to the simmering beef. Now transfer contents of pan to a big iron enamel or other fireproof casserole. Set it on top of stove and make your biscuit dough.
Set it on top of stove and make your biscuit dough.

Turn the oven up to 400°. Return casserole to oven. When the gravy in the casserole bubbles hard, thicken it, if necessary, with the seasoned flour left in the bag. Drop in frozen peas and stir them into gravy. Return to oven. When it bubbles hard again, take pieces of dough, half biscuit sized, and drop them all over the top of the casserole. Then set casserole, uncovered, into the oven and bake until the biscuits are well browned — 20-25 minutes.

I discovered a note that says this meat pie will serve 8-12. Perhaps this is so with some groups, but not if one young gentleman is present. He had six helpings when he dropped in for lunch. However, there were six other people, so perhaps arithmetically that made 12. It proves helpful to know the approximate size of your guests' appetites, and even then, the best dishes seem to disappear even after all stomachs have been filled.

Most of the recipients of this meal won't need any dessert. But if some insist, you might serve fruit and cheese, and if you like you may pass the Oatmeal Lace Cookies,* just to see if anyone will take any. I bet they will.

SHORT RIBS OF BEEF

(For 4)

When you buy a sirloin roast of beef (oh, rare occurrence) you may have the short ribs cut off. These can be very handy in the event that any unexpected epicures drop in to supper. Or, of course you may buy the short ribs on purpose.

Begin with:

- 4 *tablespoons flour*
- 8 *short ribs of beef from a 14 pound roast*
- 2 *tablespoons butter*
- 1 *onion, minced*
- 1 *teaspoon curry powder*
- ½ *teaspoon chili powder*
- ½ *teaspoon each, cloves and cinnamon*
- ½ *teaspoon pepper from the grinder*
- ¼ *teaspoon cayenne*
- ¼ *teaspoon nutmeg*
- 2 *tablespoons instant flour*
- 2 *cups hot Beef Stock**
- 2 *tablespoons tomato ketchup*
- 4 *tablespoons prepared mustard*
- 2 *tablespoons Worcestershire sauce*
- 1 *cup beef jelly from the roast, or one cup extra jellied stock*
- 2 *tablespoons beef fat and cracklings*
- 1 *tablespoon parsley, minced*

Put four tablespoons flour into a paper bag and shake ribs in the flour until they are thoroughly coated. Lay them on a platter. Pat more flour on them if necessary. You will need your largest frying pan for the ribs and a smaller one for the sauce.

First make the sauce. Melt butter. Cook onion in butter until soft. Mix dry seasonings with two tablespoons instant flour and rub them into butter over very low heat. Cook for two minutes over low heat, and pour in hot stock slowly, blending it in well. Add ketchup, mustard, Worcestershire sauce and beef jelly or stock. Cook for three minutes, then set aside in a warm place to mellow while you cook the ribs.

Try out a quarter pound of beef suet, cut into cubes, over low heat till till cracklings are golden brown. Skim them out and set aside. Put in floured beef ribs and brown them all over. This takes about eight minutes.

When serving, put ribs on a hot platter, pour sauce over them, adding more stock or a little tomato juice if it seems too thick. Sprinkle parsley and the cracklings over them. Rice, mashed potatoes or Yorkshire Pudding* are all good for soaking up the sauce. Serve slices of sautéed zucchini, a green vegetable and some of Mrs. Appleyard's Chutney* with the ribs.

HAMBURGER

Until the First World War, Mrs. Appleyard had never socially encountered a hamburger with a small H. She used to think, on occasion, that since that first meeting she never saw anything else. With all that experience, she asserted that some hamburgers were better than others. For instance, she once had a friend who flew over Germany in an English plane. The hostess remarked to him, "There's a place down below us where they serve a very good kind of roll with chopped beef in it." "What's its name?" queried the ravenous passenger.

I'll leave the guessing as to the name of that city to you, not wanting to insult your intelligence. I just hope the hamburger in that city was superior.

To begin with, it depends somewhat on the rolls. If you like them made of fine used Kapok, you had better, like Paolo and Francesca, read no farther in this book. If you make your own bread it isn't much more trouble to cut out some circular pieces and bake them for hamburger rolls. Baking Powder Biscuit* rolls, or shortcake dough are both better with hamburger than commercial rolls. I appreciate the fact however, that many modern cooks have neither the time nor the desire to bake their own hamburger rolls. For the majority I would suggest Pepperidge Farm or Paramount Farms (only in New England) rolls, or English muffins.

I often had occasion to be in attendance, invisibly yet attentively, while Grandmother was preparing hamburgers for a crowd of appreciative friends and relatives. Fortunately for me, Grandmother frequently mused to herself aloud as she absent-mindedly continued the oft-performed task at hand. This day she was heard to think back to her innocent youth. "There then was tough steak, but it was not ground. It was pounded and usually not enough. The invention of the electric grinder changed things." Mrs. Appleyard then went on record — for the benefit of stray archaeologists and inquisitive grandchildren — as considering the ground meat age superior to the pounded meat era. She did mention, however, the fact that "you can't get any better meat out of a grinder than you put into it. It may be tender but not full flavored or with a better proportion of fat to lean meat." She thought it better to "buy chuck or bottom of the round and have it ground twice. In addition, you should have any suet cut off and use it separately for cracklings and for cooking fat — or give it to the woodpeckers." She thought a hamburger ought to be of generous size and that one weighing a quarter of a pound was better than two smaller ones.

I'm thankful that my Grandmother was not exposed to the use and abuse of the hamburger in the time that quickly followed the individually owned and operated meat grinder. Many a "quarter-pounder," dissimilar to Mrs. Appleyard's juicy "hamburger weighing a good quarter of a pound" has been consumed by young and old alike in the new age of "The Quick Food Fad." A positive point arose from all of this, however. You may now buy ground beef in many forms with great ease and convenience, at any corner market or food chain outlet. For those steeped in nostalgia and longing for the time of home-ground meat, you may still buy cuts of beef and grind them twice in your own kitchen. But, enough philosophizing about the strengths and pitfalls of modernization, and on to the really important items, i.e. cooking time.

The length of time a hamburger is to be cooked is a matter of taste. I like them brown on the outside, a genial pink — but not raw — inside. I achieve this effect by cooking them two minutes on each side in a well heated iron frying pan. The cakes should be of uniform thickness — about half an inch through. In getting them ready, mix a tablespoon of cold water with a pound of ground lean meat, shape and pat each cake firmly and conceal a small lump of butter, half a teaspoonful, in the center of each.

With sliced young onions, rich red tomato slices still warm from the vines, your own piccalilli, chutney, Mustard Pickle,* Horseradish and Sour Cream,* and homemade rolls, I consider the eating of hamburgers no penance.

BROILED HAMBURG ON TOAST

(For 4)

4 slices homemade bread (if available)
Butter, soft but not melted
1 tablespoon cold water
1 pound bottom of the round, ground twice
Desired relishes

Toast bread on one side and spread the other side with softened butter. Mix cold water with ground meat. This makes it easy to spread the meat on the toast. Do so while the toast is still warm. Be sure the meat is spread right out to the crust. Broil it in a radiant electric broiler about three inches from the flame until meat is brown and sizzling. Broilers vary in their intensity but it ought not to take much over two minutes of broiling, unless you like yours very well done.

MARINATED HAMBURGER

(For 4)

In winter when my garden is asleep, I have been known to marinate hamburgers. For a pound of ground meat, chuck or bottom round, use the following marinade:

1/3 cup red wine
1/4 teaspoon oregano
1 tablespoon Dijon mustard
1 tablespoon melted butter
1 clove garlic, put through press
1 tablespoon horseradish
1/2 tablespoon sugar
Extra butter

Mix all ingredients together, mix in ground meat and let mixture stand for half an hour at room temperature. Split, toast and butter two English Muffins.* Spread each half with marinated meat and broil them until meat is brown, in a radiant electric broiler, four inches from heat.

Note: In my notebook I wrote that this quantity would serve four elderly ladies. I realize, however, that for young mountain climbers of either sex you would need at least twice as much of everything.

HAMBURGER PLANKED

It's quite possible that your best stainless steel well and tree platter has not seen many Porterhouse steaks lately. Well, at least you can use it for hamburgers.

Allow a quarter pound of meat apiece. Pat and press meat firmly into cakes with water and butter — or marinate them as above if you prefer. Brown them on one side in iron frying pan hot enough so that drops of water run around in it like mercury.

Have ready:

Slightly mashed potatoes

Sliced tomatoes broiled on one side
Onion rings
Carrot sticks, cooked but not mushy
Partly cooked, large mushroom caps, washed but not peeled
Slices of bacon, cooked but not crisp

Arrange potato around platter in a ring, score it lightly with a fork and dot with butter. Put hamburgers, cooked side down, in the middle of the platter. Arrange partly-cooked vegetables around them. Add mushrooms gill side up, dotted with butter. Dot more butter over the other vegetables. Slide platter under the broiler, three inches from flame and cook until everything is as browned as you like it. Baste once during broiling with juice that has gathered in well of platter.

Decorate the platter with sprays of watercress and parsley. You'll hardly miss that Porterhouse.

Once on an inclement and hunger-rousing winter night, Mrs. Appleyard served three friends what she meekly referred to in her notebook as:

PERFECT HAMBURGER

Use a pound and a half bottom of the round, ground twice and make it into four large cakes with a little cold water and melted butter. Heat an iron frying pan until drops of water run but don't sizzle, and brown cakes half a minute on each side. Then turn off heat, insert meat thermometer in one of the cakes, cover the pan tightly and let meat stand until thermometer registers 150°. The whole process takes 14 minutes.

With the hamburgers, Grandmother served Mushroom Sauce,* tiny frozen peas cooked in a small amount of water until there were only a few drops of water left. She combined the peas with thinly sliced onion rings which she had cooked in butter until they were translucent and straw colored. She also had a dish of Scalloped Tomatoes.* "No complaints," the note concluded. I doubt that any complaints would have been vocalized to my sometimes stern Grandmother, but I believe in the perfection of her cooking anyway, as any good grandchild should.

BROILED HAMBURGER WITH MUSHROOM SAUCE

Another good way of cooking hamburgers is to cook them in the frying pan, in the way outlined above, but remove them when the thermometer registers 140°. Have homemade rolls ready, split, toasted and buttered. On these place the partly cooked hamburgers, cover them with Mushroom

Sauce,* and toast them under the broiler until the sauce bubbles, about two minutes.

HAMBURGER PIE

For four people use an eight-inch frying pan and one and three-quarters pounds ground meat. Butter pan lightly. Put meat in, all in one thick cake, pressed down evenly. Cook for five minutes on top of the stove over high heat, then for four minutes under pre-heated gas or electric broiler. This results in a medium rare effect. Increase both times slightly if you like it more well done. Or, if you want to be sure it is rare, insert a meat thermometer carefully so it will be in the meat not too close to the pan, and cook the pie until the thermometer registers 145°.

To enhance the pie, serve either Mushroom Sauce,* poured bubbling hot over the pie, or a tomato sauce with garlic and green pepper *(Summer Kitchen,* p. 53) or Taxi Driver's Tomato Sauce.*.

And then there is the variation dubbed:

HAMBURGER PIE STROGANOFF

Who was Stroganoff? No one has been able to answer this question for Mrs. Appleyard. All anyone has ever replied is: "Well — you take some sour cream . . ."

So, she took *one cupful of sour cream,* as you well might, along with:

3 onions, thinly sliced
Butter
*2 cups hot Brown Stock**
*Hamburger Pie**
Parsley

Begin by cooking onions in butter till they just start to brown. Pour hot stock over them and leave them to simmer until liquid has almost all cooked away. Prepare Hamburger Pie in a separate pan. Meanwhile, stir sour cream in with onions and let stand until pie is ready. Next, heat sour cream and onions to the boiling point, pour the sauce around the edge of the pan where the pie has shrunk away from the edge in cooking. Sprinkle parsley on top and serve it in the pan.

The hamburger cooked this way is juicy enough so that the juice runs into the onion and sour cream mixture to make a rich gravy.

Grandmother served Corn Pudding* and Beets Appleyard* with it. Not bad, was the verdict from the professional Vermonter present. They were in New York State when she invented this chef d'ouevre, so they were naturally, perhaps more enthusiastic and outspoken than they would have been across the Green Mountains.

Mrs. Appleyard reportedly had a Russian phase at the time we were allies, and Stalingrad was being gallantly defended. She once sent two fur coats to Russia, one of which she missed forever after. It reached to the ground and was like a rug and a coat combined, great on below-zero days. She was well rid of the other one, a comparatively stylish garment. She had always wondered whether some commissars wore them and studied many pictures without detecting either one of the coats. I sometimes marvel at my Grandmother's generosity and wonder what possessed her to send fur coats to Russia. She must have had a vision of Siberia filling the whole of the country. I am grateful, however, for the following rule which arose from that same period.

RUSSIAN STEAK — APPLEYARD

(For 4)

4	*slices chuck steak*		*Pinch nutmeg*
4	*tablespoons butter*	½	*teaspoon black pepper*
2	*medium onions, minced*	½	*cup red wine*
1	*teaspoon paprika*	1	*cup Beef Stock**
½	*teaspoon garlic powder*	1	*cup sour cream*

1 *tablespoon minced parsley*

Cut steak in pieces about two by four inches and brown pieces quickly on both sides in butter in a hot iron frying pan. Do not overcook. Put half the onion in a fireproof casserole. Add steak, scattering the rest of the onion in between and sprinkling in seasonings. Pour it over the steak. Rinse out the frying pan with the red wine. Add wine and stock to the casserole. Cover and cook in the oven until tender — about two hours at 300°. Then set casserole over low heat on top of the stove and simmer uncovered until no more than half a cup of juice is left.

At serving time add thick sour cream, bring it to the boiling point but do not boil. Sprinkle the minced parsley over it.

Serve with Beet Greens and Young Beets* and small new potatoes from your garden.

MEAT LOAF

On days when you don't want to do last minute cooking for a meal, it is convenient to have something on hand that has been cooked ahead of time. Sooner or later, for everyone, this "something" will be meat loaf. Here is one version that Grandmother starred in her notebook. It was made with bottom of the round. It can also be made with regular hamburger, of course, but if it is, much of the loaf will melt away and have to be poured off before it's served, leaving a much smaller loaf than expected.

Begin with:

	Extra butter for greasing pans	1	*cup dried bread crumbs, rolled fine*
2	*eggs, lightly beaten*	2	*pounds bottom of the round, ground twice*
1	*cup rich milk*		
1	*teaspoon onion, minced*	¼	*cup extra bread or cracker crumbs*
¼	*teaspoon celery flakes*		
¼	*teaspoon mixed herbs*	1	*tablespoon butter*

Butter a bread tin thoroughly. Beat eggs and milk together, add onion, celery flakes and herbs. Pour mixture over bread crumbs and let stand five minutes. Light oven: 350°. Add ground beef and mix it thoroughly into bread mixture. Fill bread tin. Scatter extra crumbs over top and dot with butter. Bake at 350° for fifteen minutes. Reduce heat to 300°. Use a meat thermometer. Bake until it registers 150° — about an hour longer. Pour off melted fat. Serve it hot with Taxi Driver's Tomato Sauce,* or serve well chilled.

CORNISH PASTIES

The packaged pastry works well with what might be called Cornish Pasties, if Mrs. Appleyard had not tampered with their contents. The genuine sort contains a kind of beef stew mixture with vegetables cut up fine: carrots, onions and turnips. The following version embodies substances Grandmother preferred.

½ pound ham steak
½ pound veal cutlet
*1 cup Chicken Stock**
2 tablespoons white wine
½ tablespoon dried onion
¼ teaspoon nutmeg
½ pound mushroom caps
1 tablespoon butter
1 tablespoon instant flour
1 package pastry mix

Cut the ham steak and veal cutlet into small neat cubes. Put chicken stock, white wine, onion and nutmeg into an iron frying pan. Add ham and veal and simmer until meat is tender — about one hour.

Sauté sliced mushroom caps in butter for five minutes, and add them to the mixture. Add instant flour, stirring all the while to avoid lumps.

Roll out pastry. Cut it into six six-inch circles. Heap some of the mixture on half of each circle, not too near the edge. Dot mixture with butter. Moisten outer edges slightly with a pastry brush. Fold the other half circle over and press the edges together with a fork and with your fingers. Prick holes in the top of each pastie with a fork.

Have the oven at 400°. After 30 minutes, reduce heat to 350°. Put pasties on a baking sheet and bake them until they are well browned, top and bottom. It will take about 50 minutes. Serve the pasties hot, or cool them and let your guests eat them as if they were sandwiches.

VEAL

In thinking of beef, veal is often forgotten; yet there must be veal before there is beef. One of its virutes is that it is milder in flavor than other meats — beef, lamb or ham. Therefore, the flavor of vegetables and sauces served with it is readily appreciated, whether that flavor is strong, like that of cabbage or of a pungent mustard sauce, or mild, like that of Broiled Zucchini Slices* or of a Sour Cream Sauce* very lightly flavored with curry. Vegetables and sauces will be described in their own places, but I will mention some combinations I like as we go along. One of my favorite ways of serving veal is in the form of:

BRAISED VEAL CHOPS

2 tablespoons butter
4 large veal chops
*1 cup Chicken Stock**
¼ teaspoon rosemary
½ teaspoon Worcestershire sauce
¼ teaspoon garlic powder
¼ teaspoon tarragon
1 tablespoon sherry
½ cup currant jelly
Sprays of watercress and parsley

If you have an electric skillet, it will come in handy now. But an iron frying pan, used first on top of the stove, then covered in the oven at 300° will do.

Melt butter. Brown chops in it slowly for five to ten minutes, turning often. When they are well browned add stock and seasonings. Cover and turn heat down, or place covered pan in a 300° oven so that the juice just simmers, and cook until chops are tender, about one hour. Turn occasionally. Add more stock if necessary.

Just before serving, add sherry and currant jelly. Turn chops in the mixture till jelly is melted and starting to bubble. Put them on a hot platter. Wreathe them with watercress and parsley. Serve with Brown Rice* and broiled tomato au gratin.

VEAL LOAF

(Mrs. Appleyard's)

- 2 *pounds of veal and one pound of lean pork, put twice through the grinder together*
- ½ *pound calves liver*
- 2 *large onions, minced*
- ½ *cup light cream*
- 2 *eggs, well beaten*
- 6 *Cross crackers*
- 1 *teaspoon poultry seasoning*
- *Pinches of thyme, nutmeg, oregano*
- 1 *teaspoon pepper from the grinder*
- ½ *pound baked ham, cubed*
- 2 *truffles, sliced or 4 small mushroom caps, sliced*
- 1 *tablespoon butter*
- 1 *tablespoon flour*
- ¼ *cup fine dried bread crumbs*
- 4 *slices bacon*

Have the butcher grind veal and pork together for you. Cook liver the day before you use it. Simmer it until tender and chop very fine.

Chop onions fine and chop the liver into them. Mix in veal and pork thoroughly. Add cream and eggs beaten together. Roll crackers into fine crumbs. Mix seasonings with them and mix them into meat. Now add ham cubes and sliced truffles or mushrooms.

Butter a large tin bread pan and put in the mixture. Press it well into the corners. Dredge top with flour and firmly rolled bread crumbs. Cover crumbs with dots of butter and bacon cut into small strips.

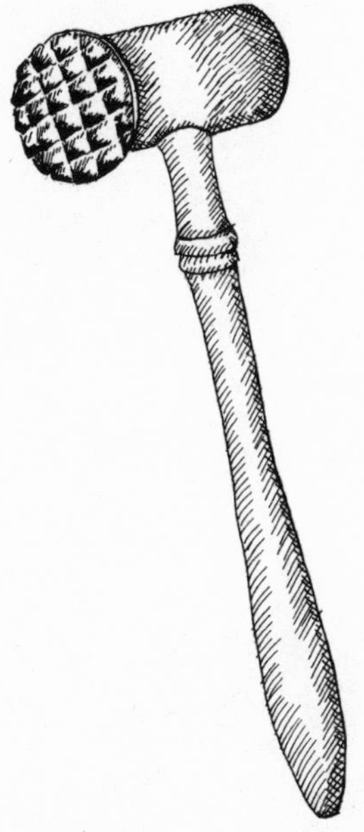

Set the pan on a rack in a covered roaster, surround it with water, and bake for two and a half hours at 350° or until a thermometer inserted in the loaf registers 165°. Add more water to the roaster if necessary. Reduce heat if the loaf seems to be browning too fast. Chill it several hours before serving.

Serve with Mushroom Sauce,* Sliced Baked Ham* and Vegetable Salad.*.

SMOTHERED VEAL

- 2 *tablespoons chopped onion*
- 2 *tablespoons butter*
- 1 *cup flour seasoned with pepper, salt, oregano, marjoram, rosemary or a combination you like*
- 4 *cups hot Chicken Stock**
- 1 *cup light cream*
- 2 *tablespoons white wine*
- 2 *tablespoons minced parsley*
- 2 *tablespoons chopped chives*
- *A pinch of fresh minced dill*
- 2 *pounds of veal cut from the leg*

Cut the veal into inch-thick slices and cut each slice into two by three-inch pieces. (Save the trimmings and use them in meat loaf.) Fry the onion in butter until translucent. Put seasoned flour in a bag and shake pieces of veal in it until they are well coated all over. Skim out onions and set them aside while you brown the veal until the coating is crisp on both sides. Put onions back in the pan with veal. Pour hot stock over it. Let meat just simmer, over a very low flame, until tender — about one hour and a quarter. Add a little water occasionally if the stock cooks away too fast. It should not cook dry.

At serving time add cream and let it cook a minute, being careful not to let it boil. Stir in the wine. Serve it in the pan in which it was cooked with parsley, chives and dill scattered over it.

I like to serve Corn Pudding* and Beet Greens with Young Beets* with it and pass some of Mrs. Appleyard's Chutney.*

VEAL AND HAM PIE

(For 6)

This is a first cousin to an aspic. Grandmother worked out an improved technique for making this masterpiece. I now impart her rule.

Begin the day before you plan to serve it with:

1½	*pound slice of ham*	*½*	*teaspoon cinnamon*
2	*pounds veal, cut from the leg*	*6*	*whole cloves*
		½	*teaspoon pepper*
	Veal bones, knuckles are best	*3*	*onions, sliced*
		1	*carrot, sliced*
1	*calf's foot*		*Celery tops*
12	*chicken wing tips*	*3*	*sprays parsley*
½	*teaspoon nutmeg*		*2,000 Layer Pastry**

4 eggs, hard boiled

Put ham on to simmer after removing fat. Put it into a big frying pan with plenty of water and add water occasionally as it cooks away. Save water for Lentil,* Black Bean* or Princess Pea Soup.*

At the same time, in a large kettle, put veal, bones, calf's foot, chicken wing tips, seasonings, onion, carrot, celery tops and parsley. Cover with water and let simmer at least three hours.

While ham and veal are cooking, make 2,000 Layer Pastry. You might like to bake the pastry on top of the pie, but it is likely to lose some of its flakiness and flavor if cooked with liquid under it. I suggest forming a pastry lid neatly tailored to fit the top of your best iron enamel or other fireproof casserole. Bake the lid separately and place it on the casserole when it is finished cooking.

After both veal and ham are tender, strain off veal broth. Cool it first in a pan set in cold water with ice cubes around it, and then in refrigerator. There should be about four cups of broth, which you should allow to jell overnight.

The next morning skim all fat from the jelly. If it is not stiffly jelled, soak one tablespoon of gelatin in some cold stock, add the white of an egg, mix it with rest of the stock and bring to a boil. Then strain it through clean cheesecloth. Even if stock does not need thickening, put in the white of an egg to clear the stock, heat and stir, leaving out the gelatin.

Cut veal and ham into neat cubes and mix them together. Arrange a layer of meat in your casserole. Slice hard-boiled eggs, put some slices around the edge. Repeat layering until the dish is full. Pour in enough stock to cover the meat. Save out a cup of stock and cook it down to half a cup.

In the meantime set the dish, loosely covered — steam should be allowed to escape — into a 350° oven and cook until meat and broth are well merged — about 40 minutes. Add the half cup of broth you cooked down. Chill thoroughly. The spaces between the meat should then be full of a sparkling ambrosial jelly. Put the baked pastry lid on top and serve with a tossed salad.

ROAST PORK

Pork should be cooked carefully because of the possibility of infection by trichinosis, but this does not mean that it has to be cooked as dry as an old shingle. Use a meat thermometer, which should register 165° when the pork is done. Long slow cooking at 300° is ideal for roast pork.

- 7 *pound loin of pork*
- ½ *cup flour*
- 1 *teaspoon poultry seasoning*
- ½ *teaspoon paprika*
- ½ *teaspoon cinnamon*
- ¼ *teaspoon cloves*
- ¼ *teaspoon nutmeg*
- *Small onions*
- *Carrots*
- *Wax and green beans*
- *Celery, cut fine*
- *Peas*

Have the butcher cut the chops almost all the way through so that the roast will be easy to carve. Sift flour and seasonings together and rub the mixture well into the surface of the meat. Place the roast on a rack in an uncovered roaster. Allow roughly 35 minutes a pound for roasting, but check the meat thermometer. A seven and a half pound roast will take about four hours.

During the last 40 minutes of roasting, cook vegetables. Put a small amount of water in a saucepan and begin with the tiny onions; in ten minutes put in the other vegetables, except for the peas which should be added in the last few minutes. Add water, if necessary, to keep vegetables from burning.

When roast is thoroughly cooked, remove it from the pan to a stainless steel serving platter. Drain water from vegetables and use it to make gravy. Arrange vegetables around roast. Return platter to the oven while you make Sour Cream Pork Gravy.*

Serve mashed potatoes and green applesauce made with early summer apples, with the roast pork.

PORK CHOPS WITH APRICOTS AND ALMONDS

(For 6)

- 6 *pork chops*
- 4 *tablespoons hot liquid (chicken stock or vegetable cooking water)*
- ½ *cup sugar*
- 3 *drops almond extract*
- 4 *tablespoons almonds, blanched and slivered*
- 2 *ounces dried apricots*

Use a large iron frying pan and place over medium high heat. When it is well warmed, take the chops singly and rub the edges of each one over the surface of the pan. This will cook the edges of the chops and grease the pan at the same time. Next, sear chops on both sides.

Insert meat thermometer into the largest chop so that the point touches neither fat nor bone. Turn heat to low and set the pan over a flame tamer. Add about four tablespoons hot liquid (use hot water if nothing else is available) to the pan and cover it. Cook chops until thermometer registers 165° — about thirty minutes. Turn chops every ten minutes and add a little more hot liquid as it cooks away.

While chops are cooking steam two ounces dried apricots for ten minutes in an Italian steamer, the kind with legs, that can be used in a covered saucepan. Put fruit in a pint jar. Cook the water used for steaming down to one cup, add sugar and cook till syrup is quite thick — about ten minutes more. Pour syrup over the fruit in the jar. Add almond extract. Let stand until needed.

When chops are done, remove them to a circular fireproof platter. Put apricots in the middle of the platter and in between chops. Set platter in the oven. Brown the blanched and slivered almonds in the fat in the frying pan. Scatter them over apricots and serve.

With this combination I suggest serving Spoon Bread* and a green vegetable plate of broccoli, peas and green beans. Serve at least one green vegetable as a contrast to the brown and russet of the chops and apricots.

SAUSAGE

The most difficult part of making your own sausage is finding a butcher who will take the time to grind the meat especially for you. Once you have found such a sympathetic person, hold on to him and arrange a convenient time for your experiments that give him a chance to display his natural virtuousity. Take a large piece of wax paper or a plastic bag with you to carry the meat home in.

For three pounds of pork also take along a small jar containing:

2 teaspoons salt
1 tablespoon sage
1 tablespoon pepper from grinder

Shake seasonings together well. Have the butcher put the pork (not too fat) through the grinder twice. During the second grinding have him add your seasonings to the meat.

Once home with your wax paper full of sausage meat, work it through the paper, without touching the meat itself, and pat and roll it out into a cylinder shape. In this form it may be frozen for future use in several tightly bound layers of wax paper. *Never* taste raw sausage or any mixture containing it due to the danger of trichinosis. Use this homemade sausage (*sans* nitrates) as you would any good commercial sausage.

It may be used immediately to make:

SAUSAGE WITH PINEAPPLE

(For 6)

1 cup homemade bread crumbs
1½ pounds homemade sausage
¼ teaspoon nutmeg
1 tablespoon butter
12 halves of canned pineapple slices

Crush well-dried bread crumbs into a fine powder. Sprinkle in nutmeg.

Cut sausage right through the wax paper into slices half an inch thick. Peel off the paper. Roll the sausage cakes in the crumbs.

Melt butter in a big iron frying pan. Put in sausage cakes. Thrust a toothpick through outer curve of each half slice of pineapple and fasten one, curved side up, to each sausage cake. Sprinkle with the remaining crumbs. Bake in a 350° oven for at least 35 minutes. Baste twice with fat from the pan. Check a sausage cake and be sure the meat has no pink color left.

With this dish serve Inside-out Potatoes* and Green Beans with Mushrooms.*

Note: Handle any sausage, your own or anyone else's, as little as possible and wash your hands thoroughly. Forgive me for dwelling on this. My Grandmother once had a friend who had trichinosis. Even after 20 years, she told the story with frightening realism.

SAUSAGE LINKS WITH APPLES

(For 4)

1 pound link sausage
3 tablespoons cold water
4 large tart apples
4 tablespoons sugar
Pinches of nutmeg and cinnamon
1 tablespoon molasses

Into a large frying pan put one pound of link sausages, separated. Add cold water. Cover. Cook over low heat — using a flame tamer — for ten minutes. Pour off fat, but save it. Turn links as they brown. Do not prick them. Continue cooking until links are brown all over, pouring off the fat at least twice.

When links are browned, put them on paper towels and keep them warm while you slice apples. Discard stem and blossom ends. Cut the rest of the apple horizontally into three slices. Put slices into hot fat in the frying pan. Mix sugar, spices and molasses and spoon some of the mixture over each apple slice. Cook slowly on top of stove until sugar melts. Return sausage links to pan. Cover, cook one minute and serve.

Corn Pudding* and Broiled Tomato Slices* go well with these.

SAUSAGE WITH YORKSHIRE PUDDING

(For 6)

Yorkshire Pudding is the classic accompaniment for roast beef, but it is also good with either sausage cakes or sausage links.

12 cakes of Vermont sausage
½ cup flour, extra
2 eggs
1 cup flour
½ teaspoon salt
1 cup milk

Dip sausage cakes into extra flour. Put them into a cold, nine-inch iron frying pan and cook slowly over very low heat until bottoms of cakes are well browned and tops show no pink — about ten minutes. Turn and cook until they are well browned underneath also.

Light oven: 450°.

Put eggs, flour, salt and milk into blender and blend for half a minute. By this time there should be plenty of fat in the pan. Remove sausage cakes, drain on paper towels and keep in a warm place. Pour the Yorkshire mixture into hot fat in the pan, set the pan into the oven and bake for ten minutes at 450°. Reduce heat to 350° and bake it until it is well puffed and brown — 25-30 minutes longer. Heat the sausage in a separate pan and serve.

SPAGHETTI WITH SAUSAGE

For those who long for a little variety in a spaghetti dish I offer the following rule:

4	*sausage cakes*	½	*cup dry bread crumbs*
3	*cups Tomato Sauce**		*Butter*
½	*pound cooked spaghetti*	½	*cup grated cheese*

Cook sausage cakes slowly on one side in an iron frying pan until they are brown underneath and the pink color disappears on the uncooked side — about ten minutes. Turn them over and brown on other side. Break into pieces and add to tomato sauce. Combine cooked spaghetti with the sauce. Put entire mixture into a casserole, sprinkle top with dry bread crumbs, dot with butter. Put in a 350° oven for 20-25 minutes, until warm. Just before serving, sprinkle grated cheese over the top of the casserole.

Sausage leads us logically and happily to the subject of ham.

VERMONT HAM

When her family had a reunion, now a less frequent happening Grandmother liked to have a Vermont ham on hand. And why not? The last time she cooked one she had an idea that worked well. Instead of simmering the ham in water and baking it later, she did the whole thing in a 200° oven. She started a ten-pound ham in the oven at ten o'clock one night, basted it twice during the next hour, then went to bed and slept peacefully. The next morning all Appleyard Center smelled sweet and smoky and the ham was cooked just right. With it Mrs. Appleyard served cauliflower in a wreath of Green Beans and Beets,* Mustard Sauce* and Popovers.*

BOILED HAM

Most hams available today need no boiling, some have already been filled with as much water as the manufacturer can legally inject into the body of the meat. However, boiling is necessary for some hams. Perhaps one may come to you that was cured two or three years ago, still in its own tough, dry, thick, salty, smoky skin. (Cheer up, there's flavor to be had underneath it all.) Such a ham is of no use to civilized man unless an enlightened cook deals with it first. If you find yourself in this situation pursue the following directions:

Scrub the ham first with a stiff brush to remove the saltpeter and smoke left from the curing process. Soak it overnight in cold water. In the morning put it into a large kettle, one that will hold five gallons, skin down. Cover it with tepid water and keep it simmering. It should not boil. The classic way of determining when a ham is done is to note when it turns over in the kettle of its own accord.

Allow about half an hour's cooking time for each pound of ham. Assuming that a ten-pound ham has room in the kettle, it will turn over in about five hours. Let it cool the rest of the day and all night in the water in which it was cooked. The next morning, skin it and bake as directed in the rule for Baked Vermont Ham.

There is bound to be ham left even after the finest part has been sliced so thin you can read a magazine through it. The less edible pieces may be used in Ham au Gratin on Toast.*

BAKED VERMONT HAM

1	*10-pound ham, cooked and skinned*	¼	*teaspoon cinnamon*
1	*cup sugar*	1	*teaspoon dry mustard*
2	*tablespoons dark molasses*	¼	*teaspoon allspice*
		¼	*teaspoon ginger*

Whole cloves

Basting sauce:

½	*cup ginger ale*	½	*cup fizzy cider*

½ *teaspoon ginger*

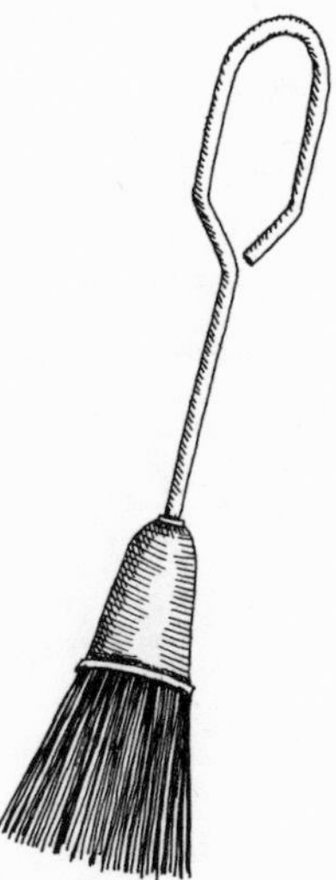

The only skin that needs to be removed from my favorite ham is a piece around the shank. Yours may need more removed. Score the fat in diagonal lines about three-quarters inch apart, making diamonds. Mix sugar, molasses and spices together and rub mixture into the surface of the ham. Press whole cloves into the intersections of scored lines. Sprinkle fine bread crumbs over the whole surface.

Mix ginger ale, cider and extra ginger and pour mixture into a roasting pan. Place the ham on a rack in the roaster. Insert meat thermometer so that it touches neither fat nor bone. Set the pan into a preheated 200° oven. Baste ham twice during the first hour, then cover with aluminum foil and forget it until morning.

The next day the thermometer should register 165° and the ham should be a golden brown. If necessary, let it go on cooking until it reaches this stage. Set in a cool place but do not refrigerate it. Serve at room temperature.

SLICED HAM — BAKED

1	*slice boiled ham, two inches thick (about 3 pounds)*	1	*cup or more ginger ale*
2	*tablespoons dry mustard*	2	*bananas*
	Whole cloves	4	*slices canned pineapple*
¼	*cup maple syrup*		*Butter*
			Parsley sprigs

Begin by rubbing the fat edge of ham over bottom and sides of an iron enameled pan. Then rub mustard all over ham and impale cloves into the fat. Dribble the maple syrup over the upper side. Pour ginger ale over it so it comes to the top of the slice.

Bake in a 350° oven until tender — 1½ to 2 hours. Turn ham after 45 minutes and add more ginger ale. Serve it hot.

Just before serving, transfer the ham to a stainless steel well and tree platter and set it in the oven. Put the pan containing the juices over the fire to simmer and cook down to about half a cup of liquid.

Halve and split bananas, halve pineapple slices. Place fruit on a lightly greased broiler pan, dot with butter and broil until brown, turning the pineapple slices once. Place the fruit around the meat, pour juice from the pan over them.

Decorate the platter with sprigs of parsley. With the ham serve freshly picked, freshly cooked corn and Cole Slaw.*

HAM AU GRATIN ON TOAST

(For 4)

4 rounds of homemade bread
1 cup chopped ham
2 tablespoons thick cream
¼ teaspoon nutmeg
¼ teaspoon cinnamon
4 tablespoons grated Vermont cheddar cheese
Butter
2 large stuffed olives, cut in halves

Toast one side of the rounds of bread lightly. Butter other side. Mix ham, cream, and seasonings. Spread mixture on uncooked side of the rounds of bread. Sprinkle cheese over the ham. Broil until cheese melts and just starts to brown. Serve each portion topped with half a stuffed olive.

HAM AND MUSHROOM ROLL

(For 6)

½ pound mushroom caps
1 teaspoon minced onion
2 tablespoons butter
2 tablespoons sherry
½ teaspoon nutmeg
1 cup finely minced ham
¼ cup cream
¼ teaspoon pepper
¼ teaspoon cinnamon
Pinch of ground cloves

For the dough you will need:

2 cups flour
½ teaspoon salt
Pinch of cloves
½ cup butter
2 eggs, beaten
⅔ cup cold milk
Flour for rolling
1 egg, separated

Start by making dough: put flour, sifted with seasonings, into a wooden bowl. Chop in the butter until it is in pieces no bigger than the top of your index finger. Beat eggs well and beat milk into them. Add eggs and milk to flour mixture. Flour a board well, toss dough on it. Knead it gently for one minute. Add more flour if necessary. Roll it out into an oblong, 12x9-inches. Chill the dough while you prepare the filling.

Wash mushroom caps and chop them, not too fine. Sauté minced onion in butter, add sherry, mushrooms and nutmeg. Cover and cook until mushrooms are tender about five minutes. Cool slightly.

Mix ham with cream, pepper, cinnamon and cloves. Spread half the dough with the mushroom mixture and the other half with the ham mixture. Leave margins at both left and right sides of dough. With a fork beat both the white and the yolk of the egg, separately, each with one teaspoonful of water. Brush the margin of the dough with some white of an egg.

Lap one half of the dough over the other and seal edges together with the rest of egg white. Brush the outside of the roll with egg yolk. Lay the roll in a teflon baking pan. Bake it at 400° until well browned — about 30 minutes. Check after ten minutes and if it has started to brown too fast, reduce the temperature to 325°. Cut the roll in slices and serve hot or cool.

HAM MOUSSE

(For 8)

1½	*tablespoons plain gelatin*	⅛	*teaspoon cayenne pepper*
2	*tablespoons cold water*	1	*teaspoon horseradish (optional)*
¾	*cup hot water*	3	*cups ground ham*
2	*teaspoons dry mustard*	¾	*cup cream*

Soak gelatin in cold water for five minutes, then add hot water to dissolve it. Stir seasonings in. Be sure there is no gristle in the ham to spoil the consistency. Put ham through a meat grinder using your finest attachment, and pound it in a mortar or in a wooden bowl until it is smooth. Add gelatin to the ham. Put ice cubes and cold water into a melon mold to chill it.

Whip cream until stiff and add it to the ham mixture, folding it in gently and thoroughly. Empty the mold. Put in the mousse. Chill it covered in the refrigerator for at least three hours.

When unmolding the mousse, uncover the mold and set it into water that feels just warm, about 100°, for about half a minute. Watch it and as soon as the mousse softens the least bit at the edge, wipe the outside dry and invert it on a serving platter. Surround it with watercress and Radish Roses.* Serve Mustard Sauce* with it.

DEVILED HAM

½	*cup hot fizzy cider*	⅛	*teaspoon cayenne pepper*
1	*cup ham cut in small pieces*	¼	*teaspoon cloves*
1	*tablespoon butter*	1	*teaspoon dry mustard*
2	*egg yolks*	¼	*teaspoon nutmeg*

Put cider in blender. Add ham, butter, egg yolks and seasonings. Run blender until the mixture is smooth and well blended. Cool. Use for sandwiches, canapés or for stuffing eggs.

HAM STEAK WITH PINEAPPLE

(For 6)

1½	*pound ham steak*	1	*teaspoon grated orange peel*
12	*whole cloves*	½	*cup orange juice*
6	*slices pineapple*	½	*cup pineapple juice*
2	*tablespoons dry bread crumbs*	2	*tablespoons sugar*
½	*teaspoon dry mustard*	1	*tablespoon molasses*

Butter

Press whole cloves into ham. Put it into a large buttered iron frying pan. Cut pineapple slices in halves and put them around ham. Mix bread crumbs, mustard and dry orange peel and sprinkle them over ham and pineapple. Mix the orange juice, pineapple juice, sugar and molasses and pour it over the contents of the pan. Dot pineapple with butter. Warm the pan on top of the stove until juice begins to bubble. Then set it in the oven at 350° and bake until ham is tender and the juice is thick — about one hour.

Variation: If you prefer, you may omit pineapple slices and use milk instead of fruit juices, dried onion chips instead of orange peel. When the ham is tender, thicken the gravy with two tablespoons of instant flour. Sauté half a pound of sliced mushroom caps in butter and add them to the sauce.

TONGUE WITH RAISIN SAUCE

1 fresh tongue weighing six pounds
*8 cups Beef Stock**

The day before you plan to serve the tongue place it on a rack in a covered roaster. Simmer for six hours in stock. When stock has cooked down to about six cups, strain three cups of it. Return vegetables used in the stock — carrots, onions, celery — to the roaster and let the tongue go on simmering until it is tender. Cook the stock down to two cups. Chill it well.

The next day remove fat from chilled stock and use the stock as a basis for:

MRS. APPLEYARD'S RAISIN SAUCE

1 cup seedless raisins
2 cups stock
¼ teaspoon nutmeg
¼ teaspoon cinnamon
*¼ cup Boiled Cider Jelly**
*½ cup Mrs. Appleyard's Tomato Conserve**
2 tablespoons lemon juice
2 teaspoons Worcestershire sauce

Simmer raisins in the stock until they are tender — about ten minutes. Add seasonings, conserve, cider jelly, lemon juice and Worcestershire sauce. Simmer until sauce is rather thick — about 15 minutes longer.

Serve the tongue hot or cold on a large platter with little heaps of vegetables around it — matchstick beets, French-cut Green Beans with Garlic Croutons,* diced carrots, Brussel sprouts, for instance. A big dish of Corn Pudding* goes well with the tongue. Serve the sauce separately.

TONGUE, HAM AND VEAL IN JELLY

This dish can be planned for as you are cooking the tongue. To the stock left in the roaster, after you've strained three cups for the raisin sauce, add a bay leaf, three whole cloves and a half teaspoon of dried oregano leaves. Let it simmer until there are two cups of it left. Strain, chill and keep it until you need it; when you have all but finished the tongue. Let us hope that by good fortune you also had a cold cooked ham and veal on hand. More likely, though, you'll have to buy one or both. In that event, cut them into small cubes and simmer them in stock until they are tender. Strain the stock and chill it, remove the fat.

Use a loaf pan. You will need:

2 tablespoons gelatin
2 cups clear stock
1 lemon
1½ cups cooked tongue, diced
¾ cup cooked veal, diced
¾ cup cooked ham, diced

Soak gelatin in half a cup of stock. Heat one and a half cups of stock, add the strained juice of a lemon. Pour it over gelatin and stir well until it dissolves. Rinse out loaf pan, glass or teflon, with cold water. Empty it. Cover bottom with stock. Put pan in the refrigerator.

Mix tongue, veal and ham. When stock in the pan begins to jell, fill pan with the mixture of meat, leaving a space around the ends and sides. Pour in the rest of the stock and set pan back in refrigerator for several hours.

At serving time, unmold the loaf on a platter. Surround it with garden lettuce, parsley, watercress, sliced fresh tomatoes, stuffed hard-boiled eggs, mounds of small green peas. Accent the decorations with Green Mayonnaise* and serve mayonnaise separately.

A loaf of hot sliced French Bread* with garlic butter is a good accompaniment to this loaf.

SWEETBREADS

In Grandmother's youth there was a meat market just around the corner where they gave away sweetbreads. Of course, you had to happen in at just the right moment and buy something else such as a large Porterhouse steak. Mrs. Appleyard, at that happy period of her life had not yet learned to boil water. She did not cook the sweetbreads herself. She simply asked her grandmother's advice and passed it on to her kitchen in which Minnie was always hoping to try something new. One day this system produced:

SWEETBREADS, BROILED WITH MUSHROOMS

(For 6)

1 *pair of fresh sweetbreads*
2 *tablespoons melted butter*
1 *teaspoon paprika*
12 *large mushroom caps*
Extra butter
2 *tablespoons sherry*
¼ *teaspoon nutmeg*
1 *teaspoon finely minced onion*
12 *triangles hot buttered toast*
Green vegetables
Parsley

Don't parboil the sweetbreads, for it makes them dry and tasteless. Rather, cut them lengthwise into half-inch slices. Remove any small bits of connective tissue as you cut them. Place on a broiling rack, brush with melted butter and sprinkle them with paprika.

Wash, do not peel, the mushrooms. Use caps only — save the stems for soup. Put four dots of butter and a little sherry on each cap. Sprinkle in a few grains of nutmeg and a little minced onion. First broil sweetbreads for ten minutes. Turn them. Brush them again with melted butter. Arrange seasoned mushrooms around them. Broil for six minutes. Remove slices of sweetbread to a well and tree platter. The mushrooms should be done, but give them an extra two minutes if necessary.

Arrange slices of toast around the platter. Also ring the platter with some cooked green vegetables — peas, green beans or asparagus — and the mushroom caps. Pour juice from the pan over the sweetbreads. Garnish with parsley.

Even if you had to buy your sweetbreads, frozen and free from tubes and membranes, as I did, they are still a tasty form of sustenance.

SWEETBREADS IN CREAM

(For 6)

2	*pounds frozen sweetbreads*	1½	*cups cream*
2	*tablespoons butter*	¼	*teaspoon nutmeg*
1	*cup water*	½	*teaspoon paprika*
½	*tablespoon lemon juice*	1½	*tablespoons instant flour*
	Small onion, minced		*Salt to taste*
1½	*pounds mushrooms, washed and sliced*	2	*tablespoons sherry*
		12	*triangles pastry, baked a delicate brown*

1 *tablespoon butter*

Thaw the sweetbreads. Put 2 tablespoons of butter into a pan. Add sweetbreads, water and lemon juice. Simmer until sweetbreads are tender — about 20 minutes. Break them into inch cubes.

In the meantime, in a separate pan, sauté the onion and mushrooms, sliced vertically, in a tablespoon of butter. When they are tender, but not soft, add cream, nutmeg and paprika and add mixture to the cooked sweetbreads. Sprinkle in instant flour and salt to taste, and cook one minute. Add sherry. Bring to the boil but do not boil. Pour the mixture into a hot shallow bowl, arrange pastry triangles around the edge and serve.

This way of serving sweetbreads may be varied in several ways:

1. Include very thin slices of green pepper and of canned pimento in the sauce.
2. Substitute toasted and buttered Holland rusks or buttered toast for the pastry.
3. Garnish the dish with slices of bacon, broiled as you like.

People who don't think they care for sweetbreads often change their minds when exposed to these combinations.

Kidneys are another food that have increased their usage and social position in recent years. Try them in:

KIDNEYS IN CREAM WITH WAFFLES

(For 6)

12	*lamb kidneys, split*	¼	*teaspoon nutmeg*
2	*tablespoons butter, melted*	1	*teaspoon dried onion*
1	*tablespoon lemon juice*	1	*cup thick cream*
⅛	*teaspoon thyme*	1	*tablespoon instant flour*

¼ *cup white wine*

Remove white membrane from kidneys. Cut each into two pieces. Melt butter, add lemon juice, thyme, nutmeg and onion and brush kidneys all over with the mixture. Heat cream. Stir in instant flour and simmer one minute. Add the white wine and keep mixture warm.

Make Waffles.* Broil kidneys five minutes on the first side. Insert a meat thermometer and broil them on the second side to a temperature of 160°. Bring cream mixture to the boil but do not boil. Add kidneys. Serve with waffles.

MIXED GRILL

In Grandmother's youth, the central feature of a mixed grill was an inch thick lamb chop for each person to be served. She began by broiling the chops on one side — about six minutes. Since they took longer to cook than the other items, after four minutes she added lamb kidneys, split. After turning the chops and the kidneys, she added bacon, mushrooms, tomatoes, slices of cooked sweet potatoes, dotted the vegetables with butter and cooked them until everything was done — about six minutes more. This was for chops that were still pink. If you liked them well done, you allowed more time on the first side and removed the vegetables and bacon as soon as they were cooked to suit you, to a hot platter.

If I acquire a chop an inch thick, I regard it as frivolous to treat it as only part of a mixture. It becomes the *pièce de résistance* of a serious meal with baked potatoes and nourishing vegetables. If I make a mixed grill, I use for each person to be served:

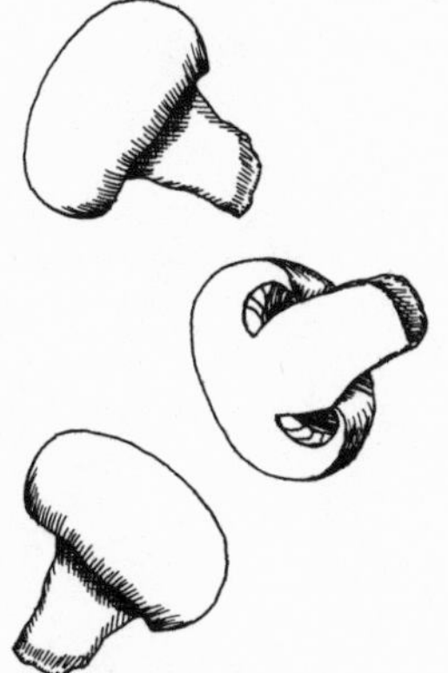

- ½ *tomato with crumbs, garlic powder, pinch of mustard*
- *Grated cheese*
- 3 *link sausages*
- 1 *lamb's kidney, cleaned and split*
- 1 *chicken liver*
- 2 *slices bacon*
- 3 *medium-sized mushroom caps*
- 1 *cooked sweet potato, sliced*
- *Dots of butter*

Begin by fixing tomato halves. Cover them with a mixture of bread crumbs, garlic powder and mustard. Sprinkle grated cheese over them and dot with butter. Set them in a shallow dish in a 350° oven and bake for ten minutes.

Now boil link sausages for seven minutes and drain them on paper towels. On the rack of an electric broiler arrange sausages, kidneys, chicken liver, bacon, mushroom caps and potatoes. Dot all but bacon with butter. Add baked tomatoes. Broil until everything is brown and sizzly — about seven minutes — turning kidneys and liver once. Remove any vegetables as soon as they are done. Transfer all to a serving dish and serve.

Another more substantial form of mixed grill may be prepared as follows:

MIXED GRILL WITH TENDERLOIN

(For 6)

- 6 *tomato halves*
- ½ *cup dry bread crumbs*
- 1 *teaspoon garlic powder*
- *Extra butter*
- 1 *pound tenderloin steak*
- ¼ *pound mushroom caps, sliced*
- 6 *lamb kidneys*
- *Watercress*
- 2 *tablespoons butter*

Use a stainless steel well and tree platter to serve this grill.

Begin by fixing tomatoes. Mix the bread crumbs and the garlic powder. Put tomato halves in a baking pan. Sprinkle them with crumbs, dot with extra butter. Bake until tomatoes are tender, at 350° — about 20 minutes.

Cut steak into six serving pieces. Broil them on one side for three minutes. Arrange them uncooked side up around the platter.

Sauté mushrooms and kidneys in butter without turning. Remove the mushrooms to platter after three minutes, kidneys after six minutes. Put them on the platter uncooked side up.

When tomato halves are ready, arrange them around the platter. Pour juice from the pan in which mushrooms and kidneys were cooked over the tomatoes. Dot them and the steak with butter and pour any gravy from the steak over the meat. Slip platter under the broiler. Broil for five minutes. Garnish with watercress.

Patties of ground round steak may be used instead of the tenderloin.

Mrs. Appleyard never acquired a fondness for tripe. Mr. Appleyard did, however, and such was his wife's devotion that she actually served it from her own kitchen. She later took the position that almost every cook has a specialty. The chef at the Parker House produced perfect tripe, according to Grandfather, so Grandmother suggested that he should eat it there. He did, and she stuck to such minor specialties as Oatmeal Lace Cookies* and Chutney.* This system worked well for them.

BROILED HONEYCOMB TRIPE

1 pound fresh, not pickled, tripe
*1 cup Chicken Stock**
2 tablespoons cider vinegar
3 tablespoons butter, melted
4 tablespoons instant flour
Salt and pepper to taste
Extra butter
1 teaspoon paprika
Juice of 1 lemon

Cut tripe into $2\frac{1}{2}$-inch squares and put in a buttered shallow pan over the lowest possible heat. Pour in heated stock, add vinegar and simmer for three and a half hours. By this time the tripe should be tender and the liquid evaporated. Remove tripe, brush it on both sides with melted butter and roll it in flour mixed with the salt and pepper. Place it on a buttered baking sheet. Sprinkle with paprika. Broil it slowly on both sides until it is delicately brown. Squeeze lemon juice over it and serve.

Tripe cooked this way can be included in a mixed grill: an ideal place for it, Grandmother thought.

LAMB

Mrs. Appleyard's daughter Cicely once had a wonderful idea. Well, as a matter of fact, like all the Appleyards she had interesting ideas every day, but this one she put into practice. She would, she said, buy two lambs and tether them in her backyard. They would keep the grass nibbled down as smooth as a billiard table. The grass would nourish them splendidly so that by the time snow came their fleece could be spun into yarn from which she could knit sweaters for the children and the rest of them (the lambs she meant) could be stored in the freezer locker in the form of roasts, chops and stew meat.

It did not work out just that way:

In the first place the lambs were fussy eaters. Grass they would eat, yes, but not dandelions or plantains or the other standard components of Vermont lawns. What they really liked was flowering plants — larkspurs, anemones, lupines, phlox. They did not care for goldenrod. They loved small children, galloping at them and knocking them down in their affection. When it was suggested that it was time to put the lambs into the freezer locker there were such sobs and wails from the children, such reproachful bleats from the lambs, that Cicely gave up the whole idea.

They grew into rather cynical looking sheep. The children fed them during the winters. In the summers they continued their selective eating thus promoting the growth of goldenrod, fireweed, milkweed and thistles. Pretty soon it was difficult to tell the lawn and the flower garden apart.

After that somewhat unsuccessful episode, when roast lamb was needed, Cicely bought it, and would say generously to her mother, "Come to dinner with us. How would you like the lamb cooked? Shall we have it boned?"

ROAST LAMB

(Old-Fashioned Method)

When time is limited this is the most expeditious method of cooking a lamb roast.

Heat oven to 450°. Brush roast with a little melted butter and then rub it all over with flour seasoned with garlic powder, thyme, oregano, paprika, and freshly ground pepper. Insert a meat thermometer, being careful not to touch fat or bones, if they've been left in. Put roast on a rack in a roasting pan and place in the 450° oven.

Be sure you know accurately what the roast weighs. If you like it slightly pink in the middle allow 18 minutes to the pound with the bones in; without bones, allow 20 minutes to the pound. If it is to be well done allow 20 minutes to the pound with the bones in; 22 minutes to the pound without bones. These figures will give you approximate times by which to calculate the cooking time of your roast. The thermometer will give you the final answer. For a slightly pink middle cook until the thermometer reaches 155°, for well done — 165°. Baste often with a baster shaped like an enormous medicine dropper.

Save the bones and trimmings to make broth for basting and making gravy to go with the roast. Serve with Roast Potatoes Around the Meat.*

ROAST LEG OF LAMB

(Slow Method)

This is certainly the most restful way to cook a roast and leads to melt-in-your-mouth meals.

The meat should be at room temperature when you begin. Brush it with melted butter. Rub it all over with flour seasoned as above — with garlic powder, thyme, oregano, paprika and pepper — or your own mixture. Insert meat thermometer so that it touches neither fat nor bones. Place roast on rack in an uncovered pan. Set into a cold oven. Light oven: 300°. Allow 25-30 minutes a pound. If you like it slightly pink, the thermometer should read 155°. If liked well done, cook until it reads 165°. If roast has not browned sufficiently when you check it 20 minutes before serving time, you may raise the oven temperature to 350° for ten minutes.

Serve with Mint Sauce* or Brown Gravy* made from stock.

SHOULDER ROAST OF LAMB

For a small family a boned shoulder roast of lamb makes a good dinner. Follow, in general, the directions for roasting the leg by the slow method (above). Start cooking at 275°. Allow 40-50 minutes a pound. Cook to 155° for rare, 165° for well done. Like the leg, it may be browned for the last ten minutes at 350°.

One advantage of the slow method is that the day after the roast is first served, you may turn it the other side up, pour gravy over it and heat it at 300° for about half an hour. It will be almost as good as when it was first roasted.

A variation for roast leg or shoulder of lamb is made by making a coating for the meat of crumbs and parsley. Use:

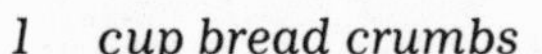

1 cup bread crumbs
½ cup Cross cracker crumbs
1 teaspoon garlic powder
½ teaspoon paprika
2 tablespoons parsley, minced
3 tablespoons butter, melted

Prepare bread crumbs by drying triangles of stale bread in a 300° oven until they are just starting to brown. Roll into fine crumbs. Roll crackers also and mix the crumbs with the bread crumbs. Add seasonings and parsley. Last of all add butter. Spread mixture evenly over roast and cook it at 300°, allowing a little longer per pound than you would without the parsley crust.

CURRY OF LAMB

(For 6)

Cooked lamb may be simmered a long time and made into curry, but it's better if you start with raw lamb from the shoulder cut into inch cubes.

1½ cups stock, from bones
2 tablespoons flour
2 tablespoons curry powder
1½ pounds lamb, cut into cubes
1 tablespoon minced onion
2 tablespoons butter
1 cup milk
1 teaspoon paprika
1 teaspoon garlic powder
1 cup seedless grapes
4 hard-boiled eggs
½ cup blanched and toasted almonds
1 tablespoon chopped parsley
½ cup cream

Make stock from bones, with celery, carrots and one teaspoon poultry seasoning, the day before you serve the curry. Strain and chill it.

The next day, mix flour with curry powder and roll lamb cubes in the mixture. Cook onion in butter until it is straw colored. Add lamb cubes and brown them. Remove fat from stock, heat it and add to the mixture. Simmer until lamb is tender — about 50 minutes. Heat milk and cream and stir them in. Add paprika and garlic powder. Simmer until sauce is quite thick. Stir in green grapes. Put curry in a shallow bowl. Decorate it with quarters of hard-boiled eggs and toasted almonds. Sprinkle with chopped parsley.

With the curry serve Kasha,* Brown Rice* or groats. Spiced applesauce and Mrs. Appleyard's Chutney* go well with it, too.

Once when Mrs. Appleyard did not feel in a mood for a roast she invented:

LAMB ROLL WITH CUMBERLAND MINT SAUCE

- *¾ pound raw lamb, ground*
- *1 small onion, minced*
- *2 tablespoons minced pimento*
- *¼ teaspoon pepper*
- *¼ cup chopped mushrooms*
- *2 teaspoons minced parsley*
- *2 tablespoons Mrs. Appleyard's Chutney**
- *¼ teaspoon dry mustard*
- *1 tablespoon soft butter*

Mix all ingredients, set them aside at room temperature while you roll out the dough. Use Bisquick if you like — or better yet, make your own dough:

- *1½ cups flour*
- *¼ teaspoon thyme*
- *Salt and pepper to taste*
- *1½ teaspoons baking powder*
- *¼ teaspoon marjoram*
- *3 tablespoons butter*
- *½ cup rich milk*
- *2 tablespoons cream*
- *Extra butter*

Sift flour and dry ingredients together three times. Cut in butter. Add milk and mix until dough is moist. Handle as little as possible. Roll into an 8x10-inch rectangle. Spread lamb mixture to within an inch of the edge. Roll up like a jelly roll. Set oven at 425°. Moisten edge of dough with cream, seal, fasten with toothpicks, and dot with butter. Put roll in a buttered pan, or in a teflon baking pan. Brush with cream. Bake at 425° for 20 minutes. Reduce heat to 350° and bake until well browned — about ten minutes longer. Serve with Cumberland Mint Sauce.*

CROWN ROAST OF LAMB

(For 8)

- *16 rib chops of lamb*
- *8 link sausages*
- *1 cup Kasha (cracked wheat or bulghur)*
- *1 pound mushrooms, caps only*
- *1 medium onion, minced*
- *3 tablespoons butter*
- *¼ teaspoon pepper*
- *Salt to taste*
- *Pinches of paprika and thyme*
- *¼ teaspoon nutmeg*
- *6 tomatoes, halved*
- *1 cup bread and cracker crumbs*
- *3 cloves of garlic, crushed*
- *1 tablespoon minced parsley*
- *Sprays of parsley, watercress and mint*
- *½ cup cream*

Have the butcher make rib chops into a crown.

Cut sausage links each into two pieces, making a slit in the cut end of each one, and slip them over the ends of the chop bones. Light oven: 300°. For a three-pound crown roast allow one and a quarter hours for medium rare, one and a half for well done. If you use a meat thermometer, insert it in the lean meat, not touching bone or fat. It should reach 160° for medium (slightly pink), 165° for well done. It is difficult to insert a thermometer into a crown roast, so you may have to depend on instinct or luck.

While the roast is cooking, make the stuffing.

Stuffing: Grandmother had a neighbor who ground whole wheat to just the right coarseness for Kasha. I substitute bulghur wheat from our food cooperative, but you may use groats, brown rice or wild rice.

Drop Kasha into 2 cups of boiling water and cook five minutes, stirring carefully. Then put the pan over hot water and cook until grains have absorbed all the water — about 20 minutes. Brown rice will take longer.

In the meantime, wash mushrooms. Button mushrooms of medium size are best for this purpose. Cut off stems at the level of the caps and slice caps vertically. Cook onion in butter until straw colored. Add sliced mushrooms, sprinkle with pepper, salt to taste, paprika, thyme and nutmeg. Mix them with Kasha and keep mixture hot. Twenty minutes before serving time, fill the center of the roast with the stuffing.

Garnish: The tomatoes are used for garnishing the roast. Slice tomatoes in halves. Cover them with bread and cracker crumbs, mixed with crushed garlic. Bake them in a shallow pan for 15 minutes at 350°. Just before serving pour a little thick cream over each one. Slide them under the broiler until crumbs are brown — about three minutes.

Now the great moment has come. Put roast on a circular platter. Arrange tomatoes around the roast. Sprinkle them with minced parsley. Put a sprig of parsley, one of mint and one of watercress on top of the stuffing. It's such a pleasant picture that it seems a pity to take a knife to it, but go right ahead, it's as good as it looks.

RAGOUT OF LAMB

1½ cups lamb stock (from bones)
Bit of bay leaf
2 cloves
1½ pounds lean lamb from shoulder
2 tablespoons flour
½ teaspoon garlic powder
½ teaspoon oregano
3 tablespoons butter
1 onion, minced
4 small carrots, sliced
½ teaspoon instant coffee
1 10-ounce package frozen tiny peas
1 teaspoon minced parsley

The day before you plan to serve the ragout, put bones on to cook with three cups of cold water, bay leaf and cloves. Simmer three hours, strain and chill.

The next day cut lamb into inch cubes. Dip in flour mixed with garlic and oregano. Melt butter in a large frying pan, add diced onion, carrot slices and lamb. Toss all in butter until the flour browns.

Remove fat from the stock. Heat it with coffee, add it to meat and simmer two hours. Cook frozen peas. Put lamb in the center of a round platter, add the small amount of gravy that is left. Arrange carrots and peas around meat. Arrange potato balls which have been dipped in butter, chives and parsley around the edge. Decorate with sprays of watercress and serve.

Pies

VERMONT is overrun with rules for pies, especially apple and other fruit pies. For before the days of reliable refrigeration, the pie was a winter staple. The back pantry, where things obliged you by freezing whether or not you wanted them to, was commonly stocked with dozens of pies made just before snow flew. Housewives needed only to pull out a pie in time for it to thaw sufficiently before supper or breakfast, and on many a breakfast table they appeared as regularly as bacon and eggs. Many women were almost saddened by the coming of spring, for it meant the pantry "deep freeze" was no longer operable and desserts must be made up from scratch. This melancholy was generally brief, lasting only as long as it took the strawberries to ripen, their promise of another season of fruit pies — strawberry, rhubarb, blueberry, raspberry, blackberry, apple: a summer calendar of pies.

Flour, salt, shortening, and water are the basic ingredients of any pastry. Other ingredients or variations of these four may be added in special instances. For example, herbs add a distinctive flavor to meat-pie crusts, and spices, grated orange or lemon rind, or chopped nuts provide a change for fruit or pumpkin pie crusts. Fruit juice may replace all or part of the water in fruit-pie crusts; sugar may be added to the pastry used for deep-dish fruit pies; and grated cheese may be substituted for part of the shortening in apple pie crusts.

Grandmother deplored the making of pies at all unless the pastry was worthy of the best filling and vice-versa. She has told in previous discourses how to make pastry that is light, tender, flaky, and delicately brown. So that you might have it at hand in the event that a yearning, or a request, for pie production strikes you, I repeat my Grandmother's rule for:

TWO THOUSAND LAYER PASTRY

The name of this pastry used to frighten me, simply because the number of layers sounded overwhelming. In reality, the method is quite simple once it is learned, and the results will be more than worth the effort. Novice pie-makers should not be frightened, for they are often more likely to enjoy success with this method than experienced pastry cooks, who may find it difficult to resist their impulses to knead the pastry and pound it with the rolling pin. Old dogs must positively foreswear those tricks if they are to succeed with this recipe.

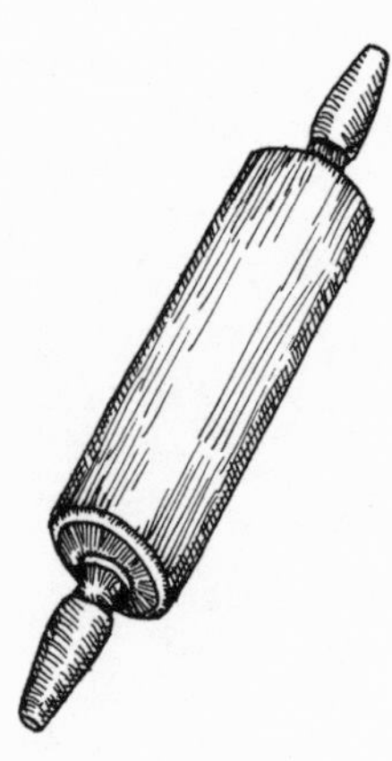

Grandmother learned this routine from her grandmother. Her own contribution was a mathematical exegesis. The essential feature of the process is that you keep cutting the gently rolled pastry into three pieces, turning the board ninety degrees, piling the pieces on top of one another, and rolling the pastry out again. The first time this is done, three layers result; the second time, nine layers. The number of layers increases so rapidly that if this is done seven times, you have 2,187 layers of pastry. Thus the name, Two Thousand Layer Pastry — a modest approximation. Grandmother has made about 20,000 layers on occasion — and once, out of curiosity, she repeated the process ten times, thus creating (she figured) 59,049 strata. She reported little difference from the mere 2,000 layer form.

To begin, chill a large bowl, preferably of wood or pottery, a chopping knife or pastry cutter, and a spatula; and the water, butter, and lard or shortening.

These are the ingredients you will need:

1 cup ice water
1 cup chilled butter
1 cup chilled lard or vegetable shortening
4 cups all-purpose flour
Salt to taste
Extra flour for rolling out — as little as possible

Sift flour three times, adding the salt during the final sifting. Measure it. Use what is left beyond the four cups for flouring the pastry board and rolling pin. Use a pastry board cloth and rolling pin stocking if you have them, or fasten lightly floured waxed paper to the board and rolling pin. *Note:* I find the cloth much more manageable.

Put sifted flour, butter, and lard into a large bowl. Chop gently with a pastry cutter until butter and lard are well distributed throughout the flour in pieces no bigger than the tip of your little finger.

Add half a cup of ice water, all at once. Work it in well with chopper. Add the rest of the water and work it in with the chopper. You now have the pastry, which you should religiously avoid touching with your hands.

That you need not wonder at this prohibition, I shall explain it to you fully in a moment. In the meantime, use the chopper and spatula — and not your hands — to get the pastry out of the bowl and onto the floured board.

Roll the pastry out gently into an oval about 12 inches long. Cut it into three pieces, the short way. Lay the two end pieces on top of the middle one. Turn the board 90 degrees. Roll pastry out again, never touching it with your hands if it can be helped. Cut into three pieces again, laying end pieces on top of the middle one. Continue until you have repeated the process seven times, at which point you will have 2,187 layers of cold air trapped within the pastry. When you finally bake it, the heat of the oven will suddenly strike the cold air trapped within the layers, and the air will expand, making the pastry rise to a fluffy lightness. The reason you must not touch the raw pastry with your hands — much less knead it or pound it with the rolling pin — is that the warmth of your hands and the pressure of the rolling pin will begin to melt the chilled butter and lard, thus gluing the fragile layers together and driving out their little cushions of air. It is air we are out to capture, and it must be netted as gently as a butterfly. This recipe will make you more than enough pastry for one pie. I cut it into three chunks, each sufficient for a single, good-sized crust. What is not needed immediately may be wrapped in waxed paper and shaped gently into a ball as you wrap. (This should be the nearest you come to touching the paste with your hands.) It may be put into the refrigerator to be used the next day — rolled out for turnovers, tarts, pies, or cheese straws as you wish. Or it may be wrapped in aluminum foil and frozen for future use, though freezing will tend to dry it out a bit.

Mrs. Appleyard was once heard to ask a man what his favorite kind of pie was. He replied rhubarb, which surprised Grandmother, and she told him so.

"I always thought men liked apple pie best," she said.

Her friend replied gallantly, "Of course I meant *next* to apple. Every man's favorite is apple, and deep-dish apple is mine. After rhubarb comes pumpkin."

That being the case, I begin with:

DEEP-DISH APPLE PIE

For one deep-dish pie to be made in a nine-inch dish, use:

	2,000 Layer Pastry for one crust	12	*McIntosh apples, washed, pared, cored, and sliced*
⅔	*cup granulated sugar*	¼	*cup butter*
¼	*teaspoon nutmeg*		*Juice and grated rind*
⅛	*teaspoon cinnamon*		*of 1 lemon*

Mix sugar and spices. Grease dish lightly with paper from a stick of butter. Put in a layer of apple slices and sprinkle them with spiced sugar, dot with butter, and sprinkle with lemon juice and rind. Repeat layers until the dish is full, heaping apples slightly toward the center of the dish.

Next, roll out a circle of pastry that is slightly larger than the dish.

Moisten the edge of the dish slightly. Put the pastry circle on top of the apples, press it down lightly, and trim it neatly. Of the trimmings, make a twisted ribbon of pastry and lay it all the way around the dish quite close to the edge. Using shears, cut openings for steam to escape.

You may make bowknots out of the last scraps of pastry to decorate the top of the pie. You needn't tie them: just lay two loops and two ends in appropriate positions, and where they join place a small strip to serve as the knot.

Chill pie in refrigerator until the oven is heated to 450°. Bake it for ten minutes, then reduce heat to 350°, and continue to bake until the crust is puffed and delicately browned — about 35 minutes longer. Serve the pie warm with Hard Sauce,* thick cream, or ice cream. Many Vermonters think a wedge of Vermont cheese is a necessity with deep-dish apple pie. Choose for yourself.

A more traditional apple pie is the two-crust variety below.

APPLE PIE

Pastry for a double crust

- 1 *tablespoon instant flour (extra)*
- 1 *tablespoon sugar (extra)*
- ⅛ *teaspoon each of cinnamon and nutmeg (extra)*
- 6 *large tart apples, peeled and sliced very thin*
- 1 *cup sugar*
- 1 *teaspoon cinnamon*
- ¼ *teaspoon nutmeg*
- ⅛ *teaspoon cloves*
- 2 *teaspoons butter*
- ½ *teaspoon lemon juice*
- ¼ *teaspoon grated lemon rind*

Line a nine-inch pie plate with 2,000 Layer Pastry or your own variety. Never grease a pie plate: good pastry does its own greasing.

Mix the instant flour, extra sugar, and extra spices carefully and scatter the mixture over the bottom crust. This mixture will help keep the lower crust from getting soggy. Preheat the oven to 450°.

Put a layer of apples into the pie plate, scattering sugar and spices over them. Repeat with layers of apple slices and sugar and spices, until the plate is full. Dot the top layer with small bits of butter and sprinkle the whole with lemon juice and rind.

Moisten the edge of the bottom crust slightly with a damp (not wet) pastry brush. Put on the top crust, trim it, and pleat its edges neatly with your fingers. Gash it in three places to let steam escape. Bake the pie at 450° for 15 minutes. Reduce heat to 350° and continue baking until the pastry is well browned — about half an hour longer.

APPLE PIE WITH A TANG

- 7 *tart apples, peeled, cored, cut in eighths*
- ½ *cup sugar*
- ¼ *cup water*
- 4 *tablespoons maple syrup*
- 1 *tablespoon lemon juice*
- 1 *tablespoon orange juice*
- *Grated rind of 1 lemon and 1 orange*
- 1 *tablespoon orange curaçao*
- 2 *tablespoons sugar*
- 2 *tablespoons instant flour*
- ⅛ *teaspoon nutmeg*
- *Pastry for two crusts*

Begin by cutting the apple slices in half and poaching them in a syrup

**See Index for pages where recipes can be found.*

made of ½ cup sugar, water, and maple syrup. Cool slightly. Add lemon juice, orange juice, grated lemon and orange rind, and orange curaçao.

Line a 9-inch glass pie plate with pastry. Scatter over it sugar and flour seasoned with nutmeg. Add apple mixture. Preheat the oven to 450°.

Cut pastry for the top crust into half-inch strips and cover filling with a lattice of pastry. When making a lattice pie crust, I first place a strip of pastry running north and south and cross it with another running east and west. I continue this alternation until the top of the pie is covered. When pie fillings are juicy, a lattice crust permits more steam to escape and thus helps to prevent the juices from bubbling over into the oven. Moisten the edges of the crust slightly and seal them with a ribbon of pastry made by twisting two strips together.

Bake pie at 450° for 15 minutes. Reduce temperature to 350° and bake until the crust is well-browned — about 25 minutes longer.

You may, of course, use the same pastry for any number of pies, with delectable results. For example:

APPLE CHEESE PIE

This is a lattice pie, put together like the one above. You will need these ingredients:

	Pastry for a bottom crust and top lattice	2	*eggs*
2	*tablespoons instant flour*	2	*tablespoons lemon juice*
2	*tablespoons sugar*	1	*teaspoon dried lemon rind*
⅛	*teaspoon cinnamon*	¼	*cup Vermont cheddar cheese*
2½	*cups applesauce*	1	*tablespoon butter*

Line a 9-inch pie plate with pastry. Scatter over it the instant flour mixed with sugar and cinnamon.

Pour applesauce into the pastry shell. Beat eggs together with lemon juice and pour this mixture over the apple sauce. Sprinkle the top with dried lemon rind and cover with thin strips of cheddar. Dot with butter and weave a lattice over all.

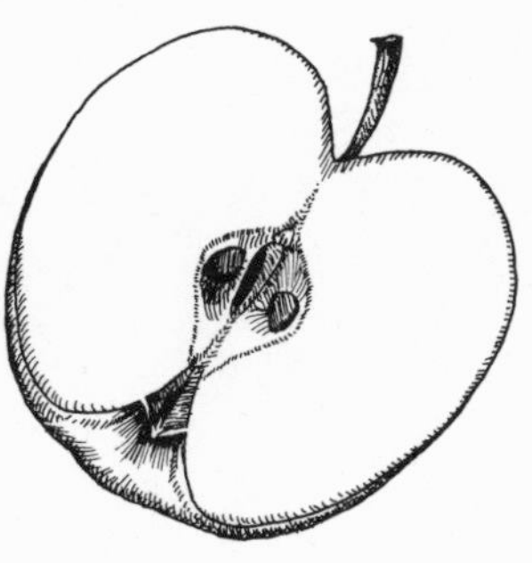

Bake the pie at 450° for ten minutes. Reduce heat to 350° and continue baking until the pastry is puffed and brown, about half an hour longer. Do not overbake, or the cheese custard will separate.

CIDER APPLE PIE

This is also made with a lattice crust, but is baked in a rather deep dish with only a top crust.

6	*large apples, cut in eighths*	½	*teaspoon nutmeg*
4	*cups real cider*	1	*tablespoon butter*
2	*tablespoons instant flour*	1	*egg yolk, beaten*
1	*cup sugar*	1	*cup thick sweet cream*
½	*teaspoon cinnamon*		*Pastry for lattice crust*

Peel, core, and cut the apples into eighths. Boil the peelings and cores in the cider until the cider is reduced from 4 cups to 1 cup. Strain the cider.

Put layers of apple slices into a well-buttered deep dish. Mix flour and sugar with spices and sprinkle over each layer of apple slices. Pour strained cider over apples. Dot top layer with butter. Beat egg and cream together with a wire whisk and pour mixture over the apples. Weave a lattice crust on top and bake at 450° for ten minutes. Reduce heat to 350° and continue baking until the crust is puffed and lightly browned — about 25 minutes longer. Serve with cheese.

BLUEBERRY PIE

I like to follow in my family's tradition of using blueberries brought home by me, my brothers, and any of the various cousins or friends who happen to be around for the annual climb to the top of Camel's Hump. I suppose that blueberries from another mountain top — or even a farm stand or grocery store — would do. If you must use cultivated berries, sprinkle them with a teaspoon of lemon juice for wildness and an extra teaspoon of sugar to restore their freshness before you cover them with the crust. When you clean blueberries, wild or domestic, remove any leaves or twigs, but leave the few red or greenish berries — they add tartness to the flavor.

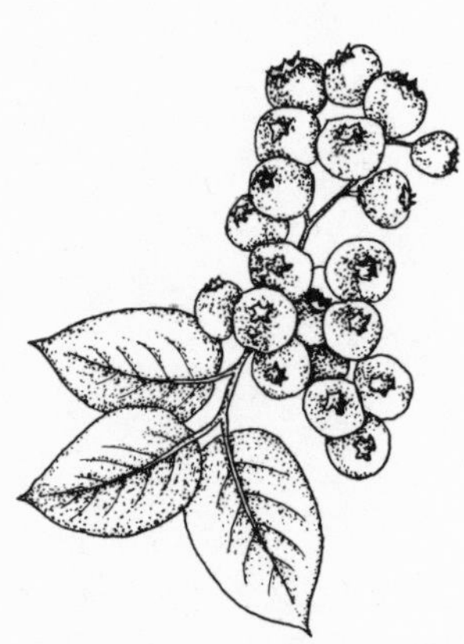

For a 9-inch pie plate of glass or teflon, use:

Pastry for a double crust
2 *tablespoons instant flour*
2 *tablespoons sugar*
3 *cups blueberries*
1 *cup sugar*
2 *teaspoons butter*

Preheat oven to 450°. Line a 9-inch pie plate with pastry. Mix instant flour and sugar together and scatter over bottom crust. Put berries into the crust in layers, sprinkling each layer with sugar, and finishing with sugar. Dot butter over the berries and sprinkle them with lemon juice if extra tartness is needed.

Moisten edge of lower crust with a damp pastry brush. Cover the pie with top crust, gashing it in three places to let the steam escape. Flute the edges carefully. There will be lots of juice — which you want to keep in the pie, not the oven — so be sure the edges are well sealed. Bind the edge with a strip of gauze or aluminum foil, if you like. This will help keep the juices inside and will also prevent the edge from browning too quickly. Another method of keeping pie juice where it belongs is to roll small cones of smooth glazed paper and insert them, points up, in the gashes in the top crust. The juice will rise in the cones while the pie bakes and go down again as the pie cools.

Bake the pie at 450° for 15 minutes. Reduce heat to 350° and bake until the crust is well browned — 30 to 35 minutes longer. Serve warm but not hot with vanilla ice cream or cheddar cheese. If the pie is served too hot, the filling will run out when the first cut is made. It would be a shame for the first recipient to get all the filling.

CRANBERRY LATTICE PIE

2 *cups cranberries*
⅔ *cup water*
1 *cup sugar*
Pastry for a double crust
2 *tablespoons instant flour*
2 *tablespoons sugar*

Put cranberries, water, and sugar — in that order — into a saucepan. Cook until all the berries pop — about ten minutes. Cool the berries while you roll out a lower pastry crust and cut half-inch strips for the lattice. Preheat the oven to 450°.

Line a 9-inch pie plate with pastry. Scatter flour and sugar mixture over the lower crust. Put in cooked cranberries. Moisten edge of crust slightly, using a damp pastry brush, and weave a lattice over the top. Bake for 15 minutes at 450°. Reduce heat to 350° and continue to bake until the crust is well-browned, about 30 minutes longer.

Other lattice pies, with a variety of fillings, may be made in the same manner. Here are some variations.

CRANBERRY-RASPBERRY PIE

2	*cups cranberries*	⅔	*cup juice drained from frozen raspberries*
1	*cup sugar*		

Cook these ingredients together until the cranberries all pop — about 10 minutes. Proceed as above with Cranberry Lattice Pie.

APRICOT CROSSBAR PIE

Serve this pie warm with thick Vermont cream in a pitcher, or with ice cream, or with cheddar cheese.

2	*12-ounce boxes dried apricots*	1¼	*cups sugar*
		2	*cups water*

Cook the apricots the day before you make the pie. Start the water boiling in a saucepan deep enough to hold an Italian folding steamer. Have the legs of the steamer long enough so that the apricots will be held above the water. Cover the saucepan tightly and steam the apricots until they are tender — about 12 to 15 minutes. Be sure the water does not boil away: there should be about 1¼ cups of it left in the saucepan when the apricots have cooked. Pack the steamed apricots into a quart jar, pressing them down if necessary. Some of the flavor of the fruit will be left in the water in the saucepan. Add the sugar to it and cook until the syrup just starts to color. Pour the syrup over the packed apricots and set the jar in a cool place until you are ready to begin the pie.

For the pie, you will need:

2 *eggs, well beaten*

2	*tablespoons syrup from apricots*	1	*pint cooked apricots, cut into half-inch pieces*
2	*tablespoons lemon juice*		*Pastry for a double crust*
	Grated lemon rind	2	*tablespoons instant flour*
1	*tablespoon undiluted frozen orange juice*	2	*tablespoons sugar*
		½	*cup blanched and slivered almonds*
1	*tablespoon Cointreau (optional)*	1	*tablespoon butter, melted*

Mix beaten eggs, syrup from apricots, lemon juice and rind, orange juice, and Cointreau. Add apricots. Line a 9-inch pie plate with pastry. Scatter flour and sugar mixture over it. Preheat oven to 450°.

Put apricot mixture into pastry shell. Sprinkle the apricots with blanched almonds that have been shredded and brushed with melted butter. Weave the lattice crossbars into place — not too close together: they will expand. Bake pie at 450° for 15 minutes. Reduce heat to 350°

and bake until the crust is puffed and lightly browned, about 30 to 35 minutes longer.

MINCEMEAT

If you have a large, hungry family, a big covered crock and a cool cellar or pantry to keep it in, you might like to make your own mincemeat. If so, use:

3	*pounds round of beef*	*2*	*pounds currants*
1	*gallon fizzy cider*	*1*	*pound seeded raisins*
	Tart apples pared, cored, and quartered: enough for 2 cups chopped apples per cup of chopped beef	*1*	*tablespoon lemon extract*
			Juice and grated rind of 2 lemons
		1½	*tablespoons nutmeg*
1	*pound suet*	*1*	*tablespoon cinnamon*
1	*pound citron, chopped fine*	*½*	*teaspoon cloves*
¼	*pound each, candied orange and lemon peel*	*2*	*teaspoons allspice*
		2	*pounds sugar*
2	*pounds seedless raisins*	*3*	*cups brandy*

Simmer the beef until tender, about 5 hours. Do not put it through a grinder. Use a wooden bowl and a chopper to chop it fine. Remove any pieces of gristle as you chop. While you are busy at the chopping bowl, cook 1 gallon of fizzy cider down to 2 quarts, and reduce to 1 quart the water in which the beef was simmered. Chop the apple into the beef. Chop in suet. Add 1 quart of cooked cider to moisten the mixture.

In the other quart of cooked cider, simmer citron and candied lemon and orange peel for 10 minutes. Skim them out and add them to the meat. Add currants, raisins, lemon extract and lemon juice, spices, and sugar. Add a cup and a half of beef stock. Put the whole mixture into a heavy kettle and simmer for two hours over very low heat. Stir occasionally from bottom and add the rest of the cider and the remainder of the beef stock.

When the mixture is quite thick and almost dry, cool it slightly and stir in the brandy. Pack it into a crock and let it stand in a cool place for at least a week. If necessary, add a little more brandy just before you make your pies.

MINCEMEAT PIE

2 cups mincemeat, preferably homemade
Pastry for a double crust

If you are not using homemade mincemeat, you may heat store-bought mincemeat in the top of a double boiler and add some brandy, raisins, chopped fresh apple, and butter the day before you plan to bake your pies.

Line a 9-inch pie plate with pastry. Fill it with mincemeat and dot with butter. Moisten the edge of the pastry, cover with the top crust, and flute the edges with your fingers. Gash the crust in three or four places to let the pungent steam escape. If you wish, you may decorate the edges with extra pastry that has been rolled and braided.

Bake at 450° on the lower shelf of the oven for 30 minutes. Then move the pie to the upper shelf and bake at 350° until it is well browned, about half an hour longer. Serve mincemeat pie warm or cold, with vanilla ice cream or wedges of Vermont cheese.

MINIATURE MINCE TURNOVERS

If you have a little pastry left over and also a little mincemeat, it is easy to make these.

Preheat the oven to 450°. Roll out the pastry into an 8-inch square about 1/6-inch thick. Cut it into 16 two-inch squares.

Place a teaspoon of mincemeat on each square, moisten the edges, fold the squares over into triangles, and crimp the edges with the back of a lightly floured fork. Put the turnovers on a teflon cookie sheet and bake them for 15 minutes. Check to see if they are puffed and delicately browned. Bake 5 minutes longer if need be.

Don't worry if the mincemeat oozes out a little at the edges: it tastes all the better. These turnovers are quite nourishing at 10° below zero whether they are served warm or cold.

If you must, use packaged pastry and mincemeat from a jar, by all means add a little brandy, fresh chopped apple, and butter.

PUMPKIN PIE

(For 8)

Begin by caramelizing the pumpkin. Butter a large iron frying pan and cook two cups of pumpkin, stirring often, till the sugar in it caramelizes and the pumpkin is as dry as good mashed potato and a deep, rich golden-brown in color. Give it your complete attention, or you will wind up with a brown speckled mess suitable for gluing down floor tiles. Start with 2 cups of pumpkin in order to finish with 1½ cups cooked.

For two 8-inch pies or one 12-inch pie, you will need:

1½	*cups caramelized pumpkin*	*1*	*teaspoon cinnamon*
	Pastry for pie shells	*½*	*teaspoon salt*
2	*tablespoons flour*	*½*	*teaspoon nutmeg*
1	*cup sugar*	*2*	*eggs*
3	*cups rich milk*	*2*	*tablespoons sugar mixed with 1 tablespoon flour*
1	*cup cream*		

½ teaspoon ginger

Put the caramelized pumpkin in a large bowl, sprinkle it with 2 tablespoons flour, stir thoroughly, then stir in the sugar.

Butter the bottom of a saucepan and scald milk in it. Add cream and seasonings to the scalded milk. Pour it into the pumpkin mixture and stir. Add well-beaten eggs. Stir everything together until the mixture is well blended.

Have your pie shells built up well around the edge and nicely fluted. Scatter the flour and sugar mixture over the bottom crust.

Fill the pie shells with pumpkin mixture to a depth of about ¾ inch. Moisten strips of gauze and put them around the edges of the pies to keep them from browning too fast. Or use strips of aluminum foil and remove them during the final 10 minutes of baking.

Bake the pies at 450° for 15 minutes, then reduce the heat to 325°

and bake about half an hour longer. The pies are done when they just shake in the center, or when a knife slipped into the middle comes out clean.

Variation: For a tangier pie, replace ½ cup of the milk with bourbon.

For a special treat made with pumpkin caramelized in the same way as above, try:

DEEP-DISH PUMPKIN PIE

For a 2-quart deep dish:

	Pastry for a top crust	*1*	*cup cream*
1	*teaspoon flour mixed with 1 teaspoon sugar and a dash of cinnamon*	*1*	*teaspoon cinnamon*
		½	*teaspoon ginger*
		½	*teaspoon nutmeg*
1½	*cups caramelized pumpkin*	*2*	*tablespoons sherry*
2	*tablespoons flour*	*1*	*cup sugar*
3	*cups rich milk*	*2*	*eggs, beaten*

First, prepare a circular pastry lid. Preheat the oven to 450°. Roll out the pastry into a circle the size of the dish you are going to use for the pie. Sift the flour, sugar, and cinnamon mixture over it and decorate it with a twisted ribbon edge and bowknot in the center.

Carefully transfer the pastry to a teflon cookie sheet. Bake at 450° for 10 minutes. Reduce heat to 350° and continue to bake until it is well browned — about half an hour longer. Remove it from the oven and cool but do not chill it.

Caramelize the pumpkin in the manner described in the recipe above. Place the caramelized pumpkin in a bowl, scatter flour over it, and stir it well. Scald but do not boil the milk and cream, add spices and sherry, and pour this mixture over the pumpkin. Add sugar and well-beaten eggs.

Butter and dust with flour a 2-quart baking dish. I inherited a brown tortoise-shell Bennington dish for great occasions such as this. Reduce oven heat to 325°. Pour the pumpkin custard — for a custard it is — into the dish and bake for half an hour or until it just shakes in the middle (175° in case you use a thermometer). Be sure the oven is not too hot, or the custard will curdle.

Chill the pumpkin custard well. When serving time comes, place the pastry lid on the dish and serve it to cries of "And how did you ever get the pastry so flaky?" You may choose to reveal the secret — or smile your best Yankee smile and leave them to wonder. A little cheese goes well with this pie.

Easier to make is:

MRS. APPLEYARD'S PUMPKIN PIE WITH SOUR CREAM

1½	*cups caramelized pumpkin*	*½*	*teaspoon nutmeg*
2	*tablespoons flour*	*2*	*tablespoons sherry*
3	*cups rich milk*	*1*	*cup sugar*
1	*cup cream*	*½*	*cup sour cream*
1	*teaspoon cinnamon*	*2*	*eggs, beaten*

This is made in the same way as the Deep-Dish Pumpkin Pie above, with ½ cup sour cream added. Follow the instructions for caramelizing pumpkin as in the recipe for Pumpkin Pie.* Put the caramelized pumpkin into a large bowl, scatter flour over it and stir well. Scald but do not boil milk and cream, add spices and sherry, and pour this mixture into the pumpkin. Add sugar, sour cream, and well-beaten eggs and mix well. Set aside to cool.

For the crust, you will need:

- ¾ *cup Cross crackers, rolled fine*
- ½ *cup homemade bread crumbs, dried and rolled fine*
- ½ *cup sugar*
- 1 *teaspoon mixed spice (cinnamon, nutmeg, allspice, cloves)*
- 1 *teaspoon dried lemon peel*

Mix together the cracker crumbs, bread crumbs, sugar, spices, and lemon peel. Thoroughly butter a deep dish — one that will hold at least 5 cups easily. Reserve ½ cup of the crumb mixture for topping and use the rest to coat the bottom and sides of the buttered dish. Chill it slightly while you wait for the pumpkin mixture to cool. Spoon the cooled pumpkin custard into the crumb crust carefully so as not to displace it. Scatter the crumb topping over the custard.

Bake at 275° for one hour, or to a central reading of 175° on the thermometer. Dust the top with sugar and run the dish under the broiler for about three minutes, or until it is rich, golden brown. Watch it! It can burn easily. Chill thoroughly before serving.

CELESTIAL PIE

To serve 12, use two 8-inch pie plates, buttered. It is good to make this up the day before you want to serve it.

- 3 *egg whites, beaten to stiff peaks*
- 1 *cup sugar sifted with 1 teaspoon baking powder*
- 1 *teaspoon vanilla*
- 1 *cup broken pecan meats, chopped*
- 1 *cup heavy cream*
- 1 *10-ounce package frozen raspberries*
- 5 *Pilot biscuits, rolled very fine*

Work the sugar and baking powder mixture slowly into stiffly beaten egg whites. Add vanilla, cracker crumbs, and chopped pecans. Divide the mixture into two buttered pie plates. Bake them at 325° for 35 minutes. Cool, then cover with waxed paper and chill for at least 3 hours.

At serving time, whip one cup heavy cream and top the pies with it. Serve thawed, frozen raspberries for your guests to spoon over their pie.

RHUBARB PIE

A Vermont cookbook would be incomplete without a rule for rhubarb pie. The showing of rhubarb is one of the first true signs of spring. While dirt roads are still making automobiles wallow in mud, and neither daffodils nor apple blossoms have yet shown their beauty, the rhubarb may be spotted in the garden patch. For pie or any other rhubarb concoction, pick the rhubarb when the first stalks come up. By the time its ivory plumes of flowers appear, it will be tough and stringy. Young "strawberry rhubarb" makes the best pie.

For a 9-inch pie, use:

	Pastry for a double crust	⅛ *teaspoon each of cinnamon and nutmeg*
3	*cups rhubarb*	1 *egg well beaten*
2	*tablespoons flour*	2 *tablespoons butter cut into 12 bits*
1½	*cups sugar*	

Use the youngest, tenderest "strawberry rhubarb" — the kind that needs no peeling. Discard leaves and lower ends of stalks and cut into ½-inch pieces.

Line a 9-inch pie tin with pastry. Leave a good margin of pastry to be turned up over the top crust and crimped with a fork so that no juice will run out. I dislike any drippings in the oven, because I resent spending time cleaning it, so I always place a cookie sheet under fruit pies just in case they drip. In my experience, they have never failed to do so.

Sift flour, sugar, and spice together. Scatter ¼ cup of this mixture over the lower crust. Add half of the rhubarb, half of the remaining sugar mixture, then the rest of the rhubarb and the last of the sugar and spice. Heap the rhubarb slightly toward the center of the pie: it will sink while baking.

Pour the beaten egg over the pie and dot it with bits of butter. Set the top crust in place and gash it well so that steam can escape. Bake at 450° for 15 minutes. Reduce the heat to 350° and continue baking until the fruit is tender and the crust is brown and puffed — about 40 minutes longer. If it browns too quickly, cover it with a tent of aluminum foil, but remove the tent during the last 10 minutes of baking. Enjoy the coming of spring!

LEMON PIE

(For 6)

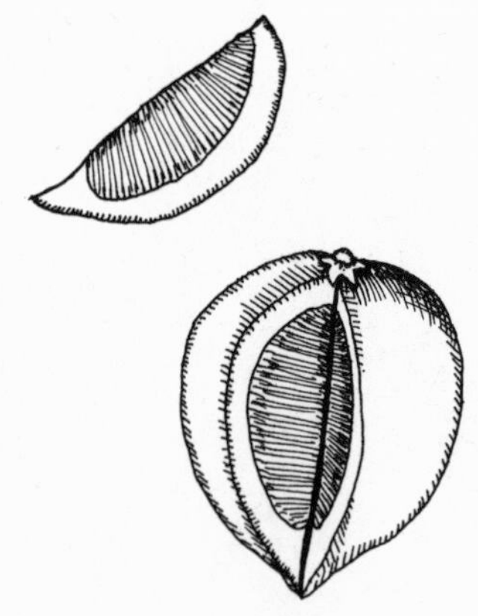

This is a lemon pie rule that has never seen cornstarch. And perhaps if cornstarch were even waved over the completed pie, it would take on the flavor of rancid glue. If you are one of those whose culinary tastes balk at the mention of cornstarch, read on.

For a 10-inch pie plate, use:

	Pastry for a single crust	1½	*tablespoons soft butter*
5	*whole eggs, separated*	3	*tablespoons frozen condensed orange juice*
1½	*cups sugar*	½	*cup lemon juice*
5	*tablespoons instant flour*		

Grated rind of 1 lemon

Prepare a bottom crust. You may bake it the usual way — on the inside of the pie tin. Prick it all over with a fork so that it will not bulge from steam trapped underneath. Build up the edges and flute them. Or you may choose to live dangerously and bake it on the back of an upside-down pie tin, from which it can theoretically be removed intact and displayed in all its glory. You are more skillful than I am if you can succeed in this endeavor.

Separate the eggs, using a strainer that lets all the white through and does not break the yolks. Reserve whites for meringue. Beat yolks slightly, beat in the sugar and flour, softened butter, orange and lemon juice, and lemon rind. Cook the custard in a double boiler for about 10 minutes or until it is creamy and thick and coats the back of a spoon. Set aside to cool.

For the meringue:

- 5 *egg whites*
- 5 *tablespoons sugar*
- ¼ *teaspoon cream of tartar*
- ½ *teaspoon vanilla*
- *Soft butter*
- 1 *tablespoon instant flour mixed with 1 tablespoon sugar*

With an electric beater, beat egg whites until they form stiff peaks. Beat in the sugar, cream of tartar, and vanilla. Use a pastry brush to brush the baked pie shell lightly with soft butter, then dust it with the instant flour and sugar mixture. Spoon in the lemon custard and swirl meringue over the top. Be sure the meringue touches the edge of the pastry all around, or it will slip back toward the center.

The oven should not be too hot: 300-325°. Bake for about 20 minutes which will make the meringue firm and crusty but not tough.

These directions are for a large pie with a lot of meringue. I think you will not find it too large when your friends appear at the kitchen door to inquire about the marvelous scent of lemon pie wafting through the neighborhood.

FUDGE PECAN PIE

(For 6)

- 2 *Cross crackers, rolled fine*
- ½ *cup dry bread crumbs, rolled fine*
- ⅓ *cup sugar*
- 6 *ounces chocolate chips*
- 1 *tablespoon instant flour*
- ¼ *cup sugar*
- 2 *cups milk*
- 3 *eggs at room temperature, beaten*
- 1 *tablespoon butter*
- 1 *teaspoon vanilla*
- ½ *cup unbroken pecan halves*
- ½ *cup heavy cream*
- 1 *tablespoon bitter chocolate shavings*

Butter a 9-inch pie plate thoroughly. Mix the cracker and bread crumbs with sugar and coat the pie plate thickly with this mixture. Chill.

Put chocolate chips with 1 tablespoonful of hot water into the top of a double boiler and melt over hot water.

Mix flour with ¼ cup sugar. Add 2 cups of milk and cook in a double boiler for ten minutes, stirring constantly. Set aside over hot water.

Beat eggs, add a little melted chocolate to them to warm them up, then stir the eggs into the rest of the melted chocolate. Add butter and vanilla to the chocolate mixture.

Stir some of the heated milk into the chocolate/egg mixture, and then stir the rest of the chocolate/egg mixture into the milk. Cook the resulting mixture until it will coat the back of a spoon — about 5 minutes. Cool slightly.

Lay some pecan halves on the crumb crust and carefully pour the chocolate mixture over them. Chill for at least two hours.

At serving time, whip heavy cream and swirl it over the pie. Decorate it with the rest of the pecans and shaved bitter chocolate.

This is less trouble but just as calorific as it sounds — and just as delicious.

WASHINGTON PIE

This is really a form of cake, but Grandmother thought of it as a pie and therefore she filed it that way. Please don't make it with a custard filling. The honorable Mr. Washington ought not be linked with an airy cake glued together with wallpaper paste.

4	*cups flour*	*3*	*cups sugar*
2	*teaspoons baking powder*	*4*	*eggs, separated*
2	*teaspoons cream of tartar*	*2*	*cups milk*
	Pinch of nutmeg		*Raspberry jam*
½	*cup butter*		*Confectioners' sugar*

Sift the flour with baking powder, cream of tartar, and nutmeg. Cream the butter, using an electric beater, and then beat in the sugar. Separate the eggs, reserving the whites. Beat egg yolks until they are lemon colored. Beat milk into them and then beat the egg and milk mixture into the butter and sugar. Add the flour gradually.

Wash the beater. Beat the egg whites to stiff peaks and fold them gently into the cake mixture. Preheat the oven to 375°. Divide the batter into three 9-inch layer cake tins that have been buttered and dusted with flour. Bake at 375° for about 20 minutes, or until the layers are delicately brown.

Assemble the "pie" while the layers are still warm. Spread raspberry jam liberally between the layers and dust the top with powdered sugar. If you have the time and inclination, you can make your own powdered sugar by whirling granulated sugar around in a small bowl with the electric mixer. Unlike commercial powdered sugar, the homemade product has no cornstarch in it and tastes the way powdered sugar did in Mr. Washington's day.

Poultry

WITH beef prices the highest we've ever seen them, and the prices of chicken and turkey much less by comparison, it seems likely that we all will be eating a good deal more poultry. So why not make it as tasty as possible and enjoy it as a treat well worth eating.

During the days when Jay and I tried our hand at farming, we thought we would economize by raising our own hens. It was our plan to use them both for the eggs they would produce and then, ultimately, for the poultry dinners with which they would provide us. Gathering eggs was a chore that took some getting used to, but when it came time for those hens to be prepared for the dinner table, we found ourselves thoroughly unprepared for the results. With any luck, at the end of eight hours of simmering, the chickens were suitably tender for making a chicken pie.

We have since decided that any hens we raise in the future will either be asked to produce eggs or expected to become chicken dinners. The double duty doesn't work.

I think it necessary to vary the method of cooking poultry from time to time. I recommend using an electric frying pan as the best way of simmering chicken so that a constant temperature is maintained without constant attention. A large iron frying pan will also work well as it retains heat. In this unharried way make:

CHICKEN IN CREAM

(For 4)

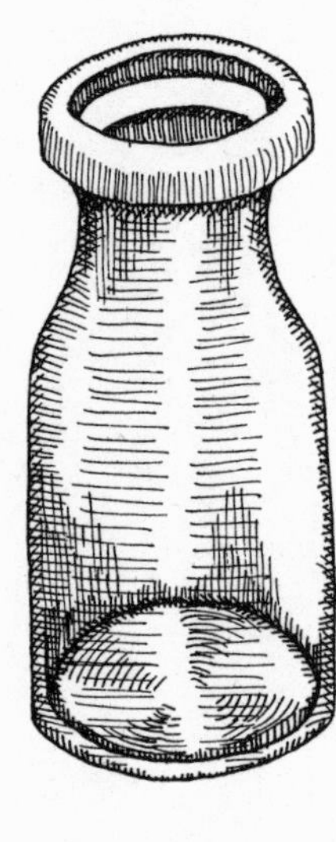

Make this in the morning and use it for supper that evening. Allow half a chicken breast for each person to be served. Using an electric skillet or a large frying pan over low heat, begin with:

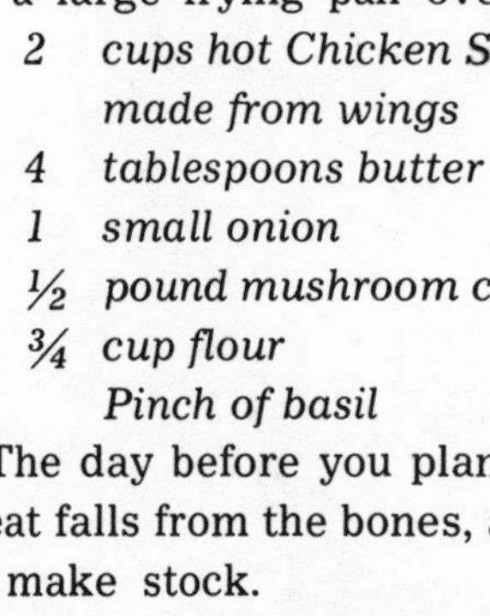

2	*cups hot Chicken Stock* made from wings*	½	*teaspoon paprika*
		¼	*teaspoon nutmeg*
4	*tablespoons butter*	4	*halves chicken breasts*
1	*small onion*	½	*cup thick cream*
½	*pound mushroom caps*	2	*pimentos*
¾	*cup flour*	2	*tablespoons white wine*
	Pinch of basil	2	*tablespoons lemon juice*

The day before you plan to serve the chicken, simmer wings until the meat falls from the bones, about 3 hours, with the carrot, onion and celery to make stock.

The next morning, cook onion in butter until yellow and transparent. Remove and set aside. Wash, do not peel, mushroom caps and slice vertically. Cook in butter until tender but not mushy — about 5 minutes. Set aside with the onion.

Mix flour and dry seasonings in a paper bag. Put chicken breasts into the bag and shake until they are well coated with seasoned flour. Put the breasts, skin side down, into buttered skillet and cook over medium heat until golden brown. Turn. Brown other side.

Remove fat from chicken stock. Heat stock and add slowly to the breasts in the pan. There should be about 2 cups of stock. Cover and simmer until breasts are tender, about an hour.

Just before serving, add cream slowly. Remove breasts to a hot platter. To the sauce, add onions, mushrooms and pimentos, cut in narrow strips. Stir well, add wine and lemon juice. Simmer a minute, but do not boil. Salt to taste. Pour hot sauce over chicken. Wreathe with watercress.

Variations:

1. Make broth with tomato juice instead of water. Add green pepper, sliced thin and sautéed in butter with mushrooms.

2. When adding wine and lemon juice, also add ½ cup sour cream, 1 tablespoon minced parsley and 1 teaspoon finely cut chives to the sauce. Add ½ teaspoon garlic powder to dry seasonings in the bag.

3. During last 15 minutes, put corn cut from six ears of Golden Bantam corn fresh from the garden. Sprinkle with minced parsley and chives. In winter, use one cup of whole corn from a can or the freezer.

4. Omit mushrooms and pimentos. To flour, add 1 teaspoon garlic powder and 1 teaspoon paprika, and to the cream in the pad add 1 tablespoon lemon juice and 1 tablespoon white wine. Brown breasts under the broiler for 5 minutes on a side. Put them in an electric frying pan, add 1 cup cream, simmer until tender — do not boil. Add ½ cup blanched shredded browned almonds.

5. Omit pimentos. Reduce stock to 1½ cups and add juice from one 6-ounce can mandarin orange sections. When adding mushrooms and onions, add mandarin orange sections and ½ cup diced, sautéed celery. Omit the lemon juice and add, instead, 3 to 4 tablespoons white wine.

**See Index for pages where recipes can be found.*

CHICKEN APPLEYARD

(For 4)

4 halves chicken breasts, wings removed
2 cups soft bread crumbs, browned in butter
*4 ounces liver Pâté**
4 tablespoons white wine
Watercress
*Bread Sauce**
2 cups chicken stock made from wings and neck with onion, carrot and celery

Butter each chicken breast well. Put them in an electric skillet, add chicken stock and wine and simmer until tender, about one hour. Brush breasts again with butter. Brown breasts under the broiler. Sprinkle browned bread crumbs over them. Top each breast with a small mound of pâté. Serve wreathed in watercress. Pass bread sauce with them or, if you prefer, thicken the gravy in the pan with instant flour. Add 2 tablespoons of white wine. Simmer until thick, about 3 minutes.

CHICKEN PLATTER

(For 8)

2 cups uncooked rice
4 cups creamed chicken
4 halved bananas, split lengthwise
2 tablespoons light brown sugar
2 tablespoons butter
6 slices canned pineapple, halved
12 cooked prunes, strained, stuffed with blanched almonds
Currant jelly

Cook rice. Put the cooked rice into a buttered ring mold. Warm creamed chicken (made the same as for Chicken Pie*) in a double boiler and keep rice warm while you fix the fruit. You will need two frying pans that will fit under the broiler. In one, put sliced bananas dotted with butter. Set this into a 350° oven. In the other frying pan put butter and brown sugar, stir them together until sugar melts. Put halved pineapple slices and stuffed prunes in and turn them over in the mixture. Broil until pineapple begins to brown. Slip the pan of bananas under the broiler and cook until brown.

Next, turn rice ring out on a large hot circular platter. Put pineapple slices around the rice. Fill holes in the pineapple with currant jelly. Put prunes and bananas in between pineapple slices. Pour any juice in the pan over the fruit. Decorate with sprays of parsley. Put creamed chicken in the center of the ring. Serve quickly while all is hot.

This hot chicken platter is for a cold evening. For a hot evening you might like:

CHICKEN PLATTER #2

6 halves boneless chicken breasts
*1 cup Mayonnaise**
1 tablespoon drained capers
1 tablespoon finely cut chives
½ teaspoon curry powder
1 teaspoon minced onion
1 pimento cut in small bits
6 pineapple slices
Seedless green grapes
Minced parsley
Watercress

Cook chicken breasts by browning in butter after shaking them in seasoned flour. Brush with butter and bake at 350° until they are tender, about 25 to 30 minutes. Cool. Into 1 cup of homemade mayonnaise stir curry powder, capers, onion, chives and pimento. Lay whole pineapple slices around on a circular platter. On each pineapple slice, place one cooked chicken breast. Mask the breasts with the seasoned mayonnaise. Put little heaps of seedless green grapes sprinkled with minced parsley between the pineapple slices. Decorate the platter with watercress.

CHICKEN PLATTER #3

(For 4)

This is another method of making "plain" chicken more interesting simply by arranging it with other good foods and is also an efficient way of using up leftovers.

For four, broil four chicken breasts slowly, far from heat. Broil bony side first, then turn skin side up, brush with butter and broil until they just start to turn brown. Place breasts on a stainless steel platter.

Arrange around the breasts: small heaps of Lima Beans with Mushrooms,* cooked mashed butternut squash, mashed potato and slices of tomato. The tomatoes should first be cooked on one side in a buttered frying pan and sprinkled with buttered bread crumbs. After arranging, dot the chicken and vegetables with butter and run the entire platter under the broiler until the squash starts to brown.

When you make creamed chicken, it isn't much more trouble to make:

REAL CHICKEN A LA KING

(For 8)

2	*frying chickens, 3½ pounds each*	½	*teaspoon pepper from the grinder*
1	*carrot*	3	*tablespoons instant flour*
1	*small onion*	½	*teaspoon paprika*
1	*teaspoon mixed herbs*	2	*cups light cream*
4	*tablespoons butter*	1	*cup heavy cream*
½	*pound fresh mushrooms, caps only*	½	*cup jellied Chicken Stock**
		3	*pimentos, cut fine*
1	*green pepper*	2	*egg yolks*
¾	*teaspoons nutmeg*	1	*tablespoon lemon juice*

½ *cup white wine*

Cook chickens the day before you plan to serve this. Put them in either an electric skillet or a large kettle. Cover with cold water and simmer slowly with carrot, onion and herbs until meat falls from the bones. Remove meat from bones and return bones and skin to the broth and simmer one hour. Strain the stock. Chill.

The next day, cut up chicken meat, not too fine. Save any small pieces for a casserole or pâté later. In a large frying pan, big enough to hold the entire mixture, melt 3 tablespoons of the butter and gently toss the washed mushrooms, sliced vertically, and finely sliced green pepper. When mushrooms are tender, sprinkle them with flour mixed with the dry seasonings and stir. Cook one minute. Reduce heat to its lowest point. First stir in light cream. Then add heavy cream. Add ½ cup of jellied stock with all fat removed. Cook until mixture begins to thicken, about 5 minutes. Add sliced chicken. Cook one minute longer. Let stand for at least one hour.

When serving time arrives, reheat mixture over low heat. Add pimentos. In a pint bowl, beat eggs lightly. Add one tablespoon of the hot cream sauce. Keep beating. (This process is called "delayering.") Add more sauce, beating all the time until you have about a cup all together. Add lemon juice and wine to the "delayered" eggs. Beat them in and then stir the egg mixture into the chicken and cream mixture. Cook over very low heat until the mixture thickens. It will separate if heat is too high.

Just before serving the chicken, slip one tablespoon of butter into it. Have a big, hot platter ready. Serve chicken on it. Garnish it with triangles of Melba Toast* or, preferably, Mrs. Appleyard's 2,000 Layer Pastry.*

It is fun to cook things sous cloche. But if you have no cloche (glass bell) you can still get the same taste results with covered pyrex dishes.

Enjoy the following rule for:

BREASTS OF CHICKEN UNDER GLASS

(For 6)

*1 quart Chicken Stock**
1 finely minced onion
2 tablespoons butter
2 tablespoons instant flour
¼ teaspoon pepper
¼ teaspoon oregano
¼ teaspoon nutmeg
½ teaspoon paprika
Breasts of 3 broilers, halved
6 slices of very dry toast
6 thin slices baked ham
2 cups cream
24 vertically sliced mushroom caps

Extra butter for toast

The day before you plan to serve this, make a stock with chicken wings, onion, celery, carrot and mixed herbs.

The next day, sauté minced onion in butter until transparent. Blend in the flour mixed with the dry seasonings. Continue cooking until flour is just lightly browned, set aside. Skim all fat from the stock. Simmer chicken breasts in it for 15 minutes. While they are simmering, butter the bottoms of six small covered pyrex dishes.

Cut rounds of bread to fit the dishes. Toast and butter them. Cover toast with sliced ham, or spread it with Underwood's deviled ham if you prefer. Remove chicken breasts and cook stock down until you have about 2 cups. Pour it slowly over the roux of butter and seasoned flour, stirring it carefully as it thickens. Add cream. Let it simmer while you put one chicken breast on each round of toast and mushroom slices around them. Pour some of the sauce over each of the chicken breasts. Cover the dishes. Seal them with freezer tape. Set in a hot oven at 475°. Cook for 30 minutes. Remove tape. Serve while sauce is still bubbling hot.

Serve the chicken with Spoon Bread,* young peas and carrots cooked together, and currant jelly. For dessert serve a wreath of dark red strawberries with their hulls on with a mound of powdered sugar in the middle and a big lemony Sponge Cake.*

If you are in an even more exotic mood, try making:

TWELVE BOY CURRY

(For 8)

2	*frying chickens, 3½ pounds each*	2	*onions*
			Sprig of parsley
1	*stalk celery*	½	*teaspoon pepper*
1	*carrot*	½	*teaspoon mixed herbs*

Have frying chickens cut up, either at the market or at home. Simmer them, covered with cold water and with vegetables and seasonings for 2½ hours. Strain the broth. Chill it. Take meat from the bones and cut it into not too small pieces. Chill. Skim fat from the stock.

For the curry sauce use:

4	*tablespoons butter*	3	*tablespoons curry powder*
4	*tablespoons flour*	4	*cups Chicken Stock**

Curry powder must always be cooked in the sauce. Much of its flavor is lost if it is simply stirred in at the last minute. In a pan big enough to hold the whole mixture, melt butter. When it bubbles, rub in flour and curry powder. Taste it. Add more curry if you like. Cook over low heat for 3 minutes. Stir 4 cups of chicken broth into the roux. Add chicken. Set the pan where it will barely simmer while you cook the rice.

If you are going to use Minute Rice, follow the directions on the package, allowing a generous amount for each person. If you wish to use brown rice, begin the cooking before you make the curry sauce.

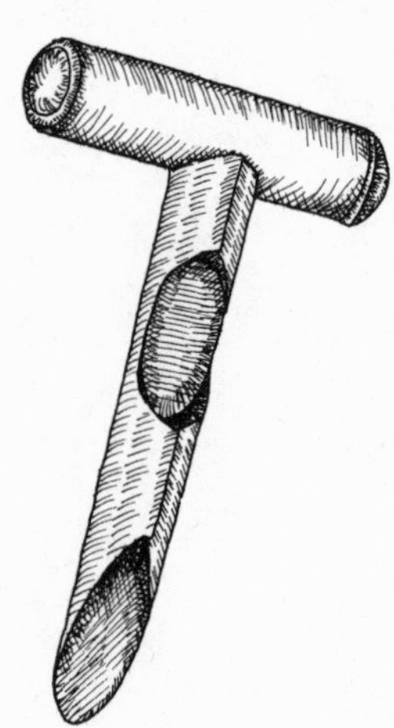

Have a big, hot platter ready when the rice is done. Place chicken in the center of the platter. Using a teacup, turn out small mounds of cooked rice around the chicken. Pour hot curry sauce over the chicken.

In the meantime, your helpers have been preparing twelve bowls, Chinese if possible, filled with the following garnishes:

- Chopped white of hard-boiled eggs.
- Grated yolk of hard-boiled eggs (allow one egg per person).
- Finely chopped parsley and chives.
- Finely minced raw onion.
- Mrs. Appleyard's Tomato Conserve.*
- Piccalilli.
- Mrs. Appleyard's Red Pepper Relish.*
- Shredded coconut (fresh if possible).
- Chopped peanuts.
- Blanched shredded, browned almonds.
- Sliced bananas.
- Chutney, Mrs. Appleyard's* or Major Grey's.

Traditionally there was a Chinese "boy" to pass each dish to the guests. But not having any available, and not approving of child labor, I encourage each guest to help himself. Each takes a mound of rice, covers it with curry and then helps himself to any combination of relishes he chooses. Generally, I've noticed, each person samples a little of everything and often returns for more of his favorites.

A cooling dessert is called for after such a repast. Lemon sherbet and Pound Cake* are rather soothing in these circumstances.

The contents of the bowls may vary. You might like to use green tomato relish, spiced candied applesauce, or orange marmalade preserves.

THE PRINCESS'S CURRY

(For 8)

2	*broilers*	4	*tablespoons curry powder*
4	*tablespoons butter*	1	*teaspoon cayenne pepper*
2½	*cups brown rice*	3	*finely chopped onions*
		1	*quart tomato juice*

Cut broilers into 4 pieces each and brown them in butter. Turn them carefully. While chicken is browning, begin cooking the rice.

Sprinkle the chicken with curry powder and cayenne pepper. Add chopped onion and tomato juice. Simmer until chicken is tender, about half an hour. Serve it with the rice, some crystallized ginger, some blanched almonds tossed in butter until delicately brown and some of Mrs. Appleyard's Chutney.*

CHICKEN BREASTS WITH CURRY

(For 4)

3	*egg yolks slightly beaten*	2	*tablespoons soft butter*
1	*tablespoon water*	2	*chicken breasts, halved, wings removed*
1	*teaspoon Dijon mustard*		
1	*teaspoon curry powder*	½	*cup fine soft bread crumbs*
1	*tablespoon chili sauce*		*Extra butter*

Use a shallow dish in which you will serve the chicken. Butter the dish well. Beat egg yolks and water with wire whisk. Beat in mustard, curry powder, chili sauce and butter. Put chicken breasts, bone side down, in the dish. Spread curry mixture over skin sides of breasts. Cover them with bread crumbs, and dot with butter.

Cover dish with aluminum foil and bake at 325° for 40 minutes. Remove foil. Run dish under the broiler, not too close to the flame, and cook until the breasts are well browned, about 5 minutes. Be sure to turn the dish so all pieces will brown evenly.

Serve with Kasha,* broiled bananas and Mrs. Appleyard's Tomato Conserve.*

The curry mixture may also be used as a barbecue sauce for chicken. Simply reduce the water to 1 teaspoon and baste chicken often while barbecuing.

PLANKED CHICKEN AND SAUSAGE

(For 4)

2	*chicken breasts, halved, wings removed*		*Butter*
		1	*teaspoon garlic powder*
4	*thin slices of ham*	8	*sausages cooked as above*
4	*tomatoes, halved, covered with crumbs*		*Ring of cooked hominy grits*
		2	*pimentos, cut in thin strips*
4	*slices pineapple*		*Currant jelly*

Arrange chicken breasts, bone side up, on a stainless steel platter on top of the slices of ham. Add tomatoes and pineapple. Dot tomatoes with butter and sprinkle with garlic powder. Dot chicken and pineapple with butter. Bake 15 minutes at 350°. Turn chicken skin side up, dot with butter. Bake 15 minutes. Arrange cooked sausages, cooked hominy grits and pimentos around the chicken. Dot hominy and pimentos with butter. Slip platter under broiler, not too near the heat. Broil until well browned, turning platter often, for 5 to 7 minutes. Put currant jelly in pineapple centers. Serve.

Another good chicken-sausage combination is:

CHICKEN AND SPAGHETTI WITH SAUSAGE

(For 16)

- 2 *5-pound fowls*
- 3 *tablespoons butter*
- 2 *large onions*
- 2 *sweet red peppers, seeded, finely sliced*
- 1 *pound sliced mushrooms*
- 3 *tablespoons instant flour*
- ¼ *teaspoon each of cinnamon, cloves, allspice, pepper*
- 2 *large cans tomatoes*
- 3 *cloves of garlic, put through the press*
- 2 *teaspoons sugar*
- *Bit of bay leaf*
- 2 *pounds small link sausages*
- 1 *pound spaghetti*
- ½ *cup finely minced parsley*
- 1 *cup dry Vermont cheddar cheese, grated*
- 1 *teaspoon paprika*

Cook fowls the day before you plan to serve this celestial stew. Simmer them in water containing sliced carrots, celery tops and a teaspoon of mixed herbs. Cook until meat slips easily from the bones, about 4 hours. Remove skin. Cut meat into serving pieces. Wrap them in wax paper and keep in refrigerator until needed. Return bones to the broth and cook until broth is thick enough to jell, about an hour. Strain into a large bowl. Add any small pieces of meat. Keep in a cool place until needed.

The next day, melt butter in a large iron skillet. Sauté onion and sweet peppers until onions are translucent. Sauté mushrooms. Skim chicken fat from broth and add a tablespoon of it to the pan. Sprinkle in flour and dry seasonings, except paprika. Blend seasoned flour into fat over low heat. Add tomatoes, garlic, sugar and bay leaf. Stir well and simmer one hour while keeping an eye on it. Add more chicken stock occasionally. Stir mixture well from the bottom of pan so it will not stick.

Half an hour before serving time, cook spaghetti and sausages in the following manner. Put the chicken stock on to heat in a large kettle. Put sausages into a frying pan. Pour warm water over them until they are almost covered and let simmer. The water should cook away in about 20 minutes. Turn them at the end of 10 minutes. Do not prick them. After the water has cooked away, leave them in the pan until they brown. At the end of 5 minutes, drain off the fat, turn them, cook 5 minutes more. Keep them warm until needed.

When chicken stock boils hard — there should be about 3 quarts — slip spaghetti into it slowly so that it curls up and the stock never stops boiling. Coil it around in the water. Cook until it is tender but not mushy, 7 to 8 minutes. Drain it, mix parsley, except for 1 tablespoon, with it and put it on a heat-proof platter. Save stock and reheat the cooked chicken in it a few minutes. Skim out the chicken and arrange the large pieces on top of the spaghetti. Add smaller ones to the tomato sauce and heat.

Arrange sausages around the spaghetti and chicken. Pour sauce over the whole thing. Set the platter into the oven while the guests are gathering. Sprinkle grated cheese over the platter. Sprinkle cheese with paprika and a tablespoon of parsley.

Note: The sausages may be substituted with chicken livers browned in butter until they are tender but not overcooked.

After such picturesque arrangements you might find it peaceful just to serve some plain broiled chicken, using an electric broiler and the slow method of cooking.

BROILED CHICKEN BREASTS OR LEGS

Put breasts, skin side down, on a rack on the broiling pan, set it as far as possible from the heat. Dot chicken with butter. Squeeze a little fresh lemon juice over them. Broil 10 minutes. Turn, dot with butter, squeeze a little more lemon juice over them. (This takes about a minute to do.) Broil 10 minutes longer. Remove to a hot well and tree platter. Add a little boiling water and more lemon juice to the pan. Boil it up, stirring well and serve as a sauce with the chicken. Serve Asparagus Country Style* and Thin Scalded Johnny Cake* with the chicken.

Chicken legs can be broiled in the same fashion but need 12 minutes cooking on each side.

One improvement in modern life is the ability to buy legs and breasts separately. For years Grandmother ate the second joint so someone else could have the breasts. She came to prefer the dark meat, as I do. I often cook nothing but legs, which I've found many of my friends like, too.

Variations:

1. Herb butter. To either breasts or legs add herb butter made by melting 2 tablespoons butter and adding 2 tablespoons minced chives, 2 tablespoons minced parsley, ½ teaspoon minced tarragon, 1 teaspoon chopped basil. Brush chicken underneath with herb butter. Broil as far as possible from the flame, 10 minutes for breasts, 12 minutes for legs, on each side.

2. With broccoli. Broil chicken 8 minutes on each side. Add 1 cup cream. Simmer until tender, about 10 minutes longer. Cook 3 cups fresh broccoli flowers until tender and crisp. Add to chicken. Add 1 tablespoon lime juice and 1 tablespoon sherry. Sprinkle with 1 cup Garlic Croutons,* ½ cup grated cheddar cheese. Simmer at 400° for 10 minutes. Slide under broiler until cheese just starts to brown.

3. With cauliflower. Prepare as for chicken with broccoli above. Substitute 3 cups cauliflower for the broccoli and add ¼ pound mushroom caps, washed, sliced vertically and browned in 1 tablespoon butter. Also shred ½ a green pepper and sauté it with mushrooms. Add 1 cup cream, 1 tablespoon lemon juice, 1 tablespoon sherry, Garlic Croutons* and grated cheese. Cook as above.

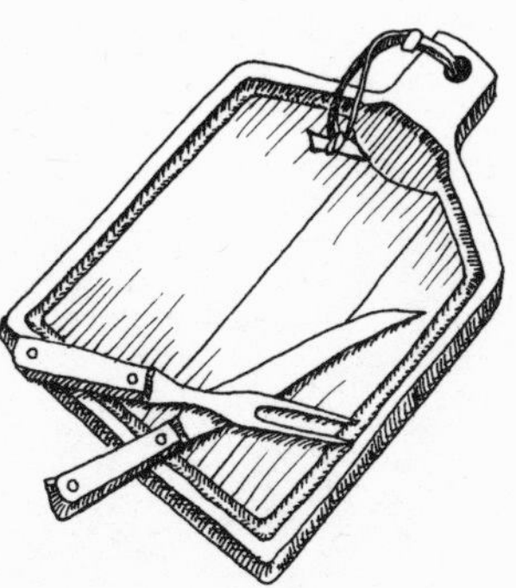

4. With bacon. Cook chicken as with broccoli. Substitute strips of bacon partly cooked and drained, for the cheese. Run pan under the broiler until bacon is crisp.

5. With giblet gravy. Cook as above. Use peas instead of cauliflower. For the cream, substitute Giblet Gravy.* Split and butter Baking Powder Biscuits.* Put chicken and gravy on a hot platter. Put a circle of tiny

cooked peas around the chicken. Put the biscuits around the edge. Sprinkle biscuits and chicken with minced parsley.

6. Planked chicken legs. Broil legs of chicken. Add Giblet Gravy.* Arrange a wall of mashed potatoes on a stainless steel platter. Dot potatoes with butter. Sprinkle with paprika, add a ring of green beans, cooked al dente. Put chicken and gravy in the center of the dish. Add ½ pound whole mushroom caps, washed, sautéed in butter, and a few tiny cooked beets. Slide entire dish under broiler and cook until potato starts to brown. Add a few sprays of watercress and serve.

When you have leftover chicken, do not forget the useful casserole. I will not try to give exact quantities because, most likely, that's what you won't have. You have to learn to be a sort of improvising computer, carrying in your mind numbers of persons to be served, sizes of dishes, lengths of time available, and what's in the refrigerator.

Grandmother looked with a certain amount of suspicion on casseroles not made by herself. She knew well that even a rare old Bennington dish might contain such substances as MSG, cornstarch or other "poisons." Here is one containing none of those things. Approximate the ingredients, or add any you have that might prove interesting.

GREEN GARDEN CASSEROLE

(For 6)

2	*minced onions*	*1*	*teaspoon minced chives*
2	*tablespoons butter*	*¼*	*teaspoon nutmeg*
½	*pound mushroom caps, washed and peeled*	*1*	*tablespoon lemon juice*
1	*cup cooked spinach*	*1*	*cup mushroom stock, from stems*
1	*cup Chicken Stock**	*1½*	*cups cooked chicken*
1½	*cups sour cream*	*1*	*cup cooked broccoli*
	Chopped sprays of watercress and parsley	*1*	*cup brown rice, cooked*
		½	*cup breadcrumbs*

Extra butter

Sauté onion in butter until pale yellow. Add mushrooms. Cover and cook slowly until they are tender but not mushy, about 5 minutes. Make mushroom stock by putting stems and ½ cup water in blender and blending. Heat the stock and simmer a few minutes. Put cooked spinach, chicken stock, sour cream, watercress, parsley, chives, nutmeg and lemon juice into blender. Run until everything is smoothly blended, about 2 minutes. Add mushroom stock. Pour this green mixture over mushrooms and onions, add chicken, broccoli and rice. Heat until it starts to bubble around the edge. Pour mixture into a Dutch iron casserole. Sprinkle with bread crumbs, dot with butter. Bake at 375° until top is well browned, about 15 to 20 minutes.

Variations:

1. No spinach? Use fresh lettuce from the garden, cooked as you would spinach.
2. No mushrooms? Use chopped livers.
3. Short on butter? Top with ¼ cup mayonnaise and ¼ cup sour cream, sprinkled with browned crumbs. Brown briefly under the broiler.

4. Cauliflower may replace the broccoli.

5. Cold capon is delicious in a green sauce. Scatter browned, blanched almonds over the top.

6. No time to get the meat off the bones? Too many people? Cut two broilers into 12 pieces. Put them in a buttered, shallow oblong pan. Pour green sauce over them. Set pan into preheated 350° oven. Make Baking Powder Biscuit* dough. When the sauce bubbles raise the temperature of the oven to 450°. Pat out dough. Do not roll it. Pinch off pieces smaller than biscuit size and put them over the meat, not quite touching each other. Bake until biscuits are well browned, about 20 minutes.

7. Cook as above but substitute Giblet Gravy* for the green sauce.

8. Fried chicken in casserole. Cut one 3½ pound chicken in serving pieces. Shake the pieces in a bag containing ½ cup instant flour, 1 teaspoon paprika, ¼ teaspoon pepper, ⅛ teaspoon nutmeg. Heat ½ cup butter and fry chicken in it until golden brown, about 10 minutes. Turn pieces often. Arrange them in a shallow casserole. Pour off all but 2 tablespoons of fat from the pan. Rub 1 tablespoon instant flour into the fat over low heat. Slowly pour 1 cup of rich milk and 2 tablespoons cream into pan, mixing all the time. Cook until it thickens over low heat. Pour sauce over chicken. Bake at 350° until tender, about 30 minutes. Serves four. If you like, sautéed mushrooms and green pepper slices with a little white wine may be added to this just before serving.

CHICKEN PIE

(For 10)

Grandmother said that Vermont chicken pies were usually made from fowls, which have more flavor than chicken. If you can obtain fowls, use them. If not, chicken is fine, but it doesn't need to cook as long.

2 5-pound fowls	*3 onions, sliced*
2 carrots, sliced	*1 stalk celery, cut up*

Celery tops

The day before you plan to serve the pie, clean your fowl and cut each into 8 pieces. Put meat and vegetables into a large kettle and cover with cold water. Bring water slowly to a boil. Set the kettle on a flame tamer over medium heat. When water starts to boil reduce heat so water will just simmer. Cook until meat slips easily from the bones, about 3 hours. Set a colander into another kettle. Put meat into colander. Strain broth and set aside. Pick over the meat, removing skin and bones. Set meat in a cold place. Return bones and skin to broth. Simmer 2 hours. Strain broth and set away to cool.

Next morning skim fat from broth, which should have jelled. If it hasn't, cook it down a little more. There should be about 2 quarts of jellied broth.

Now put the chicken into a large shallow baking dish. Mrs. Appleyard liked best a big Bennington one, like polished tortoiseshell, that had been in her pantry for a hundred years or so. But if it was busy in some other philanthropic work, she would use a four-quart milk pan. Whatever you use, grease it lightly with chicken fat and lay in the meat, cut up not too small.

Next, make a sauce using:

4 tablespoons chicken fat, skimmed from stock
4 tablespoons instant flour
2 quarts stock
Salt to taste, about 2 teaspoons
2 teaspoons sage (optional)

Melt chicken fat. When it is hot, work in the flour and cook the roux over low heat for 3 minutes. Then slowly stir in the chicken stock, letting it simmer a few minutes. Pour sauce over chicken, set the dish into a hot oven (450° to 475°) and let the pie heat while you make biscuits for the topping.

You may use either regular Baking Powder Biscuit* or Sour Cream Biscuit* dough. Whichever you use, do not roll out the dough. When the juice of the pie is bubbling hard, and not before, drop the dough in small lumps on top of the meat. The secret of having a biscuit topping of a chicken pie crisp, not soggy, is this bubbling juice.

Serve Giblet Gravy* with the pie. At the chicken pie suppers in the church at Gospel Hollow, they serve white cabbage finely shredded and mixed with boiled salad dressing, pickled beets, mashed potatoes and six kinds of pie for dessert.

Grandmother, who didn't need potato for building up her silhouette, would serve instead, thick slices of her own tomatoes with French Dressing.* She said that you had never tasted a tomato if you didn't pick it off your own vine some crisp sunny morning when there would be northern lights in the evening by which to eat it. I think beets with Cumberland Mint Sauce* and tiny frozen peas are good companions for the pie.

CHICKEN SHORTCAKE

(For 6)

Bake shortcake as for Peach and Raspberry Shortcake.* Use fowl cooked as for Chicken Pie, above. Split shortcake, butter the layers. Put cooked chicken between layers and on top. Arrange a few mushrooms, washed, sliced vertically and cooked until tender but not mushy, around the edge of the top layer. Add slices of crisply cooked bacon, a dusting of paprika and a little minced parsley. Return to a 350° oven for a minute to warm. Serve hot with Glazed Carrots* and French-cut green beans.

CHICKEN LATTICE PIE

(For 4)

2,000 Layer Pastry for lattice*
3½ pound frying chicken
2 small onions, sliced
1 carrot, sliced
1 small stalk celery, cut fine
Celery tops

Cook the chicken as you would for Chicken Pie,* with vegetables in a large kettle, covered with cold water. Bring water slowly to a boil and simmer until meat slips easily from the bones, about 2 hours. Remove the meat from the bones, return skin and bones to broth and cook down until broth starts to jell when tested on a cold saucer. There should be about one quart. Chill broth and chicken.

The next day make the sauce as for chicken pie out of:

- 2 *tablespoons chicken fat*
- 2 *tablespoons instant flour*
- 1 *quart Chicken Stock**
- *Salt to taste*
- ¾ *teaspoon sage (optional)*

Grease a shallow enamel baking dish and put the meat in it. Melt chicken fat. When hot, work in flour and cook roux over low heat for 3 minutes. Slowly stir in stock and let simmer for a few minutes. Pour sauce over chicken and set pan into a preheated 450° oven to simmer while you roll out the pastry and cut it into strips. Put the lattice strips over the pie. Twist any leftover pastry into a rope to lay around the edge. Set the dish back into the oven and bake at 450° for 15 minutes. Reduce heat to 350° and bake until pastry is puffed and golden brown, about 40 minutes longer.

Sometime when there's something you ought to do that you don't want to, the following dish is a good thing to make because it will take you a whole morning. It is called:

CHICKEN POCKETBOOKS

- 6 *second joints and drum sticks of broilers*
- ⅓ *loaf French Bread**
- ¾ *cup cream*
- ½ *teaspoon poultry seasoning*
- 6 *mushroom caps, chopped*
- 1 *small onion*
- 3 *chicken livers*
- ½ *cup sausage meat*
- 4 *tablespoons butter, melted*

Take the bones out of the second joints and drum sticks, keeping meat and skin intact for stuffing. (This sounds easy, but I've had to use three knives, the kitchen shears and poultry clippers to do it.) Slice bread, dry it in the oven at 300° and pound it into fine crumbs. Mix crumbs with half the cream, seasonings and mushrooms. Mince onion fine. Add chicken livers and keep chopping. Chop in sausage meat. Do not taste after this point. Combine the mixtures. Add more cream. The mixture should hold its shape.

Stuff drum sticks and second joints, folding skin over stuffing and tying the whole thing firmly together. A toothpick inserted here and there helps in this project. Preheat the oven to 450°. Melt butter in an enameled iron dish. Put the pocketbooks in the dish and turn them over in the butter. They should end up skin side up. Cover dish and bake for 40 minutes. Uncover the dish and put strips of partly cooked bacon over the pocketbooks. Return the dish to the oven and cook until bacon is as you like it, 5 to 10 minutes longer. Serve very hot with beets in Cumberland Mint Sauce* and lima beans.

ROAST CHICKEN

One of the most important things about roast chicken is the stuffing. It should not be a heavily seasoned mass of wet dough, but a delicately flavored trap for the juice of the roasting bird. I prefer the slow method for roasting, and the use of a meat thermometer. Know the weight of the chicken before stuffing it. Stuff it and place into a cold oven set at 275°. Allow approximately 18 minutes per pound. In 1½ hours the thermometer should register 165°. Check it and remove bird from the oven to a hot platter while you make Giblet Gravy* in the pan. Use the chicken livers, chopped, as well as the neck and giblets.

Stuffing (For 3 small chickens or 2 large):

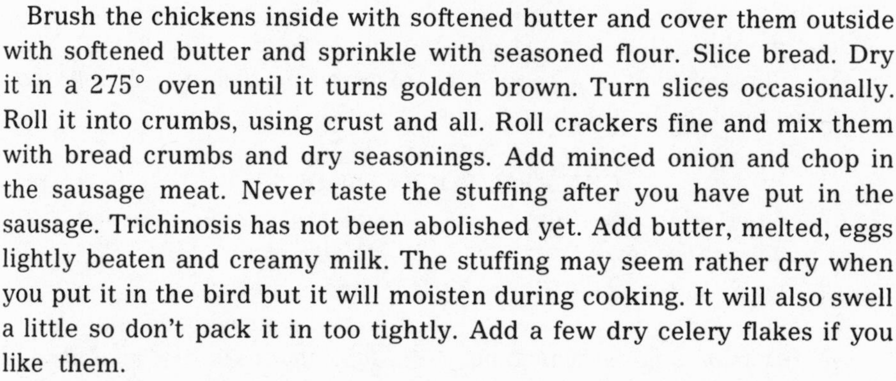

Extra butter, softened
- *½ cup flour with 1 teaspoon poultry seasoning*
- *5 cups homemade bread crumbs*
- *2 Cross crackers*
- *Salt to taste — ½ to 1 teaspoon*
- *½ teaspoon pepper*
- *¼ teaspoon nutmeg*
- *2 teaspoons poultry seasoning*
- *2 large onions, finely minced*
- *2 tablespoons sausage meat*
- *½ cup butter*
- *2 eggs, beaten*
- *½ cup milk, part cream*

Brush the chickens inside with softened butter and cover them outside with softened butter and sprinkle with seasoned flour. Slice bread. Dry it in a 275° oven until it turns golden brown. Turn slices occasionally. Roll it into crumbs, using crust and all. Roll crackers fine and mix them with bread crumbs and dry seasonings. Add minced onion and chop in the sausage meat. Never taste the stuffing after you have put in the sausage. Trichinosis has not been abolished yet. Add butter, melted, eggs lightly beaten and creamy milk. The stuffing may seem rather dry when you put it in the bird but it will moisten during cooking. It will also swell a little so don't pack it in too tightly. Add a few dry celery flakes if you like them.

Mrs. Appleyard's father liked Bread Sauce* with roast chicken. You might also like it to go with either chicken, turkey or guinea chickens.

CLUB SANDWICHES

The Appleyards prefer club sandwiches made with two pieces of toast to the triple-decker style, which always seems to consist chiefly of toast. They use the Consumer's Cooperative plan; one person makes the toast, another cooks bacon, a third slices tomatoes and onions. the chief cook slices the chicken and wreathes it in oak leaf lettuce from the garden and also sets out mayonnaise and Mrs. Appleyard's Chutney.*

Each customer puts his own sandwich together, using his favorite substances, and is soon back for another. Serve beer or cider with the sandwiches and eat them in front of an open fire.

If you're getting the idea that we think chicken is the only kind of poultry there is, it's not quite true. I'll make just a few more suggestions before moving on to ducks, geese and turkey.

CHICKEN BREASTS WITH APRICOT OR CURRANT JELLY

(For 6)

- *1 whole chicken, cut up (or 3 breasts, halved)*
- *4 tablespoons flour seasoned with salt, pepper and paprika*
- *3 tablespoons butter*
- *¼ pound mushrooms*
- *1 cup sour cream*
- *1 8-ounce jar apricot preserves or currant jelly*

Shake chicken pieces in a bag with seasoned flour until all are well coated. Brown them in butter in a large frying pan. Place chicken in a shallow buttered casserole. Slice washed mushrooms vertically and sauté in butter. Make a sauce of the sour cream, half the preserves or jelly and the mushrooms. Pour sauce over chicken. Dab the remaining jelly on the tops of breasts, poking up through sauce. Bake in a 350° oven for 25-40 minutes or until tender. This makes a good sweet-and-sour combination and is easy to assemble.

CHICKEN MOUSSE WITH ASPARAGUS

This is really a fancy chicken salad, perfect for summer luncheons or hot evenings.

- 1 *cup jellied stock from fowl, made as for stock used in Chicken Pie**
- *Salt and pepper to taste*
- 1 *teaspoon celery seed*
- 2 *tablespoons gelatin soaked in 2 tablespoons cold water and 1 tablespoon lemon juice*
- 3 *cups finely chopped cooked chicken from one fowl weighing about 3½ lbs.*
- ½ *cup neatly diced cooked ham*
- *Whites of 3 eggs*
- *Chicken fat for greasing molds, skimmed off jellied stock*
- 1 *cup thick cream*

Heat stock with seasonings and pour stock on soaked gelatin. Cool. Whip cream and mix it with chicken and ham. Add cooled stock. Beat whites of eggs to stiff peaks and fold them into the mixture. Grease small molds or a ring mold and spoon mixture in. Chill at least 3 hours. Serve hot Popovers* and cold cooked asparagus marinated with Vinaigrette Sauce.*

COQ AU VIN

(For 12)

- 1 *pound butter*
- 4 *medium onions, chopped fine*
- 2 *crushed cloves of garlic*
- 4 *teaspoons mixed herbs: basil, tarragon, rosemary*
- 1 *cup instant flour*
- *Toast triangles*
- 4 *broilers cut in small pieces (cut and set aside back bones)*
- 2 *cups Pouilly Fuissé, or other dry white wine*
- 1 *pound fresh mushroom caps, washed and sliced vertically*

Into a big well-seasoned black iron frying pan put butter, chopped onion and crushed garlic. Place pan over medium heat. Use a flame tamer. Sprinkle in herbs. Flour chicken pieces by shaking them in a bag with the flour until they are well coated. Brown chicken in herb butter. Pour in wine slowly so it comes well up around the chicken pieces. Cover pan and simmer contents slowly until tender, from 45 minutes to 1 hour and 15 minutes. Meat will usually be tender in about 50 minutes. Don't cook longer than 1 hour and 15 minutes. After 40 minutes add mushroom caps. Before serving, skim surplus butter off gravy and save it to use in a Rissotto* the next day. Put chicken and mushrooms on a hot stainless steel platter. Surround with triangles of crisp dry toast. Serve very hot with Garlic Bread* and a Tossed Green Salad.* Serve gravy in a separate tureen.

PAELLA

This is a dish of Spanish origin, very filling and with a surprising variety of tastes. It is not difficult to make once the ingredients are assembled.

Meat from 4 pork chops

2	*tablespoons fat from fowl*	*½*	*pound rice*
2	*small minced onions*	*1*	*chicken, boiled and meat removed from the bones*
4	*cups stock from fowl*	*2*	*10-ounce packages frozen peas, or 3 cups fresh peas*
½	*cup white wine*	*1*	*pound lobster meat, fresh if possible (or frozen)*
	Seasonings: bit of bay leaf, 4 cloves, salt to taste, pepper from grinder, ¼ teaspoon powdered saffron, 1 tablespoon chopped parsley	*4*	*pimentos, cut in strips*
		½	*pound pepperoni sausage, skinned and sliced*

This should be made in a large frying pan and brought to the table in the pan.

Cut pork into small cubes and fry it in chicken fat until tender. Add onion and cook until pale yellow. Add stock, white wine, seasonings (except saffron and parsley) and when stock boils, stir in rice. Add chicken and cook gently until the rice is done, about 20 minutes. In the meantime, cook peas. When rice and peas are ready, sprinkle saffron over rice and stir it in.

Over the top of the rice mixture, arrange lobster pieces, peas, pimentos and sausage in a handsome red and green design. Sprinkle in parsley. Cover pan just long enough to heat lobster through and bring to the table.

There are undoubtedly many versions of this same dish. You might find other shellfish, bacon or additional green vegetables in it. If you have difficulty locating any of the above ingredients, they are only suggestions, so feel free to substitute your own. It is essential, however, to include the saffron, some form of pork, shellfish and fowl and, of course, rice.

ROAST GOOSE

It was late in her career that Grandmother roasted her first goose. Someone else had always cooked those her family ate at Christmas time. She approached the bird with respect and a certain amount of nervousness. She was glad to report that it yielded admirably to the slow method and being spied on by a meat thermometer, thrust into the second joint near the body, not touching any bone.

Begin by stuffing the goose with chestnut stuffing. This is easier to make than it used to be because the chestnuts can now be bought in cans all cooked and ready to use.

1½	*cups crumbs from homemade bread, dried and rolled into course crumbs*	*1*	*tablespoon finely minced onion*
¼	*pound sausage meat*	*1*	*egg lightly beaten with ¼ cup milk*
12	*chestnuts, each broken into 4 or 5 pieces*	*½*	*teaspoon mixed herbs: sage, thyme, basil*
½	*cup Cross cracker crumbs*	*1*	*tablespoon chopped raw apple*

Mix all ingredients together. *Never* taste it after you have put in the raw sausage meat (remember trichinosis?). This is a rather dry dressing. Use more milk if you like yours moist. Use 2 tablespoons of butter instead of the sausage meat if you prefer.

Some people prefer their goose stuffed with a small onion and a small apple — no regular stuffing. This is considered a sophisticated gesture. I'll just note that your guests might be hungry and that there's very little meat on a goose in proportion to its size. So, I'll continue to be naive and make stuffing. Serve Giblet Gravy* separately. If you don't stuff the bird you might like it with the Orange Sauce* Grandmother served with Roast Duckling.*

After stuffing the bird, brush it all over with vegetable oil and sprinkle it lightly with flour seasoned with pinches of thyme, sage and marjoram. Allow 25 minutes to the pound in a 300° oven. Cook to 185° on the meat thermometer. For a 12-pound goose allow about 5 hours, but check it in 4 hours. When cooked, remove from the oven and let stand 10 minutes or more to facilitate the carving.

ROAST DUCKLING

You may roast a duckling in a similar fashion. Ducklings are rarely stuffed as they are smaller birds. They therefore are well suited to the sophisticated action of placing a small onion and a small apple in the cavity and roasting as above. A good deal of fat runs into the pan and should be poured off at least twice during the roasting. Remember that unstuffed birds tend to cook faster than stuffed ones, so watch the time.

DUCKS WITH ORANGES IN CASSEROLE

(For 6)

2	*young ducks*	4	*oranges, rind and juice*
6	*small sliced carrots*	1	*8-ounce jar currant jelly*
2	*cups peas*	¼	*cup red wine*
3	*sliced onions*	1	*teaspoon salt*
1	*cup lima beans*	½	*teaspoon paprika*
3	*tablespoons butter*		*Mashed potato*
2	*tablespoons flour*	6	*slices bacon*

Cut ducklings into serving pieces. Put a rack in your roaster, or roasting pan. Put a cupful of water in the bottom of it and put in the vegetables. You may use some other combination of vegetables, but have a variety. Frozen ones may be used if fresh are not available.

Brown duck pieces in butter in a frying pan for a few minutes and lay them over the vegetables. Cover the roaster and cook for 1 hour at 375°.

Have your individual casserole dishes ready — Mexican, French, pyrex glass are all good. Make a brown gravy from the juice in the roaster, using 2 tablespoons flour, well browned, the juice of the oranges and their grated rind, the currant jelly and the red wine. Add salt, paprika and a little pepper. Taste and season more highly if you wish.

Put vegetables into each casserole, put pieces of duck on top. Add sauce. Put on top, a rosette of mashed potato sprinkled with a little more orange peel and some chopped parsley. Put a partly cooked slice of bacon on top of the potato. Set casseroles into a 475° oven for a few minutes, just long enough to finish cooking the bacon and ensure that everything else has blended and the gravy is sizzling hot.

All you need to complete this meal are crusty rolls and red wine. Top it off with a lettuce salad with French Dressing* and later some toasted crackers and cheese.

A gastronomic surprise happened to Mrs. Appleyard when a French acquaintance told her she had made Pâté Maison for lunch and it turned out to be meat loaf. The experience impelled Grandmother to make something she originally called Pâté Casa Blanca, because she lived in the White House, so-called to distinguish it from the Brick House next door. After several experiments, she settled down to a formula for something she could call by its dressy name with a clear conscience.

PÂTÉ MAISON D'APPLEYARD

1 pound bottom of the round
1 pound Vermont sausage
½ pound chicken livers
2 eggs, lightly beaten
½ cup milk
¼ cup light cream
1 teaspoon minced onion
¼ teaspoon celery flakes
¼ teaspoon nutmeg
¼ teaspoon mixed herbs
6 slices homemade bread, dried and crushed
6 medium mushroom caps, washed and chopped coarsely
½ cup dry bread crumbs, rolled fine
1 tablespoon melted butter
6 thin strips suet

Have the butcher put the bottom of the round through the grinder twice. The second time get him to add the sausage and chicken livers. The mixture should all be ground together.

Mix together eggs, milk, cream, onion, celery flakes, nutmeg and herbs. Pour mixture over crushed dried bread crumbs and let it stand for five minutes.

Heat the oven to 350°. Butter a bread tin. With a pastry blending fork, combine meat mixture and soaked bread crumbs. Be sure everything is evenly distributed. Work in chopped mushrooms. Put pâté into buttered tin. Cover the top with fine bread crumbs mixed with melted butter. Lay strips of suet over top. Insert meat thermometer. Bake at 350° for 15 minutes. Reduce heat to 300° and bake until thermometer registers 150°, about an hour longer. Pour off the fat and save it. It's delicious for frying sweet potatoes or zucchini, or used with scalloped tomatoes.

This pâté is intended to be served cold with a tossed salad. Chill it overnight on the platter. When you serve the pâté, surround it with sprays of parsley and watercress. Stuffed Eggs* go well with it and look attractive around the platter.

I sometimes wish I had truffles growing under my sugar maple and a philanthropic pig to root them up for me. However, I allege that even without truffles, Pâté Maison isn't bad: high praise from this adopted Vermonter.

GOOSE LIVER PÂTÉ WITH TRUFFLES

Since we had several guests coming to supper, I eked out the goose's liver with chicken livers.

4	*tablespoons butter*	½	*teaspoon sugar*
1	*large goose liver*	½	*teaspoon onion powder*
1	*8-ounce package frozen chicken livers*	¼	*teaspoon garlic powder*
¼	*cup jellied Chicken Stock**	¼	*cup dry bread crumbs, rolled fine*
		2	*ounces truffles*

Melt 2 tablespoons of the butter over low heat. Put in the livers — goose liver cut in 6 pieces and chicken livers, slightly thawed, cut in halves. Cover pan. Cook livers for 3 minutes. Turn them over. Cook 2 minutes longer. Put livers into a blender. Add sugar, onion powder, garlic powder, bread crumbs and remaining 2 tablespoons of butter. Blend until mixture is smooth and the consistency of thick cream. It should take about 2 minutes — a minute at a time.

Now extract pâté from the blender, an annoying task made possible by a narrow rubber scraper, and stir in truffles, thinly sliced and cut in quarters. Pack the pâté neatly into the dish in which you plan to serve it. Chill at least 3 hours.

Served with Caesar salad and homemade Melba Toast,* this pate is of a poetic quality. The truffles give it a sort of idyllic perfume.

If you have neither truffles nor goose liver, you can still make a quite satisfactory substance to spread on Melba toast. It is:

CHICKEN LIVER PÂTÉ

4	*tablespoons butter*	1	*teaspoon minced onion*
½	*pound mushroom caps, cut rather fine*	¼	*teaspoon mixed herbs*
		½	*teaspoon white pepper*
1	*8-ounce package frozen chicken livers, partly thawed*	¼	*teaspoon nutmeg*
		1	*teaspoon sugar*
		½	*cup chicken stock*

Melt 2 tablespoons of the butter. Sauté mushrooms until tender. Remove them and set aside for later. Sauté onion 1 minute. Remove and set aside. Melt 2 more tablespoons butter, add livers, cut in halves. Cover. Cook over low heat for 3 minutes. Turn livers over. Cover. Cook 2 minutes longer.

Into the blender put livers, seasonings and onion. Rinse out the pan with chicken stock and add it to the blender. Blend until mixture is like thick cream. Two minutes of blending, a minute at a time, should produce this consistency. It will stiffen as it chills. Stir in — do not blend — chopped mushrooms.

Pack pâté into a wide-mouthed jar, such as a peanut butter jar. Chill several hours.

TARTS WITH LIVER PÂTÉ

From a Cordon Bleu graduate of her acquaintance, Mrs. Appleyard learned to combine her own liver pâté with packaged pastry mix. Marie Claire, as this talented chef was called, obligingly read the directions on the package in French to Grandmother so they sounded excitingly exotic. She then proceeded. Mix pastry according to package directions and roll it out lightly. Using a small curved cookie cutter, cut fluted circles from the pastry and set them on a baking sheet. These are the bottom of your tart shells. Make the same number of circles, cutting holes in the centers. A ginger ale bottle cap with two nail holes punched in it will produce fluted holes.

Moisten the bottom of the tart shells slightly with a pastry brush and place the open-centered circles on top of them. Place the small pastry circles on the baking sheet to be used later as lids for the tarts. Chill the full sheet of tarts for 5 minutes while the oven is heating to 450°.

Bake tarts for 5 minutes at 450°, then reduce heat to 375°. Bake until they are puffed and delicately browned, about 12 minutes longer.

At serving time fill some of the tarts with Pâté Maison d'Appleyard* and some with caviar. If you wish, mix some sour cream with powdered onion and place a dab of this mixture on top of the caviar. Then crumble hard-cooked egg yolks on top.

Grandmother used both fillings to show that she was broad-minded and admired the Russians for whatever was admirable about this. Of course, she knew well, that the caviar had been no nearer Russia than Gloucester, Massachusetts, where some ingenius American had dyed codfish roe black. Still, imitation is a compliment and, doctored as above, the imitation is delicious.

On more leisurely occasions, you may make 2,000 Layer Pastry,* but I find the packaged mixture quick and easy to use. The tarts may also be filled with various substances — Ham Mousse,* Goose Liver Pâté,* or used as a dessert filled with lemon cheese or cranberry and raspberry jelly.

ROCK CORNISH HENS

These can be purchased frozen, beautifully trussed, encased in oven-proof plastic bags and stuffed with wild rice. Cooking directions come with them but — oddly enough — Mrs. Appleyard had a suggestion or two.

Put the birds, one for each person to be served, into a covered roaster right in their plastic bags. Have the roaster set at 325° to 350°. After an hour remove the bags. This is not as easy as it sounds — rather like juggling a hot greased pig. After you have won the battle, pour melted butter over the chickens and dredge them with flour seasoned as you like. Now is the time that some chicken fat and jellied stock will come in handy. Put the fat into the roasting pan with the birds. There will soon be enough liquid to baste the birds. Do this every 10 minutes until they are brown and tender, about an hour longer. Remove them to a hot platter and make gravy. For 4 birds use:

2 tablespoons finely minced onion
2 tablespoons fat from the roaster
2 tablespoons instant flour
*1½ cups hot Chicken Stock**
1½ cups rich milk
Salt and pepper to taste
2 tablespoons chopped parsley

Cook onion in fat until soft. Rub flour into fat. Cook over low heat until mixture thickens and starts to brown. Turn off heat, blend in stock and milk until gravy is smooth. Add any seasoning you like: salt, pepper, paprika, oregano, nutmeg, or let the gravy lead its own life. Reheat. Sprinkle parsley over it and serve in a tureen with the birds.

ROAST TURKEY

The best turkeys for roasting are native turkeys that have never been frozen. This is true whether they and you are a native of Vermont, New Hampshire, New York or Utah. The most important thing to remember, however, with frozen or fresh turkeys, is to have them at an even temperature all the way through before attempting to stuff and roast the bird. With a frozen bird this means getting the neck and giblets out of the cavity as soon as possible so as not to have an icy spot in the middle. The thawing should be done the day before you intend to roast the turkey. This allows you time to cook and mince the giblets for gravy on that same day, leaving the roasting and serving day for other endeavors.

Grandmother has recommended two methods for roasting turkeys. For either one you will need a meat thermometer. The first is the low temperature method. This produces a very tender bird and does not require advance planning.

First, clean and stuff the bird with one of the dressings below or your own favorite. Know precisely how much the empty bird weighs. Brush it lightly all over with melted butter or vegetable oil. Have the oven at 200° and allow about 70 minutes to the pound. Cook it uncovered on a rack in a dripping pan. If it appears to be browning too rapidly, drape a tent of aluminum foil over the bird. Remove tent in the last 20 minutes. Cook with a meat thermometer deep in the second joint, touching no bone, until it registers 185°. For a 20-pound bird this will take about 24 hours of little watching. You need only baste the bird twice during the first hour and when you think of it after that. It will cook all night with no tending. If it reaches the desired temperature before you are ready to serve it, simply remove it from the oven and reheat for a few minutes before serving.

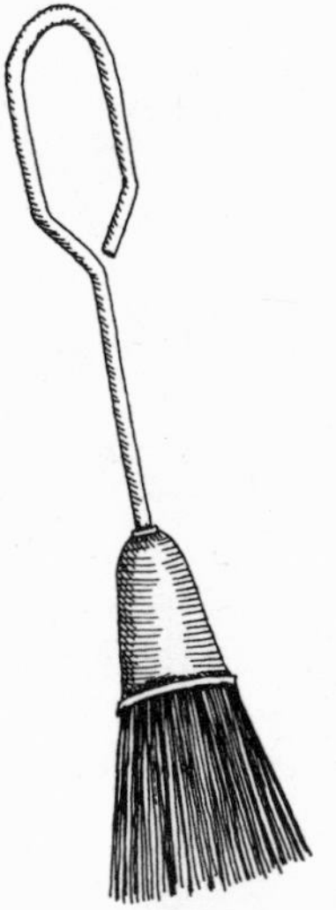

The second method is similar but the bird cooks at a higher temperature for a shorter period of time. Clean and stuff as above. Brush with oil or melted butter. With the meat thermometer inserted deep in the second joint, touching no bone, cook in a 275° oven until the thermometer registers 185°. Allow about 22 minutes to the pound. During the last 2 hours of cooking time, drape links of sausage over the bird. The sausages will help baste the bird and are tasty themselves when cooked in this way. When a turkey was thus decorated, Grandmother's English father used to call it the "Alderman in Chains." When cooked, remove the turkey to a hot platter, wreathe with parsley and serve with Giblet Gravy,* Green Beans with Mushrooms,* and other favorite Thanksgiving Day treats.

Choose from one of the following stuffings to make your turkey something special. Begin with the best homemade bread you can locate. Slice it thinly, dry it slowly in the oven and crumble it, not too fine. Or buy Pepperidge Farm packaged stuffing bread and reduce the seasonings below. Allow about ½ cup of bread crumbs per pound of turkey.

BASIC STUFFING

(For a 20-pound turkey)

- *10 cups bread crumbs*
- *3 finely minced onions*
- *½ pound melted butter*
- *1 cup milk (part cream)*
- *Salt to taste*
- *3 eggs, lightly beaten*
- *2 cups Cross cracker crumbs, not too fine*
- *4 tablespoons poultry seasoning*
- *1 teaspoon pepper from the grinder*

Mix ingredients together and stuff the turkey with them, pinning the cavity closed with skewers or sewing it closed, to keep the inside moist. This is rather a dry stuffing. If you like it moist, add more milk and another egg. Remember that stuffing tends to moisten and swell during cooking as it absorbs juice from the meat. Leave some space for it to expand. Extra stuffing may be moistened with gravy, baked in a casserole and served with cold turkey the next day.

CORN STUFFING

For half the bread crumbs in the basic rule, substitute Cornmeal Muffins,* dried and crumbled.

MUSHROOM STUFFING

For the milk in the basic rule, substitute mushroom sauce made as follows:

- *½ pound mushrooms, stems and all, cut fine*
- *2 tablespoons butter*
- *1 tablespoon flour*
- *¼ teaspoon nutmeg*
- *1 cup milk (part cream)*

Sauté mushrooms in butter. Blend in flour and nutmeg. Blend in milk. Cook until it thickens. Add to the stuffing.

CHESTNUT STUFFING

Basic Stuffing

49 chestnuts (or 1 pound whole cashews or 1 pound filberts and hazel nuts mixed)

Make basic stuffing but reduce seasonings to half so that the flavor of the nuts will be detectable. Mix all together and stuff the turkey.

OYSTER STUFFING

If your family has mixed opinions about oyster stuffing, compromise by putting oyster stuffing in the crop and plain stuffing in the other end. All should be happy.

For the above compromise method for a 20-pound bird use:

¼ cup juice from oysters

- *½ cup butter*
- *1 minced onion*
- *½ cup finely chopped celery*
- *1 cup oysters, cut in small pieces*
- *4 cups bread crumbs*
- *2 Cross crackers, rolled fine*
- *Pinch of thyme, pinch of nutmeg*
- *1 beaten egg*

In a pan big enough to hold the mixture, heat oyster liquid. Add butter and as it melts add the onion, celery and oysters. Cook until butter froths.

Remove from heat. With a pastry fork, stir in bread and cracker crumbs, seasonings, beaten egg. If you prefer it very moist, add a little thick cream.

TURKEY BUFFET

Mr. Appleyard preferred his turkey cold and Grandmother sometimes indulged him by never serving the turkey hot at all. There were, however, complaints from their descendants who wanted to see and smell a hot, well-browned turkey draped with chains of sizzling sausages. They alleged that mashed potato never tasted the same with cold turkey as it did with hot, and neither did gravy, not even Pilgrim gravy and that, after all, their father could always have his turn at cold turkey. So Grandmother varied her practice from year to year and used to argue on both sides. A cold turkey, she would say, was restful to the hostess, was easier to carve and was more subtly flavored than a hot one. Sometimes she almost convinced herself by these arguments. Not quite, though. She continued to serve most of her turkeys hot. But on occasions other than Thanksgiving and Christmas, a cold turkey is a particularly good item for a buffet supper of the following items: Cold sliced turkey and ham arranged around a bowl of Chicken Liver Pâté* with a border of Stuffed Eggs,* stuffed olives and watercress; mayonnaise; Corn Pudding;* Caesar salad; and hot Deep-Dish Apple Pie.*

Sooner or later you will be cooking the turkey bones to make stock or soup. When you have some jellied stock on hand and enough turkey meat, you might like to make:

CREAMED TURKEY AND OYSTERS

8	*ounces frozen oysters*	2	*cups light cream*
2	*cups cubed turkey meat*	1	*green pepper*
3	*tablespoons butter*	1	*cup heavy cream*
½	*teaspoon onion, minced*	2	*pimentos*
½	*pound mushrooms, caps only, washed and sliced*	2	*egg yolks*
		½	*cup dry white wine*
3	*tablespoons instant flour*	1	*tablespoon lemon juice*

½ *cup turkey stock*

Let oysters thaw out slowly in refrigerator ahead of time. Slice turkey rather thick and cut into inch squares. Measure. Melt butter. Sauté onion and sliced mushroom caps until onion is straw colored. Remove pan from heat, sprinkle in flour. Stir well. Return to low heat and cook 3 minutes, stirring gently, add milk slowly, blending it in smoothly. Increase heat and simmer 5 minutes. Add turkey, pimentos cut in inch pieces, green pepper, cleaned of seeds and cut in very thin strips. Add heavy cream. Simmer a minute longer, transfer everything to the top of a double boiler over hot, not boiling, water. Let mixture stand until just before serving time. Then beat egg yolks, add wine and lemon juice, and beat all together. Stir 3 tablespoons of hot sauce from the turkey mixture into the egg mixture, one at a time. Blend sauce well into eggs and then add this mixture to turkey mixture. Cook, stirring until it thickens — 3 minutes or more. Remove from heat. During the last cooking of the turkey, bring jellied stock to a boil in a small saucepan. Add oysters. Cook until edges curl — a minute or two. Don't overcook. Add them and the stock to the turkey mixture.

Serve with English Muffins* split, buttered and run under the broiler. Pineapple Upside-Down Cake* makes an excellent dessert.

Another way of utilizing cold turkey is in turkey salad.

TURKEY SALAD

(For 8)

3	*cups turkey meat, cubed*	2	*sliced, hard-boiled eggs*
1	*cup celery, cut very fine*	12	*large stuffed olives*
1	*cup French Dressing**		*Garden lettuce, or Boston lettuce*
½	*cup pickles, chopped fine*		
1½	*cups mayonnaise*	12	*blanched toasted almonds, slivered*
12	*slices tomato*		

Mix celery and turkey and marinate in French dressing for at least one hour. At serving time, drain off French dressing (save for use as a future marinade). Stir chopped pickle into turkey/celery mixture. Stir in half the mayonnaise. Fill custard cups ⅔ full with the mixture and unmold them on a serving platter dressed with lettuce, watercress, chicory, and parsley. Mask the molds with the rest of the mayonnaise. Decorate the platter with sliced tomatoes, sliced hard-boiled eggs, almonds and stuffed olives. Keep cool until ready (good advice for cooks as well as salads).

Another way of using leftover turkey after you have cooked the bones and made jellied stock is in:

MRS. APPLEYARD'S TURKEY PLATTER

(For 6)

2 *cups uncooked white rice*

2	*cups creamed turkey*	2	*tablespoons sugar*
6	*large slices canned pineapple, halved*	1	*teaspoon dark molasses*
		4	*bananas split and halved*
12	*cooked prunes*	3	*tablespoons currant jelly*
12	*blanched almonds*		*Paprika*
¾	*cup pineapple and prune juice*		*Extra butter*
			Parsley sprays

Cook rice and put it into a buttered ring mold that holds at least a quart. Have creamed turkey in the top of a double boiler over hot, not boiling, water. Take two frying pans, one large, one medium. Butter the large one and put into it the halved slices of pineapple. In between them lay the cooked prunes, stoned and stuffed with blanched almonds. Into the smaller pan, put pineapple and prune juices, sugar and molasses and cook until it is quite thick, about 5 minutes. Pour syrup over pineapple slices and prunes. Put banana slices, dotted with butter, under the broiler and broil until they just start to brown, about 2 minutes.

Now turn rice ring out on a large serving platter. Put halved pineapple slices around the ring. Fill holes with currant jelly. Put prunes and bananas in between pineapple slices. Fill center of mold with creamed turkey.

Dust a little paprika on the rice. Pour any syrup left over the fruit and decorate with sprays of parsley.

You'll need no dessert with this masterpiece, just a tossed salad, a few toasted Cross crackers and some Vermont cheese.

If you have a good deal of dark turkey meat left, it goes well in a casserole such as:

TURKEY WITH BROCCOLI AND MUSHROOM SAUCE

(For 4)

2	*cups dark turkey meat, cut up*		*Pinch of nutmeg*
2	*packages frozen broccoli flowers*	4	*tablespoons bread crumbs*
1	*cup Mushroom Sauce**	1	*tablespoon butter*
3	*tablespoons light cream*	2	*tablespoons grated dry cheese*
		½	*teaspoon paprika*

Cut turkey into good-sized cubes. Cook broccoli flowers until they are just cooked through but not mushy, about 5 minutes, and put them into a lightly buttered shallow fireproof baking dish. Cover them with the cubed turkey and then with mushroom sauce to which you have added the light cream and a pinch of nutmeg. Toss bread crumbs in a tablespoon of butter and spread them over the sauce. Sprinkle grated cheese and paprika over the top. Do this all well ahead of serving time. Just before you serve it, set the dish on a flame tamer over medium heat until the sauce starts to bubble. Then run the dish under the broiler until cheese just starts to brown. With it you might like squash slices and Beets Appleyard.*

If you have plenty of jellied stock and some turkey left, you can easily make:

TURKEY IN ASPIC

(For 4)

2½	*cups jellied turkey stock, melted*	3	*Stuffed Eggs**
1	*cup turkey, in small cubes*	6	*small balls liver Pâté**
½	*cup celery, cut very fine*	1	*truffle, sliced thin*
	Watercress		*Parsley*
			Mayonnaise

Skim every bit of fat off stock. Rinse out a quart ring mold with very cold water. Pour in a little stock. Set mold into freezer for a few minutes. When jelly hardens add turkey and celery mixed together and the rest of the stock. Set mold into refrigerator for several hours. At serving time set mold briefly into barely warm water. Watch it and as soon as there is the least sign of softening, unmold it on a circular platter. Put watercress in the middle. Arrange halves of stuffed eggs and balls of pâté, your own or your favorite brand, around mold. Decorate them with truffle slices, or mushroom slices if truffles aren't available. Put sprays of parsley, watercress and dabs of mayonnaise in between. Pass more mayonnaise separately.

Preserves

GRANDMOTHER always liked preserving things — fruit, friendship or furniture. "I suppose friendship is the least work," said a young friend who heard Mrs. Appleyard make this alliteration. I have doubts about that: fruits seem to have a definite advantage over friendship. They may go rotten and they may be sticky and burn to the bottom of the kettle, but they don't make heavy demands on you, except for the time needed in the beginning, and while cooking they send a heavenly aroma throughout the house. Once stacked on your pantry shelves they can give you a feeling of great accomplishment, add color to your winter interiors and spice to your meals. What more could you ask, and could you ask as much of a friend?

While leafing through a 1949 collection of Vermont recipes I came upon a quip that seems appropriate here. It was attributed to someone called "The Punster." It reads: "We eat what we can; and what we can't we can." In that statement lies the essence of New England frugality and the basis for many rules for preserves. Here I present some of the most delectable, beginning with:

MRS. APPLEYARD'S CHUTNEY

This is a three-day task. Grandmother's ambition was always to make her chutney taste like Major Grey's or Colonel Skinner's. She thought this version came rather near the products named for these revered gentlemen; I think it better. (You'll have to ignore my obvious prejudice.)

3 large cucumbers
1 cup red wine vinegar
1 cup cider vinegar
2 teaspoons cayenne
3 tablespoons curry powder
2 teaspoons cinnamon
2 tablespoons dry mustard
3 whole heads garlic, peeled, sliced
½ cup chopped mint leaves
½ teaspoon peppermint extract
2 teaspoons allspice
3 tablespoons candied ginger, cut fine
5 pounds sugar
4 tablespoons dark molasses
1 pound seedless raisins
½ pound currants
1 pound seeded raisins
8 small onions, chopped fine
3 slices canned pineapple, cut fine
4 quarts tomatoes, measured whole, skinned, quartered (or 2 quarts canned tomatoes)
1 green pepper, seeded, sliced thin
1 4-ounce can pimentos, sliced
3 oranges, sliced thin, cut fine
3 lemons, sliced thin, cut fine
24 tart early apples, cut in eighths, peeled, added 3rd day

Cut cucumbers into cubes and soak them in a salt-water brine for 2 hours while you assemble the other ingredients. In a preserving kettle that holds 5 gallons, scald vinegar with spices, sugar and molasses. Add the drained cucumbers and all of the fruit except apples. Bring contents of kettle to a boil. Set the kettle on a flame tamer. Cook 1 hour, stirring occasionally. Cover. Let stand overnight.

The next morning bring to a boil again. It will take about half an hour to reach the boiling point. Stir well from the bottom. Boil 5 minutes. Cover. Let stand overnight.

Third day, bring to the boil again, add the apples. Use the most tart apples you can find. They are theoretically to take the place of mangoes which are not often available. They really aren't much like mangoes, but they do have a good flavor and texture.

Boil the chutney until juice thickens slightly — 10 to 15 minutes. Have sterilized half-pint or pint jars ready. Using a spoon with holes in it, distribute fruit mixture in the jars, filling them ⅞ full. The syrup left in the kettle should be good and thick. Cook it down more if you have any doubt about it. Fill the jars with it, stirring contents with a sterilized silver fork. Seal jars by twisting caps on tightly and steaming jars on a rack in a covered roaster for 10 minutes. This recipe yields about 16 pints.

MRS. APPLEYARD'S TOMATO CONSERVE

4 quarts ripe tomatoes, measured whole
Sugar
3 oranges
3 lemons
1 cup seedless white Sultana raisins
½ ounce stick cinnamon
6 medium sized tart apples, peeled, cored and cubed

If you make this in the winter, substitute 2 quarts of canned tomatoes for the ripe tomatoes. Peel fresh tomatoes by holding them on a wooden-handled fork over a gas flame until the skin sizzles and pops. If you are not quite so daring, you may immerse them, *very* briefly in boiling water, then in cold water. Be careful not to let them remain in the water too long or they will become soggy. Peel off skin. Slice tomatoes and cut them up, not too fine. Pour off about a quart of the juice. Keep it to drink — chilled — or use as soup stock. But, if you are using canned tomatoes use the juice and cut the whole tomatoes into several pieces.

Measure tomatoes and measure an equal amount of sugar. Slice oranges and lemons very thin. Cut slices in eighths with scissors. Add oranges, lemons, raisins and stick cinnamon to the tomatoes and put them into a large kettle to boil. If you cannot get white (Sultana) seedless raisins, use darker seedless ones, but not the seeded kind.

Before adding sugar to the tomato mixture, heat it in a shallow pan in a 250° oven for about 10 minutes, stirring it occasionally to expose all of it to heat. When tomato mixture starts to bubble, add the heated sugar. Cook 5 minutes, stirring well from the bottom of the kettle. Cover. Turn off heat. Keep in cool place overnight.

The next day, reheat conserve and boil 5 minutes longer. Have the kettle on flame tamer to prevent scorching. Stir well while conserve is boiling. Again keep in a cool place overnight.

The third day (Cheer up — this is the last time!), reheat once more. Peel, core and cut apples into small cubes. As soon as conserve starts to boil, add apples. Cook until they begin to soften. Test a little conserve on a cold saucer. The juice should crinkle (shimmer). Cook until it does, stirring from the bottom of the kettle. Remove stick cinnamon. Pack conserve into hot sterilized jars. Steam them 10 minutes on a rack in a covered roaster to seal lids.

It used to be that the only way you could obtain the tastes and rewards of either Mrs. Appleyard's Conserve or Chutney was by going through the three-day process yourself or, of course, by knowing Mrs. Appleyard at the right time of year. Luckily for all of us, however, Hugh Appleyard recognized the demand for both of these delicacies and initiated (with his mother) the production and sale of them. The Appleyard Corporation is now a small but thriving business, located in Maple Corner, Vermont (not far from Appleyard Center), run by two energetic young couples and producing Mrs. Appleyard's Chutney and Tomato Conserve from nearly the same rules as given above. Now anyone with a mailing address can indulge in the tastes and smells of Vermont.

LEMON MINT CHUTNEY

6 large onions
8 pounds small green tomatoes
½ cup salt
Cold water
7 lemons, sliced thin and slices cut in eighths
2 cups cider vinegar
5 pounds sugar
4 tablespoons dark molasses
1 packed cup mint leaves
4 cups cubed early tart apples
2 tablespoons ginger
2 cups seedless green grapes
1 pound seedless raisins, Sultana if possible

Chop onions fine. Add tomatoes and chop fine. Cover with salt and cold water. Let stand overnight. Next morning, drain, wash thoroughly in cold water. Put in a large kettle and set on a flame tamer. Add lemons and raisins. In a saucepan heat vinegar, dissolve sugar and molasses in it and pour over mixture. Bring to a boil. Cook 15 minutes, stirring carefully.

Second day: Reheat. Cook 10 minutes, stirring well from the bottom.

Third day: Pick mint leaves (no stems). The cup should be packed solidly. Puree them in blender with ¼ cup water. Add them, the apple cubes, ginger and green grapes to the chutney. Bring mixture to the boil. Cook 5 minutes. Test juice on a cold saucer. It should shimmer. If it doesn't, cook another 5 minutes. Stir mixture up from the bottom of the kettle. Put chutney in sterilized jars. Tighten caps. Seal by steaming 10 minutes in covered roaster.

I was so pleased with the results of the above rule, that when the last jar had disappeared in mid-winter, I found myself wishing for more green tomatoes. Can you imagine wanting green tomatoes? They seem to be in unusable abundance every fall when the first frost hits, always earlier than expected. Of course, you can try to ripen the green tomatoes in many ways, but if there isn't a touch of red on them, even the most careful hanging in cellarways, or wrapping in newspaper will usually produce nothing but rotten tomatoes. Better to make chutney or conserve.

GREEN TOMATO AND LIME CONSERVE

12 medium green tomatoes | *½ cup salt*
12 limes | *6 cups sugar*

Chop tomatoes and limes in a large wooden bowl. Pour salt over them and cover with cold water. Drain the next morning, rinse and drain again. Stir in sugar and cook over medium heat on a flame tamer for 3 hours. Stir up from the bottom occasionally to prevent sticking. Spoon the conserve into hot sterilized jars. Tighten caps and seal by steaming 10 minutes on a rack in a covered roaster.

If you have an abundance of ripe tomatoes, or simply wish to have a good relish to eat with hamburgers, or anything else for that matter, why not make:

RED-PEPPER RELISH

12 red peppers | *1 lemon, sliced thin*
6 green peppers | *1 quart cider vinegar*
3 large onions | *2 cups sugar*
6 ripe tomatoes | *1½ tablespoons salt*

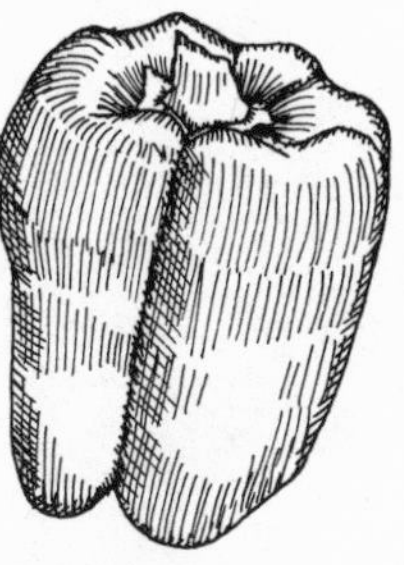

Split peppers, take out seeds and chop in a big wooden bowl. Cover with boiling water, let stand 10 minutes, drain, pour more water over, let stand 5 minutes, repeat, drain. Chop onions fine and add them. Peel tomatoes either by holding them over a gas flame until skins pop, or plunging them briefly into boiling water. Remove skins, chop tomatoes with the peppers, not too fine. Add lemon slices cut in eighths.

Heat vinegar, sugar and salt. Boil 5 minutes. Add chopped pepper mixture. Bring it to a boil. Cook 10 minutes, stirring carefully. Cover relish and let stand overnight.

In the morning, cook 10 minutes longer, stirring carefully. Test juice on a cold saucer and cook until it shimmers. Put relish into sterilized jars. Tighten caps. Seal by steaming jars 10 minutes on a rack in a covered roaster. Always check jars to be sure caps are tightly sealed. If they are not, tighten caps and steam jars an extra 5 minutes. This rule makes about 4 pints.

A relish to make on short notice to ensure that there is some to go with cold venison, is:

ONION RELISH

1 large onion, chopped fine
Grated rind and juice of 1 lemon
2 teaspoons sugar
Pepper from the grinder
Salt to taste

Mix all together and let stand in a cool place for one hour before serving. Also good with cold meat, hamburger, meat loaf and broiled fish.

A quickly-made relish:

TOMATO AND PEPPER SAUCE

2 cups peeled and chopped tomatoes
2 medium onions, sliced
1 clove garlic
2 tablespoons minced chives
2 tablespoons minced parsley
1 green pepper, seeded, minced
Pepper from the grinder
Salt to taste

Use a blender to make this. Put tomatoes, their juice, onion, and garlic into blender and run it until tomatoes are well pureed. Strain out seeds. Add chives, parsley, green peppers and a sprinkling of pepper and salt. Serve well chilled.

MUSTARD PICKLE

Wash and prepare:

1 quart small pickling cucumbers
1 quart (3 large) cucumbers, cubed
1 quart green tomatoes, cut small
1 large cauliflower, cut in small pieces
1 quart button onions, peeled

Mix 2 cups of salt with 4 quarts of water. Pour the brine over the vegetables and let it stand overnight.

Next day: bring to the boiling point and drain in a colander.

Mix:

2 quarts cider vinegar
1 cup flour
1 tablespoon tumeric
6 tablespoons dry mustard
2 cups sugar

First, slowly mix enough vinegar with the flour and spices to make a smooth paste. Then add the rest of the vinegar and the sugar. Boil until thick and smooth, stirring constantly. Add vegetables and cook until they are just heated through. Overcooking makes them mushy. You want them crisp. Pour mixture into sterilized jars. Seal immediately by steaming 10 minutes on a rack in a covered roaster. Be sure lids are tight. Makes 8 pints.

For those who like bread and butter pickles, but would welcome a variation on a theme, try the following rule. And just try to keep any on the shelves!

ZUCCHINI PICKLES

2 quarts small, unpeeled, zucchini squash, sliced thin
2 medium onions, sliced thin
¼ cup salt
2 cups sugar
2 teaspoons mustard seed
2 cups cider vinegar
1½ teaspoons celery seed
1 teaspoon tumeric
¾ teaspoon dry mustard

In a large bowl combine zucchini and onions. Sprinkle them with salt, cover with cold water and let stand 2 hours. Drain, rinse with fresh water, drain again. In a large kettle, combine remaining ingredients and bring to the boil. Cook 2 minutes. Add zucchini and onions, remove from heat, let stand 2 hours. Bring again to the boil and cook 5 minutes. Spoon into sterilized jars, tighten lids and seal by steaming on a rack in a covered roaster for 10 minutes. Make sure the seal is sound. Makes four pints.

Yes, Mrs. Appleyard has made piccallili and watermelon pickle, but I've just read a few remarks on these subjects in her private notebook such as, "Tastes like everyone else's piccallili." "Nice if you like them." "A lot of work — why not be extravagant and buy a jar?" So, I will assume that you have rules for these and other treasures of *your* great-grandmother's, and will pass on to things your great-grandmother may not have been familiar with.

BRANDIED FRUIT

Sterilize as many quart jars as you think you'l! need. You will use about half a pint of brandy for each jar, so let your supply of brandy be your guide. The assemblage of this concoction is an individual matter but goes basically as follows:

Into each jar put different kinds of fruits as they come in season, adding about half as much sugar as fruit. Begin with a few stoned sweet cherries and add, from time to time, a very little pink rhubarb cut fine, fresh pineapple finely diced (canned will do), red raspberries, red currants, black raspberries, sliced peaches, diced early apples, blackberries, a few cranberries. Cover the first batch of fruit and sugar with brandy and add a little more brandy each time you put in fruit and sugar. Part of the fun is to taste it occasionally on a piece of stale sponge cake. It should be quite sweet. The result is a fine dark reddish-purple syrup with fruit floating in it. Seal and let stand until you are ready to use it. It's good on ice cream. A little gives a trifle a special pungency. Grandmother has even been known to pass it with Pineapple Upside Down Cake.*

In the wintertime the family seems to enjoy a batch of:

*See Index for pages where recipes can be found.

MRS. APPLEYARD'S FRUIT CONSERVE

1	*package cranberries*	24	*dried apricots*
1	*8-ounce glass currant jelly*	½	*cup seedless raisins*
1	*10-ounce package frozen raspberries*	1	*cup sugar*
12	*prunes*		*Rind of 2 Temple oranges, cut fine*

Extra sugar if needed

Cook cranberries whole and use the directions and amount of sugar suggested on the package. Add jelly and frozen raspberries. In a large saucepan, put 1 cup of water. Use an Italian folding steamer and in it put prunes, apricots and raisins. Steam until prunes can be easily pitted — about 15 minutes. Set apricots and raisins aside. Cool prunes slightly and pit them. Add one cup of sugar to the liquid remaining in the saucepan to make syrup. Using a candy thermometer, cook syrup to 220°. (About this time you can relax and eat the Temple oranges.)

Put the cut-up orange peel and all the fruit into a large kettle. Pour syrup over it. Taste. Add a little more sugar if you like. Cover. Let stand overnight.

In the morning, bring conserve to the boil and cook until juice shimmers when tested on a cold saucer. Pack fruit into sterilized jars, distributing it evenly. Fill jars with syrup. Tighten lids and steam for 10 minutes on a rack in a covered roaster to seal. Be sure to check lids, tighten and steam another 5 minutes if necessary.

Another good wintertime occupation is making:

CONSERVED APRICOTS

2	*12-ounce packages dried apricots*	12	*blanched almonds (optional)*
2	*cups water*	¼	*teaspoon almond extract (optional)*
1¼	*cups sugar*		

Start the water boiling in a saucepan large enough to hold a folding Italian steamer. Put the legs of steamer out long enough so apricots will be above the water. Cover tightly and steam until apricots are tender and have increased in bulk, about 15 minutes. Be sure water does not cook away. There should be about 1¼ cups left in the pan and it will contain some of the apricot flavor. Pack apricots and almonds, if used, into a quart jar, pressing them down if necessary. Add sugar to the water in the pan and cook until syrup just starts to color. Add the almond extract, if used. Pour syrup over the packed apricots.

Eat these apricots with ice cream and sponge cake. Use them in a trifle. Eat them with yogurt and Paradise Jelly (rule given below). Bake them in Apricot Crossbar Pie.* You will have to make more sooner than you think.

CIDER APPLE JELLY

This is a somewhat more flavorful apple jelly than most, as the cider adds a resounding apple flavor.

Start with good tart apples — Wealthies if you can get them — because of the red color of their skins. Wash, but do not peel or core, them. Cut into quarters. Cover with sweet cider (as fresh as possible). Boil apples in the cider until they are very soft. Put them in a jelly bag and let juice drip through. Do not press the bag or the jelly will be cloudy. Measure the juice. To each pint of juice add a pound of sugar warmed in a shallow pan in the oven a few minutes. Bring liquid and sugar to a boil and boil until it jells on a cold saucer — from 20 minutes to half an hour. It should be a full rolling boil and at a temperature of 220°. Skim it carefully and pour into hot sterilized glasses. Let it cool slightly. Either cover glasses with paraffin, 2 thin layers, or use self-sealing jelly glasses. Cover, label and date them.

BOILED CIDER

This becomes a rather thick, dark, adhesive liquid, not quite jelled, but pleasantly tart in flavor and versatile in its uses.

Pour 1 gallon of fresh unpasteurized cider into a two-gallon kettle and cook it down, over medium heat, to about 2 quarts. At this stage the cider can be used in making mince pie, giving extra flavor to hot spiced cider, glazing fried apple rings to go with sausage, added to baked apple filling and making many apple dishes more intensely flavored. It even tastes good on pancakes.

If you wish a substance closer to jelly, simply continue cooking the cider until it reaches 220°, is quite thick and jells on a cold saucer. The result will be a pungently tart jelly, delicious with meat, hot or cold, or as a spread on bread.

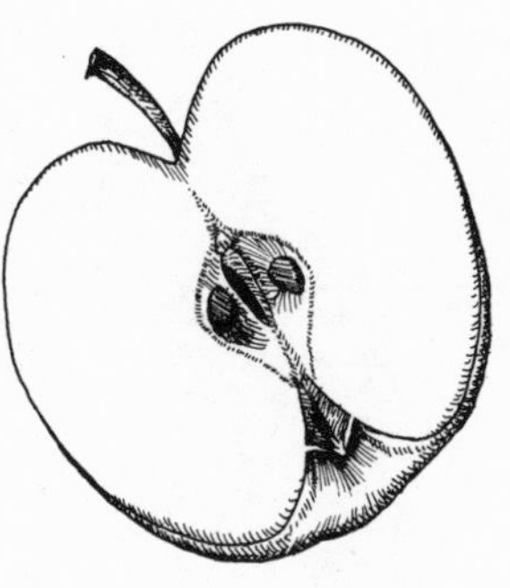

CIDER APPLES

- 2 *cups cider with a little fizz*
- 1 *cup sugar*
- 6 *whole cloves*
- ½ *teaspoon cinnamon*
- 12 *tart apples, peeled and cut in eighths*

Bring cider, sugar and spices to a boil. Stand right there, peeling the apples and dropping in the pieces. Adjust the number of slices you use according to the size of the apple. Cook the slices until tender but not mushy. As the apple slices begin to look translucent, skim them out with a spoon with holes in it and pack them into hot sterilized quart jars. Pour syrup over them. Tighten caps and seal by steaming 10 minutes on a rack in a covered roaster.

Variations:

1. Fresh pineapple cut in ¾-inch chunks is delicious done in the same way as the apples. The chunks take a little longer to cook than do the apples.

2. Fresh peaches, peeled after being doused in very hot water, and sliced, are also good done this way. The cooking time is a little shorter than for apples.

PARADISE JELLY

- 6 *large apples*
- 9 *large quinces*
- 1 *quart cranberries*
- *About 2 quarts water*
- *Sugar — equal in volume to juice*

Wash apples and quinces. Remove blossom ends, stems and cores. Pick over and wash cranberries. Cut up quinces and apples, add water and cranberries. Boil until mushy. Put fruit in a jelly bag and let the juice drain off overnight. In the morning boil the juice 20 minutes, skimming it carefully. Measure. For each cup of juice, add 1 cup sugar, heated in a 250° oven. Cook until it jells when tested on a cold saucer. Fill sterilized jelly jars not quite full. Cover with melted paraffin — first a very thin layer, and when that hardens another one. Put on sterilized covers.

Some jelly looks handsome but has little flavor. This is different.

STRAWBERRY FREEZER JAM

This is another recipe acquired in a somewhat roundabout method. It came via my brother-in-law's mother. It doesn't matter whether or not you followed that relationship, enjoy the jam.

2 cups finely mashed strawberries
4 cups sugar
1 envelope powdered pectin
1 cup water

Combine berries and sugar. Let stand 20 minutes, stirring occasionally. Stir pectin into water. Bring to boiling and boil for 1 minute, stirring. Remove from heat. Add berries and stir for about 2 minutes. Pour the jam into freezer containers, plastic or glass. Cover and let stand at room temperature for 24 to 48 hours. Store in the freezer. This makes six jelly glasses. Once opened, this jam keeps in the refrigerator for several weeks. It has a very fresh taste and is a special treat on chilly winter mornings.

Puddings

WHEN Grandmother first mentioned to a food expert of her acquaintance that she was going to include puddings in her next book, the expert tersely said: "Don't bother — puddings are extinct."

This statement aroused a combination of obstinancy and nostalgia in the general region where Grandmother usually kept her amiability. She was determined to include puddings and set about collecting her most exciting and palatable rules. After sampling many of the included rules, I am very glad that my Grandmother did not decide to throw it all to the winds of time and give up on the unfashionably outdated puddings. This section is incorporated here for more than simple historic purposes, for the rules are both nutritious and savory.

I begin with an appropriately old recipe which, I believe, Grandmother herself hadn't made in 20 years. Enjoy her rule for:

QUEEN PUDDING

5 eggs, separated
4 cups milk
⅛ teaspoon nutmeg
½ cup raspberry jam
5 tablespoons sugar
3 drops almond extract
2 cups rather dry bread crumbs, from homemade bread if possible

Beat egg yolks until thick and lemon colored. Beat in milk and nutmeg. Stir in bread crumbs. Butter a straight-sided French soufflé dish. Pour in the mixture. Bake at 350° until top just starts to brown, about 25 minutes. Wash the beater. Remove pudding from the oven and spread raspberry, strawberry jam or orange marmalade on top. Increase oven heat to 450°. Leave pudding in a warm place while you beat egg whites to stiff peaks and beat in almond flavoring and the sugar, about a tablespoon at a time. Spread meringue over top of pudding and bake until it is a delicate creamy tan. Serve either hot or cold.

Another "fashionable" pudding that is relatively easy to make is:

NESSELRODE PUDDING

1½	*tablespoons gelatin*	2	*teaspoons vanilla*
½	*cup cold water*	¼	*pound macaroons*
2	*cups milk*	¾	*cup Sultana raisins*
½	*cup sugar*	½	*cup almonds, blanched, slivered*
5	*eggs, separated*		

Whipped cream

Soak gelatin in cold water. Mix milk and sugar and bring just to the boiling point. Keep warm over hot, not boiling, water while you beat egg yolks thick and lemon colored. Add vanilla to the hot milk and pour slowly over the egg yolks, beating all the time until cool, saving out ¾ cup of milk. Pour the ¾ cup of milk on the soaked gelatin and beat it in. Beat in the rest of egg yolk mixture, add the macaroons, broken in small pieces, the raisins and slivered almonds. Wash beater. Beat egg whites to stiff peaks and fold gently and thoroughly into the mixture. Pour into a salad mold rinsed out with very cold water. Chill several hours. Unmold. Serve with whipped cream. When unmolded, this pudding forms three distinct layers, one of foamy lightness, one of vanilla custard and the treat of macaroons, raisins and almonds on the top.

In the days when pudding was always part of a meal, it would be served first, especially in boarding schools where the children would be told "He who eats the most pudding will get the most meat."

I don't know what kind of pudding was served before meals, but I know a good one to serve after. It is:

STEAMED BLUEBERRY PUDDING

2	*cups flour*	2	*tablespoons butter*
4	*teaspoons baking powder*	1	*cup milk*
½	*teaspoon salt*	1¼	*cups blueberries*

Sift flour and measure it. Sift it three times more with baking powder and salt. Work butter in with your fingertips. Add milk and berries — which you have shaken with a little flour — alternately. Put batter into a buttered tin that has a tight cover. A one-pound coffee can is a good shape and size. Vacuum-packed cans are no good.

Steam the pudding 1½ hours. Steaming is easy if you have the mold (or a coffee can), a kettle with a tight cover, a rack to set the mold on, and something heavy — an old stovelid retired from active service — to put on top of the can containing the pudding so it will not tip over. If the pudding stands upright and the water never stops boiling, the pudding should fill the mold and be fluffy inside and a delicate biscuit-tan outside with rich purple spots through it.

Do not fill the mold more than two-thirds full. Be sure the water comes halfway up around the can and that it doesn't cook away. The pudding is made with biscuit dough, not cake batter. The richness is in the sauce with which you serve it. Try Foamy Sauce.*

PLUM PUDDING

This Christmas pudding can be made several weeks ahead of time. It keeps well in a cool place right in the molds in which you cooked it and needs only a short period of steaming when you serve it.

- *2 cups dried French bread crumbs*
- *1 pound beef suet, ground fine*
- *½ pound almonds, blanched and ground*
- *½ pound citron*
- *½ pound seedless raisins*
- *¼ pound candied cherries*
- *½ pound currants*
- *1 teaspoon ground nutmeg*
- *1 teaspoon each cloves, cinnamon, allspice*
- *2 tablespoons rose water (hard to find — omit if necessary)*
- *2 tablespoons lemon juice*
- *1 cup sherry*
- *2 tablespoons rum*
- *10 eggs*
- *2 cups sugar*
- *1 cup flour*

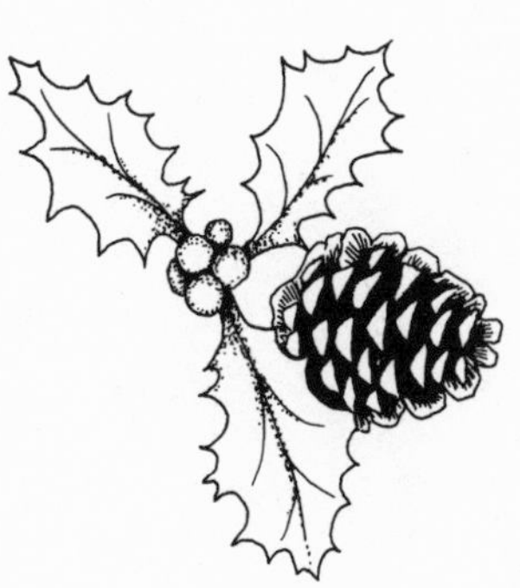

Dry the bread crumbs (from inside of loaf only) and roll into very fine crumbs. Mix them with suet, ground almonds and fruit. Sprinkle spices over mixture. Pour over rose water, lemon juice, sherry and rum and let mixture stand overnight.

Next day, separate eggs. With an electric beater, beat yolks thick. Beat in sugar. Sprinkle in flour a little at a time and beat it in. Wash beater. Beat egg whites to stiff peaks and fold them, using rubber scraper, into mixture.

This makes several small, or two large, puddings according to the size cans you steam them in. Use coffee cans, brown bread tins, melon molds — anything with a really tight-fitting cover. Most cans have either a cover that is damaged in being opened or a projecting edge that makes it impossible to get the pudding out intact. A melon mold is the best container.

Butter the molds well. Fill no more than two-thirds full. The pudding expands as it steams. Set molds on a rack in a large kettle. Pour in boiling water almost to the level of the rack. Cover kettle tightly, put a flatiron or other heavy object on the lid to hold it down. Steam pudding 5 or 6 hours (5 for small cans, 6 for larger ones). Add boiling water as needed during cooking. Serve warm with Hard Sauce.*

If you can steam a plum pudding, you might want to try steaming a:

STEAMED GRAHAM PUDDING

- *½ cup butter*
- *½ cup sugar*
- *1 egg, beaten*
- *1 cup sour milk*
- *½ cup white flour*
- *1 teaspoon cinnamon, cloves, allspice, nutmeg*
- *1 heaping cup graham or whole wheat flour*
- *1 teaspoon baking soda*
- *1 cup raisins*

Cream butter and sugar together. Beat in egg, milk and flour sifted with other dry ingredients. Add raisins. Put into a buttered mold with

*See Index for pages where recipes can be found.

a tight-fitting lid. Put the mold on a rack in a covered pan, pour in boiling water and steam, covered, for 2 hours. Serve warm with Hard Sauce,* or cool with whipped cream flavored with powdered sugar and vanilla, or a sauce made of:

1 cup brown sugar	*1 tablespoon butter*
2 tablespoons flour	*1 teaspoon vanilla or lemon extract*
2 tablespoons cider vinegar	
1 cup hot water	

Mix sugar and flour together. Add vinegar, hot water and butter. When mixture is cool, add flavoring.

PRUNE SOUFFLÉ

1 cup prune pulp (in blender)

4 egg yolks	*1 teaspoon vanilla*
Juice and grated rind of 2 lemons	*4 egg whites*
	½ cup sugar

Butter top pan of a double boiler. Put enough pitted prunes through blender to make 1 cup. Add egg yolks, lemon juice and rind, and vanilla. Beat egg whites to stiff peaks. Fold in sugar and then fold egg whites gently into prune mixture. Put all into top of double boiler, cover and cook over simmering, not boiling, water until firm, about 50 minutes. Serve with Foamy Sauce* with brandy.

ORANGE MARMALADE SOUFFLÉ

(For 6)

¾ cup egg whites	*6 tablespoons orange marmalade*
4 tablespoons sugar	*2 tablespoons whiskey*
Grated rind of 1 orange	

Beat egg whites to stiff peaks. Mix rest of ingredients and fold egg whites into the mixture carefully. Put all in a lightly buttered top of a double boiler and cook over simmering, not boiling, water for at least an hour. An extra 5 minutes does no harm. It may be kept warm over hot, not boiling, water for a short time if necessary.

Make a sauce of:

2 teaspoons butter	*2 tablespoons sugar*
2 tablespoons orange marmalade	*2 teaspoons lemon juice*
	2 tablespoons whiskey

Soften butter, add sugar and marmalade. Heat over medium heat until mixture just starts to bubble. Add lemon juice and whiskey. Cointreau may be used instead of whiskey if you prefer.

Turn soufflé out on a large warm platter. Pour sauce over it and serve.

Variation: Use 1 tablespoon orange marmalade and 5 tablespoons Apricot Pulp,* pureed in blender. Add 2 tablespoons Cointreau, 4 tablespoons sugar, grated rind of one Temple orange. Beat egg whites to stiff peaks. Mix the rest of ingredients together and fold in egg whites. Cook over simmering, not boiling, water for at least 1 hour.

Make the sauce with Cointreau instead of whiskey. Have a dozen blanched almonds ready. When you turn the soufflé out on the warm platter, scatter almonds over it and then pour on the sauce.

ORANGE CUSTARD CREAM

Thin peel of orange and lemon
½ *cup orange juice*
1 *tablespoon lemon juice*
1 *cup powdered sugar*
5 *eggs, separated*

Put peel, juice, and sugar into blender and blend until rind is finely minced. Add egg yolks. Blend briefly. Pour mixture into top of double boiler and cook until mixture coats the back of a spoon. Cool while you beat egg whites to stiff peaks. Fold them into custard. Pour into custard cups and chill well. Or use the custard in the making of a Pin Wheel Pudding.*

UPSIDE DOWN CARAMEL CUSTARD

(For 6)

1 *cup white sugar*
1 *quart milk, part cream*
4 *eggs, well beaten*
1 *teaspoon vanilla*

Put a few drops of water in each of six glass custard cups. In an iron frying pan, caramelize sugar over medium heat. Have milk heating over hot, not boiling, water. (Do not scald milk or you will have trouble when you add the caramel). Stir sugar constantly as you caramelize it and get all the lumps out of it. It should be a rich dark golden brown syrup. Put a little into each custard cup, leaving enough to pour very slowly into the warm milk. If you are not careful, it will foam up and caramelize your stove! Stir well. When there is no undissolved caramel in the milk, set mixture aside to cool while you beat the eggs. Beat well. Keep beating as you pour in the caramel mixture. Add vanilla.

Preheat oven to 350°. Put a rack and some hot water into a baking pan. Fill custard cups with the mixture. Set them on the rack. Bake until custard is set, about 25 minutes. If you put the mixture all in one dish it will take about 50 minutes to bake. Serve cold. The caramel in the bottom of the cups makes the sauce. You may unmold each one, upside down on a small glass dish, or eat them as they are from the custard cups.

While I'm on the subject of custards, a good one to make as a light dessert is:

COFFEE CUSTARD

2 *cups milk*
2 *tablespoons instant coffee*
3 *egg yolks*
¼ *cup sugar*
½ *teaspoon vanilla*

Scald milk and dissolve coffee in it. While milk is cooling, beat egg yolks, add sugar and vanilla and beat again. Pour the coffee milk over egg mixture and mix well by hand. Pour custard into buttered custard cups and bake in a preheated 350° oven on a rack in a baking pan of warm water. Bake until custard sets, about 40 minutes. These may be served either warm with meringue baked on, or chilled with whipped cream. If meringue is to be used, increase oven heat to 425°, cover custard with meringue and continue baking until meringue is a delicate tan. If served chilled, whip 1 pint cream with ⅓ cup powdered sugar and ½ teaspoon vanilla. Spoon on top and serve.

CREAM CHEESE CUSTARD

This is a good custard to serve cold for lunch with a green salad, Deviled Biscuits* and Mrs. Appleyard's Chutney.*

6	*ounces cream cheese*	4	*eggs, beaten*
¾	*cup rich milk*	½	*teaspoon dry mustard*

Soften cream cheese over hot water. Remove from heat. Beat together milk, eggs and mustard and beat in softened cheese. Pour into buttered custard cups. Set on a rack over hot water and bake in a preheated 350° oven until knife comes out clean, about 25 minutes.

SAVORY CUSTARD

This custard is meant to be the garnish for hearty bowls of Onion Soup with Custard* or simple beef bouillon.

1	*egg*	¼	*teaspoon pepper*
	Yolk of another egg	4	*tablespoons cream*
2	*tablespoons Portable Soup* or Beef Stock**	½	*teaspoon salt*
			Pinch of nutmeg

Beat all ingredients together. Have a small buttered mold ready. An old baking powder tin, 2½ inches in diameter, with a lid that fits over the edges, works well for this. Fill the mold two-thirds full of custard, put it on a rack in a rather deep pan and surround it with boiling water. Cook in a 350° oven until it is set and a knife comes out clean, 10 to 12 minutes. Chill thoroughly.

Before serving the soup, unmold the custard, put a slice of toasted French bread in each soup plate. Cover the bread with a slice of custard. Slicing it is slippery business. Be firm but not rash. Pour steaming hot soup over this. Pass some more cheese and toasted bread with the soup.

CHOCOLATE CREAM

(For 8)

This was invented by Grandmother for her chocolate loving friends when she had some paper cups and instant potato flakes on hand.

1	*cup boiling water*	3	*egg yolks*
2	*teaspoons instant coffee*	1½	*cups sugar*
5	*squares unsweetened chocolate*	¾	*cup butter*
		2	*tablespoons rum (optional)*
1⅓	*cups instant potato flakes*	3	*egg whites (beaten stiff)*
1	*cup heavy cream, whipped*		

Into the top of a double boiler put ½ cup boiling water. Add instant coffee. Stir well. When it dissolves add chocolate and cook over low heat or over hot water until chocolate is melted. Into blender put the other ½ cup boiling water and potato flakes. Press them down well and run blender half a minute. Then add egg yolks, sugar, butter, rum and melted coffee/chocolate mixture. Blend until mixture is smooth, about half a minute. Remove from blender. Fold in beaten egg whites and all but 4 tablespoons of whipped cream. Pour mixture into paper cups. Decorate tops with the remainder of the whipped cream. Chill and serve.

This is probably the only palatable use for instant potato flakes, and is, in fact, quite good.

CASTILLIAN PUDDING

This is the type of old-fashioned pudding likely to be found in the 1949 vintage Vermont cookbook that has recently come into my possession. It contains such items as Stonewall Jackson Pudding and a mincemeat rule from Mrs. Calvin Coolidge. Some of the ingredients are hard to come by, but the results are well worth the extra effort.

1 pound cooked chestnuts
1½ cups sugar
1 cup water
2 ounces gelatin
1 cup cold water
1 quart milk
8 egg yolks
2 teaspoons vanilla
1 pound French fruit (angelica, citron, cherries, etc.)
1 cup sherry

Wash cooked chestnuts. Break them up and mix with 1 cup sugar and 1 cup water cooked together 5 minutes. Soak gelatin in 1 cup cold water. Make a boiled custard with milk, eggs, vanilla, and the remaining ½ cup sugar. Add gelatin and strain it into chestnut mixture. Set bowl into a pan of ice water and beat with wire whisk until mixture begins to thicken. Add chopped fruit which has been soaking in sherry. Drain it first and put it into the mold alternately with chestnut custard. Chill until set and serve with whole marrons glacé.

BARLEY CREAM

(For 8)

1 gallon water
½ pound barley
2 quarts milk
2 eggs
2 tablespoons flour
½ cup sugar
2 tablespoons sherry
½ cup cream, whipped

Boil water in a kettle and when it reaches a full boil, drop barley into it. Cook until mixture is thick and barley is tender like boiled rice. Drain. Put milk in the top of a large double boiler. Scald it. Beat eggs, beat in flour. Add a little of the hot milk and beat it in. Keep adding milk and beating it until you have about a cup of the egg/flour/milk mixture. Add this to the hot milk. Set pan over hot water. Stir. Add hot barley, then sugar. Cook until mixture thickens, about half an hour. Taste. Add more sugar if you like. Stir in sherry or use vanilla, lemon or almond flavoring if you prefer. Chill thoroughly. Serve in glasses with whipped cream on top.

CRÈME BRÛLÉE

1 quart light cream
2 tablespoons sugar
2 teaspoons vanilla
8 egg yolks
1 cup light brown sugar, more or less

The amount of brown sugar you will need depends on the size of pan you use. One cup will be enough for a 9x13-inch pyrex one. This gives enough top in proportion to the depth.

Heat cream but do not scald. Add white sugar and vanilla and pour mixture over well-beaten egg yolks and then into the buttered pyrex dish. Set dish into a pan of warm water and bake at 350° until a knife slipped into the center comes out clean, about 20 minutes. Chill the custard for several hours or overnight. When it is very cold, cover it ¼-inch deep with light brown sugar which is well sifted and free from lumps.

Now the broiling. Light either gas or electric broiler ahead of time: gas — 5 minutes, electric — 1 minute. The idea is to briefly expose the sugar to intense heat. Slide the pan of custard under the broiler, watching it every second until the sugar melts. The center usually melts first so it is a good idea to slide first one end of the pan and then the other under the flame. The whole melting process takes about 3 minutes, perhaps less. When it begins to brown, remove at once. Now chill the Brûlée again. The top should be like golden ice and when tapped with a spoon should give forth a pleasant resonance.

CRACKER PUDDING

Cracker pudding is a dish that frequently shows up at pot luck suppers from the hands of an ex-Canadian lumber expert turned gardener and guardian of historical properties in the Appleyard Center region. Mr. Beecher has his finger in every pie in the community and is a welcome sight at pot luck suppers.

If you are going to serve this for supper, start in the morning.

6 Cross crackers
¼ cup butter
6 eggs
6 tablespoons sugar
3 cups milk
1 cup cream
½ teaspoon nutmeg
¼ teaspoon cinnamon
½ teaspoon almond extract

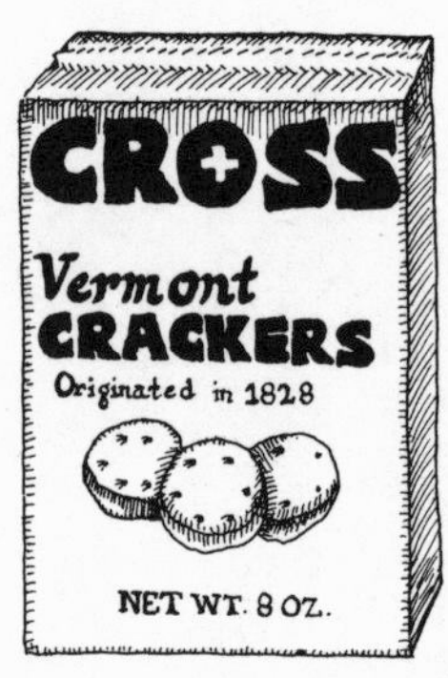

Split and butter crackers. Pile them in a buttered casserole. Beat the eggs with sugar, add milk, cream and seasonings. Pour this mixture over the crackers. Set dish in refrigerator for at least 3 hours. Before supper preheat oven to 425°. Set dish of pudding in oven and bake for 15 minutes. Reduce heat to 350° and bake until it is well puffed and brown, about 30 minutes longer.

Serve hot with vanilla ice cream sprinkled with small pieces of candied lemon or orange peel.

INDIAN PUDDING

This rule was weaseled out of a cook from a small Vermont inn not far from the Connecticut River. It was the best Indian pudding Mr. and Mrs. Appleyard had ever tasted. The difference from other rules is that the cornmeal has already been cooked in the form of johnny cake.

Square of cold johnny cake 6x8 inches (Spider Corn Cake may be used)*
1 quart milk
½ cup molasses
½ teaspoon salt
½ teaspoon nutmeg
½ teaspoon cinnamon
2 eggs

Crumble johnny cake very fine. Pour milk over it and soak it well. Add molasses and seasonings, mix well and let stand on back of stove for a while. Beat 2 eggs and add them. Taste it and add more molasses if you like. Put mixture into a buttered baking dish and bake it for 1½ hours at 350°. Stir it three times the first hour, slipping the spoon in at the side and taking care not to break the skin.

Serve the pudding with thick cream and powdered maple sugar or vanilla ice cream. As a variation you might like to add ½ cup raisins before you bake the pudding.

RICE PUDDING

There are two kinds of rice pudding enthusiasts; those who like the milder, more subtly flavored variety and those who like the richer version made with eggs and raisins. I've included one rule of each variety for both classes of fans.

MILD RICE PUDDING

¾ cup sugar
2 tablespoons soft butter
1 quart rich milk
3 level tablespoons rice

Butter a straight-sided quart casserole. Mix sugar and butter. Stir in milk, then rice. Put mixture into a casserole and bake at 300° for 3 hours. At least 3 times, oftener if you feel like it, stir pudding thoroughly so that top "skin" is well distributed throughout the mixture. Leave it alone the last hour. When it is ready, the top will be a rich golden light brown in color. Chill pudding. Serve it cold with cream. It will be the consistency of cream itself. If you like, you may mix in ½ cup sherry before baking.

RICH RICE PUDDING

(For 8)

3 beaten eggs
⅓ cup honey
2 cups cooked brown rice
3 cups milk
1 tart apple with skin, grated
1 cup raisins
½ teaspoon cinnamon
1 teaspoon grated orange rind
½ cup walnuts, chopped

Beat eggs, stir in warmed honey, then all other ingredients. Pour into buttered custard cups or a buttered casserole. Bake at 350° until custard is set, about 30 minutes in cups and longer if all in one dish. Chill. Serve with cream or yogurt. This is a substantial dessert, best eaten following a light supper.

MARLBOROUGH PUDDING

(For 6)

1 cup Cross cracker crumbs
1¼ cup sugar
¼ teaspoon nutmeg
6 tart apples
½ cup butter
2 tablespoons lemon juice
Grated lemon rind
6 eggs, well-beaten
½ cup thick cream

Butter a baking dish thoroughly. Roll cracker crumbs very fine. Mix them with ½ cup of the sugar and nutmeg. Coat inside and bottom of the baking dish with crumb mixture.

Pare and core apples, and grate or chop them fine. Cream butter and extra sugar together, stir in lemon juice and rind, add the eggs, well beaten, and cream. Stir in grated apple. Old rules for this suggest adding rose water (made by pouring brandy over rose petals) extra nutmeg and cinnamon. Add a tablespoon of brandy if you like. I prefer it with just the apple and lemon flavors. Pour mixture into baking dish. Bake at 350° for 1 hour. It is done when a knife slipped into the middle comes out clean. Chill and serve cold.

BREAD AND APPLE PUDDING

This is a rather general rule but perfect for late fall or winter, when your cellar is still full of apples and you need a different way of making them into a dessert.

Peel tart apples, grate them into a buttered baking dish. Grate in as much stale bread. Beat 2 eggs in a pint or so of milk and make it quite sweet with sugar. Flavor with rose water or grated lemon or orange peel. Mix the liquid well into apple and bread crumbs. Bake in a 350° oven until set, about 30 to 40 minutes. Serve hot as a pudding for dinner, or cold with cream at tea time. If you happen to have quinces on hand, grate in ⅓ quince, add some extra sugar and you will have a great improvement.

PUMPKIN PUDDING

(For 4)

This is really intended to use up extra pumpkin pie filling when you are in the process of making pies. Of course, you may make it on purpose.

- *1 cup caramelized pumpkin (see Pumpkin Pie* for directions)*
- *2 eggs, well beaten*
- *½ cup sugar*
- *1 tablespoon mixed spices (nutmeg, ginger, cinnamon)*
- *1 cup milk*
- *2 Cross crackers*
- *2 tablespoons light brown sugar*

Butter a small casserole. Mix all ingredients, except crackers and brown sugar, with a wire whisk until well blended. Pour mixture into casserole. Roll Cross crackers into fine crumbs and mix them with 2 tablespoons light brown sugar. Scatter over pumpkin mixture. Dot with butter. Bake at 350° for 10 minutes. Reduce heat to 325°. Bake about 20 minutes longer, until a knife slipped into the center comes out clean and crumbs are golden brown. Serve hot if you like, or cold with whipped cream or sour cream, or even plain.

SWEET POTATO PUDDING

- *1 pound sweet potatoes, boiled and peeled*
- *1 pound sugar*
- *¼ pound butter*
- *6 eggs, well beaten*
- *Grated rind and juice of 1 lemon*
- *2 tablespoons sherry*

Mash potatoes through sieve. Add sugar, softened butter, beaten eggs, rind and juice of lemon and sherry. Put entire mixture into a buttered baking dish. Sprinkle with granulated sugar and bits of citron. Bake at 350° until set. Goes well with baked ham, or cold as a nutritious dessert.

Even if you rarely indulge in the making of pudding from scratch, occasionally experiment with one of the above rules, if only for historical purposes and to compare with modern "improvements."

Salads

As fruits and vegetables have become available year round in every climate, the salad has gained an increasingly prominent position in the American diet. As well it should, for salads may contain any variety of ingredients and may be served virtually any time of the day. They may be served at any lunch, supper or dinner as the main course, as an accompaniment to or as a first course with other main dishes or as a grand finalé to a meal.

I've often thought that ruminants had a great advantage over humans in that they are able to consume potentially any green vegetable (if grass might be called a vegetable) and turn that into good, solid protein, satisfying all but a small bit of their nutritive needs.

The key to making a successful salad lies in obtaining the freshest and most tasteful ingredients. The greens must be washed, thoroughly dried and well-crisped. Meat, fish and cheese should be cut into bite-sized pieces of uniform size, and fruits and vegetables must be well-drained. The salad bowl may be a platter and might be made of wood, glass, pottery or china, although for most green salads, wood is the best material. A wooden salad bowl should never be washed, but simply have the oil rubbed from it after use, with paper towels or a piece of bread, making sure to clean out the crumbs. It must be cared for almost as a part of the salad, being rubbed with olive or other oil prior to having greens laid in it. If you are partial to garlic, you might want to rub a split clove over the surface of the bowl after the warm oil has been rubbed in.

Ideally, any oil and vinegar dressing should be made with olive oil, but as that is not always practical or desirable, other oils, preferably one with a light delicate taste, notably safflower, may be used. The vinegar gives the zip to the dressing and may be mild cider vinegar, the most versatile, or your own tarragon, basil or wine vinegar. If you're using tarragon vinegar, you may need little else as it tends to flavor the dressing well on its own. You can make your own by pouring some mild cider vinegar over fresh tarragon leaves, stopping the bottle tightly and leaving it for at least a week.

The secret to Mr. Appleyard's wonderful French dressing was the clove of garlic curing in the bottle of red wine vinegar. Of course, if you don't like garlic, you'll not want to take up this peculiarity, but if you do, it adds an almost unidentifiable zing to the dressing.

In putting together everyday salads, it is the dressing that makes the salad. Therefore, I will include a number of suggestions for dressings here. Also included are rules for varying combinations of main course, dinner, buffet and fruit salads. Remember to obtain the best ingredients, or there will be no point in making a salad at all. Be imaginative in your selection of ingredients and throw new combinations together for spice and variety.

The best place to begin is with combinations to be used in a:

TOSSED GREEN SALAD

Of course, you may put in any vegetables that are available or that come to mind. Some suggestions for combinations are:

Combination One: Lettuce, chicory, asparagus tips, tomatoes. Serve with French Dressing* into which you have mixed 1 teaspoon finely chopped pickled beets, 1 teaspoon minced parsley, and 1 teaspoon chopped onion.

Combination Two: Lettuce and watercress with finely chopped herbs — fresh tarragon, chives, parsley, chervil, thyme, very little sage. French Dressing.*

Combination Three: Curly bronze lettuce, romaine, plain iceberg, sliced cucumbers, radishes. French Dressing* with chives. Serve with this: toasted Cross crackers and frozen cheese made by blending ½ pound cottage cheese, ¼ pound Roquefort or Argentine blue cheese, 2 teaspoons minced chives, ½ teaspoon paprika and ¼ cup cream. Chill mixture and toss with salad.

Combination Four: Shredded iceberg lettuce, shredded white cabbage, romaine, chicory, sliced tomatoes, small cubes of tongue or chicken and ham, crisp chopped bacon, sliced stuffed olives. French Dressing.*

Combination Five: Iceberg lettuce sliced in rounds, thin onion rings, mung bean sprouts. Serve with Yogurt Dressing with Dill.*

Combination Six: 1 head iceberg lettuce, 4 stalks sliced celery, 5 large hothouse tomatoes, half a carrot, sliced, ¼ pound Danish blue cheese, 1 cup raw cauliflower flowerets, 2 green peppers — one sliced, one in rings. Sour Cream Dressing.*

Combination Seven: Watercress, chicory, lettuce, sliced radishes, purple onion, thinly-sliced cucumber, sliced tomatoes, bacon (crisply cooked and crumbled), toasted sesame seeds.

There are various other combinations of vegetables that might be used in assembling a green salad. Listed below are ingredients from which to choose:

Greens

Lettuce — all kinds
Spinach
Cabbage, red, white, Savoy or Chinese
Romaine
Chicory
Escarole
Celery tops
Swiss chard
Endive
Watercress
Collards
Comfrey
Beet greens
Scallions
Broccoli leaves
Cauliflower leaves

Wild Greens

Milkweed, young
Salsify and tops
Purslane
Lamb's quarters (pigweed)
Nasturtium leaves and buds
Fiddleheads

Other Vegetables

Carrots, thinly sliced, or julienned
Celery, thinly sliced
Avocado, sliced
Asparagus tips
Green pepper slices or rings
Red pepper slices or rings
Fresh green peas or pods
Green beans, cooked or raw
Radish slices
Broccoli flowerets
Cauliflower flowerets
Tomatoes — all kinds
Onion rings, thinly sliced
Eggplant, raw
Turnip, raw grated
Beets, raw grated
Bean sprouts — all kinds
Cucumber slices

Garnishes

Garlic Croutons (see below)
Cheese Cubes*
Sunflower seeds
Toasted sesame seeds
Hard-boiled egg slices
Radish Roses (see below)
Carrot curls
Nuts, whole or slivered
Cottage cheese
Ripe or green olives
Dried fruits
Fresh fruit
Crisp bacon, crumbled
Egg Water Lilies (see below)
Tomato Flowers*

Egg Water Lilies: Cut hard-boiled eggs in halves. Remove yolks and powder them fine with a fork. Cut the white of each half into pointed petal shapes. Cut them only about two-thirds of the way to the base of the egg. Cut a small slice from the base so that the egg will rest upright on the plate. Put powdered yolk back into the halves to represent the centers of the lilies.

Radish Roses: Wash radishes, cut off stems so radish will stand evenly on a plate. Cut off tops. Score the radish in lines to make petal shapes and cut thin petals back about two-thirds of the way to the base of the radish. Put in a bowl with ice cubes until serving time.

Garlic Croutons or Crumbs: Cream ¼ pound butter. Peel 4 cloves of garlic. Put them through a garlic press. Stir the crushed pulp into the butter. Add — if you like — 2 tablespoons minced parsley and 1 tablespoon minced chives. Melt mixture in an iron frying pan. Toss croutons or crumbs in it until lightly browned, about 5 minutes. If you feel conservative about garlic, use 1 teaspoon garlic powder to ¼ pound butter.

I'm sure that you might come up with additional components to go into your salads. Use any mixture you desire, and at least look over the succeeding suggestions.

VEGETABLE SALAD

(For 6)

1	*cup raw baby carrots*	1	*tablespoon chopped nasturtium stems*
¼	*cup chopped cucumber*	1	*tablespoon chopped chives*
6	*young onions, chopped*		*French Dressing**
1	*cup cooked green beans*	4	*slices crisp bacon, crumbled*
½	*cup young beets, cooked, cubed*		*Garden lettuce, several kinds*
1	*cup new peas, cooked*	⅔	*cup sour cream*
	Green onion tops, sliced	⅓	*cup chili sauce*

Mix vegetables except lettuce and marinate them with French Dressing, using just enough dressing to moisten vegetables slightly. At serving time mix in crumbled bacon. Arrange lettuce in a large wooden bowl, add vegetables. Mask vegetables with salad dressing made of ⅔ cup sour cream, ⅓ cup chili sauce.

APPLEYARD CENTER VEGETABLE SALAD

This salad is a variable one, mostly dependent upon the contents of the garden at Appleyard Center. One year the cauliflower may not come up, or it may all be consumed by the friendly neighborhood deer. The next, heavy rains may drown all but a few vines of peas. In general the ingredients are:

Cauliflower	*Carrots*
Beets	*Tomatoes*
Celery	*Green peas*
Green and wax beans	*Onions*
Curly lettuce	*Hard-boiled eggs, sliced*
Potatoes	*Chopped chives and parsley*

First, cook separately: whole cauliflower, diced carrots, small new beets, beans, cut fine, and cubed potatoes. Drain and marinate in French Dressing* to which 3 teaspoonfuls of grated onion have been added. Vegetables should marinate for at least an hour before being served.

Drain vegetables, and into a large wooden bowl put first the whole cooked cauliflower, then a ring of tiny beets. Follow these with a ring of small carrots, and then a ring of small heaps of different kinds of vegetables: raw celery, green peas, yellow and green beans, cubed potatoes mixed with chopped chives and parsley. Surround with sliced tomatoes and last of all a border of green and bronze lettuce.

Scatter some Mayonnaise,* to which some sour cream has been added, in small heaps among the vegetables.

Variations:

1. Set a small dish of mayonnaise into the center of a round wooden bowl. Surround it with the following vegetables which have been marinated in French Dressing* with plenty of minced onion in it: cooked beets, asparagus tips, peas, raw carrot and cucumber cut into matchstick pieces, finely cut celery, sliced purple onions, sliced red tomatoes, yellow tomatoes — peeled and left whole. Make a border of chicory and watercress. Scatter bean sprouts over.

2. In this variation the ingredients are all mixed together, then marinated in French Dressing,* drained and mixed with mayonnaise. It consists of: raw cauliflower, separated into flowerets, raw carrot, cooked beets, cooked potato, string beans, chopped onion, finely shredded white cabbage, minced green pepper, cubes of baked ham and tongue. Place all into a big pottery bowl and surround with curly lettuce.

VEGETABLE SALAD DELUXE

1 cup cooked carrots, cubed
1 cup cooked potatoes, cubed
1 cup cooked peas
1 cup cooked lima beans
1 cup cooked beets, cubed
1 cup raw celery, cut fine
1 onion, minced
Lettuce
Watercress
2 tablespoons minced parsley
Smoked salmon
Anchovy fillets
2 hard-boiled eggs
2 tablespoons red caviar

Put vegetables in separate bowls, marinate them with French Dressing* and add a little chopped onion to each bowl. In the middle of a large deep platter put a silver bowl or glass dish of Russian Dressing.* Arrange lettuce and watercress around edge of platter and make wedge-shaped sections of vegetables around the bowl of dressing, alternating bright ones with green and white ones. Divide sections with lines of minced parsley. Garnish two sections with smoked salmon, two with anchovy fillets (or sardines, if you prefer), one with chopped egg white, one with grated egg yolk. Dot a little red caviar here and there. This attractively arranged salad is especially good served with Baked Ham.*

HOT VEGETABLE "SALAD"

This is a mixture of garden vegetables. It goes well with Roast Lamb* with new potatoes roasted around it and Mint Sauce* served with it.

1 red bell pepper, seeded, cut fine
1 cup green beans, cut diagonally
1 green pepper, seeded, cut fine
4 carrots, cut in matchstick pieces
4 stalks celery cut in ½ inch pieces
12 scallions, cut in inch pieces
4 tablespoons butter
4 tablespoons light brown sugar
Pinches of cinnamon, nutmeg and allspice
4 tablespoons cream

Toss vegetables in butter. Do this in a fireproof dish in which they can be served. Sprinkle on the sugar and spices. Almost cover with hot water. Cook until carrots are tender but not mushy. Add water if necessary but it should all cook away. At the last minute add the cream. Salt to taste. Stir well and serve very hot with Garlic Croutons.*

GREEN GARDEN SALAD

This is a local version of Caesar salad and is made as soon as there are several kinds of lettuce ready in the garden.

1 cup olive oil (part salad oil if you prefer)
4 cloves garlic
1 large bowl of various kinds of lettuce including romaine
4 slices bread ¾ inch thick, crusts cut off
Chopped chives and minced parsley
½ cup dry grated cheese
1 teaspoon dry mustard
Salt to taste
¼ teaspoon cayenne
1 teaspoon paprika
¼ teaspoon sugar
1 whole raw egg
Peppercorns in a grinder
2 tablespoons lemon juice

Begin several hours before you are going to mix the salad by making some garlic oil. Do this by pouring a cup of oil over the peeled and sliced cloves of garlic and leaving it in a cool place. Wash lettuce thoroughly, dry it and crisp it in the refrigerator. Slice bread into ¾-inch cubes, chop chives and mince parsley. Mix dry grated cheese with mustard and other dry seasonings, except pepper and sugar. If you have real Parmesan, use it. Just before your guests come, gently fry croutons in garlic oil, using about half of it, and then put them into a slow oven for a little while to dry out and crisp.

When everyone is sitting down and ready to eat, break the raw egg over the greens. The purpose of this is not to shock your guests but to help the dressing coat every leaf. Toss leaves gently, until the egg disappears. The French call this "fatiguing" the salad, an unattractive term for a necessary activity. Sprinkle in chives and parsley. Keep tossing. Grind in plenty of pepper. Toss some more. Now add oil and lemon juice, mixed together. There should be 6 tablespoons of oil to 2 tablespoons of lemon juice. Keep lettuce moving. Every leaf should be coated and there should be no excess dressing in the bottom of the bowl. Mix in cheese and other seasonings, still tossing. Last of all add garlic croutons. Serve immediately.

COLESLAW

(For 6)

4 hard-boiled eggs
4 cups finely chopped cabbage
1 tablespoon butter
2 tablespoons sugar
1 teaspoon celery seed
2 teaspoons dry mustard
1 teaspoon onion, put through garlic press
1 tablespoon Worcestershire sauce
Salt and pepper to taste
1 cup cider vinegar

Chop whites of hard-boiled eggs. Add them to cabbage. Cream butter, work in egg yolks with a fork. Add sugar, celery seed, onion, Worcestershire sauce, mustard, salt and pepper. Bring vinegar to a boil. Stir in spice mixture and pour it slowly over chopped cabbage, stirring well.

Chill for at least 2 hours. Serve cold. For added color, use part red cabbage.

A simple cabbage salad that goes well with sausage, roast pork or pork chops is the following.

CABBAGE AND RAW CARROT SALAD

White cabbage	*Onion*
Raw carrots	*Mayonnaise*

Grate cabbage and raw carrot until you run out of energy. Grate a little raw onion and mix the whole thing together with mayonnaise or part mayonnaise and part sour cream dressing.

CUCUMBER SALAD WITH YOGURT DRESSING

2	*large cucumbers*	2	*tablespoons parsley, minced*
1	*clove of garlic*	1	*cup yogurt*
¼	*teaspoon white pepper*	½	*teaspoon paprika*
	Salt to taste		

Mint leaves

Peel cucumbers. Slice them paper thin. Add garlic, put through the press, pepper, salt and parsley to the yogurt. Toss sliced cucumbers in the mixture. Sprinkle paprika over all. Decorate with sprays of fresh mint leaves.

WINTER SALAD SUGGESTIONS

There are a number of different amalgamations that may be put together when days are short and cold and you have some French Dressing* on hand. Below are a few.

Suggestion One: Cooked shrimp, hothouse tomatoes, torn romaine and Boston lettuce, ripe olives.

Suggestion Two: Crabmeat, sliced avocado, celery, watercress. Make dressing with lemon juice instead of vinegar.

Suggestion Three: Iceberg lettuce in thin rounds, red onion rings, watercress, bean sprouts.

Suggestion Four: Jerusalem artichokes, cooked, peeled and chilled, marinated in French Dressing* to which 2 cloves of garlic crushed through the press have been added. Serve with a mixture of salad greens — romaine, endive, watercress — and toss well in marinade.

Suggestion Five: Frozen tiny peas and French-cut green beans. Cook vegetables al dente. Pour on French Dressing while they are hot. Chill. Serve with watercress, red onion rings and Garlic Croutons.*

Suggestion Six: Cauliflower flowerets, sliced avocado, hothouse tomatoes, Boston lettuce, French Dressing to which 1 tablespoon Roquefort cheese, crumbled, is added for each 4 tablespoons of dressing.

Among the great and glorious collection of cookbooks I seem to have collected by some means or other, there is a book unadornedly called *American Cookery,* "The Art of Cookery made Plain and Easy, written by a Ladie" in 1760. She seems to have a higher purpose to her collection which she freely discusses in her forward. "The great cooks have such a high way of expressing themselves, that the poor girls are at a loss to know what they mean; and in all receipt books yet printed there are such an odd jumble of things as would spoil a good dish." My salad rules have the same purpose, to lay out simply, and in a way even I might understand, manners of putting differing things together to their, and your, best advantage.

Having vaguely explained myself, I'd best get on with the business of making suggestions. A particularly tasty salad to have in winter when citrus fruits, especially Temple oranges and ripe avocados, are available is an avocado salad. It is one of the pleasant things about winter, along with flocks of Evening Grosbeaks and Pine Grosbeaks.

AVOCADO SALAD

This is one of those combinations for which there is no definite rule. It is essentially ruled by your tastes in putting it together.

Slice the avocado and put it in the bottom of a salad bowl. Squeeze lemon juice over it and cover with seeded sections of grapefruit and orange and very thin slices of mild onion. The avocado should not turn dark. Since there is plenty of fruit juice in the bowl, the dressing should be only oil mixed with whatever seasonings you like. You might add a little ginger, some mustard and paprika and decorate the bowl with crystallized ginger. Form a wreath of watercress or chicory around the bowl and serve chilled.

FILLED AVOCADO HALVES

A good way to serve avocados, either as an appetizer or as a last course, is to brush halves with lemon juice and pack them with cubes of pineapple and grapefruit sections or with cooked, chilled shrimp; or with orange sections, lime juice and sprays of mint; or with cream cheese and garnished with candied ginger. For a luncheon special, fill avocado halves with French Dressing* made with lemon juice instead of vinegar and serve with finger sandwiches, curried chicken sandwiches and rolled asparagus or watercress sandwiches.

AVOCADO AND ARTICHOKE SALAD

(For 6)

- 1 *package frozen artichoke hearts*
- ½ *cup garlic French Dressing,* with pinches of ginger and nutmeg*
- ½ *pound raw button mushrooms*
- 1 *tablespoon lemon juice*
- 2 *ripe avocados*
- ¼ *cup Garlic Croutons**

Cook artichoke hearts, drain them, and while still hot, pour garlic dressing over them. While artichokes are cooling, slice mushroom caps, umbrella style, in ⅛-inch slices. Mix them with the artichokes, dressing and lemon juice.

When serving time comes, slice avocados in ¼-inch slices, add the other mixture. Taste. Add more lemon juice and 1 tablespoon undiluted frozen orange juice, if desired. Put all in a bowl. Sprinkle garlic croutons over all. Surround with chicory. Serve at once with Cornmeal Muffins,* split, buttered and toasted.

GUACAMOLE

This may be made as a before dinner dip or served as individual salads on beds of lettuce. The traditional dipping materials are Mexican corn chips, but thin fingers of Thin Scalded Johnny Cake* work well also. If served as a salad, you may want to serve tortilla pieces with melted cheese with it. Don't try to make this unless you can get some really ripe hothouse tomatoes, the best obtainable in the winter.

This may be made in the blender, but doesn't have to be.

- 2 *hothouse tomatoes, peeled, seeded, chopped*
- 1 *tablespoon onion, finely chopped*
- 2 *canned chili peppers, chopped*
- 1 *tablespoon very hot chili sauce*
- ¼ *teaspoon ginger*
- *Pinches of salt, pepper, sugar*
- 2 *large ripe avocados*
- *Crystallized ginger*

Make this just before you serve it. It doesn't take long if you have all the materials combined except the avocados and crystallized ginger — so that the avocados won't have a chance to turn dark.

Peel avocados and mash them. Add the other mixture. Decorate with crystallized ginger.

A traditional summertime favorite that may also be eaten at other times of the year is:

POTATO SALAD

- 4 *cups cooked potatoes, diced*
- 1 *tablespoon cider vinegar*
- 2 *teaspoons mustard*
- ⅛ *teaspoon pepper*
- 2 *tablespoons parsley*
- ½ *teaspoon celery seed*
- 1½ *cups diced celery*
- 1 *tablespoon finely minced onion*
- ¼ *cup sliced radishes*
- 1 *cup Mayonnaise**
- *Hard-boiled eggs*
- *Tomato slices*
- *Green or ripe olives*
- *Lettuce*
- *Radish Roses**

As soon as potatoes are cooked, slice or dice them into a mixing bowl. Sprinkle over them the vinegar mixed with seasonings and onion. Stir in celery, sliced radishes and mayonnaise. Pack the salad into a lightly oiled ring mold and chill. Unmold on a circular platter and surround with slices of hard-boiled eggs, tomatoes and whole olives. Fill the center of the mold with oak leaf lettuce and radish roses. Serve. Small cooked, chilled beets are a good addition if added at the last minute so as not to color the entire salad pink.

BEAN SALAD WITH TARTAR SAUCE

- 1 *package frozen green beans*
- 1 *package frozen wax beans*
- 1 *package frozen lima beans*
- 2 *cups garlic French Dressing**
- 1 *medium onion, sliced thin*
- *Tartar Sauce**
- *Watercress*
- 2 *hard-boiled eggs, sliced*
- *Green olives, sliced*

Cook beans in a little water, drain, and while they are still hot pour the dressing over them. Mix in the sliced onion. Chill at least half an hour. Drain dressing from beans and mix the tartar sauce into the beans. Put salad on a platter, wreathe with watercress, hard-boiled egg slices and slices of olives.

Another substantial salad for hot evenings is a:

SHELL BEAN SALAD

(For 4)

2 cups cooked shell beans
½ cup diced celery
Lettuce
*⅓ cup Mrs. Appleyard's Chutney**
2 tablespoons minced chives
1 teaspoon chopped mint
2 tablespoons chopped parsley
½ cup mayonnaise
2 tablespoons chili sauce

For the garlic oil marinade:

½ cup oil
2 cloves garlic
¼ cup vinegar
1 teaspoon mustard
1 teaspoon sugar
Salt and pepper to taste
½ teaspoon paprika

Make the marinade and pour it over the shell beans and celery and let stand in a cool place at least ½ hour. Arrange lettuce in a shallow wooden bowl. Add chutney, chives, mint, and parsley to the beans. Mix well. Put the mixture into the center of the bowl, mask with ½ cup mayonnaise into which you have stirred 2 tablespoons chili sauce. Serve with cold ham and Corn Dodgers.*

TOMATO FLOWERS

Peel whole tomatoes and cut in five sections almost to the stem end. Stuff centers with raw cauliflower flowerets, with green beans cooked al dente or with chicken salad. Marinate with French Dressing* and top with mayonnaise. An attractive way to serve salad or for use as a garnish, simply spread "petals" and sprinkle grated egg yolk in the center.

TRIPLE DECKER TOMATOES

Cut a hollow from the center of tomatoes. Fill hollows with cream cheese mixed with chives. Chill. Just before serving time, slice stuffed tomatoes, put on a bed of lettuce and dress with French Dressing.* Serve with the main course.

RIPE OLIVE SALAD

(For 6)

A good salad to serve with Greek dishes such as Eggplant Casserole* and broiled lamb patties.

Garlic mayonnaise
Garden lettuce
½ cucumber, sliced
18 ripe olives, pitted
2 pimentos, cut in strips
1 cup cottage cheese
⅓ cup sour cream

To make garlic mayonnaise mix Mayonnaise in the Blender* with 2 cloves of peeled garlic. In a shallow bowl arrange lettuce. Slice cucumber very thin, remove pits from olives. Cut pimentos into very thin strips. Mix cheese and sour cream and heap in the center of the lettuce. Surround cheese with a ring of olives, then one of cucumber slices. Decorate cheese with pimento strips. Pass mayonnaise in a separate bowl.

MAIN DISH SALADS

Salads can often serve as the main part of a light lunch or supper, especially in hot weather. Meat, seafood or poultry frequently form the basis of these salads, which need only Parker House rolls, or corn muffins and a light dessert to make up a complete meal.

COUNTRY CHICKEN SALAD

(For 8)

"What are you composing — a still life by an old Dutch master?" Nicholas Appleyard asked his grandmother. "Need any help?"

Grandmother neatly draped a lettuce leaf over the place where some Appleyard boy — a century ago — had cut a piece out of the edge of the big pewter platter. He just wanted to make a few bullets, the rascal whimpered, while his mother shook him by the scruff of his neck.

"Why that old platter," he sobbed, "it must be more'n a hundred years old . . ."

After two hundred years it can still hold a summer salad. I served this one hot evening while hummingbirds buzzed in and out of the larkspurs and ice tinkled in tall glasses. First make the chicken salad:

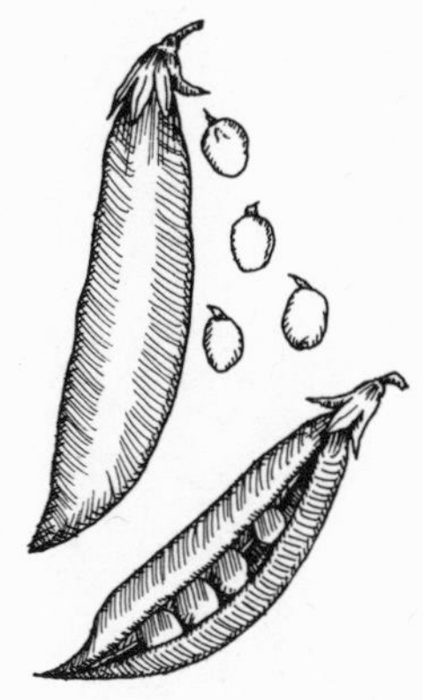

- 6 *chicken quarters, all white meat*
- 1 *carrot, sliced*
- 1 *onion, sliced*
- *Pinches of thyme, basil, oregano*
- *Hearts of 2 bunches celery*
- 1 *quart cooked new peas*
- 12 *broccoli flowers*
- 1 *green pepper*
- 4 *large tomatoes*
- 4 *hard-boiled eggs*
- *Garden lettuce, several kinds*
- ½ *cup almonds, slivered and toasted (optional)*
- 4 *young raw carrots*

Start this the day before you plan to serve it. Simmer chicken, carrot, onion and seasonings until meat slips easily from bones, about 1½ hours. An electric frying pan or an enamel Dutch oven are both good for this purpose. Remove meat and skin from bones. Return bones and skin to broth and cook half an hour. Strain broth. Chill.

The next day cut chicken into neat pieces, not too small. Also cut the celery into ¼-inch strips, then across into ¼-inch cubes. Skim fat from broth and use 3 tablespoons of it in the marinade:

- ½ *teaspoon dry mustard*
- ¼ *teaspoon garlic powder*
- ¼ *teaspoon curry powder*
- ¼ *teaspoon nutmeg*
- ½ *teaspoon paprika*
- ¼ *teaspoon black pepper*
- ½ *teaspoon grated lemon peel*
- *Salt to taste*
- 2 *tablespoons cider vinegar*
- 1 *tablespoon mayonnaise*

Mix this in a bowl big enough to hold chicken and diced celery. There should be 4 cups of chicken, loosely packed, and 2 cups of celery. Put dry seasonings in a large wooden bowl, pour vinegar over them, mixing vigorously with a wooden fork. Stir briskly while you add mayonnaise and chicken fat to make a rather thick marinade. Add chicken and celery, turning them over gently until well coated with marinade. Cover bowl with plastic wrap and chill for at least 3 hours.

In the meantime, shell, cook and chill enough peas to make a quart. Dice young carrots, cut broccoli flowers from stem, seed and slice green pepper and skin and slice tomatoes. Cook, shell and slice hard-boiled eggs. All this can be done in the morning so that at serving time all you need do is cover a large platter with several kinds of lettuce and unmold the salad on the lettuce. Arrange prepared vegetables and eggs around the salad, mask it with mayonnaise. Decorate with strips of green pepper. Pass mayonnaise with the salad and serve.

If you make this in the wintertime, and there is no fresh garden lettuce to use as a background, you might want to add the toasted almonds to the mixture. Pack the salad into custard cups, one for each person to be served, and unmold it on pineapple slices, having first filled the centers with some of the mixture. Wreathe with watercress. Pass Lemon Mint Chutney* and Curried Bread* with it. Happy silence often greets this combination.

TURKEY SALAD WITH AVOCADO

Make Turkey Salad.* Brush avocado halves with lemon juice and fill with salad. Set on beds of oak leaf lettuce, mask with mayonnaise and serve with Baking Powder Biscuits* with cheese and Mrs. Appleyard's Chutney.*

On those rare occasions in summer when you are able to get hold of Gaspé salmon, grab a two-pound chunk and make:

SALMON SALAD PLATTER

2 pounds Gaspé salmon
1 cup cooked young beets, cubed
2 cups green beans, cooked
2 cups green peas, cooked
Garden lettuce
3 hard-boiled eggs, chopped
1 cup sour cream
3 tablespoons chili sauce
¼ cup young onions, chopped fine
1 tablespoon minced chives
2 tablespoons finely-chopped cucumber (peeled and seeded)
12 perfect tomato slices, big ones
1 cup tiny carrots, sliced
2 tablespoons minced parsley

Wrap the salmon in cheesecloth and steam to an internal temperature of 150° — about 20 to 30 minutes. Cool. Chill at least 2 hours. Chill cooked vegetables. Peas may be fresh from your garden or tiny frozen peas. Beans should be cut in long diagonal slices and cooked as soon as picked in the smallest amount of water. On a large platter arrange different kinds, shapes and colors of crisp garden lettuce. Put the boned chunk of salmon in the center of platter and arrange vegetables around it in little heaps.

Stir chopped hard-boiled eggs into sour cream. Add chili sauce, onion, chives, parsley and cucumber. Mix well. Mask salmon with the mixture.

Garnish with tomato and carrot slices. Sprinkle with minced parsley. Put spoonfuls of dressing among the heaps of vegetables. Parker House rolls go well with this combination.

SEAFOOD SALAD

(For 8)

- 2 *12-ounce frozen haddock fillets*
- 1½ *pounds cooked lobster meat*
- 2 *pounds cooked crabmeat*
- 2 *pounds cooked shrimp*
- ½ *cup diced celery*
- *French Dressing**
- *Mayonnaise*
- *Boston lettuce*
- *Watercress*
- 2 *hard-boiled eggs*
- 6 *large stuffed olives*

Cut frozen haddock fillets into quarters and cook them in a folding steamer until they flake easily. Cooking time will depend on how much they have thawed: 4 to 6 minutes should be enough. Break into flakes and chill. Mix lobster and crabmeat, both cut up, not too fine; shrimp left whole; celery and flaked haddock. Marinate in French Dressing for several hours. When serving salad, arrange it on a large platter. Mix some mayonnaise with the fish and make it into individual mounds, each resting on lettuce, surrounded by watercress, masked with more mayonnaise and decorated with sliced hard-boiled eggs and olives.

HALIBUT AND FLOUNDER SALAD

(For 4)

- ½ *pound flounder fillets*
- ½ *pound slice of halibut*
- 2 *hard-boiled eggs, chopped*
- ½ *cup Mustard Pickle**
- *Boiled Dressing**
- *Garden lettuce*
- *Green peas, cooked and cooled*
- *Radish Roses**
- *Egg Water Lilies**
- *Celery stalks*
- *Tomato Flowers**

Steam the fish to an internal temperature of 150° or until it flakes. Cool. Flake it and stir into it the chopped eggs and Mustard Pickle. Pack it into a bowl rinsed out with cold water and chill in refrigerator for at least 2 hours. At serving time turn fish out on a round platter. Cover with Boiled Dressing or mayonnaise. Surround with garden lettuce, heaps of green peas, Radish Roses, Egg Water Lilies, celery stalks, and Tomato Flowers.

CRABMEAT AND SHRIMP SALAD

(For 4)

- ½ *pound crabmeat, cooked*
- ½ *pound shrimp, cooked*
- ½ *cup finely cut celery*
- ½ *cup French Dressing**
- 3 *hard-boiled eggs, stuffed*
- 1 *teaspoon crushed onion*
- ½ *cup mayonnaise*
- *Lettuce*
- *Radish Roses**
- *Tomato slices*

Mix crabmeat, shrimp and celery and marinate in French Dressing* for at least ½ hour. Cut hard-boiled eggs in halves. Mash yolks with crushed onion and mayonnaise. Stuff the whites with the mixture. Arrange garden lettuce on a platter. Heap crabmeat mixture in the center. Mask it with mayonnaise. Arrange stuffed eggs, Radish Roses, and tomato slices around the platter. Pass extra mayonnaise.

MEAT AND VEGETABLE SALAD

(For 4)

This may be made of many combinations of meat and vegetables. For instance:

1 cup each, tongue, chicken, ham, cut in neat cubes
½ cup diced celery
½ cup shredded white cabbage
*French Dressing**
Mixture of salad greens
2 tablespoons crisp bacon, crumbled
2 tablespoons chopped ripe olives

Marinate meat, celery and cabbage in French Dressing. At serving time toss the mixture in a bowl with greens, bacon and chopped olives. With it serve French Garlic Bread.*

MOLDED SALADS

For a different kind of salad, especially good when a cooling substance is needed to round out a meal, try one of the following molded or jellied salads.

SALMON IN TOMATO ASPIC

As this is a substantial salad, and therefore a time-consuming task, I'd suggest starting the day before you plan to serve it for lunch, or early morning if you will be serving it for dinner. Grandmother invented this one day with a large copper mold in the shape of a fish as her inspiration. For a large mold you will need:

1 carrot
1 onion
Small piece of bay leaf
Sprig of thyme
Parsley, salt and pepper to taste
Salmon bones
3 pounds Penobscot or Gaspé salmon
1 quart tomato juice
Peppercorns
Egg shells for clearing soup, or 2 egg whites
2 envelopes (tablespoons) plain gelatin
Juice of 1 lemon
Fresh tarragon leaves
2 eggs, hard-boiled
Oak leaf lettuce
Sliced lemon
*Green Mayonnaise**

Make Court Bouillon* (fish stock) using carrot, onion, thyme, bay leaf, parsley, salt and pepper, salmon bones and two quarts of water. Cook all together for half an hour. Strain through cheesecloth over fish in a kettle large enough to hold the fish. Simmer fish over low heat for 40 minutes or until it flakes easily. Remove fish and put aside to cool. Add tomato juice to the bouillon and cook it down until there is about one quart. Add peppercorns the last few minutes of cooking; they turn bitter if cooked too long. Add egg shells. If there is no white clinging to them, add one or two extra whites. When whites are cooked hard, strain bouillon again through cheesecloth.

Soak gelatin in the juice of the lemon and a little cold water for a few minutes. Pour hot bouillon over mixture and stir until gelatin is dissolved. Wet the mold with cold water. Pour in a little of the jellied bouillon, sprinkle tarragon leaves on top of it and set mold into refrigerator. While it is stiffening, remove skin and any remaining bones from the fish and peel and slice hard-boiled eggs.

When jelly is stiffened, lay egg slices around the sides of the mold and put in the fish. You might try to make it look as if the fish came in one piece. Now pour in the rest of the jellied bouillon and set the mold in the refrigerator. The big problem now is to get the salad out of the mold intact when serving time comes. When that time arrives, have your best platter ready and plenty of fresh parsley and sliced lemon at hand. Set fish mold in a pan of warm, not hot, water. Watch it. In a minute you will see the first softening of the jelly around the edge. Remove the mold immediately from the water. Wipe it dry. Put the platter over it and turn the whole thing upside down. If the jellied fish does not leave the mold immediately, wring out a wet, hot cloth and apply it to the top of the mold. Just when you think it is never coming out, it will. Lift off the mold. Surround the fish with oak leaf lettuce, parsley, sliced lemon, and Green Mayonnaise.* Put it where it will keep cold and relax for a short while before you serve your guests.

JELLIED SHRIMP AND COLESLAW

A somewhat less filling salad than the salmon aspic, but refreshing.

- *1 3-ounce package lemon or lime jello*
- *1 cup mayonnaise*
- *1 cup finely shredded carrot*
- *1 cup finely shredded cabbage*
- *½ cup crushed pineapple*
- *1 cup small cleaned shrimp*

Prepare jello according to the directions on the package. When it is partly chilled, stir in mayonnaise, cabbage, carrot and pineapple. Rinse a ring mold with cold water or brush with oil. Put in one quarter of the mixture. Distribute the shrimp around the ring. Fill with remaining mixture. Chill, turn out of the mold, and arrange on a platter with leaf lettuce.

TOMATO ASPIC

- *4 tablespoons plain gelatin*
- *1 cup cold water*
- *2 large onions, chopped fine*
- *1 teaspoon grated lemon rind*
- *1½ teaspoons pepper*
- *4 cloves*
- *Salt to taste*
- *7 cups tomato juice*
- *4 tablespoons lemon juice*
- *1 tablespoon Worcestershire sauce*
- *2 teaspoons sugar*

Soften gelatin in cold water. Simmer the onion, lemon rind, pepper, cloves and salt with tomato juice for half an hour. Strain some of the juice over the soaked gelatin and stir well. Strain the rest of it into another kettle and add gelatin, lemon juice and Worcestershire sauce. Rinse a 2-quart mold with cold water. Pour in tomato mixture. Set mold into refrigerator. Stir the aspic twice before it sets. Chill until set.

When it is time to unmold it, have ready a round platter. Put a little water on it, less than a teaspoonful, and spread it around evenly with a pastry brush. In the event that you do not center the mold exactly on the plate, the moisture will allow you to tease the aspic into place without completely disrupting it. Set the mold in warm, not hot, water for 5 or 6 seconds. Don't leave it too long. Loosen the aspic around the edges with a dinner knife. Put the platter over the mold. Reverse the whole thing. Wait patiently for the gentle plop of the aspic's falling onto the platter. Keep cool (both the aspic and yourself) while you make the following filling to go in the center.

1 cucumber

1 small onion, thinly sliced
1 green pepper
2 tablespoons chives cut fine
1 tablespoon fresh parsley, minced
Lemon rind, grated
*¼ cup French Dressing**
Lettuce or watercress
½ cup sour cream
*½ cup Mayonnaise**

Peel cucumber. Engrave the edges by drawing the tines of a fork down the outside of it. Slice it thin. Add onion slices. Slice the green pepper in very thin rings. Remove seeds and pith and add rings to cucumber mixture. Sprinkle with chives, parsley and lemon rind. Add French Dressing and toss until the vegetables are well coated with it. When serving time comes, put sprays of watercress or leaves of Boston lettuce around the aspic. Put cucumber mixture into center of ring. Mix sour cream and Mayonnaise and mask cucumber mixture with this dressing.

Pass Danish Blue or Roquefort cheese with the aspic. Serve with Seafood Chowder* and Souffléd Cross Crackers* or sesame crackers.

MOLDED CUCUMBER SALAD

(For 6)

For a light salad to go with cold sliced roast beef and Baking Powder Biscuits* on a hot summer night.

1 8-ounce package cream cheese
1 cucumber, peeled, seeds removed, chopped
¼ cup sour cream
1 tablespoon minced chives
Lettuce
6 large ripe tomato slices
Mayonnaise

Moisten cream cheese with sour cream. Add the chopped cucumber and chives. Stir well. Arrange lettuce on a platter. Lay tomato slices on it. Pack the cream cheese and cucumber mixture into a custard cup and unmold it on a tomato slice. Repeat until all the slices are covered. Pass mayonnaise with the salad.

CHICKEN IN JELLY

1 5-pound fowl, cut in 8 pieces
4 cups water
1 large onion
1 stalk celery
1 carrot, sliced
Bay leaf
1 tablespoon gelatin
*1 cup Green Mayonnaise**
Watercress
Oak leaf lettuce

The day before you plan to serve salad, simmer fowl in water with onion, celery and carrot. Simmer until meat slips easily from bones — about 2½ hours. Add bay leaf during last 15 minutes of cooking. Remove meat and skin from bones. Return bones and skin to broth. Cook broth down to about 2 cups. Cut meat into pieces, not too small. Chill overnight. Strain broth and chill overnight.

In the morning, remove fat from broth, heat broth and pour it over gelatin. Stir well. Brush a ring mold with olive oil. Put in a little broth. Chill until it jells. Put pieces of chicken in mold. Pour cool broth over chicken. Chill until mold is set. Unmold on a circular platter. Fill center with Green Mayonnaise. Wreathe with watercress, oak leaf lettuce and small tomatoes.

GINGER ALE ORANGE RING

2½	*tablespoons gelatin*	2	*cups orange sections or thinly-sliced peaches*
¼	*cup cold water*	3	*ounces cream cheese*
2	*cups ginger ale*	½	*cup mayonnaise*
½	*cup sugar*		*Watercress*
2	*tablespoons lemon juice*		*Sprigs of mint*
½	*cup frozen lemonade diluted with ½ cup water*	¼	*cup crystallized ginger, cut rather fine*
1¼	*cups orange juice*		

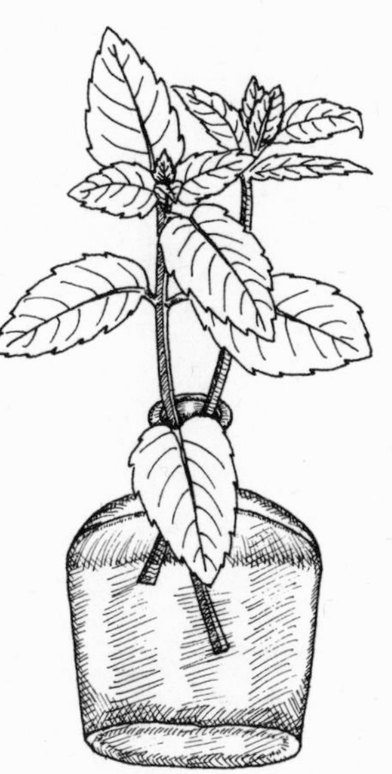

Soak gelatin in ¼ cup cold water. Heat a little of the ginger ale with the sugar. Pour it over the gelatin and stir until gelatin is dissolved. Add lemon juice, frozen lemonade, orange juice and the rest of the ginger ale. Rinse out a 2-quart ring mold with cold water. Pour in a little of the mixture. Chill. When it hardens, distribute the fruit sections evenly around the ring and pour in the rest of the mixture. Chill overnight. At serving time set the ring into lukewarm water, 98°, for 30 seconds. Wipe it dry. Turn a large platter over it, center it carefully and reverse it.

Have ready the cream cheese mixed with the mayonnaise, or use cottage cheese for extra protein. Put it in the middle of the mold. Wreathe the mold with watercress and sprigs of mint. Sprinkle crystallized ginger over the dressing. A good salad to serve as part of a buffet.

JELLIED GRAPE JUICE AND FRUIT

1	*3-ounce package grape jello*	3	*cups fruit cocktail or the equivalent in fresh cut-up fruit (no pineapple)*
1	*6-ounce can frozen grape juice*		*Mayonnaise*
½	*cup chopped walnuts*	½	*cup whipped cream*
			Sugar

Prepare grape jello according to the directions on the package, substituting the concentrated grape juice for part of the required liquid. When partly chilled stir in fruit and nuts. Place in a fancy mold, complete chilling and unmold on a glass platter. Serve with mayonnaise into which ½ cup whipped cream and a little sugar have been stirred.

TOSSED FRUIT AND SCALLION SALAD

1 grapefruit, sectioned
1 orange, sectioned
1 green pepper, sliced thin
1 avocado, diced
1 bunch scallions, finely cut

Toss all together with French Dressing.*

FRUIT SALAD WITH CREAM CHEESE BALLS

Use fruit that comes frozen in glass jars or fresh fruit cut in bite-sized pieces. Drain fruit and add to it: 1 sliced banana, 4 canned pears, halved, and some fresh whole strawberries. Marinate it in Fruit Salad Dressing:

1 tablespoon lemon juice
3 tablespoons salad oil
½ teaspoon paprika
Salt to taste
2 drops peppermint extract
1 tablespoon honey
¼ teaspoon mustard
½ teaspoon white pepper
1 teaspoon lemon extract

While the salad is marinating make the Cream Cheese Balls:

2 tablespoons powdered sugar
1 3-ounce package cream cheese
1 teaspoon thick cream
2 tablespoons candied ginger, cut fine
1 tablespoon chopped blanched almonds

Sprinkle a small cutting board with powdered sugar. Mix cream cheese, cream and candied ginger. Sugar your fingers slightly and form the mixture into balls. Sprinkle chopped almonds on sugared board and roll balls in the mixture.

Line salad bowl with watercress or Boston lettuce. Toss fruit gently a few times in dressing and heap into bowl. Put cheese balls around the edge. Serve, garnished with sprays of fresh mint.

Other combinations of fruit that may be served in the same fashion are:

1. Pineapple cubes, grapefruit sections, sliced bananas, served in hollowed out grapefruit halves.
2. Diced red apples, celery, pear halves, alfalfa sprouts.
3. Diced red apples, sliced bananas, raisins, fresh shredded coconut.
4. Six sliced bananas, ½ cup pitted and chopped dates, ½ cup chopped walnuts, sprays of fresh mint.

ORANGE AND ONION SALAD

Peel seedless oranges down to the pulp and cut out orange sections. Allow one orange for each person to be served. For four oranges, thinly slice 1 medium onion and combine with oranges. Cover with French Dressing.* Put fruit in a bowl with sprays of watercress arranged around it. Toss just before serving. An excellent combination to be served with roast duck.

SALAD DRESSINGS

"To make a perfect salad there should be a spendthrift for oil, a miser for vinegar, a wise man for salt, and a mad-cap to stir the ingredients and mix them well together." — Anonymous

I think you need a mad-cap for mixing as well as for experimenting with a variety of ingredients in making a new salad dressing. Here are a few of the results of such experiments I think the best.

FRENCH DRESSING

You may have noticed that this dressing is called for on numerous occasions and even more frequently on salads. It is the best of the basics: oil, vinegar, and seasonings. You may make endless changes in the format by simply changing one or two ingredients. For instance, for fruit or avocado salads, substitute lemon juice for the vinegar. If you find, as I do, that you use it quite often, simply make up the mixture of dry spices ahead of time, keep them in a glass jar until needed. At dressing time you'll be all set. If you have access to fresh herbs, please use them rather than the dried ones. The taste will be so much richer.

This is the basic herb mixture. Multiply it as many times as you need to fill your bottle. When mixed, this quantity seasons about four-fifths of a cup of dressing.

1 teaspoon dry mustard
½ teaspoon pepper from grinder
¼ teaspoon thyme
½ teaspoon mixed herbs
⅛ teaspoon curry powder
½ teaspoon sugar
½ teaspoon paprika
¼ teaspoon oregano
1 teaspoon garlic powder

In mixing your salad allow 2 teaspoons of this mixture to:

⅓ cup olive oil
⅓ cup salad oil
1 tablespoon chopped chives
3 tablespoons red wine vinegar
1 tablespoon chopped parsley
½ teaspoon salt

Put all ingredients in a screw-top jar. Tighten cover and shake well. Dip a crust of bread into the mixture and taste it. Add more vinegar if you like, or more of any of the other ingredients if your palate so dictates.

To "properly" dress the salad you have two choices. You may pour some of the dressing into a wooden bowl. Lay a wooden fork and spoon over the dressing and put whatever combination of greens or vegetables you like to rest on the fork and spoon. Then ask one of your guests to carefully toss exactly twenty-seven times so that every leaf is coated and there is no dressing left in the bowl.

Or, you may assemble the dry ingredients you like in a large spoon, rub the bowl with peeled and cut garlic, fill the spoon, stirring well with the fork, once with vinegar and three times with oil. Then put in the salad greens and toss mixture until every leaf is coated. This sounds simpler but really isn't, because it has to be done at the last minute. Choose whatever method best suits your way of life, or make up another one.

Variations of French Dressing:

With Roquefort. Add 1 tablespoon crumbled Roquefort Cheese after you add the oil. Argentine or Wisconsin Blue cheese may be used instead of Roquefort.

With garlic. Soak a clove of garlic in your bottle of red wine vinegar and proceed with the rule for French Dressing.

With anchovy. Omit ¼ teaspoon salt and add 1 tablespoon anchovy paste before adding the oil. If there is oil with the anchovies, use it in the dressing. This dressing goes well with a salad of lettuce hearts garnished with strips of anchovy fillets.

With olives. To a double quantity of French Dressing add: 1 tablespoon chopped ripe olives, 1 tablespoon chopped green stuffed olives, half a green pepper — minced, 1 hard-boiled egg — white chopped and yolk grated — 1 tablespoon chopped chives. Put all ingredients into a jar, pour the dressing over them, cover jar tightly and shake it hard. Very good with a simple salad of lettuce and tomatoes.

With chutney. Add 2 tablespoons of Mrs. Appleyard's Chutney* or Major Grey's Chutney, minced fine, to French Dressing. Mix well and serve with plain lettuce. A great addition to toasted cheese sandwiches or Welsh Rabbit.*

With chili sauce. Add 2 tablespoons finely-minced green pepper, 1 tablespoon minced green onion and 2 tablespoons chili sauce.

Thousand Island style. Add 1 tablespoon chopped stuffed olives, 1 teaspoon grated onion, 1 tablespoon minced green pepper, 1 chopped hard-boiled egg, 1 tablespoon minced parsley.

GARLIC SALAD DRESSING

1 clove garlic, put through press
1 teaspoon sugar
Salt and fresh pepper to taste
1 teaspoon mustard
1 cup red wine vinegar (part lemon juice)
1½ cups oil (1 cup salad oil, ½ cup olive oil)
½ teaspoon paprika

Mix garlic with dry seasonings with the back of a wooden spoon. Pour in vinegar and oil and mix well. Use on a salad of lettuce, endive, chicory and romaine.

BOILED DRESSING

This is one of the two dressings used in Appleyard Center when Grandmother first arrived there. The other was a mixture of vinegar and sugar over lettuce. This is the one worth remembering.

2 tablespoons lemon juice (or vinegar)
1 teaspoon dry mustard
½ teaspoon white pepper
1 teaspoon sugar
½ teaspoon paprika
1 teaspoon salt
4 egg yolks (large eggs)
1 cup thick cream

Into a double boiler over hot, not boiling water, put lemon juice and dry seasonings. Stir until seasonings are mixed and dissolved. Then with a wire whisk, beat in the egg yolks. Beat well and then beat in the cream, a third cup at a time, beating well after each addition. Keep beating until the mixture coats the beater. Remove from fire. Chill.

This dressing serves multiple purposes. Made with lemon juice, it is good on fruit salads. Made with vinegar, it is great on potato salad, and either way may be used on tossed salads.

CREAM DRESSING

(For Shredded Cabbage)

¼	*cup mild vinegar*	¼	*teaspoon pepper*
1	*teaspoon mustard*	½	*teaspoon paprika*
1	*teaspoon powdered sugar*	1	*whole egg, beaten*
½	*teaspoon salt*	¼	*cup thick sour cream*

Mix vinegar and dry seasonings. Beat egg and beat cream into it. Just before serving beat the two mixtures together and mix them thoroughly with shredded cabbage. You might like to add grated carrot and a little grated onion to the cabbage.

SOUR CREAM DRESSING

(For Potato Salad)

½	*cup thick sour cream*	½	*teaspoon paprika*
½	*teaspoon salt*	¼	*teaspoon pepper*
½	*teaspoon powdered sugar*	1	*tablespoon chopped chives*
1	*tablespoon lemon juice*	1	*tablespoon minced parsley*

Mix all together and beat well. Use tarragon vinegar in place of lemon juice if you prefer.

COLESLAW DRESSING WITH HONEY

This is a somewhat sweeter and more flavorful dressing than plain mayonnaise to go with shredded cabbage.

1	*cup sour cream*	2½	*teaspoons lemon juice*
¼	*cup honey*	½	*teaspoon salt*
1	*tablespoon poppy seeds*		

First mix sour cream and honey together. If your honey needs to be warmed in order to be in a liquid state, best let it cool before adding sour cream to it, or all will be liquid. Then add remaining ingredients and blend well.

MAYONNAISE

This is for those who either have no blender, or simply enjoy the effort it takes to make mayonnaise by hand. Use a bowl with a rounded bottom, a wire whisk or a rotary beater and have the bowl, beater and eggs well chilled.

1	*teaspoon powdered sugar*	1	*teaspoon dry mustard*
1	*teaspoon salt*	2	*raw egg yolks*
¼	*teaspoon pepper*	3	*tablespoons vinegar or lemon juice*
½	*teaspoon paprika*		
2	*cups salad oil*		

Mix dry ingredients together, add them to the egg yolks, beat well and add vinegar or lemon juice and beat some more. Then add oil, drop by drop at first, later in larger amounts, beating all the time. If the dressing begins to curdle, start over again with a third yolk, beat a little of the remaining oil into it and then work in the curdled dressing. Mix until all the oil is well blended into the dressing.

Mayonnaise should be kept in a cool, but not too cold, place. It separates if it gets too cold. It will also separate if you mix it with the salad too far ahead of time.

MAYONNAISE IN THE BLENDER

This rule is simpler than the one above and will be more useful for most people with a blender.

1 whole egg
1 teaspoon dry mustard
½ teaspoon salt
½ teaspoon paprika
Pepper (optional)
Grated rind of 1 lemon
1 tablespoon lemon juice or vinegar
1 teaspoon sugar
1 tablespoon olive oil
1 cup salad oil (or ½ cup salad, ½ cup olive)

Break egg into the blender. Add mustard, salt, paprika, pepper, grated lemon rind, lemon juice (or vinegar), and sugar. Blend for 5 seconds. The mixture should now be fairly thick. Next add the salad oil, ¼ cup at a time, blending for 10 seconds after each addition.

Use lemon juice in mayonnaise for fruit salads and vinegar for meat and fish salads. Tarragon or basil vinegar may also be used to impart a particular flavor.

LEMON MAYONNAISE

(For Fruit Salads)

Make Mayonnaise* with lemon juice. Take peel off one lemon in thin strips and let the peel stand in ½ cup of thick cream for half an hour. Remove lemon peel, whip the cream and add to the mayonnaise.

GREEN MAYONNAISE

Put into the blender:

2 tablespoons lemon juice
¼ cup chopped greens — a little watercress, parsley, a leaf or two of spinach, and a slice or two of scallion or a slice of onion

Run the blender until you have a bright green pulp. Add:

1 whole egg
¼ cup oil (olive or part salad oil)
Dry seasonings: mustard, sugar, pepper, salt to taste

Run blender about 5 seconds or until everything is well blended. Now add, a small amount at a time, ¾ cup oil. Run 5 seconds after each addition. Run a few seconds after the last oil is in.

SOUR CREAM DRESSING WITH HORSERADISH

1 cup sour cream
½ teaspoon curry powder
1 teaspoon horseradish
½ teaspoon sugar

Blend all together and serve with shrimp salad.

CREAM CHEESE DRESSING

*3 ounces cream cheese, thinned to desired consistency with French Dressing**
2 pimento strips, cut fine
1 hard-boiled egg, chopped
1 tablespoon minced parsley

Mix all together and serve with plain lettuce.

YOGURT DRESSING WITH DILL

1 cup plain yogurt
2 tablespoons cider vinegar
½ small onion, finely chopped
½ teaspoon salt
1½ teaspoon dill weed
¼ teaspoon dry mustard
¼ teaspoon garlic powder
Pepper to taste

Mix all ingredients and serve on a green salad or sliced cucumbers.

ROQUEFORT DRESSING

¾ cup yogurt or sour cream
3 tablespoons mayonnaise
3 tablespoons Roquefort cheese, crumbled
3 tablespoons cottage cheese
1 tablespoon minced chives
Salt and pepper to taste

Blend all ingredients in blender until smooth. If you prefer a dressing with chunks of cheese in it, simply crumble cheese fine and mix together with a spoon. Especially good on a simple salad of rounds of iceberg lettuce and cherry tomatoes.

RUSSIAN DRESSING

*1 cup Mayonnaise**
2 tablespoons chili sauce
1 teaspoon Worcestershire sauce
1 tablespoon chopped chives
1 teaspoon chopped green pepper
½ teaspoon paprika

Mix seasonings together and stir well into the mayonnaise. This surely is a misnomer for this dressing, as no one knows where the habit of putting tomato sauce and mayonnaise together came from, but most likely not from Russia. At any rate, it is good on a salad of raw cauliflower and tomato, or served as a dip for raw vegetables.

GREEN ONION DRESSING

¼ cup green onions, minced
¼ cup tarragon vinegar
1 tablespoon lemon juice and rind
1 cup sour cream
2 cloves garlic, put through press
Pepper to taste
1½ teaspoons sugar
*2 cups Mayonnaise**

Put all but mayonnaise in blender and blend briefly. Add mayonnaise. Blend a few seconds more. Serve with broiled fish or on a vegetable salad.

CURRANT CREAM DRESSING

2 tablespoons currant jelly
1 tablespoon juice from frozen raspberries
½ cup sour cream
½ cup mayonnaise

Beat jelly and juice together with a wire whisk until you have a smooth mixture. Stir in cream and mayonnaise. Serve with fruit salad.

SOUR CREAM DRESSING

(For Fruit)

1 teaspoon lemon juice with 1 tablespoon chopped mint soaked in it
½ teaspoon powdered sugar
1 cup sour cream (or yogurt)

Mix all together and serve with fruit salads.

CREAM CHEESE DRESSING

(For Fruit)

3 ounces cream cheese
¼ cup orange juice
1 tablespoon lemon juice
1 teaspoon orange rind, grated
1 teaspoon sugar
1 teaspoon lemon rind, grated

Soften cream cheese with orange juice. Blend in other ingredients and serve on fruit salad.

Sauces & Gravies

SAUCES are often a food of disguised virtue, as they are frequently used to camouflage an otherwise uninteresting meal. There are those who attempt to cover up meats, vegetables and fruits of inferior quality with rich and often paste-like sauces. The true virtue of a sauce lies in the fact that it may be made with the best ingredients becoming a sauce of truly exceptional quality, either adding a subtle variety to a familiar dish, or imparting a strong contrast of flavors to an otherwse delicately seasoned dish.

For the most part, sauces are not difficult to put together. Once you have learned the basics of combining butter and flour for most cooked sauces, and are careful to continue stirring at certain crucial times to prevent lumps, it is only a matter of proportion and seasoning.

It seems that the logical place to begin is with a sauce that becomes the basis for many other sauces and dishes of other kinds; soufflés, soups and scalloped dishes. It is a simple sauce to make, once you know the routine, and it opens up ever new possibilities.

WHITE SAUCE

Use at least as much butter as flour and try to use at least part cream, or you will have a mass resembling wallpaper paste. Your rule may call for thin, medium or thick white sauce. Use these proportions:

THIN WHITE SAUCE

1 tablespoon butter
1 tablespoon flour
¼ teaspoon salt
⅛ teaspoon pepper
½ cup milk
½ cup cream

MEDIUM WHITE SAUCE

2 tablespoons butter
2 tablespoons flour
¼ teaspoon salt
⅛ teaspoon pepper
½ cup milk
½ cup cream

THICK WHITE SAUCE

3-4 tablespoons butter
3-4 tablespoons flour
¼ teaspoon salt
⅛ teaspoon pepper
½ cup milk
½ cup cream

This may be made successfully in a heavy pan over direct low heat, but I prefer using a double boiler, over hot, not boiling, water: The results are much more consistent.

Melt the butter. When it bubbles and froths, rub in flour sifted with seasonings. (You might want to add a little paprika or other seasonings at this point.) Reduce heat and cook the roux (mixed flour and butter) very slowly for three minutes — that is how the taste of raw flour leaves the sauce. Stir carefully and be sure it does not get any darker than a deep rich ivory color. Next, using a wire whisk, or gravy whisk, stir in the cool milk, a little at first. Rub it to a smooth paste. Be sure to get all the lumps out at this stage, or you will run into them again later. When this paste is perfectly smooth, blend in the rest of the milk and then the cream. Cook it slowly for another ten minutes below the boiling point. Taste it and add more seasoning if you like. The results should be smooth and evenly colored.

If by some off chance, you upon occasion allow a few lumps to creep into your white sauce, there is a solution. All you need do is strain the sauce through a fine sieve, rubbing all you can of the flour through. It will be as good as new.

CREAM SAUCE

Make as you would Thin White Sauce, using all cream.

1 tablespoon butter
1 tablespoon flour
¼ teaspoon salt
⅛ teaspoon pepper
1 cup cream

Add chicken, eggs, a vegetable or whatever you are creaming, the seasoning you like, a little onion, some paprika, and let the sauce and its contents mellow and blend for 20 minutes in the double boiler while you move on to something else.

OYSTER SAUCE

For each cup of Thick White Sauce heat half a pint of oysters in their own juice, with a slice of onion. Cook them until the edges curl, add to the sauce. When you serve it, sprinkle some paprika over it and remove the onion. Good served with boiled fowl.

CHEESE SAUCE

To one cup of Medium White Sauce add:

⅛ teaspoon mustard	*½ teaspoon paprika*
½ teaspoon grated onion	*½ cup grated cheese*

Stir grated cheese into warm white sauce and continue stirring until all is melted.

EGG SAUCE

To one cup Medium White Sauce add one hard-boiled egg, chopped; half a teaspoon grated onion. Or add sliced onion and remove the onion when you serve the sauce.

ONION SAUCE

For each cup of Medium White Sauce, mince three large onions fine. Cook them with butter until they are tender. Add more butter to make two tablespoons butter and work in the flour. Cook, then work in milk and cream. Add about a teaspoon of minced parsley. Good with fish.

BÉCHAMEL SAUCE

(Chicken Cream)

*1 cup Cream Sauce**	*2 egg yolks, beaten*
*1 cup Chicken Stock**	*Pinch of nutmeg*
3 slices onion	*1 tablespoon minced parsley*

Mix warm cream sauce and chicken stock together. Sauté the onion in butter and add to sauce. Beat egg yolks. Spoon three tablespoons of sauce over egg yolks, mix together and put mixture back into sauce, blending well. Cook in top of double boiler. Add nutmeg. When serving, remove onion and add parsley.

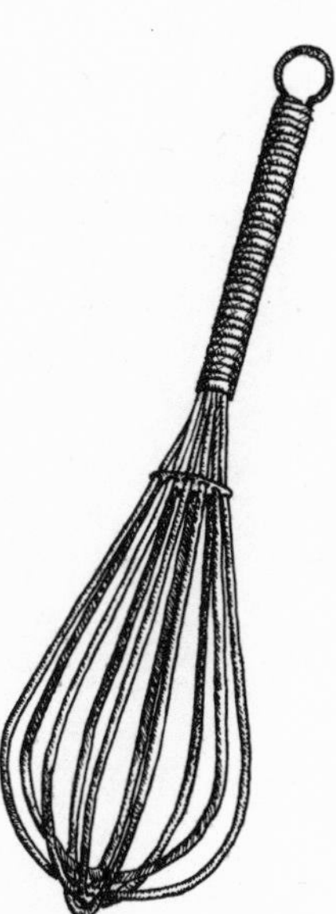

HOLLANDAISE SAUCE

This sauce is frequently looked on as a frightening commodity that only confident cooks make. In fact, it is quite simple to make and less trouble than many other sauces. The most important thing you'll need in making it, besides courage, is a French wire whisk. You'll probably want to make it in the top of a double boiler, over hot, not boiling, water. You may try it over direct heat if your burner can be counted on to keep a steady very low heat. Otherwise, don't risk it.

½ cup cold butter	*½ teaspoon grated lemon rind*
Yolks of 2 large eggs	*¼ teaspoon salt*
1 tablespoon lemon juice	*⅛ teaspoon cayenne pepper*

Divide butter into three pieces. Put unbeaten egg yolks, lemon juice and rind, salt and cayenne into top of a double boiler over hot water. Start beating with a wire whisk and add the first piece of butter. Keep beating and as the butter melts, add the second piece. The sauce will start to thicken. As the second piece of butter disappears add the third one. Here's the danger point. Just as the last piece of butter melts — keep beating all the time — remove sauce from heat. It will curdle if left a minute too long. But, if you should happen to leave it too long anyway, simply bring it back by beating a teaspoon or more of cream into it. Be sure

**See Index for pages where recipes can be found.*

cream is well chilled. Put sauce into a warm bowl and serve immediately with broccoli, asparagus, fish or any other dish your heart desires.

This rule makes a rather thick sauce. It may be thinned by adding two teaspoons of cream and one teaspoon of hot water mixed together so that they are not too hot. Always make plenty of Hollandaise while you are at it and never cast aside any that is left over. You might work it into salad dressing, sandwiches, or some other sauce.

BÉARNAISE SAUCE

This is very much like Hollandaise. Use the following ingredients and follow the same path as with Hollandaise, above.

1 tablespoon chopped shallots, or onion
1 teaspoon tarragon leaves
1 tablespoon white wine vinegar (approx.)
½ cup cold butter
Yolks of 2 eggs
¼ teaspoon salt
Pinch of cayenne pepper
1 teaspoon minced parsley

Cook shallots or onions and tarragon leaves in enough vinegar to cover the leaves. Cook down to one tablespoon. Strain it. Divide butter into three pieces. Put unbeaten egg yolks, vinegar, salt and cayenne into top of a double boiler over hot water. Start beating with wire whisk and add the first piece of butter. Keep beating and as the butter melts, add the second piece. The sauce will start to thicken. As the second piece melts, add the third one. Keep beating all the time, and as last piece of butter melts, remove from heat. Stir in parsley and serve with lamb chops, steak or fish.

HOLLANDAISE TOMATO SAUCE

You can make this sauce to go with white fish, by adding two tablespoons of condensed tomato soup to Hollandaise. Have the soup warm, not hot, and beat it in just before the last piece of butter melts. It has a rich, warm color, but I still prefer plain Hollandaise.

TOMATO CHEESE SAUCE

1 teaspoon minced onion
2 tablespoons butter
2 tablespoons flour
¼ teaspoon pepper
½ teaspoon salt
1 cup cream
½ cup grated cheese
2 cups condensed tomato soup
½ teaspoon mustard
6 drops Worcestershire sauce

Fry onion in butter, make a roux of the butter and flour which has been sifted with pepper and salt. When it is thoroughly cooked add cream slowly. Blend until there are no lumps in the sauce. Add cheese. Stir until it melts and add the tomato soup, mustard and Worcestershire sauce. Beat thoroughly. Serve with spaghetti or rice.

MUSHROOM SAUCE

When I was a small child summering in Appleyard Center, Grandmother, Aunt Cicely and numerous siblings and cousins would make a frequent pilgrimage to neighboring horse pastures, well nibbled down, to pick mushrooms. Despite all my early training, I still have not learned with confidence which varieties of fungii are safe to consume, and must go picking with my cousin, Jane, in order to trust the species enough to eat them. I would not recommend that anyone else eat wild mushrooms unless you are absolutely sure of their edibility. Fortunately for those of us without ready access to fresh, wild mushrooms, there are still fresh, imported ones from Delaware that show up on our grocer's shelves.

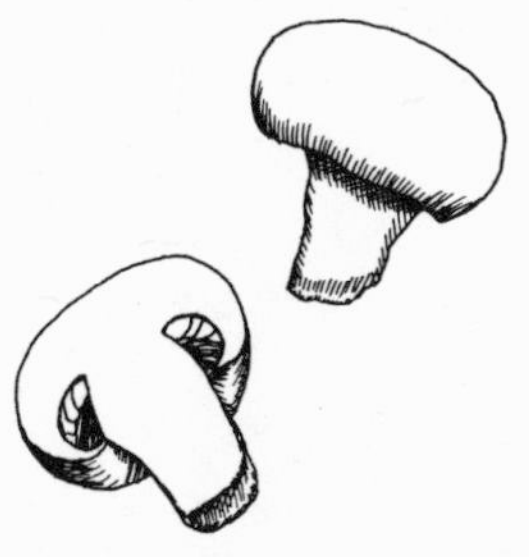

- *1 pound mushrooms, peeled, caps only*
- *1 teaspoon minced onion*
- *2 tablespoons butter*
- *2 tablespoons flour*
- *1 cup light cream*
- *Salt to taste*
- *½ teaspoon paprika*
- *¼ teaspoon pepper*
- *¼ teaspoon nutmeg*
- *Piece of bay leaf*
- *1 cup heavy cream*
- *1 tablespoon sherry*

Save mushroom skins and stems for soup. Slice caps vertically. Sauté onion in butter until translucent, then add mushrooms and cook until tender — about five minutes. Remove with a slotted spoon to top of a double boiler. In first pan, rub flour into butter, adding more butter if necessary; there should be at least two tablespoons in the pan. Remove pan from heat while you are doing this. Return it to very low heat and cook the roux for three minutes. Now add the light cream, slowly at first, stirring well to make a thin paste free from lumps. Add dry seasonings. Add heavy cream, stirring all the while. Let sauce simmer gently but not boil, for five minutes. Pour it over mushrooms in the double boiler. Let mellow for about an hour, if possible, before using it. At serving time, remove bay leaf, heat the sauce and add sherry.

This sauce may be served with a large variety of foods, from Meat Loaf,* to Omelettes,* to baked or broiled fish. Use your ingenuity.

Below are several sauces that go well with fish of different sorts.

SOUR CREAM SAUCE

- *½ tablespoon vinegar*
- *½ tablespoon lemon juice*
- *3 egg yolks*
- *Salt, pepper, paprika — whatever seasonings you like*
- *1 cup sour cream*

Put vinegar and lemon juice into top of a double boiler over boiling water. Beat in egg yolks, then cream, a third at a time. Season to taste. Remove from heat at once and serve with green beans, Fish Mousse* or asparagus.

EGG AND CREAM SAUCE

- *2 tablespoons butter*
- *½ teaspoon onion, put through garlic press*
- *2 tablespoons flour*
- *½ teaspoon salt*
- *½ teaspoon paprika*
- *¼ teaspoon pepper*
- *1 cup milk*
- *1 cup cream*
- *2 hard-boiled eggs*

Melt butter and cook onion in it until straw colored. Lower heat and rub in flour mixed with dry seasonings. Cook very slowly for three minutes. Do not let it brown. Remove from heat. Stir in half the milk, a little at a time, rubbing the mixture smooth with the back of a spoon. When you have a smooth paste, stir in the rest of the milk and the cream. Return to the fire and cook until sauce just starts to bubble. Put sauce in top of a double boiler and leave over hot water until serving time. Add eggs, chopped not too fine. If sauce seems too thick, add a little more milk.

EGG AND BUTTER SAUCE

¼ pound butter
1 tablespoon lemon juice
1 teaspoon grated lemon rind
2 hard-boiled eggs

Melt butter over low heat, add lemon juice and rind. Add the whites of the eggs cut up in quarter-inch pieces and the yolks flaked fine with a fork. Serve hot with baked halibut.

FISH SAUCE

*1 cup Court Bouillon**
2 tablespoons butter
2 tablespoons flour
½ cup heavy cream
1 cup light cream
2 egg yolks
2 tablespoons white wine
Salt and pepper to taste

The bouillon should be jelled. If it is not, take 1½ cups and cook it down to one cup. Melt butter. When it bubbles, rub in flour smoothly. Cook gently for three minutes. It must not brown. Remove from heat. Add bouillon, slowly at first, and then the cream. Return to low heat. Beat egg yolks. Mix the hot sauce into them a tablespoon at a time until you have half a cup of the mixture. Pour mixture back into sauce. Stir it well until it thickens. Add wine and seasonings. Do not let it boil. Sprinkle with minced chives or parsley. Serve with Fish Mousse.*

SAUCE RAVIGOTE

*1 cup Thin White Sauce**
1 tablespoon tarragon vinegar
2 green onions, with stems
1 tablespoon parsley
1 tablespoon watercress
1½ teaspoons fresh tarragon leaves
1 tablespoon butter
1 tablespoon lemon juice
1 teaspoon chopped capers

Warm white sauce. Put vinegar, onions, parsley, watercress and tarragon into the blender. Blend until well mixed. Stir into sauce. Add butter, lemon juice and capers. Serve cold on Fish Mousse.* If sauce is too thick add more cream. Or reheat in top of a double boiler, thin with milk and serve with Gaspé salmon.

OYSTER COCKTAIL SAUCE

1 cup tomato ketchup
1 cup tomato cocktail sauce
1 cup tomato juice
1 tablespoon Worcestershire sauce
2 tablespoons prepared horse-radish
2 drops Tabasco sauce
1 small onion, minced fine
Thin peel and juice of half lemon

Mix all together and chill. Serve as a cocktail sauce with oysters or shrimp or a combination of the two. Allow six oysters for each person.

Fill cocktail glasses half full with sauce. Stir in oysters or shrimp and let the glasses stand in refrigerator until serving time.

GARLIC SAUCE

¼ pound butter
2 cloves garlic, put through press
1 tablespoon lemon juice
3 tablespoons minced parsley
1 tablespoon minced chives

Melt butter and gently simmer garlic in it until butter browns a bit. Stir in lemon juice, parsley and chives and serve hot with broiled fish.

TARTAR SAUCE

*1 cup Mayonnaise**
½ tablespoon chopped capers
½ tablespoon olives
½ tablespoon tarragon
½ tablespoon chopped dill pickles
1 tablespoon chopped shallot

Mix all together and serve with fresh pan-fried fish; smelt or trout.

SAUCES FOR MEATS AND VEGETABLES

MUSTARD SAUCE

½ cup sugar
1 pint heavy cream
4 tablespoons dry mustard
Salt to taste
⅔ cup vinegar
2 egg yolks

Heat the sugar and half the cream over hot water. Add mustard and salt mixed with vinegar. Beat egg yolks slightly. Add about three tablespoons of the sauce to yolks, one tablespoon at a time, mixing well. Add egg mixture to the sauce. Stir it in carefully and cook until it thickens slightly — two or three minutes. Cool. Before serving, whip the remaining cream and fold it in. Serve with Ham Mousse* or with hot or cold sliced ham.

Baked ham occasionally needs a variation from mustard sauce. Either of the two following sauces will do well.

RAISIN SAUCE

To half a cup pan juice add:

*1 cup clear Beef Stock**
1 cup seedless raisins
1 tablespoon Worcestershire sauce
3 tablespoons vinegar
¼ teaspoon cinnamon
½ teaspoon nutmeg
½ cup orange marmalade

Mix all together. Cook slowly until marmalade is melted. Serve in a separate bowl with either Baked Ham* or Tongue.* Or make:

CHAMPAGNE SAUCE

2 tablespoons butter
2 tablespoons flour
*2 cups hot clear Chicken Stock**
1 cup champagne

Melt butter, let it brown a little. Remove pan from fire, blend in flour. Return to low heat and stir for two minutes. Blend stock in gradually, stirring constantly. Cook three minutes. Let it come to the boil but do not boil. If sauce is not perfectly smooth, strain it through a fine sieve, reheat to the boiling point, add champagne and serve. If you think this is a waste of champagne, you may substitute white wine or just add flour and stock to juices in the pan.

CIDER MINT SAUCE

(For 4)

1 cup mint leaves, stripped from stem
¼ cup sugar
2 tablespoons cider vinegar
¾ cup fizzy apple cider

Put all ingredients in blender. Blend until mint is finely cut. Remove to a saucepan. Simmer until liquid cooks down to about half a cup. Turn off heat. At serving time, reheat and serve very hot. Serve with lamb of any variety.

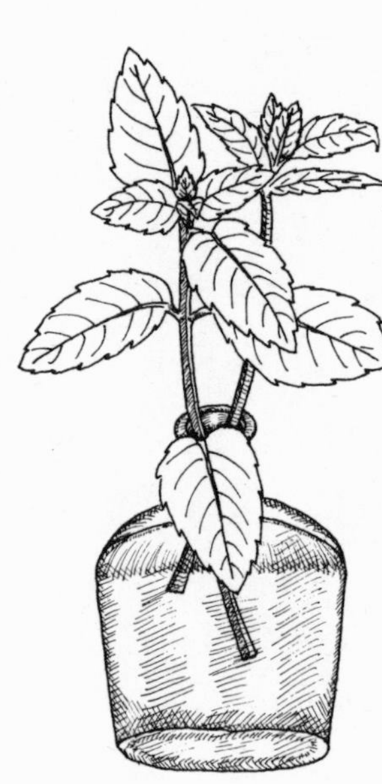

MINT SAUCE — SHORTCUT

½ cup water
½ cup vinegar
1 8-ounce glass apple-mint jelly
4 tablespoons finely chopped mint

Boil water and vinegar, add jelly. Stir until it melts. Add mint. It is ready to serve whenever you are. Another great addition to roast lamb.

CUMBERLAND MINT SAUCE

½ cup fresh mint leaves
¾ cup red wine vinegar
1 cup currant jelly

Heat mint leaves in half a cup of vinegar and simmer five minutes. Put the mixture through blender. Heat a quarter cup more vinegar, add currant jelly and the blended mint. Cook until it bubbles hard. Serve with Lamb Roll,* roasted potatoes, baked butternut squash and sliced tomatoes.

CURRANT-ORANGE SAUCE

1 cup red wine
1 tablespoon thin orange peel, finely cut
Juice of one orange
1 tablespoon thin lemon peel, finely cut
½ cup orange marmalade
1 8-ounce glass currant jelly

Mix wine, orange juice and lemon peel. When it boils over medium heat, add marmalade and currant jelly and stir until they melt. Set aside in a warm place until needed. Excellent with roast venison, lamb, or duck. For sauce to go with duck, substitute consommé for wine.

CURRANT-MINT SAUCE

½ cup consommé
Thin peel of one orange
Thin peel of one lemon
Juice of one orange
1 teaspoon lemon juice
2 tablespoons finely minced mint leaves
1 8-ounce glass currant jelly

Mix consommé, peel, lemon and orange juice and mint leaves. Heat over medium heat. When it starts to boil, add currant jelly and let it melt. Set aside to keep warm. Remove peel and serve very hot with Roast Leg of Lamb.*

CURRANT-RAISIN SAUCE

- 1 *cup seedless raisins*
- 1 *cup consommé*
- 3 *cloves*
- ⅛ *teaspoon cinnamon*
- 1 *thinly sliced lemon*
- 2 *tablespoons orange marmalade*
- 1 *8-ounce glass currant jelly*

Cook raisins in consommé until tender. Add the rest of ingredients and serve when jelly is melted and sauce is very hot. Good with smoked shoulder, pork or tongue.

BREAD SAUCE

An excellent sauce to pass with poultry of any kind, particularly Chicken Appleyard* or roast partridge.

- 3 *cups milk*
- ¼ *teaspoon pepper from grinder*
- ⅛ *teaspoon nutmeg*
- 1 *teaspoon salt*
- 1 *small onion, stuck with eight cloves*
- ½ *cup dry bread crumbs rolled fine*
- 5 *tablespoons butter*
- ¾ *cup coarse bread crumbs*

Put milk, seasonings and onion in top of a double boiler. Add the fine bread crumbs. Cook over gently boiling water for 30 minutes. Remove onion. Add half the butter and stir well. Keep warm. In an iron pan, melt rest of butter over medium heat. Add coarse bread crumbs. Toss and stir until crumbs are brown. Put sauce in a bowl or gravy tureen and sprinkle browned crumbs over it. The sauce should be about the consistency of whipped cream.

CRANBERRY SAUCE

The Appleyards like cranberry sauce with the berries popped and the sauce not strained. Simply buy fresh cranberries and cook them exactly as the package directs. For eight people cook two packages the day before they are to be served. Heap them in your best glass serving dish and set it in a cool place.

A Thanksgiving tradition started by my mother was the serving of:

CRANBERRY ORANGE RELISH

- 1 *package (4 cups) cranberries*
- 2 *large oranges*
- 1½ *cups sugar*

Wash and pick over cranberries. Cut oranges in quarters and remove seeds. Put both fruits through a food grinder, or carefully through a blender, not chopping too fine. Add sugar, mix thoroughly. Chill an hour or more.

HORSERADISH SAUCE

- ½ *cup heavy cream*
- 2 *tablespoons prepared horseradish*
- ½ *teaspoon pepper*
- ½ *cup sour cream*
- 1 *tablespoon minced parsley*

Whip cream until it just starts to thicken. Stir in horseradish and pepper. Stir in sour cream. Put in a bowl and sprinkle with minced parsley. Serve with Braised Beef* or Country Chicken Salad.*

SPANISH STEAK SAUCE

½	*cup butter*	½	*teaspoon mustard*
1	*tablespoon ketchup*	½	*teaspoon sugar*
1	*tablespoon paprika*	1	*clove pricked garlic*

2 *teaspoons vinegar*

This sauce is meant to be made immediately after you have broiled a steak. Melt butter in broiler pan. In a cup blend ketchup, paprika, mustard and sugar. Add mixture and garlic to melted butter. As sauce begins to bubble over medium heat, turn down heat, remove garlic and add vinegar. Stir vigorously and remove from heat at once or it will separate. Serve immediately with steak. This is Cicely's favorite steak sauce, and certainly worth a try. While we're on the subject of Spanish sauces I might tell how to make:

SPANISH SAUCE FOR OMELETTE

1	*tomato*	6	*mushrooms*
1	*green pepper, seeded*	½	*teaspoon salt*
1	*small onion*	½	*teaspoon paprika*
2	*sprigs parsley*	⅛	*teaspoon cayenne*
1	*stalk celery*	4	*tablespoons butter*

Chop vegetables together. Add seasonings. Simmer in butter until pepper is tender. Put half the sauce inside the omelette, pour the rest on top and sprinkle grated cheese over all. Serve hot.

TOMATO SAUCE

This rule was given to Grandmother by an Armenian friend. I don't know whether it makes it more acceptable to serve with eggplant or stuffed grape leaves, but it is good with both of these as well as with meat loaf, spaghetti or rice.

6	*tablespoons olive oil*	2	*onions, chopped*
4	*tablespoons butter*	½	*teaspoon each white pepper, red pepper*
1	*stalk celery, chopped*	½	*teaspoon powdered thyme*
2	*cloves of garlic, pressed*	1	*teaspoon salt*
1	*green pepper, seeded, chopped*	4	*tablespoons flour*
¼	*teaspoon cinnamon*	2	*quarts peeled ripe tomatoes*
⅛	*teaspoon cloves*	2	*tablespoons light brown sugar*
2	*carrots, sliced*		

2 *tablespoons minced parsley*

This is best made with fresh tomatoes at their garden best. But if you haven't tomatoes at their reddest and juiciest, use canned tomatoes — two large cans.

Put oil in a large frying pan and add butter and everything else except the tomatoes, flour and sugar. Stir carefully over low heat until onions and green pepper are soft. Push vegetables to one side, remove pan from heat and blend flour into the hot fat. When it is well mixed, return pan to the fire and add four cups hot water, slowly, stirring it well. Add tomatoes, peeled and quartered, and sugar. Mix well, set the pan, covered, on lower rack of the oven at 300° and let cook for an hour. Uncover it, stir well from the bottom. Let it cook half an hour longer. Strain through a fine strainer. May be served immediately, or refrigerated or even frozen for future use.

TAXI DRIVER'S TOMATO SAUCE

All taxi drivers have their pet subject. This particular man was especially congenial with Grandmother because his topic was cooking. While they were stalled in traffic he told her how his mother makes tomato sauce. I think you'll agree with the results. This is a simpler sauce than the preceding version.

8 large tomatoes, peeled and mashed or one large can tomatoes
⅓ cup sugar
1 clove garlic crushed or one teaspoon garlic powder
1 teaspoon mixed herbs: rosemary, basil, thyme, oregano
2 tablespoons butter
2 tablespoons olive oil
2 ounces tomato paste (⅓ of a 6-ounce can)
1 tablespoon molasses

Cook everything but tomato paste in butter and oil, stirring often until the mixture begins to brown around the edges of the pan. Stir in tomato paste and cook three minutes. Set aside and reheat at serving time. Excellent with a casserole of zucchini, summer squash and chicken.

Sometimes vegetables need a little cheering up, and one of the following sauces goes a long way in such a mission.

VINAIGRETTE SAUCE

6 tablespoons olive oil
2 tablespoons salad oil
1 tablespoon tarragon vinegar
2 tablespoons cider vinegar
1 tablespoon minced piccalilli
1 tablespoon minced green pepper
1 teaspoon minced parsley
1 tablespoon minced chives
Seasonings to taste: salt, teaspoon paprika, pepper from the grinder, ½ teaspoon mustard

Put all ingredients in a jar and shake well. Use sauce for marinating vegetables to be used as appetizers. For example, asparagus tips, broccoli spears, green beans or sliced mushrooms. Or marinate vegetables a short time and include them in a salad.

LEMON BUTTER FOR ASPARAGUS

Melt two tablespoons butter, add one tablespoon lemon juice and three tablespoons asparagus liquid. Pour over hot asparagus, or serve separately in a bowl.

GRAVIES

Gravy is a form of sauce made from the juices and pan drippings that escape a piece of meat during its cooking, flour, browned in butter or fat, and hot liquid. The flavor comes from the pan drippings and is as strongly flavored as are the juices.

BROWN GRAVY

The success of brown gravy depends on the thorough browning, not burning, of the flour. If the fat you use comes from a roast, it is usually sufficiently brown in itself. When your roast has finished cooking, pour the juices off into a glass measuring cup and separate the fat from the rest of the juices. Use two tablespoons fat to two tablespoons flour. First heat the fat in a shallow pan, then work in the flour with the back of a spoon or, better yet, a gravy whip. Cook the roux well before adding any additional liquid. Have the liquid, juices, consommé, or boiling water hot when you add it, using one cup for each two tablespoons of fat. Add liquid slowly at first, stirring well to a smooth paste, then add the rest of liquid, stir well and let simmer until thickened, watching carefully. Taste the gravy and add more seasoning, if you like; salt and pepper and paprika, a few drops of Worcestershire sauce or even a teaspoon of instant coffee (to add a richer brown). Strain gravy if there are any lumps and serve from a gravy boat, very hot.

GIBLET GRAVY FOR TURKEY

The day before you plan to make the gravy, simmer gizzard, heart and neck until they are tender, 2 to 3 hours. The liver should be added in the last 20 minutes of cooking. Mince all the meat fine, discarding any bones and gristle. A wooden bowl and chopping knife are useful for this task. Set giblets in a cool place. Save water in which they were cooked in a separate bowl.

The next day, when the turkey is almost cooked, take:

4 tablespoons fat from the roaster
1 finely minced onion
Minced giblets and meat from neck
4 tablespoons flour
Salt, pepper and paprika to taste
Pinch of nutmeg
2 cups stock from giblets
2 cups rich milk
2 tablespoons minced parsley

Put fat in a big iron frying pan. Sauté onion and giblets over low heat until onion begins to brown. If mixture has absorbed all fat, add another tablespoonful. Blend in flour and seasonings. Stir in stock. Blend until smooth. Add milk slowly, stirring all the while. Cook until it thickens and serve immediately, or let cool and reheat at serving time. Put in gravy tureen and sprinkle with parsley.

ORANGE SAUCE FOR ROAST DUCKLING

2 tablespoons duck fat
2 tablespoons flour
Pan drippings
1½ cups orange juice
Juice and grated rind of one orange
1 tablespoon Cointreau

Heat fat in a heavy pan over low heat. Work in flour over medium heat and cook for three minutes. Add pan juices and cook for another three to four minutes, stirring to keep gravy smooth.

Add juice and rind of orange, stirring all the while. Cook over medium heat until thickened. Add Cointreau at the last minute, do not allow gravy to boil after it is added. Serve hot with Roast Duckling.*

SOUR CREAM PORK GRAVY

2 tablespoons pork fat
2 tablespoons flour
1 cup light cream
Pinch of nutmeg, and paprika
1 cup sour cream

Put pork fat into a heavy iron pan over low heat and blend in flour mixed with seasonings. Cook for three minutes, or until flour begins to brown. Stir in light cream, slowly at first, making a smooth paste. Stir in sour cream, stirring all the time. Cook without boiling until thick — about five minutes. Serve with a pork roast.

FRUIT AND DESSERT SAUCES

HARD SAUCE

½ cup butter
1 cup powdered sugar, sifted
1 teaspoon vanilla
½ teaspoon cinnamon
½ teaspoon nutmeg

Butter should be at room temperature. Cream it and work in powdered sugar. Add vanilla. Beat well, using a pastry blending fork. Put sauce into a glass serving bowl, swirl into an attractive pattern and sprinkle with spice. Chill so sauce will hold its shape, removing from refrigerator ahead of serving time. Serve with Plum Pudding.*

For those who like a touch of brandy to go with their flaming plum pudding, simply mix one teaspoon brandy into sauce with the vanilla. It adds a special touch.

BRANDIED HARD SAUCE

This hard sauce combines brandied fruit, butter and sugar and is delicious served with puddings of all sorts, plain cake or plum pudding.

½ cup butter
1 cup powdered sugar
*½ cup Brandied Fruit**
1 well beaten egg

Cream butter, add sugar gradually, stir in brandied fruit and egg. Beat all together with a wire whisk. You can control the consistency of the sauce by the amount of fruit juice you add, according to whether you prefer a thick or thin sauce. This makes a rather thin one.

MOTHER'S CHOCOLATE SAUCE

There comes a time in the life of every hostess, host or cook when dessert must consist of ice cream with chocolate sauce. The mother in this title is my mother-in-law's mother. The rule has been around for a good long while and is foolproof to make as well as tasty to consume.

¼ cup butter
1½ squares unsweetened chocolate
¼ cup cocoa
¾ cup sugar
½ cup evaporated milk
Pinch of salt
½ teaspoon vanilla

In the top of a double boiler melt butter and chocolate. Stir in the cocoa, sugar, milk and salt. Mix until sugar is well dissolved. Add vanilla. Keep warm over hot water until serving time. Or refrigerate and use at a later date.

BUTTERSCOTCH PECAN SAUCE

Another sweet sauce to serve with ice cream.

2 cups light brown sugar
½ cup heavy cream or evaporated milk
1 tablespoon honey
⅓ cup butter
¼ cup chopped pecans

Mix all, except pecans, in a saucepan and boil for two minutes, stirring well to keep sugar from crystallizing on the sides. Add pecans and serve.

APRICOT SAUCE

1 cup apricot pulp
½ cup sugar
Juice and grated rind of half lemon

Use blender in making apricot pulp. Tenderize dried apricots by soaking them in water overnight. Put small amounts of apricots in their water into the blender one at a time and blend until they form a pulp.

Stir sugar with apricot pulp, warmed slightly, until sugar is thoroughly dissolved. Add lemon juice and rind. Taste and add more sugar if you like it sweeter. Serve as a sauce for orange sherbet or vanilla ice cream.

APRICOT GLAZE

(For Cakes or Cream Puffs)

6 tablespoons apricot preserves
1 tablespoon lemon juice
½ pint cream, whipped

Melt jam over low heat, strain into another pan. Stir in lemon juice. Use as a glaze between layers of a Washington Pie* or on top of custard filled Cream Puffs.* If used with the pie, brush bottom layer with glaze, cover with sliced fresh peaches and cream. Repeat on the next layer and swirl cream around the edge.

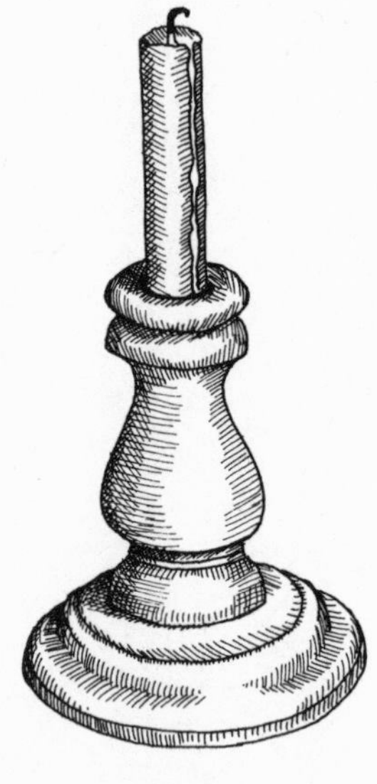

FOAMY SAUCE

½ cup butter
1 cup powdered sugar
3 egg yolks
2 tablespoons sherry or brandy, or 1 teaspoon vanilla, or ½ teaspoon almond extract
1 egg

This must be made at the last minute, but the butter, softened slightly, sugar and flavoring may be combined beforehand in the top of a double boiler. When serving time comes, beat egg yolks and egg together well, add them to the butter and sugar mixture and cook over hot water, beating all the time, until mixture thickens. It takes only a few minutes. Serve with Orange Marmalade Soufflé* or any of a number of other desserts.

RHUBARB SAUCE

This needs to be made in early summer when the rhubarb is young and tender. Make enough to freeze and you will have it all winter long.

4 cups strawberry rhubarb cut in half-inch pieces
3 cups sugar

Never add water to rhubarb, it makes its own juice. Mix fruit and sugar in a large shallow enamel pan. It should not be more than half full. Set into a 350° oven and cook until fruit is tender but not mushy — about an hour. Taste for sweetness. Add more sugar if you like. Eat warm as it is, serve on ice cream, or mixed with plain yogurt.

ORANGE MARMALADE SAUCE

1 cup orange marmalade
2 tablespoons lemon juice
2 tablespoons frozen orange juice, not diluted
1 teaspoon grated lemon rind

Mix all together. Simmer, stirring carefully, until marmalade melts. Bring to the boil but do not boil. Serve as a sauce with candied yams, or with an Orange Marmalade Soufflé.*

MRS. APPLEYARD'S ICEBOUND RASPBERRY-CRANBERRY SAUCE

Grandmother invented this one evening at Cicely's, during which time all were icebound and the electricity was off. She records it as a fine relaxing time of silence from the typical bellowing of power driven machines.

1 pint frozen raspberries
1 8-ounce glass currant jelly
½ package cranberries, cooked whole

Thaw raspberries by setting package in warm, not hot, water. Cook cranberries until berries are all popped. Remove from heat, add currant jelly, stir until it is melted. Cool slightly. Add the partly thawed raspberries. Stir well. Keep in a cool place until needed. Serve with vanilla ice cream.

Soups

SOUPS, what a magnificent invention! For us, they frequently serve as a main course accompanied by a salad and rolls or muffins of some variety. But they might just as easily become a first course or even a dessert, in the case of fruit soups. Soup making happens to be one of my favorite pastimes. I'm living under no delusions, however, about the frequency of soup making from scratch that presently exists in this country. I'm surprised that more house-persons don't come down with sprained wrists from the constant activity of cranking can openers over difficult circular surfaces. As you can see, I am still tremendously in favor of making soups from scratch. Yes, that does mean simmering bones and vegetables for hours, straining the broth and then beginning with the assemblage of the actual soup. It does take hours, but is usually worth the time and they are hours requiring little attention.

If you just don't have the time, or the inclination to do all that work, then I would suggest taking a few liberties with canned soups. Rarely eat them just as they come from the can. Add a little braised celery, a few whole cloves and a stick of cinnamon to commercial tomato soup, for instance, for an increase in flavor. Make changes — add vegetables, or stock, or leftovers you might have around to an otherwise uninteresting can of soup.

Most of the rules in this section do require a certain amount of work. For many of them, substitutions may be made in order to facilitate the making. So, if you need to, use canned consommé or chicken broth as a basis and soar from there. And for those of you with the time, energy and desire, enjoy yourselves with the rules worthy of the label — SOUP.

The obvious starting point for any good homemade soup is the stock from which variations are made. The fullbodiness of the stock goes a long way in determining the quality of the finished product. If you can't produce your own stock that will enhance the finished soup or stew, better to buy canned consommé, either beef or chicken as the case may be, and start from there.

I've told already how to make excellent Beef Stock.* Refer to that rule for any of the following recipes that call for beef stock or consommé. (The terms are virtually interchangeable.) Another type of basic broth that may be used in any of a number of rules, both here and elsewhere, instead of that despicable substance innocently referred to as a bouillon cube, is:

PORTABLE SOUP

5 pound shinbone of beef
2 medium onions, sliced
1 carrot, sliced
1 teaspoon salt
Pinches of thyme, rosemary, cinnamon, cloves and basil

Cover all with cold water. Simmer until meat falls from bone, replacing water as needed to prevent scorching. Simmer for about 5 hours. Strain broth, cool, remove fat. Cook broth down until it is the consistency of thick jelly. Spread it in flat pans to cool. Score in squares of uniform size about 1½-inch square and set where it will dry. When you finally cut this into pieces it will be the consistency of horn.

These seemingly useless squares may be used any place broth, stock, consommé or bouillon is called for. Simply pour one cup of boiling water over a square to dissolve it.

This rule was written down by a Mrs. Gardiner of Gardiner, Maine in 1763. She was the wife of Dr. Sylvester Gardiner who had to ride for miles on horseback to visit patients. He would often carry squares of Portable Soup with him to relieve his thirst, hunger or fatigue along the trip. You may not wish to go through the time it takes to make these old-time squares, but the process takes little attention, and if done on a day you plan to be home anyway, it is an interesting experiment as well as being tasty. Another frequently used base for soups, hot or cold, is:

CHICKEN STOCK

1 pound wing tips and necks of chicken, carcass of roast chicken with scraps of meat and stuffing
3 pounds veal bones
2 stalks celery with tops cut fine
4 carrots, washed and sliced
1 tablespoon minced parsley
2 onions, peeled and sliced
1 bay leaf
¼ teaspoon thyme
Pinches of basil, rosemary, oregano

Put all ingredients in a large kettle. Add 2 gallons cold water. Bring to boiling point and simmer 4 hours. It will cook down so that you have

*See Index for pages where recipes can be found.

about 2½ quarts of liquid. Strain it, chill it, skim fat off when chilled. Pour into pint jars. It will jell and keep well in the refrigerator.

When making fish stews or soups, or fish balls for that matter, you will want to have a supply of court bouillon on hand. This is simply a fancy name for fish stock.

COURT BOUILLON

Bones and head of 4-pound haddock
1 *onion*
12 *peppercorns*
1 *bay leaf*
1 *carrot, sliced*
2 *tablespoons lemon juice*
1 *tablespoon tarragon vinegar*
3 *cloves*
Pinches of herbs
1 *cup white wine*

Put bones and head of fish into a kettle and cover with cold water, about two quarts. Add remaining ingredients. Cover, bring to a boil. Simmer for 1 hour. Strain and use immediately in the making of quenelles or Seafood Chowder,* or chill for future use. This stock will not keep as long as beef or chicken stock. Better plan to use it fairly soon.

CONSOMMÉ CARDINAL WITH PEARLS

(For 6)

One of the best canned soups, and the hardest to reproduce at home, is the clear garnet jelly known as consomme cardinal. On a hot evening you might serve it cold, jellied with just a slice of lemon, or hot on a cool evening. To serve hot:

6 *tablespoons pearl tapioca*
1 *cup cold water*
2 *cups boiling water*
4 *cans consommé cardinal*
4 *tablespoons sherry*
6 *slices lemon*

Soak tapioca in cold water for at least 2 hours. It must not be the instant kind. Drain it, add the boiling water, cook in a double boiler until tapioca is transparent. This will take about half an hour. Be sure tapioca is really clear. Nothing is worse than half-cooked tapioca. Add the soup and sherry and let it cook a few minutes longer. Add more consommé if it seems too thick. Serve it hot with a slice of lemon in each soup plate.

LIGHT SOUPS

The next few soups are of a light nature, suitable as first course soups or as an accompaniment to sandwiches and salad at lunch time. Of course, virtually any soup may be used as a main course depending on the size of the portions ladled out. These are intended to be served in fairly small portions.

HARTWELL FARM CHICKEN SOUP

2 *fowls, about 3 pounds each*
3 *quarts cold water*
4 *tablespoons chicken fat*
4 *tablespoons flour*
½ *teaspoon salt*

Put fowls into a large kettle, cover with cold water and cook until the meat falls from the bones. The liquid should cook down to about 2 quarts. Remove chickens, cool, remove meat and skin from bones (use meat for

Chicken Salad*), put bones and skin back in with stock and let it cook down to about 1½ quarts of liquid. Put the jelly that forms around the chicken on the platter back into the soup. Strain soup into a bowl and let cool overnight.

The next day, skim off fat. Melt 4 tablespoons of fat in a kettle over low heat and make a roux with 4 tablespoons of flour. Cook slowly for 3 minutes. Add a little warmed stock and work it in with the back of a spoon or a wire whisk. Add the rest of the stock and cook gently for a few minutes. Taste it and add a little salt to increase flavor if you like. Cook a while longer over low heat to mellow flavor and serve very hot.

This rule comes from Hartwell Farm in Lincoln, Massachusetts, where they use seven or eight chickens to make a gallon of soup. It is full-bodied chicken soup. You may make variations on it if you wish, such as adding a carrot and an onion to the simmering chicken, or including a few pinches of herbs. I happen to like it just this way, with simply the smooth, honest taste of chicken.

GREEK EGG AND LEMON SOUP

(For 6)

- 3 *cans chicken soup, or 4 cups Chicken Stock* or Hartwell Farm Chicken Soup (above)*
- 1 *cup instant rice*
- 4 *eggs*
- 4 *tablespoons lemon juice*

Bring soup to the simmering point. Add rice and cook for 3 minutes. Beat eggs and add lemon juice slowly. Turn soup off and add egg and lemon mixture very slowly, stirring constantly. Serve at once with Cross crackers, buttered and toasted.

TURKEY SOUP

Turkey soup is an unavoidable happenstance for any conscientious cook who has used up all the leftover turkey meat in salads and casseroles. Make it a delight in this way:

- *Carcass of 20-pound turkey (including pan juices and stuffing)*
- 2 *onions*
- 2 *carrots, sliced*
- *Celery tops and outer stalks*
- *Leftover Giblet Gravy**
- 2 *tablespoons turkey fat*
- 1 *onion, finely grated*
- *Stems from 2 pounds mushrooms, sliced thin*
- 2 *tablespoons flour*
- 1 *teaspoon burnt onion powder*
- ⅛ *teaspoon each: pepper, cloves, cinnamon, allspice*
- 1 *teaspoon instant coffee (optional)*
- ½ *teaspoon paprika*

The day before you plan to make the soup, break up carcass and put bones and any meat and stuffing that clings to them into the roaster. Add wing tips, all the skin, onions, carrots, celery tops and stalks. Cover bones with cold water and simmer for 5 to 6 hours. Strain off liquid — there should be about 2 quarts. Remove any scraps of meat from bones and add to the broth. Chill well.

The next day skim fat from broth and save it. Simmer skimmed broth down to 1½ quarts. Add gravy to it. Melt fat and sauté onion and mushroom stems in it. Mix flour with seasonings. Sprinkle it in, blend over very low heat. Add broth gradually, stirring well until soup is smooth. Simmer until it thickens. Serve.

If you would rather have a clear soup, like a turkey consommé, omit gravy, fat and flour. Add 2 tablespoons of sherry just before serving.

If you like a more bland soup, add 1 cup of rich milk to the mixture just after adding broth. Any one of these versions, as well as your own adaptations, may make you feel that the holiday was actually worth having.

GAZPACHO

(For 6)

This is a perfect soup for hot summer evenings, and a good way to make use of what bounty your garden produces.

- 4 *tablespoons mixed chopped fresh herbs: parsley, dill, chives, basil, marjoram, savory*
- 6 *large ripe tomatoes, skinned and chopped*
- 2 *cloves of garlic, chopped fine or pressed*
- *Juice of 2 lemons*
- 2 *peppers, seeded and chopped fine*
- 1 *cup olive oil*
- 6 *cups Chicken Stock**
- *Salt and fresh pepper to taste*
- 2 *cups cucumbers, peeled, seeded and chopped fine*
- 1 *Bermuda onion, chopped fine*
- 2 *celery hearts, chopped fine*

With a potato masher crush together herbs, tomatoes, garlic and peppers. Gradually add lemon juice and oil until mixture is a paste. Stir in chicken stock. Season with salt and pepper. Add cucumbers, onion, and celery. Mix all together and chill at least 4 hours before serving. Serve cold topped with parsley sprigs.

SHRIMP SOUP

(For 4)

- 4 *tablespoons butter*
- 3 *tablespoons flour*
- 1 *teaspoon paprika*
- ½ *teaspoon pepper from grinder*
- ¼ *teaspoon nutmeg*
- ¼ *teaspoon garlic powder*
- 2 *cups milk*
- 1 *pound frozen shrimp*
- 1 *tablespoon grated onion*
- 6 *tablespoons white wine*
- 1 *pimento, cut rather fine*
- 2 *cups heavy cream*
- 1 *tablespoon finely cut parsley*
- 1 *tablespoon chopped chives*
- *Lemon slices*

This is prepared most easily in an electric skillet but may be made in a large frying pan.

Melt 3 tablespoons of the butter over medium heat. Blend in flour mixed with dry seasonings. Reduce heat to its lowest point and pour milk in slowly, stirring all the time until mixture is smooth. Leave over very low heat while you puree shrimp with onion and wine. Add this mixture and pimento to skillet mixture. Cook covered over very low heat for 20 minutes, stirring several times. At serving time add cream. Bring to a boil, but do not boil. At the last minute slip in 1 tablespoon butter. Pour soup into hot bowls, sprinkle with parsley and chives. Add lemon slices. You may add a few whole cooked shrimp to each bowl if you like.

This soup makes an excellent luncheon soup followed by omelettes and a green salad.

OYSTER AND CELERY SOUP

(For 4)

This is made possible and easy with the help of a canned soup.

1 *cup cream*
Bit of bay leaf
Slice of onion
1 *can condensed cream of celery soup*
½ *teaspoon celery salt*
½ *cup oyster liquor*
1 *cup oysters*
4 *large mushroom caps*
1 *tablespoon butter*
1 *tablespoon white wine*
⅛ *teaspoon nutmeg*

Scald cream with bay leaf and onion and strain it over celery soup, to which you have added ½ cup of hot water and celery salt. Set this where it will simmer. Heat oyster liquor and cook oysters in it until their edges curl. Meanwhile cook mushroom caps in butter. Add oysters to soup. Add wine and nutmeg. Put mushroom caps into heated soup plates and pour soup over them. Serve.

SOUPS FOR A MEAL

If a soup or stew is to be the main dish around which the rest of the meal is arranged, it must be a soup of some character rather than a simple consommé or broth. The following soups are intended to be the hearty center of a meal or, if served in small portions, first courses.

LAMB SOUP

1 *5-pound leg of lamb bone with scraps of meat left on*
2 *carrots, sliced*
3 *large onions, sliced*
Pinches of herbs: rosemary, basil, tarragon
½ *teaspoon Worcestershire sauce*
½ *teaspoon instant coffee (optional)*
Pinch of curry powder
2 *tablespoons fat from broth*
2 *tablespoons flour seasoned with: pinches of cinnamon, cloves, pepper, garlic powder*
1 *cup tomato juice*

This is to be made after you have had a roast leg of lamb and you need something to do with the leftover bone. Simply leave the bones in the roaster (with some meat left on) and cover with hot water. Add the carrots, one onion, herbs, tomato juice, Worcestershire sauce, coffee and curry powder. Let simmer until the meat falls from the bones — about 3 hours. Remove and discard the bones. Pour soup, carrots and all, into a large bowl and set in a cold place for fat to rise.

When you make the soup, skim all fat from broth. Melt 2 tablespoons of it in a large pan and sauté 2 onions, sliced thin, in it until straw colored. Sprinkle in seasoned flour and blend in well. Cook slowly for 3 minutes. Remove pan from heat, spoon in cold broth, stirring well until you have a smooth mixture. Add remainder of broth, meat and carrots. Taste. Add more tomato juice and a little lemon juice if you like. Serve hot with Cross crackers split, buttered, sprinkled with sesame seeds and toasted until lightly browned. You might also like a green salad and a cool dessert to finish the meal.

For special occasions, or those rare instances when lobster is in season and not too outrageously expensive, serve:

LOBSTER SOUP

1	*3-pound haddock*	3	*cups milk*
1	*small onion, sliced*	2	*cups cream*
2	*teaspoons salt*	6	*toasted and buttered Holland rusks*
½	*teaspoon paprika*	2	*tablespoons sherry*
⅛	*teaspoon nutmeg*	2	*tablespoons cream*
3	*small lobsters*	2	*egg yolks*
6	*tablespoons butter*	½	*tablespoon cold butter*
6	*tablespoons flour*		

Have the haddock cut for chowder and cook it all, including head, until fish slips from bones. Remove fish from bones. (It serves to bring out lobster flavor.) Return bones to broth, add onion and seasonings, lobster shells and claws. Let this cook for an hour. It should cook down so you have about 2 cups of strong fish stock.

Cut lobster meat up neatly but not too fine. Make a white sauce with butter, flour, milk and cream. Put it into top of a double boiler to keep hot and add lobster. When you are ready to serve soup, put a toasted rusk into each soup plate, stir strained fish bouillon into white sauce, add sherry and 2 tablespoons cream. Then add beaten egg yolks, first diluting them with some of the soup (delayering) and then stirring them into the soup. Slip in the ½ tablespoon butter — it should be cold and hard. Stir sauce until butter melts. Put some of the lobster meat on each rusk, pour soup over rusk boats with their cargo of lobster, and serve.

SEAFOOD CHOWDER

(For 8)

¼	*pound beef suet*	3	*tablespoons cold water*
3	*medium onions, minced*	1	*8-ounce tin frozen lobster, thawed*
6	*medium potatoes, sliced thin*	1	*pound shelled, cleaned and frozen shrimp, thawed*
1½	*quarts boiling water*	2	*8-ounce tins minced clams*
½	*teaspoon garlic powder*	3	*cups rich milk*
1	*teaspoon mixed herbs*	2	*cups light cream*
¼	*teaspoon nutmeg*	2	*tablespoons parsley, minced*
1	*teaspoon paprika*		*Sliced lemon*
3	*pounds frozen haddock fillets, thawed*		*Cross crackers*
2	*tablespoons flour*		

An electric skillet is good to make and serve this in, but a large brightly colored enameled frying pan will also work well.

Dice suet and try it out in frying pan over low heat until pieces are crisp and a light golden brown. Remove them with a slotted spoon and drain on paper towels until needed. Cook minced onions in suet fat until they are transparent and straw colored. Pare potatoes. Slice them less than ¼-inch thick. Pour 1½ quarts of boiling water into skillet. Put in potatoes and mix well with onions. Sprinkle in seasonings, except parsley. Lay in haddock fillets cut into four-inch pieces. Cover pan but let some steam escape. Cook about 15 minutes. Water should cook down to about a quart. Turn off heat. Put flour in a cup. Add cold water to it, stirring until smooth. Salt to taste. Strain through a fine strainer into mixture. Stir it in well.

The basis of the chowder is now ready. It may be set aside in a cool place to mellow. Several hours will do it no harm. Just before serving, heat it to the boiling point and add lobster and shrimp, which have slowly defrosted in the refrigerator. Cut largest pieces of lobster in medium-sized pieces. Leave shrimp whole. Add minced clams. Check the time. When liquid boils again, cook mixture 5 more minutes. Heat milk and cream so they are just scalding. Add to the mixture. Do not let mixture boil after this point or it will separate. Taste and add more seasoning if you like. Put in suet cubes and minced parsley.

Pass lemon slices and Cross crackers, split, well buttered and delicately browned.

LORD BALTIMORE SOUP

This soup can be made in three different manners. The first is made with a certain disregard for expense and time. All three are worthy of the original appellation.

LORD BALTIMORE SOUP

(19th Century Version)

1 quart oysters
*1 quart Chicken Stock**
4 tablespoons butter
4 tablespoons flour
1 teaspoon chopped parsley
Few grains cayenne pepper
1 teaspoon Worcestershire sauce
1 cup heavy cream

Pick over oysters, removing any pieces of shell. Parboil them for 10 minutes in their own juice. Press them through cheesecloth and drain. Add a quart of clear strong chicken stock to oysters. Make a roux of butter and flour, blend in oyster and stock mixture. Add seasonings, Worcestershire sauce and cook gently 5 minutes. Just before serving add heavy cream. Bring to the boil but do not boil. Serve with Souffléd Cross Crackers.*

LORD BALTIMORE SOUP

(20th Century Version 1)

*2 cups leftover Seafood Chowder**
2 cups milk
*2 cups jellied Chicken Stock**
½ cup breast meat of chicken
½ cup heavy cream

Put fish chowder through blender or chop fine and puree by hand. If you use a blender, do it in 2 batches, adding a cup of milk to each batch. Put puree in top of a large double boiler over hot, not boiling, water. Add chicken stock. While soup is heating, cut breast meat into neat cubes and add them to soup. At serving time add cream and bring soup to boiling over direct heat. Put into a hot tureen and serve in well-heated soup plates. Serves four generously with second helpings.

LORD BALTIMORE SOUP

(20th Century Version 2)

- 1 *chicken breast*
- 1 *carrot*
- ½ *teaspoon mixed herbs*
- ½ *teaspoon paprika*
- ¼ *teaspoon pepper, salt to taste*
- 3 *medium onions, sliced*
- 2 *tablespoons butter*
- 3 *potatoes, sliced very thin*
- 1 *frozen haddock fillet (12 ounces), thawed*
- 2 *cups Chicken Stock**
- 2 *cups milk*
- 1 *cup heavy cream*
- 8 *ounces oysters, frozen*
- *Sherry*
- *Lemon slices*

Cook chicken breast with carrot, herbs and seasonings in about 3 cups water. Cook this stock down to 2 cups. Strain, chill, skim off fat. Sauté onions in butter until pale yellow and transparent. Do not let them brown. Add sliced potato and haddock. Cover with boiling water and cook until potatoes are done, 10 to 20 minutes. Put mixture through blender in 2 batches. Put puree into a large pan over low heat. Add 2 cups of chicken stock and half a cup of cubed breast meat. Dilute flour with a little cold water and rub it through a fine sieve into the soup. Stir well. Scald milk and cream in another pan. Be careful not to scorch. Bring chicken and fish mixture to the boil. Drop in oysters and cook until edges curl, about 3 minutes. Add scalded milk and cream and bring soup to the boil but do not let it boil. Put a dash of sherry and a slice of lemon into each hot soup plate and serve immediately.

A good one-dish meal to serve on a cool evening in the middle of corn season, or in winter using canned or frozen corn is:

CHICKEN AND CORN SOUP

(For 4)

- 4 *tablespoons flour*
- *Pinch of nutmeg*
- 1 *teaspoon mixed herbs*
- ½ *teaspoon garlic powder*
- 1 *3-pound frying chicken, cut up*
- 4 *tablespoons butter*
- 1 *large onion, minced*
- *Tops from bunch of celery*
- ½ *cup minced parsley*
- 1 *quart fresh tomatoes*
- 1 *cup white wine*
- 2 *cups corn, cut from cob (canned or frozen)*
- 2 *tablespoons sherry*

Mix flour and seasonings in paper bag. Shake pieces of chicken in it until well coated. Melt butter in a large iron frying pan. Add onion and chicken pieces and cook over low heat until chicken is lightly browned, turning often. Add celery tops, parsley, tomatoes, peeled and cut up (canned may be used), wine and enough hot water to come well up around the chicken. Simmer for about 2 hours, adding more hot water if necessary. Just before serving, remove chicken from bones, discard bones, put chicken pieces in a fireproof dish and keep them hot. Sprinkle corn into the pan, add sherry. Cover pan and cook until corn is done — 10 to 12 minutes if fresh, less if canned or frozen. Pour soup over chicken and serve hot with Thin Scalded Johnny Cake.*

MULLIGATAWNY SOUP

(For 6)

This is a New England version of an eighteenth century East Indian soup. It seems to have been around long enough to be called a traditional New England soup. Whoever claims this soup, it is a good hearty one and sufficiently filling to satisfy any New Englander, or midwesterner for that matter.

3 tablespoons chicken fat or butter
3 large onions, chopped
1 small carrot, sliced thin
4 stalks celery, cut fine
2 pounds veal, in cubes
3 tablespoons flour
8 cups water
1 3-pound frying chicken, cut up
2 tablespoons curry powder

Melt chicken fat in a large frying pan. If there isn't enough, add butter to make 3 tablespoons. Cook onions, carrot and celery in it over low heat until onions are straw colored. Put in veal cubes and toss for 5 minutes. Put vegetables aside and make a roux with flour, adding extra butter if needed. Over very low heat, add water and stir until there are no lumps. Put in pieces of chicken, cover pan tightly. Simmer until veal and chicken are tender — about 3 hours. Remove chicken, remove bones and skin and cut into medium pieces. Return chicken pieces to the soup. Mix curry powder with some of the broth and stir mixture into soup. Let simmer half an hour longer. It is best if left to mellow all day in a cool place after having been made in the morning. Pass boiled brown rice with it.

BAKED BEAN SOUP

(For 4)

A hearty soup to serve the family, following Saturday night Baked Beans,* needing only brown bread and cream cheese sandwiches and a dessert of fruit and cheese to complete the repast.

*2 cups Vermont Baked Beans**
4 cups water
1 tablespoon minced onion
1 teaspoon instant coffee (optional)
4 cooked frankfurters
1 lemon, sliced
2 hard-boiled eggs
2 tablespoons sherry

This is easier made in a blender, but may be made by heating beans slightly with a cup of water and pressing them through a fine sieve or food mill.

If using a blender, puree beans in two batches, 1 cup of beans, 1 cup of water and some onion in each batch. Put puree into a large casserole, from which you can serve it. Add the rest of water, coffee and sliced frankfurters. Heat carefully, stirring well until mixture starts to bubble.

In each soup plate put slices of lemon and hard-boiled egg. Add sherry to soup and ladle it into soup plates. The coffee won't affect the taste much — it simply gives the soup color and the flavor blends into the mixture, but leave it out if you wish. Do not make this with excessively sweet baked beans. Too much molasses and ketchup flavor will spoil the soup.

BLACK BEAN SOUP

This is a more sophisticated version of the above soup and a traditional one for the New England area, especially fitting on cold winter afternoons.

1	*pound black beans*	*¼*	*teaspoon thyme*
2	*quarts water*	*1*	*onion, sliced*
1	*ham bone*	*1*	*stalk celery, cut fine*
½	*teaspoon garlic powder*	*3*	*tablespoons butter*
¼	*teaspoon allspice*	*1½*	*tablespoons flour*
4	*cloves, whole*	*6*	*tablespoons sherry*
1	*bay leaf*	*2*	*lemons*

3 hard-boiled eggs

Soak the beans overnight in the water. In the morning put them on to cook with ham bone and dry seasonings. Slice the onion, cut up celery and sauté in 1½ tablespoons of butter. Add them to soup and simmer for 4 hours. Add hot water from time to time to prevent scorching. When beans are soft, strain off liquid and set aside, remove ham bone and cloves, put the rest of mixture through blender and run until smooth. Make a roux of rest of butter and flour, add liquid slowly, stirring well over very low heat until it reaches desired thickness. Cook 2 minutes, add bean puree. You might want to add 2 tablespoons of tomato ketchup at this point, for color. I prefer it without. Keep soup in a double boiler until ready to serve, or over a flame tamer on low heat. At serving time, have plates very hot. In each one put 1 tablespoon of sherry, 2 slices of lemon. Chop hard-boiled eggs to sprinkle over top of the soup. Serve with crackers, a green salad and Gingerbread* for dessert.

LENTIL SOUP

(For 10)

2 cups lentils

2	*quarts water*	*1*	*clove garlic, put through press*
1	*medium onion, sliced*	*2*	*teaspoons salt*
2	*slices bacon, uncooked, cut in pieces*	*¼*	*teaspoon pepper, from the grinder*
¼	*cup chopped celery*	*½*	*teaspoon oregano*
¼	*cup chopped carrots*	*1*	*pound canned tomatoes*
3	*tablespoons chopped parsley*	*2*	*tablespoons wine vinegar*

Rinse lentils and put them into a large kettle with water, onion, bacon, celery, carrots, parsley, garlic, salt, pepper and oregano. Cover pan and simmer until lentils fall apart, about 1½ hours. Stir in tomatoes, breaking them up with the back of a spoon, stir in vinegar and simmer half an hour longer. Serve with hot Sour Cream Graham Bread* and a fruit salad.

DANISH HAM SOUP

- 1 *ham bone with some meat on it*
- 2 *potatoes*
- 1 *bunch green onions with tops*
- 3 *stalks celery with tops*
- 2 *cups chopped green cabbage*
- 2 *carrots*
- ¼ *cup chopped parsley*
- 3 *tablespoons flour*
- 1 *cup cream*

Boil ham bone until meat falls from bone, at least 1 hour. Remove bone. There should be about 2 quarts of liquid left. Put in all the vegetables, chopped, not too fine, and parsley. Cook until vegetables are tender, about 40 minutes. Pour cold water slowly on flour, mixing well, and rub through a fine strainer into soup. Bring soup to boil, add cream. Cool for several hours. Reheat when you serve it. It should be quite thick — you may add a little hot water to thin it if you like.

At serving time, add the seasonings you like; freshly ground pepper, a pinch of mixed herbs, a pinch of cinnamon. It is even better the next day, if you are lucky enough to have any left. Grandmother was introduced to this soup by a young Dane, a guest of Cicely's, who helped make an international meal for New Year's dinner. Serve with Garlic Bread* and a tossed salad.

CREAMED SOUPS

Although cream soups are scattered throughout this section I would like to present a number of others here. There are vast differences of opinion concerning cream soups. Some think them too heavy, or too rich to be served as a first course in a full meal. But if served in small portions, they seem to me to be just the right touch with which to begin a meal.

They are all made in the same basic way with the making of a roux or white sauce to which other ingredients are added or blended. A good one to begin with is:

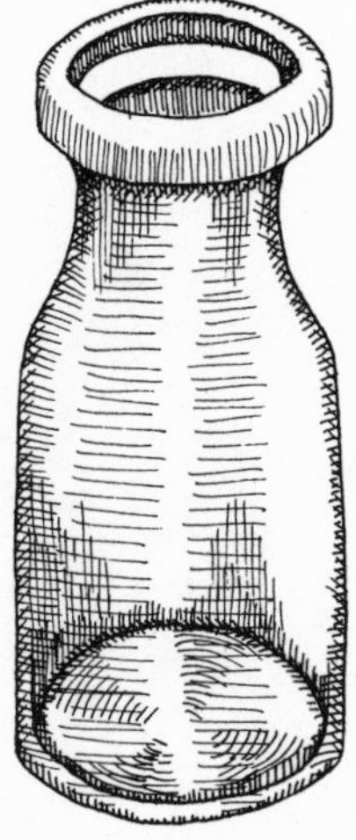

VERMONT CHEESE SOUP

This was originally intended to be made with real Vermont cheddar, but might just as well be put together with New York or Wisconsin dairy cheese. Please don't use that artificial substance called "processed American cheese," for you can only end up with a taste as fine as the ingredients that went into the making allow.

- ½ *cup celery, cut fine*
- ½ *cup onion, minced*
- ½ *cup fresh carrots, cut fine*
- ½ *cup green pepper, cut fine*
- ¼ *cup butter*
- 2 *cups Chicken Stock**
- 6 *tablespoons butter*
- 6 *tablespoons flour*
- 1 *quart milk (part milk, part cream)*
- 1 *cup grated cheese*
- *Salt and pepper to taste*
- *Mixed herbs: pinch of tarragon and basil*

Cook vegetables in ¼ cup butter or chicken fat until onion is tender and pale gold in color. Add 2 cups chicken stock and let vegetables simmer.

While vegetables are cooking make the sauce. Melt butter, blend in flour. Cook 3 minutes. Reduce heat. Blend in milk and cook several minutes until sauce starts to thicken. Stir in cheese and seasonings — salt, pepper and mixed herbs. Continue cooking over hot water until cheese melts. The vegetables should be slightly crisp, not mushy. When the sauce is ready, put the two mixtures together in an iron enameled dish to heat. Stir and serve. In corn season, just before serving, add a cup of Golden Bantam Corn cut from the ears and cooked in a little water for 10 minutes. Serve with Garlic French Bread.*

CRÈME SENEGALESE

(For 4)

*2 cups Chicken Stock**
Pinches of marjoram, thyme, oregano
1 teaspoon dried onion flakes
3 tablespoons chicken fat
3 tablespoons flour
¼ teaspoon nutmeg
½ teaspoon curry powder
½ teaspoon paprika
2 cups heavy cream
2 tablespoons minced chives
*Garlic Croutons**

Heat chicken stock with marjoram, thyme, oregano and onion flakes. Melt fat and make a roux with flour seasoned with nutmeg, curry powder and paprika (and a little salt if you wish). Strain stock through a fine sieve. Remove roux from heat and work in stock. Cook until it thickens — about 5 minutes. Chill. Set in refrigerator. At serving time stir in cream. Pour soup into chilled bowls, and set them into freezer for 5 minutes. Serve sprinkled with minced chives and Garlic Croutons.

You might want to serve this hot for a change, adding 1 cup of cubed white chicken meat and serving with Baking Powder Biscuits* or Parker House rolls.

PRINCESS PEA SOUP

(For 6)

4 tablespoons butter
4 tablespoons flour
4 cups rich milk
1 cup fresh or frozen peas, cooked
¼ teaspoon nutmeg
½ teaspoon paprika
⅛ teaspoon curry powder (optional)
¼ teaspoon mixed herbs
½ teaspoon parsley flakes
1 cup jellied Chicken Stock cooked with 1 small onion*
¾ cup light cream
½ cup breast of chicken, cubed

Melt butter over low heat, rub in flour. Remove from heat. Add 1 cup milk, slowly, stirring carefully until smooth. Cook over low heat, stirring all the time until it thickens, about 3 minutes. Put into blender with half the cooked peas and seasonings. Blend 2 minutes. Put mixture into top of a double boiler. Put rest of peas and chicken stock into blender, blend 2 minutes and add to contents of double boiler. Add rest of milk and cook over boiling water at least 20 minutes. At serving time add cream and chicken cubes. Serve very hot with Kolacky Bread.*

CREAM OF PEA AND SHRIMP SOUP

Make Princess Pea Soup (above), omitting chicken breast. For 4 people make a quart of soup. Allow one six-ounce package frozen cleaned shrimp to each quart of soup. Put soup in top of a double boiler over hot, not boiling, water. Cook shrimp, tightly covered, in a very small amount of water, until tender — about 5 minutes. Add shrimp and any liquid left with the shrimp to the soup. Bring to the boil but do not boil. Serve at once.

CREAM OF WATERCRESS SOUP

(For 8 to 10)

Watercress is not as readily available today as it was in Grandmother's day, but it can be found and makes a delicious cream soup. Look around nearby ponds and streams for it — you might be surprised.

- 1 *quart fresh crisp watercress, carefully washed*
- 1 *quart Chicken Stock**
- 3 *tablespoons butter*
- 3 *tablespoons flour*
- *Pinch of nutmeg*
- *Pinch of cayenne pepper*
- *Salt to taste (up to 1 teaspoon)*
- 3 *cups rich milk*
- 1 *cup thin cream*
- 3 *egg yolks*

Put washed watercress and one cup of stock into blender and blend until you have a smooth bright green puree. Melt butter, rub in flour mixed with seasonings, cook until smooth — about 1 minute. Remove from heat, stir in rest of stock a little at a time. Stir in puree. Cook over hot water for 15 minutes. Scald milk and cream. Stir into watercress mixture. At serving time, beat egg yolks. Add some of the soup to them, a little at a time, stirring well until you have about 1 cup of egg and soup mixture. Stir into soup. Cook until thickened — about 2 minutes. Do not overcook or it will curdle. You may leave it to stand over hot, but not boiling, water until ready to serve. Sesame crackers are good with this soup.

CREAM OF SPINACH SOUP

Make this just as you would Cream of Watercress Soup (above), substituting spinach for the watercress. You may make this the day before you plan to serve it, leaving out the egg yolks. Reheat in a double boiler and delayer the egg yolks, adding them to the mixture just before you serve it.

CREAM OF SPRING SOUP

(For 4)

- 3 *tablespoons butter*
- 1 *medium onion, sliced*
- 3 *tablespoons flour*
- *Salt to taste*
- *Pinch of nutmeg*
- 1 *cup milk*
- 2 *cups Chicken Stock**
- 2 *cups fresh watercress (or spinach)*
- 1 *10-ounce package frozen peas, cooked*
- 6 *stalks asparagus, cooked*
- ½ *cup cream*
- 2 *egg yolks*
- 1 *tablespoon minced parsley*

Melt butter. Cook onion in it until transparent, rub in flour mixed with salt and nutmeg. Remove pan from heat. Slowly stir in milk. Add chicken stock. Cook until it melts and sauce starts to thicken — about 5 minutes.

Put 1 cup of sauce, the watercress, half the peas, and asparagus into blender and run for half a minute. Pour puree into top of a large double boiler and blend in rest of stock and vegetables. Add cream and cook over hot water for at least half an hour.

At serving time beat egg yolks in a small bowl. Add soup mixture to them, a tablespoon at a time, until you have about 1 cup of the mixture. Stir this back into soup and cook over hot water until it thickens slightly, about 5 minutes. Stir it carefully. Add a little more milk if it seems too thick. Serve hot, sprinkled with parsley, with Souffléd Cross Crackers,* or pour into jars to be served cold with hot French Garlic Bread.*

CREAM OF ARTICHOKE AND WATERCRESS SOUP

Make as for Cream of Spring Soup (above), but substitute 2 cups cooked Jerusalem artichokes for peas and asparagus. Just before serving, stir in 1 tablespoon lemon juice and 1 tablespoon butter. Serve either hot or cold with Cornmeal Muffins.*

CREAM OF ASPARAGUS SOUP

Make like Cream of Spring Soup (above), substituting 3 cups cooked asparagus for the other vegetables. A delicately tasteful flavor, great for a first course.

CREAM OF LEEK SOUP

1 bunch leeks
6 tablespoons butter
6 tablespoons flour
1 teaspoon salt
¼ teaspoon pepper
½ teaspoon paprika
3 cups milk
1 cup cream
Yolk of 1 egg
1 teaspoon minced parsley
Grated cheese

Slice leeks thin, using both green and white parts. Sauté them slowly in butter. Remove leeks to top of a double boiler and make a white sauce in the pan of butter, flour, seasonings and milk. Pour sauce over leeks, stir in cream and cook 40 minutes in a double boiler. Just before serving time add egg yolk, first beating it lightly and diluting it with some of the soup, then stirring it into the soup. Serve soup with parsley and paprika sprinkled over each plateful and pass grated dairy cheese with it. Excellent with sandwiches made of buttered toast spread with deviled ham and lightly broiled.

CREAM OF PUMPKIN SOUP

If your family is like mine and has taken to asking for mince or cranberry or blueberry pie to go with the traditional fixings at Thanksgiving time, you might want to begin the meal with small portions of this soup. It is quite rich, so if you want there to be room for the Turkey,* Chestnut Stuffing,* Giblet Gravy,* Green Beans and Mushrooms,* Cranberry-Orange Relish,* baked butternut squash, mashed potatoes, baby onions in cream, three kinds of pie and whatever else happens to be on the table that glorious day, you had better allow only small portions even if some beg you for more.

By this time of the year I generally still have an ample supply of pumpkins on hand from the garden, for they always seem to do quite well even if other crops barely make a showing. If you haven't fresh pumpkins, it is not considered a sin to begin with canned pumpkin and brown it as follows.

Butter a large frying pan lightly, and in it put 1½ cups of stewed and strained pumpkin which you will cook down to 1 cup. Do this over medium heat on top of the stove, stirring it often and turning the whole mass from time to time so that all of it comes in contact with the pan. The purpose is to brown the pumpkin just slightly and bring out its own natural sweetness. Drying it in the oven will not achieve this same happy effect. When the pumpkin is golden brown, thick and smooth, you might use it in various ways, one of which is Cream of Pumpkin Soup.

- 2 *tablespoons butter*
- 1 *slice onion, minced*
- 2 *tablespoons flour*
- ¼ *teaspoon nutmeg*
- ½ *teaspoon paprika*
- 2 *cups Chicken Stock**
- 2 *cups milk*
- 1 *cup pumpkin, browned as above*
- 1 *egg yolk*
- 1 *cup cream*
- ½ *teaspoon garlic powder*
- 2 *tablespoons sherry (optional)*

Melt butter. Cook onion in it until onion is straw colored. Remove pan from heat. Put onion aside and blend flour, mixed with spices, with the butter. Return to heat. Work in chicken stock, then milk. Cook until it bubbles around the edge — about 3 minutes. Stir in pumpkin. Pour mixture into top of double boiler and cook uncovered for 20 minutes, stirring occasionally.

At serving time, beat egg yolk and cream lightly together in a small bowl. Stir 4 tablespoons hot soup, one tablespoon at a time, into the mixture, then stir this mixture into the soup. Cover and let it cook until soup is well heated. It should then be the consistency of thick cream. If you use sherry, add it at the last minute, or add it to the bowls of those individuals who would like it. It will be the color of frosted sugar maples. Serve with Cheese Biscuits.*

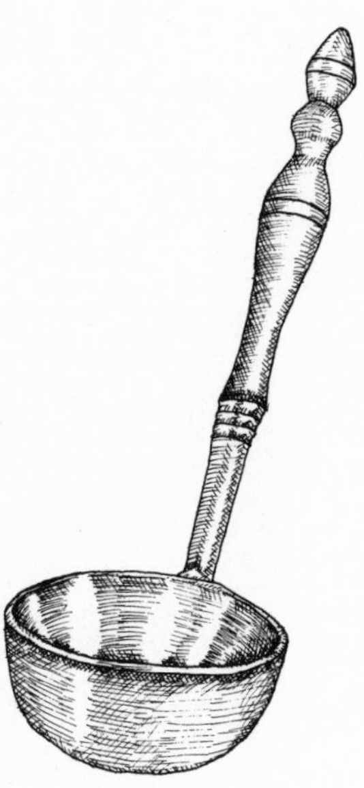

CREAM OF MUSHROOM SOUP

(For 6)

- *Skin and stems of 2 pounds mushrooms*
- 1 *teaspoon salt*
- 1 *bay leaf*
- ½ *small onion, sliced*
- 4 *tablespoons butter*
- 2 *tablespoons flour*
- 2 *cups milk*
- 1 *cup cream*
- ⅛ *teaspoon nutmeg*
- *Caps of 6 mushrooms*
- 1 *tablespoon sherry*

Start this the day before you serve it. Chop stems of mushrooms fine, add skins, salt, bay leaf and onion, cover with cold water, and simmer for at least 1 hour — 2 hours are even better. You should end with 1 cup of strong mushroom broth. (Add a bouillon cube and a little Worcestershire sauce if it is not strong enough.)

The next day make a white sauce of butter, flour and milk. Add the cream, mushroom stock and nutmeg. Put soup in a double boiler and cook 40 minutes. If it seems too thick, dilute with a little cream or rich milk. If it is too thin, thicken with an egg yolk, first blending yolk with a tablespoonful of soup and then stirring it well into the soup. Add sherry and serve at once. Into each plate put one of the mushroom caps, which has been either broiled or fried in a little butter.

CREAM OF CLAM AND CHICKEN SOUP

(For 4)

2 cups strong chicken stock
1 tablespoon butter
1 tablespoon flour
8 ounces minced clams
Salt and pepper to taste
2 tablespoons white wine
½ cup milk
½ cup heavy cream

Make chicken stock ahead by cooking a fowl with a carrot, large onion, celery tops, 1 teaspoon mixed herbs. Remove meat from bones, use it as you wish, in salad, creamed chicken or sandwiches. Return bones to broth and cook them at least an hour. Strain. Stock should jell when chilled. Skim fat from top.

In a frying pan melt butter, blend in flour, remove pan from heat and slowly stir in 1 cup of stock. Cook until it starts to thicken, about 3 minutes. Put it into blender with clams and blend to a smooth puree, about half a minute. Put it into top of double boiler with rest of stock, then cook over hot water for about 20 minutes. Add salt and pepper. At serving time, add wine, milk and cream. Bring to the boil but do not boil. Serve immediately in hot soup plates.

CREAM OF CLAM AND CELERY SOUP

(For 6)

2 tablespoons butter
1 small onion, minced
2 tablespoons flour
Salt to taste
¼ teaspoon mace
½ teaspoon paprika
½ teaspoon pepper
2 cups milk
1 bunch celery
*1 cup jellied Chicken Stock**
1 cup cream
2 cups clam juice
2 tablespoons minced parsley
2 tablespoons minced chives

Melt butter. Add onion and cook until straw colored. Mix flour and seasonings and blend it smoothly into butter over very low heat. Remove from heat, add milk slowly, stirring until smooth. Cook over low heat 5 minutes. Into blender put celery, washed and cut up. Include the best and most crisp celery leaves. Add chicken stock and blend until mixture is thick and smooth. Add mixture to soup, simmer for 5 minutes. Put soup into a top of a large double boiler and let stand over hot, not boiling, water until serving time. Then add cream. Bring mixture to the scalding point. Heat clam juice separately and stir it in. Do not let soup boil after adding clam juice or it will curdle. Serve with minced parsley and chives scattered over it. Serve with brown bread and cream cheese sandwiches.

There was a time, several years ago, when it seemed as if I had just discovered the vegetable eggplant. I tried anyway I could to make it more interesting to eat. My mother and I happened to be in one of our inventive frames of mind when we assembled a surprisingly delicious soup, hence called:

CURRIED EGGPLANT SOUP

(For 8)

8	*cups stock, chicken and vegetable*	2	*onions, finely chopped*
1	*cup red lentils*	2	*small eggplants, peeled and diced*
4	*medium potatoes, peeled and diced*	3	*tablespoons butter*
¼	*teaspoon garlic powder*	4	*tablespoons lemon juice*
2	*teaspoons celery leaves*	2	*cups milk*
2	*tablespoons parsley*	4	*tablespoons grated Parmesan cheese*
3	*teaspoons curry powder*	6	*tablespoons white wine*

Heat stock to the boiling point in a large kettle. Stir in lentils and add potatoes, garlic powder, celery leaves, parsley and curry powder. While potatoes are cooking, dice onions and eggplant and simmer them over medium heat in butter and lemon juice until onion is transparent and eggplant is tender but not mushy. Put potato and lentil mixture through blender in two batches, blending until smooth. Pour back into kettle. Slowly stir in milk and cheese, stirring until cheese melts. Salt to taste. Add eggplant and onion, cook over medium heat until all is warmed through, not letting it boil. Add the wine at the last minute and serve hot with parsley sprinkled over the top — good with hot, buttered Sour Cream Graham Bread.* This soup may serve as a delicate first course, or as the main course for lunch with open-faced chicken sandwiches.

A soup that may be made without stock, quickly and easily is:

CREAM OF POTATO AND ONION SOUP

6	*potatoes*	1	*tablespoon salt*
3	*large onions*	¼	*teaspoon pepper*
4	*tablespoons butter*	3	*cups milk*
2	*tablespoons flour*	1	*cup cream*

Chopped peanuts

Pare potatoes and slice thin. Slice onions thin, also. Cook both in water, covered, until tender and water has all but cooked away. Make a white sauce of butter, flour, seasonings and milk. Put onions and potatoes into top of double boiler, pour white sauce over them, mix well, add cream. You might want to rub soup through a fine strainer, but I prefer having pieces of onions and potato to bite into. Pour into hot soup plates, sprinkle chopped peanuts over each one and serve.

VEGETABLE SOUPS

Although many of the soups already listed in this chapter might be considered vegetable soups, the following ones can really be considered nothing else. In making vegetable soups there are a few things to remember. Always cook the vegetables until tender before adding large amounts of water, or the vegetables will taste rather like soggy pancakes.

If you are going to puree cooked vegetables, sauté them in butter, before putting them through the blender. The same follows for making whole vegetable soups. Sauté them before adding the stock. Theoretically vegetables should be sautéed even if you are going to use them in the making of stock, but only the strongest of characters take the time and energy to do this. Grandmother did, but I'm afraid I'm a bit lazier than she.

CABBAGE SOUP

(For 10)

2 *pounds beef chuck, cut in inch cubes*	2 *pounds tomatoes*
Bones from beef chuck	6 *potatoes*
2 *pounds chicken necks and wings*	1 *stalk celery*
3 *quarts water*	2 *minced onions*
½ *teaspoon mixed herbs*	4 *tablespoons fat from stock*
	6 *cups cabbage, shredded and chopped*

½ *teaspoon mixed spices*

Put beef, bones and chicken necks and wings into a deep kettle with water. Add herbs and spices and let simmer for 2 hours. Skim fat from top from time to time. Prepare vegetables while stock is cooking. Peel tomatoes by holding them over a gas flame or plunging them into boiling water for a brief time. Cool and cut into eighths. Peel potatoes. Use either small new ones, freshly dug, or potato balls made from larger ones, or dice into half-inch pieces. Cut celery fine and mince onions. An hour before serving time, remove bones from stock. Sauté celery and onions in fat until onions are transparent and add to the soup. Then sauté cabbage for 5 minutes and add to the soup. Add potatoes and cook until potatoes are done, 2 to 5 minutes. Add tomatoes a short time before serving. Rinse out frying pan with a little soup to get all the flavor from the pan. Salt to taste. Serve in a large bowl or tureen and pass sour cream or yogurt with it.

BEET BORSCHT

(For 10)

3 *large onions, sliced*	1 *pint beet juice*
½ *cup shredded cabbage*	1 *cup tomato juice*
3 *tablespoons butter*	6 *small beets, finely chopped*
2 *cans consommé or strong soup stock*	2 *cans condensed vegetable soup*
2 *cups water*	1 *cup sour cream*

Begin by frying onion and cabbage in butter, using a large iron frying pan and adding more butter if necessary. Cook, stirring constantly until onion is a light straw color. Add consommé, water, beet juice, tomato juice, chopped beets, and vegetable soup. If you have small amounts of other cooked vegetables on hand, such as carrots, peas, string beans or celery, you might want to add them at this time, depending on how "pure" you would like your borscht. Let the whole thing simmer for 40 minutes.

Serve hot in bowls and pass sour cream for those who like it. The soup itself is a deep crimson, the cream changes it to a fine cranberry pink. Brown bread and cream cheese sandwiches go well with this.

MUSHROOM AND BARLEY SOUP

- ¾ *cup pearl barley*
- 1 *quart Beef Stock**
- 2 *medium onions, chopped*
- ½ *pound mushrooms, sliced vertically*
- 1 *cup vegetable stock*
- 2 *tablespoons wheat germ*
- 1 *small carrot, diced*
- 1 *small stalk celery, diced*
- 1 *tablespoon green pepper, minced*
- *Salt and black pepper to taste*
- *Pinch of nutmeg*

Wash barley and cook in half the beef stock until soft. Sauté onions and mushrooms in butter until soft. Cook the remaining ingredients, except for seasonings, for 20 minutes in the vegetable stock and remaining beef stock. Put all ingredients together with salt, pepper and nutmeg. Heat through. Serve hot with Bran Muffins.* This is a delicately flavored soup of interesting texture.

VICHYSSOISE

Most people either like vichyssoise tremendously or find it repulsive. If you enjoy it, you will want to try Grandmother's rule for it.

- 4 *leaks (white stalks only)*
- 1 *stalk celery*
- ½ *cup butter*
- 4 *raw potatoes, sliced very thin*
- 2 *cups Chicken Stock**
- 2 *cups water*
- 1 *sprig parsley, chopped fine*
- 1 *teaspoon salt*
- ¼ *teaspoon pepper*
- ⅛ *teaspoon nutmeg*
- 1 *cup cream*
- 1 *tablespoon chives, chopped*

Mince leeks and celery fine and cook them slowly in butter for 10 minutes. Do not let them brown. Stir constantly. Add sliced potatoes, chicken stock, water and seasonings. Cook over medium heat for ½ hour. At this point you have two choices.

If you want to serve it hot, add the cream, chopped chives and serve hot with croutons.

To be served cold, strain it through a sieve, stir in cream, pour into cups, chill and serve it very cold with chives sprinkled over it. The soup looks especially attractive in brightly-colored cups.

If you haven't any thick cream on hand the soup may be made richer with the addition of 2 egg yolks. With hot vichyssoise add eggs after the cream, just before serving. Beat egg yolks slightly, spoon 2 tablespoons hot soup into them, beat and then stir mixture back into soup. Never cook soup after doing this, or it will separate.

ONION SOUP WITH CUSTARD

(For 4)

This is the old-fashioned kind of onion soup, made with rich beef stock and made extra special by serving it with custard. Make Savory Custard* early in the day.

For the soup, use the following ingredients:

- *4 large onions*
- *4 tablespoons butter*
- *3 cups jellied Beef Stock**
- *3 cups water*
- *4 tablespoons red wine*
- *4 slices French Bread,* toasted*
- *½ cup grated cheddar cheese or real Parmesan*

Slice onions and sauté them gently in butter. They should cook to a delicate straw color, not brown. Stir well so they will cook evenly. Add the stock and water and let soup simmer for an hour. At serving time, add wine. Toast bread lightly on both sides. Put a slice of toast into each hot soup plate. Remove custard from mold, slice it and lay a slice on each piece of toast. Ladle soup over toast. Sprinkle grated cheese over custard and pass extra cheese in a small bowl.

ONION SOUP COUNTRY STYLE

(For 4)

- *½ teaspoon garlic powder*
- *¼ pound creamed butter*
- *3 large onions*
- *3 tablespoons butter*
- *3 tablespoons flour*
- *2 cups milk*
- *1 cup jellied Chicken Stock**
- *2 cups light cream*
- *French bread, sliced and toasted*
- *Pinch of nutmeg*
- *½ teaspoon pepper from grinder*
- *Pinch dried tarragon*
- *Salt to taste*
- *1 cup grated cheddar cheese*

First make garlic butter by creaming garlic powder with butter.

Chop onions and cook in the plain butter until they are transparent and straw colored, about 5 minutes. Blend in flour over low heat. Remove pan from heat and stir in milk. Add chicken stock. Cook, stirring, over low heat for 5 minutes. Turn off heat and let stand until serving time. Toast bread, sliced one inch thick, on one side. Spread other side with garlic butter and brown lightly under broiler. Have soup plates hot. Put one slice of toast in each plate. Add cream and seasonings to soup, heat to the scalding point and pour soup over toast. Pass grated cheese and extra slices of toast.

Vegetables

If there is any country with a worse reputation for cooking and serving vegetables than the United States, it must surely be England, the home of my ancestors. Word has it that they know how to cook only three vegetables, two being cabbage. Now I doubt whether there is a great deal of truth to that for even the English must be learning to cope with the increased availability of fresh and carefully frozen vegetables. My brief experience in England would lead me to believe that most of the country has far to go in learning how to produce truly palatable and enticing vegetable dishes. But then, I was not staying at the best of inns or eating at the most discerning of restaurants.

Actually, there is no great mystery about cooking vegetables that are both nutritious and sumptuous. Most important is starting with the freshest produce possible (be it straight from your own garden or canned or frozen directly from someone else's). Cook uniform size pieces in as little water as possible (steaming is the most efficient method) and cook only until they are tender but not overcooked and mushy. Save any water that might be left over to be used in soups, stews or other future cooking projects. Never add baking soda to the vegetables to increase the color for, yes, the color may be brilliant, but the flavor will be of soda and the vitamins destroyed. Try to prepare a variety of vegetables, from deep green to yellow and orange, thus obtaining a balance of the vitamins and minerals inherently available in the vegetables.

I will include the basics of vegetable cookery as well as a number of more unusual dishes. It is better to eat vegetables simply, yet carefully prepared, than to serve a tired combination of tasteless vegetables in the aim of being fancy.

Let us begin with:

ARTICHOKES HOLLANDIASE

Wash artichokes in cool water, place on a rack over boiling water, cover and steam for about half an hour, or until the leaves pull out easily but the artichokes have not turned army green. While they are cooking, make the Hollandaise Sauce.* Serve artichokes hot in individual dishes with separate dishes of Hollandaise, or lemon butter, for each person.

JERUSALEM ARTICHOKES

(For 6)

These are deceptively homely looking. They are a member of the sunflower family, and a root vegetable. They have a deliciously delicate flavor and haven't the fluff that usually chokes the unwary eater of the French Globe artichoke.

1 pound Jerusalem artichokes
¼ cup butter
Juice and rind of one lemon
2 tablespoons minced parsley
¼ teaspoon salt
½ teaspoon paprika
⅛ teaspoon pepper

Wash and peel artichokes. Drop them as you peel them into a quart of cold water with half a cup of vinegar in it to keep them from darkening. Drain. Cook in boiling water until soft — about 25 minutes. Check them often during cooking and remove from heat as soon as they are soft. They may get hard again if they cook too long. Melt butter, add lemon juice and rind, parsley and seasonings. Drain artichokes. Put them in a hot dish and pour the sauce over them.

MARINATED JERUSALEM ARTICHOKES

1 pound Jerusalem artichokes
2 tablespoons tarragon vinegar
6 tablespoons olive oil
½ teaspoon salt
1 teaspoon dry mustard
½ teaspoon pepper
⅛ teaspoon curry powder
1 teaspoon garlic powder
½ teaspoon paprika
½ teaspoon sugar

Wash, peel and cook artichokes as above. Put all other ingredients in a jar and shake them well together. Pour marinade over artichokes while they are still hot. Chill thoroughly. Use for hors d'oeuvres or in a salad. Use cider vinegar and safflower oil if you prefer.

Artichokes are also good garnished with Garlic Crumbs.*

ASPARAGUS

Pick asparagus fresh from your own garden or get it as fresh as possible from a roadside stand. Break off the tough ends and throw them away. Cut stalks into inch pieces. Keep tips in a separate dish. Cook the lower parts of the stalks in rapidly boiling water for 15 minutes. Add the tips,

*See Index for pages where recipes can be found.

cover, and cook until tips and stalks are tender — about five minutes longer. Drain. Serve with melted butter, lemon butter, Hollandaise Sauce* or with the following:

HORSERADISH AND SOUR CREAM

1	*tablespoon powdered horse-radish*	1	*cup sour cream*
	Sweet cream		*Salt and pepper to taste*
		¼	*cup coarse bread crumbs*

2 *tablespoons butter*

Mix horseradish with a little sweet cream to make a paste. Heat sour cream over hot, not boiling, water. Add salt and pepper to taste and stir in horseradish. Brown bread crumbs in butter. Put the sauce in a bowl and sprinkle bread crumbs over.

ASPARAGUS COUNTRY STYLE WITH BUTTER AND EGG SAUCE

(For 12)

3	*large bunches asparagus*		*Juice of 1 lemon*
¼	*pound butter*	2	*hard-boiled eggs*

Salt and pepper to taste

Cook asparagus. Have rounds of buttered toast ready on a hot platter. Make sauce by heating butter and lemon juice and adding hard-boiled eggs, cut up rather fine, and the seasonings. Drain water left in asparagus. Cook it down to one tablespoon and add to the sauce. Heap asparagus on toast. Bring sauce to a boil and spoon some over each heap of asparagus. There will be no extra.

Grandmother has told in the *Vermont Year Round Cookbook* how to freeze asparagus and numerous other vegetables. I will leave out that information, as it can be gotten in proliferation from a number of other sources, notably, *Putting Food By*, by Beatrice Vaughn. If you follow her information, you will be in good shape.

GREEN OR LIMA BEANS WITH MUSHROOMS

(For 8)

2	*10-ounce packages frozen French-cut beans or lima beans*	1	*tablespoon flour*
		½	*teaspoon nutmeg*
		½	*teaspoon paprika*
1	*teaspoon minced onion*		*Salt to taste*
2	*tablespoons butter*	½	*cup cream*
1	*pound mushrooms, caps cut vertically, stems sliced thin*	2	*tablespoons sherry (optional)*

Make this dish ahead of time and keep in a double boiler until serving time. It improves with standing.

Cook beans in small amount of water until tender but not mushy. Do not overcook. Put them in top of a double boiler. Sauté onion in butter until straw colored. Add mushroom caps and stems and cook four or five minutes, stirring well. Sprinkle flour mixed with seasonings over mushrooms and onions. Blend it in. Do this over very low heat. Add cream, let it get hot but do not boil. Add mixture to the beans and stir well. Just before serving, reheat, add more cream if necessary. Add sherry and serve. An excellent dish to serve with turkey at Thanksgiving or Christmas time.

Variation: In addition to making this combination with green or lima beans, the mushroom sauce may be added to either brussel sprouts, broccoli, or shell beans with tasty results. Simply mix the mushroom sauce with the cooked vegetable. Let mixture stand over hot water until serving time. You might want to add sherry just before serving, but I think the sprouts and shell beans are better without.

GREEN BEANS AND BEETS

(For 8)

- *2 10-ounce packages frozen French-cut beans*
- *4 tablespoons butter*
- *1 1-pound can matchstick cut beets*
- *½ cup blanched almonds*

Cook beans until tender but not mushy in smallest possible amount of water. Add one tablespoon butter during last few minutes cooking. Heat beets in their own juice with one tablespoon butter. Watch them: they burn easily and suddenly. Toss the blanched almonds in two tablespoons of butter until they start to brown. On a hot circular dish, heap beans and surround with a ring of beets. Scatter almonds over beans and serve.

GREEN BEANS WITH GARLIC CROUTONS

(For 8)

This may be made with your own frozen beans or packaged French-cut frozen beans.

- *2 10-ounce packages frozen beans*
- *½ cup heavy cream*
- *2 tablespoons sour cream*
- *Salt, pepper, paprika to taste*
- *Garlic Croutons**

Cook beans in top of a double boiler in small amount of boiling water, about two tablespoons to a package. Keep stirring with a fork so that ice in them will melt as fast as possible. After six or seven minutes the water should have all cooked away. Add heavy cream. Set beans over hot water until serving time. They improve while standing.

At serving time add sour cream and seasonings to beans. Put them in a hot dish, serve with croutons sprinkled over them.

GREEN BEANS WITH CREAM AND BEEF CRACKLINGS

- *¼ pound beef cracklings made from fat of roast beef or steak*
- *1 pint frozen or fresh green beans*
- *Cream*

Begin by cutting beef fat into half-inch cubes and setting them over a very low flame to fry. Stir occasionally and pour off some of the fat. Save in a marked jar for browning hashed brown potatoes. The cubes should shrink to half their size and be a delicate tan in color.

Slice the beans on the diagonal. Cook them in a small amount of rapidly boiling water. When water has cooked away, add a little thick cream. Before serving them, heat the cracklings briefly, skim them out of the

pan, using a spoon with holes in it, and sprinkle over the beans. Serve.
Also good are green beans with Sour Cream Sauce.*

GREEN BEANS AND SAUSAGE

This dish was originated as an unplanned combination by an ingenious friend of the family. For a family of eight use:

½	*pound link sausages*	2	*10-ounce packages frozen French-cut green beans*
1	*tablespoon butter*		

Bake sausages in a 350° oven for 40 minutes. Toward the end of baking time, cook beans in smallest amount of hot water possible. Watch them carefully and cook until they are tender but not mushy, and water has nearly cooked away — about 12 minutes. Add butter. Put beans in a hot vegetable dish. Drain sausages on paper towels, cut them in halves widthwise. Thrust the halves, cut end down, into the beans, leaving the top half an inch above the beans. Serve.

SHELL BEANS WITH TOMATOES

2	*cups shell beans*	*Salt and pepper to taste*
1	*cup heavy cream*	*Beef cracklings*

*Broiled Tomato Slices**

Start beans cooking in boiling water. Cover. Cook until tender — about 25 minutes. Spoon out beans into top of a double boiler. Cook liquid down to about two tablespoons. Add cream, bring just to boiling point, pour mixture over beans. Add salt and pepper to taste.

While beans are cooking, try out small cubes of beef suet to a golden brown, drain them on paper towels. At serving time heap the beans in center of a hot circular platter. Sprinkle cracklings over them and surround with Broiled Tomato Slices.*

VERMONT BAKED BEANS

4	*cups yellow-eye beans*	1	*teaspoon dry mustard*
1	*pound salt pork*	½	*teaspoon ginger*
2	*small onions*	4	*tablespoons maple syrup*

Soak beans overnight. Drain them in the morning, cover with cold water and heat slowly. Keep water below boiling point and cook beans for about 40 minutes until skins crack when you take them out on a spoon and blow on them.

Drain beans, saving the water. Cut a thin slice of pork and put it in bottom of a bean pot. Put onions in whole. They will vanish during cooking leaving the flavor as a memory. Mix seasonings with maple syrup — or brown sugar if you've no maple syrup — with a cup of boiling water. Put some beans on top of onions. Make several gashes about an inch deep in rind of salt pork. Put it into the bean pot. Surround with rest of the beans, letting rind show on top. Then pour over seasoned reserved water and add enough more water to cover beans. Put a lid on the pot and set into a 300° oven for eight hours. Occasionally add a little water. Uncover beans after seven hours so rind of pork will get brown and crisp. Serve for supper with Boston brown bread and Mrs. Appleyard's Chutney.*

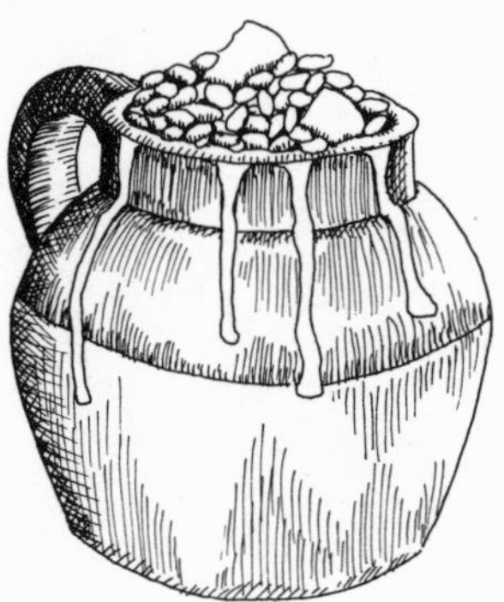

MRS. APPLEYARD'S OWN BAKED BEANS

(For 6)

This is for those who either should not or do not want to eat salt pork. Grandmother used to make these for herself to take along to community suppers, but she would usually find a few friends to share them with her. Perhaps you would like to.

- 2 *cups yellow-eye beans*
- 4 *tablespoons butter*
- ¾ *cup light brown sugar*
- 1 *teaspoon granulated sugar*
- ¼ *teaspoon ground pepper*
- 1½ *teaspoons dry mustard*
- *Pinches of rosemary, basil, marjoram, oregano, curry powder, nutmeg*
- *Bit of bay leaf, scalded in water and removed*
- 1 *onion, minced*
- 2 *cloves of garlic, crushed*
- ¼ *pound beef suet in half-inch cubes*
- 1 *cup light cream*
- 1 *tablespoon brown sugar (extra)*

Soak and parboil beans as above. Mix butter, sugar, dry seasonings, onion and garlic and combine them with beans. Put them into a small bean pot or casserole with the reserved liquid to cover. Bake tightly covered for six hours at 300°. Try out suet cubes until golden brown. Drain. Uncover beans. Pour in cream and stir beans so that different ones are on top. Scatter suet cubes over beans. Sprinkle extra brown sugar over top. Cook half an hour or until beans are tender and have absorbed most of the liquid. For a special touch, you might want to scatter half a cup of cheddar cheese over the top in the last ten minutes of cooking.

BEAN SPROUTS

Bean sprouts are an excellent source of vitamins (particularly B-complex), protein and energy during the months when it is sometimes hard to get fresh vegetables. Since they are sprouted from the seed of the plant, they contain the heart of the future plant and given moisture and heat will supply you with low-calorie, high energy food. Oh, I should also mention, for those unaccustomed to the ingestion of bean sprouts, they are delicious in salads, added to casseroles or eaten plain as a nutritious snack. Kids love them, too.

The following whole beans and peas, when treated correctly, can be sprouted with little trouble:

mung beans	lima beans	kidney beans
lentils	chick peas	pinto beans
soybeans	green peas	

Seeds and whole grains may also be sprouted successfully, including wheat, rye, alfalfa, oats, corn, unhulled sunflower and sesame seeds.

There are numerous containers suitable for sprouting, from an old mayonnaise jar to an unglazed pottery pie pan purchased especially for the purpose. The important thing to remember in choosing a container is that it be able to provide drainage of some sort and that you can easily fit it into a dark cupboard where you won't forget to check on it regularly. I use a large mayonnaise jar, thoroughly cleaned out, with several layers of cheesecloth held over the top with rubber bands. Discard the jar lid.

Begin by selecting clean, whole seeds, beans or grains. Remove any foreign matter that may be mixed in with them and place a quarter cup of dry beans into your sprouting jar. Cover with water and soak overnight. They expand substantially during the sprouting process. One quarter of a cup of dried beans will sprout to a full two cups.

Next morning, drain off the water and rinse with cool water. Put the cheesecloth or other cover (providing plenty of ventilation) over your container and invert it in a glass measuring cup or any other container large enough to hold it well above the bottom. Keep container upside down for drainage. Place in a warm, dark cupboard and rinse once or twice a day, frequently enough to keep them moist. They will be ready to eat in three to six days, depending on the type of bean, seed or grain and the room temperature. My favorite, mung bean sprouts, are ready to eat when the sprout is one and a half to three inches long.

Use sprouts as soon as possible after they are ready, keeping any unused ones in a covered container in the refrigerator. Serve in salads, as a garnish for soup or stew, blended into beverages, in casseroles, mixed with grated cheese or deviled ham, moistened with mayonnaise and used as a sandwich spread. Use your imagination! They are especially popular when combined with other vegetables and stir-fried in a wok.

Just a note about trying to sprout soybeans. They tend to be more difficult to sprout successfully than are other beans, especially in warm weather. Don't forget them for days at a time or you will open your cupboard to find a moldy mess. Try to remove any that are rotting as the rest are sprouting and rinse them often.

BEETS APPLEYARD

Start with beets that are young and tender, or the best canned shoestring beets. If using your own, cook beets in plenty of boiling water until tender, and save juice. Slip them out of their skins, slice and set where they will keep warm. You should have about two cups.

2 cloves of garlic
Grated rind of 1 lemon
1 cup beet juice
⅓ cup red wine
2 tablespoons cider vinegar
3 tablespoons sugar
2 tablespoons butter
1 tablespoon minute tapioca
2 cups beets, fresh and cooked as above or canned
1 tablespoon lemon juice

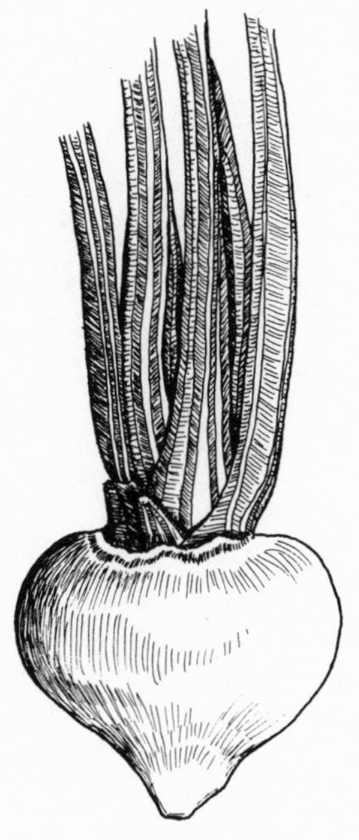

Soak garlic and lemon rind in beet juice, wine, vinegar and lemon juice for one hour. Strain juice, add sugar, butter and tapioca. Cook in top of a double boiler until sauce is thick and clear. Add beets. Set aside until serving time. Reheat. Add a little more hot wine if sauce seems too thick.

BEETS WITH BROCCOLI

This is a rule of indeterminate proportions. Use the amount of vegetables you need or have on hand to form a handsome array.

Cook beets and glaze them as above or just add butter to them if you prefer. Heap in the middle of a hot round platter and surround with a ring of cooked broccoli flowers. Pass a sauce of lemon juice and melted butter — two tablespoons of lemon juice to four of butter.

BEET GREENS AND YOUNG BEETS

These are one of my favorite green vegetables. But they are only good when the greens are fresh and thoroughly cleaned.

Cut off all the roots of fresh young beets, scrub them well in several changes of water and remove all the strings. Cut and wash the thick red stems from the greens and cut into quarter inch pieces and put on to steam with the young beets. Steam for 25 minutes or until tender. Meanwhile wash the leaves, cut them with scissors and put them on to cook with just the water that clings to them with two tablespoons of butter. Cook for five minutes, chopping them all the time. Add the cooked beets and stems and cook for three more minutes. Most of the liquid will have been absorbed. Both the beets and greens should be tender and well-colored. Serve with sour cream.

STIR-FRIED BROCCOLI

2	*pounds broccoli*	*1½*	*teaspoons salt*
2½	*tablespoons peanut oil*	*1*	*teaspoon sugar*
3	*thin slices fresh ginger root*	*1*	*cup water*

Break small branches of broccoli from the stem, one at a time. Peel the tough skin from the stem and cut stem diagonally into thin slices. Wash slices and flowers.

Heat the oil in a Chinese wok or large frying pan. Add ginger slices and stir for one minute. Remove ginger and add broccoli and stir for one minute over medium heat. Add salt, sugar, and water, cover and cook for three minutes. Remove cover and stir every half minute for about five minutes. The broccoli should be tender, crisp and a lovely color of green. Excellent with poultry of any kind.

BROCCOLI WITH GARLIC CROUTONS

(For 4)

1	*10-ounce package chopped broccoli*	*1*	*tablespoon butter*
		¼	*cup cream*

*Garlic Croutons**

Follow directions on package for cooking frozen broccoli. Cook uncovered after water is boiling hard. If water has not all cooked away by the time broccoli is tender but not mushy, remove broccoli to a hot dish and cook water down to two tablespoons. Add butter and cream, heat well and pour over broccoli. Sprinkle garlic croutons over.

BRUSSEL SPROUTS

(For 4)

1 pound Brussel sprouts	*1 cup dried bread crumbs*
4 tablespoons melted butter	*1 tablespoon lemon juice*

2 hard-boiled eggs, chopped

If you are using fresh Brussel sprouts soak them for 15 minutes in salted water to be sure there are no cabbage worms in them. Remove any worms that emerge, drain and rinse sprouts, steam until tender in an Italian folding steamer over boiling water — about 15 minutes.

Melt butter and let it brown slightly. Add bread crumbs, tossing them in the butter. Add lemon juice and chopped egg. Add more butter if necessary. Put sprouts in a hot dish, scatter the mixture over them and serve.

CABBAGE WITH CREAM CHEESE AND CREAM

2 tablespoons butter
2 cups shredded white cabbage
½ cup boiling water
3 ounces cream cheese
¼ cup cream
½ teaspoon paprika
Salt and pepper to taste
1 tablespoon minced parsley

Melt butter. Sauté cabbage in it, stirring well until cabbage is tender yet crisp. Add boiling water. Cover. Cook about five minutes longer. Most of the water should have cooked away. Mix cream cheese and cream. Stir it in, let it melt and come to the boil, but do not boil. Add seasonings and parsley. Serve.

CARROTS

The best carrots are those that you pull out of your garden when they are small and sweet, but even packaged carrots you buy at the grocery store can be made palatable. For the best way to serve fresh carrots simply cut them into rather thin slices, or if they are very small cook them whole, just trimming off the ends. Cook them in as little water as possible and cook every drop of water out of them. Watch carefully or they will scorch and stick to the bottom of the pan. When they are tender but not mushy, add thick cream and let them stand awhile in the top of a double boiler, or add soft butter and serve at once.

CARROTS AND PEAS

For a very short time in the middle of the summer the carrots are young and tender and the peas are still ripening. This is the time to serve these two delectable vegetables in combination.

Start the carrots first. When they are almost finished cooking, drop in the peas. Stand right over them while they are cooking. Five minutes later the water should be all cooked out, the peas tender and a lovely emerald green amidst the orange and gold of the carrots. Add either butter or thick cream to them and serve at once. If you must add salt, do it after they are cooked. If the vegetables are truly fresh they will require little.

CARROTS AND GREEN PEPPERS

1 onion, minced
2 tablespoons butter
6 medium carrots, thinly sliced
2 green peppers, seeded, thinly sliced lengthwise
1 tablespoon brown sugar
1 cup hot water

Sauté onion in butter until straw colored. Add carrots and peppers. Sauté five minutes. Add more butter if necessary. Be sure peppers touch the pan so they can brown a little. Sprinkle brown sugar over them and add water. Cover and cook ten minutes. Uncover and cook until all water has gone. The vegetables should be quite crisp and slightly browned.

GLAZED CARROTS

(For 6)

12	*small carrots*	3	*tablespoons light brown sugar*
1	*onion, minced*	¼	*teaspoon nutmeg*
3	*tablespoons butter*		*Salt to taste*
1	*cup hot water*	2	*tablespoons chopped mint*
1	*teaspoon lemon juice*		

Scrub carrots, slice them. Sauté carrots and onion in butter. Add water and sugar, cover and simmer ten minutes. Uncover and cook 10 to 15 minutes longer. Add lemon juice, nutmeg and salt if you use it. Stir occasionally turning carrots over in the glaze. Add mint and serve. Maple syrup or honey may be used in place of brown sugar.

For a change of pace in glazed carrots, try:

GLAZED CARROTS WITH PINEAPPLE

1	*small onion, cut fine*	6	*tablespoons water*
3	*tablespoons butter*	½	*cup brown sugar*
2	*cups garden carrots, sliced, or 24 whole baby carrots*	1	*cup pineapple chunks*
		1	*cup pineapple juice*

Sauté onion in butter until yellow, add carrots and cook five minutes. Add water, brown sugar, pineapple and juice. Turn carrots and pineapple over in syrup until well coated. Bake in a 350° oven for ten minutes or until carrots and pineapple are well glazed. Baste twice and turn carrots over in syrup. Serve hot.

CAULIFLOWER AND BROCCOLI WITH GARLIC CRUMBS

(For 6 to 8)

1	*large head cauliflower*	4	*tablespoons butter*
2	*bunches fresh broccoli*	½	*teaspoon garlic powder*
1	*cup bread crumbs*		*Salt and pepper to taste*

Yolks of 2 hard-boiled eggs

Remove stalk and leaves from head of cauliflower, soak in salted water ten minutes. Use flowers of broccoli, not stems, and put flowers also in salted water. Drain and rinse well. Have water boiling hard in a large saucepan. Set folding steamer into it. Place cauliflower in center of steamer and broccoli in a ring around it. Cover tightly and cook until vegetables are tender but not mushy — about 20 minutes.

Meanwhile toss bread crumbs in butter until golden brown. Add garlic powder and other seasonings. Mix well. Grate cooked egg yolks. When vegetables are ready, place cauliflower in center of a shallow dish, surround it with broccoli flowers, sprinkle bread crumbs over all and the powdered egg yolk over broccoli. This makes a very festive looking dish.

CAULIFLOWER AND GREEN BEANS HOLLANDAISE

1	*large head cauliflower*	½	*cup bread crumbs*
2	*cups green beans*	3	*tablespoons butter*

*Hollandaise Sauce**

Remove stalk and stem from cauliflower and soak in salted water for ten minutes. Cut beans in half-inch pieces on the diagonal. Place cauliflower in folding steamer over boiling water and steam, covered, for 20 minutes, or until tender. Add the beans after eight minutes cooking. Make the Hollandaise just before serving, or it will curdle. While vegetables are cooking, brown the bread crumbs in butter.

At serving time, place cauliflower in center of a circular platter or dish. Make a garland of beans around it. Pour Hollandaise over the cauliflower and sprinkle bread crumbs over beans. Serve.

CAULIFLOWER BAKED IN TOMATO

- 2 *tablespoons butter*
- 2 *tablespoons flour*
- 2 *cups condensed tomato soup or tomato sauce*
- ½ *teaspoon salt*
- ⅛ *teaspoon pepper*
- ½ *teaspoon mustard*
- 1 *tablespoon light brown sugar*
- ⅛ *teaspoon Worcestershire sauce*
- 1 *teaspoon grated onion*
- ½ *cup grated cheese*
- 1 *head cauliflower, parboiled*

Buttered bread crumbs

Melt butter. When it bubbles, work in flour, cook three minutes over low heat, add soup (or sauce), seasonings, onion and grated cheese. Cook until cheese melts — about two minutes. Grease a shallow casserole. Put cauliflower into it, pour sauce over, top with buttered bread crumbs and more grated cheese. Bake for half hour at 400° or until top is well browned.

CAULIFLOWER IN CHEESE PUFF

- 1 *large head cauliflower*
- 1½ *cups Medium White Sauce**
- ¾ *cup grated cheddar cheese*
- 4 *egg yolks*
- 1 *teaspoon sugar*

Salt and pepper to taste

Trim cauliflower and break into flowerets. Cook over boiling water until just tender. Put flowerets in buttered shallow baking dish, reserving a few for garnish. Make the white sauce, add cheese and stir until it melts. Beat egg yolks, sugar, salt and pepper together. Add to white sauce, turn off the heat. Pour sauce over cauliflower. Bake in preheated 350° oven for 20 minutes or until sauce is firm. Garnish with remaining flowerets.

This is a very filling dish, suitable for serving with cold sliced lamb or beef and a green salad on a cool summer evening.

CELERY

Most often, we eat celery raw, as sticks for dipping, stuffed as appetizers or sliced as part of a salad. If you would like to try cooked celery, it does have a good flavor and is not much trouble.

Cut celery in small pieces, using green as well as white parts. Cook in salted boiling water to cover and either cook out all the water or save some for soup stock. When celery is tender, not mushy, drain it and add either butter or some thick cream. If you use cream, put celery, cream and a little paprika into top of a double boiler and allow them to become blended.

BRAISED CELERY

(For 8)

4	*bunches, best part only, crisp celery*	¼	*pound butter*
1	*cup jellied Chicken Stock* or Beef Stock,* well seasoned with herbs and spices*	½	*cup coarse bread crumbs*
		3	*tablespoons extra butter*
			Grated cheese
			Minced chives and parsley

Cut celery in pieces four inches long. Wash well. In a shallow enameled iron pan in which celery can be served, melt butter and toss celery in it so that all sides are exposed to the heat. Cover and cook over very low heat for seven to eight minutes. Add stock and simmer over medium heat until celery is tender — about 20 minutes. You may bake it in the oven at 375° if more convenient. Just before serving, brown crumbs in extra butter. Sprinkle them and grated cheese over celery. Run pan under broiler until cheese melts. Sprinkle with chives and parsley and serve. Good served with broiled fish and a brightly colored vegetable such as candied sweet potatoes.

CREAMED CELERY

(For 4)

2	*tablespoons butter*	½	*cup hot water*
1	*tablespoon minced onion*	½	*cup thick cream*
	Best stalks of two heads celery cut in half-inch pieces		*Pinch of nutmeg*
		1	*tablespoon sherry*
2	*egg yolks*		

Melt butter, add onion and celery and toss them in butter for five minutes. Do not let butter brown. Add water and cook until celery is tender and most of the water has cooked away — 10 to 15 minutes longer. Add cream and nutmeg. Heat. Beat sherry and egg yolks together with a fork. Dilute yolks with a tablespoon of hot cream, repeat twice, stirring well. Add mixture to cream in the pan. Cook over low heat until mixture thickens, stirring all the time. Serve from pan in which it was cooked. This can have a delicate, tender taste, if it is allowed to cook thoroughly but is not overcooked.

CORN ON THE COB

The best way to cook corn is over an open fire, still in the husks, having just picked it a few minutes earlier. If you've a good bed of coals, it takes about 15 minutes for the tassels to burn off and the husk at the tassel end to turn black. Then all you need is plenty of butter, salt and a healthy appetite.

Even if you haven't an open fire you can still cook some pretty good corn in your own kitchen.

Begin by boiling water in a large kettle. Fill the kettle about one-third full of water. When water is boiling hard, pack the kettle full of husked corn. Cover and watch it carefully to check the time the water begins to boil again. This will vary with the amount of corn in the kettle. After the kettle is steaming hard again, five minutes is long enough to cook the corn. For a big kettle of corn, picked on a cool evening, the whole thing may take 15 minutes. Have a hot platter ready, drain the corn and serve immediately with butter and salt. There is nothing better.

When you can no longer enjoy corn straight off the stalk, you might still want the flavor of fall brought back with:

GOLDEN BANTAM CORN, BAKED

1 package frozen Golden Bantam corn
½ teaspoon paprika
Salt to taste
¼ teaspoon pepper
1 teaspoon sugar
4 tablespoons butter

Heavily butter a shallow, enameled iron, baking dish in which corn will be served. Mix seasonings with corn, spread it out in the dish, dot all over with butter. Bake at 375° until golden brown around the edges — 20 to 30 minutes.

BAKED CORN WITH CRACKLINGS

8 ears freshly picked Golden Bantam corn
1 teaspoon sugar
½ teaspoon salt
¼ teaspoon pepper
1 tablespoon minced parsley
4 tablespoons butter
½ cup light cream
½ cup beef suet cracklings (diced and lightly browned)
¼ teaspoon garlic powder

Score and scrape uncooked corn from the cob. Add seasonings. Melt two tablespoons butter in a casserole. Put in corn and rest of butter cut in small pieces. Pour cream over it. Bake at 350° to 375° until corn is crusty brown around edge of dish — 35 to 40 minutes. Scatter with cracklings and serve. This is good served with toasted mushroom sandwiches and a tossed salad.

CORN AND PEPPERS

(For 6)

Make this in a chafing dish or double boiler. Serve on English Muffins,* split, buttered and browned under the broiler.

3 tablespoons butter
1 tablespoon minced onion
1 green pepper, seeded and shredded
1 cup corn
2 pimentos, cut fine
1 cup milk
½ cup cream
½ teaspoon salt
½ teaspoon paprika
½ teaspoon mustard
1 cup grated cheddar cheese
3 egg yolks, beaten with a fork

Melt butter. Add onion and green pepper and sauté until onion is straw colored. Add corn and pimentos. Cook until corn is tender — about three minutes after ice melts if using frozen corn. Add milk and cream. Do not let mixture boil after this point or it will separate. Add seasonings and cheese. When cheese melts, add some of the mixture to beaten eggs. Keep adding and stirring with a fork until you have about three-quarters of a cup of the mixture. Stir it into the corn and pepper mixture. Cook one minute and pour over toasted muffins on hot plates. This is very good served with Mrs. Appleyard's Chutney* and an Avocado Salad.*

BAKED CORN AND CHEESE PUFF

(For 6)

This is really closer to a soufflé but may be served as a vegetable with roast beef or even with Planked Shad.*

3	*tablespoons butter*	*¼*	*teaspoon pepper*
½	*teaspoon minced onion*	*½*	*teaspoon paprika*
2	*slices minced green pepper*	*1*	*cup rich milk*
1	*pimento, cut fine*	*1½*	*cups cream-style corn*
2	*tablespoons flour*	*½*	*cup grated mild cheese*
	Salt to taste	*3*	*eggs, separated*

Melt butter over medium heat in a fireproof enamel dish. Add onion, green pepper and pimento and sauté until onion is straw colored. Sprinkle in flour, mixed with seasonings, and blend thoroughly. Remove pan from heat, pour in milk and stir until smooth. Cook three minutes over low heat. Remove from heat and allow to cool. Add corn, grated cheese and egg yolks, beaten light, and mix well. Preheat the oven 350°. Beat egg whites to stiff peaks. Fold gently into corn and cheese mixture. Set dish into the oven and bake until puff has risen well and is nicely browned — about 35 minutes. Serve hot.

CUCUMBER SANDWICHES

These are the kind of sandwiches which polite society serves with tea, along with a number of other delicacies, including Cheese Biscuits.* They are not sandwiches for filling up the hollow legs of adolescent boys, although even they will put away a good number of them.

Start with young green, freshly picked cucumbers, not more than seven inches long. Peel them and score with a sharp tined fork, lengthwise, all around the surface. Slice cucumbers very thin. Cut small rounds of bread, just bigger than the cucumber slices, using a cookie cutter. If the bread is homemade, slice it very thin. Save crusts and corners for bread crumbs.

Spread rounds of bread lightly with softened creamed butter, then with a very thin coating of mayonnaise. Lay cucumber on one round of bread and cover with another. Keep covered until serving time to keep them from drying out.

MARINATED CUCUMBERS

These are really more of a salad than a hot vegetable. Good with any kind of broiled fish.

¼	*cup vinegar*	*1*	*tablespoon minced parsley*
½	*cup olive oil*	*1*	*clove of garlic*
1	*bay leaf*	*½*	*teaspoon fresh thyme*
½	*teaspoon salt*	*¼*	*teaspoon freshly ground pepper*
2	*small onions and tops, chopped fine*	*1*	*small cucumber, peeled, scored, sliced thin*
½	*tablespoon minced tarragon*		

Mix all ingredients but cucumber together. Pour over cucumber and let stand in marinade at least an hour. At serving time remove bay leaf and garlic.

DANDELION GREENS

These are an inexpensive, nutritious vegetable to be readily found on just about any lawn or field in early summer. The greens must be picked before blossoms come, or they will be bitter. Actually, they should be dug. Cut off the roots, buds and coarse outside leaves. Wash greens thoroughly. Even when they are young and tender, dandelions are quite bitter, therefore they need to be cooked thoroughly.

Put greens into a vegetable cooking basket and lower into rapidly boiling water. Cook greens 15 minutes, change water, bring to boiling again and cook until greens are tender — about 10 minutes longer. Drain, chop and reheat. Serve sprinkled with crisp bacon or tried out cubes of salt pork or beef suet and sliced hard-boiled eggs. The dandelion season is short, so take advantage of them while available.

EGGPLANT CASSEROLE

(For 8)

- 2 *medium eggplants*
- *Olive oil*
- 2 *large onions*
- 1 *1-pound can tomatoes*
- 2 *bay leaves*
- 3 *tablespoons tomato paste*
- 2 *cloves garlic, crushed*
- 1 *tablespoon sugar*
- ½ *teaspoon each basil, tarragon, oregano*
- ⅛ *teaspoon cinnamon*
- ½ *cup burgundy*
- *Salt and pepper to taste*
- 1 *cup cottage cheese*
- 2 *large eggs*
- ½ *cup sour cream*
- *Salt and pepper*

Peel and slice eggplant in half-inch slices. Brush slices with olive oil. Brown over medium heat and cut in one-inch squares. Drain on paper towels. Sauté chopped onions in olive oil until straw colored. Add tomatoes, bay leaves, tomato paste, garlic, sugar, basil, tarragon, oregano, cinnamon, burgundy and salt and pepper. Simmer for half an hour. Discard bay leaves.

Grease a large casserole and alternate layers of eggplant and sauce, ending with sauce. Blend cottage cheese, eggs and sour cream together with salt and pepper to taste. Pour over eggplant. Bake casserole at 350° for about 45 minutes, or until topping is lightly browned and set. Delicious as a taste of Greek cuisine with lamb patties or Roast Lamb* and a Ripe Olive Salad.*

EGGPLANT WITH ALMONDS

(For 6)

Eggplant is a particularly interesting vegetable, especially when combined with other vegetables and seasonings. This is excellent served with roast chicken.

- ⅓ *cup butter*
- 1½ *pounds eggplant, peeled, sliced ⅜ inch thick*
- 1 *cup cream*
- 1 *slice onion*
- *Pinch of nutmeg*
- ½ *cup almonds, blanched, peeled and sliced*
- 1 *bay leaf*

In a big iron enamel pan in which you will serve it, melt the butter and brown slices of eggplant in it. Scald cream with bay leaf, onion and nutmeg. Remove onion and bay leaf, pour cream over eggplant and sprinkle with blanched sliced almonds. Bake at 325° until eggplant is tender and almonds lightly browned — about 45 minutes.

You might also like to serve a tossed salad with several kinds of lettuce and a dessert of avocado halves filled with lemon sherbet and topped with crystallized ginger.

EGGPLANT RATATOUILLE

This dish is to be found all through the Middle East, but originated in the south of France. There are as many versions as there are people preparing it. The basics include eggplant, tomatoes, onions and olive oil. You may want to add more vegetables or tomatoes depending on what you have on hand. Be careful not to eat too much, it is surprisingly rich!

4 tablespoons olive oil

2 cloves garlic, crushed
2 green or red peppers, seeded, cut in wide strips
2 medium onions, chopped
1 large eggplant, cut in cubes
4 large tomatoes, quartered, or one small can tomato paste
1 medium zucchini, cubed
¼ teaspoon basil
¼ teaspoon thyme
¼ teaspoon marjoram
Pinch rosemary
1 teaspoon salt
⅛ teaspoon pepper from grinder

Heat olive oil in a large frying pan. Sauté garlic in it until soft. Add all the ingredients and simmer, covered, until vegetables are the desired texture for you. Some people like their vegetables soft, while I prefer them somewhat crisp. Serve hot with cooked Brown Rice* or cook uncovered to a puree and spread on cooked buttered pastry cut in squares and served as an appetizer. You'll like the response you get.

Variation: If you'd like to serve this as a main dish, simply add half cup dried soybeans, cooked, in the last 15 minutes of cooking. Served with Wild or Brown Rice* and a salad, Eggplant Ratatouille is a vegetarian's delight.

FIDDLEHEADS

Fiddleheads, the coiled tops of the ostrich fern, are readily available in early spring if you know where to look for them. They are to be found in abundance in standing water such as on the bank of a stream, in the shade, usually under overhanging trees. If you pick them at their prime, they are tender with a delicate flavor all their own. Some people say fiddleheads are like asparagus, but their flavor is distinctly unique.

Fiddleheads must be picked before they unroll and the shortest time possible before they are cooked. Carefully rub off the brown scales on the ferns before cooking them. Also remove the tough ends. Allowing six fiddleheads per person to be served, heap them into a folding steamer above rapidly boiling water. Cover kettle and cook for half an hour. Serve on buttered toast with Cream Sauce* or with Egg and Butter Sauce.*

MILKWEED SHOOTS

(For 6)

These are ready approximately the same time as are fiddleheads. They must be picked when only a few inches high and can be found in virtually any field that has been allowed to "go to seed."

24 milkweed shoots	*2 tablespoons flour*
6 slices buttered toast	*Salt and pepper to taste*
1 hard-boiled egg	*½ cup milk*
2 tablespoons butter	*½ cup light cream*

Rub shoots between your hands to loosen wooly covering and wash shoots in several changes of water. Have a large pan of boiling water ready and have more hot water in your teakettle. Boil shoots until tender — about half an hour. Change the water twice during cooking period, to rinse away the bitterness of the milkweed juice.

Make toast and butter it. Chop hard-boiled egg, not too fine. Melt butter and make a roux with flour and seasonings. When roux is well blended and smooth, remove pan from heat and work in first the milk, then cream. Return to heat. Cook over low heat, stirring constantly for at least five minutes. Add chopped egg, turn off heat. At serving time, drain milkweed shoots, put them on toast, bring sauce to the boiling point and pour over milkweed.

MUSHROOMS SAUTÉED

(For 4)

This is a very simple way in which to prepare mushrooms to be served with a thick, juicy steak.

1 pound mushrooms	*2 tablespoons butter*
1 large onion, chopped	*2 tablespoons sherry*

Minced parsley

Wash mushrooms and drain. Slice vertically. Chop onions. Melt butter in a frying pan, toss onions and mushrooms in butter and sherry until onion is straw colored — about three minutes. Sprinkle parsley over all and serve with steak while hot.

STUFFED MUSHROOM CAPS

Make a smooth mixture of cream cheese, thick cream, chopped chives and minced parsley. Stuff medium-sized mushroom caps, washed but not peeled, with the mixture and dust with paprika. Serve as appetizers.

MUSHROOMS IN CREAM

(For 6)

For this, it is best to use small individual glass casseroles. A large one may be used, but it is really better in smaller ones.

2 pounds mushrooms	*¼ teaspoon nutmeg*
3 tablespoons butter	*2 teaspoons minced onion*
2 teaspoons salt	*1 bay leaf, cut into bits*
½ teaspoon paprika	*3 cups heavy cream*
¼ teaspoon white pepper	*3 tablespoons sherry*

Use only the caps, saving the stems for soups or casseroles. Into each buttered dish put mushroom caps, skin side down. Dot butter between layers of mushrooms and over them. Put seasonings, except sherry, into a saucepan with cream and heat until it starts to bubble around the edges. Pour it over the mushrooms and put dishes into a 425° oven. Cover each one tightly and cook until mushrooms are tender — about half an hour. Add the sherry just before serving.

If the mushrooms are to be served in the dishes in which they are cooked, have ready rounds of thin, dry toast, cut to fit the bottom of the dishes. When you add the sherry, slip the toast under the mushrooms and serve. If the mushrooms are to be taken out of the dishes, bring the dishes in on separate plates and have a pile of hot buttered toast to serve with them. Each person takes a piece of toast and spoons the mushrooms and hot juice onto it.

Another way to serve mushrooms to make plain meat, or Meat Loaf,* more interesting is in the form of:

GRILLED MUSHROOMS

Peel large mushroom caps. Into each one put a small lump of butter, two drops of Worcestershire sauce, quarter teaspoon sherry, and a dash of salt. Place on a buttered pan and broil for about two minutes. Allow two or three large caps for each person to be served. Pour the juice in the pan over meat loaf and put caps around it. Serve.

ONIONS SIMMERED IN CREAM

Use only small onions, peeled, for this. Cook until tender in rapidly boiling salted water — about 15 minutes. Drain. Add thin cream, one cup for three cups of onions, and cook in top of a double boiler until soft. Add salt and pepper to taste when onions are almost done. Serve hot with Vermont scrapple and Green Beans with Garlic Croutons.*

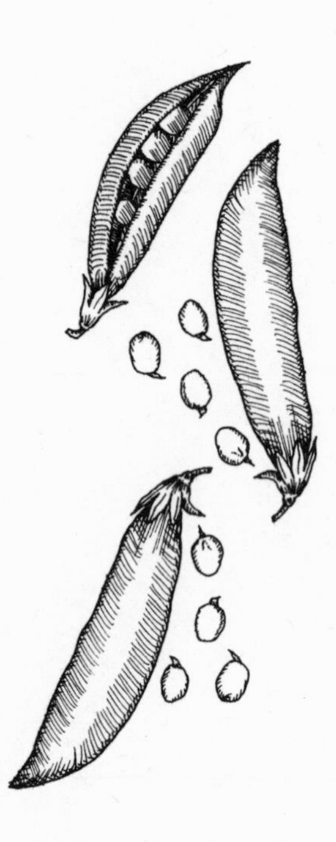

GREEN PEAS

Peas are the jewel of any Vermont garden and often the rule by which gardeners measure the bounty of their own garden. During the middle of summer when peas come in in full force, you might hear comments in the general stores such as, "I can hardly keep up with my peas now, I've got so many — froze 15 pints just yesterday." Or, "Have you seen so-and-so's garden, of course the only reason he has so many peas is that he spends all his time out there, I wish *I* had that much time." Or, "I was expecting to have a bumper crop of peas this year, but the deer found them before I could get them picked." "Haven't you heard of using blood-meal to keep them away?" I generally don't enter into such discussions as my bounty of peas has yet to be bountiful, and I've enough pride to not want to expose myself.

When I do happen to grow enough peas to serve at more than one meal, and I keep trying, the best way to serve them is freshly picked and shelled and cooked in as little water as possible. Or you may put them directly into the refrigerator, unshelled, and shell them just before cooking.

Use only enough water to cover the bottom of the pan. Have it boiling when you put the shelled peas in. Stir them during cooking. Taste them (this is the best part). Remove from the fire as soon as they are soft — about 5 minutes. Ladle out with a spoon with holes in it and stir lumps of butter into them. Cook remaining liquid down to two tablespoons and pour over peas. Serve hot with just about anything, salmon is especially good.

PEAS AND NEW POTATOES IN CREAM

(For 8)

This is an excellent combination when peas are in abundance and small new potatoes are just ready to be dug.

- 4 *quarts of unshelled peas*
- 2 *quarts tiny, freshly dug potatoes*
- ½ *pound salt pork, or beef suet, diced*
- 1 *small onion, finely minced*
- 1 *cup thick cream*

Shell peas. Scrub potatoes well but do not peel them. Have water boiling in a fireproof casserole big enough to hold both peas and potatoes. Drop potatoes into just enough boiling water to cover them. Cook about 20 minutes while you are trying out pork or suet cubes until they are a delicate straw color. Skim them out and cook chopped onion in fat until straw colored. The potatoes should now be done. Don't overcook them or they will be mushy. Most of the water should have cooked away. Add the suet and onions to potatoes.

In a separate pan have half a cup boiling water. Add peas and cook three minutes after water boils again. Add them with their juice to the casserole. Simmer a few minutes over a low flame so that everything will blend well. Add cream. When it just begins to bubble around the edges, it is time to serve.

PEAS AND PEARL ONIONS WITH FRENCH MUSTARD SAUCE

Allow one can very small onions to two packages frozen tiny French peas. Cook peas as directed on package until not quite soft. Drain peas and onions and put into top of double boiler over hot water. Stir in two tablespoons of butter. Pass French Mustard Sauce with them.

- 2 *tablespoons butter*
- 2 *tablespoons flour*
- *Salt to taste*
- *Few grains cayenne*
- 1 *tablespoon Dijon mustard au vin blanc*
- ½ *teaspoon crushed garlic*
- 1 *tablespoon grated Parmesan cheese*
- ¾ *cup light cream*
- 1 *egg yolk*
- 2 *teaspoons butter (extra)*

Melt two tablespoons butter. As soon as it starts to foam, remove pan from fire and rub in flour mixed with salt and cayenne. Add mustard, garlic, Parmesan and then cream, slowly stirring all the time until mixture is smooth. Return pan to low heat and add one tablespoon of warm sauce to beaten egg yolk, stir well and add another tablespoon of sauce. Mix thoroughly and stir mixture back into sauce. Add extra butter dot by dot, and cook until sauce begins to thicken. Remove pan from heat, cover it and set aside where it will keep warm, not hot, until serving time.

GREEN PEPPERS WELLFLEET

The most difficult part of preparing this dish is the skinning of the peppers. At least 24 hours before you plan to serve them, skin peppers by putting them into a very hot oven for about ten minutes, or plunging them into boiling water, or holding them over a hot flame. Whichever way you choose, it is a messy job. Having gotten the skins off, slice peppers lengthwise, about half an inch wide. Prepare a simple French Dressing* with olive oil, wine vinegar and two or three cloves of garlic. Cover peppers with this and set aside to absorb the flavor and dressing. The slices will be limp and delicious.

GREEN AND RED PEPPERS SAUTÉED

The red peppers give some cheering color to this dish. Green peppers which are partly ripe work well. Allow half a good-sized sweet pepper for each person to be served. Split peppers, clean out seeds and pulp. Cut peppers with scissors into long narrow strips. Toss in melted butter, or part butter and part olive oil, until edges are brown. Do not overcook. They should be slightly crisp. Serve hot.

SMOTHERED POTATOES

(For 4)

- 4 *medium or 8 small potatoes*
- ¼ *pound butter*
- *Pepper from the grinder*
- 1 *teaspoon onion, put through garlic press*
- *Salt to taste*

Peel potatoes and slice them. Cut butter into small bits. Mix butter and onion with potato. Add seasonings. Wrap in aluminum foil. Put package in a heated iron frying pan. Set pan in 450° oven and bake for ten minutes. Reduce heat to 350° and bake until done — about an half hour longer. Serve in a very hot dish with cold sliced lamb.

POTATOES APPLEYARD

(For 6)

- 7 *good-sized potatoes*
- ¼ *pound butter*
- ¼ *pound mild cheddar cheese, crumbled*
- 1 *large onion, minced*
- ½ *teaspoon pepper*
- 1 *teaspoon paprika*
- *Salt to taste*
- ½ *cup milk*
- ½ *cup cream*

Peel potatoes. Slice them thin. Melt two tablespoons butter in a large iron frying pan. Put a layer of potatoes into pan. Dot with butter, sprinkle with cheese, onion and seasonings. Repeat until you have four layers. Put extra butter on top layer. Now pour milk and cream into pan. The liquid should come up to the top layer but not cover it. It is somewhat difficult to give precise amounts of ingredients because size of potatoes and pans vary. If you're in doubt, be generous.

Bake all in a preheated 450° oven for ten minutes. Reduce heat to 350° and bake 35 to 40 minutes longer. The potatoes should absorb all the liquid and be brown on top and a glazed brown underneath. Cut into pie-shaped wedges on a hot platter. If the pan is thoroughly buttered to begin with the wedges will come out with no trouble.

INSIDE-OUT POTATOES

(Baked Potatoes with Sour Cream)

Allow one medium-sized potato for each person to be served. Bake for 15 minutes in a preheated 450° oven. Reduce heat to 350° and bake 35 minutes longer. Check at 25 minutes. If potatoes are soft and fall easily from the tines of a fork, they are done.

Cut a slice from the side of each potato and remove contents to a heated bowl. For each potato allow half a tablespoon butter, two tablespoons sour cream, a quarter teaspoon paprika, salt and pepper to taste and finely chopped parsley.

Mash potato with butter, seasonings and half the sour cream. Beat until light and pile into potato shells. Use rest of the cream to top each potato. Set potatoes on a baking sheet and run briefly under broiler until cream just starts to brown. Sprinkle with parsley and serve.

Variations: Use thick, sweet cream in place of sour cream. Or top each potato with thin strips of cheddar cheese, or top each one with bacon cooked on one side, drained, and cut into small pieces, cooked side down.

POTATOES HASHED IN CREAM

(For 6)

These are for those who claim, "But I never eat potatoes." Try this dish and I bet they will.

- 6 *baking size potatoes*
- 6 *tablespoons butter*
- 1½ *cups thin cream*
- 1 *tablespoon finely minced onion*
- *Salt and pepper to taste*
- *Parsley sprigs*

Bake the potatoes for half an hour at 450°. Peel them and chop rather fine. Melt two tablespoons butter in an iron frying pan. Warm the cream. Add rest of the butter, onion and seasonings. Stir in chopped potatoes. Put mixture in pan and cook over very low heat until cream is absorbed and you see brown around the edges. This will take about 20 minutes longer. Loosen potato mixture around the edges. Treat like an omelette: make a fairly deep cut across at right angles to the pan handle. Turn top half over the other half. Slide the folded "omelette" out, bottom side up on a hot platter. Garnish with parsley and serve.

SWEET POTATOES

These are one of the most delicious vegetables I know of, and tasty even when prepared simply. I usually bake them starting in a 450° oven, reducing the heat to 350° after ten minutes and baking for 20 to 30 minutes longer. They come out a sweet, moist and golden-colored delight that needs only sweet butter and a little salt to complete the taste.

A very simple method of serving sweet potatoes to go with duckling is as:

BOULES D'OR

These are potato balls scooped out from sweet potatoes. Steam over boiling water until they are soft but not mushy — about 20 minutes. Serve with butter and salt. Surround a Roast Duckling* with them and pass Orange Sauce.*

You occasionally might want to serve sweet potatoes in a more elaborate manner, in which case try:

GLAZED SWEET POTATOES

(For 6)

6	*good-sized sweet potatoes*	*½*	*cup hot water*
½	*cup butter*	*¼*	*cup sherry*
¾	*cup light brown sugar*	*½*	*cup chopped peanuts*

Steam potatoes without peeling until a sharp knife can be pushed into one rather easily — about 25 minutes. They should not be mushy. Cool slightly and holding a potato on a fork, peel off the skin. Cut crosswise into ⅜-inch slices. Butter a shallow baking pan and put potato slices in one layer. Dot generously with butter, sprinkle with brown sugar. Pour hot water around them. Set pan into a preheated 375° oven and bake until syrup is quite thick and potatoes are tender — about half an hour. Baste three times with the syrup. Just before serving, tip pan and pour sherry into syrup and baste potatoes with it again. Scatter coarsely chopped peanuts over potatoes, set pan back into oven for five minutes and serve. The sherry is optional. You might want to use half a cup of maple syrup in place of the brown sugar and occasionally stir in a little rum. If you do this, omit the peanuts, for the syrup will not be tasted in the presence of peanuts.

SPINACH RING WITH PEAS

(For 8)

2	*10-ounce bags washed spinach*	*¼*	*teaspoon pepper*
1	*tablespoon chopped onion*	*½*	*cup cream*
¼	*cup water*	*4*	*eggs*
1	*cup milk*	*1*	*10-ounce package frozen peas*
3	*tablespoons butter*		*Croutons made from two slices bread (lightly browned in two tablespoons butter)*
3	*tablespoons flour*		
1	*teaspoon nutmeg*		
	Salt to taste		

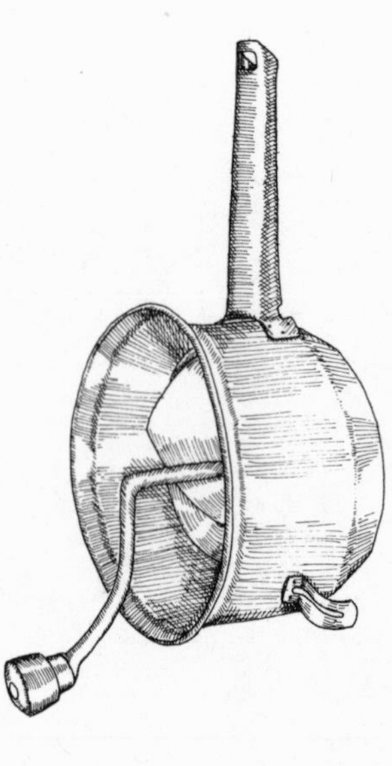

Chop spinach and onion with water until spinach is limp. Keep chopping. It takes about four minutes. Put one third of the milk, water from spinach and half of the spinach into blender and puree it. Add the rest of spinach in two more lots. Melt butter, work in flour and seasonings slowly. Remove from heat und stir in the rest of milk, making sure there are no lumps. Stir in cream. Cook over low heat until it thickens. Remove from heat. Add spinach puree. Mix well. Add eggs one at a time. Beat well after each addition. Put mixture into a well-buttered one and a half quart ring mold. Have oven at 325° with a pan containing hot water on lowest shelf. Set the ring on the shelf above it. Bake ring until knife comes out clean — about 35 minutes. Cook peas during last six or seven minutes. Do not overbake spinach or it will separate.

To remove spinach from the mold, let it stand for a minute. Run a spatula around the edge of ring and a small knife around the inner edge. Invert on a circular dish. Fill center with peas. Cook remaining liquid from peas down to half a teaspoonful. Add one tablespoon butter and one tablespoon of thick cream. Season to taste. Pour over peas. Scatter croutons over spinach and serve.

SPINACH APPLEYARD

1	*teaspoon finely minced onion*	¼	*cup hot water*
2	*10-ounce bags washed spinach*	2	*tablespoons thick cream*
		2	*tablespoons butter*
			Pinch of nutmeg

For the croutons:

4	*slices homemade bread (¼ inch thick)*	2	*tablespoons butter*
		¼	*teaspoon garlic powder*

Begin by making croutons. Cut crusts off bread. Cut into quarter-inch cubes. Melt butter. Toss croutons in butter until golden brown. Sprinkle garlic powder over them. Remove and set aside until needed.

In the same pan cook onion until transparent and yellow. Rinse out the pan with a quarter cup hot water. Swish it around to get all the flavor and pour it into the kettle in which you plan to cook spinach. Chop spinach rather coarsely. Put just enough water in the kettle to cover bottom. Have it boiling hard. Add chopped spinach. Cook five minutes, chopping while it cooks. When it is tender and a bright green color remove it from pan to a hot dish, leaving the water in the kettle.

Cook water down to about one tablespoon. Add cream, butter and nutmeg, heat and pour over spinach. Sprinkle croutons over and serve. Good with Turkey Salad* and Mrs. Appleyard's Tomato Conserve.*

SPINACH COUNTRY STYLE

16	*very small beets*	4	*tablespoons butter*
2	*teaspoons salt*	1	*tablespoon light brown sugar*
16	*young carrots*		
1	*slice of onion*	2	*hard-boiled eggs*
4	*quarts young spinach*	1	*tablespoon chopped parsley*

Begin by cooking beets with half a teaspoon salt until tender. While they are cooking start carrots with onion, and another half a teaspoon of salt. When they are almost done, start spinach, well-washed, and cook it with only the water that clings to it and the rest of the salt. Chop it fine as it cooks. It will only take a few minutes, so stand right there while it cooks.

By the time the spinach is nearly done, the water should be cooked out of the carrots. Add two tablespoons butter and the sugar to them and set them to simmer gently.

Put the spinach into the center of a hot platter with the rest of the butter. Make a depression in the middle of it and put half the beets into it. Put rings of hard-boiled eggs on the spinach and surround with the rest of beets and carrots, alternating them. Sprinkle all with parsley and serve.

BAKED SQUASH

You may bake any of a number of types of squash. Particularly good varieties are acorn, buttercup and butternut.

Allow half a medium-sized squash for each person to be served. Split, clean out seeds and strings, lay face down on a well-buttered baking sheet. Bake at 350° until tender — about 40 minutes. Cut small pieces from the curved sides of squash so they will stand evenly. Turn them over in the pan. Prick upper sides all over with a fork. Dot with butter. Sprinkle each piece with a grating of orange and lemon rind. Mix two tablespoons lemon juice, two tablespoons orange juice and two tablespoons sherry. Pour some of the mixture over cut side of the squash and into the center. Cook 15 minutes longer. Baste once with liquid in center. If you like a sweeter squash fill the cavity with a small amount of maple syrup or brown sugar and dot with butter and then return to oven for 15 minutes.

SQUASH WITH SAUSAGE

(For 4)

2 squash | *1 pound sausage*

Hollow out center well of squash and bake as described above, leaving out the final filling and baking. Cook sausage meat over medium heat, breaking it up with a fork and tossing until it shows no pink color — about ten minutes. Drain off the fat. Heap meat in the centers of squash. Return squash to the oven and bake ten minutes longer. With it, serve broccoli with lemon butter sauce and Broiled Tomato Slices.* For dessert serve fruit cup and Madeleines.*

BROILED ZUCCHINI SLICES

Pick zucchini when they are not over eight inches long. Slice them ⅜-inch thick and dip them lightly in flour seasoned with mixed herbs. Put three tablespoons olive oil in frying pan and toss two cloves of peeled and sliced garlic in it. Put in zucchini slices. Brown them on both sides. Set pan in a 350° oven for 10 to 15 minutes. Slice a seeded green pepper thin. Cook slices in a little olive oil for three or four minutes. Add them to pan of zucchini. Cover vegetable slices with thin slices of sharp cheddar cheese and run pan under broiler until cheese melts.

Summer squash may be prepared in the same way, or served with plenty of Taxi Driver's Tomato Sauce.*

BROILED TOMATO SLICES

12 good sized tomato slices
1 cup homemade bread crumbs
2 tablespoons light brown sugar
4 tablespoons melted butter
1 tablespoon garlic powder
Pinch of mixed herbs
1 teaspoon paprika
12 slices cheddar cheese

Place tomato slices in a buttered fireproof pan. Mix together bread crumbs, butter, sugar, garlic powder, herbs, paprika. Spread mixture on tomato slices. Put pan into a 350° oven and bake 20 minutes. Then top each slice with a thin slice of cheese. Run pan under broiler until cheese melts.

SCALLOPED TOMATOES

- 2 *quart jars tomatoes*
- ⅓ *cup sugar*
- 2 *tablespoons molasses*
- ½ *teaspoon instant coffee (optional)*
- 1 *tablespoon dried onion flakes*
- ¼ *teaspoon nutmeg*
- ¼ *teaspoon cinnamon*
- ½ *teaspoon dried oregano*
- ½ *teaspoon dried basil*
- *Salt to taste*
- 2 *tablespoons butter*
- 3 *slices homemade bread, cubed*
- ½ *teaspoon garlic powder*

Heat tomatoes in a buttered deep frying pan, stirring often to break them up. When they come to the boil, add sugar, molasses, coffee, onion flakes, nutmeg, cinnamon, oregano, basil and salt. Simmer over low heat until mixture is quite thick — about half an hour — scraping it occasionally from the sides of the pan. While it is cooking, melt butter in another frying pan. Toss bread cubes in butter over low heat until they are lightly browned all over. Turn off heat. Sprinkle them with garlic powder and toss them in it.

Butter a shallow dish. Pour in some of the tomato mixture; sprinkle with some of the croutons. Repeat twice. End with a sprinkling of croutons on top. Bake at 350° until top croutons are well browned — about half an hour. Serve hot.

Glossary

Brewer's Yeast Powder. A source of high-quality protein by itself, Brewer's Yeast also increases the protein quality of other foods. It does not have the rising properties of baking yeast.

Burnt Onion Powder. A bottled spice obtainable in gourmet shops.

Calcium Lactate. A white powder obtained from milk and used as a dietary supplement providing calcium.

Caramelized Sugar. Sugar which has been melted over low heat to a liquid state of a golden brown color.

Citron. A fruit like the lemon in appearance and structure but larger. The preserved rind of the citron is used in fruitcake.

Cointreau. A liqueur made from bitter oranges.

Coulibiac Tart. A traditional Russian fish pie originally made with pike and perch, now commonly made of salmon or turbot. Coulibiac is derived from its Russian name: Kulebyaka.

Cracklings. The crisp bits of beef or pork fat that remain after "trying out."

Cross Crackers. Sometimes known as Montpelier Crackers because the bakery was located in Montpelier, Vermont (10 miles from Appleyard Center). These dry, round and puffy crackers are now made at the Cross Baking Company in Claremont, New Hampshire.

Delayer. The process of adding eggs to a hot mixture by beating eggs and adding a small amount of hot mixture to the eggs, beating continuously, adding more by small amounts and putting the egg mixture into the hot mixture. See page 227.

Democratic Baking Powder. On one occasion, Mrs. Appleyard ran out of baking powder and so made her own with the following ingredients: 4 tablespoons cream of tartar, 2 tablespoons bicarbonate of soda and 2 tablespoons instant flour. She sifted all the ingredients together three times through a small triple sifter, sifted them into a baking powder can and put on a label giving the contents and the date the baking powder was made.

Farina. A finely ground meal, usually wheat, but the term may be applied to meal made of other grains. The form in which it is now commonly met is Cream of Wheat.

Flame Tamer. An asbestos or metal device placed over a gas or electric burner to distribute the heat more evenly. It is excellent for preventing sticking in long, slow cooking.

Fizzy Cider. Unpasteurized cider will turn fizzy, or tart, after a few days, especially if not refrigerated. Under the right conditions, and after a longer period of time, it will become hard cider (alcoholic). But watch out — you may have cider vinegar instead (which also has many good uses).

French Baskets. Made of metal or wicker, these baskets are used primarily for cheesecake to drain through. See the rule for Coeur a la Crème on page 111.

Graham Flour. Whole wheat flour.

Holland Rusk. A sweet raised bread oven dried to a golden brown crispness. Used as an appetizer for dipping, or under sauces such as Welsh Rabbit, or rolled fine for bread crumbs.

Horehound. An extract or confection made from the bitter mint plant called horehound.

Instant Flour. A flour that is finer than pastry flour. "Gold Medal Wondra" by General Mills is an instant flour, but regular flour may be substituted if care is taken with the mixing. (Regular will tend to lump.)

Italian Steamer. A perforated container with collapsible sides and adjustable legs that allow it to fit into any saucepan or kettle. Used mainly to steam vegetables.

Kirsch. A dry, colorless brandy distilled from the fermented juice of the black morello cherry.

Kolacky Nut Bread. A Slovack nut bread.

Kumquats. Any of several small citrus fruits with sweet spongy rinds and somewhat acid pulp used chiefly for preserves.

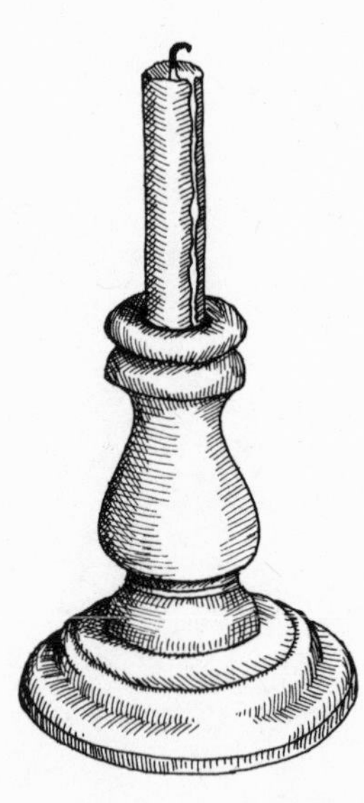

Magnesium Oxide. A white powdered dietary supplement providing elemental magnesium.

Mixed Herbs. Any combination of compatible dried or fresh herbs suitable to the dish being made. Variations are subject to the chef's discretion. See Herb chapter for suggestions. Fines Herbes are finely chopped herbs such as parsley, chives, tarragon and marjoram. They are used as a seasoning in omelettes, soups, stews, sauces and as a garnish.

Monosodium Glutamate. A white crystalline chemical food additive used extensively as a seasoning in commercial food processing. It may be purchased as a seasoning. Like table salt, it is known to increase blood pressure if used over a long period of time.

Orange Bitters. A bitter orange flavored liquid, usually alcoholic, made with herbs and roots and used in beverages.

Orange Curaçoa. A liqueur flavored with the dried peel of the sour orange.

Pilot Biscuits. A flat cracker sometimes referred to as hardtack. "Sea Toast" by the Keebler Company is one brand available.

Poultry Seasoning. Any combination of herbs for poultry such as "Bell's Poultry Seasoning."

Rose Water. Made by pouring brandy over rose petals, used as a flavoring.

Roux. A cooked mixture of flour and fat or butter used for thickening sauces, gravies and soufflés.

Saffron. An autumn-flowering crocus dried for its deep yellow color. Frequently used in Indian dishes such as curries, and occasionally in pickles or preserves.

Sour Milk. To make sour milk add one tablespoon vinegar or lemon juice to one cup (minus one tablespoon) of milk. Let stand 5 minutes.

Soya Lecithin. A food supplement obtained from soybeans, helpful in the body's utilization of cholesterol.

Stoned. To have removed the large pit or stone from fruits such as cherries or prunes.

Sultana Raisins. A pale yellow seedless raisin from the Sultana grape which is grown for both raisins and wine making.

Sweetbreads. The thymus gland of a young animal, lamb or calf, used for food.

Tripe. Stomach tissue of beef or lamb which may be purchased either fresh or pickled. See page 204.

Truffles. The usually dark and rugose edible subterranean fruiting body of European fungi. Very popular in France where pigs are used to find and rout out this delicacy.

Try Out. To melt the solid fat of beef or pork over medium heat, stirring the pieces. The fat will be rendered out leaving, when done, the cracklings.

Index

ACKNOWLEDGMENTS

I hope the following people and businesses will accept, individually and collectively, my lasting appreciation: the Cross Baking Company, Claremont, N.H. for permission to use Cross Crackers by name throughout the book; Donna Fitch, Linda Paradee and Penny Candy for extensive help in all the details of production; Edith Joslin, Carol Ellingwood and Donald Lefebvre; as well as Carbur's Restaurant, La Patisserie, Kitchen Korner and Shelburne Museum for their help in background material for illustrations.

Special thanks to my family members for tolerating and supporting my work, and sampling my cooking, both successful and not. My mother, Edith; brothers, Bruce, Tim and Nick; sister, Maggie; in-laws, Dottie, Jim, Connie, Woody, Kathy, Jack, Ed, Margy, Karan, Kevin and Tom. And to my aunts, Elizabeth Kent Gay and Rosamond Kent Sprague, for their material contributions and moral support.

— P.K.C.